D0561288

CONTINUED ON BACK END PAPER

English Grammar and Composition

REVISED EDITION

WITH SUPPLEMENT

COMPLETE COURSE

JOHN E. WARRINER

FRANCIS GRIFFITH

SPECIAL CONTRIBUTORS

Donald W. Lee
vocabulary

Peter M. Miller and
Orville Palmer
college entrance examinations

HARCOURT, BRACE & WORLD, INC.

New York   Chicago   San Francisco   Atlanta   Dallas

THE SERIES:

English Grammar and Composition 7

English Grammar and Composition 8

English Grammar and Composition 9

English Grammar and Composition 10

English Grammar and Composition 11

▶ English Grammar and Composition: Complete Course

Test booklet and teacher's manual for each title above

CORRELATED BOOKS OF MODELS FOR WRITING:

Composition: Models and Exercises 7

Composition: Models and Exercises 8

Composition: Models and Exercises 9

Composition: Models and Exercises 10

Composition: Models and Exercises 11

Advanced Composition: A Book of Models for Writing

AUTHORS: John E. Warriner has taught English for 32 years, in junior and senior high schools and in college. He is also a coauthor of the *English Workshop* series. Francis Griffith, who holds a doctor's degree in education from Columbia University, was for many years Chairman of English and Speech in a Brooklyn, New York, high school.

SPECIAL CONTRIBUTORS: Donald W. Lee, Associate Professor of English at the University of Houston, is a coauthor of the *Harbrace Vocabulary Workshop*. Peter M. Miller, who wrote the material on College Entrance and Other Examinations, was formerly on the staff of Educational Testing Service and is now Associate Director of Admissions at the California Institute of Technology. Orville Palmer, who assisted in the planning and editing of the chapter on examinations, is a member of Educational Testing Service.

ISBN 0-15-312000-2

Preface

The teacher of senior English occupies a difficult but challenging position. Because the course he teaches is in large part a summary of all the English courses that have preceded it, he feels obligated to review, or reteach, everything. Two thoughts impress upon him the magnitude of his responsibilities. The first is the image of the college English instructor lurking in the future of his college-bound students, ready and, it often seems, eager to find weaknesses in their high school preparation. The other is the even more sobering knowledge that for his terminal students the senior English class may be the last chance to master language skills that will help them meet the speaking and writing demands of a lifetime.

Although teaching literature may be more interesting and less wearing than teaching writing, the experienced teacher recognizes that the latter is the more critical responsibility. This is so because, in a practical sense, a person is more handicapped in college and in life by failures in self-expression than by ignorance of literature. Writing faults are specific and easily detected; literary ignorance is less apparent and more easily overcome with effort. Relatively few college students fail because of inadequate preparation in literature compared to the number who fail because they cannot write.

In teaching expository writing, a teacher must deal with four kinds of composition problems: the problem of the word; the problem of the sentence; the problem of the paragraph; and the problem of the longer composition. A teacher may at times choose to deal with one kind of problem in isolation—sentence structure, for example—over a stretch of several lessons, and he may at other times deal with all four kinds of problems in the course of a single class period. The order in which he takes them up during the course will be dictated by the needs of his class or the sequence of his local course of study. But whatever plan and order he chooses, he must cover these four kinds of composition problems.

Problems of word usage involve three areas of study. First, the study of grammatical correctness in the use of inflected forms (agreement, pronoun usage, verb usage, etc.); second, the study of the conventions of usage and of appropriateness in word choice; third, the study of vocabulary and diction as a means to a more powerful style. Seniors should begin to have a sophisticated view of language. They should know about the changes that are constantly occurring in their language. They should understand usage levels. They should be able to use formal standard English when it is appropriate, and they should be trained to use common reference tools efficiently.

The attack on problems of sentence structure in the senior year should include training in the writing of sentences that are both clear and smooth. The words in a sentence may be correct grammatically and appropriate in a usage sense, but the sentence itself may still be unclear. Also, a sentence may be correct and clear but unfelicitous or awkward in its structure. The efficient way to provide this training in sentence building is to teach students to recognize and correct those sentence structure faults which commonly cause confusion or awkwardness. Specific terms for sentence faults may eventually be forgotten, but extensive practice in revising poor sentences to produce good sentences gives the student an understanding of the difference between a good sentence and a poor one.

The most important and perhaps most difficult thing to achieve in teaching expository writing is good organization. Organization can be most concretely taught through the paragraph which, in small compass, demands most of the important writing skills. No matter how many times students may have been taught the topic sentence, the methods of developing a paragraph, the common transitional devices both within and between paragraphs, they can still profit from more experience in organizing and writing the single-paragraph composition. More demanding than the single-paragraph composition is the longer paper of many paragraphs. Planning and organization again are the important goals. Students should be given experience in writing many kinds of exposition: exposition that defines; exposition that informs; exposition that explains. In learning to write opinion and argument, they should be instructed in the elements of clear thinking. They will benefit from practice in writing such specific expository forms as the précis, the factual report, the business letter, and the research paper.

Sometimes referred to as the "kitchen work" of composition teaching, instruction in mechanics is frequently necessary in the senior course. Manuscript form, capitalization, punctuation, and spelling are areas in which competence is rightfully expected of high school graduates. Here again, the senior must be mature enough to find in reference books the answers to questions of technique. The composition teacher urges him to become independent to the extent that he can use his own textbook in this way.

Students write best when they have something interesting and important to say. The competent composition teacher realizes that he must help his students with the subject matter as well as the techniques of writing. When literature and composition are taught in the same class, a large part of the writing can and should be about the literature being studied, especially about ideas derived from it. Nevertheless, a very considerable proportion of the subject matter of student themes should come from the students' experience and special interests. Showing students that they do have information, ideas, and experiences worth writing about is one of the teacher's most important tasks. The new supplement, "Making Writing Interesting," shows students how to use narrative, attractive introductions, and concrete words to make their writing come alive.

The teacher of writing must never lose sight of his goal, which is the improvement of his students' writing ability as shown in their compositions. The carry-over from classroom instruction and practice exercises to the student theme is not automatic. It can be assured only if the teacher insists on it. Composition assignments, made regularly and motivated carefully, are the indispensable features of any course in writing. In them the student applies all that he has learned in class; through them his teacher both evaluates the student's achievement and, by judicious criticism, helps him to display more and more effectively the major writing skills which he has been taught.

In his endeavor to bring his seniors up to a high level of competence in written English, the good teacher needs and deserves the best available tools. Most important of these is a good textbook. It is the intent and the hope of authors, editors, and publishers of *English Grammar and Composition: Complete Course* that this book will serve both students and teachers in their important work.

J. W.

The authors and publishers wish to acknowledge the valuable critical help given by the many teachers who contributed suggestions for this book. Special thanks are due to Mr. Henry Aronson, International School of The Hague, Netherlands; Dr. John R. Arscott, Coordinator, Senior Division, West Essex High School, North Caldwell, New Jersey; Mrs. Margaret R. Bonney, Lexington High School, Lexington, Massachusetts; Miss Jean E. Crabtree, Garden City Senior High School, Garden City, New York; Mr. Raymond E. Kavanagh, Levittown Memorial High School, Levittown, New York; Mrs. Gladys Kronsagen, Glenbard Township High School, Glen Ellyn, Illinois.

Contents

Preface

vii

PART THREE: COMPOSITION: SENTENCE STRUCTURE

PART FOUR: COMPOSITION: PARAGRAPHS AND LONGER PAPERS

PART FIVE: AIDS TO GOOD ENGLISH

PART SIX: SPEAKING AND LISTENING

PART SEVEN: MECHANICS

PART ONE

Grammar

The Parts of Speech

Their Identification and Function

By this time in your educational career, you understand the importance of being able to speak and write effectively. A principal goal of instruction in English is to increase your competence in speaking and writing. Every year your English course takes you further along the road to mastery of language skills.

Since English is a cumulative subject, some things that you encounter each year are bound to be familiar. Among these is grammar, which you have probably been studying since elementary school. There is a good chance that by now you already know enough English grammar to meet your needs. You may, however, find your knowledge of grammar somewhat tarnished and in need of polishing.

Grammar is important. By giving names to the kinds of words and the parts of a sentence, it provides the vocabulary you need in your study of language. By making you aware of the basic patterns of English sentences, it helps you to develop a varied and interesting style. You should, therefore, find out early in the school year whether your knowledge of grammar is adequate. The way to do this is to test yourself and then review what you still need to learn.

Chapter 1 deals with the most fundamental grammatical knowledge—the parts of speech, or the names of words according to their function in the sentence.

Diagnostic Test

Number your paper 1–33. After the proper numbers, copy the numbered words in the following passage. Note the way each of the words is used and after it write what part of speech it is, using abbreviations: *n.*, noun; *pron.*, pronoun; *adj.*, adjective; *v.*, verb; *adv.*, adverb; *conj.*, conjunction; *prep.*, preposition; *inter.*, interjection.

Nouns used as adjectives or adverbs (*house* paint, come *tomorrow*) should be called adjectives or adverbs. Pronouns in the possessive case preceding a noun (*my* book, *her* friend, etc.) should be labeled pronouns unless your teacher prefers to have you label them possessive adjectives.

Higher education in (1) *this* country is (2) *rapidly* becoming higher. (3) *More* people than ever before (4) *graduate* from high school (5) *and* go (6) *to* college. (7) *Many* spend five, instead of four, years in (8) *college*. (9) *Today* a bachelor's degree is (10) *more* common than a (11) *high school* diploma was (12) *sixty* years ago. (13) *Graduate* study (14) *is* as common as undergraduate study was (15) *then*. (16) *Because* man's knowledge has increased, there is more for (17) *us* to learn. (18) *Our* fields (19) *of* specialization (20) *grow* narrower. (21) *Although* the successful, self-educated man (22) *who* did not graduate from (23) *high school* (24) *still* exists in America, (25) *he* is a rare exception. (26) *His* kind will (27) *soon* be extinct. (28) *Anyone* who wishes to achieve high position in (29) *today's* world had better get a (30) *college* degree. (31) *Alas*, twenty years of schooling may be (32) *necessary* for success in the (33) *future*.

THE NOUN

1a. A *noun* is a word used to name a person, place, thing, or idea.

Nouns may be classified in three ways: *proper* or *common;* *abstract* or *concrete;* and *collective*.

A *proper noun* is the name of a particular person, place,

or thing. Proper nouns are capitalized: *Tom, Miami, White House.*

A *common noun* is a noun that does not name a particular person, place, or thing. Common nouns are not capitalized: *man, city, building.*

An *abstract noun* names a quality, a characteristic, an idea: *beauty, strength, love, courage.*

A *concrete noun* names an object that can be perceived by the senses: *hat, desk, book, box.*

A *collective noun* names a group: *crowd, team, class.*

♦ NOTE A *compound noun* is a noun of more than one word: *Chase Manhattan Bank, Ringling Brothers Circus, high school.*

THE PRONOUN

1b. A *pronoun* is a word used in place of one or more nouns.

EXAMPLES Fishermen complained about the weather forecast. **They** said **it** had not warned **them** of the storm. [The pronouns *they* and *them* take the place of the noun *fishermen.* The pronoun *it* takes the place of the noun *forecast.*]

A car and a truck collided near the school. **They** ran over the lawn. [The pronoun *they* takes the place of two nouns, *car* and *truck.*]

Sometimes a pronoun takes the place of another pronoun.

EXAMPLE **One** of our planes is missing. **It** was last heard from over four hours ago. [The pronoun *it* takes the place of the pronoun *one.*]

The word to which a pronoun refers (whose place it takes) is the *antecedent* of the pronoun. In the preceding example *one* is the antecedent of *it.*

There are several kinds of pronouns: *personal, relative, interrogative, demonstrative,* and *indefinite.*

1 a-b

PERSONAL PRONOUNS

| I, me | he, him | it | they, them |
| you | she, her | we, us | |

POSSESSIVE FORMS OF THE PERSONAL PRONOUNS

| my, mine | his | its | their, theirs |
| your, yours | her, hers | our, ours | |

Some of the possessive forms—*my, your, his, its, our, their*—are used before a noun in the same way adjectives are used to limit the meaning of a noun: *my* parents, *your* home, *his* coat, etc. They are possessive pronouns functioning as adjectives. In this book these words are called pronouns. Your teacher may, however, prefer to have you call them possessive adjectives. Follow your teacher's instructions in labeling these words.

REFLEXIVE AND INTENSIVE PRONOUNS

myself	ourselves
yourself	yourselves
himself, herself, itself	themselves

Personal pronouns combined with *–self, –selves* may be used in two ways:

1. They may be used *reflexively.*

   Barry hurt **himself.**

2. They may be used *intensively* for emphasis.

   Barry **himself** was not hurt.

RELATIVE PRONOUNS

| who | which | whose |
| whom | that | |

Relative pronouns are used to introduce subordinate clauses (see page 56).

EXAMPLES   The people **who** live there are on vacation.
            The copy **that** I read was from the library.
            Do you know that man **whose** car was stolen?

INTERROGATIVE PRONOUNS

who	which	whose
whom	what	

Interrogative pronouns are used in questions.

EXAMPLES **Who** lives in that house now?
What was the name of the book?

DEMONSTRATIVE PRONOUNS

this	these	that	those

Demonstrative pronouns are used to point out persons or things.

EXAMPLES **That** is the one.
This seems to be my lucky day.

MOST COMMONLY USED INDEFINITE PRONOUNS

all	each	most	other
another	either	neither	several
any	everybody	nobody	some
anybody	everyone	none	somebody
anyone	few	no one	someone
both	many	one	such

Pronouns that do not fall into the classifications above are called *indefinite pronouns*. Most indefinite pronouns express the idea of quantity: *all, few, none*.

EXAMPLES **All** of us are here.
Few of the cars were new.

● EXERCISE 1. Number your paper 1–7. After the number of each sentence, write in order the pronouns in the sentence.

1. Solving the traffic problems of a great city taxes the imagination of those who have the responsibility for it.
2. When they need new streets for through traffic, engineers sometimes construct them above existing streets.
3. Elevated highways like these are costly; they are also objectionable to merchants who have stores below them.

4. You hear the same objections that were raised against the elevated railways, which are now outmoded by subways and buses.
5. When the George Washington Bridge became too crowded, engineers showed us how resourceful they were by building a lower deck doubling its capacity.
6. Neither of my parents likes to drive downtown, but I myself am ready to drive Dad to work whenever he wants me to.
7. Father says anyone who enjoys driving under today's traffic conditions must be crazy; others, like me, think it is fun.

THE ADJECTIVE

1c. An *adjective* is a word used to modify a noun or a pronoun.

To modify means "to limit," or to make more definite the meaning of a word. Adjectives may modify nouns or pronouns in any one of three different ways.

1. By telling *what kind:*
   blue eyes, **large** city, **strong** wind

2. By pointing out *which one:*
   this man, **that** suggestion

3. By telling *how many:*
   several reasons, **ten** players

As the preceding examples show, the normal position of an adjective is directly before the word it modifies. Occasionally, for stylistic reasons, a writer may use adjectives after the word they modify.

EXAMPLE   The night, **cold** and **foggy**, drove us indoors.

A *predicate adjective* [1] (see page 31) is separated from the word it modifies by a verb.

---

[1] A predicate adjective is one kind of subject complement. The other kind is the predicate nominative.

EXAMPLES   Stephen is **capable.**
He looks **tall.**
The food tasted **good.**
His hand felt **cold.**

The Same Word as Adjective and Pronoun

A word may be used as more than one part of speech. This is especially true of the words in the list below, which may be used both as pronouns and as adjectives.

all	either	one	these
another	few	other	this
any	many	several	those
both	more	some	what
each	neither	that	which

ADJECTIVE   **Which** pen do you want?   [*Which* modifies the noun *pen*.]

PRONOUN   **Which** do you want?   [*Which* takes the place of a noun previously mentioned.]

ADJECTIVE   I like **this** picture.   [*This* modifies the noun *picture*.]

PRONOUN   I like **this.**   [*This* takes the place of a noun previously mentioned.]

Nouns Used as Adjectives

Nouns are sometimes used as adjectives.

barn dance   **dog** house
house paint   **table** tennis

When you are identifying parts of speech and you encounter a noun used as an adjective, label it an adjective.

● EXERCISE 2.   Some of the nouns, pronouns, and adjectives in the following sentences are italicized. For each sentence, list these words in order in a column, numbering as in the example. After each word, tell what part of speech it is. If a word is an adjective, write after it the word the adjective modifies.

1c

EXAMPLE   1. A *hobby* is something *you* like to do in your *spare*
time.
      1. *hobby*   n.
        you   pron.
        spare   adj. (*time*)

1. *Some* people take up a hobby because *it* is fun; *others* seek
in hobbies relief from the *tensions* of life.
2. In *this* complex culture of *ours*, *everyday* living imposes stresses
and strains *which* affect many people adversely.
3. A hobby offers *them* a release from strain and a chance to
share *enjoyment* and relaxation with *other* hobbyists.
4. In *their* hobbies Franklin Roosevelt and Dwight Eisenhower
found relaxation from the *arduous* responsibilities of the
Presidency.
5. President Roosevelt's hobbies were stamps and *ship* models;
President Eisenhower took up painting after *he* met Sir Winston Churchill, *who* was also a painter, during World War II.
6. *All* hobbies provide fun and relaxation, but *some* are also
educational.

THE VERB

**1d. A *verb* is a word that expresses action or
otherwise helps to make a statement.**

All verbs help to make a statement. Some help to make a
statement by expressing action. The action expressed may
be physical, as in the case of such verbs as *hit*, *play*, *blow*,
and *run*, or it may be mental, as in *think*, *know*, *imagine*,
believe.

Transitive and Intransitive Verbs

Action verbs may or may not take an *object*—a noun or
pronoun that completes the action by showing *who* or *what*
is affected by the action. Verbs that have an object are
called *transitive*. The verbs in the following examples are
transitive:

The catcher **dropped** the ball. [*Ball* is the object of *dropped*.]

The people **believed** the politician. [*Politician* is the object.]

The waiter **ignored** the customers. [*Customers* is the object.]

Verbs that can express action without objects are called *intransitive*.

The catcher **shrugged.**

The people **chuckled.**

The waiter **quit.**

Although some verbs are transitive only (*ignore, complete*) and some intransitive only (*arrive, sleep*), most verbs in English can be either.

EXAMPLES   The judges **explained** the contest rules. [transitive]

Patiently, the judges **explained.** [intransitive]

The contestants still **misunderstood** them. [transitive]

The contestants still **misunderstood.** [intransitive]

♦ NOTE   Most dictionaries group the meanings of verbs according to whether they are transitive (*v.t.* in most dictionaries) or intransitive (*v.i.*). Remembering the difference will help you to find readily the meaning you want.

Linking Verbs

Some intransitive verbs help to make a statement not by expressing action, but by expressing a state or condition. These verbs link to the subject a noun, pronoun, or adjective that describes or identifies it. They are called *linking verbs*. The word that is linked to the subject is called a *subject complement*.

EXAMPLES   The butler **is** the main suspect. [The subject complement *suspect* refers to the subject *butler*.]

This **is** he. [*He* refers to the subject *this*.]

He **looks** guilty. [*Guilty* refers to the subject *he*.]

The subject complement always refers to the subject of the linking verb. It may identify the subject, as in the first

1d

two examples, or describe the subject, as in the third one.

The most common linking verb is the verb *be*,[1] which has the following forms: *am, is, are, was, were, be, being, been* (and all verb phrases ending in *be, being,* or *been,* such as *can be, is being,* and *could have been*). Other common linking verbs are listed below.

COMMON LINKING VERBS

appear	grow	seem	stay
become	look	smell	taste
feel	remain	sound	

Many of the verbs in the preceding list can also be used as action verbs—that is, without a subject complement.

LINKING   The detectives **looked** puzzled.
ACTION   The detective **looked** for clues.

In general, a verb is a linking verb if you can substitute for it some form of the verb *seem*.

EXAMPLES   The detectives **looked** [seemed] puzzled.
            Everyone in the stadium **felt** [seemed] cold.
            All of the passengers **remained** [seemed] calm.

The Helping Verb and the Verb Phrase

A *verb phrase* is made up of a main verb and one or more *helping verbs*.[2] Helping verbs are so called because they help the main verb to express action or make a statement. The helping verbs in the following phrases are printed in bold-faced type:

has played	**will be** coming
should have paid	**must have been** injured

In other words, a verb phrase is a verb of more than one word.

---

[1] The verb *be* can also be followed by certain adverbs and adverb phrases: We were *there;* the men were *at work.* In this situation, *be* is not considered a linking verb.

[2] The helping verb is sometimes called an *auxiliary* verb.

COMMON HELPING VERBS

am	has	can (may) have
are	had	could (would, should) be
is	can	could (would, should) have
was	may	will (shall) have been
were	will (shall) be	might have
do	will (shall) have	might have been
did	has (had) been	must have
have	can (may) be	must have been

The parts of a verb phrase may be separated from one another by other words; i.e., the helping verb may be separated from the main verb.

EXAMPLES   **Did** you **hear** me call?
I **am** not **going** with you.
We **had** finally **completed** our work.

● EXERCISE 3.   List in order the verbs and verb phrases in the following sentences, placing before each the number of the sentence in which it appears. After each verb, tell whether it is transitive, intransitive, or (intransitive) linking. You may use abbreviations: *v.t.*, *v.i.*, or *l.v.* (linking verb). Be sure to list all words in a verb phrase.

1. The modern shopping center is a response to the migration to the suburbs that began after World War II and is continuing.
2. Although we have nearly seven thousand shopping centers in this country, many more are on the architects' drawing boards.
3. With art galleries, theaters, concerts, and festivals, the big shopping centers are also cultural centers.
4. A typical center contains acres of parking space and scores of stores where one can buy almost anything.
5. A whole town may rapidly develop around a new shopping center, and the center then becomes the downtown area of the community.
6. Because most shoppers are women, architects design the centers for them.

7. Parking spaces are ample, and the management offers baby-sitting service.
8. The variety of stores interests women shoppers who enjoy bargain hunting, but because most stores in a shopping center cater to people of the same income level, prices actually do not vary greatly.
9. Although the primary aim of shopping centers is convenience, they also provide recreation and entertainment.

THE ADVERB

1e. An *adverb* is a word used to modify a verb, an adjective, or another adverb.

The adverb is used most commonly as the modifier of a verb. It may tell *how*, *when*, *where*, or *to what extent* (how often or how much) the action of the verb is done.

EXAMPLES   He drives **carefully**.   [*Carefully* tells *how* he drives.]

He drives **early** and **late**.   [*Early* and *late* tell *when* he drives.]

He drives **everywhere**.   [*Everywhere* tells *where* he drives.]

She can **almost** drive.   [*Almost* tells *to what extent* she can drive.]

She drives **daily**.   [*Daily* tells *how often* she drives.]

An adverb may modify an adjective.

EXAMPLE   He is an **unusually** good driver.   [*Unusually* modifies the adjective *good*, telling how good or to what extent he is good at driving.]

An adverb may modify another adverb.

He behaved **very** well.   [The adverb *very* modifies the adverb *well*, telling how well.]

◆ NOTE   To avoid possible confusion, you should know that *not* is classified as an adverb. Because it is so commonly used, you may ignore it in doing the exercises on parts of speech.

Nouns Used as Adverbs

Some nouns may be used adverbially.

I called him **yesterday.**
He is leaving **tomorrow.**
We expect them **Monday.**

In identifying parts of speech, label nouns used in this way as adverbs.

● EXERCISE 4.   On your paper, list in order the adverbs in the following sentences, placing before each the number of the sentence in which it appears. After each adverb, write the word or words it modifies, and state whether the adverb tells how, when, where, or to what extent.

1. Dr. Simon, a chemist, spoke interestingly in assembly today, but he talked too long.
2. He described some recent advances in chemistry and boldly predicted some sensational results.
3. British biochemists recently announced that they will soon produce milk synthetically.
4. Scientists are working very hard here and abroad to learn more about man and nature.
5. Modern air travel depends heavily on scientific instruments that were completely unknown before 1940.
6. Although they can't change the weather very much, meteorologists can certainly predict it quite accurately.
7. Fog, which has always been a hazard to mariners, is now a hazard to aviators.
8. Once a plane landed safely in very heavy fog and then could not find its way to the passenger terminal.

● EXERCISE 5.   Copy in a column on your paper the numbered, italicized words in the following paragraphs. After each word, tell what part of speech it is; then after each adjective or adverb, tell what word or words it modifies.

Mr. Johnson's (1) *new* car is so (2) *long* that (3) *he* cannot get (4) *all* of (5) *it* into his garage. (6) *Someone* suggested (7) *once*

1e

that he (8) *buy* a (9) *smaller* car, but he (10) *had set* his (11) *heart* on (12) *this* (13) *model*, a (14) *very* impressive sedan with (15) *plenty* of status. (16) *This* is why (17) *you* (18) *always* see his (19) *overhead* (20) *garage* door lowered (21) *only* halfway. The tail of the big (22) *white* sedan (23) *protrudes* beneath the half-lowered door; the only (24) *time* Mr. Johnson can lock his garage is when the car is not (25) *there*.

(26) *Yesterday* masons and carpenters (27) *arrived* to correct the awkward (28) *situation* by extending the (29) *front* of the garage (30) *three* feet beyond its present position. When Mr. Johnson (31) *eventually* gets the bill for his garage, he may reflect (32) *sadly* upon the (33) *high* cost of status.

THE PREPOSITION

1f. A *preposition* is a word used to show the relation of a noun or pronoun to some other word in the sentence.

In the following sentences the prepositions are shown in bold-faced type. The words between which the prepositions show relationship are underscored.

I enjoy working **in** the laboratory more than listening **to** lectures.
The oriental rug **in** the hall is a Sarouk.
Grass will not grow **under** these trees.
Put your paper **on** my desk.
Both **of** us bought the same gift **for** you.

Object of a Preposition

A preposition always appears in a phrase, usually at the beginning (see page 36). The noun or pronoun at the end of a prepositional phrase is the *object* of the preposition that begins the phrase.

EXAMPLES   before **lunch**
in the **hall**

COMMONLY USED PREPOSITIONS

about	between	over
above	beyond	past
across	but (meaning "except")	since
after	by	through
against	concerning	throughout
along	down	to
amid	during	toward
among	except	under
around	for	underneath
at	from	until
before	in	unto
behind	into	up
below	like	upon
beneath	of	with
beside	off	within
besides	on	without

A group of words may act as a preposition: *on account of,*
in spite of.

● EXERCISE 6.   Write ten sentences each containing a different one of the following prepositions. Draw a line under
the phrase which each preposition introduces, and draw a
circle around the object of each preposition.

1. above	3. below	5. during	7. into	9. until
2. against	4. by	6. for	8. of	10. up

THE CONJUNCTION

**1g.   A *conjunction* is a word that joins words or
groups of words.**

In the following sentences the conjunctions are printed
in bold-faced type; the words or groups of words that the
conjunctions join are underscored.

Bring your <u>lunch</u> **and** one <u>dollar.</u>
You must <u>pass</u> every subject **and** <u>maintain</u> a good average.

1
f-g

We placed an ad, **but** no one responded.
I can use the truck **or** the jeep.
You can **either** stay here **or** come with us.
She invited both Martin **and** me.
I will let you know **when** I hear from him.
He succeeds **because** he works hard.

There are three kinds of conjunctions: *coordinating* conjunctions, *correlative* conjunctions, and *subordinating* conjunctions.

COORDINATING CONJUNCTIONS

and   but   or   nor   for

Correlative conjunctions are always used in pairs.

EXAMPLES   The work is **not only** profitable **but also** pleasant.
Do you know **whether** he is coming alone **or** with his parents?

CORRELATIVE CONJUNCTIONS

either . . . or   not only . . . but (also)
neither . . . nor   whether . . . or
both . . . and

Subordinating conjunctions are used to begin subordinate clauses (see page 63), usually adverb clauses.

In the following sentences the subordinate clauses are printed in bold-faced type, and the subordinating conjunctions that introduce them are underscored.

There is no use arguing, **since you have already made your decision.**
We stayed indoors **until the storm abated.**
You may stay **where you are.**

A subordinating conjunction need not come between the sentence parts that it joins. It may come at the beginning of the sentence.

Although speed is important, accuracy is more important.
When I take an examination, I become frightened.

COMMONLY USED SUBORDINATING CONJUNCTIONS [1]

after	before	provided	unless
although	how	since	until
as	if	than	when
as much as	in order that	that	where
because	inasmuch as	though	while

THE INTERJECTION

1h. An *interjection* **is a word that expresses emotion and has no grammatical relation to other words in the sentence.**

EXAMPLES   Oh!   My goodness!   Hurry!   Ah!   Ouch!   Alas!

THE SAME WORD AS DIFFERENT PARTS OF SPEECH

You have already learned that there are many words in English which can be used as more than one part of speech. For example, *these* may be an adjective (these books) or a pronoun (I want these); *blue* may be an adjective (the blue car) or a noun (Blue is my favorite color); *Tuesday* can be a noun (Tuesday is my birthday) or an adverb (Come Tuesday). There are thousands of words like these which can be classified by part of speech only when you see them in sentences.

EXAMPLES   The toy soldier was really made of **iron.** [*Iron* names a metal; it is a noun.]

We usually **iron** clothes on Tuesday.   [*Iron* expresses action; it is a verb.]

The **iron** gate clanged shut.   [*Iron* modifies *gate;* it is an adjective.]

[1] Some of these words may be used as prepositions: *after, before, since, until;* others may be used as adverbs: *how, when, where. That* is often used as a relative pronoun.

1h

● EXERCISE 7.   This is an exercise in identifying the same word when used as different parts of speech. Copy on your paper the italicized words in the following sentences. After each word, write what part of speech it is. Be prepared to explain your answers.

1. The manager likes to hear the *ring* of the cash registers as the salesgirls *ring* up their sales.
2. According to the *daily* schedule, the boat makes three trips *daily*.
3. She packed an especially large *box* to take to the *box* social.
4. Be sure to turn *right* at the *right* corner; our house is the first one on the *right*.
5. *That* shows you didn't read *that* explanation carefully.

Summary of Parts of Speech

RULE	PART OF SPEECH	USE	EXAMPLES
1a	noun	names	man, Iowa, corn, wealth
1b	pronoun	takes the place of a noun	you, we, himself, them
1c	adjective	modifies a noun or pronoun	red, large, two
1d	verb	shows action or helps to make a statement	is, does, have wanted
1e	adverb	modifies a verb, an adjective, or another adverb	rapidly, well, somewhat, too
1f	preposition	relates a noun or a pronoun to another word	into, below, from, of
1g	conjunction	joins words or groups of words	and, but, or, for, after, as, until
1h	interjection	shows strong feeling	ouch!

● REVIEW EXERCISE.   Copy in order in a column on your paper the italicized words in the following paragraphs. Consider carefully the use of each word, and write after it what part of speech it is.

(1) *Our* new neighbors, the Whartons, moved (2) *into* (3) *that* vacant house (4) *across* the street (5) *today.* I (6) *enjoyed* watching and helping (7)*whenever* I could. The (8) *enormous* moving van arrived (9) *about* eleven o'clock, followed (10) *closely* by Mr. and Mrs. Wharton, (11) *their* four children, (12) *and* their dog in a station wagon loaded above the windows.

(13) *Moving* is (14) *like* an exhibition exposing (15) *all* of your secrets to the public, for neighbors (16) *like* to gather (17) *around* and inspect each bed, table, chair, and lamp as the workmen carry (18) *it* into the house. (19) *Other* delivery trucks arrived. (20) *Soon* movers, delivery men, Mr. and Mrs. Wharton, the (21) *four* children, the dog, and (22) *others* were getting in one another's way as (23) *they* rushed into and out of the house. I (24) *offered* to help unload the (25) *wagon.* I wanted to do (26) *this* (27) *not only* (28) *because* I was feeling friendly (29) *but also* because I wanted to see what the Whartons were bringing with (30) *them.*

Mrs. Wharton became more and more (31) *distraught* as she directed the placing (32) *of* furniture and rugs, (33) *cautioned* the movers about marring the (34) *freshly* (35) *painted* walls, and tried (36) *vainly* to keep the children out of the way. The children (37) *barely* missed destruction a (38) *dozen* times. (39) *At* seven o'clock, as the evening was growing dark and the van was finally pulling away, I heard the youngest Wharton saying to his mother, (40) "*Hey*, Mom, why can't we go home now?"

The Parts of a Sentence

The Function of Subjects, Predicates, and Complements

In order to achieve an understanding of English sentences, you need terms to use in referring to the basic parts of the sentence. With only two terms—*subject* and *predicate*—you could begin to describe most sentences. After you had started, however, you would find out that you need to know the name and function of some other important sentence elements: *object, predicate nominative,* and *predicate adjective,* to name only the most important. You have encountered all of these terms in previous English classes. To find out how well you remember them, take the following diagnostic test to see which terms, if any, you need to review.

Diagnostic Test

From each of the following sentences, copy the subject, verb, and complement, if there is one. After each complement, tell what kind it is: indirect object (*i.o.*), direct object (*d.o.*), predicate nominative (*p.n.*), predicate adjective (*p.a.*).

EXAMPLE   1. His employers gave my father a bonus.
　　　　　　1. *employers, gave, father (i.o.), bonus (d.o.)*

1. Some of your classmates will succeed.
2. This experience taught me a valuable lesson.

3. Out of the darkness came a huge, lumbering creature.
4. To everyone's surprise, Jane and I were not late.
5. The water in the bay seemed very cold.
6. The only people in the water were the children.
7. This morning the mailman left this letter for you.
8. He gave me this one, too.
9. Mr. Munson is our most popular coach.
10. Mechanics had just assembled and checked all parts of the motor.

2a.   A *sentence* is a group of words expressing a complete thought.

SENTENCE   The importance of the minority party in American politics must be understood.

NOT A SENTENCE   The importance of the minority party in American politics . . .

SENTENCE   This third political party will appeal to the dissatisfied in both of the established parties.

NOT A SENTENCE   This third political party, appealing to the dissatisfied in both of the established parties . . .

SUBJECT AND PREDICATE

2b.   A sentence consists of two parts: the *subject* and the *predicate*. The *subject* of the sentence is that part about which something is being said. The *predicate* is that part which says something about the subject.

SUBJECT	PREDICATE
Faculty and students	planned a new class schedule.

PREDICATE	SUBJECT
At the end of the day comes	our activity period.

These two main parts of sentences may consist of single words or many words. The whole subject is called the *complete subject;* the whole predicate, the *complete predicate.*

2
a-b

However long a subject or predicate may be, it always has a core—an essential part.

The Simple Subject

2c. The *simple subject* is the principal word or group of words in the subject.

EXAMPLES   A large computing machine in constant use requires two hours of servicing every day. [subject: *A large computing machine in constant use;* simple subject: *machine*]

The University of North Carolina at Chapel Hill has a Univac computer. [subject: *The University of North Carolina at Chapel Hill;* simple subject: *University of North Carolina*]

◆   NOTE   Throughout this book the term *subject,* when used in connection with the sentence, refers to the simple subject; the term *verb* refers to the simple predicate.

The Simple Predicate, or Verb

2d. The principal word or group of words in the predicate is called the *simple predicate,* or the *verb.*

EXAMPLE   Faculty and students planned a new class schedule. [predicate: *planned a new class schedule;* simple predicate, or verb: *planned*]

Compound Subjects and Verbs

2e. A *compound subject* consists of two or more subjects that are joined by a conjunction and have the same verb. The usual connecting words are *and* and *or*.

EXAMPLE   The **White House** and the **Pentagon** denied the charges against them. [compound subject: *White House . . . Pentagon*]

2f. A *compound verb* consists of two or more verbs that have joined by a conjunction and have the same subject.

EXAMPLE   The assistant principal **handles** attendance and **enforces** discipline. [compound verb: *handles . . . enforces*]

How to Find the Subject of a Sentence

To find the subject of a sentence, first find the verb (the simple predicate); then ask yourself the question "Who or what . . .?" For instance, in the sentence "Outside the wall walked an armed guard," the verb is *walked*. Ask the question, "Who or what walked?" You find the answer to be *guard walked*. *Guard* is the subject of the sentence.

In addition to this simple formula for locating the subject, you should keep in mind the following facts:

1. In sentences expressing a command or a request, the subject is always *you*, even though the word *you* may not appear in the sentence.

(You) Stamp the envelopes before mailing them.
(You) Please run some errands for me.

2. The subject of a sentence is never in a prepositional phrase.

Neither of the rivals survived the duel.   [verb: *survived*.   Who survived? *Neither*.   *Neither* is the subject. *Rivals* is not the subject. It is in the phrase *of the rivals*.]

Knowledge of grammar is an aid to good writing.   [verb: *is*. What is? *Knowledge*.   *Knowledge* is the subject. *Grammar* is not the subject. It is in the phrase *of grammar*.]

3. To find the subject in a question, turn the question into statement form.

QUESTION   Into which drawer did you put the box of pencils?
STATEMENT   You did put the box of pencils into which drawer. [subject: *you;* verb: *did put*]

2
c-f

4. *There* or *here* is not usually the subject of a verb.

Except in a statement like rule 4, *there* and *here* are either adverbs or expletives.

Here is the book. [verb: *is;* subject: *book.* In this sentence the word *here* is an adverb telling where.]

There are arguments on both sides. [verb: *are;* subject: *arguments.* In this use *there* is called an *expletive*, a word used to get the sentence started. The word *it* may also be used as an expletive: *It* is useless to argue.]

● EXERCISE 1. Number your paper 1–20. Write after the proper number the subject and the verb in each sentence. Underline subjects once and verbs twice. Be careful to include all parts of compound subjects and verbs, as well as all words in a verb phrase.

1. This kind of argument is hard to answer.
2. In October the colorful foliage and scenic drives attract thousands to Vermont.
3. There are many good reasons for our policy.
4. At the cliff edge there came over me an urge to jump.
5. What were the British doing during Paul Revere's ride?
6. Rocket travel may supersede plane travel and render costly airline equipment obsolete.
7. Where have the years gone?
8. How ridiculous some of these suggestions are!
9. The largest ocean in the world is the Pacific.
10. Take your time and do your best.
11. College courses in many subjects are given on television.
12. Most of our professional basketball players played in college.
13. Almost all of the commonly misspelled words in English are simple, everyday terms.
14. What were the principal objections to the plan?
15. There will be plenty of time for club meetings after school.
16. In what part of Africa is the Congo?
17. From whom did most of this information come?
18. Into the thick of the brawl strode two state troopers.
19. With the wet weather came hordes of mosquitoes.
20. How many African nations are there?

COMPLEMENTS

Some sentences express a complete thought by means of a subject and verb only.

S V	S V
He thinks.	Everybody left.

Most sentences, however, have in the predicate one or more words that complete the meaning of the subject and verb. These completing words are called complements.

Frank caught	a large **tuna.**
She handed	**me** a **note.**
Jerry is	the class **president.**
The best ones are	**these.**
She seems	**happy.**
He called	**me lazy.**
Who appointed	**him chairman?**

◆NOTE   An adverb modifying the verb is not a complement. Only nouns, pronouns, and adjectives act as complements.

Mrs. Clark is **here.** [The adverb *here* modifies the verb *is.* It is not a complement.]

Mrs. Clark is a **teacher.** [The noun *teacher* is a complement.]

Mrs. Clark is **young.** [The adjective *young* is a complement.]

Direct and Indirect Objects

Complements that receive or are affected by the action of the verb are called *objects.* They are of two kinds: the *direct object* and the *indirect object.*

2g. The direct object of the verb receives the action of the verb or shows the result of the action. It answers the question "What?" or "Whom?" after an action verb.

I took **him** with me.   [I took *whom?*]

Jean has written her **composition.**   [Jean has written *what?*]

2g

Except when it ends in *–self* (*myself*, *himself*), the object of a verb never refers to the same person or thing as the subject.

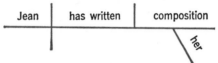

◆   NOTE   The diagrams are included as an aid to those students who have already studied diagraming. No attempt is made in this book to teach diagraming or to give practice in diagraming. However, a review explanation may be appropriate. On the main line the subject comes first, then a vertical line crossing the main line, then the verb. Between the verb and the direct object is a vertical line which does not cross the main line. Between the verb and a predicate adjective or a predicate nominative (see pages 31–32) is a similar line slanted to the left. The indirect object occupies a lower horizontal line joined to the verb by a slanted line. Single-word modifiers slant downward from the words they modify.

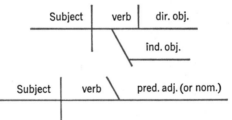

2h. The *indirect object* of the verb precedes the direct object and usually tells to whom or for whom the action of the verb is done.

If the word *to* or *for* is used, the noun or pronoun following it is part of a prepositional phrase; it is not an indirect object. Like subjects, objects of verbs are never part of a prepositional phrase.

Father promised **me** the car.   [*Me* is an indirect object.]
Father promised the car **to me.**   [*Me* is part of phrase *to me.*]

EXAMPLES He gave **us** his permission. [gave *to* us]

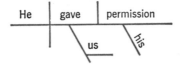

Bob made his **mother** a writing desk. [made *for* his mother]

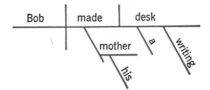

Objects of the verb may be compound.

Mrs. Spiers praised the stage **crew** and the **cast.**

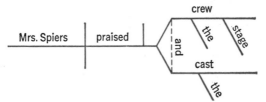

She gave **George** and **me** several suggestions.

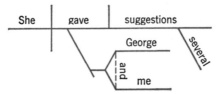

The Objective Complement

To complete their meaning, some action verbs require an additional complement following their objects. This additional complement is called an *objective complement* because it refers to the object; it may be a noun or an adjective.

21

They elected Mary **chairman.** [The noun *chairman* refers to the direct object *Mary* and helps to complete the meaning of the verb *elected*. It is an objective complement.]

You made her **angry.** [The adjective *angry* modifies the direct object *her* and helps to complete the meaning of the verb *made*. It is an objective complement.]

Only a few verbs meaning "make" or "consider" take an objective complement: *elect, appoint, name, choose, render, make, consider,* etc.

The dog licked the dish **clean.**   [*made* the dish clean]
The barber cut my hair **short.**   [*made* my hair short]
We thought the clown **funny.**   [*considered* the clown funny]

● EXERCISE 2.   Number your paper 1–10. Copy after the proper number the objects of the verb or verbs in each sentence. After each object, write *i.o.*, for indirect object, or *d.o.*, for direct object. If a sentence has no object, write *0* after the number on your paper.

1. Please leave a forwarding address with the postman.
2. Someone must have told her the story.
3. There was so much to do in a short time that we worked under great pressure.
4. The governor had promised the people a reduction in taxes.
5. The governor signed the new tax bill under protest.
6. Coach Sullivan used his second team throughout the game.
7. If you know any of the answers, tell them to me.
8. Mr. Green gave us a surprise test.
9. He remembered me very well, but he did not recognize Jim.
10. For my birthday, Joe bought me a box of candy.

Subject Complements

Complements that refer to (describe, explain, or identify) the subject are *subject complements*. There are two kinds: the *predicate nominative* and the *predicate adjective*.

Subject complements follow linking verbs only.[1]

2i. A *predicate nominative* is a noun or pronoun complement that refers to the same person or thing as the subject of the verb. It follows a linking verb.

New York is our largest **city.**   [*City* refers to the subject *New York*.]

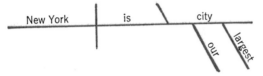

My best friends were **Agnes** and **she.**   [Compound predicate nominative; *Agnes* and *she* refer to the same persons as the subject *friends*.]

2j. A *predicate adjective* is an adjective complement that modifies the subject of the verb. It follows a linking verb.

This book is **dull.**   [The predicate adjective *dull* modifies the subject *book*.]

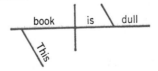

[1] The common linking verbs are the forms of the verb *be* (see page 12), and the following: *become, seem, grow, appear, look, feel, smell, taste, remain, sound, stay.*

2
i-j

His speech seemed **repetitious** and **tiresome.**   [compound predicate adjective modifying the subject *speech*]

In the normal order of an English sentence, complements follow the verb. However, a complement may precede the verb.

This futile **course** he finally abandoned.   [*Course* is the direct object of the verb *abandoned*.]

Happy and **healthy** was our life in the open.   [*Happy* and *healthy* are predicate adjectives modifying the subject *life*.]

● EXERCISE 3.   Number your paper 1–20. After the proper number, write the predicate nominatives or predicate adjectives in each of the following sentences; identify each with the abbreviation *p.n.* or *p.a.* Some sentences contain more than one complement.

1. Summer is my favorite season.
2. His speech before the committee seemed effective.
3. About noon the sky became dark and ominous.
4. The loss of his fortune was a fatal blow.
5. Before a match I always feel extremely nervous.
6. Pete has been an excellent captain.
7. A reliable worker he always was.
8. Some of the new regulations seem quite unfair.
9. Tall and handsome was the bridegroom.
10. It was Helen who appeared happy at the news.
11. The outcome of the election was uncertain for a long time, and both candidates nearly became nervous wrecks.
12. Although the teacher was absent, the class remained orderly.
13. You can be sure that your anonymous benefactor is either he or Mr. Graham.
14. If you had been ready, no one would have been late.
15. After she lost weight, Aunt Jo looked better and felt better.
16. In spite of many corrupting influences, he remained honest.
17. The ocean mist smelled fishy and tasted salty.
18. The older boys grew tall, but the youngest stayed short and fat.
19. If you were president, you would not be so dictatorial.
20. Shortly after graduating, he became a pilot.

Summary of Sentence Patterns

You have learned that every sentence has two basic parts—subject and predicate. Within the subject there is a simple subject, commonly called just the subject; within the predicate there is a simple predicate, commonly called the verb. The pattern of some sentences consists of subject and verb only.

$$\overset{\text{S}}{\text{Children}} \quad \overset{\text{V}}{\text{play.}}$$

Modifiers may be added to the subject and verb without changing the basic pattern of such a sentence.

$$\overset{\text{S}}{\text{Many children}} \text{ from this neighborhood } \overset{\text{V}}{\text{play}} \text{ in the park every day.}$$

You have learned also that certain additions to the predicate create other sentence patterns. These additions are complements, which complete the meaning begun by the subject and verb. The different kinds of complements produce the different sentence patterns. The seven common sentence patterns are

S	V		
Children	play.		

S	V	D.O.	
Children	play	games.	

S	V	I.O.	D.O.
He	gave	the children	toys.

S	V	D.O.	OBJ. COMP. (ADJ.)
This	made	the children	happy.

S	V	D.O.	OBJ. COMP. (NOUN)
They	made	him	director.

S	V	P.N.	
He	is	director.	

S	V	P.A.	
He	seems	competent.	

● REVIEW EXERCISE.   Number your paper 1–15. Write after the proper number the subject, the verb, and the complements in each sentence. After the complement, tell what kind it is, using abbreviations as follows: direct object, *d.o.;* indirect object, *i.o.;* predicate nominative, *p.n.;* predicate adjective, *p.a.*

1. O. Henry is the pseudonym of the American writer William Sydney Porter.
2. Although born in Greensboro, North Carolina, this author is most famous for his stories about New York City.
3. As a result of his frequent, long walks through the city streets, he knew all aspects of the rapidly growing metropolis.
4. Through his writing, he gave us a clear, if romantic, picture of the city in the early 1900's.
5. The *New York World* paid O. Henry one hundred dollars for each of his weekly stories.
6. Many of his characters were people in poor or modest circumstances.
7. In O. Henry's time, the population of New York City was four million.
8. O. Henry describes the troubles, hardships, and joys of the "four million" in his short stories.
9. The vivid description in his stories gives the reader a sympathetic understanding of the characters.
10. The typical O. Henry story is sentimental and full of stereotyped characters.
11. His best-known story is "The Gift of the Magi."
12. In "The Gift of the Magi," a young husband sells his prized watch, and his wife sells her beautiful long hair.
13. With the proceeds he buys her a set of combs for Christmas, and she buys him a fob for his watch.
14. The stories usually have a surprise ending.
15. In spite of their faults, they are interesting, and they re-create for us the New York of two generations ago.

CHAPTER 3

The Phrase

Kinds of Phrases and Their Functions

Words in a sentence act not only individually but also in groups. The grouped words act together as a unit which may function as a modifier, a subject, a verb, an object, or a predicate nominative. The most common group of related words is the phrase. In Chapter 1 you learned about the verb phrase, which is a verb of more than one word (*is coming, might have been*). This chapter provides a review of the makeup and function in the sentence of other kinds of phrases.

Diagnostic Test

To determine which parts of this chapter you need to study in your review of phrases, take the following two-part test.

A. Number your paper 1–6. Copy in order the ten prepositional phrases in the following sentences. After each phrase, tell whether it is an adjective or an adverb phrase.

1. Allen and I are in the same math class, but his assignment is different from mine.
2. When traffic in town is heavy, walking downtown is faster than driving the car.
3. When you confer with your guidance counselor, he will give you information about several colleges which are suitable for you.

4. Accepting his suggestions, I wrote immediately to several colleges in the Middle West.
5. The President, facing a difficult decision, called a meeting of the Security Council.
6. To raise your grades during the last quarter is more difficult than to maintain them all year.

B. Copy on your paper two participial phrases, two gerund phrases, and two infinitive phrases from the test sentences in Part A. Label each phrase and give before it the number of the sentence in which it appears.

3a. A *phrase* is a group of words not containing a verb and its subject. A phrase is used as a single part of speech.

Five kinds of phrases are explained on the following pages: *prepositional phrases, participial phrases, gerund phrases, infinitive phrases,* and *appositive phrases.*

THE PREPOSITIONAL PHRASE

3b. A *prepositional phrase* is a group of words beginning with a preposition and usually ending with a noun or pronoun.

for Peg and you	**in** the classroom
after the exam	**to** bed

The noun or pronoun that concludes the prepositional phrase is the object of the preposition that begins the phrase.

on the **steps**	from **Hazel** and **me**
with a **grin**	for **Jim** or **Mary**

Prepositional phrases are usually used as modifiers—as adjectives or adverbs. Occasionally, a prepositional phrase is used as a noun:

After dinner will be too late.   [The prepositional phrase is the subject of the sentence; it is used as a noun.]

The Adjective Phrase

3c. An *adjective phrase* is a prepositional phrase that modifies a noun or a pronoun.

Tucson has been the locale **of many Westerns.**

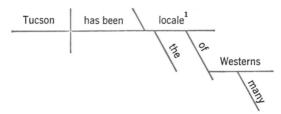

Tourists **from the East** visit the old frontier towns **in the West.**

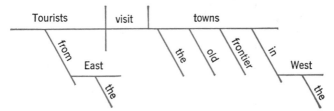

Many **of the tourists** like historical places.

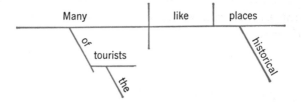

---

[1] In a diagram the preposition which begins the phrase is placed on a line slanting downward from the word the phrase modifies. The object of the preposition is placed on a horizontal line extending to the right from the line with the preposition. Single-word modifiers are diagramed in the usual way.

3
a-c

● EXERCISE 1.   Copy in a column the adjective phrases in the following sentences. Before each phrase, place the number of the sentence in which it appears. After each phrase, write the noun the phrase modifies.

1. Once inhabited by Indians and dreaded by pioneers, the deserts of the Southwest are now popular areas for business and recreation.
2. Caves beneath the rims of desert canyons were once the homes of small bands of Indians.
3. These lofty homes provided protection from enemies, but life in a cliff dwelling was hard and tedious.
4. The flatlands below the abandoned ruins were once irrigated by a system of canals.
5. A visit to the desert intrigues tourists from states without deserts.
6. Man's survival on the desert is a problem of the past now that he has impounded rivers to irrigate the land.
7. The desert is a thing of great beauty, especially under the glow of the setting sun.
8. A remarkable fact about the Southwestern desert region between Los Angeles and west Texas is the growing popularity of its climate.

The Adverb Phrase

3d. An *adverb phrase* is a prepositional phrase that modifies a verb, an adjective, or another adverb.

The following sentences show the ways in which an adverb phrase can modify a verb.

He practices **with diligence.**   [*how* he practices]
He practices **before a concert tour.**   [*when* he practices]
He practices **in his studio.**   [*where* he practices]
He practices **for weeks.**   [*to what extent* he practices]
He practices **for his own good.**   [*why* he practices]

See the diagram on the following page.

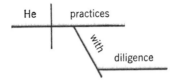

In the sentence below, the adverb phrase modifies an adjective.

He was true **to his word.**

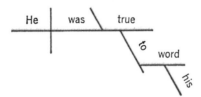

The following sentence illustrates an adverb phrase modifying an adverb.

He threw the ball far **to the left.**

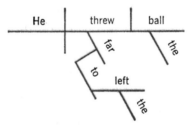

● EXERCISE 2. Number your paper 1–10. After the proper number, list the adverb phrases in each of the following sentences. After each phrase, write the word the phrase modifies.

1. After the concert everyone praised Gail for her performance.
2. At our school every student spends one period daily in study hall.
3. When you are flying above the clouds in bright sunshine, you forget that heavy rain may be falling on the ground below.

3d

4. Although Janet can sing like an opera star, she is lazy about her voice training.
5. Some students go far beyond the requirements of the assignment, but others are content with a minimum performance.
6. After we had been studying for several hours, we went into town for a pizza.
7. If people live on Mars, they must be quite different from us.
8. Overdosage of vitamin A may be harmful to the bone structure.
9. Charlie, the best pitcher in the league, eyed the pinch hitter with disdain.
10. When I talked with Howard before the meeting, he agreed to give us his support.

●EXERCISE 3.   Demonstrate your understanding of the way a prepositional phrase functions as an adjective or an adverb by using the following phrases, as indicated, in complete sentences.

EXAMPLE   1. with quiet pride   [Use as an adverb phrase.]
         1. *George spoke with quiet pride of his forty merit badges.*

1. in great haste   [Use as an adverb phrase.]
2. of surprising value   [Use as an adjective phrase.]
3. for his own good   [Use as an adverb phrase.]
4. without actually cheating   [Use as an adverb phrase.]
5. with a generous nature   [Use as an adjective phrase.]
6. of unexpected courage   [Use as an adjective phrase.]
7. to success   [Use as an adjective phrase.]
8. by fair means or foul   [Use as an adverb phrase.]
9. of the joke   [Use as an adjective phrase.]
10. after another disappointment   [Use as an adverb phrase.]

PHRASES CONTAINING VERBALS

Less common than the prepositional phrase but still very useful to a writer are the verbal phrases: the *participial phrase*, the *gerund phrase*, and the *infinitive phrase*. They are called verbal phrases because the most important word in them is a verbal. Verbals are so called because they are formed from verbs. In some respects they act like verbs. They may express action; they may have modifiers; and they may be followed by complements. In one important respect, however, they are not like verbs: verbals are not used as verbs in a sentence. They are used as other parts of speech —as nouns, as adjectives, or as adverbs.

Before you can understand verbal phrases, you must understand the verbals on which the phrases are based. On the following pages you will find an explanation of each kind of verbal, followed by a discussion of the verbal as it is most commonly used—in a phrase.

The Participle and the Participial Phrase

3e. A *participle* is a verb form that is used as an adjective.

The rapidly **developing** storm kept small boats in port.
Developing rapidly, the storm kept small boats in port.
The storm, **developing** rapidly, kept small boats in port.

In these sentences, *developing*, which is formed from the verb *develop*, is used as an adjective, modifying the noun *storm*.

In the following sentence the participle *crying*, which is formed from the verb *cry*, is used as an adjective, modifying the pronoun *her*.

I found her **crying.**

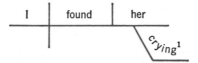

There are two kinds of participles: *present participles* and *past participles*. A present participle, like those in the pre-

---

[1] In a diagram the participle is written on a bent line drawn downward from the word the participle modifies.

3e

ceding examples, ends in *–ing.* A past participle may end in *–ed, –d, –t, –en,* or *–n:* ask*ed,* sav*ed,* deal*t,* eat*en,* see*n.*

PRESENT PARTICIPLE He heard his sons **arguing.**
PAST PARTICIPLE   The boys, **angered,** began to fight.

Although participles are formed from verbs, they are not used alone as verbs. A participle may, however, be used with a helping verb to form a verb phrase.

PARTICIPLE   The **moving** car gathered speed rapidly. [*Moving* modifies *car.*]
VERB PHRASE   The car **was moving** rapidly. [The verb phrase *was moving* consists of the helping verb *was* plus the present participle *moving.*]

When participles are used in verb phrases, they are considered part of the verb and are not considered adjectives.

3f. A *participial phrase* is a phrase containing a participle and any complements or modifiers it may have.[1]

Removing his coat, Jack rushed to the river bank. [The participial phrase is made up of the participle *removing* and the complement *coat,* which is the direct object of *removing.* Like verbs, participles may take an object.]

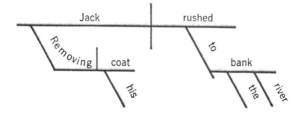

[1] For work on the participial phrase as a sentence fragment, see page 199. For exercises on the dangling participle, see pages 233–35.

Hesitating there for a moment, he quickly grasped the situation. [The participial phrase is made up of the participle *hesitating* plus its modifiers—the adverb *there* and the adverb phrase *for a moment*.]

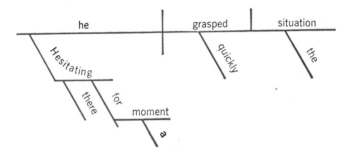

The participle usually introduces the phrase, and the entire phrase acts as an adjective to modify a noun or pronoun.

Sid, **watching the Late Show,** fell asleep.

Getting up at five, we got an early start.

Destroyed by fire, the church was never rebuilt.

● EXERCISE 4.   List on your paper the participial phrases in the following sentences. Be sure to include all complements and modifiers. Before each phrase, write the number of the sentence in which it appears. After each phrase, write the word the phrase modifies.

1. High school graduates replying to a questionnaire about their college courses often mention freshman English as the course giving them the most trouble.
2. Facing college standards, the graduates realize that they did not work hard enough on the themes assigned in high school.
3. Statistics reported by the National Education Association revealed that seventy percent of American colleges offer remedial English classes emphasizing composition.

3f

4. Handicapped by their writing deficiencies, graduates seeking employment or advancement in their vocations are often denied desirable opportunities.
5. Recognizing the importance of practice, teachers of composition, imitating the athletic coach, conduct regular practice sessions.

● EXERCISE 5.   For each of the following sentences, copy in order on your paper the phrases which are numbered and italicized. Place each phrase on a separate line, and number it. After each phrase, write the word it modifies, and tell whether it is a *participial* phrase, an *adjective* prepositional phrase, or an *adverb* prepositional phrase. Do not list separately the prepositional phrases within a larger italicized phrase.

EXAMPLE   (1) *Gathering my courage,* I mentioned (2) *to my father* my need (3) *for a car.*

     1. *gathering my courage, I, participial*
     2. *to my father, mentioned, adverb*
     3. *for a car, need, adjective*

a. (1) *Being an Army officer,* Karen's father was frequently transferred (2) *to different posts,* and so Karen attended schools (3) *of many kinds.*
b. (4) *By 1975* one half of the students (5) *attending college* will be (6) *in junior colleges.*
c. Ambitious persons (7) *struggling for success* usually equate success (8) *with either wealth or prestige.*
d. Of the 20,000 new books (9) *published annually in this country,* only twenty percent are books (10) *of fiction.*
e. The public (11) *of today,* (12) *interested primarily in biography and current affairs,* buys fewer novels than people bought (13) *in the past.*
f. (14) *Persuaded by her husband,* Mrs. Sears, (15) *showing perhaps more bravery* than wisdom, invited thirty boys and girls (16) *to a party* which she gave (17) *for her daughter.*
g. (18) *Left in charge of the class,* a student, (19) *receiving good cooperation from his classmates,* taught an excellent lesson.

h. The trip to Canterbury (20) *taken by Chaucer's pilgrims* was a religious pilgrimage (21) *made customarily in the spring.*

i. (22) *Lacking sufficient time*, we could not prepare a special election issue (23) *of the school paper.*

j. A student must know not only the colleges (24) *having the desired courses* but also the colleges (25) *accepting students with his qualifications.*

The Gerund and the Gerund Phrase

3g. A *gerund* is a verb form ending in –*ing* that is used as a noun.

Traveling is fun. [*Traveling* is formed from the verb *travel* and, as the subject of the sentence, is used as a noun.]

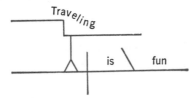

A gerund is a verbal noun. It may be used in any way that a noun may be used.

Good writing comes from much practice. [gerund used as subject]

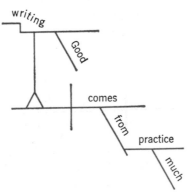

3g

They do not appreciate my **singing**.   [gerund used as object of verb]

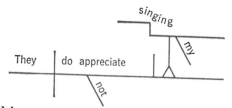

By **studying**, you can pass the course.   [gerund used as object of a preposition]

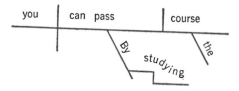

3h.   A *gerund phrase* is a phrase consisting of a gerund and any complements or modifiers it may have.

Finding a needle in a haystack is a traditional example of the impossible.   [The gerund *finding* has *needle* as its direct object and is modified by the adverb phrase *in a haystack*.]

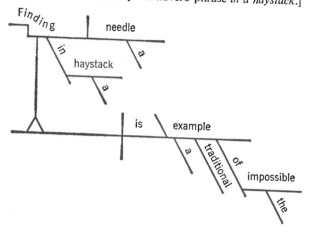

Like the gerund alone, the gerund phrase may be used in any place that a noun would fit:

Telling your father was a mistake. [gerund phrase as subject]

The college advises **sending applications early.** [gerund phrase as object]

He won the game by **kicking a field goal.** [gerund phrase as object of preposition]

Her most important achievement was **winning the national championship.** [gerund phrase as predicate nominative]

The Infinitive and the Infinitive Phrase

3i. An *infinitive* is a verb form, usually preceded by *to*, that is used as a noun or a modifier.

to go   to speak   to believe   to be

An infinitive is generally used as a noun, but it may also be used as an adjective or an adverb.
The infinitive used as a noun:

To wait for the bus is tiresome. [infinitive as subject]

Everyone wanted **to go.** [infinitive as object of the verb]

His ambition is **to fly.** [infinitive as predicate nominative]

The infinitive used as an adjective:

He lacked the strength **to resist.** [infinitive modifies *strength*]

The infinitive used as an adverb:

We study **to learn.** [infinitive modifies the verb *study*]

◆ NOTE Do not confuse the infinitive, a verbal of which *to* is a part, with a prepositional phrase beginning with *to*, which consists of *to* plus a noun or pronoun.

INFINITIVES	PREPOSITIONAL PHRASES
to fly	to him
to draw	to school

3
h-

The word *to*, called the sign of the infinitive, is sometimes omitted.

He made me [to] **leave.**
Help me [to] **do** my homework.

3j. An *infinitive phrase* consists of an infinitive and any complements or modifiers it may have.[1]

We intend **to leave early.**   [*Early* is an adverb modifying the infinitive *to leave.*]

I have a paper **to write before class.**   [*Before class* modifies *to write.*]

No one wants **to help us.**   [*Us* is the object of *to help.*]

Like infinitives alone, infinitive phrases can be used as nouns or as modifiers:

We tried **to reason with him.**   [The infinitive phrase *to reason with him* is the object of the verb *tried.*]

To save money became his obsession.   [*To save money* is the subject of the sentence.]

There must be a way **to solve this problem.**   [The infinitive phrase modifies the noun *way.*]

I am too busy **to go to the movies tonight.**   [The infinitive phrase modifies the adjective *busy.*]

His plan is **to go to college for two years.**   [The infinitive phrase is a predicate nominative, referring back to *plan.*]

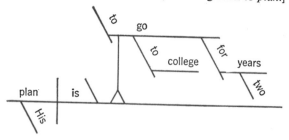

---

[1] For exercises on the use of the infinitive phrase to reduce wordiness, see pages 258–65.

The Infinitive Clause

Unlike other verbals, an infinitive may have a subject as well as complements and modifiers.

I expected **John to vote for me.** [*John* is the subject of the infinitive *to vote*.]

I asked **him to help me.** [*Him* is the subject of the infinitive *to help*.]

I believe **it to be John.** [*It* is the subject of the infinitive *to be*, and *John* is a predicate nominative referring back to *it*.]

I believe **it to be good.** [*It* is the subject of the infinitive *to be*, and the adjective *good* is a predicate adjective referring back to *it*.]

When an infinitive has a subject, as in the preceding examples, the construction is called an *infinitive clause*. Notice that the subject of an infinitive is in the objective case.[1]

● REVIEW EXERCISE A. Number your paper 1–20. In the following sentences most prepositional, participial, gerund, and infinitive phrases are numbered and italicized. Study the entire phrase, and after the corresponding number on your paper, tell what kind of phrase it is. In the case of a prepositional phrase, tell whether it is an adjective phrase or an adverb phrase.

a. (1) *Writing fiction* requires different talents from (2) *writing nonfiction.*
b. (3) *Watching the crowds*, I was impressed (4) *by the similarity* (5) *between people and cattle.*
c. Although few people really want (6) *to be leaders* themselves, nearly all people enjoy (7) *criticizing their leaders.*
d. Overconfidence which comes from (8) *underestimating one's opponents* is the cause (9) *of many unexpected defeats.*
e. (10) *Speaking to a citizens' committee*, Mayor Wilson explained that municipal costs are met primarily (11) *by taxes* (12) *on real property.*

[1] For rules concerning the use of the objective case, see pages 108–12.

3j

f. (13) *Realizing they have more* (14) *to take into account* than village taxes, residents are interested (15) *in county, state, and school tax levies* (16) *on their homes.*

g. (17) *Designed with the most modern devices,* the new incinerator, which will be completed (18) *in the spring,* will use heat (19) *from burning waste* (20) *to heat the building.*

THE APPOSITIVE [1]

3k. An *appositive* is a noun or pronoun — often with modifiers — set beside another noun or pronoun to explain or identify it.

Your friend **Bill** is in trouble.

The *Daily News,* a **tabloid,** has the largest circulation in the city.

An *appositive phrase* is a phrase consisting of an appositive and its modifiers.

My brother's car, **a sporty red convertible with bucket seats,** is the envy of my friends.

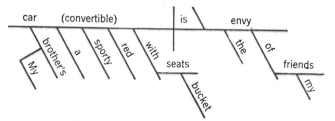

An appositive phrase usually follows the word it explains or identifies, but it may precede it.

A beautiful **collie,** Skip was my favorite dog.

● REVIEW EXERCISE B.   Number your paper 1–25. In the following sentences most of the phrases have been numbered and italicized. Write after its number on your paper the

---

[1] For rules on the punctuation of appositives, see page 636. For the use of the appositive in subordination of ideas, see page 219.

The Adjective Clause

Like a phrase, a subordinate clause acts as a single part of speech—as an adjective or an adverb or a noun.

4b. An *adjective clause* is a subordinate clause that, like an adjective, modifies a noun or a pronoun.

EXAMPLES   The house **where he was born** has been made a national shrine.

He is one **who earned his honors.**

This composition, **which I wrote last year,** received a grade of *C*.

Since a subordinate clause, like a sentence, has a verb and a subject and may contain complements and modifiers, it is diagramed very much like a sentence. Adjective and adverb clauses are placed on a horizontal line below the main line. An adjective clause begun by a relative pronoun is joined to the word it modifies by a slanting dotted line drawn from the modified word to the relative pronoun.

EXAMPLES   Students **whose work represents their second-best** are not real students.   [The subordinate clause *whose work represents their second-best* modifies the noun *students.*]

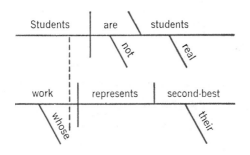

4b

Bob spent on an old car all the money **that he had earned during the summer.**   [The subordinate clause *that he had earned during the summer* modifies the noun *money.*]

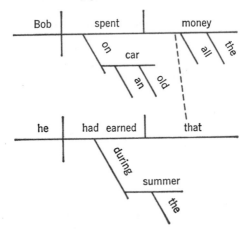

Relative Pronouns

Adjective clauses often begin with the pronouns *who, whom, which,* or *that.* These pronouns refer to, or are *related* to, a noun or pronoun that has come before.

4c. A *relative pronoun* is a pronoun that begins a subordinate adjective clause and is related to a noun or a pronoun already mentioned or understood. The word to which the relative pronoun is related is its *antecedent.*

A relative pronoun does three things.

1. It refers to a preceding noun or pronoun:

Tebbetts is a man **whom** we can trust.

The joke was one **that** I had heard before.

2. It connects its clause with the rest of the sentence:

I don't admire anyone **who acts like that.**   [The subordinate clause is joined to the independent clause by the relative pronoun *who*.]

You need a watch **that keeps time.**   [The subordinate clause is joined to the independent clause by the relative pronoun *that*.]

3. It performs a function within its own clause by serving as the subject, object, etc., of the subordinate clause:

The principal appointed George, **who is a reliable student.** [*Who* is the subject of the verb *is* in the adjective clause *who is a reliable student*.]

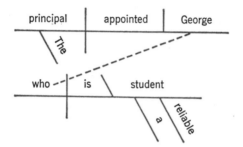

These are the assignments **for which you are responsible.** [*Which* is the object of the preposition *for*.] [1]

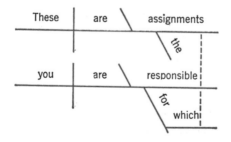

---

[1] In this sentence two words—*for* and *which*—begin the clause. Other two-word combinations of a preposition and a relative pronoun to begin a clause are *in which, by whom, for whom, from whom,* etc.

4c

Show me the book **that** you read. [*That* is the object of the verb *read* (read *what?*)]

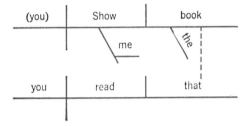

An adjective clause may also begin with the relative adjective *whose* or with the relative adverb *where* or *when*.

He is a coach **whose record has been amazing.** [*Whose,* the possessive form of the relative pronoun *who,* functions as an adjective modifying *record.*]

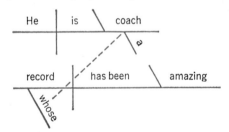

Do you remember the restaurant **where we ate lunch?** [*Where* acts as an adverb modifying *ate,* the verb in the clause. The antecedent is *restaurant.*]

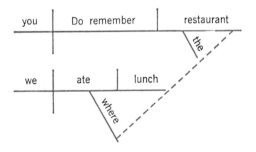

●EXERCISE 2.   Copy in order on your paper the adjective clauses in the following sentences. After each clause, write the noun or pronoun that the clause modifies. Your teacher may ask you to indicate whether the word which begins the clause is used as a subject, an object of a verb, an object of a preposition, or a modifier.

1. There are people who enjoy this kind of humor.
2. That was the moment when he made his great mistake.
3. At the record store there is a new jazz album that I want for my birthday.
4. We appreciate your order, which exceeded our expectations.
5. Send us a list of the people whom you would recommend.
6. It is sometimes good to meet people whose opinions differ from yours.
7. Write an essay about the character who interests you most.
8. There are books that you can read rapidly and others on which you must concentrate.
9. The skirt that I ordered from Hanley's was mailed by mistake to my father, who was very much surprised.
10. Bruce owns several old guns for which he paid very little.
11. Mr. McCauley's book, which appeared twenty years ago, is still the best book that has been published on its subject.
12. It was an experience that I did not enjoy and one that I shall never forget.
13. Our library, which contains ten thousand volumes, can provide material on almost any subject that you want.
14. A friend whose loyalty shifts frequently is not one whom you trust.

The Noun Clause

4d. **A *noun clause* is a subordinate clause used as a noun.**

In diagraming, a noun clause is pictured as a unit by being placed at the top of a vertical line, that rises from the part of the diagram (subject, object, predicate nominative) to which the clause belongs.

4 (

EXAMPLE **Whoever wins the election** will have many problems.

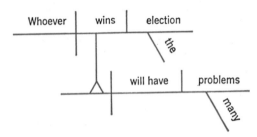

The entire noun clause *whoever wins the election* is the subject of the verb *will have*. Study the following pairs of sentences to see how a noun clause functioning in the same way that a noun functions may be a predicate nominative, an object of a verb, or an object of a preposition.

> This is his **job.** [*Job* is a noun used as a predicate nominative after the linking verb *is*.]
>
> This is **what he does.** [*What he does* is a noun clause used as a predicate nominative.]
>
> Do you know the **score?** [*Score* is a noun used as the object of the verb *do know*.]
>
> Do you know **what the score is?** [*What the score is* is a noun clause used as an object of a verb.]
>
> Here is a copy of my **speech.** [*Speech* is a noun used as the object of the preposition *of*.]
>
> Here is a copy of **what I said.** [*What I said* is a noun clause used as an object of a preposition.]

A noun clause may begin with an indefinite relative pronoun—*that, what, whatever, who, which, whoever, whichever.* Unlike a (definite) relative pronoun, an indefinite relative pronoun does not have an antecedent in its sentence.

EXAMPLE He told me **what he wanted.**

A noun clause may also begin with an indefinite relative

adjective—*whose, which, whatever*—or an indefinite relative adverb—*where, when, how*, etc.

I know <u>**whose**</u> **car this is.**

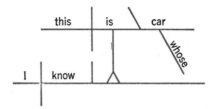

I know <u>**where**</u> **she went.**

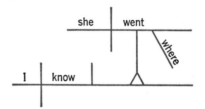

♦ NOTE Adjective and noun clauses are sometimes used without an introductory word. Note that the introductory word is omitted in the second sentence in each of the following pairs.

I found a friend **whom I could trust.**
I found a friend **I could trust.**

She says **that I am right.**
She says **I am right.**

● EXERCISE 3. List in order on your paper the subordinate clauses in the following sentences. Before each clause, place the number of the sentence in which it appears. After each clause, tell what kind it is—adjective or noun. Be prepared to tell what word each adjective clause modifies and how each noun clause is used in the sentence—as a subject, an object of a verb or of a preposition, or a predicate nominative.

1. The processes that are explained in the text are hard to understand.
2. Ask someone who knows Bill what he looks like.
3. Whatever you say will be recorded on the tape recorder that is on the table.
4. This is the prize that I chose, but that is what Jerry chose.
5. No one who attended the meeting objected to what I said.
6. Whoever talks during the final examination will be asked to leave.
7. The glare of light in the fieldhouse where we played was what affected our scoring.
8. Remember how you came, and you will know by which route you should return.
9. Someone asked us when we were leaving, but we did not tell him what he wanted to know.
10. I could not tell whose voice spoke the words that I heard.
11. We agreed with what he said, but we objected to the manner in which he said it.

The Adverb Clause

4e. An *adverb clause* is a subordinate clause that, like an adverb, modifies a verb, an adjective, or an adverb.

In the following examples each adverb clause illustrates one of the typical adverbial functions of telling *how, when, where, why, to what extent,* or *under what conditions.*

He plays golf **as though he were in a hurry.**   [*how* he plays]

He plays golf **whenever he can.**   [*when* he plays]

He plays golf **wherever he travels.**   [*where* he plays]

He plays golf **because he enjoys it.**   [*why* he plays]

He plays golf more **than I do.**   [*how much* more]

He plays golf **if the weather permits.**   [*under what conditions* he plays]

In diagraming, an adverb clause is written on a horizontal line below the main line of the diagram. The subordinating conjunction beginning the clause is written on a slanting dotted line which links the verb of the clause to the word the clause modifies.

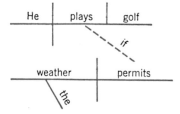

Adverb clauses may also modify adjectives and other adverbs.

> He is confident **that he will win.** [The adverb clause *that he will win* modifies the adjective *confident.*]
>
> He played better **than I did.** [The adverb clause *than I did* modifies the adverb *better.*]

The Subordinating Conjunction

Adverb clauses often begin with a word like *after, because,* or *when* that expresses the relation between the clause and the rest of the sentence.

4f. **A conjunction that begins an adverb clause is called a subordinating conjunction. It joins the clause to the rest of the sentence.**

The following words are subordinating conjunctions.

COMMON SUBORDINATING CONJUNCTIONS [1]

after	because	so that	whenever
although	before	than	where
as	if	though	wherever
as if	in order that	unless	whether
as long as	provided that	until	while
as though	since	when	

[1] Many of these words may also be used as other parts of speech.

4
e-f

The Elliptical (Incomplete) Clause

Sometimes in our writing and speaking, we do not complete the adverb clauses we use.

EXAMPLES   I am stronger than you [are].

While [I was] waiting for the dentist, I read a magazine.

In these adverb clauses the part of the clause given in brackets has been omitted. The missing part, however, could be readily supplied. Such incomplete clauses are said to be "elliptical." [1]

● EXERCISE 4.   Copy on your paper the adverb clauses in the following sentences. Before each clause, write the number of the sentence in which it appears. Draw a line under the subordinating conjunction that introduces the clause. After each clause, write what the clause tells: *how, when, where, why, to what extent, under what conditions.*

1. The entire audience rose in acclaim as the final curtain fell.
2. When Mason had discovered the true murderer, the State's principal suspect went free.
3. Whenever he traveled, Morgan collected works of art as though he had an unlimited amount of money to spend.
4. Since the Lions had had a poor season, the Indians mistakenly expected them to be weaker than they really were.
5. Because Marcia's family rented a car in Europe, they were able to travel farther than we did.
6. If you take my advice, you will read the preface before you read the book.
7. So that military discipline can be maintained, a soldier must go wherever the army sends him.
8. As long as magazines attract a large audience, national advertisers will support them.

---

[1] The definition of *ellipsis*, as applied to grammar, is an omission of one or more words, obviously understood, but necessary to make the expression grammatically complete. For the correct usage of pronouns in elliptical clauses, see page 118.

9. Because strikers and employers were equally determined, the dispute could not be settled until the hardships suffered by both had become unbearable.

10. If homework were abolished, parents would complain, because they think that children waste their time when they have no work to do.

● REVIEW EXERCISE. Each of the following sentences contains one or more subordinate clauses. Copy the clauses in order on your paper. Before each, write the number of the sentence in which it appears. After each, write what kind it is—adjective, noun, adverb.

1. When you drive a car, you must carry liability insurance, which pays for any damage or injury that you may inflict on others.

2. Insurance in some places is cheaper than it is in others.

3. How much insurance costs depends on how congested traffic is in the area.

4. If you live in a rural community, you probably pay much less than you would if you did most of your driving in or near a city.

5. An unmarried male who is under twenty-five pays the highest premium because statistics show that he is the worst risk.

6. Drivers who have a record of accidents must also pay a high premium since they have cost their insurance companies a great deal of money.

7. Although bad risks pay more, this does not necessarily mean that good risks pay proportionately less.

8. Insurance companies divide accidents into two categories: those that happen because of unforeseeable events and those that are made to happen.

9. When a tire blows out while you are driving in heavy traffic, the resulting accident is classed as unforeseeable.

10. If a driver passes another car on a turn, the resulting accident is one that was made to happen.

11. What is most alarming about our accidents is that four fifths of them are made to happen.

12. Insurance is costly for all of us because so many drivers make accidents happen.

SENTENCES CLASSIFIED BY STRUCTURE

4g. Classified according to their structure, there are four kinds of sentences: *simple, compound, complex,* and *compound-complex.*

(1) A *simple sentence* is a sentence with one independent clause and no subordinate clauses.

Great literature stirs the imagination.

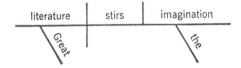

(2) A *compound sentence* is a sentence composed of two or more independent clauses but no subordinate clauses.

Great literature stirs the imagination, and it challenges the intellect.

Great literature stirs the imagination; moreover, it challenges the intellect.

♦ NOTE   Do not confuse the compound predicate of a simple sentence with the two subjects and two verbs of a compound sentence.

Study the following diagrams.

Great literature **stirs** the imagination and **challenges** the intellect.   [simple sentence with compound predicate]

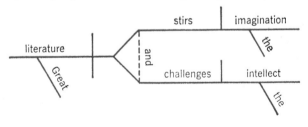

Great **literature stirs** the imagination, and **it challenges** the intellect. [compound sentence with two subjects and two verbs]

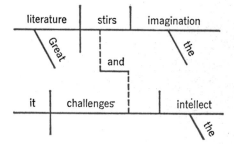

Independent clauses may be joined by coordinating conjunctions:

and   but   nor   or   for   yet

or by conjunctive adverbs:

also	furthermore	nevertheless	therefore
besides	however	otherwise	thus
consequently	moreover	then	still [1]

(3) A *complex sentence* is a sentence that contains one independent clause and one or more subordinate clauses.

Great literature, which stirs the imagination, also challenges the intellect.

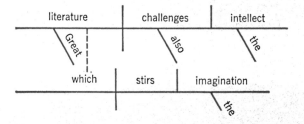

[1] For rules concerning the punctuation of compound sentences, see pages 628 and 645.

4 g

(4) A *compound-complex sentence* is a sentence that contains two or more independent clauses and one or more subordinate clauses.

Great literature, which challenges the intellect, is sometimes difficult, but it is also rewarding. [The independent clauses are *Great literature is sometimes difficult* and *it is also rewarding.* The subordinate clause is *which challenges the intellect.*]

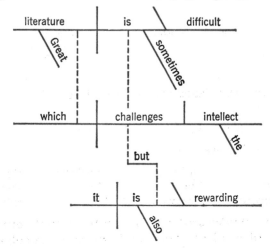

SENTENCES CLASSIFIED BY PURPOSE

4h. Classified according to their purpose, there are four kinds of sentences: *declarative*, *imperative*, *interrogative*, and *exclamatory*.

(1) A *declarative sentence* is a sentence that makes a statement.

In 1945 the United Nations had fifty-one members.

(2) An *imperative sentence* is a sentence that gives a command or makes a request.

Stop talking and open your books.
Please write to me.

(3) An *interrogative sentence* is a sentence that asks a question.

Which book did you like most?

(4) An *exclamatory sentence* is a sentence that expresses strong feeling.

How beautiful it is!

● EXERCISE 5.   After the proper number, classify each of the following sentences in two ways: (1) according to its structure and (2) according to its purpose.

EXAMPLE   1. Let me have your order tomorrow if you can.
   1. *complex*   *imperative*

1. According to the dictionary, the word *speliology* is formed from a Greek word meaning "cave" and the suffix *–logy*, meaning "study of" or "science of."
2. Speliology, which, then, is the scientific study of caves, is the pursuit of the National Speliological Society, which sponsors exploration of caves.
3. If a scientific explorer of caves is a speliologist, what do we call the many amateurs for whom cave exploration is just an exciting hobby?
4. These men, whose primary interest is adventure, are called *spelunkers*, and this word is derived from *spelunca*, the Latin word for cave.
5. Read a book on spelunking and enjoy vicariously some of the excitement of underground exploration.
6. Did you know that the techniques and equipment used by spelunkers are similar to those used by mountain climbers?
7. In limestone ice caves, where water seeps through ceilings and walls, surfaces are glazed and very slippery.
8. How perilous an adventure such a cave offers!
9. In the eight hundred feet of explored passages in Wyoming's Fossil Mountain Ice Cave, the temperature is 30 degrees.
10. Dripping water is transformed into sparkling icicles and columns of ice, and where water drops have splashed and frozen, the floor glitters as if it were covered with diamonds.

PART TWO

Usage

Levels of Usage

Because we are members of a civilized society, there are a number of matters we do not decide independently for ourselves. Instead, we more or less willingly comply with social conventions—customary ways in which things are done. The clothing we wear involves one such set of conventions; our notion of manners involves another. This chapter is about the conventions that govern our use of language. But before we come to language customs, let's consider the more obvious and familiar conventions that govern the way we dress.

Although everyone knows the expression "clothes make the man," few really believe it. We like to think that we can recognize the qualities we admire in a person whether he is wearing coveralls or a business suit. Yet we cannot truthfully say that a person's clothes make no impression at all on us. We may not pay particular attention to what a person wears as long as his clothes are more or less what we would expect him to be wearing under the circumstances. We expect to see bathing suits at the beach and suits and party dresses at a dance. We would be quite startled to see on the dance floor the costume that is right for the beach, and vice versa. In other words, it is only when clothing is obviously inappropriate that we are likely to form unfavorable impressions of the wearer.

APPROPRIATE LANGUAGE

It is much the same with the language a person uses. As long as it is appropriate to the situation, we do not pay special attention to the way in which people form their sentences or to the words they choose. Instead we concentrate on what they have to say to us. However, when a person's use of language strikes us as unsuitable for the situation, we are likely to become distracted from what he is saying and begin to think mainly about how he is saying it. Language that calls attention to itself gets in the way of communication instead of making communication easier.

The words you use and the way you put them together convey other messages besides the ideas you are talking about. If you speak to someone in a stiffly formal way, you are likely to give the impression of being standoffish, whether you mean to or not. On the other hand, if you speak as casually in an interview with a prospective employer or the admissions officer of a college as you do in conversation with your friends, you may create an impression of immaturity or lack of seriousness. In casual conversation with your friends after school, it is quite acceptable to say "Who are you going to the game with?" In a formal report, however, you might write something like this: "With *whom* is the President going to confer?"

THE VARIETIES OF ENGLISH

We can distinguish several different kinds of English, partly by the situations in which each is used and partly by the educational level of those that use each kind. To begin with, we can distinguish two very large varieties of English: *standard* and *substandard*.

Standard English

Standard English is the language of educated people—those who write for newspapers and magazines, authors of books, teachers, lawyers, government officials, doctors, businessmen. Although standard English differs, as we shall see, in different situations, it has certain conventions that are observed regularly by all the people who use it. And because the people who use standard English are the ones who carry on the important affairs of the world, their language conventions are respected. That is why this variety of English is called *standard*—a term that implies that something is an example or model for others to follow.

Remember that standard English is associated with educated people. Since we do not have a class that produces all of our leaders and professional people, we do not call the language they speak "upper-class English" or "English for leaders." The one thing all of the speakers of standard English have in common is likely to be education, and so we take the language they use to be a sign of education.

Substandard English

Those who do not observe the conventions of standard English, or who observe a different set of standards, are judged to be either uneducated or unwilling or unable to profit by their educational opportunities. Although there are several different terms for this kind of language, all of them mean approximately the same thing—*substandard*. Speakers of substandard English can, and often do, rise to positions of importance in business, government, and elsewhere. But to do so, they generally have to master standard English. Of course, standard and substandard English are not different languages; while there are some words that appear only in one or the other, most of the words in English can appear in either kind of English. The main differences appear in the use of pronouns and certain verb forms. Where a speaker of standard English would use *brought*, a speaker of substandard might use *brung*. Similarly:

STANDARD	SUBSTANDARD
He did it **himself.**	He did it **hisself.**
You and **he** fight all the time.	You and **him** fight all the time.
He **doesn't** trust me.	He **don't** trust me.
He **ran** right into me.	He **run** right into me.

Sentences like those in the right-hand column above are spoken by thousands of native speakers of English. But these speakers do not have the prestige and influence of the speakers of standard English; the use of such forms is almost always associated with the uneducated. It occasionally happens that a speaker of substandard English makes his language his trademark. Dizzy Dean, a famous pitcher for the St. Louis Cardinals and later a radio and television sports broadcaster, is one of the few who have actually made substandard speech an asset. The following excerpt from an interview in the *New York Times* gives you an idea of what substandard English is like. (It also gives you Dizzy Dean's opinions about usage matters.)

And I reckon that's why that now I come up with an *ain't* once in a while, and have the Missouri teachers all stirred up. They don't like it because I say that Marty Marion or Vern Stephens *slud* into second base. What do they want me to say —*slidded?*

Me and Paul [Dizzy's brother, also a pitcher for the Cards] didn't have to worry about that sort of stuff when we were winning games for the old Gas House Gang. And I don't know why I should get a sweat up now.

Paul, he'd win one game and I'd win the next.

Didn't nobody come around after the game and ask whether we'd throwed or threw the ball in there to make a play.

We won 'em, no questions asked.[1]

Two Kinds of Standard English

All of this book, and the following pages in particular, is intended to help you understand the conventions of standard English—the language of educated people.

Standard English is used in so many different ways— ranging from casual telephone conversations to formal speeches—that it would be impossible to name a particular kind that would be appropriate for each situation. But we

[1] From "Dizzy Dean." The *New York Times*, July 26, 1946. © 1946 by The New York Times Company. Reprinted by permission.

can distinguish two varieties of standard English: *formal* and *informal.*

Formal English

Formal English, like formal dress and formal manners, is language for special occasions. Sometimes referred to as "literary English," it is usually written. It is the English appropriate to serious essays, essay answers on examinations, formal reports, research papers, literary criticisms, and addresses on serious or solemn occasions.

As you might expect, formal English is likely to use words that would never come up in ordinary conversation. The sentences are likely to be more elaborately constructed and longer than those of ordinary writing. Contractions are rarely used. Formal English pays close attention to refinements in usage, and seldom admits slang. It is language in formal dress.

In the following example of formal English, note the long and carefully constructed sentences, which employ parallelism and repetition for rhetorical effect. Notice also the formal vocabulary: *fatuous, legitimate, detriment, grotesque, anachronism,* etc.

No one asks for a naïve and childlike confidence; no one asks for a fatuous enthusiasm for all that is foreign; no one asks that the genuine and legitimate differences of interest which have always marked, and will always continue to mark, the relations between peoples be ignored. We must expect Russian national interests not only to continue to exist but to be vigorously and confidently asserted. But in a [Russian] regime that we could recognize as an improvement over what we know today, we would expect that this would be done in an atmosphere of emotional sanity and moderation: that the foreign representative would not continue to be viewed and treated as one possessed of the devil; that it would be conceded that there might be such a thing as innocent and legitimate curiosity about a foreign country, which could be permitted to be gratified without fatal detriment to that country's national life; that it would be recognized that there might be individual foreign business aspirations which did not aim at the destruction of the Russian state; that it would be admitted, finally, that persons desirous of traveling across international borders might have, and are even apt to have, motives other than "espionage, sabotage, and diversion"—such trivial motives, in fact, as the enjoyment of travel or the peculiar impulses that move people to wish to visit relatives from time to time. In short, we may ask that the grotesque system of anachronisms known as the Iron Curtain be lifted from the world, and that the Russian people, who have so much to give and so much to receive as mature members of the world community, cease to be insulted by a policy that treats them as children, too immature to have normal contact with the adult world, too undependable to be let out alone.[1]

Informal English

Informal English is the language that most educated people use most of the time. It is the language of magazines, newspapers, and most books, and of business letters and talks intended for general audiences.

The conventions of informal English are less rigid than those of formal English. Sentences may be long or short and they are likely to sound more like conversation than the stately rhythms of formal English. Contractions often appear in informal English and sometimes a slang expression is admitted. Here is an example of written informal English.

It is ten o'clock on a Saturday morning in Spruce Manor, our flowery suburb. The month is May, the sun is shining, and the air smells sweet of lilac and lily of the valley and Weed Killer 2–4–D. Outside the windows of the kitchen, where my husband and I are lazily pouring ourselves a cup of coffee, we see the world at work—the bee raiding the hyacinth, the robin advancing on the worm, all our soil-colored, grass-stained neighbors in their regular weekend fury of pruning, snipping,

[1] From *American Diplomacy, 1900–1950* by George F. Kennan. Copyright © 1951 by The University of Chicago.

dividing, spraying, heeling-in, grubbing out, and propping up. Automatically my husband reaches as if for his gardening shears. I shake my head warningly, whereat he relaxes and butters another slice of toast.

For this year the Saturday fever is not for us. After eighteen years we are giving up a habit as wasteful as drink, nearly as obsessive as drugs. We are now charter members in good standing of Horticulturists Anonymous, Local Chapter Number 1; reformed addicts in the process of reducing our garden to not much more than a "green thought in a green shade."

Later in the morning we will perhaps give the lawn mower a brisk spin. We may even lean across the fence to commend the man next door, whose peonies show such prosperous buds. But we will not linger too long at any such outdoor pastime. Since we can't take it calmly, we're leaving it alone.[1]

Summary

STANDARD ENGLISH	TYPICAL USES	TYPICAL FEATURES
Formal	research papers, serious speeches, books and articles for special audiences	words little used in ordinary speech; longer sentences; few contractions; no slang
Informal	conversations of educated people; most writing in books, newsapers, and magazines; business letters, lectures to general audiences, politica! speeches, most textbooks	wide variety of sentence length; less difficult vocabulary than formal; sentences that sound like good conversation, even when written; contractions; some slang

[1] From *The Province of the Heart* by Phyllis McGinley, The Viking Press, Inc., 1959.

SUBSTANDARD ENGLISH	TYPICAL USES	TYPICAL FEATURES
	conversations of people of little education; dialogue intended to represent the speech of the uneducated in movies, books, comic strips, and on radio and television	verb and pronoun forms not appearing in Standard English (<u>dassent</u>, <u>slud</u>, <u>you was</u>, <u>he don't</u>, <u>hisself</u>, etc.); adverbs without the –<u>ly</u> ending (She sings <u>bad</u>); frequent use of slang words and localisms

● EXERCISE 1. Read each of the following passages carefully and identify the level of English to which it belongs—formal, informal, or substandard. Note the particular words and constructions that cause you to label the passage as you do.

1

In a few weeks, you will each receive a copy of the treasurer's report. Anyone who wants to gripe about the way we're spending the club's money will get his chance at next Saturday's business meeting.

2

If I'd of known they was goin' to let you feed the elephants I'd of went with you.

3

Those actions of his former subordinates that the General was now powerless to oppose, he elected to support. In his eagerness to anticipate any new mischief that might occur to the junta, he promulgated a series of new laws, each more harshly repressive than the last, which even the most rabid of the young officers would not have dared to propose.

4

One thing is, he don't take long walks like he used to. Every morning we used to see him out there, takin' those big long steps. Just as fast! You'd of thought there was something after him. And if you was to meet him, he'd never stop to say nothing to you. Just bob his head at you and go right on. Now that he ain't comin' by anymore, we sort of miss it. When you get used to something, you kind of want it to keep on.

5

I passed all the other courses that I took at my university, but I could never pass botany. This was because all botany students had to spend several hours a week in a laboratory looking through a microscope at plant cells, and I could never see through a microscope. I never once saw a cell through a microscope. This used to enrage my instructor. He would wander around the laboratory pleased with the progress all the students were making in drawing the involved and, so I am told, interesting structure of flower cells, until he came to me. I would just be standing there. "I can't see anything," I would say. He would begin patiently enough, explaining how anybody can see through a microscope, but he would always end up in a fury, claiming that I could *too* see through a microscope but just pretended that I couldn't. . . .[1]

● EXERCISE 2. Each of the following brief passages is written, as indicated, in a kind of English typical of a certain level and certain circumstances. Rewrite each of the passages in English suited to the level and circumstances specified.

1. *Substandard English used in an oral summary of an article. Rewrite in standard informal English.*

    The President finally got his dander up and told them Russians to get their stuff out of Cuba fast or else! He said the Navy would search ships headed for Cuba and if they didn't stop they'd be sorry.

2. *A student reports to his friends in the lunchroom a conversation*

[1] From "University Days" from *My Life and Hard Times*. Copyright © 1933, 1961 by James Thurber. Published by Harper & Row. Originally printed in *The New Yorker*. Reprinted by permission of Helen Thurber.

he has had with the school principal. Rewrite in language he would use if reporting the same conversation to his class.

Yeah, old Sherlock Holmes told me that any guys caught sneaking out of assembly would get kicked out of school.

3. *Substandard English used in relating an incident. Rewrite in standard informal English.*

When Dad and me come home, we seen right away they'd been somebody messing around with the car.

4. *The mayor talking informally to the City Commission. Rewrite in the kind of English he would use in making the same explanation to an audience of citizens.*

In a couple of weeks you'll all receive the report recommending a new high school. You can bet that there'll be plenty of moaning from those people up on the Hill.

IMPROVING YOUR USAGE

While we can speak generally about three kinds of English —formal standard, informal standard, and substandard— the lines between them are not always easy to draw. One level of usage shades into another; an expression we think of as being informal may turn up in a formal address; a slang word that originates in substandard English may become an acceptable part of the informal vocabulary; many words and constructions that we think of as belonging to educated speech may come into use among speakers of substandard English. The great majority of our words and our ways of putting them together are common to all three levels.

Sources of Usage Information

If your usage habits conform to the conventions of standard English, your main concern will be in suiting your language to the occasion in which you speak or write. If you are in a conversation, the usage of those you are talking with will give you valuable clues. If you are writing, keeping your audience in mind should help.

There will be times, however, when you cannot be sure whether a particular word or expression is suitable for a particular situation. Or there may be a few substandard forms that crop up from time to time in your writing and speaking. You can deal with these problems by studying a textbook like this one, by referring to a dictionary, or by consulting a special book on usage like those listed on page 83. Most important of all, you can develop the habit of noticing the usage preferences of careful users of English.

You will find the rules of grammar a useful but not invariably reliable guide to usage. Grammar describes the system of a language; usage is concerned with appropriate forms of expression. The two are not always the same, for language is a living and growing thing, and life and growth are not always logical. Changes are brought about by the people who use a language, and grammar rules, which can only be stated when the changes have occurred, necessarily come afterward. The rules of grammar describe the way the language works. When the system changes, the rules change.

The Importance of Good English

Using English according to the conventions established by educated users of the language and adapting it to the circumstances in which we use it will not, of course, make us effective speakers and writers. Conventional usage is only one of the qualities of good speech and good writing. Perhaps it is not even the most important. It is not so important, for example, as clarity or forcefulness of expression. It is not so important as honesty or originality or freshness. Yet good usage is important, nevertheless. We like to be noticed for things that are worthwhile and admirable, not just for things that are different. The one man who is out of step in a parade attracts more attention than all the rest of those marching, but we do not usually seek that kind of notice.

People will judge you by your usage. If you deviate from

the conventions of standard English, they will think more about how you are expressing yourself than they will about what you are saying. This may seem unfair, but it is true. In matters of usage as well as in dress, you will not go far wrong by following this advice of Lord Chesterfield's:

> Take great care always to be dressed like the reasonable people of your own age, in the place where you are; whose dress is never spoken of one way or the other, as either too negligent or too much studied.[1]

● EXERCISE 3. The words and expressions listed below present usage problems that trouble many people. Look them up in this and whatever other textbooks are available to you—most of these problems will be listed in the index. Consult also the usage books listed below if they are in your library.

1. *It's me.* [pronoun usage]
2. *shall* or *will*
3. *imply* or *infer*
4. double negatives
5. *between* or *among*
6. (*the*) *reason is because* . . .
7. split infinitive
8. *due to*

Guides to Usage

The following books contain accurate and up-to-date information about usage problems. You will find additional information on usage in your dictionary (see page 530). Neither the books listed below nor your dictionary can tell you exactly what to say or write in a particular situation. What they can do is help you to make up your own mind.

Evans, Bergen and Cornelia, *A Dictionary of Contemporary American Usage*, New York, Random House, 1957.

Bryant, Margaret M., *Current American Usage*, New York, Funk & Wagnalls, Inc., 1962.

Nicholson, Margaret, *Dictionary of American-English Usage*, New York, Oxford University Press, 1957.

[1] *Letters*, October 9, 1746.

Agreement

Subject and Verb,
Pronoun and Antecedent

Some words in English have matching forms to show grammatical relationships. Forms that match in this way are said to *agree*. For example, a subject and verb agree if both are singular or both plural. Pronouns also agree with their antecedents — the words pronouns stand for.

AGREEMENT OF SUBJECT AND VERB

6a. A word that refers to one person or thing is *singular* in number. A word that refers to more than one is *plural* in number.

SINGULAR	PLURAL
book	books
child	children
this	these
either	both
he, she, it	they

6b. A verb agrees with its subject in number.

(1) Singular subjects take singular verbs.

A young **man lives** in the future.
This **exhibit was prepared** by the art department.

84

(2) Plural subjects take plural verbs.

Young **men live** in the future.
These **exhibits were prepared** by the art department.

You will find it helpful to remember that *is, was, has,* and most verbs ending in a single *s* are singular: he *thinks,* she *works,* it *counts,* etc. *Are, were, have,* and most verbs not ending in a single *s* are plural: they *think,* they *work,* they *count.* The exceptions, which should cause you little difficulty, are verbs used with *I* and singular *you:* I *think,* you *work,* etc.

Notice that all the verbs given as examples in the preceding paragraph are in the present tense. All past tense verbs have the same form in the singular and plural except for the verb *be,* which has a special form *was* that is used with *I, he, she,* and *it,* and all singular nouns.

SINGULAR	PLURAL
I went	they went
he carried	we carried
I was	we were
it was	they were

If English is your native language, you probably have little trouble in making verbs agree with their subjects when they directly follow the subjects as in the examples above. You will encounter sentences, however, in which it is not so easy to identify correctly the subject or determine whether it is singular or plural. These constructions, which create most agreement problems, are taken up separately below.

Intervening Phrase

6c. The number of the subject is not changed by a phrase following the subject.

A phrase that comes between a singular subject and its verb can easily mislead you if it contains a plural word.

**6
a-c**

Remember that the verb agrees with its subject, not with any modifiers the subject may have.

EXAMPLES The **performance was** very funny.

The **performance** of the first three clowns **was** very funny. [*Performance*, not *clowns*, is the subject of the sentence.]

The **decision has been reversed.**

The **decision** of the contest judges **has been reversed.** [*decision has*, not *judges have*]

In formal writing, singular subjects followed by phrases beginning with *together with*, *as well as*, *in addition to*, and *accompanied by* take singular verbs.

EXAMPLE The captain, as well as the coaches, **was** disappointed in the team.

● EXERCISE 1. Number your paper 1–20. Write after the proper number the subject of each sentence. After the subject, write the one of the two verbs in parentheses that agrees in number with the subject. Check your answers before going on to the next exercise.

1. The construction of fallout shelters (was, were) being encouraged.
2. Your contribution, in addition to other funds, (assures, assure) the success of our campaign.
3. A combination of these methods (is, are) sure to succeed.
4. The standards of behavior in our crowd (changes, change) with our mood.
5. Poe's stories of mystery and imagination (appeals, appeal) most to me.
6. Trespassing on these grounds (is, are) prohibited.
7. The north wing, like the south and east wings, (has, have) six rooms.
8. His answers to our question (changes, change) everything.
9. Employees of the mill (lives, live) in bunkhouses.
10. The winner of both races (was, were) from Central.
11. Bill, like many of his relatives, (thinks, think) conservatively.
12. Clearness in writing and speaking (is, are) essential to success.

13. The wing span of these planes (is, are) so narrow that the planes can be launched from bombers.
14. Her shyness in the presence of strangers (is, are) quite surprising.
15. The time for courage and decision (is, are) here.
16. His objections to our program (seems, seem) trivial.
17. The depth of some of these lakes (has, have) never been measured.
18. His use of dissonance and strange harmonies (does, do) not appeal to me.
19. Working under these unfavorable conditions (is, are) exasperating.
20. The boxes of dishes, together with the lamps and all of the silverware, (was, were) put on a truck going to the wrong city.

Indefinite Pronouns as Subjects

Pronouns like *everybody*, *someone*, *everything*, *all*, and *none*, all of which are more or less indefinite in meaning, present some special usage problems. Some of them are always singular, some are always plural, and some others may be singular or plural, depending on the meaning of the sentence. In addition, such pronouns are often followed by a phrase. Therefore, you must first determine the number of the pronoun and then remember the rule about phrases that come between subjects and verbs.

6d. The following common words are singular: *each, either, neither, one, no one, every one, anyone, someone, everyone, anybody, somebody, everybody.*

EXAMPLES **Each has** his own motorcycle.
Each of the boys **has** [not *have*] his own motorcycle.
Everyone wants more money.
Every one of the workmen **wants** [not *want*] more money.

6d

6e. The following common words are plural: *several, few, both, many.*

EXAMPLES   **Several** of the regular members **were** absent.
Few of my family really **understand** me.
Both of your excuses **sound** plausible.
Many were surprised at the final score.

6f. The words *some, any, none, all,* **and** *most* **may be singular or plural, depending on the meaning of the sentence.**

When these words are used to refer to an amount or quantity that is considered as a unit, they are singular. When the amount is considered as a number of separate units, these words are taken to be plural. Compare the following examples:

Some of the money **was** missing.   [*Money* is thought of as a unit.]

Some of the dimes **were** missing.   [The dimes are thought of as separate units.]

All of the fruit **looks** ripe.

All of the cherries **look** ripe.

Most of the book **was** interesting.   [an indefinite part of a book]

Most of the books **were** interesting.   [a number of separate books]

Has any of this evidence been presented?

Have any of my friends called me?

None of the evidence **points** to his guilt.

None of our students **were** involved.

◆ USAGE NOTE   *Was* could have been used in the last example, but modern English usage prefers a plural verb in this situation. If you want the subject to be singular in such a sentence, use *no one* or *not one* instead of *none.*

●EXERCISE 2.   Number your paper 1–10. Write after the proper number on your paper the subject in each sentence. After it, write the one of the two verbs in parentheses which agrees in number with the subject.

1. Each of these dresses (has, have) a wide belt.
2. One of my best friends (was, were) playing against me.
3. All of our study periods (is, are) spent in the library.
4. Some of these errors (is, are) preventable.
5. Ford, as well as Chrysler and General Motors, (was, were) willing to compromise.
6. Every one of my summer dresses (is, are) too small.
7. A few of the guard (was, were) left behind.
8. The loss of his sons (was, were) a cruel blow.
9. Everybody living in these states (pays, pay) a state income tax.
10. An amateur in competiton with these professionals (hasn't, haven't) a chance.

● EXERCISE 3.   Rewrite these ten sentences, following the instructions that appear in brackets after each of them. Sometimes the addition will affect agreement. Be sure to make the subject and verb of the new sentence agree. Underline each subject once and each verb twice.

EXAMPLE   1.   Every one of the new buildings was damaged in the earthquake.   [Change *every one* to *all*.]

1. *All* of the new buildings *were damaged* in the earthquake.

1. This group sings better than any of the others.   [Add *Two members of* before "This group."]
2. A porpoise swims near the surface.   [Add *like whales and sharks* after "porpoise." Put a comma before and after the added phrase.]
3. Apples were shipped from New York State to Chicago.   [Add *One carload of* before "Apples."]
4. Several were unfairly treated.   [Add *of our group* after "Several."]
5. Every one of the offices has been equipped with electric typewriters.   [Change *Every one* to *All but three*.]

6
e-f

6. Each of the other witnesses agrees with my account of the accident.   [Change *Each* to *All*.]
7. All of the money has been used up.   [Change *money* to *tickets*.]
8. His struggle to overcome illness was finally successful.   [Add *and financial reverses* after "illness."]
9. The sky looks promising.   [Add *as well as the wind and the water* after "sky." Set off the addition with commas.]
10. Morgan, one of our regular pinch hitters, usually strikes out. [Change *one* to *like the rest*.]

● EXERCISE 4.   *Oral Drill.*   The following oral drill sentences are of the kind that come up in ordinary conversation. These sentences should be read *aloud* many times to fix the habit of using the correct form. Ear training is important in correcting usage. In reading aloud, stress the italicized words.

1. *One* of the girls *was* late.
2. The *cause* of both fires *was* the same.
3. *Does either* of them have any money?
4. *Each* of the boys *is* dependable.
5. *All* of my friends *have* left.
6. Not *one* of the teachers *approves* our conduct.
7. *Both* of the cars *were* damaged.
8. *Every one* of us *is* hungry.
9. The *result* of his efforts *seems* uncertain.
10. The *number* of *A*'s *was* disappointing.

● EXERCISE 5.   Number your paper 1–20. Read each of the following sentences aloud. If the verb in a sentence agrees with its subject, write a + after the proper number on your paper; if the verb does not agree, write the correct form on your paper.

1. Each of the students are responsible for one lesson.
2. The goal of their efforts were to raise one million dollars.
3. Neither of the stories were good enough to publish.
4. Every one of the stations was out of gasoline.
5. Some of the crops have been ruined by frost.

6. The height of the office buildings are unusually great.
7. One of the club members has not yet voted.
8. The Russian ambassador, together with the Polish and Hungarian ambassadors, has called a press conference.
9. All of the mines has been closed.
10. The principal, as well as the school board and the faculty, was enthusiastic.
11. The desire for property and great riches ruin many lives.
12. Some of the criminal's motives were apparent.
13. The result of so many attempts was disappointing.
14. Each of the salesmen have a definite territory to cover.
15. The ocean, as well as the gulf and the bay, provides good fishing.
16. Neither of his paternal grandparents are living.
17. Several of our best news sources have been cut off.
18. Few members of the party approve the chairman's appointments.
19. A sophomore, as well as a freshman, is allowed to take public speaking.
20. The vessel, with its entire crew and cargo, were lost.

Compound Subjects

As you will recall from Chapter 2, two words or groups of words may be connected to form the subject of a verb. These words, usually joined by *and* or *or*, are called a *compound subject*. Compound subjects may take singular or plural verbs, depending on whether the words joined are singular or plural and **on** what the connecting word is.

6g. Subjects joined by *and* take a plural verb.

EXAMPLES A **truck and** a **convertible were** in the ditch.

Gerald and his twin **brother** naturally **look** a lot alike.

The **walls and** the **ceiling were** beautifully decorated.

6g

EXCEPTION   When the parts of a compound sentence are considered as a unit or when they refer to the same thing, a singular verb is used.

Macaroni and cheese is the cafeteria special again today.

The Stars and Stripes is our national emblem.

His **friend and** fellow **author was** cool to the idea of collaborating on a new cookbook.

6h. Singular subjects joined by *or* or *nor* take a singular verb.

EXAMPLES   My **brother or** my **sister is** likely to be at home.

Neither the **president** of the company **nor** the **sales manager is** a college graduate.

Either **John or Jim is** sure to know the answer.

6i. When a singular and a plural subject are joined by *or* or *nor*, the verb agrees with the nearer subject.

ACCEPTABLE   Either the judge or the lawyers **are** wrong.

It is usually possible to avoid this awkward construction [1] altogether:

BETTER   Either the judge is wrong or the lawyers are.

♦ USAGE NOTE   The rules in this chapter are consistently followed in formal written English but are often departed from in informal speaking and writing. Formal usage is likely to call for a singular verb after a singular subject in a strictly logical way.

[1] Another reason for avoiding this construction is that the subjects may be different in person. In this case, the verb must agree with the nearer subject in person as well as number. In the following example, the verb must not only be singular to agree with *I*, it must also have the form that matches *I* as a subject:

ACCEPTABLE   Neither my brothers nor I am going to summer camp.
BETTER   My brothers are not going to summer camp, and neither am I.

Informal usage, on the other hand, often permits the use of a plural verb, whatever the logical number of the subject, if the meaning is clearly plural. Compare the following examples of formal and informal practices:

FORMAL   Neither Lucy nor Carol has any money left.

INFORMAL   Neither Lucy nor Carol have any money left. [Although joined by *nor*, which strictly calls for a singular verb, the meaning of the sentence is essentially plural: both Lucy and Carol have spent all of their money.

FORMAL   Every one of the campers was hungry.

INFORMAL   Every one of the campers were hungry. [Strictly speaking, the subject *one* is singular and takes a singular verb. However, the meaning is essentially the same as that expressed by "All the campers were hungry." Informal usage permits a plural verb in such cases.]

FORMAL   My aunt, along with my uncle and three of my cousins, is coming to our house this weekend.

INFORMAL   My aunt, along with my uncle and three of my cousins, are coming to our house this weekend. [Although the construction logically calls for a singular verb, the meaning is clearly plural—all of them are coming, not just the aunt. It is usually wise to avoid constructions that set up a conflict between logic and meaning. In this case it would be better to write "My aunt, my uncle, and my three cousins *are . . .*"]

In some of the exercise sentences in this chapter, you will encounter such differences between formal and informal usage. For the purposes of these exercises, follow the rules of formal usage.

● EXERCISE 6.   Number your paper 1–25. Read each of the following sentences aloud. If the verb in a sentence agrees with its subject, write a + after the proper number.

6
h-

If the verb does not agree, write the correct form of the verb on your paper. Follow the practices of formal usage.

1. Neither the crates nor the plastic boxes were damaged in the accident.
2. One of the islands appear to be inhabited.
3. The extent of his injuries have not been determined.
4. Neither the milk nor the groceries have been delivered.
5. Some of her jewels look valuable.
6. Either Pete or his father are going to pick us up.
7. Both the funds appropriated by the legislature and the income from the sales tax were exhausted.
8. Have each of the stowaways been questioned by immigration officials?
9. One of our best suggestions was vetoed by the council.
10. Not one of these cases have ever been solved.
11. Both private ownership and free competition is characteristic of capitalism.
12. Neither of these reference books contain the information I need.
13. Not one of her children have offered to help her financially.
14. Neither Ken nor Sid have enough energy to walk such a distance.
15. Several of his best stories have been sold for very small amounts of money.
16. The chemistry teacher, as well as his students, was nervous during Charles' demonstration experiment.
17. Speaking and writing involves different skills.
18. The ambassador, accompanied by his family and aides, is returning to Washington.
19. Every one of the culprits has decided to plead guilty.
20. The results of yesterday's election has not yet been made public.
21. Sam and his brother have a new sailboat.
22. Either the students or the teacher are wrong.
23. Neither the junior high nor the senior high has enough teachers.
24. Either Friday or Saturday appears to be the best time.
25. The curtains and the rug match.

Other Problems in Agreement

6j. When the subject follows the verb, as in questions and in sentences beginning with *here* and *there*, be careful to determine the subject and make sure that the verb agrees with it.

WRONG   There's three routes you can take.
RIGHT   There **are** three **routes** you can take.

WRONG   Where's your mother and father?
RIGHT   Where **are** your **mother and father?**

6k. Collective nouns may be either singular or plural.

A collective noun names a group: *crowd, committee, jury, class.* A collective noun takes a plural verb when the speaker is thinking of the individual members of the group; it takes a singular verb when the speaker is thinking of the group as a unit.

The **crowd were fighting** for their lives.   [The speaker is thinking of the individuals in the crowd.]

The **crowd was** an orderly one.   [The speaker is thinking of the crowd as a single thing, a unit.]

The **team were** talking over some new plays.

The **team was** ranked first in the nation.

The **family have** agreed among themselves to present a solid front.

The **family is** the basic unit of our society.

SOME COMMON COLLECTIVE NOUNS

army	crowd	orchestra
audience	flock	public
class	group	swarm
club	herd	team
committee	jury	troop

6
j-k

6l. Expressions stating amount (time, money, measurement, weight, volume, fractions) are usually singular when the amount is considered as a unit.

EXAMPLES   **Three years** in a strange land **seems** like a long time.

Ten dollars is not enough.

Three fourths of the money **has** been recovered.

However, when the amount is considered as a number of separate units, a plural verb is used.

EXAMPLES   These last **three years have** been full of surprises.

There **are two silver dollars** in each of the stockings.

6m. The title of a book or the name of an organization or country, even when plural in form, usually takes a singular verb.

EXAMPLES   *The Adventures of Huckleberry Finn* was published in 1884.

The **Knights of Columbus is** sponsoring a carnival.

The **United States remains** the leader of the Western bloc.

EXCEPTION   Some names of organizations (Boy Scouts of America, New York Yankees, Chicago Bears, etc.) customarily take a plural verb when you are thinking of the members and a singular verb when you mean the organization:

The **Boy Scouts of America wear** this uniform.

The **Boy Scouts of America is** a nonprofit organization.

6n. A few nouns, such as *mumps, measles, civics, economics, mathematics, physics,* although plural in form, take a singular verb.

EXAMPLES   **Measles is** a disease to take seriously.

World **economics bears** directly on world peace.

The following similar words are more often plural than singular: *athletics, acoustics, gymnastics, tactics.* The word *politics* may be either singular or plural, and *scissors* and *trousers* are always plural.

For more information on the use of words ending in *–ics,* look up *–ics* in your dictionary.

6o. When the subject and the predicate nominative are different in number, the verb agrees with the subject, not with the predicate nominative.

ACCEPTABLE The most appreciated **gift was** the clothes that you sent us.

ACCEPTABLE The **clothes** that you sent us **were** the most appreciated gift.

BETTER Most of all we appreciated the clothes that you sent us.

Although the first two examples are acceptable, the third is clearly better. Avoid writing sentences in which the subject and predicate nominative are different in number.

6p. *Every* or *many a* before a word or series of words is followed by a singular verb.

EXAMPLES **Every man, woman,** and **child was** asked to contribute.

Many a college **student wishes** to return to the easy days of high school.

Many a boy in these circumstances **has** hoped for a lucky break.

6q. *Don't* and *doesn't* must agree with their subjects.

With the subjects *I* and *you,* use *don't* (*do not*). With other subjects, use *doesn't* (*does not*) when the subject is singular and *don't* (*do not*) when the subject is plural.

6
l-q

EXAMPLES   **I don't** remember the score.
You don't look happy.
It [He, She, This] doesn't run fast enough.
They don't swim.

By using *doesn't* after *it*, *he*, and *she*, you can eliminate most of the common errors in the use of *don't*.

6r. In formal English, verbs in clauses that follow *one of those* are always plural.

One of the most troublesome constructions in English, as far as agreement is concerned, consists of clauses that follow *one of those* . . . . Even though informal usage often permits a singular verb in the following clause, the plural verb is always correct. Therefore, if you always use a plural verb in such construction you cannot go wrong.

EXAMPLES   That is **one of those** remarks that **are** intended to start arguments.

Joan **is one of those** people who **go** out of their way to be helpful.

● EXERCISE 7.   Number your paper 1–25. After the proper number, write the correct one of the two verbs in parentheses in each sentence.

1. The cost of his explorations (was, were) paid by scientific societies.
2. Neither the President nor the FBI (was, were) willing to release any information.
3. Every one of his sons (has, have) been successful.
4. *The Case of the Missing Butler* is one of those books that (is, are) easy to put down.
5. The question of taxes (doesn't, don't) belong in this discussion.
6. Neither our car nor the cars of the others (was, were) able to plow through the drifts.
7. Fifteen minutes (is, are) enough time for this exercise.

8. There (seems, seem) to be many arguments on both sides.
9. Every planet, including the earth, (revolves, revolve) around the sun.
10. *The Magnificent Ambersons* (is, are) worth reading.
11. Most of the Roosevelt papers (has, have) been made available to the public.
12. The mayor of the city and the governor of the state (has, have) been in conference.
13. It (doesn't, don't) matter to me where you go.
14. Neither his secular music nor his religious compositions (appeals, appeal) to the popular taste.
15. Probably some of the oranges (doesn't, don't) ripen until April.
16. The fruit on the outdoor stands (looks, look) tempting.
17. Neither the doctor nor the nurse (was, were) in the patient's room when the crisis came.
18. College life and high school life (is, are) vastly different.
19. (There's, There are) not many selfish people in the world.
20. Two weeks (is, are) enough for a trip of that length.
21. She is one of those people who (is, are) never ready on time.
22. The acoustics in this room (has, have) always been bad.
23. Each of the cheeses (was, were) sampled by the inspector.
24. Few members of the scientific world (is, are) able to explain Professor Von Faber's new theory.
25. Measles (is, are) not exclusively a children's disease.

● EXERCISE 8. *Oral Drill.* To fix the agreement habit in your mind, read each of the following sentences aloud several times, stressing the italicized words.

1. *Neither Barbara nor Louise was* with me.
2. *Every one* of my brothers *is* tall.
3. *Both Joe and Bob are* smart.
4. *It doesn't* look like him.
5. Where *are* your *books?*
6. *Four dollars is* more than I can afford.
7. *One* of the roads *has* been resurfaced.
8. *Has Ellen or Dorothy* seen you?
9. *Each* of the boys *plays* a different kind of game.
10. There *were seven* of us in the car.

6r

AGREEMENT OF PRONOUN AND ANTECEDENT

6s. A pronoun agrees with its antecedent in number and gender.[1]

All that you have learned about agreement of subject and verb will be useful to you in making pronouns agree with their antecedents. The antecedent of a pronoun is the word to which the pronoun refers. Study the following examples, in which the antecedents and the pronouns referring to them are printed in bold-faced type. Notice that the pronoun is singular when the antecedent is singular, and plural when the antecedent is plural. Notice, too, that the pronoun is masculine (*he, him, his*) when the antecedent is masculine; feminine (*she, her, hers*) when the antecedent is feminine; neuter (*it, its*) when the antecedent is neither masculine nor feminine. This kind of agreement is agreement in *gender*.

> **Mr. Jameson** did **his** best.
>
> **One** of the boys injured **his** ankle.
>
> **Neither** of the girls achieved **her** purpose.
>
> The **women** in the League expressed **their** opinions forcefully.
>
> The **city** is proud of **its** parks.
>
> I recognized **one** of the boys, but I didn't speak to **him**.

(1) The words *each, either, neither, one, everyone, everybody, no one, nobody, anyone, anybody, someone, somebody* are referred to by a singular pronoun—*he, him, his, she, her, hers, it, its*.

The use of a phrase after the antecedent does not change the number of the antecedent.

---

[1] Pronouns also agree with their antecedents in *person* (see page 105):

> I should have thought of it **myself.**
> **You** will be late for **your** appointment.
> **George** is devoted to **his** aged mother.

Agreement in person rarely presents usage problems.

EXAMPLES   **Each** of the men had removed **his** parachute.

Nobody in a position of authority had given **his** approval of the bill.

If **anyone** calls, tell **him** I'll be back later.

◆ USAGE NOTE   When the antecedent may be either masculine or feminine, as in the example directly above, use the masculine pronoun in referring to it. Avoid the awkward use of two pronouns: "If *anyone* calls, tell him or her I'll be back later."

Strict adherence to the general rule of agreement between pronoun and antecedent may lead to a construction so absurd that no one would use it:

ABSURD   Did *everybody* leave the dance early because *he* wasn't enjoying *himself?*

In instances of this kind, use the plural pronoun or recast the sentence to avoid the problem:

BETTER   Did **everybody** leave the dance early because **they** weren't enjoying **themselves?**

or

Did the **guests** leave the dance early because **they** weren't enjoying **themselves?**

(2) Two or more singular antecedents joined by *or* or *nor* should be referred to by a singular pronoun.

Neither Jack **nor** Dick had **his** keys with **him**.

(3) Two or more antecedents joined by *and* should be referred to by a plural pronoun.

Jack **and** Dick came with **their** uniforms on.

◆ USAGE NOTE   Like some of the rules for agreement of subject and verb, the rules for agreement of pronoun and antecedent show variations between formal and informal usage. Standard informal usage follows meaning rather than strict grammatical agreement. The sentences below marked "informal" are acceptable in informal writing and speaking. In exercises, however, follow the practices of formal English.

6s

FORMAL   **Neither** of the girls had brought **her** skis with **her.**

INFORMAL   Neither of the girls had brought their skis with them.

FORMAL   **Every one** of the campers had been advised to put **his** name on everything belonging to **him.**

INFORMAL   Every one of the campers had been advised to put their names on everything belonging to them.

● REVIEW EXERCISE A.   This exercise covers errors in agreement of verb and subject and of pronoun and antecedent. Number your paper 1–25. If a sentence is correct, write a + after the proper number; if it is incorrect, write a 0. One error makes a sentence incorrect. Be prepared to revise all incorrect sentences.

1. One out of every twenty students are dropped from the course each term.
2. At this point the law of diminishing returns begins to operate.
3. The effect of the comics on young people are not so drastic as some believe.
4. Neither of the proposed bills were accepted in their entirety.
5. Each of the papers read in class were good.
6. Two thirds of the estate was left to the children.
7. Has either of the orders been sent?
8. When an employer is interviewing you, one of the first things they ask about is experience.
9. After a person retires, they usually prefer to live in the city.
10. A certain degree of privacy and security seem desirable.
11. Neither the Department of Agriculture nor the farmers were sure of their position.
12. He was one of those advisers who were with Roosevelt at Yalta.
13. Each of these suggestions must be taken only for what they are worth.
14. Every member of the crew was decorated for his part in the rescue.
15. Everyone needs a few spare moments to themselves to do as they wish.
16. This is one of those pens that writes under water.

17. Everybody who enters politics knows that he will have to take criticism.
18. The frequency of fatal traffic accidents are rising.
19. In the past, close cooperation among nations have brought many improvements to the world.
20. Is there any old magazines in the cellar?
21. Assault and battery is a criminal offense.
22. Are you one of the boys who were tardy?
23. Anyone who does not get their parents' permission will not be permitted to make the trip.
24. Only one of his objections were sensible.
25. After the government has chosen somebody for an important position, they should consider carefully before turning it down.

● REVIEW EXERCISE B. Rewrite the following sentences according to the directions given for each. Be sure to make changes or additions in verb forms, pronouns, etc., if necessary.

1. Some students fail to work up to their ability. [Change *Some students* to *Many a student.*]
2. Where's Mary? [Add *and Helen* after "Mary."]
3. The rivers have reached the flood stage. [Add *Neither of* before "The rivers."]
4. We expected her to be nominated. [Add *one of the girls who* (*was* or *were*) after "be."]
5. The senior high has its full complement of teachers. [Add *Neither the junior high nor* at the beginning of the sentence.]
6. People need goals if they are to be successful. [Change *People* to *A person.*]
7. A catalogue is supposed to be in the morning mail. [After "catalogue" add *together with an order form and a covering letter.* Put a comma before *together* and another after *letter.*]
8. The students are wrong about the answer. [At the beginning of the sentence, add *Either the teacher or.*]
9. This book is difficult to understand. [At the beginning of the sentence, add *All of the poems in.*]
10. A day is not much time for a trip like that. [Change *A day* to *Two weeks.*]

CHAPTER 7

Correct Use of Pronouns

Nominative and Objective Case; Special Problems with Pronouns

The function of a pronoun in a sentence is shown by the case form of the pronoun. Different functions demand different forms. For instance, a pronoun that acts as a subject is in the *nominative case;* a pronoun that acts as an object is in the *objective case;* and a pronoun that shows possession is in the *possessive case.* The following examples illustrate these three functions of pronouns:

PRONOUN AS SUBJECT   **I** paid the manager.
PRONOUN AS OBJECT   The manager paid **me.**
POSSESSIVE PRONOUN   This is **my** money.

Observe that the pronoun has a different form (*I, me, my*) in each case.

♦ NOTE   Since they are used in the same ways that pronouns are used, nouns may also be said to have case. The nouns in the following sentence illustrate the three cases of nouns:

The *people's vote* will decide the *issue.*

people's   noun in the possessive case
vote   noun in the nominative case—subject
issue   noun in the objective case—direct object

However, since nouns have identical forms for the nominative and objective cases and form the possessive in a regular way, case presents no problems as far as nouns are concerned.

7a. Learn the case forms of pronouns and the uses of each form.

Personal pronouns are those pronouns which change form in the different persons. There are three persons—first, second, and third—which are distinguished as follows:

First person is the person speaking: *I* (*We*) go.

Second person is the person spoken to: *You* are going.

Third person is a person or thing other than the speaker or the one spoken to: *He* (*She, It, They*) will go.

PERSONAL PRONOUNS

Singular

	NOMINATIVE CASE	OBJECTIVE CASE	POSSESSIVE CASE
FIRST PERSON	I	me	my, mine
SECOND PERSON	you	you	your, yours
THIRD PERSON	he, she, it	him, her, it	his, her hers, its

Plural

	NOMINATIVE CASE	OBJECTIVE CASE	POSSESSIVE CASE
FIRST PERSON	we	us	our, ours
SECOND PERSON	you	you	your, yours
THIRD PERSON	they	them	their, theirs

Since *you* and *it* do not change their forms, ignore them. Memorize the following lists of nominative and objective forms.

NOMINATIVE CASE	OBJECTIVE CASE
I	me
he	him
she	her
we	us
they	them

USES OF NOMINATIVE FORMS

7b. The subject of a verb is in the nominative case.

This rule means that whenever you use a pronoun as a subject, you should use one of the pronouns from the left-hand column on page 105. Ordinarily, you do this without thinking about it. When the subject is compound, however, many persons do make mistakes in their selection of pronouns. Whereas they would never say "Me am seventeen years old," they will say "John and me are seventeen years old." Since the pronoun is used as a subject in both sentences, it should be in the nominative case in both: *"John and I* are seventeen years old."

(1) To determine the correct pronoun in a compound subject, try each subject separately with the verb, adapting the form as necessary. Your ear will tell you which form is correct.

WRONG   Her and me are good friends.   [*Her* is a good friend? *Me* is a good friend?]

RIGHT   **She** and **I** are good friends.   [*She* is a good friend. *I* am a good friend.]

WRONG   Neither Bill nor him was in school today.   [*Him* was in school today?]

RIGHT   Neither **Bill** nor **he** was in school today.   [*He* was in school today.]

(2) When the pronoun is used with a noun (*we boys, we seniors,* etc.), determine the correct form by reading the sentence without the noun.

EXAMPLE   **We boys** will do the job.   [*We* (not *Us*) will do the job.]

● EXERCISE 1.   *Oral Drill.*   Read aloud several times the following sentences, stressing the italicized words.

1. Sally and *I* have a date.
2. *He* and Mother will be home later.
3. Our family and *they* were neighbors for years.
4. Either *she* or Jerry will write to you.
5. Have Joe and *she* written to you?
6. When are you and *he* going?
7. *We* juniors won the contest.
8. Neither Ed nor *they* can come.

7c. A predicate nominative is in the nominative case.

A predicate nominative is a noun or pronoun in the predicate that refers to the same thing as the subject of the sentence. For the present purpose, think of a predicate nominative as any pronoun that follows a form of the verb *be*.

COMMON FORMS OF BE		PREDICATE NOMINATIVE
am is, are was, were may be, can be, will be, etc. may have been, etc. want to be, like to be, etc.	are followed by	I he she we you they

EXAMPLES Are you sure it was **they?**
It might have been **she.**
This may be **he** coming up the walk.

♦ USAGE NOTE It is now perfectly acceptable to use *me* as a predicate nominative in informal usage: *It's me.* (The construction rarely comes up in formal situations.) The plural form (*It's us*) is also generally accepted. However, using the objective case for the third person form of the pronoun (*It's him, It's them*) is still often frowned on in written English. When you encounter any of these expressions in the exercises in this book or in the various tests you take, you will be wise to take a conservative attitude and use the nominative forms in all instances.

7
b-c

● EXERCISE 2. Number your paper 1–15. After the proper number, write the personal pronoun that can be substituted for each italicized expression. In those sentences calling for [1st person pron.], use the appropriate one of the following pronouns: *I, we, me, us.*

EXAMPLES 1. George and *Sally* are late again.
  1. *she*

  2. Only Jean and [1st person pron.] know our secret.
  2. *I*

1. Allan and *his brother* are going out for basketball.
2. He and *Betty* are related in some way.
3. [1st person pron.] students will support the team.
4. That might have been *the Browns.*
5. Did you think that Sally and *Helen* were close friends?
6. Can you or *Mr. Graham* do these problems?
7. Are [1st person pron.] boys invited too?
8. I wish that I were *that girl.*
9. Neither Sandra nor *Agnes* was chosen.
10. Stan and [1st person pron.] won our matches.
11. You and *the boys* are wrong.
12. Either *your teacher* or the guidance counselor will advise you.
13. First she thought she had seen the lost children; then she said she wasn't sure it was *the lost children.*
14. Mildred and *Jane* borrowed my homework paper.
15. If *John* or Bill is absent, I'll get the assignment.

USES OF OBJECTIVE FORMS

7d. **The object of a verb is in the objective case.**

The object of a verb answers the question "What?" or "Whom?" after an action verb.

EXAMPLE I saw **her.** [Saw whom? Answer: *her,* which is the object.]

As their name suggests, the objective forms (*me, him, her, us, them*) are used as objects.

EXAMPLES   I caught **him** by the shoulder.

She greeted **me** cordially.

Him I remember very well.

Since both direct and indirect objects are in the objective case, there is no point in distinguishing between them in applying this rule.

EXAMPLES   I saw **him.**   [direct object]

I told **him** the story.   [indirect object]

Like the nominative forms of pronouns the objective forms are troublesome principally when they are used in compounds. Although you would hardly make the mistake of saying, "I caught *he* by the shoulder," you might say, "I caught *Jim and he* by the shoulder." Trying each object separately with the verb will help you to choose the correct pronoun for compound objects: "I caught *him* by the shoulder."

Remember that when a pronoun is used with a noun (*we boys*, *us boys*), we determine the correct form by omitting the noun.

They blame **us** pedestrians.   [They blame *us*, not *we*.]

● EXERCISE 3.   Referring to the list of objective forms, supply the correct pronouns for the italicized words in the following sentences. In sentences calling for [1st person pron.], use the appropriate one of the following: *I, we, me, us.*

1. Have you seen *the principal* or the janitor?
2. Calvin and *George* I refused to believe.
3. Leave [1st person pron.] girls alone for a while.
4. The paper mentioned both you and [1st person pron.].
5. I'll take Janet and *Bob* in my car.
6. I reminded both the boss and *his secretary* of the meeting.
7. Will you please help Susan and *Phyllis and me?*
8. Mr. Heater sent *Frank* and Jack to the office.
9. She left Ray and [1st person pron.] behind.
10. Why are you always blaming [1st person pron.] criminals?

7d

● EXERCISE 4.   *Oral Drill.*   Read each of the following sentences aloud several times, stressing the italicized words.

1. *Ask* Dick and *him.*
2. Did he *mean* Pauline and *me?*
3. *Take* Louis and *her* with you.
4. Have you *met* the Whites and *them?*
5. Couldn't your *hear us* girls?
6. I *admire* Carl and *him.*
7. *Show* Ellen and *me* your essay.
8. I'll *give* you and *her* one more chance.
9. The officer *caught* Tom and *him.*
10. She *called them* and *us.*

● EXERCISE 5.   This exercise covers the use of personal pronouns as subjects of verbs, predicate nominatives, and objects of verbs. Number your paper 1–20. Write after the proper number the correct one of the two forms in parentheses in each sentence.

1. Who told Sam and (she, her)?
2. Have you and (she, her) had an argument?
3. That was probably Steve and (they, them).
4. Mr. Thompson said that (we, us) girls were late.
5. Tell the headmaster and (he, him) what you did.
6. Are you expecting Jean and (she, her)?
7. I don't believe it was (he, him).
8. Did you know that Bill and (she, her) are engaged?
9. Please tell (we, us) girls where you were.
10. Do not annoy (I, me) or the driver.
11. Certainly you must remember Edna and (I, me).
12. You misunderstood the teacher and (I, me).
13. Who will drive Peggy and (she, her) to the airport?
14. That must be (he, him).
15. I'll send you and (he, him) by different routes.
16. The doctor offered to treat her husband and (she, her).
17. We didn't want to leave Anne and (she, her) behind.
18. Our callers were probably (they, them).
19. Ray and (I, me) don't need advice.
20. We know it was (he, him).

● EXERCISE 6.   Write three sentences of your own, each containing a pronoun as part of a compound subject; three sentences, each containing a pronoun as part of a compound predicate nominative; and four sentences, each containing a pronoun as part of a compound object.

7e. The object of a preposition is in the objective case.

Prepositions, as well as verbs, take objects. The noun or pronoun at the end of a prepositional phrase is the object of the preposition which begins the phrase. In the following prepositional phrases the objects are printed in bold-faced type:

at **home**	in the **morning**	from **him**
to **Chicago**	under the **house**	for **George** and **him**

Errors in the use of the pronoun as the object of a preposition, like those made when it is the object of a verb, usually occur when the object is compound. Since you would not say "I had a letter from *she*," you should not say "I had a letter from *Geraldine* and *she*." By omitting the first of the two objects in a compound object, you can usually tell what the correct pronoun is.

WRONG   Give the message to either Belle or she.
RIGHT   Give the message **to** either Belle or **her**.   [to *her*]

WRONG   I begged a ride with Frank and he.
RIGHT   I begged a ride **with** Frank and **him**.   [with *him*]

WRONG   Dad bought the typewriter for my brother and I.
RIGHT   Dad bought the typewriter **for** my brother and **me**.   [for *me*]

● EXERCISE 7.   Number your paper 1–10. Select the preposition from each sentence, and write it after the proper number on your paper. After the preposition, write the correct one of the two pronouns in parentheses. Remember

7e

to choose the objective form. When you have checked your answers, use the sentences for an oral drill.

1. I played against Sam and (him, he).
2. He showed a friendly attitude toward my sister and (me, I).
3. How long did you work with (they, them) and John?
4. I addressed the card to both Carol and (her, she).
5. Bill came in after Joan and (me, I).
6. She put the blame on (us, we) boys.
7. Did you sit beside Bob and (he, him)?
8. A dispute arose between (they, them) and their leader.
9. Miss Sprague is looking for you and (her, she).
10. Were they talking about the girls or (we, us)?

● EXERCISE 8.   This exercise covers four uses of the personal pronouns: a. subject of a verb; b. predicate nominative (after a form of *be*); c. object of a verb (direct or indirect); d. object of a preposition. Number your paper 1–25. Select the correct one of the pronouns in parentheses in each sentence and write it after the proper number on your paper. After each pronoun, write the letter of its use as listed above.

EXAMPLE   1. Please ask Tommy and (she, her) for supper tonight.
   1. *her, c*

1. I will ask Carter and (he, him).
2. Have you heard from the Whites or (they, them)?
3. Bruce and (I, me) did our homework in school.
4. They thought it was (she, her).
5. Tell Mr. Clark and (he, him) what you want.
6. It might have been (they, them).
7. (He, Him) and (I, me) are on our way to the movies.
8. The book was written by (he, him) and Mr. Hall.
9. You can count on (we, us) students.
10. (She, Her) and (I, me) volunteered to help.
11. It was (he, him) who invented the electric light.
12. If (we, us) seniors support the production, others will, too.
13. Have you ever worked for either Miss Berger or (she, her)?

14. Did you leave the baby and (she, her) together?
15. Do I look like my father or (she, her)?
16. Don't go without (we, us) girls.
17. When Gene and (I, me) saw what was coming, we ran.
18. How do you know it was (he, him)?
19. When do you expect your family and (they, them)?
20. Bring Isabel and (she, her) with you.
21. Neither you nor (I, me) was right.
22. The trouble with Bob and (I, me) is that we are lazy.
23. The Browns and (they, them) are coming together.
24. She thought it was (they, them) who owned the house.
25. I talked to Dan and (he, him) for twenty minutes.

USES OF WHO AND WHOM

Like the personal pronouns, the pronouns *who* and *whoever* have three different case forms:

NOMINATIVE	OBJECTIVE	POSSESSIVE
who	whom	whose
whoever	whomever	whosever

Who and Whom as Interrogative Pronouns

Who and *whom* are interrogative pronouns when they are used to ask a question. The four rules on pages 106–11 governing the case forms of the personal pronouns apply also to *who* and *whom*.[1]

EXAMPLES **Who** left his books here? [The nominative form is required because *who* is the subject of *left*.]

Whom did Mary call? [The objective form is required because *whom* is the object of *did call*.]

[1] You may find it helpful, at first, to substitute *he, she—him, her* for *who—whom*, respectively. If *he* or *she*, nominative pronouns, fits the sentence, then *who*, also nominative, will be correct. If *him* or *her* fits, then *whom* will be correct.

(*Who, Whom*) left his books here? [*He* left his books here. Hence, *Who* left his books here?]

(*Who, Whom*) did Mary call? [Mary did call *him*. Hence, Mary did call *whom*. *Whom* did Mary call?]

Interrogative pronouns appear in both direct and indirect questions. A direct question uses the exact words of the speaker and is followed by a question mark. An indirect question does not use the exact words of the speaker and is not followed by a question mark.

DIRECT QUESTION **Who** is the captain?
INDIRECT QUESTION He asked **who** the captain was.
DIRECT QUESTION **Whom** did he meet?
INDIRECT QUESTION They asked **whom** he had met.

When the interrogative pronoun is used immediately after a preposition, *whom* is always the correct form.

EXAMPLES **To whom** were you speaking?
With whom did you go?

♦ USAGE NOTE In informal usage, *whom* is not usually used as an interrogative pronoun. *Who* is used regardless of the case.

INFORMAL **Who** do you know in Toledo?
Who does the manager want?

In formal usage, the distinction between *who* and *whom* is still recognized:

FORMAL **Whom** do you know in Toledo? [*Whom* is the object of the verb *do know.*]

Whom does the manager want? [*Whom* is the object of the verb *does want.*]

Who and Whom as Relative Pronouns

When *who* and *whom* (*whoever* and *whomever*) are used to begin a subordinate clause, they are relative pronouns. Their case is governed by the same rules that govern the case of a personal pronoun. Although *whom* is becoming increasingly uncommon in spoken English, the distinction between *who* and *whom* in subordinate clauses is usually observed in writing. Study the following explanations and refer to them whenever you need help with relative pronouns in your own writing.

7f. The case of the pronoun beginning a subordinate clause is determined by its use in the
clause that it begins. The case is not affected
by any word outside the clause.

In order to analyze a *who–whom* problem, follow these
steps:

1. Pick out the subordinate clause.
2. Determine how the pronoun is used in the clause—
subject, predicate nominative, object of verb, object of
preposition—and decide its case according to the rules.
3. Select the correct form of the pronoun.

PROBLEM	The new teacher, (who, whom) has taken Mr. Green's position, came from the South.
Step 1	The subordinate clause is (*who, whom*) *has taken Mr. Green's position.*
Step 2	In this clause the pronoun is used as the subject of the verb *has taken;* as a subject it should be, according to rule, in the nominative case.
Step 3	The nominative form is *who.*
SOLUTION	The new teacher, **who** has taken Mr. Green's position, came from the South.
PROBLEM	The new teacher, (who, whom) I met today, came from the South.
Step 1	The subordinate clause is (*who, whom*) *I met today.*
Step 2	In the clause the subject is *I;* the verb is *met;* and the pronoun is the object of the verb *met* (*I met whom*). As an object it is in the objective case according to rule.
Step 3	The objective form is *whom.*
SOLUTION	The new teacher, **whom** I met today, came from the South.
PROBLEM	Does anyone know (who, whom) the new teacher is?
Step 1	The subordinate clause is (*who, whom*) *the new teacher is.*

7f

Step 2   In the clause, *teacher* is the subject, *is* is the verb; the pronoun is a predicate nominative (*the new teacher is who*). As a predicate nominative it is in the nominative case according to rule.

Step 3   The nominative form is *who.*

SOLUTION   Does anyone know **who** the new teacher is?

In writing the preceding sentence, one might tend to use *whom*, thinking it the object of the verb *know*, but *know* is outside the clause and cannot affect the case of a word in the clause. The object of the verb *know* is the entire clause *who the new teacher is.*

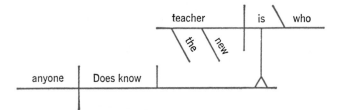

PROBLEM   I do not remember (who, whom) I lent the book to. [Following the three steps, you will find that the pronoun here is used as the object of the preposition *to;* it should be in the objective case, hence *whom.*]

SOLUTION   I do not remember **whom** I lent the book to.

SOLUTION   I do not remember **to whom** I lent the book.

◆ USAGE NOTE   In determining whether to use *who* or *whom*, do not be misled by a parenthetical expression like *I think, he said,* etc.

EXAMPLES   They are the people **who,** I think, are the foundation of society.   [*who* are the foundation of society]

He is the man **who** Mr. Bryan thinks should be rewarded.   [*who* should be rewarded]

● EXERCISE 9.   Number your paper 1–20. Using the three steps described on page 115 for determining the case of a relative pronoun, determine the correct form for each of the following sentences and write it on your paper after the proper number. Take plenty of time. Don't guess.

1. In *Hamlet* the two characters (who, whom) I most admire are Hamlet and Horatio.
2. If I had known (who, whom) he was, I would have been more cordial.
3. Next month's chairman will be (whoever, whomever) the delegates elect.
4. Since I did not know (who, whom) the caller wanted, I instructed him to return later.
5. Everybody (who, whom) received an invitation sent a reply.
6. The club members (who, whom) have paid their dues are qualified to vote.
7. He was one of the men (who, whom) the politicians could not influence.
8. No one has figured out to (who, whom) the teacher was referring.
9. The church is looking for someone (who, whom) it can assign to lead the young people's group.
10. John Wallace is a boy (who, whom), I think, is well qualified for the work.
11. The poets (who, whom) the reading public takes to its heart are not always great poets.
12. Everyone in the courtroom wondered (who, whom) the mysterious witness would be.
13. Many men (who, whom) are on strike would prefer to be working.
14. She is one of those students (who, whom), I believe, would make the most of an opportunity to study abroad.
15. The two men (who, whom) the police arrested for a parking violation were wanted for robbery in three states.
16. He couldn't plan his strategy until he knew (who, whom) his opponents would be.
17. You may tell anyone (who, whom) you think is interested that our fight has just begun.
18. The reporters must rely for information on certain persons (who, whom) they know well and whose trust they have obtained.

19. The coach's reply to the grandstand strategists (who, whom) were criticizing him was an undefeated season.
20. He is a man (who, whom) nobody trusts.

PRONOUNS IN INCOMPLETE CONSTRUCTIONS

An "incomplete construction" occurs most commonly after the words *than* and *as*. To avoid repetition, we say "The captain played better than he." (*Played* is omitted.) "Are you as tall as she?" (as she *is*). The interpretation of the sentence may depend upon the form of the pronoun used.

EXAMPLES   I like Fred better than **he.**   [than he likes Fred]
I like Fred better than **him.**   [than I like him]

7g. **After *than* and *as* introducing an incomplete construction, use the form of the pronoun you would use if the construction were completed.**

● EXERCISE 10.   Number your paper 1–10. Write after the proper number the part of each sentence beginning with *than* or *as*, using the correct pronoun and completing the sentence to show that the pronoun is correct. In several sentences either pronoun may be correct, depending on how the sentence is completed.

EXAMPLE   1. Philip is more popular than (he, him).
             1. *than he is.*

1. Did you stay as long as (they, them)?
2. I don't know Pat as well as (she, her).
3. Sam is much stronger than (I, me).
4. You played harder than (they, them).
5. Mr. Eldred was more helpful than (he, him).
6. Is he older than (I, me)?
7. The race proved that Mason could not stand the pace as well as (he, him).

8. Are you willing to trust Carl more than (I, me)?
9. Are they as fast as (we, us)?
10. I can understand him better than (she, her).

MINOR PROBLEMS IN THE USE OF PRONOUNS

7h. **In standard formal English the pronouns ending in** *–self, –selves* **are usually used only to refer to or to emphasize another word in the sentence.**

EXAMPLES   I hurt **myself.**   [*Myself* refers to *I.*]

He told me the whole story **himself.**   [*Himself* emphasizes *he.*]

The **boys themselves** made the suggestion.   [*Themselves* emphasizes *boys.*]

Avoid the use of pronouns ending in *–self, –selves* in place of other personal pronouns used as subjects.

EXAMPLES   John and **I** [not *myself*] are seventeen years old.
Did anyone take longer than **you** [not *yourself*]?

7i. **An appositive is in the same case as the word with which it is in apposition.**

WRONG   Two freshmen, Abe and him, made the best speeches.
RIGHT   Two freshmen, **Abe and he,** made the best speeches.

Abe and *he* are in apposition with *freshmen*, the subject of the sentence. Since the subject of a verb is nominative, the appositive is also nominative; hence, *he* is correct.

RIGHT   The truant officer was chasing two boys, **Abe and him.**

In apposition with *boys*, which is the object of *was chasing*, *Abe* and *him* are also in the objective case; hence, *him* is correct.

7
g-

7j. Use the possessive case of a noun or a pronoun before a gerund.

This use of the possessive case will appear reasonable if you understand that a gerund is a noun form.

EXAMPLES   I was surprised by the **child's question.**
I was surprised by the **child's asking** such a question.
Do you object to **my presence?**
Do you object to **my being** present?

Sometimes a participle ending in *–ing* may be confused with a gerund. The following use of the objective case before a participle is correct.

EXAMPLE   I watched **him running** down the street.

The use of the possessive *his* in this sentence would change the meaning to a far less likely idea: *I watched his running down the street.*

Whether or not you should use the possessive form of a word preceding a word ending in *–ing* often depends on which word you wish to emphasize. If you wish to emphasize the action in the *–ing* word, you use the possessive. If you wish to emphasize the preceding word, you do not use the possessive.

What do you think of Helen's singing?   [In this sentence the emphasis is on the kind of singing Helen does.]

Can you imagine Helen singing?   [In this sentence the emphasis is on Helen, who apparently is not likely to be a singer.]

7k. The subject of an infinitive is in the objective case.

An infinitive is a verb form consisting of *to* followed by a verb: *to go, to see, to play.*

I wanted you and him **to help** me.

In this sentence the words *you* and *him* may seem to you to be objects of the verb *wanted;* actually they are subjects of the infinitive *to help,* the whole infinitive clause being the object of *wanted.*

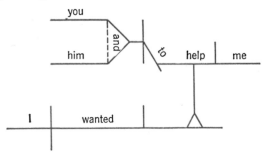

In most sentences like this one, since the subject of the infinitive is in the same case as the object of the verb, you will encounter little difficulty in using the correct pronoun. In one instance, that of the infinitive *to be,* the distinction between the subject of the infinitive and the object of the verb is important. In this rather involved construction, you find a pronoun following the infinitive.

EXAMPLE   I believed **it** to be **him.**

The explanation of the use of *him* in this construction is that the same case follows a form of *to be* as precedes it. Since *it,* the subject of the infinitive, is in the objective case, the pronoun following the infinitive *to be* is also in the objective case, hence *him.* In other words, when you wish to determine the case of a pronoun following *to be,* look to see whether a noun or pronoun immediately precedes *to be.* If it does, use the objective case of the pronoun after *to be.*[1]

---

[1] When the infinitive *to be* does not have a subject, it is followed by the nominative case. See rule 7c, page 107.

FORMAL   I wouldn't like to be **he.**   [no subject before *to be*]

Strict adherence to this rule is rare except in the most formal English.

INFORMAL   How would you like to be me?

7
j-l

FORMAL   **Whom** did you think me to be?   [You did think *me* to be *whom*].

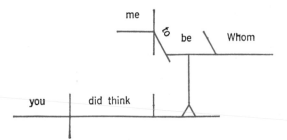

● EXERCISE 11.   Number your paper 1–10. Write a + after the proper number for each correct sentence; write a 0 for each incorrect sentence. After each 0, write the correct form.

1. The school's being open on a holiday surprised us.
2. Jean and myself did not have dates.
3. I do not enjoy his playing.
4. No one could understand Bob failing a math course.
5. The best players, Carl and him, were too ill to play.
6. After him warning us, we decided to study for the test.
7. Somebody, either Harold or he, answered the question.
8. I had not been notified of their coming.
9. His brother and himself were offered the job.
10. The class's taking the test without preparing for it was a mistake.

● REVIEW EXERCISE A.   Number your paper 1–33. Select the correct one of the pronouns in parentheses in each sentence and write it after the proper number on your paper. Be prepared to explain your answers.

1. Helen and (I, me) stayed after school.
2. Have you seen Sally and (she, her)?
3. No one could be sure that it was (they, them).
4. Today I had letters from both Nancy and (she, her).

5. The Senator (who, whom) I talked with objected to the bill.
6. He is a boy (who, whom), I think, has always had his own way.
7. You should have seen Dick and (I, me).
8. I do not know (who, whom) he had in mind.
9. He said that you and (I, me) are his best friends.
10. How can anyone be sure (who, whom) it was?
11. He could not cook as well as (she, her).
12. These are the students (who, whom), I think, Mr. Langley meant.
13. The disagreement between John and (he, him) was easily settled.
14. My sister and (I, me) did most of the cooking.
15. I do not know (who, whom) it was.
16. He knows that it might have been (she, her).
17. His sister is handsomer than (he, him).
18. Please call on either Mr. Nash or (I, me) if you need help.
19. (He, Him) and (I, me) have been in the same homeroom for three years.
20. The flowers came from Harry and (I, me).
21. You go ahead and (we, us) girls will follow later.
22. Why do you dislike Tom and (he, him)?
23. That was the girl (who, whom) John wanted him to meet.
24. Bob and (he, him) have their driver's licenses.
25. He refused to let (we, us) boys drive his car.
26. Ask the co-editors, Roy and (she, her), when the yearbook will be published.
27. It was (his, him) whistling that annoyed us.
28. Two teachers, Mr. Bryce and (she, her), are sponsoring the Ski Club.
29. Did you hear about (Howard, Howard's) breaking his leg?
30. Sue and (I, me, myself) did the homework together.
31. I do not approve of (their, them) habitually talking in class.
32. Herb and (I, me) took turns at the wheel.
33. An investigation uncovered the story of the (congressman, congressman's) refusing a bribe.

● REVIEW EXERCISE B.   Some of the following sentences contain errors in the use of pronouns. Others are correct.

Number your paper 1–20. If a sentence is correct, write a +
after the proper number. If it is incorrect, write the correct
form of the pronoun.

1. He was older than her.
2. No one knew who the winner was.
3. I can't tell her sister and her apart.
4. Please wait for Andy and I.
5. Are him and Maggie going to the movies?
6. Consult Dr. Faust, who, I think, will advise you wisely.
7. Is the captain him or Tom?
8. You can never depend on him being anywhere on time.
9. Sally, Sue, and me are giving a party.
10. He is a man who comes highly recommended.
11. Jim and me had lunch downtown with our fathers.
12. We have some members whom I have never met.
13. I will talk with whoever gets the assignment.
14. Two priests, Father Dalton and he, are in charge.
15. Get Harry and he to finish the job.
16. Whom did he say is the best-qualified candidate?
17. I want to know who you elected.
18. I was glad to hear about you winning an award.
19. It's easy to mislead gullible people like you and he.
20. There is a man whom prosperity ruined.

Correct Form and Use of Verbs

Principal Parts; Tense, Voice, and Mood

A verb is a word that expresses action or otherwise helps to make a statement.

KINDS OF VERBS

All verbs help to make statements about their subjects. Those that do so by expressing action performed by the subject are called *action verbs.*

ACTION VERBS Bob **dived** into the icy water.

Anne gingerly **tapped** the egg against the rim of the bowl.

He **thought** at length about the problem.

Some verbs help to make statements by linking with the subject a word in the predicate that explains, describes, or in some other way makes the subject more definite. Such verbs are called *linking verbs.*

LINKING VERBS Our prospects **looked** good. [*Good*, an adjective, modifies the subject *prospects*.]

Martin **is** my brother. [*Brother*, a noun, identifies Martin.]

George **became** a professional ball player. [*Ball player* identifies George.]

Some verbs can be either action verbs or linking verbs:

ACTION VERB   We **looked** everywhere for the missing puppy. [*Looked* expresses action.]

LINKING VERB   The test **looked** hard. [This time, *looked* links the subject, *test*, with a word that describes it, *hard*.]

There are many fewer linking verbs than action verbs. (You will find a list of the most common linking verbs on page 12.) The verb used most often as a linking verb is *be*, whose forms are *am, is, are, was, were*, and all verb phrases ending in *be, being*, or *been: may be, was being, has been*, etc.

In addition to functioning as a linking verb, *be* can also be followed by an adverb or adverb phrase:

She was **there.**
The house is **in the country.**

Although it resembles an action verb in this use, *be* is not generally classified as one. Just remember that *be* is always a linking verb except when followed by an adverb instead of a subject complement.

There are, then, two main classes of verbs: action and linking. Some verbs belong to both classes and some only to one. The verb *be* is a special case.

THE PRINCIPAL PARTS OF A VERB

Every verb has four basic forms called principal parts: the *infinitive, present participle, past*, and *past participle*. All other forms are derived from these principal parts.

INFINITIVE	PRESENT PARTICIPLE	PAST	PAST PARTICIPLE
work	(is) working	worked	(have) worked

The words *is* and *have* are given with the present participle and past participle forms to remind you that these forms are used with a helping verb: *am, is, are, was, were, has been, will be, have, has, had*, etc.

Regular Verbs

A regular verb is one that forms its past and past participle by adding *-d* or *-ed* to the infinitive form.

INFINITIVE	PAST	PAST PARTICIPLE
live	lived	(have) lived
play	played	(have) played

Irregular Verbs

An irregular verb is one that forms its past and past participle in some other way than a regular verb.

This "other way" may involve changing the spelling of the verb or making no change at all.

INFINITIVE	PAST	PAST PARTICIPLE
swim	swam	(have) swum
write	wrote	(have) written
hit	hit	(have) hit

The major problem in the correct use of verbs is the choice of the correct past and past participle forms of irregular verbs. Since irregular past tenses and past participles are formed in a variety of ways, you must know the principal parts of each irregular verb.

Three principal parts of common irregular verbs are given in the following alphabetical list. Use this list for reference. For the principal parts of other irregular verbs, consult a dictionary. Drill exercises on irregular verbs frequently misused are given following the list.

PRINCIPAL PARTS OF IRREGULAR VERBS

INFINITIVE	PAST	PAST PARTICIPLE
bear	bore	(have) borne
beat	beat	(have) beaten *or* beat
begin	began	(have) begun
bite	bit	(have) bitten
blow	blew	(have) blown

INFINITIVE	PAST	PAST PARTICIPLE
break	broke	(have) broken
bring	brought	(have) brought
burst	burst	(have) burst
catch	caught	(have) caught
choose	chose	(have) chosen
come	came	(have) come
creep	crept	(have) crept
dive	dived [1]	(have) dived
do	did	(have) done
draw	drew	(have) drawn
drink	drank	(have) drunk
drive	drove	(have) driven
eat	ate	(have) eaten
fall	fell	(have) fallen
fling	flung	(have) flung
fly	flew	(have) flown
freeze	froze	(have) frozen
get	got	(have) got *or* gotten
give	gave	(have) given
go	went	(have) gone
grow	grew	(have) grown
know	knew	(have) known
lay	laid	(have) laid
lead	led	(have) led
lend	lent	(have) lent
lie	lay	(have) lain
lose	lost	(have) lost
ride	rode	(have) ridden
ring	rang	(have) rung
rise	rose	(have) risen
run	ran	(have) run
say	said	(have) said
see	saw	(have) seen
set	set	(have) set
shake	shook	(have) shaken
shine	shone *or* shined	(have) shone *or* shined
sing	sang *or* sung	(have) sung

[1] Informal, *dove*.

INFINITIVE	PAST	PAST PARTICIPLE
sink	sank *or* sunk	(have) sunk
sit	sat	(have) sat
speak	spoke	(have) spoken
steal	stole	(have) stolen
sting	stung	(have) stung
swear	swore	(have) sworn
swim	swam	(have) swum
swing	swung	(have) swung
take	took	(have) taken
tear	tore	(have) torn
throw	threw	(have) thrown
wear	wore	(have) worn
write	wrote	(have) written

8a. Learn the principal parts of common irregular verbs.

To help you learn the correct use of irregular verbs, those which are commonly misused are presented on the following pages in four groups. Memorize the principal parts of the verbs in each group and do the exercises. In doing the exercises, remember that the past participle is used with helping, or auxiliary, verbs: *is, are, was, were, have, has, had, have been,* etc. As you say the principal parts, place *have* before the past participle: *begin, began, have begun.*

GROUP I

INFINITIVE	PAST	PAST PARTICIPLE
beat	beat	(have) beaten *or* beat
begin	began	(have) begun
blow	blew	(have) blown
break	broke	(have) broken
burst	burst	(have) burst
choose	chose	(have) chosen
come	came	(have) come
do	did	(have) done

8a

● Exercise 1.   Number your paper 1–20. After the proper number, write either the past or the past participle of the verb given at the beginning of each sentence, whichever will fill correctly the blank in the sentence.

1. *begin*   I had already —— to work.
2. *blow*   The wind has —— hard all day.
3. *come*   He —— in last night at ten o'clock.
4. *choose*   Has everyone —— a partner?
5. *beat*   We —— them three times least season.
6. *do*   Jack —— the best he could.
7. *break*   Was his arm ——?
8. *burst*   Thousands died when the Johnstown dam ——.
9. *do*   We —— what was expected of us.
10. *begin*   You should have —— earlier.
11. *blow*   His boat had been —— out to sea.
12. *choose*   They —— Dr. Harzog as the keynote speaker.
13. *burst*   They thought the water pipes had ——.
14. *come*   We watched as the band —— slowly up the street.
15. *choose*   I wished we had —— the other route.
16. *break*   He has —— his promise.
17. *come*   I —— along right after the accident happened.
18. *do*   The actors —— well in last night's performance.
19. *begin*   When the news came, I —— to regret my choice.
20. *come*   She has —— to get your advice.

GROUP II

INFINITIVE	PAST	PAST PARTICIPLE
draw	drew	(have) drawn
drink	drank	(have) drunk
drive	drove	(have) driven
fall	fell	(have) fallen
fly	flew	(have) flown
freeze	froze	(have) frozen
give	gave	(have) given
go	went	(have) gone

● Exercise 2.   Number your paper 1–20. After the proper number, write either the past or the past participle of the verb, whichever will fill correctly the blank in the sentence.

1. *drink* Have you —— all the milk?
2. *fall* If I hadn't ——, I'd have caught him.
3. *freeze* The water hasn't —— yet.
4. *go* He has —— to Chicago.
5. *give* She —— me a make-up test yesterday.
6. *fly* Have you —— the Atlantic?
7. *drive* George has —— since he was fourteen.
8. *draw* Marilyn —— the cartoons for the yearbook last year.
9. *go* Mac has —— to the library.
10. *give* I —— him the money last week.
11. *freeze* All of us were nearly ——.
12. *fly* You could have —— up here in two hours.
13. *draw* No child could have —— that picture.
14. *drink* Although I had worked hard, he —— more soda than I did.
15. *drive* We have —— more than 500 miles today.
16. *fall* I thought he had —— from the tree.
17. *give* He —— me only a dollar.
18. *drive* If you had —— a little farther, you would have found us.
19. *go* He has —— home already.
20. *give* He should have —— me more time for the test.

● EXERCISE 3. *Group* i and *Group* ii. Number your paper 1–33. After the proper number, write a + for each sentence in which the italicized verb is correct; for each sentence in which the verb is incorrect, write the correct form of the verb.

1. Janet *drew* the picture for us.
2. I *begun* to think you had forgotten me.
3. No one *drunk* very much.
4. The boys *have broke* the window.
5. He has *drove* this road hundreds of times.
6. You *should have chosen* Jimmy.
7. She *had* not *fell* very far.
8. The boys *done* the heavy work.
9. I *had flown* as far as St. Louis.
10. She *come* home an hour ago.
11. The food *must be frozen* immediately.

12. During the heavy rain the ripest cherries *had bursted* open.
13. He *give* me what I wanted.
14. Strong winds *blowed* us off our course.
15. We *could* not *have gone* any further.
16. Rice Lake *was froze* to a depth of two feet.
17. His plow *was drawed* by a team of mules.
18. *Have* you ever *drunk* papaya juice?
19. He *had chose* her for his partner.
20. You *could have flew* to Newark.
21. As I reached the car, the bag of groceries suddenly *burst* open.
22. You *should have went* earlier.
23. Since then he *has* never *been beaten*.
24. Who *give* you the pearls?
25. Pete *come* in third in the first race.
26. You *might have fallen* on your head.
27. The axle *must be broke*.
28. The game *begun* about two o'clock.
29. He *had drunk* too much soda.
30. We *had driven* for miles in the fog.
31. Who *done* it?
32. The river *had frozen* solid.
33. The bus driver *come* after us about noon.

GROUP III

INFINITIVE	PAST	PAST PARTICIPLE
grow	grew	(have) grown
know	knew	(have) known
ride	rode	(have) ridden
ring	rang	(have) rung
run	ran	(have) run
see	saw	(have) seen
sing	sang *or* sung	(have) sung
speak	spoke	(have) spoken

● EXERCISE 4. Number your paper 1–20. After the proper number, write either the past or past participle of the verb given at the beginning of each sentence, whichever will fill correctly the blank in the sentence.

1. *ring*   The bell has ——.
2. *run*   When the rain came, everyone —— for shelter.
3. *sing*   Had she —— in the choir before?
4. *speak*   If I had recognized you, I'd have —— to you.
5. *see*   The boys —— some rattlesnakes last summer.
6. *ride*   The messenger had —— twenty miles.
7. *know*   You should have —— better.
8. *grow*   He has —— too fast.
9. *see*   I —— him at the drugstore.
10. *know*   We found that no one —— the correct answer.
11. *ride*   Barry had —— over to see us.
12. *grow*   In one year the trees had —— a foot.
13. *speak*   Have you —— to her yet?
14. *sing*   Has anyone here ever —— this song?
15. *run*   We —— home as soon as school was out.
16. *ring*   Has she —— the bell?
17. *speak*   I wish I hadn't —— so severely.
18. *see*   Who —— me last night?
19. *ring*   The telephone has —— ten times in the past hour.
20. *run*   He —— as fast as he could in the last race.

GROUP IV

INFINITIVE	PAST	PAST PARTICIPLE
spring	sprang *or* sprung	(have) sprung
steal	stole	(have) stolen
swim	swam	(have) swum
swing	swung	(have) swung
take	took	(have) taken
tear	tore	(have) torn
throw	threw	(have) thrown
write	wrote	(have) written

● EXERCISE 5.   Number your paper 1–20. After the proper number, write either the past or past participle of the verb given at the beginning of each sentence, whichever will fill correctly the blank in the sentence.

1. *spring*   The lock had been —— by force.
2. *swim*   I could not have —— another foot.
3. *tear*   Have you —— your coat?

4. *write*   Has she —— to you?

5. *throw*   Jackie —— him out at first base.

6. *take*   She should have —— the children with her.

7. *swing*   Last year they —— in the playground swings nearly every day.

8. *steal*   They thought their car had been ——.

9. *throw*   The first ball Gary —— was a wide curve.

10. *write*   My uncle has —— several books.

11. *tear*   You have —— my homework paper.

12. *swim*   Yesterday she —— alone to the raft.

13. *spring*   In a moment he had —— into the saddle and galloped away.

14. *take*   I should have —— a course in typing.

15. *swing*   All morning the balloon —— back and forth on its cable.

16. *steal*   I'm sure no one has —— your wallet.

17. *write*   If you had —— to me, I'd have helped you.

18. *swim*   Where were you when we —— the channel?

19. *throw*   A sudden lurch of the boat —— everyone overboard.

20. *write*   When you have —— your essay, show it to me.

● EXERCISE 6.   *Group* III and *Group* IV.   Number your paper 1–33. After the proper number, write a + for each sentence in which the italicized verb is correct; for each sentence in which the verb is incorrect, write the correct form of the verb.

1. You *have growed* much taller this year.

2. Who *had rang* the bell?

3. He *has ran* his last race.

4. We *have sung* that number in every concert.

5. He *has spoke* at our school several times.

6. They *swam* until they were tired.

7. I *had tore* my shirt.

8. You *have* never *wrote* a better story.

9. *Had* I *known* your number, I'd have called you.

10. I *had* not *rode* horseback for years.

11. He thinks I *seen* him there.

12. Who *throwed* you out?

13. We *should have taken* more money with us.
14. Several pages *have been torn* from this book.
15. The acrobat *swung* himself over the swinging bar.
16. Someone *must have stolen* my watch.
17. On both plays they *threw* us for a loss.
18. Mr. Maxwell *seen* at once what the trouble was.
19. Dad thought we *had ridden* far enough.
20. He *would have knowed* what to do.
21. *Have* you *wrote* your composition yet?
22. The gale *had tore* both sails.
23. No one *could have swum* that far.
24. I *have* not *spoken* to Everett.
25. She *has sung* her way to stardom.
26. When Mr. Stoltz appeared, the boys *run* away.
27. I did not know the bell *had rang*.
28. This town *has grown* rapidly.
29. You *should have knowed* better.
30. Nothing *had been stolen*.
31. She *had tore* her new gloves.
32. You *could have took* Jane to the dance.
33. I *shall have written* my letter by that time.

● EXERCISE 7. *Groups* I–IV. Number your paper 1–50. After the proper number, write either the past or past participle of the verb at the beginning of each sentence, whichever will fill correctly the blank in the sentence.

1. *burst*　In the bus station my suitcase suddenly —— open.
2. *freeze*　The doctor said I had —— both feet.
3. *break*　Were any bones ——?
4. *fly*　We'd be home now if we had ——.
5. *blow*　The storm had —— down a telephone pole.
6. *fall*　She could not have —— more than six feet.
7. *begin*　We —— the job yesterday morning.
8. *know*　You should have —— what to do.
9. *beat*　We —— them twice last season.
10. *ring*　Someone had —— the bell.
11. *drive*　How far have you —— today?
12. *ride*　Spot had never —— in the back seat before.
13. *drink*　During the 1962 flood, we —— bottled water.

14. *run*   When I saw him pass the house, I —— after him.
15. *do*   She —— her homework before school was out.
16. *swim*   When I called for help, Helen —— out to me.
17. *come*   He —— in about an hour ago.
18. *steal*   Jack thought someone had —— his bicycle.
19. *choose*   The council could have —— a better representative.
20. *sing*   You should have —— louder.
21. *grow*   The school has —— beyond capacity.
22. *speak*   How many times have I —— to you about that?
23. *go*   Alice had —— to the movies.
24. *see*   I'm sure Raymond —— me as I left the room.
25. *give*   Who —— you the black eye?
26. *take*   I wish he had —— me with him.
27. *tear*   The trainer said I had —— a ligament.
28. *throw*   We lost the game when Bob —— the ball over Ben's head.
29. *tear*   Someone had —— the draperies.
30. *write*   Why haven't you —— to your mother?
31. *throw*   Who —— away this fountain pen?
32. *go*   We could not have —— any earlier.
33. *see*   How do you know they —— you last night?
34. *freeze*   If he had not been rescued promptly, he would have ——.
35. *run*   The truck —— into us as we parked at the curb.
36. *come*   Last night, Don —— over to hear some records.
37. *write*   You should have —— more.
38. *drink*   Who —— the Coke I left here?
39. *know*   I had —— June when she was a little girl.
40. *break*   Two convicts had —— away from the work gang.
41. *begin*   A little later I —— to see what he meant.
42. *swim*   During last week's cold wave we —— in the pool.
43. *fall*   We thought he must have —— through the ice.
44. *beat*   The defendant claimed his jailers —— him.
45. *see*   I —— him at the dance last night.
46. *throw*   That horse has never —— a rider.
47. *run*   Mr. Smith —— for mayor last year.
48. *speak*   I wish he had —— about his travels.
49. *come*   I couldn't find the family when I —— home.
50. *write*   Both men have —— an autobiography.

THREE TROUBLESOME PAIRS OF VERBS

Three pairs of verbs require special study and drill because they are more difficult to use correctly than any other verbs. These special verbs are *lie*, *lay*, *sit*, *set*, *rise*, and *raise*. Most difficult to use correctly are the verbs *lie* and *lay*.

Lie and Lay

The verb *lie* means "to assume a lying position" or "to be in a lying position." Its principal parts are *lie*, (*is*) *lying*, *lay*, (*have*) *lain*.

The verb *lay* means "to put" or "to place something." Its principal parts are *lay*, (*is*) *laying*, *laid*, (*have*) *laid*.

The verb *lie* is intransitive (see page 11); that is, it never has an object. You never "lie" anything down.

The verb *lay* is transitive; that is, it may have an object, or be in the passive voice. (See page 10.)

INTRANSITIVE	The metal **lies** in a mold until thoroughly cooled. [no object]
TRANSITIVE	Workers **lay** the molds in a cooling chamber. [object: *molds*]
TRANSITIVE	The molds **are laid** in a cooling chamber. [passive voice]

Memorize the principal parts of these verbs:

INFINITIVE	PRESENT PARTICIPLE	PAST	PAST PARTICIPLE
lie (to recline)	(is) lying	lay	(have) lain
lay (to put)	(is) laying	laid	(have) laid

If you do not habitually use these verbs correctly, you must begin your work on them slowly and thoughtfully. Only by taking time to think through each form you use can you eventually establish the habit of using the verbs correctly. When faced with a *lie–lay* problem, ask yourself two questions:

1. What is the meaning I intend? Is it "to be in a lying position," or is it "to put something down"?

2. What is the time expressed by the verb and which principal part is required to express this time?

PROBLEM After the alarm had awakened me, I (lay, laid) in bed too long.

Question 1 Meaning? The meaning here is "to remain in a lying position." The verb which means "to remain in a lying position" is *lie*.

Question 2 Principal part? The time is past and requires the past form, which is *lay*. [lie, *lay*, lain]

SOLUTION After the alarm had awakened me, I **lay** in bed too long.

PROBLEM Mac (lay, laid) his coat on the table.

Question 1 Meaning? The meaning here is "to put." The verb which means "to put" is *lay*.

Question 2 Principal part? The time is past and therefore requires the past form, which is *laid*. [lay, *laid*, laid]

SOLUTION Mac **laid** his coat on the table.

PROBLEM How long had it (lain, laid) there?

Question 1 Meaning? The meaning here is "to be in a lying position." The verb which means "to be in a lying position" is *lie*.[1]

Question 2 Principal part? The time requires the past participle with *had*. The past participle of *lie* is *lain*. [lie, lay, *lain*]

SOLUTION How long had it **lain** there?

PROBLEM The dog is (lying, laying) on the doormat.

Question 1 Meaning? The meaning here is "to be in a lying

---

[1] You should be warned against two fairly common misconceptions about *lie* and *lay*. The first is that only people and animals *lie*. A moment's thought, however, will make clear that inanimate objects may also be in a lying position. The second misconception is that because an inanimate object in a lying position must have been put there, one should use *lay*, the verb meaning "to put," to say that the object is at rest. Regardless of its having once been put down, the object *lies* (not *lays*) there.

position." The verb which means "to be in a lying position" is *lie.*

Question 2   Principal part? The time here requires the present participle, which is *lying.*

SOLUTION   The dog is **lying** on the doormat.

It will pay you to use this two-question formula each time you are in doubt about a problem in the use of *lie* and *lay.* Although slow at first, the process will speed up after a few trials, and you will be able to select the correct verb quickly. Of course, you must memorize the principal parts of the verbs before you can use the formula.

Two facts about the use of *lie* and *lay* may be of additional help.

1. Most errors in the use of these verbs are made when the speaker means "to assume or to be in a lying position." When this is the meaning you intend, be especially cautious.

2. When you wish to express the idea of "putting or placing something" in the past tense, always use *laid.*

● EXERCISE 8.   Number your paper 1–10. After the proper number, write the correct one of the two words in parentheses. Use the two-question formula.

1. He spent the summer just (lying, laying) around home.
2. Someone (lay, laid) the dictionary on my glasses.
3. He had (lain, laid) a burning cigar on the edge of the table.
4. Jimmy (lay, laid) down on the back seat of the car.
5. I saw your hat (lying, laying) on the hall table.
6. She had just (lain, laid) down when the telephone rang.
7. Have they (lain, laid) the cornerstone yet?
8. Not feeling well, he (lay, laid) in his sleeping bag all day.
9. She (lay, laid) her sewing aside and went to the door.
10. Don't leave any money (lying, laying) in plain sight.

● EXERCISE 9.   Choose the correct form of *lie* or *lay* to fill the blank in each sentence. Use the two-question formula.

1. The book —— open to page 231.
2. —— on your back and stretch yourself.

3. An hour ago I —— down for a nap.
4. The tiger was —— asleep near the tree.
5. Have they —— the flooring yet?
6. I think he is —— in the hammock.
7. He —— the boxes on the porch yesterday.
8. She had —— there only a short time.
9. The dog was —— in the shade.
10. She —— the dress pattern on the material.

● EXERCISE 10. Number your paper 1–20. After the proper number, write the correct one of the two verbs in parentheses. Use the two-question formula.

1. The wreck (lay, laid) in twenty feet of water.
2. The cat loves to (lie, lay) on the window sill.
3. The missing book was (lying, laying) on the top shelf.
4. Do you remember where you (lay, laid) my pen?
5. You shouldn't have (lain, laid) there so long.
6. Jack was (lying, laying) on the deck.
7. Here the coal (lies, lays) near the surface.
8. We gathered driftwood while Doug (lay, laid) a fire.
9. I planned to (lie, lay) down for only ten minutes.
10. Gently she (lay, laid) down the injured child.
11. Sandy usually (lies, lays) near the fire.
12. I could not persuade him to (lie, lay) down.
13. Yesterday Dad and I (lay, laid) the new carpet.
14. The cat never (lies, lays) in the bed we made for her.
15. Someone had (lain, laid) a paintbrush on the chair.
16. His clothes were (lying, laying) about the room.
17. Frank had (lain, laid) his camera on the railing.
18. The fossils had (lain, laid) there for a million years.
19. Beneath his rough exterior (lies, lays) a kind heart.
20. I keep forgetting where I have (lain, laid) the hammer.

Sit and Set

Sit usually means "to assume or to be in an upright, sitting position." [1] The principal parts of *sit* are *sit*, (*is*)

---

[1] Such expressions as "Sit the baby in his high chair" or "Sit him up" really mean "to put" or "to place," and these expressions, which are acceptable, are exceptions to the general rule.

sitting, sat, (have) sat. Sit is almost always an intransitive verb; it rarely takes an object.

Set usually means "to put, to place something." The principal parts of *set* are *set, (is) setting, set, (have) set.* Like *lay, set* is a transitive verb; it may take an object.

Since all forms of *set* are made without changing the vowel, the problem of using these two verbs is rather simple. You need only keep in mind the fact that when you mean "to put something down," you use *set* or *setting.* For all other meanings use *sit* or *sat* or *sitting.*[1]

Memorize the principal parts of these verbs:

INFINITIVE	PRESENT PARTICIPLE	PAST	PAST PARTICIPLE
sit (to rest)	(is) sitting	sat	(have) sat
set (to put)	(is) setting	set	(have) set

● EXERCISE 11. Number your paper 1–10. After the proper number, write the correct one of the two verbs in parentheses in each sentence.

1. She has been (sitting, setting) by the telephone all evening.
2. Bill just (sat, set) still and said nothing.
3. In what row were you (sitting, setting)?
4. Extra chairs were (sat, set) in the aisles by the ushers.
5. Had you (sat, set) there longer, you would have caught a fish.
6. We decided to (sit, set) quietly and await results.
7. Passengers (sitting, setting) in the rear seats were not injured.
8. If you (sit, set) on the damp ground, you may catch a cold.
9. He plans to (sit, set) the new cabin on the beach.
10. Someone had (sat, set) in the fresh paint.

Rise and Raise

The verb *rise* means "to go up." Its principal parts are *rise, (is) rising, rose, (have) risen.* In other words, when the subject of the verb is itself moving upward, use *rise.* Like *lie, rise* is intransitive; it never takes an object.

---

[1] The expressions "The sun sets," "the setting hen," and "Wait for the cement to set" are exceptions to the rule.

The verb *raise* means "to force something to move upward." Its principal parts are *raise*, *(is) raising*, *raised*, *(have) raised*. When the subject of the verb is acting on something, forcing it upward, use *raise*. Like *lay* and *set*, *raise* is transitive; it may take an object.

Memorize the principal parts of these verbs:

INFINITIVE	PRESENT PARTICIPLE	PAST	PAST PARTICIPLE
rise (to go up)	(is) rising	rose	(have) risen
raise (to force up or be forced up)	(is) raising	raised	(have) raised

● EXERCISE 12. Number your paper 1–10. After the proper number, write the correct one of the two verbs in parentheses in each sentence.

1. The river has been (rising, raising) all night.
2. The effect of the controversial law was to (rise, raise) prices again.
3. Our hopes (rose, raised) and fell in the same instant.
4. We saw a column of smoke (rising, raising) above the farmhouse.
5. The moon (rises, raises) about nine o'clock.
6. If taxes (rise, raise) any higher, we shall have to move.
7. With its extra load of fuel, the plane would not (rise, raise) from the runway.
8. Workmen (rose, raised) the house six feet.
9. Clouds were (rising, raising) on the horizon.
10. Rents are (rising, raising) rapidly.

● EXERCISE 13. For each of the following verbs, write a brief sentence in which the verb is correctly used.

1. lie	6. raised	11. rising
2. raising	7. rises	12. rose
3. laying	8. have lain	13. setting
4. set	9. lay (past tense)	14. risen
5. lying	10. has laid	15. sat

● EXERCISE 14. Number your paper 1–25. After the proper number, write the correct one of the two words in parentheses in each sentence. Work slowly. Try for 100 percent.

1. A film of oil (lay, laid) on the water.
2. Can't you (sit, set) a while longer?
3. If his temperature (rises, raises), call the doctor.
4. The dog had been (lying, laying) in my bed.
5. We hardly (sat, set) down at all during the final quarter of the game.
6. Your letter was (lying, laying) at the bottom of the pile.
7. The waves (rose, raised) to mountainous height.
8. I had (lain, laid) the flashlight on the car seat.
9. From where we were (sitting, setting), the stage was barely visible.
10. She forgot where she had (lain, laid) her gloves.
11. Piles of books and papers were (lying, laying) on the desk.
12. Clouds of black smoke were (rising, raising) from the hills behind us.
13. If we (sit, set) here much longer, we'll be late.
14. (Lie, Lay) down, Butch!
15. Boulders and jagged rocks (lay, laid) across the highway.
16. Since the election, stocks have been (rising, raising) steadily.
17. The dog must have been (lying, laying) under the car.
18. We spent the afternoon just (sitting, setting) and talking.
19. Where do you want to (sit, set)?
20. The child refused to (lie, lay) under the beach umbrella.
21. Beyond this point the road (rises, raises) sharply.
22. Who (lay, laid) out this tennis court?
23. No one expected the tide to (rise, raise) so high.
24. We were (sitting, setting) before the fireplace.
25. The ties on which the track (lies, lays) must be firm and level.

TENSE

Verbs change in form to show the time of their action or of the idea they express. The time expressed by a verb (present, past, future) is its tense. There are six tenses. As the following conjugations of the verbs *go* and *be* will show you, the six tenses are made from the principal parts of the verb. Study these conjugations and use them for reference in your work on tense.

8b. Learn the names of the six tenses and how the tenses are formed.

CONJUGATION OF THE VERB <u>GO</u>

Present infinitive: *to go*   Perfect infinitive: *to have gone*

PRINCIPAL PARTS

INFINITIVE	PRESENT PARTICIPLE	PAST	PAST PARTICIPLE
go	going	went	gone

PRESENT TENSE

Singular	*Plural*
I go	we go
you go	you go
he, she, it goes	they go

Present progressive: *I am going*, etc.

PAST TENSE

Singular	*Plural*
I went	we went
you went	you went
he, she, it went	they went

Past progressive: *I was going*, etc.

FUTURE TENSE

(*will* or *shall* + infinitive [1])

Singular	*Plural*
I will (shall) go	we will (shall) go
you will go	you will go
he, she, it will go	they will go

Future progressive: *I will be going*, etc.

[1] For a discussion of the use of *shall* and *will*, see page 190.

PRESENT PERFECT TENSE

(*have* or *has* + the past participle)

Singular	Plural
I have gone	we have gone
you have gone	you have gone
he, she, it has gone	they have gone

Present perfect progressive: *I have been going*, etc.

PAST PERFECT TENSE

(*had* + the past participle)

Singular	Plural
I had gone	we had gone
you had gone	you had gone
he, she, it had gone	they had gone

Past perfect progressive: *I had been going*, etc.

FUTURE PERFECT TENSE

(*will have* or *shall have* + the past participle)

Singular	Plural
I will (shall) have gone	we will (shall) have gone
you will have gone	you will have gone
he, she, it will have gone	they will have gone

Future perfect progressive: *I will have been going*, etc.

CONJUGATION OF THE VERB BE

Present infinitive: *to be*   Perfect infinitive: *to have been*

PRINCIPAL PARTS

INFINITIVE	PRESENT PARTICIPLE	PAST	PAST PARTICIPLE
be	being	was, were	been

PRESENT TENSE

Singular	Plural
I am	we are
you are	you are
he, she, it is	they are

Present progressive: *I am being*, etc.

8b

PAST TENSE

Singular	*Plural*
I was	we were
you were	you were
he, she, it was	they were

Past progressive: *I was being*, etc.

FUTURE TENSE

(*will* or *shall* + the infinitive)

Singular	*Plural*
I will (shall) be	we will (shall) be
you will be	you will be
he, she, it will be	they will be

Future progressive: *I will be being*, etc.

PRESENT PERFECT TENSE

(*have* or *has* + the past participle)

Singular	*Plural*
I have been	we have been
you have been	you have been
he, she, it has been	they have been

PAST PERFECT TENSE

(*had* + the past participle)

Singular	*Plural*
I had been	we had been
you had been	you had been
he, she, it had been	they had been

FUTURE PERFECT TENSE

(*will have* or *shall have* + the past participle)

Singular	*Plural*
I will (shall) have been	we will (shall) have been
you will have been	you will have been
he, she, it will have been	they will have been

8c. Learn the uses of each of the six tenses.

Each of the six tenses has its own particular uses, some of which require explanation. Study the following explanations of these uses; learn rules for the uses of the tenses; do the exercises. Use these pages for reference when you are confronted by a problem in tense in your own writing.

(1) The *present tense* is used to express action (or to help make a statement about something) occurring now, at the present time.

EXAMPLES   **I work** here.

          I am working now. [progressive form]

          I do work. [The verb with *do* or *did* is called the emphatic form.]

◆ NOTE In all tenses, as in the second example, continuing action may be shown by the use of the progressive form, which ends in *–ing*. The third example illustrates the emphatic form, consisting of a form of *do* plus the first principle part of a verb. The normal way of making a sentence emphatic is to pronounce the helping verb with unusual stress. When there is no helping verb, *do* or *did* is added to carry this stress. These emphatic forms can be used in the present and past tense only.

The present tense is also used to indicate habitual action.

EXAMPLE He **works** every evening.

The present tense is often used to express a general truth, something which is true at all times.

EXAMPLES He apparently thought that seeing **is** [instead of *was*] believing.

          I did not know that Salem **is** [instead of *was*] the capital of Oregon.

The present tense is also used occasionally to achieve vividness in writing about past events. This use of the present tense is known as the *historical present.*

EXAMPLE Napoleon promptly **senses** the danger to his left flank and **dispatches** reinforcements.

8 c

(2) The *past tense* is used to express action (or to help make a statement about something) that occurred in the past but did not continue into the present. The past tense is formed regularly by adding *–d* or *–ed* to the verb.

EXAMPLES   I **worked** there during the holidays.
            I **was working** there during the holidays.

◆ NOTE   Past action may be shown in other ways.
EXAMPLES   I **used to work** there.
            I **did work** there.   [emphatic form]

(3) The *future tense* is used to express action (or to help make a statement about something) occurring at some time in the future. The future tense is formed with *will* or *shall*.

EXAMPLES   I **will work** in the library after school.
            I **will be working** in the library after school.

◆ NOTE   The future may also be indicated in other ways.
    EXAMPLES   I **am going to work** there.
                I **am about to work**.
                I **work** there **tomorrow**.   [present with another word indicating future time]

(4) The *present perfect tense* is used to express action (or to help make a statement about something) occurring at no definite time in the past. It is formed with *have* or *has*.

EXAMPLE   He **has worked** for us many times.

The present perfect tense is also used to express action (or to help make a statement about something) occurring in the past and continuing into the present.

EXAMPLES   I **have worked** here for six weeks.   [I am still working here.]
            I **have been working** here for six weeks.   [I am still working here.]

(5) The *past perfect tense* is used to express action (or to help make a statement about something) completed in the past before some other past action or event. It is formed with *had*.

EXAMPLES   When I **had worked** for a week, I asked for my pay. [The working preceded the asking.]

When I **had been working** for a week, I asked for my pay.

(6) The *future perfect tense* is used to express action (or to help make a statement about something) which will be completed in the future before some other future action or event. It is formed with *will have* or *shall have*.

EXAMPLES   By the time school **opens, I will have worked** here eight weeks. [The working precedes the opening of school.]

By the time school **opens, I will have been working** here eight weeks.

● EXERCISE 15.   Explain the difference in meaning between the sentences in the following pairs. The sentences are correct. Name the tense used in each sentence.

1. Katherine went to high school for two years.
   Katherine has gone to high school for two years.
2. How long has she been here?
   How long was she here?
3. What has been going on here?
   What went on here?
4. Have the ballots been counted?
   Had the ballots been counted?
5. We learned that he had been there for three hours.
   We learned that he has been there for three hours.
6. I suppose Mary will have finished college when they return from abroad.
   I suppose Mary will finish college when they return from abroad.

SPECIAL PROBLEMS OF TENSE USAGE

The Past Perfect Tense

The past perfect tense requires special consideration because young writers frequently fail to employ it in expressing two actions which happened at different times in the past. The function of the past perfect tense is to make clear which of the actions preceded the other.

8d. Use the past perfect tense for the earlier of two past actions.

WRONG   Suddenly he remembered (past) that he promised (past) to meet her at eight. [The same tense has been incorrectly used for two actions which did not happen at the same time. Since the forgetting preceded the remembering, the past perfect form of *forget* should be used.]

RIGHT   Suddenly he **remembered** (past) that he **had promised** (past perfect) to meet her at eight.

WRONG   Everything he told (past) me I heard (past) before. [The hearing preceded the telling.]

RIGHT   Everything he **told** (past) me I **had heard** (past perfect) before.

WRONG   There was (past) a beautiful park where the city dump was (past). [Since the two verbs in this sentence are in the same tense, the sentence suggests that the park and the dump were there together.]

RIGHT   There **was** (past) a beautiful park where the city dump **had been** (past perfect). [The past perfect *had been* makes it clear that the dump was there before the park.]

RIGHT   There **had been** (past perfect) a beautiful park where the city dump **was** (past). [Making the other verb past perfect reverses the time order; the park preceded the dump.]

8e. Avoid the use of *would have* in "if clauses" expressing the earlier of two past actions. Use the past perfect.

WRONG   If he would have worked harder, he'd have made the honor roll.

RIGHT   If he **had worked** harder, he'd have made the honor roll.

WRONG   If I would have thought of it, I'd have called for you.

RIGHT   If I **had thought** of it, I'd have called for you.

● EXERCISE 16.   Correct the following sentences, which contain errors in the use of tenses. Refer, if necessary, to the rules on pages 147–51 for the uses of the various tenses.

1. The class officers canceled the party after I made all arrangements for it.
2. Gerald based his decision on the old proverb that honesty was the best policy.
3. By the time I graduate, my brother will be practicing law for five years.
4. Even though his innocence was previously proved, he was not released.
5. If you would have been here earlier, you'd have met Joe.
6. When the police finally arrived, the thief already vanished with the loot.
7. The company hired Mr. Littmann because he lived for many years in Arabia.
8. We thought that Bill went already.
9. We especially enjoyed a speech given by a man who was in Communist China.
10. When I introduced them, they acted as if they never met before.
11. He already lost confidence in himself a long time before he was fired.
12. By that time we will withdraw all our occupation troops.
13. If she would have asked me, I could have helped her.
14. The police said they thought we probably imagined the whole incident.

8
d-e

15. If we had matches, we could have built a fire.
16. When I was doing my homework last night, I was sure I took down the assignment correctly in class.
17. By the end of the summer I will be working here two years.
18. When we totaled the scores, we found that we won by twenty points.
19. If we would have stayed at home, we'd have missed a good show.
20. The receptionist thought that Dr. Berg has been out of town until this morning.
21. I was surprised to learn that the world's highest mountains were in Asia.
22. I expect that when I am twenty-one, I will be in college five years.
23. If he would have applied himself, he would have made the honor roll.
24. Next Saturday my father and mother will be married twenty-five years.
25. He would have done better in college if he was better prepared in high school.

Having with the Past Participle

8f. In participial phrases, use *having* with the past participle to express action completed before another action.

WRONG   Being tardy three days in succession, I was kept after school today. [The present participle *being* is incorrectly used to express an action which had obviously been completed *before* the second action in the sentence.]

RIGHT   **Having been** tardy three days in succession, I **was** kept after school today.

WRONG   Making his decision, Martin stuck to it. [The decision had to be made *before* he could stick to it.]

RIGHT   **Having made** his decision, Martin **stuck to it.**

The Present and the Perfect Infinitives

8g. Use the present infinitive (*to go, to see,* etc.) to express action following another action.

WRONG   The children were disappointed because they had hoped to have gone with us. [What had the children hoped, *to have gone* or *to go?* The present infinitive *to go* should be used because the action it expresses follows the action of the verb *had hoped.*]

RIGHT   The children were disappointed because they **had hoped to go** with us.

WRONG   He intended to have written to all of us. [Was his intention *to have written* or *to write?*]

RIGHT   He **intended to write** to all of us.

8h. Use the perfect infinitive (*to have gone, to have seen,* etc.) to express action before another action.

EXAMPLE   I am glad **to have seen** that movie. [The perfect infinitive is correct because the action it expresses came before the time of the other verb *am.*]

● EXERCISE 17. The sentences in this exercise contain errors in the use of tense and in the use of the present participle and the infinitive. Correct the sentences according to the rules you have just studied. Discuss your corrections in class before doing Exercise 18.

1. Listening to the committee argue for two hours, we finally left.
2. I should have liked to have seen the races.
3. In the afternoon woodsmen trimmed the trees which they cut in the morning.
4. The date of the opening of school has always varied because Labor Day was not on the same date every year.
5. We did not wish to have become involved in any scandal.

8
f-h

6. By the time Jimmy has grown up, I shall be practicing medicine for many years.
7. I already finished my homework when I asked Barbara and Chris to come over.
8. Every boy has at some time wished to have been a fireman.
9. If I knew your address, I would have written to you.
10. By the time he called me, I finished my homework.

● EXERCISE 18.   The following sentences contain errors in the use of tense and in the use of the present participle and the infinitive. Correct the sentences.

1. I had hoped to have been a successful writer.
2. Receiving a four-year, all-expense scholarship, Dick did not work during the summers.
3. Nancy was shocked to have learned that a diamond was merely a form of carbon.
4. If the team won, we would have celebrated.
5. Becoming ill during the morning, I went home at noon.
6. I hoped to have seen you on my trip to Chicago.
7. By Saturday I will be working here three weeks.
8. We should have liked to have met your sister.
9. If I didn't eat breakfast this morning, I'd have been on time.
10. By the time George returned my book, I already bought a new one.

ACTIVE AND PASSIVE VOICE

A verb is in the *active* voice when it expresses an action performed *by* its subject. A verb is in the *passive* voice when it expresses an action performed *upon* its subject or when the subject is the result of the action.

ACTIVE VOICE   Lightning struck the barn.   [subject acting]

PASSIVE VOICE   The barn was struck by lightning.   [subject acted upon]

All transitive verbs (those that take objects) can be used in the passive voice. Instead of the usual case in which the verb expresses an action performed by the subject and affecting the object, a passive construction has the subject receiving the action. Compare the following sentences.

ACTIVE VOICE   On the third strike the catcher dropped the ball.

PASSIVE VOICE   On the third strike the ball was dropped by the catcher.

On the third strike the ball was dropped.

As you can see, to form the passive construction, the object of the active sentence is moved ahead of the verb and becomes the subject. A form of *be* is added to the verb, and the subject of the active sentence is either expressed in a prepositional phrase or dropped.

Notice that in the passive voice the main verb is always a past participle and that the tense is expressed by an appropriate form of *be*.

ACTIVE   Experienced pilots **fly** these planes.

PASSIVE   These planes **are flown** by experienced pilots.

ACTIVE   The sexton usually **rang** the church bell.

PASSIVE   The church bell **was** usually **rung** by the sexton.

The Retained Object

Active sentences that have direct objects often have indirect objects as well. When they do, either the direct or indirect object can become the subject in a passive construction:

ACTIVE   The manager gave them free tickets.

PASSIVE   They were given free **tickets** (by the manager).

PASSIVE   Free tickets were given **them** (by the manager).

In both of the passive sentences above, one of the objects has been made the subject and the other continues to function as a complement of the verb. In the first sentence the direct object is retained as a complement; in the second it is the indirect object that is retained. The object that continues to function as a complement in a passive construction is called a *retained object*.

U*e of Passive Voice

The choice between the active or passive voice of any particular verb is usually a matter of taste, not of correctness. However, it is important to remember that a passive verb is usually less forceful than an active one and that a long succession of passive verbs usually produces an awkward and unpleasant effect.

AWKWARD PASSIVE   At the beginning of his senior year, a secondhand typewriter was purchased by Bill, and a course in typing was signed up for by him.

ACTIVE   At the beginning of his senior year, Bill purchased a secondhand typewriter and signed up for a course in typing.

WEAK PASSIVE   The game was won when a home run was hit by Jerry.

ACTIVE   Jerry won the game by hitting a home run.

WEAK PASSIVE   An exciting game was expected by everyone, but a victory was predicted by no one.

ACTIVE   Everyone expected an exciting game, but no one predicted a victory.

SUCCESSION OF PASSIVES   We *were invited* by Dr. Rowland to see his famous collection of precious stones. A large table *had been placed* in the center of his study. The green cloth by which the table *was covered was removed* by Dr. Rowland, and a glittering collection of exquisite jewels *was revealed* beneath the glass top of the table. Although we *were delighted* by the display, there were so many precious stones that they *could* not *be* fully *appreciated* by us. It *was concluded* by all of us that we *would be* more *impressed* by one beautiful ruby than by a dozen.

8i. Use the passive voice sparingly. Avoid weak and awkward passives. In the interest of variety, avoid long passages in which all the verbs are passive.

There are, however, some qualifications of this general rule which should be mentioned. The passive voice is particularly useful in two common situations.

(1) Use the passive voice to express an action in which the actor is unknown.

EXAMPLE   The door **had been closed** before we arrived.

(2) Use the passive voice to express an action in which it is desirable not to disclose the actor.

EXAMPLE   A mistake **has been made** in issuing this order.

In some instances the passive voice is more convenient and just as effective as the active voice. The following passive sentences are entirely acceptable.

America **was discovered** in 1492.

We **were drenched** by the rain and **frozen** by the icy wind.

Miss Green, who **is** very well **liked** by the students, **has been invited** to act as chaperon.

Remember, however, that, in general, the active voice is stronger than the passive and less likely to get you into stylistic difficulties.

● EXERCISE 19.   Revise the following sentences by changing the passive verbs to active verbs wherever you think the change is desirable. If you think the passive is preferable, copy the sentence unchanged.

1. After the car had been washed by us, it was waxed and polished by the garage man.
2. We were held spellbound by Lieutenant Douglas as a number of his harrowing experiences in the Air Force were related by him.

8i

3. A formal protest against the location of the new school building has been presented by the Student Council, which was urged on by the entire student body.
4. The rules of the school must be understood and followed by every student.
5. Since dinner had been prepared by the girls, the dishes were washed by the boys.
6. Gunpowder was invented by the Chinese long before its use was known in Europe.
7. Her new, high-heeled shoes were worn by her to the dance.
8. The new surprise play which had been taught to the team on Thursday was completely forgotten by them in the game on Saturday.
9. Mr. James was known and liked by everybody.
10. Because proof of his accusations could not be provided by Mr. Brown, the case against the accused man had to be dropped by the FBI.

THE SUBJUNCTIVE MOOD

Verbs may be in one of three moods: *indicative, imperative,* or *subjunctive.* Almost all the verbs you use are in the *indicative mood.* The *imperative mood* is used to express a request or a command.

IMPERATIVE **Form** a single line along the left wall.
Please **reply** to this letter as soon as possible.

The only common uses of the subjunctive mood in modern English are to express a condition contrary to fact and to express a wish. These uses occur mainly in formal written English and usually apply to only one verb form—*were.* The following partial conjugation of *be* will show how the subjunctive mood differs from the indicative.

PRESENT INDICATIVE		PRESENT SUBJUNCTIVE	
Singular	*Plural*	*Singular*	*Plural*
I am	we are	(if) I be	(if) we be
you are	you are	(if) you be	(if) you be
he is	they are	(if) he be	(if) they be

The present subjunctive is used only in certain rather formal situations.

EXAMPLES   I suggested that he **be** admitted to membership.

Mr. Black insists that I **be** punished.

I move that he **be** reprimanded.

PAST INDICATIVE		PAST SUBJUNCTIVE	
Singular	*Plural*	*Singular*	*Plural*
I was	we were	(if) I were	(if) we were
you were	you were	(if) you were	(if) you were
he was	they were	(if) he were	(if) they were

8j. The subjunctive *were* is usually used in contrary-to-fact statements (after *if* or *as though*) and in statements expressing a wish.

CONTRARY TO FACT   If I **were** [not *was*] you, I'd save the money. [I am not you.]

If he **were** [not *was*] taller, he'd be a champion. [He is not taller.]

He talked as though he **were** [not *was*] my father. [He is not my father.]

WISH   I wish it **were** [not *was*] true.

I wish he **were** [not *was*] my adviser.

● REVIEW EXERCISE A.   Some of the following sentences contain errors in the use of verbs. Others are correct. Number in a column on your paper 1–25. If the verbs in a sentence are correct, place a plus (+) after the corresponding number on your paper. If a verb is incorrect, write the correct form after the proper number.

1. If I was his father, I'd give him a thrashing.
2. We lay logs under the boat and used them as rollers.
3. I had forgotten that February 22 is a holiday.
4. Instead of working, I would have preferred to have gone to the game.
5. If he weren't so lazy, he'd be a good student.

8j

6. When he entered the bank, the custodian discovered that the vault was opened during the night.

7. If you would have told the truth, you would have been forgiven.

8. The pilot of a search plane spotted wreckage laying at the bottom of a ravine.

9. As the warm air rises, the cool air pushes in beneath it.

10. If I was a year older, I could get a driver's license.

11. Survivors swum to the raft and pulled themselves up on it.

12. If you had taken your time, you would not have had an accident.

13. The driver did not see the second of the two children who run into the path of his car.

14. Would you have preferred to go to the movies?

15. When his new orders come through, Captain Martin was on his way overseas.

16. When I opened my locker, I discovered that somebody took my notebook.

17. Her mother found her lying at the foot of the stairs.

18. If he were a more liberal thinker, I'd vote for him.

19. I am not sure whether she seen us.

20. As we stepped through the door we realized that someone entered the house ahead of us.

21. I had just lain down when I heard the doorbell.

22. Mr. Stern told us that the Mississippi was the largest river in the United States.

23. If the judge would have listened to me, I'm sure he would not have fined me.

24. When we added our profits, we found we made more than a hundred dollars.

25. Was it Jean who give you the assignment?

● REVIEW EXERCISE B.   Some of the following sentences contain errors in the use of verbs. Others are correct. Number your paper 1–25. If the verbs in a sentence are correct, make a + after the proper number. If a verb is incorrect, write the correct form after the proper number.

1. Both armies laid down their arms willingly.

2. He couldn't remember where he had lain the book.

3. Several of us were setting on the stairs.
4. I thought the sharp blow had broke my watch.
5. If I was Bill, I'd let well enough alone.
6. The pond has not yet frozen over.
7. It wasn't until the third quarter that the team begun to play better.
8. If you would have called, we would have picked you up.
9. When I graduate from college, she will be married for three years.
10. He was still living in the house where he lived since 1950.
11. Please set the phonograph in the corner.
12. When I got to the station, I found the bus already left.
13. Were you at home when Tom come to the house?
14. I just laid down for a short nap when the phone rang.
15. Would you have preferred to have flown back?
16. If you had time, how would you have answered the question?
17. We laid a fire but did not light it.
18. The cost of living seems to raise every year.
19. We swum for an hour before lunch.
20. You should have lain there until help came.
21. I would like to have seen the performance.
22. As we were chasing him, he run into a man carrying a basket of feathers.
23. At the time you met him, he recently broke his leg and was using crutches.
24. We finally found our way back to the corner at which we made the wrong turn.
25. We found it laying at the foot of the stairs.

Correct Use of Modifiers

Form of Adjectives and Adverbs, Comparison

An adjective modifies a noun or a pronoun. An adverb may modify a verb, an adjective, or another adverb. These are familiar statements, but applying them to usage is sometimes difficult. Should you say "left quick" or "left quickly," "tastes strong" or "tastes strongly," "played good" or "played well"? These and other usage problems are discussed in this chapter.

ADJECTIVE AND ADVERB FORMS

Before reviewing the usage of adjectives and adverbs, you should make sure that you are able to tell which is the adjective form of a word and which is the adverb form. The fact that most adverbs end in *–ly* (*clearly, happily, eagerly*) will be helpful if you understand that not *all* adverbs end in *–ly* and that a few common adjectives do end in *–ly*. Some words have the same form whether used as an adjective or as an adverb.

The list that follows includes a number of common adjectives and adverbs with identical forms. It also includes some adjectives ending in *–ly*. Remember that the *–ly* ending is not always a sign that a word is an adverb.

ADJECTIVES	ADVERBS	ADJECTIVE ENDING IN −LY
a *fast* ball	He ran *fast*.	*daily* practice
a *slow* trip	Go *slow*.	*friendly* people
hard candy	He works *hard*.	*early* bird
a *tight* fit	Hold *tight*.	*kindly* gentleman
a *long* job	He worked *long*.	*lively* child
a *loud* noise	He sang *loud*.	*homely* dog
a *late* train	He came *late*.	*lovely* island
a *low* bridge	Swing *low*.	*elderly* person
a *straight* road	Go *straight*.	

9a. Linking verbs, especially the verbs of sense (*taste, smell, feel*, etc.), are often followed by an adjective. Action verbs are often followed by an adverb.

EXAMPLES   The dinner tasted **delicious.** [The adjective *delicious* is correct after the linking verb *tasted*. It modifies the subject *dinner*.]

Everyone felt **happy.** [The adjective *happy* is correct after the linking verb *felt*. It modifies the subject *everyone*.]

Some verbs may be used as either linking or action verbs. When they are used as action verbs, the modifier which follows modifies the verb rather than the subject and is, therefore, an adverb; for example, *looked* may be used as a linking verb and as an action verb.

EXAMPLES   He looked **sleepy.** [After the linking verb *looked*, the adjective *sleepy* is correct. It modifies *he*.]

He looked **sleepily** in my direction. [After the action verb *looked*, the adverb *sleepily* is correct. It modifies *looked*.]

When you are in doubt as to whether a verb is a linking verb or not, try substituting for it a form of *seem*, which is always a linking verb. If the substitution can be made with-

9a

out greatly changing the meaning of the sentence, the verb is a linking verb and should be followed by an adjective.

EXAMPLES He looked sleepy. [*He seemed sleepy* gives about the same meaning; hence *looked* is a linking verb.]

He looked sleepily in my direction. [*He seemed sleepily in my direction* does not make sense; hence *looked* is not a linking verb in this sentence.]

9b. In making a choice between an adjective and an adverb, ask yourself what the word modifies. If it modifies a noun or pronoun, choose the adjective. If it modifies a verb, choose the adverb.

PROBLEM We built the raft (strong, strongly) enough to hold us.

SOLUTION We built the raft **strong** enough to hold us. [The adjective *strong* modifies the noun *raft*.]

PROBLEM Has he been playing golf (regular, regularly)?

SOLUTION Has he been playing golf **regularly**? [The adverb *regularly* modifies the action verb *has been playing*.]

● EXERCISE 1. Number your paper 1–20. Select the correct one of the two words in parentheses in each sentence and write it after the proper number. If the word modifies the subject, select the adjective; if it modifies the verb, select the adverb. Remember that a linking verb is followed by an adjective.

1. Soon the engine was running (smooth, smoothly) again.
2. She feels (miserable, miserably).
3. Do your work as (careful, carefully) as you can.
4. His story sounded (suspicious, suspiciously) to me.
5. I can't forget how (cold, coldly) he looked at me.
6. The fruit tastes (bitter, bitterly).
7. What are you feeling so (sad, sadly) about?
8. Apparently Sam was feeling (angry, angrily) about his bad luck.

9. Judy does her homework (regular, regularly).
10. He slunk very (quiet, quietly) around the corner.
11. The whole orchard smelled (fragrant, fragrantly).
12. The play ended (abrupt, abruptly) and (disappointing, disappointingly).
13. The plane appeared very (sudden, suddenly).
14. He did not act as (brave, bravely) as his brother.
15. The first batch of fudge proved (poor, poorly).
16. If you just speak (firm, firmly), the dog will behave.
17. I was driving very (careful, carefully).
18. Finish the test as (quick, quickly) as you can.
19. I can finish this job (easy, easily) within an hour.
20. It cannot be accomplished so (rapid, rapidly) as you think.

Bad and Badly

Bad is an adjective modifying nouns and pronouns. *Badly* is an adverb, modifying verbs, adjectives, and adverbs. Since the verbs of sense—*feel, smell, taste, sound*—are followed by an adjective (not an adverb) modifying their subjects, it is standard English to say *feel bad, smell bad,* etc.

She feels very bad about her failure.

The stockyards smell bad.

The common expression *feel badly,* however, has, through usage, become acceptable English, although ungrammatical. Used with other verbs of sense, *badly* is not yet standard: *smell badly, taste badly,* etc.

Well and Good

Well may be used as either an adjective or an adverb. As an adjective, *well* has three meanings.

1. *To be in good health:*

He feels **well.** He seems **well.**

2. *To appear well-dressed or well-groomed:*

She looks **well** in that dress.

9b

3. *To be satisfactory:*

All is well.

As an adverb, *well* means to perform an action capably.

She sang very **well**.

Good is always an adjective. It should never be used to modify a verb.

WRONG   The team played good today.
RIGHT   The team played **well** today.

WRONG   They work very good together.
RIGHT   They work very **well** together.

Slow and Slowly

Slow is used as both an adjective and an adverb. *Slowly* is an adverb. Except for the expressions *Drive slow* and *Go slow*, which have become acceptable because of their wide use on highway signs, you will be on the safe side if you use *slow* only as an adjective.

● EXERCISE 2.   Number your paper 1–25. If the *italicized* modifier in a sentence is correct, write a + after the proper number on your paper. If it is incorrect, write the correct form, and after the correct form write the word it modifies.

1. The old car held up fairly *good.*
2. We were surprised to find the patient looking so *well.*
3. I always do my homework as *speedy* as I can.
4. Some of the food tasted *bad.*
5. Work *slow*, and you will make fewer mistakes.
6. Jean appeared quite *happy.*
7. I can do these errands *easy.*
8. Was George feeling very *bad?*
9. His clothes never fit him very *good.*
10. The family felt *bitterly* about Uncle Fred's will.
11. Drive *careful.*
12. Nancy looks *well* in blue.
13. I was afraid you had been hurt *bad.*
14. Their voices blended *beautiful* with one another.

15. We couldn't hear very *good* because of the storm.
16. Isn't it possible for you to drive *slowly?*
17. He looked *hopefully* in my direction.
18. The prisoners said they had been treated very *unfair.*
19. If the food smells *bad*, throw it away.
20. Each of us wrote the assignment down *separate.*
21. Before the game, things looked *badly* for our team.
22. He speaks French too *rapid* for me.
23. Mr. Ames always speaks *sharp.*
24. I crept *cautiously* up the stairs.
25. The class had been behaving very *bad.*

COMPARISON OF ADJECTIVES AND ADVERBS

9c. *Comparison* is the name given to the change in the form of adjectives and adverbs when they are used to compare the degree of the qualities they express. There are three degrees of comparison: *positive, comparative,* and *superlative.*

POSITIVE	COMPARATIVE	SUPERLATIVE
big	bigger	biggest
anxious	more anxious	most anxious
cheaply	more cheaply	most cheaply
fast	faster	fastest
easily	more easily	most easily

Comparative and Superlative Forms

(1) Most adjectives and adverbs of one syllable form their comparative and superlative degrees by adding –er and –est.

POSITIVE	COMPARATIVE	SUPERLATIVE
long	longer	longest
hard	harder	hardest
cold	colder	coldest

9c

(2) Some adjectives of two syllables form their comparative and superlative degrees by adding *–er* or *–est*; other adjectives of two syllables form their comparative and superlative degrees by means of *more* and *most*.

When you are in doubt as to how a word is compared, consult an unabridged dictionary.

POSITIVE	COMPARATIVE	SUPERLATIVE
happy	happier	happiest
eager	more eager	most eager

(3) Adjectives of more than two syllables and adverbs ending in *–ly* usually form their comparative and superlative degrees by means of *more* and *most*.

POSITIVE	COMPARATIVE	SUPERLATIVE
capable	more capable	most capable
rapidly	more rapidly	most rapidly

(4) Comparison to indicate less or least of a quality is accomplished by using the words *less* and *least* before the adjective or adverb.

POSITIVE	COMPARATIVE	SUPERLATIVE
bright	less bright	least bright
excited	less excited	least excited
willingly	less willingly	least willingly

Irregular Comparison

Adjectives and adverbs that do not follow the regular methods of forming their comparative and superlative degrees are said to be compared irregularly.

POSITIVE	COMPARATIVE	SUPERLATIVE
bad	worse	worst
good well	better	best
many much	more	most

● EXERCISE 3. Write the comparative and superlative forms of the following words. Use a dictionary.

1. tall	6. satisfactory	11. bad	16. humble
2. beautiful	7. ill	12. casually	17. dear
3. few	8. little	13. reckless	18. stealthy
4. short	9. industrious	14. clear	19. diligently
5. graceful	10. bravely	15. good	20. small

Use of Comparatives and Superlatives

9d. Use the comparative degree when comparing two things; use the superlative degree when comparing more than two.

COMPARISON OF TWO THINGS

Although both the plaintiff and the defendant presented strong arguments, those of the defendant were **stronger** [not *strongest*].

The doctors tried both penicillin and sulfanilamide; the penicillin proved to be the **more** [not *most*] **effective** drug.

Gail is the **more** capable one of the twins.

COMPARISON OF MORE THAN TWO THINGS

I chose this book because it was the **shortest** [not *shorter*] of the **three.**

Of the **three** branches of the armed services, the Air Force has been the **most** [not *more*] **favored** in recent years.

Which of the **twenty-eight** flavors is the **most** popular?

◆ USAGE NOTE Rule 9d describes a practice generally observed by writers of formal English. In informal speech and writing, however, the superlative is often used for emphasis, even though only two things are being compared:

INFORMAL Which book did you like best, *Moby Dick* or *The Scarlet Letter?* [formal: *better*]

Of the two readings of *Hamlet* Gielgud's interpretation is the most interesting to me.

9d

9e. Include the word *other* or *else* when comparing one thing with a group of which it is a part.

WRONG   At the end of the war, the United States was stronger than any country in the world. [Since the United States is one of the countries in the world, this sentence says illogically that it was stronger than itself.]

RIGHT   At the end of the war, the United States was stronger than any **other** country in the world.

WRONG   He has better marks than anyone in his grade. [He is a member of his grade; he cannot have better marks than himself.]

RIGHT   He has better marks than anyone **else** in his home room.

9f. Avoid double comparisons.

A double comparison is one in which the degree is formed incorrectly by both adding *-er* or *-est* in addition to using *more* or *most*.

WRONG   She is a more prettier girl than I.
RIGHT   She is a **prettier** girl than I.

WRONG   He is the most happiest child I know.
RIGHT   He is the **happiest** child I know.

● EXERCISE 4.   Number your paper 1–25. For each correct sentence, write a + after the proper number; revise each incorrect sentence and write the sentence correctly.

1. Speak to him gentle.
2. I played as good as he did.
3. Bill works harder than any boy in his group.
4. Whatever she does, she does well.
5. If negotiations proceed too slowly, the work will not be completed this year.
6. Since there were two recommended procedures, the committee had to decide which one would be best.
7. To our palates the highly seasoned food tasted strangely.

8. Try to speak as convincingly as you can.
9. Albert arrived unexpectedly and took charge of the meeting.
10. His greeting was more friendlier than hers.
11. When the tide is in, the water is many feet more deep.
12. Although he writes badly, his books are popular.
13. *Gone with the Wind* sold better than any American novel.
14. The judges were given ten manuscripts and asked to select the best one.
15. Eat moderate, and you will lose weight.
16. The tiger rushed menacing toward me.
17. I found Mr. Trumbull the most cooperative of the two men.
18. Has he been working regular?
19. The entire menu looked good to us.
20. Three jobs faced us, and we did the easier one first.
21. Pine Lake has the most clearest water.
22. I didn't believe he could act so stubborn as that.
23. She makes up her mind too slow.
24. Jack is a lot truthfuller than his brother.
25. When he ran out of money, he felt too proudly to borrow.

CHAPTER 10

Glossary of Usage

The writing and speaking habits of educated people determine what is acceptable or unacceptable English usage. Chapters 6 through 9 of this book describe the preferences of educated users of the language in matters of agreement, and in verb, pronoun, and modifier usage. In addition to vocabulary, these are the major areas in which the language of the educated differs from that of the uneducated.

There are, however, a number of special usage problems which require separate treatment. These are treated here in the glossary. To use this glossary properly, you will need to be familiar with the terms *standard* and *substandard*, *formal* and *informal*.

Summary: Levels of Usage

STANDARD ENGLISH

Informal   The everyday language of educated people, suitable for all but the most formal occasions.

Formal   The language of educated speakers when they take special pains to say the correct thing; appropriate in any situation; but mostly found in serious writing and speaking.

SUBSTANDARD ENGLISH

The language of the uneducated; generally inappropriate to educated speakers.

If you are not sure of these terms after reading the brief summary, review Chapter 5, in which they are discussed in detail.

In working the exercises in this chapter, as well as those in other parts of the book, follow the conventions of formal English.

The items in this glossary are arranged in alphabetical order, with exercises interspersed. Problems of spelling such as the difference between *already* and *all ready* and similar words often confused are taken up on pages 683–91, following the chapter on spelling.

accept, except   *Accept* is a verb; it means "to receive." *Except* as a verb means "to leave out"; as a preposition it means "excluding."

> We **accept** your invitation with pleasure.
>
> If you **except** his freshman grades, he has a good scholastic average.
>
> My grades are satisfactory in every subject **except** English.

adapt, adopt   *Adapt* means "to change in order to fit or be more suitable, to adjust." *Adopt* means "to take something and make it one's own."

> To survive, an animal must **adapt** to its environment.
>
> Some adult novels have been **adapted** for young readers.
>
> They **adopted** their physician's suggestion and **adopted** a baby.

affect, effect   *Affect* is usually a verb; it means "to impress" or "to influence (frequently the mind or feelings)." *Effect* as a verb means "to accomplish, to bring about." *Effect* as a noun means "the result of some action."

> How did the defeat **affect** the team?
>
> A number of improvements were **effected** [brought about] by the new student council.
>
> **Effects** [results] of the strike were felt everywhere.

all the farther, all the faster   Used informally in some parts of the country to mean "as far as, as fast as."

DIALECT   I did not know that was all the faster the car would go.

STANDARD   I did not know that was **as fast as** the car would go.

allusion, illusion   An *allusion* is a reference to something. An *illusion* is a mistaken idea.

His writing is full of classical **allusions.**

In spite of the evidence, he clung to his **illusions.**

alumni, alumnae   *Alumni* (pronounced ə·lum′nī) is the plural of *alumnus* (male graduate). *Alumnae* (pronounced ə·lum′nē) is the plural of *alumna* (female graduate). The graduates of a coeducational school are referred to (as a group) as *alumni.*

It was a stag party; **alumnae** were not invited.

I attended a reunion of Princeton **alumni.**

Every high school should keep track of its **alumni.**

amount, number   *Amount* refers to "quantity thought of as a unit." *Number* refers to "quantity thought of as several things." Use *amount* with a singular word; use *number* with a plural word.

This **amount** of money (singular) will buy a large **number** of tickets (plural).

and etc.   Since *etc.* is an abbreviation of the Latin *et cetera*, which means "and other things," you are using *and* twice when you write "and etc." The *etc.* is sufficient.

STANDARD   We carry a complete stock of newspapers, magazines, stationery, school supplies, tobacco, candy, **etc.**   [not *and etc.*]

and which, but which The expressions *and which, but which, (and who, but who)* should be used only when a *which* (or *who*) clause precedes them in the sentence.

SUBSTANDARD   The public was shocked by the council's revelations and which the commissioner had tried to suppress.

STANDARD   The public was shocked by the revelations **which** the council published **and which** the commissioner had tried to suppress.

STANDARD   The public was shocked by the council's revelations **which** the commissioner had tried to suppress.

anywheres, everywheres, nowheres Use these words and others like them without the final *s*.

We looked **everywhere,** but the children were **nowhere** in sight; they could not be found **anywhere.**

apt, likely, liable These words are used interchangeably in standard English, but some writers of standard formal English prefer to observe the following distinctions:
Apt is used to mean "habitually inclined" toward something or "naturally good" at something.

Bill is **apt** to worry about his school work, which is surprising in such an **apt** student.

Likely is used to express simple probability.

She is **likely** to answer your letter promptly.

Liable is used to express probability with a suggestion of harm or misfortune: it is also used to mean "responsible" or "answerable."

If you swim here, you are **liable** to be attacked by sharks. Is a father **liable** for his son's debts?

at Do not use *at* after *where*.

SUBSTANDARD Where were you staying at?
STANDARD **Where** were you staying?

● EXERCISE 1. The sentences in this exercise contain usage problems presented on the preceding pages in the glossary. Number your paper 1–20. Write after the proper number on your paper the correct one of the two words in parentheses.

1. He found it difficult to (adapt, adopt) to life in college.
2. What do you think the (affect, effect) of the decision will be?
3. I did not understand his (allusions, illusions) to my brother.
4. The (alumni, alumnae) of a local school for girls are holding a reunion today.
5. We have sold an unusually large (number, amount) of fountain pens this year.
6. On tour we met friends (everywheres, everywhere) we went.
7. Everyone agreed with me (accept, except) you.
8. His expectation of a large fortune proved to be only an (allusion, illusion).
9. I was surprised when he (adopted, adapted) my suggestion.
10. All (alumni, alumnae) of our high school are very loyal.
11. This is (all the farther, as far as) the bus goes.
12. How did her son's departure (affect, effect) Mrs. French?
13. Everyone (accept, except) George and me finished the assignment on time.
14. You should not (accept, except) money for doing a good deed.
15. Do you know any (alumnae, alumni) of a woman's college?
16. How was the team (effected, affected) by the loss of their captain?
17. After our panel discussion, the audience asked a large (amount, number) of questions.
18. Milton's poetry is full of obscure classical (allusions, illusions).
19. If you can't (accept, except) my invitation, please let me know.
20. I was surprised at the (affect, effect) of his words on the audience.

bad, badly   See page 165.

because   The use of *because* after *reason is* ("The reason is because . . .") is common in informal English, but it is generally avoided in formal writing. In a sentence beginning "The reason is . . .," the clause following the verb is a noun clause used as a predicate nominative. A noun clause may begin with *that* but not with *because*, which usually introduces an adverb clause.

ACCEPTABLE   The reason she refused to go was **that** [not *because*] she had no money.

BETTER   She refused to go **because** she had no money.

being as, being that   Poor English when used for *since* or *because.*

SUBSTANDARD   Being as my mother was away, I had to do the housework.

STANDARD   **Because** my mother was away, I had to do the housework.

beside, besides   *Beside* means "by the side of" someone or something. *Besides* means "in addition to."

Who sits **beside** you in English class?
Besides my homework, I have to write a letter.

between, among   The distinction in meaning between these words is usually observed in formal English. Use *between* when you are thinking of two items at a time, regardless of whether they are part of a group of more than two.

The ball went **between** Phil and him.

Do you know the difference **between** a Pomeranian, a Pekingese, and a Chihuahua? [*Between* is correct because the speaker is thinking of one dog and another dog—*two* at a time.]

What is the difference **between** the four plans?

Use *among* when you are thinking of a group rather than of separate individuals.

> She is never at ease **among** strangers.
> Petitions were circulated **among** the voters.
> We had ten dollars **among** the five of us.

bring, take   Use *bring* when the meaning is to convey something *to the person speaking*. Use *take* when the meaning is to convey something *away from the person speaking. Bring* is related to *come; take* is related to *go.*

> When you **come** back, **bring** your textbooks, pencils, and paper.
> Will you please **take** [not bring] this note to your father when you **go** home.

can't hardly, can't scarcely   See *Double negative* (page 192).

can't help but   See *Double negative* (page 192).

could of   Sometimes carelessly written for *could have.* Do not write *of* for *have.* Similar expressions frequently written incorrectly are *ought to of, might of, must of.*

SUBSTANDARD	He could of warned me about the dangerous roads.
STANDARD	He could **have** warned me about the dangerous roads.

credible, creditable, credulous   Sometimes confused because of their similarity, these words have quite different meanings.

Credible means "believable."

> Such a ridiculous story is hardly **credible.**

Creditable means "praiseworthy."

> For a beginner, she gave a **creditable** performance.

Credulous means "inclined to believe almost anything."

> Being **credulous,** she is often taken in by lies.

data The plural form of the Latin *datum.* In standard informal English, *data* is frequently used, like a collective noun, with a singular pronoun and verb.

> INFORMAL   This data was collected by the investigating committee.

However, since *data* has only recently become acceptable as a singular word, you will be safer if, in your writing, you use the word as a plural. See **phenomena.**

> FORMAL   **These data were** collected by the investigating committee.

discover, invent Do not use *invent* to mean "discover." *Invent* means "to make something not known before, to bring something into existence." *Discover* means "to find something which has been in existence but unknown."

> Edison **invented** the electric light.
> Astronomers **are** still **discovering** new stars.

done Not the past form of *do. Done* always needs a helping verb: *has done, was done, will be done,* etc. The past form of *do* is *did.*

> SUBSTANDARD   The doctors done all they could.
> STANDARD   The doctors **did** all they could.
> STANDARD   The doctors **had done** all they could.

don't A contraction of *do not, don't* should not be used with a singular noun or the third person of singular pronouns (*it, he, she*). Use *doesn't.* See page 97.

SUBSTANDARD   It don't matter to me.
STANDARD   It **doesn't** matter to me.

effect, affect   See **affect, effect.**

emigrate, immigrate   *Emigrate* means "to go from a country" to settle elsewhere. *Immigrate* means "to come into a country" to settle there.

> Residents of crowded countries have been advised to **emigrate** from their homelands to less crowded regions.
> His parents **immigrated** to this country in 1910.

etc.   See **and etc.**

except, accept   See **accept, except.**

famous, notorious   Learn the specific meaning of these words. *Famous* means "well and widely known." *Notorious* means "widely known" but is used in an unfavorable sense.

> Washington and Lincoln are the most **famous** Americans.
> Jesse James is probably America's most **notorious** outlaw.

farther   See **all the farther.**

fewer, less   In standard formal English *fewer* (not *less*) is used before a plural noun. *Less* is used before a singular noun.

> There were **fewer** [not *less*] guests at the last party.
> We took in **less** money tonight.

good, well   See pages 165–66.

● EXERCISE 2.   The sentences in this exercise contain usage problems explained on pages 177–80. Double negatives and the listed items explained elsewhere in this text are not covered. Number your paper 1–25. Write after the proper number the correct one of the two words in parentheses.

1. You can fool him easily because he is so (credulous, credible).
2. (Beside, Besides) the excellent meals, the hotel provides superb recreational facilities.
3. (Bring, Take) your cousin with you when you come to my house tonight.
4. I'll (take, bring) your letters to the post office when I go downtown.
5. It took courage to (emigrate, immigrate) from an established home and settle in the American wilderness.
6. There are (fewer, less) students enrolled here this year than last year.
7. Do you intend to divide the work (among, between) the four of us?
8. (Being that, Because) Father was tired, I did the driving.
9. We have (fewer, less) honors classes this year.
10. In what year was the atom bomb (invented, discovered)?
11. (Among, Between) the six of us we could raise the money.
12. Please (bring, take) this card to the library when you go.
13. Has anyone (beside, besides) you been in the room?
14. You have (fewer, less) friends than she.
15. We (done, did) the lessons according to instructions in the textbook.
16. His schoolwork (don't, doesn't) bother him very much.
17. To me this is not a (credulous, credible) tale.
18. With better equipment they could (of, have) completed the job sooner.
19. Our government found it necessary to discourage (immigration, emigration) into this country.
20. Will you please (take, bring) these books to Mr. Barrett when you go to see him?
21. Eisenhower became (famous, notorious) as commander of the Allied forces.
22. Who (discovered, invented) the telephone?
23. (Being as, Since) they are identical twins, they are frequently confused.

24. Shakespeare is the most (famous, notorious) dramatist ever to write in English.
25. She was promoted because of the (creditable, credible) job she had done as a secretary.

● EXERCISE 3.   This exercise covers all usage items explained in the glossary to this point. Number your paper 1–33. If a sentence does not contain a usage error, write a + after the proper number on your paper. If it does contain a usage error, write the correct form. It will not be necessary to copy whole sentences.

1. He has less friends than his brother.
2. Being as the mayor was going away, he appointed an assistant to handle emergencies.
3. How will the new laws affect the school?
4. Besides my teachers, my parents have been making me study.
5. The reason for the failure of our campaign was because we didn't work hard enough.
6. Mr. Standish threatened to sue the newspaper because of its unflattering allusions to his private life.
7. We asked directions of a very articulate policeman and who advised us to take Route 4.
8. Both of the women on the platform are alumni of a famous women's college.
9. The reward money was divided between the four men.
10. Is that all the faster you can work?
11. Please take this briefcase to your father.
12. Mrs. Corbin hunted everywheres for her lost book.
13. In the confusion no one knew exactly where he was at.
14. Doctors are studying the effects of this new drug.
15. I found the people full of allusions about the real causes of the strike.
16. I am sure I could of done better on my test if I had had more time.
17. Without family or a job, Francis had no other choice than to emigrate.
18. I hope you will take your family when you come East this summer.

19. As you grow older, you will encounter less opportunities to change jobs.
20. He excepted our gifts with thanks.
21. Milton expected us to use the camera which he had given us but which we had lost.
22. The amount of hot dogs one boy can eat is incredible.
23. There is growing dissatisfaction among the students.
24. With three jobs offered to him, Paul could not decide which one to except.
25. The dance on June 20 was sponsored by the high school alumni.
26. She complains about everything: health, taxes, government, weather, children, and etc.
27. I found the new statistics almost incredible.
28. The animals seemed unable to adapt to their new environment.
29. The librarian complained about the amount of books that students had lost.
30. He made a fortune by discovering a new type of automatic motor.
31. A notorious and widely admired athlete, he represented his country three times in the Olympic games.
32. Anyone so credulous is an easy mark for swindlers.
33. Being as it is supposed to be a democratic country, it should have free elections.

had of   The *of* is superfluous.

SUBSTANDARD	If I had of known him better, I'd have spoken to him.
STANDARD	If I **had known** him better, I'd have spoken to him.

had ought, hadn't ought   Do not use *had* with *ought*.

SUBSTANDARD	You had ought to read more carefully.
STANDARD	You **ought** to read more carefully.
SUBSTANDARD	You hadn't ought to stay out so late.
STANDARD	You **ought not** to stay out so late.

he, she, they, etc. Do not use unnecessary pronouns after a noun. This error is sometimes called the *double subject*.

SUBSTANDARD   My uncle he lives in California.
STANDARD   My uncle lives in California.

hisself, theirselves These words are sometimes incorrectly used for *himself, themselves*.

SUBSTANDARD   He did the work hisself.
STANDARD   He did the work **himself.**

illusion, allusion See allusion, illusion.

immigrate, emigrate See emigrate, immigrate.

imply, infer *Imply* means "to suggest something." *Infer* means "to interpret, to get a certain meaning from a remark or an action."

The speaker **implied** that he was a friend of the President's.
I **inferred** from the speaker's remarks that he was a friend of the President's.

in, into In standard formal usage observe the difference in meaning between these words. *In* means "within"; *into* suggests movement from the outside to the inside.

FORMAL   At two o'clock we walked **into** [not *in*] the principal's office.
INFORMAL   His final act was throwing a lighted match in a can of gasoline.
FORMAL   His final act was throwing a lighted match **into** a can of gasoline.

invent, discover See discover, invent.

kind, sort, type   In standard formal usage the adjectives *this, these, that, those* are made to agree in number with the words *kind, sort, type: this kind, these kinds; that sort, those sorts.*

> I like **that kind** of oranges.
> I like **those kinds** of oranges.

kind of, sort of   In standard formal usage, avoid using these expressions to mean "rather" or "somewhat."

INFORMAL   I feel kind of tired.
FORMAL   I feel **rather** [*somewhat*] tired.

kind of a, sort of a   The *a* is superfluous.

> What **kind of** [not *kind of a*] pen are you using?

lay, lie   See page 137.

learn, teach   *Learn* means "to acquire knowledge." *Teach* means "to dispense knowledge."

> I **learn** more when he **teaches** [not *learns*] me.

leave, let   *Leave* (*left*) means "to go away." *Let* means "to allow, to permit."

SUBSTANDARD   Leave me work by myself.
STANDARD   **Let** me work by myself.

SUBSTANDARD   You should have left him go.
STANDARD   You should have **let** him go.

The expressions "Leave me alone" and "Let me alone" are both correct and are commonly used interchangeably. Strictly speaking, "Leave me alone" suggests that you want somebody to go away, leaving you by yourself. "Let me alone" suggests that you want somebody to stop bothering you.

less, fewer   See **fewer, less.**

liable   See **apt, likely, liable.**

lie, lay   See page 137.

like, as   *Like* is a preposition and introduces a prepositional phrase. *As* is usually a conjunction and introduces a subordinate clause.

> He walks **like his father.**   [prepositional phrase]
> He walks **as his father walks.**   [subordinate clause]

Like as a conjunction is commonly heard in informal speech, but it is unacceptable in formal English.

INFORMAL   She cooks spaghetti like the Italians do.
FORMAL   She cooks spaghetti **as** the Italians do.

like, as if   *Like* should not be used for *as if* or *as though*, which are conjunctions used to introduce clauses.

INFORMAL   The boys acted like they were tired.
FORMAL   The boys acted **as if** [*as though*] they were tired.

likely   See **apt, likely, liable.**

myself, ourselves   Most careful writers of English avoid using pronouns ending in *–self*, *–selves* as subjects. See page 119.

> Henry and **I** [not *myself*] almost always do our homework together.

● EXERCISE 4.   The sentences in this exercise cover usage problems explained in the part of the glossary that follows Exercise 3. Number your paper 1–20. If a sentence contains no error in usage, write a + after the proper number; if it contains an error, write a 0.

1. In his novels Dickens implied that the poor were not responsible for their poverty.
2. As the procession came in the stadium, the crowd roared.

3. The Beals did all the work on the new house theirselves.
4. Mother is learning us how to play bridge.
5. I asked them to leave me go along with them.
6. Parents had ought to visit school more often.
7. For hours the troops had felt as if they could march no longer.
8. His comments inferred that he did not believe in socialism.
9. Tom finished the job himself.
10. If the bus had of been on time, she would have missed it.
11. Is an author to blame for what the public infers from his work?
12. The team hadn't ought to object to playing night games.
13. If he had behaved like he should, he would not be in trouble now.
14. Allan and myself made the decision.
15. In his remarks about the test, Mr. Jordan inferred that the class had not been very well prepared.
16. The coach let us use the gym after practice.
17. My parents they always want to know where I have been.
18. I did not mean to imply that you are incompetent.
19. Leave the girls come with us if they want to.
20. He sang like he intended to shatter the windows.

nauseated, nauseous These words do not mean the same thing. *Nauseated* means "sick." *Nauseous* means "disgusting, sickening."

> After eating too much rich food, the child became **nauseated.**

> The **nauseous** odor of dead fish overwhelmed us.

none *None* may be either singular or plural. See page 88.

notorious, famous See **famous, notorious.**

number, amount See **amount, number.**

of Do not use *of* unnecessarily. See **could of, had of.**

off of   The *of* is unnecessary.

> Never jump **off** [not *off of*] a moving train.

Do not use *off* or *off of* for *from*.

SUBSTANDARD	I got some money off Dad.
STANDARD	I got some money **from** Dad.
SUBSTANDARD	I borrowed the book off of my English teacher.
STANDARD	I borrowed the book **from** my English teacher.

or, nor   Use *or* with *either;* use *nor* with *neither.*

> **Either** John **or** Helen is mistaken.
> **Neither** John **nor** Helen is mistaken.

ought   See **had ought.**

persecute, prosecute   Distinguish between these words, which have quite different meanings. *Persecute* means "to attack or annoy someone," often for his beliefs. *Prosecute* means "to bring legal action against someone for unlawful behavior."

> Hitler **persecuted** people who opposed the Nazi government.
> Trespassers will be **prosecuted.**

phenomena   If you use this word, use it correctly. *Phenomena* is the plural form of the word *phenomenon.* Do not use it as a singular noun.

> **These** [not *this*] natural **phenomena are** [not *is*] most interesting.
> This natural **phenomenon** is most interesting.

politics, mathematics, athletics   For the number of these words and other similar words, see pages 96–97.

reason is because   See **because.**

respectfully, respectively *Respectfully* means "with respect" or "full of respect." *Respectively* means "each in the order given."

> Although hostile, the audience listened **respectfully.**
>
> *David Copperfield*, *Vanity Fair*, and *Adam Bede* were written by Dickens, Thackeray, and George Eliot, **respectively.**

Reverend, Honorable These titles should never be used with a person's last name alone. The word *the* commonly precedes the titles.

SUBSTANDARD	Reverend Hiller, the Reverend Hiller, Honorable Wagner
STANDARD	the Reverend Kenneth Hiller, the Reverend K. H. Hiller, the Reverend Mr. Hiller, the Reverend Dr. Hiller, the Honorable Robert F. Wagner

rise, raise See page 141.

same, said, such Avoid such artificial uses of these words as the following:

> The crew worked all day on the boat and had *same* ready to sail by sundown.
>
> We spent our summers at my uncle's ranch, and we became very fond of *said* uncle.
>
> Jerry always wants me to let him copy my homework, but I don't approve of *such.*

says Commonly used incorrectly for **said.**

SUBSTANDARD	Jane stopped me and says, "I know where you're going."
STANDARD	Jane stopped me and **said,** "I know where you're going."

scarcely See *Double negative* (page 192).

shall, will The old distinction between these words is no longer observed by most Americans. *Shall*, which was once considered the only correct form for the expression of the simple future in the first person, has been replaced by *will* in the speech and writing of most educated persons.

STANDARD I **shall** consider your offer.
I **will** consider your offer.

In a few expressions *shall* is the only form ever used and so presents no usage problem: *Shall we go? Shall I help you?* To use *will* in these expressions would change the meaning. With the exception of these special uses, *will* is as correct as *shall*.

sit, set See page 140.

slow, slowly See page 166.

so Because this word is usually overworked, avoid it in your writing whenever you can.

POOR The weather cleared, so we put up the sail and headed out to sea.

BETTER When the weather cleared, we put up the sail and headed out to sea.

BETTER Since the weather had cleared, we put up the sail and headed out to sea.

In writing, do not use *so* for *so that*.

We worked hard in the morning **so that** [not *so*] we could go to the game in the afternoon.

some, somewhat Use *somewhat* rather than *some* as an adverb.

FORMAL Conditions in Europe next year will be **somewhat** [not *some*] better.

take, bring   See **bring, take.**

this here, that there   The *here* and the *there* are unnecessary.

SUBSTANDARD   This here book is easy to read.
STANDARD   **This** book is easy to read.

these kind, those kind   See **kind, sort, type.**

ways   Sometimes incorrectly used for *way* in referring to distance.

INFORMAL   Although Silver Peak seemed close enough to touch, it was actually a long ways off.

FORMAL   Although Silver Peak seemed close enough to touch, it was actually a long **way** off.

well, good   See pages 165–66.

when, where   Do not use *when* or *where* in writing a definition.

WRONG   A pop foul is when the batter hits a high, short fly into foul territory.

RIGHT   A pop foul is a high, short fly that is hit into foul territory.

WRONG   An atlas is where maps are printed.

RIGHT   An atlas is a book of maps.

where   Do not use *where* for *that.*

SUBSTANDARD   I read where you are going to move away.
STANDARD   I read **that** you are going to move away.

where . . . at   See **at.**

which, that, who *Which* should be used to refer to things only. *That* may be used to refer to both things and people. *Who* should be used to refer to people only.

> This is a book **which (that)** you would enjoy.
> There is a girl **who** [not *which*] has talent.
> There is a girl **that** has talent.

who, whom See page 113.

The Double Negative

A double negative is a construction in which two negative words are used where one is sufficient. Formerly, double negatives were quite acceptable, but now they are considered substandard.

can't hardly, can't scarcely The words *hardly* and *scarcely* are negatives. They should never be used with negative *not*.

> SUBSTANDARD I can't hardly tell the difference between this year's cars and last year's.
>
> STANDARD **I can hardly** tell the difference between this year's cars and last year's.
>
> SUBSTANDARD There wasn't scarcely enough food for everyone.
>
> STANDARD There **was scarcely** enough food for everyone.

can't help but In standard formal English avoid this double negative.

> FORMAL **I cannot help admiring** [not *can't help but admire*] his courage.

haven't but, haven't only In certain uses *but* and *only* are negatives. Avoid using them with *not*.

> FORMAL We **had** [not *hadn't*] **but** a few cents in our pockets.
> We **had** [not *hadn't*] **only** a few cents in our pockets.

no, nothing, none   Not to be used with another negative word.

SUBSTANDARD	Haven't you no ticket?
STANDARD	**Haven't** you a ticket?
STANDARD	**Have** you **no** ticket?
SUBSTANDARD	She hasn't nothing to do.
STANDARD	She **has nothing** to do.
STANDARD	She **hasn't anything** to do.
SUBSTANDARD	He didn't give me none.
STANDARD	He **gave** me **none**.
STANDARD	He **didn't give** me **any**.

● EXERCISE 5.   The sentences in this exercise cover usage problems explained in the section of the glossary that follows Exercise 4. Number your paper 1–20. Write after the proper number the correct one of the two words in parentheses.

1. You may disagree with your teachers if you do so (respectfully, respectively).
2. You (can, can't) hardly afford to go to the movies every week.
3. Prospects for peace looked (some, somewhat) better.
4. Mary lives only a little (way, ways) from here.
5. Throughout history certain minorities have been cruelly (prosecuted, persecuted).
6. After he had heard our side of the story, he (says, said) we were all wrong.
7. We (haven't, have) no reason to question your honesty.
8. Neither the steamship (or, nor) the railroad has been outmoded yet.
9. We were only a little (ways, way) from home when the accident happened.
10. (This, These) strange phenomena puzzled the geologists.
11. The refugees (could, couldn't) hardly find food and shelter.
12. He insists that he (has, hasn't) done nothing wrong.
13. I (have, haven't) only a short time for my homework.
14. The French Club and the German Club will meet (respectively, respectfully) in rooms 112 and 203.

15. He would neither let me go with him (or, nor) let me follow him in my car.
16. We (had, hadn't) but one choice to make.
17. I acquired a great respect for the Romans (whom, which) we studied in Latin class.
18. The superintendent said there wasn't (any, no) reason for closing school.
19. An hour after dinner I felt (nauseous, nauseated).
20. The boys insisted they (had, hadn't) nothing to do with the crime.

● REVIEW EXERCISE. The sentences in this exercise cover problems explained in the entire glossary. Number your paper 1–33. If a sentence does not contain a usage error, write a + on your paper after the proper number. If a sentence does contain a usage error, write a 0. Your teacher may ask you to write the correct form after each 0.

1. Bring a camera with you when you go to Europe.
2. Doris has made a large amount of friends.
3. War usually results from causes such as greed and selfishness and which the world seems powerless to remove.
4. The applause showed how deeply the music had affected the audience.
5. There are less reasons for alarm now than there were a year ago.
6. I can't hardly read your writing.
7. The trustees did not accept his resignation.
8. You would of had a bad time driving in the mountains with those brakes.
9. A good speaker adapts his address to his audience.
10. His talk implied that he favored the Labor party.
11. As soon as you graduate, you are one of the alumni.
12. Unfortunately, we cannot except your invitation.
13. There are many different types of poetry, such as the ballad, the sonnet, the ode, the elegy, the simple lyric, and etc.
14. I have little sympathy with that kind of people.
15. Leave me give you a little good advice.
16. Beside having a great interest in photography, Frank is an enthusiastic artist.

17. In my opinion, his explanation was entirely credible.
18. Forty miles an hour is all the faster his car will go.
19. The volcano had been acting like it might erupt.
20. Everywhere the king went he was welcome.
21. Dichotomy is when a thing is divided into two parts.
22. What effect will the new law have on taxes?
23. There isn't nothing else to do.
24. The mayor's speech inferred that the water shortage was serious.
25. Being as the winter is nearly over, the stores are having sales on heavy apparel.
26. He resented his parents' frequent allusions to his poor grades.
27. The boys invented a new route through the swamp, which no one had ever known about.
28. They asked him less questions than he had expected.
29. These phenomena, of course, are most unusual.
30. The committee members which I talked with were pessimistic.
31. The district attorney prosecuted three gamblers last year.
32. You will be disappointed if you try to borrow money off Jack.
33. An overpopulated country will place strict limitations on emigration.

PART THREE

Composition: Sentence Structure

CHAPTER 11

Sentence Completeness

Fragments and Run-on Sentences

Two kinds of sentence errors sometimes persist in the writing of high school seniors. The first is the writing of part of a sentence, a *fragment*, as though it were a whole sentence, able to stand by itself with a capital letter at the beginning and a period at the end. The second kind of error is the writing of two or more sentences as though they were one sentence. The writer makes the mistake of using a comma, or no punctuation at all, between the sentences. You may think of these two sentence errors as opposites. The fragment is not complete; the run-on sentence is more than complete.

SENTENCE FRAGMENTS

A group of words is a complete sentence when it has a subject and a verb and expresses a complete thought.

COMPLETE   After the flood the barn roof lay in the yard.

INCOMPLETE   After the flood the barn roof in the yard

INCOMPLETE   After the flood the barn roof lying in the yard

Because they lack a verb, the last two examples do not express a complete thought. Words ending in *–ing*, like *lying*, are not verbs when they are used alone. Such words may, of course, be used with a *helping verb* to form a verb phrase (see page 12). Unless a word ending in *–ing* does have a helping verb, it cannot be used as the verb in a sentence.[1]

NO VERB   the barn roof lying in the front yard
VERB PHRASE The barn roof **was lying** in the front yard.

NO VERB   Jane going with us
VERB PHRASE Jane **will be going** with us.

11a. A *sentence fragment* is a group of words that does not express a complete thought. Since it is part of a sentence, it should not be allowed to stand by itself, but should be kept in the sentence of which it is a part.

The Phrase Fragment

A phrase is a group of words acting as a single part of speech and not containing a verb and its subject.

There are many kinds of phrases (participial, gerund, prepositional, infinitive) but regardless of their kind, they all have one important characteristic—they are parts of a sentence and must never be separated from the sentence in which they belong. When a phrase is incorrectly allowed to stand by itself, it is referred to as a fragment.

Study the way in which the unattached phrase fragments in the following examples are corrected.

FRAGMENT   On the school steps I saw Alice. Waiting for her mother to pick her up. [This participial phrase fragment modifies the word *Alice*. It should be included in the sentence with the word it modifies.]

---

[1] The following helping verbs may be used with words ending in *–ing* to form a verb phrase:

am	were	can (may) be
are	will (shall) be	could (would, should) be
is	has been	will (shall) have been
was	had been	might have been

11a

FRAGMENT CORRECTED   On the school steps I saw Alice, **waiting for her mother to pick her up.**

FRAGMENT   The largest sailing ship afloat is the 3,800-ton Argentine frigate *Libertad.* Used by the Argentine navy as a training ship. [This participial phrase fragment modifies the word *frigate.* It should be included in the sentence with the word it modifies.]

FRAGMENT CORRECTED   The largest sailing ship afloat is the 3,800-ton Argentine frigate *Libertad*, **used by the Argentine navy as a training ship.**

FRAGMENT   The new cottage is on the north side of the lake. At the edge of a grove of pine trees. [This prepositional phrase fragment modifies the verb *is*, telling where the cottage is. These phrases belong in the sentence.]

FRAGMENT CORRECTED   The new cottage is on the north side of the lake **at the edge of a grove of pine trees.**

FRAGMENT   My parents finally gave me permission. To go with Bill to the game at West Point. [Here an infinitive phrase fragment has been separated from the word *permission*, which it explains. It should be included in the same sentence with the word it explains.]

FRAGMENT CORRECTED   My parents finally gave me permission **to go with Bill to the game at West Point.**

FRAGMENT   Uncle Frank came bearing gifts. A wrist watch for Jean and a ring for me. [This appositive phrase fragment belongs in the sentence preceding it, separated by a comma from *gifts*, the word to which it refers.]

FRAGMENT CORRECTED   Uncle Frank came bearing gifts, **a wrist watch for Jean and a ring for me.**

The Subordinate Clause Fragment

A second type of fragment is the subordinate clause that is incorrectly separated from the sentence in which it belongs. A clause is a group of words containing a subject and predicate and used as a part of a sentence. A subordinate clause does not express a complete thought and cannot stand alone.

FRAGMENT   I was grateful for his financial assistance. Which enabled me to go to college.

FRAGMENT CORRECTED   I was grateful for his financial assist-ance, **which enabled me to go to college.**

11b. **Do not separate a phrase or a subordinate clause from the sentence of which it is a part.**

● EXERCISE 1.   Some of the items in this exercise consist of one or two completed sentences; others contain sentence fragments. Number your paper 1–20. If all the parts of an item are complete sentences, write *C* after the proper number. If an item contains a fragment, rewrite it to include the fragment in the sentence.

1. After a vote, the minority should abide by the decision. Until, by the same process, the consensus can be changed and the decision reversed or modified.
2. Shortly after the puff of flame came a tremendous explosion.
3. History shows few men as versatile as Franklin. Who was an inventor, scientist, public benefactor, writer, statesman, and philosopher.
4. In everything Franklin undertook, he showed the same dominant character trait. An almost ruthless determination to excel.
5. A student gradually learns the danger of putting off home-work until the next morning. Interruptions are always crop-ping up at the last minute.
6. You could not make a better choice for captain, Jack being the conscientious boy he is.
7. Although the editors resented the criticisms of their paper, they frankly admitted that some of the criticisms were fair.
8. Labor insists that management cannot arbitrarily throw workers out of their jobs. That the livelihood and purchasing power of millions of workers are at stake.
9. Committees composed of teachers and parents met every

week during the year. To discuss the school program and plan a new building.

10. Construction work on the express highway will not begin until fall. Because traffic is heaviest during the summer.

11. One automobile insurance company has reached a surprising decision. Not to insure drivers under twenty-five years of age.

12. His training gave him a good background for research. First at the university and later at the Rockefeller Institute.

13. Standing on this huge boulder, a relic of the glacial era, one commands a striking view of the entire valley.

14. At the end of the street stands a dilapidated home. Its windows broken and its porches crumbling.

15. The hero of *The Red Badge of Courage* is Henry Fleming. A young man of limited experience who is forced to face the realities of war.

16. There was no excuse for his refusing to cooperate. Knowing as he did that his services were desperately needed.

17. Team play is as important on the stage as on the athletic field. Every actor must work for the total effect, not just to show himself off.

18. During the bad years when crops were poor and starvation threatened, bands of robbers sprang up. Plundering the countryside and destroying property.

19. Each student was asked to write down what he considered his worst fault. As far as appearance is concerned.

20. Conflicts at home should be settled in the same way as conflicts among nations. By talking the problem over.

RUN–ON SENTENCES

When a comma (instead of a period, a semicolon, or a conjunction) is used between two complete sentences, the result is referred to as a "run-on sentence." One sentence is permitted to "run on" into the next. In high school writing, this type of sentence error is more common than the fragment error. Usually it is the result of carelessness in punctuation rather than of lack of understanding. Because the error involves the misuse of a comma—to separate sentences—it is sometimes referred to as the "comma fault." A worse, but less common, kind of run-on sentence results from omitting all punctuation between sentences.

11c. Avoid the run-on sentence. Do not use a comma between sentences. Do not omit punctuation at the end of a sentence.

RUN-ON SENTENCE   The choice of a camera is difficult, there are many good ones on the market.

These two sentences should either be separated by a period or joined into one sentence by a conjunction or a semicolon. There are four ways of correcting the error:

1. The choice of a camera is difficult. There are many good ones on the market.
2. The choice of a camera is difficult, **but** there are many good ones on the market.
3. The choice of a camera is difficult **because** there are many good ones on the market.
4. The choice of a camera is difficult; there are many good ones on the market.

As you grow older and do more and more writing, you develop a "sentence sense," which is the ability to recognize at once whether a group of words is or is not a complete sentence. Reading your compositions aloud, so that your ears as well as your eyes can detect completeness, will help you find any run-on sentences in your own writing.

◆ NOTE   Do not be surprised, after being warned against sentence fragments and run-on sentences, if you find them being used occasionally by writers in the best newspapers and magazines. Professional writers (who have a strong sentence sense, or they would not be professionals) do at times write fragments and use the comma between sentences, especially when the ideas in the sentences are very closely related. Leave this use of the comma and the use of the fragment to the experienced judgment of the professional.

11c

● EXERCISE 2. The items in this exercise are run-on sentences. Copy after the proper number on your paper the final word in the first sentence in each item and follow it with the first few words of the second sentence. Indicate how you would eliminate the faulty comma. You may use a semicolon, a comma and conjunction, or a period and a capital letter, or other appropriate punctuation. Do not be satisfied with using a period and a capital letter in every case; to make clear the relationship between ideas, some of the items should be corrected in other ways.

EXAMPLE 1. Ford didn't hear about the party until Thursday, he had to get a date in a hurry.

1. *Thursday; therefore he had . . .*

1. In social studies this year we are studying our major national problems, so far we have covered highways, conservation, and education.
2. The West that Mark Twain describes was a wild, lawless place, a man was not respected until he had killed someone.
3. Galileo discovered that most substances expand when heated, but contract when cooled, this was an important step in the scientific study of heat.
4. Every young person should learn one important fact about life, you do not have to be beautiful to have an attractive personality.
5. Milton took an art elective and discovered he had talent, now he spends his afternoons in the art room.
6. At an advanced age she began to write the story of her colorful life, at least she thought her life had been colorful.
7. The astounding scientific developments of one generation are accepted commonplaces in the next generation, the airplane and the telephone, for instance, are taken for granted by everyone today.
8. A new club is being formed for the study of social behavior, instead of just reading an etiquette book, students will give and attend teas, receptions, and dinner parties.
9. A large suggestion box has been placed in the hall just outside the principal's office, students can, by this means, express

their pet peeves about the school, names should not be signed to the suggestions.

10. First try to do the assignment by yourself, if you can't do it, ask your teacher for help.

● EXERCISE 3.   The following exercise contains sentence fragments and run-on sentences. Prepare to explain to the class how you would eliminate the sentence errors. Use the chalkboard when giving your explanation.

1. I have never known anyone who was a better worker than Paul. Who always did his homework in half the time I took, he usually had it done twice as well, too.

2. Concentration was the secret of his success. Although he undoubtedly had a keen mind.

3. I asked Paul to help me with my math once. When I was particularly desperate, I hadn't been getting good grades for several weeks.

4. He could do the problems easily, but he couldn't explain them to me. So that I could understand them, anyway, I didn't ask him again.

5. Mr. Rehman urges all musicians to continue to study their instruments in high school. Because he knows that as they get busier and busier, many students stop taking lessons, sports and other activities cut in on their practice time.

6. Each member of the family has certain duties, the father earns the money, the mother takes care of the home, and the child is expected to get good grades, school is the job of the child.

7. A mammoth crane was brought here to lift into place the steel girders. Huge orange-colored beams that were easily set into place. Almost as though they were matchsticks.

8. The time when a radio station may broadcast is determined by its license, some stations must go off the air at sundown.

9. Everyone was asking me about Fred. Where he was and what he was doing, wild rumors had been circulating.

10. The city's water supply has been threatened. Very little rain or snow having fallen during the past weeks.

11. I learned to like poetry when I read Kipling, his poems

appealed to me. Because of their strong rhythm and their rhyme.

12. I have learned to recognize several kinds of customers. Especially the kind that likes to argue about the merchandise, when I see one of these coming, I duck out of sight, she takes too much time, rarely buys anything, and invariably makes me angry.

13. Most teenagers spend an allowance foolishly, they don't know the value of money. Until they have to work for it.

14. Comic books and detective and confession magazines are examples of modern sensational journalism, they may have an unwholesome effect on the younger generation.

15. Women's colleges were established in America in the nineteenth century. During the Victorian period. When girls were considered frail flowers to be kept safe at home.

16. The way a girl dresses, the makeup she wears, and the way she walks are parts of her outward look, her personality is something quite different. The way she thinks and reacts to a situation and how she carries on a conversation.

17. Audiences appeared to enjoy the play, the reviews in the papers, however, were unfavorable.

18. A back-to-school night for parents convinced the taxpayers of the inadequacy of our building, consequently the bond issue for a new building was passed by a large vote. When it was presented later in the year.

CHAPTER 12

Coordination and Subordination

Relationship Between the Ideas in a Sentence

COORDINATE IDEAS

When a sentence contains more than one idea, the ideas may be equal in rank or unequal in rank. Ideas that are equal in rank are *coordinate*. (*Co–* means "equal"; *–ordinate* means "kind" or "rank"; hence *coordinate* means "of equal kind or rank.")

COORDINATE IDEAS   Mr. Carter is an architect, **and** Mr. Murphy is a contractor.

Today the country is suffering from too much prosperity, **but** thirty years ago it was suffering from too little.

The writer of the preceding sentences considered the two ideas in each sentence of equal rank; he gave them equal emphasis by expressing them in independent clauses. The clauses are coordinate clauses.

Clear Relationship Between Coordinate Ideas

The relationship between coordinate ideas (equal in rank) is made clear by means of the word used to connect the two ideas. Different connectives may be used to express different relationships. The common kinds of relationship between coordinate clauses are *addition, contrast, choice,* and *result.*

Addition

The following connectives are used to indicate that what follows is supplementary to what precedes.

EXAMPLE   I wrote to him, **and** he wrote to me.

also	furthermore
and	likewise
besides	moreover
both . . . and	then

Contrast

The following connectives are used to introduce an idea that in some way conflicts or contrasts with what has gone before.

EXAMPLE   I wrote to him, **but** he did not write to me.

but	still
however	yet
nevertheless	

Choice

The following connectives are used to introduce an alternate possibility.

EXAMPLE   You write to him, **or** I will write to him.

either . . . or	or, nor
neither . . . nor	otherwise

Result

The following connectives are used to state a result or consequence of the preceding statement.

EXAMPLE   I wrote to him; **therefore** he wrote to me.

accordingly	hence
consequently	therefore

19. They were both amazed at the high price of canoes   they paid the bills promptly.
20. Parents are put to a great deal of trouble and expense by their sons   they are usually patient and generous with us.

SUBORDINATE IDEAS

When ideas in a sentence are unequal in rank, the ideas of lower rank are subordinate. (*Sub–* means "under" or "lower.") If the idea of lower rank is expressed in a clause, the clause is a *subordinate* clause.[1] The main idea of the sentence is expressed in an *independent* clause.

EXAMPLES   The pilot, who was a veteran flyer, brought his crippled plane down safely. [Independent clause— greater emphasis: *The pilot brought his crippled plane down safely;* subordinate clause—lesser emphasis: *who was a veteran flyer.*]

Because each of them was politically ambitious, the council members rarely supported one another's proposals. [Main clause—greater emphasis: *the council members rarely supported one another's proposals;* subordinate clause—lesser emphasis: *Because each of them was politically ambitious.*]

Adverb Clauses

12b. **Make clear the relationship between subordinate adverb clauses and independent clauses by selecting subordinating conjunctions which express the relationship exactly.**

The relationship between the idea in a subordinate adverb clause and the idea in an independent clause is made clear by the subordinating conjunction that introduces the sub-

---

[1] For a more detailed explanation of subordinate clauses see pages 53–64.

12b

ordinate clause. The common kinds of relationship between subordinate adverb clauses and independent clauses are *time, cause* or *reason, purpose* or *result,* and *condition.*

Some of the conjunctions can be used in more than one way and so appear in more than one list.

Time

The following subordinating conjunctions introduce clauses expressing a time relationship between the idea in the subordinate clause and the idea in the independent clause.

EXAMPLE   Several guests arrived **before** we were ready.

after	before	until	whenever
as	since	when	while

Cause or Reason

The following subordinating conjunctions introduce clauses expressing the cause or reason for the idea expressed in the independent clause. The subordinate clause tells *why.*

EXAMPLE   We stopped **because** the light was red.

as	since
because	whereas

Purpose or Result

The following subordinating conjunctions introduce clauses expressing the purpose of the idea in the independent clause or the result of the idea in the independent clause.

PURPOSE   Astronauts undergo the most rigorous training **so that** they will be able to handle any emergency.   [The subordinate clause states the purpose of training described in the independent clause.]

RESULT   Extreme differences of opinion developed in the committee **so that** agreement seemed unlikely.   [The subordinate clause states a result of the committee's differences of opinion.]

that	in order that	so that

Condition

The following subordinating conjunctions state the condition or conditions under which the idea in the independent clause is true. Think of *although, even though, though,* and *while* as meaning "in spite of the fact that." They introduce a condition in spite of which the idea in the independent clause is true.

EXAMPLES   **Although** (in spite of the fact that) <u>it was raining</u>, we went to the game.   [The clause states the *condition* under which we went to the game.]

If <u>you pass the examination</u>, you will pass the course. [The clause states under what condition you will pass the course.]

although	though	provided	if
even though	while	unless	

● EXERCISE 2.   Number your paper 1–20. From the preceding lists choose a subordinating conjunction to fill the blank in each sentence and write it after the proper number on your paper. Make sure the conjunction you choose fits logically the meaning of the sentence. After the conjunction, tell what relationship it expresses: *cause* or *reason, condition, purpose* or *result, time.*

1. —— Jane wants to go with us, she must be ready to leave at ten o'clock.
2. —— our team had not won a game all season, no one expected them to win their final game.
3. —— our holiday was a long one, we managed to do only half the things we had planned.
4. —— I had read his latest book, I changed my opinion of him.
5. —— many boys and girls do not know what to do after graduating, the guidance teachers help them to decide.
6. John was advised to take a post-graduate course —— he could prepare for West Point.
7. We ought to wait —— the boys get home.

8. We stood in line all morning —— we could get good seats for the game.

9. —— Colonel Brandon has traveled widely in the Orient, he knows a great deal about China and Japan.

10. I will write a letter to you —— I receive one from you.

11. —— George is older than I, he is in the same grade.

12. He said he would take the job —— the pay was high enough.

13. —— the rain was freezing on the windshield, we had to stop frequently.

14. We will eat dinner at the hotel —— you prefer some other place.

15. —— I had become better acquainted with Alex, I liked him very much.

16. Halstrom's store is being enlarged —— it will accommodate a cafeteria.

17. —— our train is going to be late, I will try to send you a telegram.

18. —— ground transportation was temporarily cut off by the deep snow, the city had to be supplied by air.

19. The President called a special session of Congress —— emergency legislation could be passed.

20. —— the judge had heard the testimony, he ordered a new trial.

● EXERCISE 3.   Join the statements in each group into one sentence in which the relationship between the subordinate clause and the main clause will be shown by a logical subordinating conjunction. You will have to decide what the relationship is—*cause* or *reason*, *condition*, *purpose* or *result*, *time*. Be sure to place a comma after an adverb clause coming first in the sentence.

EXAMPLE   1. Sally did her best.
              She was unable to win the prize.

          1. *Although Sally did her best, she was unable to win the prize.*

1. It is true that you learn to do by doing.
   It is obvious that you learn to write by writing.

2. You should not make up your mind.
   You have studied all the evidence.
3. Money is undoubtedly important.
   It has never made anyone happy.
4. All students should learn standard English.
   They will never be embarrassed by their usage.
5. This critic recommends a new book.
   The book becomes a best-seller.
6. He will invest his money with you.
   You can prove that the investment is safe.
7. We raised our prices.
   Our business increased.
8. He wanted to graduate in January.
   He could join the Navy.
9. You train rigorously.
   You will be able to do well in cross-country.
10. She was ill.
    She insisted on going ahead with the show.
11. The committee members could not agree.
    The whole matter was referred to the president.
12. The president took the responsibility.
    He wanted to settle the matter himself.
13. He decided to carry the issue before the entire club.
    Everyone could express an opinion.
14. There was a great deal of talk.
    Nothing was decided.
15. A decision is reached today.
    The donors will not give us the money.
16. The City Council offered to give us money for a clubhouse.
    We would let the public use it.
17. We had never admitted the public to our meetings.
    We didn't want to admit them to our clubhouse.
18. We would not lose the chance for a new clubhouse.
    Some of us favored admitting the public.
19. I agreed with those in favor of admitting the public.
    I sympathized with the others.
20. No agreement was reached.
    The money went to another club.

Adjective Clauses

The subordinate clauses in the preceding exercises are *adverb* clauses. Subordinate *adjective* clauses are especially helpful in making clear the relationship between sentence ideas because they permit a writer to emphasize one idea above another.[1] A writer may, for instance, wish to express the following ideas in one sentence: *Abraham Lincoln became President of the United States. He was a self-educated man.* The writer, for his purposes, wishes to emphasize the fact that Lincoln became President. He emphasizes this idea by placing it in the independent clause of his sentence and by placing the other idea in an adjective clause.

Abraham Lincoln, who was a self-educated man, **became President of the United States.**

On the other hand, for a different purpose, the writer may wish to change his emphasis from one of these ideas to the other. He can do this by reversing the positions of the ideas.

Abraham Lincoln, who became President of the United States, **was a self-educated man.**

12c. Make clear the relative emphasis to be given ideas in a complex sentence by placing the idea you wish to emphasize in the independent clause and by placing subordinate ideas in subordinate clauses.

● EXERCISE 4.   Change the emphasis in each of the following sentences by placing in the independent clause the idea which is now in the subordinate clause and by placing in the subordinate clause the idea which is now in the independent clause.

[1] Adjective clauses may begin with *who, whom, whose, which, that,* and *where.*

1. Mr. Briggs, who was a famous lawyer, was defeated in the election.
2. Harvard University, which was founded in 1636, is the oldest university in the United States.
3. The plane which took us to Chicago was very comfortable.
4. Our friends, who had agreed to meet us at six o'clock, did not show up.
5. The old elm that had stood at the edge of the park was destroyed by a hurricane in 1954.
6. The canoe trip, which was one of the highlights of our camping season, lasted two weeks.
7. The committee chairman, who was appointed by the president, presides over all meetings.
8. My dog, which is a beautiful Irish setter, was given to me by Uncle Al.
9. This classroom, which is the largest in the school, will accommodate nearly one hundred pupils.
10. The idea that was proposed by Jerry was liked most by the council.

Correcting Faulty Coordination

Faulty coordination occurs when two unequal ideas are placed in coordinate clauses as though they deserved equal emphasis.

FAULTY COORDINATION The Governor was a native of Ohio, and he was elected for a third term.   [ideas of unequal rank]

The two ideas in this sentence are vastly different. It is unlikely that a writer would wish to give them equal rank. The faulty coordination can be corrected by placing one of the ideas in a subordinate position. Which idea the writer puts in the subordinate clause will depend on his purpose.

FAULTY COORDINATION CORRECTED **The Governor,** who was a native of Ohio, **was elected for a third term.**

or

The Governor, who was elected for a third term, **was a native of Ohio.**

12c

12d. **Faulty coordination may be corrected by placing ideas of lesser emphasis in a subordinate position. An idea may be given less emphasis by being expressed in a subordinate clause or a modifying phrase or an appositive.**[1]

(1) Subordination may be accomplished by means of a subordinate clause.

FAULTY COORDINATION The books are on the new-book shelf, and they may be borrowed for a week.

CORRECTED BY AN ADJECTIVE CLAUSE The books **that are on the new-book shelf** may be borrowed for a week.

CORRECTED BY AN ADVERB CLAUSE **If the books are on the new-book shelf,** they may be borrowed for a week.

● EXERCISE 5. Clarify the relationship between ideas in the following examples of faulty coordination by placing one of the ideas in a subordinate clause, either an adverb clause or an adjective clause. Choose carefully the subordinating conjunctions which introduce your adverb clauses.

1. These experiences will be valuable to me in social work and I shall have to work with people from all walks of life.
2. The region is covered with forest and dotted with small lakes, and it will be developed as a resort area.
3. Baker Brothers will build a new factory on the west side of town, and they manufacture pharmaceuticals.
4. There are only two senators from each state, and the Senate is smaller than the House of Representatives.
5. Columbia University was originally King's College, and it is situated in New York City.
6. The constant roar of machinery nearly deafened us, and we enjoyed our trip through the factory.
7. The heavy fog made flying hazardous, and it did not lift until noon.

[1] For the use of subordination in achieving sentence variety, see page 273. For the use of subordination in correcting stringy sentences and choppy sentences, see page 275.

8. The school needs another driver-training car, and more students can learn how to drive.
9. A Future Teachers of America Club was formed at our school, and the number of students planning to be teachers nearly doubled.
10. The junior college occupies the same building as the high school, and it has an enrollment of 300 students.

(2) Subordination may be accomplished by means of a modifying phrase.

FAULTY COORDINATION   The house is at the end of the street, and it is very modern in design.

CORRECTED BY A MODIFYING PHRASE   The house **at the end of the street** is very modern in design.

(3) Subordination may be accomplished by means of an appositive.

An appositive is a word, with or without modifiers, which follows a noun or pronoun and helps to explain it.

FAULTY COORDINATION   Mr. Fitch is the manager of the store, and he is tall and handsome.

CORRECTED BY AN APPOSITIVE   Mr. Fitch, **the manager of the store,** is tall and handsome.

● EXERCISE 6.   Correct the faulty coordination in the following sentences in the ways prescribed.

Correct by a subordinate clause:

1. Millions know cigarette smoking is a cause of cancer, and they continue to smoke.
2. Franklin was a scientist as well as a statesman, and he invented a new kind of stove.
3. September has always been a pleasant month, and it surprised us this year with storms and cold weather.
4. A newspaper costs far more than the public pays for it, and it is supported by the sale of advertising space.
5. The American Constitution went into effect in 1789, and it is one of the great governmental documents of the world.

12d

Correct by a modifying phrase:

6. Our final game was with Parkerville, and it was rained out.
7. For years American tourists have been inundating Europe, and they go during the summer months.
8. He told me to look in the dictionary, and it was on his desk.
9. The pocketknife had two dull blades, and it was the only weapon the shipwrecked men had.
10. The truck contained explosives, and it narrowly missed a collision with an oil truck.

Correct by an appositive:

11. Mr. Shapiro is the custodian of our building, and he came to this country only three years ago.
12. The new ruler is a man of great experience in government, and he should be able to reconcile the factions in the country.
13. The violin was an instrument with a beautiful tone, and it belonged to my grandfather.
14. This plane is the fastest passenger plane in the world, and it will take you to Europe in record time.
15. His new book is a volume of poetry, and it received very favorable reviews.

Summary

(1) Make clear the relationship between ideas in a sentence by using connectives that express the relationship exactly.
(2) Correct faulty coordination by placing ideas of lesser emphasis in a subordinate position. Use a subordinate clause or a modifying phrase or an appositive.

● Exercise 7. The relationship between ideas in the sentences is not clear: the conjunctions used are not exact, or the sentences contain faulty coordination. Rewrite the sentences. Some may be improved in more than one way.

1. The Bay Challenge Cup represents the highest achievement in sailing, and it was first put up for competition in 1903.
2. The principle that government employees shall not strike has been seldom challenged, and it applies to both federal and state employees.

3. High school graduates are better educated today than ever before, and they have a hard time finding jobs.
4. The final chapters of this book outline a constructive program dealing with the problem, and they are the most important.
5. Every business has several ambitious competitors, and no business can afford to stand still.
6. The new regulations call for the opening of school at 7:30 every morning, and they are unpopular with both students and teachers.
7. Mr. Greenberg was a high school coach for many years, and he is now coaching college teams in Ohio.
8. Representatives came from more than fifty countries, and they met in the United Nations Building in New York City.
9. The title of the book was very interesting, and the book itself was very dull.
10. Because their principal crop was potatoes and the potato season was poor, the farmers managed to avoid going into debt.
11. Miss Lang had not directed many plays, and she knew how to manage an inexperienced cast.
12. Helen may go to Wellesley next year, and she may go to Barnard.
13. Carl has taken piano lessons for only three years, and he is already a good pianist.
14. Mr. Stark has never paid back the money he borrowed, and he wants me to lend him more.
15. We waited on the corner for an hour, and the bus didn't come.
16. The Commercial High School is a large stone building on Market Street, and it is attended by students from all over the city.
17. Stewart Harrison was a famous detective, and he could not solve the arsenic murder case.
18. Mr. Armstrong has been selling advertising for many years, and he has been made advertising director of the *Herald*.
19. I am going to the airport to meet a friend, and he is coming from Chicago.
20. Professor Drake has been head of the chemistry department for twenty years, and he died yesterday.

CHAPTER 13

Clear Reference

Pronouns and Antecedents

The meaning of a pronoun is clear only when you know what it refers to. The word to which a pronoun refers is its antecedent. For example, the sentence, "He was talking with them," has little meaning unless you know to whom the pronouns *he* and *them* refer. Similarly, the pronoun *it* is meaningless in the sentence, "It chased me all the way home," unless you know to what *it* refers—a dog, a monster, etc.

In the following sentences, arrows connect the pronouns and their antecedents.

I asked Mr. Jordan for the answer but he didn't know it.

The Potters have a new sailboat on which they intend to cruise.

Handing George the coat, the salesman said, "Try this on for size."

13a. A pronoun must refer clearly to the right antecedent. Avoid *ambiguous* reference, *general* reference, and *weak* reference.

One simple way of testing pronoun reference is to substitute the antecedent for the pronoun.

Charlie is always thinking about cars. *It* [*cars?*] is his only interest.   [The antecedent cannot be substituted; the reference is faulty.]

Charlie is always thinking about cars. They [*cars*] are his only interest.   [The antecedent fits.]

AMBIGUOUS REFERENCE

(1) Avoid *ambiguous reference*. Ambiguous reference occurs when a pronoun refers confusingly to two antecedents so that the reader does not know at once which antecedent is meant.

AMBIGUOUS   The President appointed Senator Moore as chairman because he was convinced of the importance of the committee's work.

Here the pronoun *he* can refer to either the President or Senator Moore. The context in which such a sentence appears will ordinarily provide the reader with the clues he needs to identify the antecedent. Occasionally, however, the use of a pronoun that can refer to more than one antecedent causes momentary confusion. Such ambiguous reference can usually be avoided by rephrasing the sentence.

CLEAR   The President, convinced of the importance of the committee's work, appointed Senator Moore as chairman.

CLEAR   Because Senator Moore was convinced of the importance of the committee's work, the President appointed him as chairman.

Occasionally, the only way to avoid ambiguity is to replace the pronoun with the appropriate noun:

AMBIGUOUS   The partnership between Jones and Potter ended when he drew the firm's money from the bank and flew to Brazil.

CLEAR   The partnership between Jones and Potter ended when Jones drew the firm's money from the bank and flew to Brazil.

13a

● Exercise 1.   Find the ambiguous pronoun in each of the following sentences. Make the sentence clear either by revising it or by replacing the pronoun with a noun.

1. As soon as the students had left the classrooms, the custodians cleaned them.
2. Phil was arguing with Jim, and he looked unhappy.
3. One of the passengers told the bus driver that he didn't know the route very well.
4. We unpacked our dishes from the barrels and then returned them to the moving company.
5. When the accountant was studying the treasurer's report, he became very much alarmed.
6. George noticed that the principal was smiling in an odd way as he came into the office.
7. Senator Mills conferred with the Secretary of State when he was touring the East.
8. Our job was to remove the labels from the old bottles and wash them.
9. The policeman chased the thief for several blocks; then, however, he hid in an abandoned cellar.
10. International goodwill is essential to successful international trade. It will help to make a peaceful world.

GENERAL REFERENCE

(2) Avoid *general reference*. General reference occurs when a pronoun refers confusingly to a general idea that is only vaguely expressed.

The pronouns *which*, *this*, *that*, and *it* are commonly used in a general way.

GENERAL   The boys wore ski boots to their classes which the principal disapproved of.

In this sentence the pronoun *which* refers to the general idea, *the wearing of ski boots to class;* furthermore, the pronoun is so placed that it appears to refer to *classes.* The writer did not mean that the principal disapproved of the classes. The sentence can be corrected by revision.

CLEAR   The principal disapproved of **the boys' wearing** ski boots to their classes.

In the following example, the pronoun *this* does not have a clear antecedent.

GENERAL   The trip to town was strenuous. The car broke down; a tire blew out; and Father sat on the basket of eggs. This put us in a poor frame of mind.

The pronoun *this* should be replaced with a definite noun, making clear the reference to a number of misfortunes.

CLEAR   These **misfortunes** put us in a poor frame of mind.

In the next example, the pronoun *it* does not have a clear antecedent. A definite noun makes the meaning clear.

GENERAL   Great ships were moving slowly up the harbor; tugs and ferryboats scurried in and out among them; here and there a white cabin cruiser sliced sharply through the blue water under the suspension bridge. It was thrilling to a farm boy.

CLEAR   The **sight** was thrilling to a farm boy.

Although general reference can sometimes be corrected by merely substituting a noun for the unclear pronoun, it is often necessary to revise the entire sentence.

GENERAL   During class Tom tapped his pencil on the desk, scraped his feet on the floor, and dropped his books. This annoyed the teacher.

CLEAR   Tom annoyed the teacher by tapping his pencil on the desk, scraping his feet on the floor, and dropping his books.

● EXERCISE 2.   The following sentences contain examples of general, or vague, reference of pronouns. Revise the sentences or replace the unclear pronouns with nouns.

1. The Chinese were bitter when Russia withdrew her technical assistance; they said it would harm the Chinese economy.
2. Macbeth's mind was constantly imagining horrible things, and that frightened him.

3. He is a conscientious, hard-working man with an engaging personality, but it doesn't make him any richer.
4. A number of people gathered around the speaker and his microphone, which was due to curiosity.
5. I enjoyed the author's style and the type of characters he wrote about. It made me want to read his other books.
6. Father Meyer came to the house daily, from which a sturdy friendship grew.
7. A great deal of effort went into planning the expedition, hiring the right sort of men, and anticipating every emergency, which accounts for the success of the undertaking.
8. Chicago stretches along the shore of Lake Michigan, which makes a beautiful shore drive possible.
9. School gymnasiums will be open every Saturday during the winter, and school playgrounds will be supervised during the summer months. Other school facilities, such as the shops and the little theater, will be available to hobbyists. This will cost money, but the Board of Education thinks the public will be glad to meet the expense.
10. Even students with season tickets had to pay admission to the post-season games. We thought it wasn't fair.

WEAK REFERENCE

(3) Avoid *weak reference*. Weak reference occurs when the antecedent has not been expressed but exists only in the writer's mind.

WEAK   We spent the day aboard a fishing boat, but we didn't catch a single one.

In this sentence there is no antecedent of the pronoun *one*. The adjective *fishing* is not the antecedent, since it is fish, not fishing, that *one* refers to. The writer meant the pronoun to stand for the noun *fish*.

CLEAR   We spent the day aboard a fishing boat, but we didn't catch a single **fish**.

CLEAR   We spent the day aboard a fishing boat trying to catch some **fish**, but we didn't catch a single **one**.

In other words, the antecedent of a pronoun should be a noun. When the antecedent is "hidden" in a modifier or a verb form, the reference is weak.

WEAK   The people want honest public servants, but that has not always been a virtue of politicians.

In this sentence the antecedent should be the noun *honesty*, but the noun is "hidden" in the adjective *honest*. The sentence may be corrected by replacing the weak pronoun with a noun.

CLEAR   The people want honest public servants, but **honesty** has not always been a virtue of politicians.

In the next sentence, the antecedent of *it* should be the noun *writing*, which is "hidden" in the verb *wrote*.

WEAK   Louis wrote whenever he could find the time, but none of it was ever published.

CLEAR   Louis wrote whenever he could find the time, but none of **his writing** was ever published.

In the next sentence the pronoun *they* does not have an antecedent. The writer had *witches* in mind as the antecedent, but he did not use the word at all.

WEAK   He is a great believer in witchcraft, but he doubts that they ride on broomsticks.

CLEAR   He is a great believer in **witches,** but he doubts that **they** ride on broomsticks.

CLEAR   He is a great believer in witchcraft, but he doubts that **witches** ride on broomsticks.

Correct weak references by replacing the weak pronoun with a noun, or by giving the pronoun a clear antecedent.

● EXERCISE 3.   Correct the weak reference in each of the following sentences.

1. I love horses and believe it to be an enjoyable sport.
2. When you are ready to ice the cake, put some in the center of the top and spread it smoothly toward the edges.

3. Friendship is a basic need in everybody's life, for without them we wouldn't be happy very long.
4. The jewelry salesman tried to make us believe they were genuine.
5. He had written a great deal of poetry during his life, but he had never had any of them published.
6. After watching the fireman's daring exploits, all the little boys in the crowd decided that that is what they would be.
7. He is a very wealthy man, but he never spends any of it.
8. When we finally reached a gas station, the attendant told us he didn't have any.
9. She likes Indian lore although she has never seen one.
10. When we boarded the bus for Tulsa, we learned that it would take fourteen hours.

INDEFINITE USE OF PRONOUNS

13b. In writing avoid indefinite use of the pronouns *it*, *they*, and *you*.

The indefinite use of these pronouns in sentences like the following occurs in ordinary conversation but is not acceptable in writing.

INDEFINITE   In the final chapter it implies that the hero died a martyr's death.

BETTER   **The final chapter** implies that the hero died a martyr's death.

INDEFINITE   On planes that are in flight at mealtime, they serve meals without charge.

BETTER   On planes that are in flight at mealtime, **meals** are served without charge.

INDEFINITE   In some countries, you don't dare express political views openly.

BETTER   In some countries, **the people** don't dare express political views openly.

◆ NOTE   The expressions *it is raining*, *it seems*, *it is late* are, of course, entirely correct.

● EXERCISE 4. The sentences in this exercise contain examples of ambiguous, general, and weak reference. There are some examples of the indefinite use of *it*, *they*, and *you*. Correct the sentences either by replacing a faulty pronoun with a noun, or by revising the sentence. Make the meaning unmistakably clear.

1. Western farmers today can produce more because of machines and the many men working under them.
2. Nancy rode home from school with Suzie, but she didn't tell her anything.
3. We had a long assignment, an inadequate library, and insufficient time, which was very frustrating.
4. Golf wouldn't cost me so much if I didn't lose so many in the rough.
5. The radiator was leaking badly; it ran all over the garage floor.
6. In the cabin he reloaded his gun. In those days this might mean the difference between life and death.
7. He overcame his hip injury which doctors had said was impossible.
8. His spelling and sentence structure are not good, but most of it is due to carelessness.
9. Ruth saw Julie when she was in town last week.
10. In yesterday's editorial, it says the mayor has failed to live up to his campaign promises.
11. We talked with the other passengers as though we had had years of flying experience, but we had never been up in one before.
12. If the prospective buyer learns that the heating system in the house is unsatisfactory, he had better not buy it.
13. The witness testified that he had seen the accused when he was eating dinner in the dining car, which convinced the jury of his presence on the train.
14. The library does not have enough copies of some of the books in greatest demand by students writing research papers, which makes it hard for you.
15. In Washington they are skeptical about the success of the new farm program.

13b

CHAPTER 14

Placement of Modifiers

Misplaced and Dangling Modifiers

A sentence may be confusing for one of two quite different reasons. It may be confusing because the ideas, although clearly stated, are hard to understand. This kind of sentence does not represent faulty writing. But a sentence may also be confusing because of the clumsiness of the writer in arranging the modifiers in the sentence. A modifier should clarify or make more definite the meaning of the word it modifies. If the modifier is placed too far from this word, the effect of the modifier may be either lost or diverted to some other word.

MISPLACED MODIFIERS

14a. Place phrase and clause modifiers as near as possible to the words they modify.

A misplaced modifier may force the reader to reread the sentence in order to be sure what it says. Sentences like the following examples may be clear on first reading; on the other hand, because of a misplaced word or group of words, they may mislead the reader or force him to take a second look.

CONFUSING   Two meetings have been held to make arrangements for a return bout in the office of the State Athletic Commission.

Although any reader knows that the return bout is not likely to be held *in the office of the State Athletic Commission,* he may be momentarily distracted by this interesting thought. Placing the phrase next to *held,* the word it modifies, makes the sentence clear.

CLEAR   Two meetings have been held in the office of the State Athletic Commission to make arrangements for a return bout.

CONFUSING   Mr. Richman presented a cabin cruiser to his family, which, it later developed, he was unable to pay for.

The reader of this sentence will probably assume that Mr. Richman did not have to pay for his family. Nevertheless, the clause *which he was unable to pay for* should be next to cruiser, which it modifies.

CLEAR   Mr. Richman presented to his family a cabin cruiser, which, it later developed, he was unable to pay for.

CONFUSING   The thief decided to make a run for it when he saw the policeman, abandoning the stolen car and dashing into the woods.

This sentence would be clearer if it did not on first reading give the impression that the policeman was abandoning the stolen car and dashing into the woods. Moving the adverb clause *when he saw the policeman* to the beginning of the sentence makes it clear that the thief, not the policeman, ran away.

CLEAR   When he saw the policeman, the thief decided to make a run for it, abandoning the stolen car and dashing into the woods.

The usual way to clarify a sentence containing a misplaced modifier is to move the modifier next to the word it modifies. Some sentences, however, cannot be clarified so easily. In the sentence above, for example, moving the participial phrases next to thief, the word they modify, changes the meaning of the sentence: The thief, abandoning

14a

the car and dashing into the woods, decided to make a run for it when he saw the policeman.

Often, you can improve a sentence by moving an adverbial modifier (in this instance *when he saw the policeman*) to the beginning of the sentence. Indeed, regardless of how it may fit elsewhere in the sentence, an adverbial modifier is often better placed at the beginning.

The point of this discussion of the placement of modifiers is that a careful writer recognizes the importance of making himself clear at first reading. He does not try to hide behind the weak explanation, "You know what I mean."

● EXERCISE 1.   The following sentences may be confusing on first reading because of a misplaced phrase or clause. Improve the sentences by placing modifiers near the words they modify. You may find that placing an adverbial modifier first often improves the sentence. Doing the exercise orally in class will save time.

1. The students deserved the severe reprimand they received for their misbehavior in the cafeteria in the principal's office on Monday.

2. Commander Richardson was decorated for his action, but he was haunted by the memory of the men he had had to sacrifice for years after.

3. The company is now running a late bus for skiers leaving at 6:15.

4. The big schooner was sailed through the narrow channel by a daring skipper without running lights or motor about midnight.

5. One of our observers sighted a plane through his binoculars that he could not identify.

6. The minister announced that next Sunday's sermon would be an explanation of the nature of sin, in which he hoped the congregation would take great interest.

7. The causeway has a drawbridge to permit the passage of fishing boats from which all fishing is prohibited.

8. The mystery has been solved after ten years of the missing portrait.

9. The new house was built by Mrs. Borden, who later became Mrs. Gruber, at a cost of $200,000.
10. The suspect tried to make the police believe that he had found the wallet in his car that didn't belong to him.
11. Detectives narrowed the number of the houses where the robbers might strike by deduction.
12. Mike made the mistake one afternoon of running and diving when the pool was empty into the deep end.
13. I'll check the manuscript when you finish for accuracy.
14. He worked hard in his fields, raising crops that would bring in money without complaint.
15. Judge Hart asked for the submission of briefs before handing down a decision on the alleged criminal actions which were to be prepared by the opposing lawyers.
16. If what the directions say is true on the package, this is a powerful insecticide.
17. Father bought a gadget for his new car from a fast-talking salesman that was guaranteed to reduce gas consumption.
18. He wore a straw hat on the back of his head which was obviously too small.
19. Mr. Buck, the explorer, described his trips through the jungle in our social studies class.
20. Uncle Jim brought a new carriage for the baby that was named "Boodle Buggy."

DANGLING MODIFIERS

14b. A modifying phrase or clause must clearly and sensibly modify a word in the sentence. When there is no word that the phrase or clause can sensibly modify, the modifier is said to dangle.

DANGLING MODIFIER   Carrying a heavy pile of books, his foot caught on the step.

An introductory participial phrase modifies the noun or pronoun following it. In this example, the phrase *carrying a heavy pile of books* appears to modify *foot*. Since

14b

a foot could not carry a pile of books, the phrase cannot modify it sensibly. In fact, there is no word in this sentence which can be sensibly modified by the introductory phrase. The phrase, therefore, is a dangling modifier. The sentence can be corrected in two ways:

1. By adding a word that the phrase can sensibly modify.

   Carrying a heavy pile of books, **he** caught his foot on the steps.

2. By changing the phrase to an adverb clause.

   While he was carrying a heavy pile of books, his foot caught on the steps.

Study the following examples of dangling modifiers and the ways in which they have been corrected.

DANGLING MODIFIER Representing the conservative point of view, the liberals attacked him.

CORRECTED Representing the conservative point of view, he was attacked by the liberals.

CORRECTED Since he represented the conservative point of view, the liberals attacked him.

DANGLING MODIFIER After standing up well under the two-year exposure test, the manufacturers were convinced that the paint was sufficiently durable.

CORRECTED After the paint had stood up well under the two-year exposure test, the manufacturers were convinced that it was sufficiently durable.

DANGLING MODIFIER Absorbed in an interesting discussion, the time passed quickly.

CORRECTED Absorbed in an interesting discussion, we found that the time passed quickly.

CORRECTED Because we were absorbed in an interesting discussion, the time passed quickly.

It is only fair to point out that examples of dangling modifiers may sometimes be found in the works of the best authors. These examples, however, are either so idiomatic as to be entirely acceptable, or they are so clear that no possible confusion can result. The following are not objectionable:

> Generally speaking, the cost of living has remained static for several years.

> To get the best results, the oven should be preheated.

It is important, however, that you realize the absurd meanings into which danglers can lead you so that you will avoid them in your own writing.

● EXERCISE 2. Each of the following sentences contains a dangling modifier. Remove the danglers by revising the sentences.

1. Coming up the front walk, the bouquet in the picture window looked beautiful.
2. Left alone in the house, the thunderstorm terrified him.
3. Enormous and architecturally striking, everyone is impressed by the new building.
4. When selecting a college, the social life seems to interest some students more than education.
5. After considering the proposal for several hours, it was rejected by the council.
6. While talking with friends recently, the topic of dentistry came up.
7. After spending Saturday morning working in the library, a feeling of righteousness possessed me.
8. After flying in darkness for two hours, the moon rose, and navigation became less difficult.
9. While driving at high speed on a deserted highway, two deer leaped in front of our car.
10. Living in this coastal town for many years, the fishing boats and their skippers were well known to him.
11. After working in the fields all day, little strength was left for social activities.
12. When only a youngster in grade school, my father instructed me in the manly art of boxing.
13. Yielding to the temptation to look at a classmate's paper, the proctor caught her cheating.

14. While working in California, his family was living in New York.
15. Having run off the road while passing a car, my father told me I did not know how to drive.
16. Having promised to be home by midnight, the family was annoyed when I came in at two o'clock.
17. While playing in the high chair, I was afraid the baby would fall out.
18. Riding in the glass-bottomed boat, hundreds of beautiful tropical fish could be seen.
19. Being very shy, strangers terrify my little sister.
20. After being wheeled into the operating room, a nurse placed a mask over my nose.

TWO–WAY MODIFIERS

A third way in which a careless writer sometimes confuses his reader is by placing a modifier in such a way that it may be taken to modify two words. As a result, the reader cannot be sure which of the two possible meanings is intended. Such a modifier is called a *two-way*, or a *squinting*, *modifier*.

EXAMPLE   Mary said *during the meeting* Jo acted like a fool.

Since the phrase *during the meeting* may be taken to modify either *said* or *acted*, this sentence is not clear. Did Mary say this during the meeting, or did Jo act like a fool during the meeting? The sentence should be revised to make it say one thing or the other.

CLEAR   **During the meeting** Mary said Jo acted like a fool.

CLEAR   Mary said Jo acted like a fool **during the meeting.**

Study the following examples of two-way modifiers:

NOT CLEAR   Mrs. Stewart asked us *before we left* to call on her.

CLEAR   **Before we left,** Mrs. Stewart asked us to call on her.

CLEAR   Mrs. Stewart asked us to call on her **before we left.**

NOT CLEAR   Tell Fred *when he comes home* I want to see him.

CLEAR   **When he comes home,** tell Fred I want to see him.

CLEAR   Tell Fred I want to see him **when he comes home.**

● EXERCISE 3. The sentences in this exercise contain misplaced, dangling, and squinting modifiers. Revise each sentence so that its meaning will be clear on first reading.

1. Mr. and Mrs. Gray chose a village for their new home with about 4000 residents.

2. Rounding the corner of the house, his fears were confirmed.

3. Tell the driver if you wish to get to school early.

4. By Saturday all members of the cast must have their lines learned that are in the first act.

5. Having required several pints of blood from the blood bank, the patient's family and friends were asked to replenish the supply.

6. The new school building wing was described by the school board, which consists of four classrooms, a laboratory, industrial arts rooms, and a fallout shelter.

7. Having fallen heavily during the night, Sorenson found that the snow had reached the eaves of his cabin.

8. After urging so many ridiculous reforms, the voters refused to reelect Mr. Cooper.

9. The auditors discovered upon their arrival at the bank the cashier had fled.

10. From talking to others, the prevalent opinion favors us.

11. While watching the ball game, Sid's horse ran away.

12. Hotels hold all articles for a year that are found on the premises.

13. Preferring the mountains to the seashore, the Great Smokies were chosen as our vacation spot.

14. After working in Washington for twenty years, the methods of lobbyists were familiar.

15. This bank approves loans to reliable individuals of any size.

16. Did you know when you were in Chicago I was living in Highland Park?

17. While lighting a cigar, the car swerved dangerously toward a telephone pole.
18. Being completely untamed, George warned us that the animals were dangerous.
19. One can see more than a hundred lakes, flying at an altitude of several thousand feet.
20. Jack bought a book of shorthand lessons along with his new typewriter which he read and studied diligently.
21. Living constantly under the eyes of the police, his nervousness increased.
22. A new highway has finally been completed after three years of frustration through the mountains and across California by the federal government.
23. Phil wanted to know before the game began what the referees said to the two captains.
24. Believing that freedom was more important than security, homes, relatives, and countries were abandoned by these emigrants.
25. Rounding a sharp curve, a detour sign warned us of danger.

CHAPTER 15

Parallel Structure

Structures of Equal Rank; Correcting Faulty Parallelism

Parallelism in sentence structure exists when two or more sentence elements of equal rank are similarly expressed. Stating equal and closely related ideas in parallel constructions often adds clarity and smoothness to writing.

KINDS OF PARALLEL STRUCTURE

15a. Express parallel ideas in the same grammatical form.

There are three sentence elements which commonly require parallel treatment: coordinated ideas, compared and contrasted ideas, and correlative constructions. A sentence reads smoothly when the writer has taken the trouble to put parallel ideas in the same form.

Coordinate Ideas

Coordinate ideas are equal in rank. They are joined by coordinate connectives. The coordinate connectives most often used in parallel structure are *and, but, or, nor.*

15a

239

To express parallel ideas in the same grammatical form, pair one part of speech with the same part of speech, a verbal with the same kind of verbal, a phrase with a phrase, a clause with a clause. Do not pair unlike grammatical forms.

FAULTY   The committee studied all aspects of the problem— humane, political, and cost.   [The adjectives *humane* and *political* are paired with the noun *cost*.]

PARALLEL   The committee studied all aspects of the problem— **humane, political,** and **financial**.   [All three coordinate elements are adjectives.]

FAULTY   In camp a group of us tried to improve our physiques by daily calisthenics, special diets, and following a strict sleeping schedule.   [two nouns paired with a phrase]

PARALLEL   In camp a group of us tried to build up our physiques by daily **calisthenics,** special **diets,** and a strict sleeping **schedule**.   [three nouns]

FAULTY   The firm's annual report revealed a growth in productive capacity but that sales had dropped.   [noun paired with a clause]

PARALLEL   The firm's annual report revealed a **growth** in productive capacity but a **drop** in sales.   [noun paired with noun]

PARALLEL   The firm's report revealed **that productive capacity had grown** but **that sales had dropped**.   [clause paired with clause]

Compared or Contrasted Ideas

FAULTY   Water-skiing no longer interests me as much as to go scuba diving.   [gerund *water-skiing* paired with infinitive *to go*]

PARALLEL   **Water-skiing** no longer interests me as much as **scuba diving**.   [gerund paired with gerund]

PARALLEL   **To go water-skiing** no longer interests me as much as **to go scuba diving**.   [infinitive paired with an infinitive.]

FAULTY   His novel was praised more for its style than for what
          it had to say.   [noun paired with a clause]

PARALLEL His novel was praised more for its **style** than for its
          ideas.   [noun paired with a noun]

Correlative Constructions

Correlative constructions are formed with the correlative
conjunctions *both . . . and, either . . . or, neither . . . nor, not
only . . . but (also).*

FAULTY   To gain entrance they tried both persuasion and to
          force their way in.   [noun paired with an infinitive]

PARALLEL To gain entrance they tried both **persuasion** and
          force.   [noun paired with a noun]

FAULTY   The new clerk soon proved himself to be not only
          capable but also a man who could be trusted.   [ad-
          jective paired with a noun]

PARALLEL The new clerk soon proved himself to be not only
          capable but also **trustworthy.**   [adjective paired with
          an adjective]

COMPLETED PARALLELISM

15b. Place correlative conjunctions immedi-
ately before the parallel terms.

WRONG   Mr. Sayers is not only president of the National Bank
         but also of the Chamber of Commerce.   [*Not only . . .
         but also* should precede the parallel terms *of the Na-
         tional Bank* and *of the Chamber of Commerce*, not the
         word *president.*]

RIGHT   Mr. Sayers is president **not only** of the National Bank
         but also of the Chamber of Commerce.

WRONG   The team both felt the satisfaction of victory and the
         disappointment of defeat.

RIGHT   The team felt **both** the satisfaction of victory **and** the
         disappointment of defeat.

15b

15c. In parallel constructions repeat an article, a preposition, or a pronoun whenever necessary to make the meaning clear.

Note that the omission or inclusion of a word in the paired sentences below changes the meaning.

Before the meeting I talked with the secretary and treasurer. [The sentence may mean that I talked with one person who holds the double office of secretary and treasurer.]

Before the meeting I talked with the secretary and **the** treasurer. [This sentence indicates that I talked with two persons.]

The weather was a greater handicap to the invading army than their enemy. [This sentence means that the invaders would rather fight the enemy than the weather.]

The weather was a greater handicap to the invading army than **to** their enemy. [This sentence means that the invaders had the harder job.]

We feel certain that he is capable, he will succeed, and you will be proud of him. [In a series of parallel *that* clauses, the meaning is usually clearer if the introductory word is repeated in each clause. Omission of the introductory *that* from the clauses may give the impression that this is a run-on sentence, the first sentence ending with *capable*.]

We feel certain that he is capable, **that** he will succeed, and **that** you will be proud of him.

● EXERCISE 1.   Improve the following sentences by putting parallel ideas into the same grammatical form. Correct any errors in the placement of correlatives and in the omission of a necessary article, preposition, or pronoun.

1. He had finally decided on his college and what profession he would enter.
2. Critics agreed that the movie was unrealistic and it was too long and that it wasn't interesting.
3. The firm can either reduce expenses by curtailing its working force or postpone factory renovations.

4. The music was written by a German, but an American did this arrangement.

5. In September the atmosphere of the school is exciting and charged with enthusiasm, but in February the feeling about the place is one of dullness and dreariness.

6. The gulf between us and the British in mannerisms of speech, the vocabulary we use, and intonation is growing narrower every year.

7. Come to the meeting prepared to take notes and with some questions to ask.

8. Passing the oral test is usually more difficult than to pass the written test.

9. The politicians not only were convinced that their platform was sound but popular.

10. Our cabinetmaker did a better job on our furniture than theirs.

11. Tell me where you have been and an account of your activities there.

12. He regarded all natives as sly, ignorant, and not to be depended upon.

13. The traffic judge told his teen-age audience that adolescents are selfish, they drive recklessly, and that they do not respect adults.

14. The audience neither understood the speaker's words nor what his purpose was.

15. Mud wasps had not only hung their cones under the porch but also the eaves.

16. The poem makes you feel the rolling of the cannon, the running of the horses, and how afraid the inexperienced soldiers were.

17. The new models will be expensive to buy, but their cost of operation will be low.

18. At one time Coleridge tried preaching but later turning to poetry and the fine arts.

19. In his lecture today Professor Hobbs explained both the causes of World War I and how the war affected the economy of Western Europe.

20. The President not only is head of the nation but his political party.

15c

15d. Include in the second part of a parallel construction all words necessary to make the construction complete.

Occasionally in your haste you may fail to include in one part of a parallel construction all the words necessary to make the construction complete.

INCOMPLETE   She wore clothes that were better than the other girls.

COMPLETE   She wore clothes that were better than **those of** the other girls.

In the first of these sentences you feel that something has been omitted because the sentence compares *clothes* with *girls*.

● EXERCISE 2.   Correct the parallelism in each of the following sentences by inserting the words that have been omitted.

1. My experience was not half so exciting as the people who didn't get home until dawn.
2. As time passed, she was torn between her love for her parents and her husband.
3. This author's style is not much different from other writers of this time.
4. Highway signs in Europe employ symbols much more than the United States.
5. Compare your grades for this quarter with last quarter.
6. Statistics prove that prices this year are lower than last year.
7. You will find the information in the second edition more up-to-date than the first edition.
8. Little children are more trouble in the boat than the beach.
9. The trail on the north side of the mountain is steeper than the south side.
10. The amount of money his wife received in the will was much smaller than the children.
11. The classrooms on the second floor are always cleaner than the first floor.

12. The inexpensive overcoat which I bought last week looks exactly like the more expensive stores.
13. Cats can catch rabbits as easily as dogs.
14. The damage done by this year's forest fires was greater than last year's.
15. The reaction of the students to the new regulations was more violent than the faculty.

● EXERCISE 3. The following sentences contain faulty parallelism. Rephrase the sentences so that the parallelism will be correctly and logically expressed. You will do well to review the various kinds of faulty parallelism before doing the exercise.

1. One of the accident victims suffered a broken arm, several broken ribs, and one of his lungs was punctured.
2. He not only was industrious but he could be depended on.
3. As we were leaving the harbor, the radio weather report predicted gale-force winds, heavy rain, and that tides would be abnormally high.
4. A cloudy day is better for a game than sunshine.
5. He spoke about his experience in Australia and several predictions about the country's future.
6. To the inexperienced soldier, war may be a romantic adventure, but a dull and dirty business is the way the combat veteran regards it.
7. The unexpected cooperation of China was a greater surprise to Russia than the United States.
8. The skipper had a harsh voice, a weatherbeaten face, and was very stocky in build.
9. We were not sure that our request for a raise was fair or it would be granted.
10. The speech of cultivated Englishmen is not so different as it used to be from Americans.
11. The public's attention has been centered on the need for more teachers, adequate classrooms, and there isn't enough new equipment.
12. This was a much harder assignment for me than Betty.
13. The ambassador did not know whether the President had sent for him or the Secretary of State.

15d

14. His friends not only were shocked by his failure but they felt a great disappointment.
15. The players were annoyed not so much by the decisions of the officials as the hostile crowd.
16. The company announced a bonus for all five-year employees and that deserving new employees would be given additional benefits.
17. The headmaster insisted that all boys return by ten o'clock and the housemasters must check them in.
18. High school programs have been accused of being too closely tied in with college education and that they neglect the average teen-age boy or girl.
19. Pioneers came with hopes of being happy and free and to make their fortunes in the new world.
20. All delegates to the convention were advised that on their return they would both have to make a written and oral report.

UNNECESSARY SHIFT   Volunteers made [active verb] the dangerous journey after dark, but no wolves were encountered [passive verb].

SHIFT AVOIDED   Volunteers **made** [active verb] the dangerous journey after dark but **encountered** [active verb] **no** wolves.

UNNECESSARY SHIFT   Since he knew that ability to speak well before a group is important, a course in public speaking was taken by him.

SHIFT AVOIDED   Since **he knew** that ability to speak well before a group is important, **he took** a course in public speaking.

(2) Avoid unnecessary shifts in the tense of verbs.

Changing without reason from one tense to another within a sentence creates an awkward and confusing effect. Stick to the tense you start with unless there is an excellent reason for changing.

UNNECESSARY SHIFT   At this point the President reads [present tense] a prepared statement but refused [past tense] to answer any questions.

SHIFT AVOIDED   At this point the President **read** [past tense] a prepared statement but **refused** [past tense] to answer any questions.

SHIFT AVOIDED   At this point the President **reads** [present tense] a prepared statement but **refuses** [present tense] to answer any questions.

UNNECESSARY SHIFT   She made [past tense] some flippant remark and rushes [present tense] off down the hall.

SHIFT AVOIDED   She **made** [past tense] some flippant remark and **rushed** [past tense] off down the hall.

SHIFT AVOIDED   She **makes** [present tense] some flippant remark and **rushes** [present tense] off down the hall.

In correcting unnecessary shifts in subject and verb, you will often find the best method is to omit the second subject. This can usually be done by using the second verb in the same voice as the first and making the verb compound.

**16
a-b**

UNNECESSARY SHIFT   A good driver has complete control of his car at all times, and allowance is made for the carelessness of other drivers.

SHIFT AVOIDED   A good **driver has** complete control of his car at all times **and makes** allowance for the carelessness of other drivers.   [The use of the compound active voice for both verbs corrects the awkward shift.]

● EXERCISE 1.   Most of the following sentences contain unnecessary shifts from one subject to another or from one verb form to another. By revising these sentences orally in class, show how these shifts may be avoided. Four of the sentences contain acceptable shifts. Identify these.

1. If a student does his homework daily, your tests will be passed easily.
2. Firemen rushed to the scene, but only a pile of ashes was found.
3. If the whole committee votes, George will be elected.
4. When a boy reaches the age of twenty-one, you should be willing to assume a man's responsibilities.
5. Some seniors expect special privileges, but equivalent responsibilities are not always accepted by them.
6. Since nearly every city has its own zoo, supplying wild animals to zoos has become a profitable business.
7. Young people not only enjoy a few weeks away from home at a summer camp, but many valuable things are learned from the experience.
8. The flour and the butter should be mixed into a paste, and add a small amount of milk.
9. A high school student can often earn his own spending money, and his family is thus relieved of at least one of its financial responsibilities.
10. The stringer first cut the old strings from the racket, and then the restringing begins.
11. When his father spoke to him about going to college, Walter says that he doesn't want to take so much money from the family at a time when living expenses were so high.

12. Economists were aware of the dwindling oil reserves, and a steady rise in the price of fuel is predicted by them.
13. Sam drove the ball deep into the left-field bleachers, and the game was ended.
14. In the last chapter the author takes us back to the early scenes, and we learn how much conditions have changed.
15. Properly equipped men can survive for months in the Arctic and no ill effects will be suffered.
16. Although we could not see the planes, their motors could be clearly heard.
17. Ruth achieved fame as the home-run king, but a fine record as a pitcher and an outfielder was also made by him.
18. If a person wishes to succeed in a writing career, you must have patience and the capacity for hard work.
19. Bellevue Hospital once operated a city medical school, but the school was later taken over by New York University's medical college.
20. It was a clear December morning when my friend Joe called and asks me to go for a plane ride with him. I always liked Joe, and so you are glad to go anywhere with him. I accepted the invitation and Joe says he'll meet me at the airport in an hour. This was the simple beginning of the most frightening experience of my life.

● EXERCISE 2.   In the following passage the tense of the verbs is frequently shifted from past to present and from present to past. Decide in what tense (past or present) it should be written. Prepare to read aloud in class, changing the verb forms to remove the unnecessary shifts in tense.

1   Mr. Sampson, who had been for ten years faculty adviser
2 of the high school annual, sat calmly at his desk after school,
3 watching the autumn sun light the empty room, while he
4 waited for the first meeting of the new yearbook staff. A
5 veteran like Mr. Sampson could hardly be expected to show
6 much emotion over the repetition of an event he had taken
7 part in so many times. He is not particularly disturbed when
8 the door opens and Jane Billings led a noisy group of boys
9 and girls into his room.

10   Following a general falling over desks and slumping
11 into seats, Jane called the meeting to order. This year, she
12 explains, the staff would produce the finest yearbook East
13 High has ever had. Someone wanted to know, first of all,
14 what kind of cover the book would have. A great preference
15 is expressed for a thick and heavy leather cover, suitably
16 embossed, and bearing the seal and colors of the school.
17 Mr. Sampson smiles, for he had never yet known a new
18 staff that did not begin with a discussion of the cover.

19   Complete agreement about the cover having been so
20 quickly reached, Win Thompson wants to know why last
21 year's book was so dull. Here Mr. Sampson smiles again.
22 Everything's going to be just fine, he thought, remembering
23 that no staff in the past had ever had a good word to say for
24 its predecessors. "Let's have twice as many pictures, a bigger
25 sports section, not so much writing that nobody ever reads."
26 These weighty matters agreed upon, everyone wanted to
27 know whether the seniors aren't entitled to more space in
28 the book. "How about three or four instead of ten senior
29 pictures to a page? After all, it's our book."

30   Mr. Sampson listened and said nothing. He is quietly
31 thinking about next January, when the supply of snapshots
32 will be disappointingly small, when the budget will be
33 alarmingly inadequate, when compromise after compromise
34 will be frantically made in order to get a yearbook out at all.
35 But he doesn't say much. He knows it is better for the staff
36 to find out for itself why last year's book and all the books
37 before it had been such complete "failures."

● EXERCISE 3.   The sentences in this exercise are awkward
because of unnecessary shifts in the subject and in the verb.
Revise the sentences to eliminate these shifts.

1. Adolescents naturally rebel against authority, but the authority of the law must be respected by them.
2. Lonely students should participate in an extracurricular
activity so that new friendships can be made.
3. A senior must not only pass his courses and graduate, but
also plans for your future must be made before the year is
over.

4. My brother frequently procrastinates, and a tendency toward laziness is occasionally shown.

5. My father has some amusing peculiarities which are not recognized by him.

6. The Russian demands were unacceptable even though some concessions were contained in them.

7. If a teacher wants to be liked, you must treat students impartially.

8. Coach Martin always insisted on long practice sessions and strict training, but his winning teams justify his methods.

9. The Vice-President flew to the Paris Conference, but few concrete results were accomplished by him.

10. A good student can win a college scholarship, and thus his parents are relieved of part of the cost of his college education.

11. When you buy a car, a man should be sure he can afford the upkeep.

12. In the end Robert stays with his mother, and the girl he loves is lost to him forever.

13. The cement and sand are first mixed thoroughly; then add the water.

14. The experienced yachtsman is aware of the danger of fire, and, when filling the gas tank, great precautions are taken not to spill gasoline in the bottom of the boat.

15. As district attorney he successfully handled the Tammany Hall cases, and the backing of the Republican party was won.

16. As the bus careens toward the edge of the road, we thought our time had come, and we grab our seats in desperation.

17. Many doctors recognize the value of health insurance, but the particular kind we should have is something they could not agree on.

18. Driven backward, Guy felt the ropes burning his back for a moment before he lunges forward with his right, and Hammer Joe's comeback was brought to an abrupt end.

19. Sammy had just finished his bitter denunciation of all teachers and of one chemistry teacher in particular, when he turns around and Mr. Lerner was seen in the laboratory doorway.

20. An explorer must study his maps very carefully so that you will be able to plan your trip efficiently.

CHAPTER 17

Sentence Conciseness

Avoiding Wordiness and Overwriting

It is a mistake to believe that the more words a theme contains the better. The professional writer who is paid according to the number of words he writes may find wordiness profitable, but he would never claim that it improves his articles. Most good writing is effective because it is not cluttered with unnecessary words.

Do not think, however, that wordiness appears only in long compositions. A long piece of writing may contain no superfluous words, whereas a short piece may be full of them. Studying the principles in this section and doing the exercises will make you aware of wordiness in writing and help you to avoid it in your own compositions.

SUPERFLUOUS WORDS AND UNNECESSARY REPETITION

The following example of wordiness was the opening paragraph of a high school student's composition about an overnight hike. Lines have been drawn through the superfluous words.

When ~~in the course of human events, when~~ a man finds it necessary to rest his weary bones, he packs up and goes on what

254

is inappropriately called a vacation. Last summer I had the good fortune to go ~~during the summer~~ to a mountain camp in ~~the mountains of~~ eastern Pennsylvania. On the day that I arrived, ~~when I got to camp,~~ I found that the camp had been quarantined because of the measles that one of the younger campers had brought in, ~~and no one who was in the camp could leave.~~ After we had spent a week in camp, the prospect of an overnight hike in the mountainous wilds looked especially good to us campers who had been so long confined ~~to camp by the quarantine.~~

17a. Avoid wordiness by eliminating superfluous words and the unnecessary repetition of ideas.

WORDY   The game is played with tiny, little round balls, which, in my opinion, I think are made of steel.

BETTER   The game is played with tiny balls, which, I think, are made of steel.

WORDY   After descending down to the edge of the river, we boarded a small raft which was floating there on the surface of the water.

BETTER   After descending to the edge of the river, we boarded a small raft.

WORDY   The first story in the book is a masterpiece in itself and quite a story.

BETTER   The first story in the book is a masterpiece.

● EXERCISE 1.   Revise the following sentences, eliminating superfluous words.

1. We watched the big, massive black cloud rising up from the level prairie and covering over the sun.
2. Far away in the distance, as far as anything was visible to the eye, the small, diminutive shapes of the settlers' huts were outlined in silhouette against the dark sky.
3. Modern cars of today, unlike the old cars of yesterday, can be driven faster without danger than the old ones.

17a

4. When what the speaker was saying was not audible to our ears, I asked him to repeat again what he had said.

5. It was in this mountain wilderness that the explorers found there the examples of wildlife for which they had been looking for.

6. During this year's current baseball season, all home games and many away games in other cities may be watched at home on your television screen as they are brought to you over station WPIX.

7. The mediator said that if both parties would give in a little that a satisfactory settlement could be reached that would satisfy both parties.

8. In spite of the fact that the danger was neither tangible to the touch nor visible to the eye, it was very real to all the dwellers and inhabitants of the village in the foothills which circled around the base of Mt. Wilson.

9. The drive over to Cross Village follows and winds along the top of a great, huge bluff above the lake.

10. When at last the pounding finally began to stop, I stretched myself out prone upon the bed and attempted to try to go to sleep.

11. The world in its present state of affairs today is in great and dire need of statesmen who will work hard to prevent the recurrence again of a disastrously destructive world war.

12. During the hours in the morning before noon, there is a variety of radio programs of different kinds to which you may listen to.

13. As you continue on in the book a little further, you will be surprised and amazed by the clever skill of the writer of the book in weaving in together the many previously unrelated threads of his story.

14. At the final end of the picture, the villain abruptly and suddenly does an about-face and changes completely into a good man with admirable characteristics.

15. His mental thought processes puzzled his school teachers and made them despair of his future success in the years after his graduation from school.

16. I am always as a rule surprised to find out that a currently popular hit tune was also a popular number years ago in

the past when my parents were both going to high school.

17. He was firmly determined to combine together both of the two divisions of the firm in order to achieve a stronger company eventually in the long run.

18. Circling around his adversary with a menacing look on his face, Broadhurst bided his time and waited for an opening through which he could connect up with his mighty right.

19. The President's struggle with Congress ended up in a victory for the President when the public voted at the November election to reelect him again to the Presidency for another term of four years.

20. The final conclusion of the novel on which he had been working on for more than five years was disappointing to everyone who read the manuscript, and he decided to revise and change the story.

● Exercise 2.   Revise the following wordy paragraphs. Eliminate all unnecessary words but keep the ideas of the paragraphs clear.

1

When we were two hundred yards away from our objective, which was a small little grove of pine trees on the sloping side of a hill, we were confronted by a vast, wet swamp. I remembered that during the last two weeks we had had, out of fourteen days, ten days of rain, and decided in my own mind to send out a few scouts who might discover a way by means of which we could reach the grove without getting our feet wet. Then, when the scouts reported back that their efforts to try to find a dry path through the swamp had been unsuccessful, we gave up and resigned ourselves to sloshing knee-deep through the muddy water.

2

When, after eight years of education in school, the student enters the ninth grade and becomes a freshman, then he begins to find out what seniors are really like. Up until this point, seniors have been heroes to him, admired from a respectful distance away as though they were gods, unless he has happened to know one personally, of course. But now, however, his conception undergoes a change. The senior becomes an ogre whose one and only purpose in life seems to the freshman to be to make life as miserable as possible for each and every freshman. Every way the freshman turns in the school corridors, a senior hall cop, with a great big letter on his chest, grabs him with huge talons and tells him with hot and fiery breath that he cannot go down an up stairway. He is enticed into joining clubs which are ruled over and presided over by seniors who use him mainly for the performance of unpleasant errands beneath the dignity of a senior. Whenever the freshman cannot be of use, he is ignored. His former ambition to be a senior fades out and wanes until one day he begins to think thoughts of getting his revenge. In his frenzied brain the idea dawns on him if he is patient, he too will someday enjoy the privilege of molding the lives and characters of ninth-graders. This idea accounts for the fanatic fixed stare which is to be seen in the eyes of so many freshmen.

CONCISENESS THROUGH REDUCTION

The opposite of wordiness is conciseness. In your effort to write well, you will profit from a study of some ways to make your writing more concise. Of course, there is a danger in being too economical in your use of words; writing which is too concise will not be clear and will not achieve its intended effect. Nevertheless, the following rule will call to your attention some helpful methods of avoiding wordiness.

17b. Avoid wordiness by reducing clauses to phrases, and phrases to single words. This process is known as *reduction.*

1. *Clauses reduced to participial, gerund, or infinitive phrases*

CLAUSE   When he was left alone on the sinking vessel, the captain made an inspection of the ship.

PARTICIPIAL PHRASE   **Left alone on the sinking vessel,** the captain made an inspection of the ship.

CLAUSE **Since he believed the ship could be saved,** he called for volunteers to help him.

PARTICIPIAL PHRASE **Believing the ship could be saved,** he called for volunteers to help him.

CLAUSE **If you leave at noon,** you can get to Chicago at three o'clock.

GERUND PHRASE **Leaving at noon** will get you to Chicago at three o'clock.

CLAUSE We decided **that we would get an early start.**

INFINITIVE PHRASE We decided **to get an early start.**

2. Clauses reduced to prepositional phrases

CLAUSE The teams **which had come from the Far West** were not scheduled to play the first day of the tournament.

PHRASE The teams **from the Far West** were not scheduled to play the first day of the tournament.

CLAUSE **When the sun sets,** the street lights come on.

PHRASE **At sunset** the street lights come on.

CLAUSE **After you have graduated,** you will be looking for a job.

PHRASE **After graduation,** you will be looking for a job.

CLAUSE My cousin **who lives in Mexico** speaks Spanish fluently.

PHRASE My cousin **in Mexico** speaks Spanish fluently.

3. Clauses reduced to appositives

CLAUSE Dr. Brown, **who is the chief surgeon,** will operate.

APPOSITIVE Dr. Brown, **the chief surgeon,** will operate.

CLAUSE His two dogs, **one of which is a collie and the other a spaniel,** perform different duties on the farm.

APPOSITIVE His two dogs, **a collie and a spaniel,** perform different duties on the farm.

4. Clauses and phrases reduced to single words

CLAUSE The troops **who had been captured** were sent to a prison camp.

WORD The **captured** troops were sent to a prison camp.

171

CLAUSE	Henry is a runner **who never tires.**
WORD	Henry is a **tireless** runner.
CLAUSE	We met a man **who is a native of France.**
WORD	We met a **Frenchman.**
PHRASE	His career **in the movies** was brief.
WORD	His **movie** career was brief.
PHRASE	She greeted everyone **in a cordial manner.**
WORD	She greeted everyone **cordially.**

From these examples of reduction you can see how to make your own writing more concise. Usually the time for such reduction is during revision of your papers. Revising the sentences in the following exercises will give you practice in writing more concisely.

● EXERCISE 3. The following sentences can be made more concise by reducing the italicized groups of words according to the directions given. Rewrite each sentence according to the directions.

1. (a) *Since he is an automobile dealer*, Mr. Holmes has promised his sons a car as a gift (b) *when they reach their seventeenth birthday*. [(a) Reduce clause to an appositive; (b) reduce clause to a prepositional phrase.]

2. After (a) *he had looked* everywhere for an old place (b) *that he could renovate*, Mr. Dayton bought the house (c) *that was deserted* on the edge of town. [(a) Reduce *he had looked* to a gerund (–*ing*); (b) reduce clause to an infinitive phrase (*to* + verb); (c) reduce *that was deserted* to an adjective.]

3. The orchard (a) *of apple trees* which stood (b) *in the area behind the house* yielded no fruit during his first year there, but it bore bushels and bushels (c) *when the second season came*. [(a) Reduce phrase to an adjective; (b) reduce to one prepositional phrase; (c) reduce clause to a prepositional phrase.]

4. (a) *Since we were sitting in seats* (b) *which were near first base*, we were able to judge the accuracy of the decisions (c) *of the umpire*. [(a) Reduce clause to a participle (–*ing*),

omitting *in seats;* (b) reduce clause to a prepositional phrase; (c) reduce phrase to a possessive.]

5. (a) *Because it was necessary for her to be away from home* (b) *in the afternoon and in the evening* for many days, Mrs. Stein, (c) *who is the president of the Parent-Teacher Association,* hired a succession of baby-sitters (d) *who were to take care of her children* (e) *while she was absent.* [(a) Reduce clause to a participial phrase (*Having to be . . .*); (b) reduce two phrases to two words telling when; (c) reduce clause to an appositive; (d) reduce clause to an infinitive phrase (*to* + verb); (e) reduce clause to a prepositional phrase.]

● EXERCISE 4. The italicized clauses and phrases in the following sentences can be reduced. Revise the sentences, reducing the clauses to phrases or appositives or single words, and the phrases to single words. You may omit unnecessary words, and you may occasionally find it necessary to change the word order.

1. We decided to wait for the bus *in order that we might save money.*

2. After I had finished the assigned reading, I read three novels *which were written by Dickens.*

3. This small hotel, *which is situated in Connecticut,* is patronized mainly by *people from Boston.*

4. *After he lost a leg in an accident which occurred while he was hunting,* Monty Stratton, *who was a pitcher for the White Sox,* made a comeback in professional baseball *which was amazing.*

5. Our seats *in which we sat at the Army-Navy game* were almost on the forty-yard line, *and they were at the top of the stadium.*

6. The poetry *of France* has had an influence *which is notable* on the poetry *of England.*

7. *While he was inspecting his new house, which is in the suburbs,* Mr. Doyle stumbled over a piece of flooring and fell down the stairs *leading to the cellar.*

8. Our days *that we spent in the north woods* would have been perfect if it had not been for the mosquitoes *that were enormous and hungry.*

9. Inez, *who is an ambitious young actress*, found that the acting *that she did in a stock company in the summer* gave her the experience *which she needed*.

10. The most common complaint *that is made by students* is that every teacher chooses Friday *on which to give examinations*.

● EXERCISE 5.   The following sentences are unnecessarily wordy. Make them more concise by eliminating redundant expressions and by reducing clauses and phrases. In your revisions do not omit any ideas.

1. Arnold prefers to work alone by himself in his own room where he has combined together a study and a bedroom.

2. In spite of our efforts to try to keep the overturned boat afloat on the water, it sank down to the bottom.

3. We took the elevator up to the second floor and roamed up and down through the long aisles which extended endlessly between glass cases which were filled and bulging with the most beautiful works of art.

4. The headmaster said that he hoped we would take and accept his suggestions which concerned the conduct of us boys when we are off campus and away from the school on vacation.

5. My brother he is taking golf lessons, but my sister, who is an expert swimmer, she is taking lessons in diving.

6. Johnny Long's six-piece orchestra will return again to play a repeat engagement at the Soph Hop, which will be held in the gym at the high school this Saturday night of this week.

7. Proposed plans that have been suggested for a new field house which is to be constructed at the local college here have been approved and acted favorably upon by the legislature, which today voted funds that are necessary for the project.

8. Because of the fact that I can borrow free, without charge, the latest, most recent books from the public library, if I simply have patience enough to wait my turn, I do not usually as a rule use the lending library which is in the bookstore which charges a daily fee of so much per day.

10. The majority of the American people do not continue their education beyond high school at the present time.
    In the future they may continue in school two more years.
    They will attend two-year community colleges.
    They will receive vocational training in the community colleges.

THE OVERWRITTEN STYLE

In their efforts to write impressively, high school students sometimes produce writing that is so artificial, flowery, and cumbersome as to be absurd. Such a style is the result of the mistaken notion that big words, unusual words, and figures of speech, no matter how commonplace, are literary. Unlike mistakes made through carelessness or laziness, a mistake of this kind is made through trying too hard to sound like a great writer. The resulting style is said to be "overwritten." It is sometimes called "fine writing."

17c. Avoid an overwritten style. Write naturally without straining after a "literary" effect.

The following example of overwriting will make you aware of the fault. Doing Exercise 7 on page 266 may help you correct overwritten passages in your own work.

Harbor Fog

The fog slowly crept in and covered the metropolis with its sinister cloak of impressive quietude. An entire day of heavy rain had drenched the surrounding municipality, forming puddles in the thoroughfares which reflected the shimmering images of the gleaming street lights and the illumination emanating from multitudes of office windows.

As I stood on the magnificent man-made span which arched above the swirling waters, the mournful warnings of the anchored ships pierced the dense fog. The constant beat of the harbor bell buoys and the gentle lapping of the murky water on the piling of this bridge combined to permeate the night air with a mystic tenseness.

The harbor boats moved tediously through the night, and their wakes left grotesque trails which slowly dissolved and enveloped themselves in the depths of the blackness.

Although it was late, the never-ceasing rumble of activity from the nearby city could still be apprehended. The penetrating night air was heavy with moisture and with each soft puff of breeze the salt of the sea could be detected.

During World War II Representative Maury Maverick, of Texas, became impatient with the overwritten style of some government writing and branded this sort of writing with the descriptive term "gobbledygook." Here is an example of the gobbledygook that troubled Mr. Maverick: "Illumination is required to be extinguished upon vacating these premises." You can see how much more effective would be, "Turn out the lights when you leave."

● EXERCISE 7.   Each of the following sentences represents the fault of overwriting. In simpler words write your version of the idea which is here expressed in a forced and unnatural style.

1. In a vast explosion of frozen precipitation, Thor shot through the feathery drift, maintaining without apparent effort his equilibrium upon the fragile strips of ash strapped to his pedal extremities.

2. My exploration of the intriguing heights of the science of economics left me with the firm conviction that *Homo sapiens* is impotent when it comes to exerting any detectable influence on the fundamental operation of supply and demand.

3. The bitterest irony of our fevered time is the oft-repeated concept that only by creating more magnificent and more deadly instruments of explosive destruction can mankind bring to this whirling planet the era of tranquillity for which it has longed since the beginning of time.

4. The sharp impact of wood upon the little white sphere was followed by a sudden emanation of sound, like an explosion, from the throats of the assembled multitude in the tiered stands as the soaring pellet arched over the greensward and came to rest beyond the masonry in the left field.

5. Nothing so impresses one with the warm security and pleasing restfulness of one's native surroundings as extensive peregrinations into foreign realms and among the exotic areas on the surface of our world.

6. Following our educational endeavors of the day, several of us conscientious seekers after knowledge relaxed our weary cerebrums by lending our ears to the latest discs at Jacobsen's music emporium.

7. Laying aside for the nonce the tomes of wisdom, I selected from the periodical rack the current issue of my favorite pictorial publication and, elongated upon the resilient davenport, slowly perused the photographic narrative of the week's outstanding occurrences.

8. In order to forestall the embarrassment of a refusal, I preceded my request for Helen's company upon an excursion to the local cinema by inquiring of her nearest of kin as to what Helen's social calendar held for the Friday evening in question.

9. Bent upon a week's tour by the time-honored expedient of thumbing accommodations from altruistic motorists, I bade a fond farewell to my anxious mater, and, with my earthly possessions ensconced in a cardboard brief case, embarked upon my great adventure.

10. Lifting the pigskin from the water-soaked gridiron with his trusty toe, Harvey booted it with mathematical precision directly between the white uprights silhouetted against the setting sun.

CHAPTER 18

Sentence Variety

Interest and Emphasis

18a. **Experiment with the length and structure of your sentences to achieve greater interest and variety.**

The great majority of English sentences—both spoken and written—begin with the subject. Any piece of writing in which most of the sentences depart from this normal order will strike a reader as artificial. However, an unbroken sequence of subject-predicate sentences may result in another stylistic fault—monotony. Such a sequence of sentences is monotonous because it lacks the logical connections and special emphasis that variations in sentence structure can provide. For example, the following sentences are perfectly clear:

> The two friends quarreled violently over a matter of slight importance.
>
> They never spoke again from that time on.

But a closer connection can be made between these two sentences by moving the adverb phrase, which refers to the quarrel, up to the beginning of the second sentence:

> The two friends quarreled violently over a matter of slight importance.
>
> **From that time on** they never spoke again.

Similarly, an important idea expressed by a modifier can be emphasized:

> George was not impressive in the classroom.
> **On the football field,** however, he came into his own.

The contrast is less striking when the second sentence begins with its subject:

> George was not impressive in the classroom.
> He came into his own, however, on the football field.

The normal order of sentences should not be shunned merely for the sake of variety. However, it is a good idea to remember that beginning a sentence with an important modifier may sometimes increase the force and clarity of your thought as well as provide a pleasing variation.

The exercises that follow are intended to give you practice in using different kinds of sentence openers. Used sparingly, these devices will improve your writing. Used too much, they will give it an unpleasantly artificial sound.

AVOIDING MONOTONY

(1) Begin some of your sentences with a transposed appositive or with one of these modifiers: single-word modifier; phrase modifier; clause modifier.

APPOSITIVES

> The human brain, an enormously complex mechanism, contains about ten billion nerve cells. [subject first]
>
> **An enormously complex mechanism,** the human brain contains about ten billion nerve cells. [transposed appositive first]

SINGLE-WORD MODIFIERS

> The book is long and badly written, and it failed to hold my interest. [subject first]

Long and badly written, the book failed to hold my interest. [single-word modifiers first]

A number of changes have been made here recently. [subject first]

Recently, a number of changes have been made here. [single-word modifier first]

The house was deserted and dilapidated and made a depressing picture. [subject first]

Deserted and dilapidated, the house made a depressing picture. [single-word modifiers first]

PHRASE MODIFIERS

He was almost unbeatable on the tennis court. [subject first]

On the tennis court, he was almost unbeatable. [prepositional phrase first]

Joe tired rapidly during the second set and decided to save his strength for the third set. [subject first]

Tiring rapidly during the second set, Joe decided to save his strength for the third set. [participial phrase first]

Tony worked late every night to win the essay prize. [subject first]

To win the essay prize, Tony worked late every night. [infinitive phrase first]

CLAUSE MODIFIERS

Investigators of the cause of the crash had to depend on evidence found in the wreckage because there were no survivors or witnesses. [subject first]

Because there were no survivors or witnesses, investigators of the cause of the crash had to depend on evidence found in the wreckage. [clause first]

Our leading lady, when she heard the orchestra playing the overture, suffered a severe attack of stage fright. [subject first]

When she heard the orchestra playing the overture, our leading lady suffered a severe attack of stage fright. [clause first]

● EXERCISE 1. This exercise will give you practice in beginning sentences in a variety of ways. Revise each sentence according to the instructions.

1. The Marine Historical Society has recreated a nineteenth-century coastal village at Mystic, Connecticut. [Begin with a prepositional phrase.]

2. Traveling, eating, and shopping with credit cards seems wonderfully easy until you receive your bill at the end of the month. [Begin with a subordinate clause.]

3. Some people are selfish and materialistic and are never happy with what they have. [Begin with single-word adjective modifiers.]

4. Ken worked part-time at a gas station during his senior year in high school and managed to save a thousand dollars toward his college expenses. [Begin with a participial phrase: *Working* . . .]

5. The most glamorous of all the new professions created by the space age is that of the astronaut. [Begin with a prepositional phrase.]

6. Belmer, one of the oldest players in professional football, makes up in experience what he lacks in speed. [Begin with a transposed appositive.]

7. The college president stated at the alumni luncheon the immediate financial needs of the college. [Begin with a prepositional phrase.]

8. A university's primary responsibility is to its resident students, although it should encourage educational programs for its alumni. [Begin with a subordinate clause.]

9. This seems to be a highly technical book, to the casual reader. [Begin with a prepositional phrase.]

10. The first ships of the expedition will sail in October, if present plans are approved. [Begin with a subordinate clause.]

11. Navy divers expertly and rapidly repaired the damaged hull. [Begin with single-word adverb modifiers.]

12. The firm lacked funds for expansion and so attempted to borrow money. [Begin with a participial phrase: *Lacking* . . .]

13. The skin on the average adult weighs 8.8 pounds and occupies an area of 20 square feet. [Begin with a participial phrase.]

14. The expedition was led by Colonel Walter H. Wood of New York and spent several weeks at its camp on Seward Glacier. [Begin with a participial phrase.]

15. One can see at first glance that modern office furniture uses more metal than wood. [Begin with a prepositional phrase.]

● EXERCISE 2. Rearrange each sentence so that it will begin with a single-word, phrase, or clause modifier or an appositive.

1. A bowling team was formed this winter for the first time in the history of the school.

2. A sinister figure stepped cautiously into the dark room.

3. Candidates for a driver's license must take a written examination to prove their knowledge of traffic regulations.

4. The children, when their mothers are working, are cared for in nursery schools.

5. The audience, tired and hot, soon became impatient.

6. We were frightened by the explosion and dared not move from our places.

7. More than half of the 90,000 acres under cultivation had been ruined by the recent drought.

8. Jim, a merchant sailor for ten years, knew every important port in the world.

9. The new houses, although they look exactly alike from the outside, have very different interiors.

10. Competition has been growing more and more intense in the transportation industry.

11. A small boy, sobbing bitterly, ran toward me.

12. Music is to me an excellent tranquilizer when it is soft and rhythmic.

13. A man, when striving for the highest spiritual goals, will frequently become discouraged.

14. More and more people are rushing to local gymnasiums and health clubs either to reduce their weight or to improve their physical fitness.

15. Nothing is more satisfying than producing your own music, even if you cannot play an instrument well and are not musically inclined.

(2) **By means of subordination, vary the structure of your sentences. Avoid the exclusive use of simple and compound sentences.**[1] **Skillful use of the complex sentence is an indication of maturity in style.**

(3) **Vary the length of your sentences. Avoid the choppy style caused by using too many short sentences. Combine short sentences into longer sentences.**

Study the following examples to see how several short simple sentences may, by subordination, be changed into one longer complex sentence.

SIMPLE SENTENCES   More and more high schools are offering advanced placement courses for seniors. These are college level courses. The students in them have to be able to do college work.

COMPLEX SENTENCE   More and more high schools are offering college-level, advanced placement courses for seniors who are able to do college work.   [In this sentence subordination was accomplished by means of an adjective and the subordinate clause *who are able to do college work.*]

SIMPLE SENTENCES   The great earthquake in Ecuador in 1949 was caused by a shift in the Andes Mountains. It took over six thousand lives. It was the worst quake in South American history.

COMPLEX SENTENCE   Caused by a shift in the Andes Mountains, the great earthquake in Ecuador in 1949, which took over six thousand lives, was the worst quake in South American history.   [In this sentence subordination was accomplished by means of a beginning participial phrase and a subordinate clause, *which took six thousand lives.*]

SIMPLE SENTENCES   A very old man may write an inaccurate autobiography. He tends to embellish imaginatively his account of distant events. He is finally unable to distinguish between the imagined and the actual.

[1] For a review of subordination, see pages 211–20. For an explanation of the kinds of sentences, see pages 66–68.

COMPLEX SENTENCE   A very old man may write an inaccurate autobiography because he tends to embellish imaginatively his account of distant events, being finally unable to distinguish between the imagined and the actual.   [In this sentence subordination was accomplished by means of a subordinate clause, *because he tends to embellish imaginatively his account of distant events,* and a participal phrase, *being finally unable to distinguish between the imagined and the actual.*]

● EXERCISE 3.   By using various means of subordination (participial phrase, appositive, subordinate clause, etc.) combine the short sentences in each group into one long, smooth sentence.

1. Engineers reported that a tunnel would be more practical than a bridge. The City Commission authorized the construction of a tunnel.
2. The students complained that they could not study in Miss Baker's study hall. There was too much confusion. They did not realize that they were responsible for the confusion.
3. John Buchan was both versatile and talented. He wrote some very successful mystery stories. One of them was *The Thirty-nine Steps.* He was at one time Governor General of Canada.
4. Dr. Brown diagnosed the case as appendicitis. He called an ambulance, rushed the patient to the hospital, and removed the appendix. He is head surgeon at the City Hospital.
5. Twenty-five students attended reading classes during the first term. All improved not only in reading but in spelling and vocabulary. Twenty raised their reading level two years.
6. Race officials decided to hold the races in spite of the rough water. Three boats were smashed. Two participants were seriously injured. The officials were severely criticized.
7. Helen did not want another extracurricular job. She accepted the presidency of the Girls' Athletic Association. She was more interested in sports than in anything else.
8. The Pulaski Highway in Maryland and the Pulaski Skyway in New Jersey were named after General Casimir Pulaski. He was an exiled Polish count. He served under Washington in the Revolution.

9. Marilyn's illness lasted three months. She was confined to her home during this time. Nevertheless, she kept up in her studies. She graduated with her class.

10. Mr. Sampson's will named his secretary as principal beneficiary and his business partner as executor. The will disappointed his relatives. They had expected to find themselves in one or the other of those positions.

AVOIDING "STRINGY" STYLE

18b. Give variety to your writing by avoiding the "stringy" style which results from the overuse of *and* and *so*.

In everyday conversation we tend to string our ideas out, one after another, by means of the simple conjunctions *and* and *so*. In writing, however, this sort of thing appears childish and monotonous. As you can see from the following examples, "stringiness" is an obvious fault which can be easily corrected. There are three ways to correct it.

(1) Correct a stringy sentence by subordination of ideas.

STRINGY SENTENCE College admission standards continue to rise, *and* tension and anxiety build to a ridiculous point in college preparatory seniors, *and* this spoils their final year in high school.

IMPROVED As college admission standards continue to rise, tension and anxiety build to a ridiculous point in college preparatory seniors, spoiling their final year in high school. [One *and* has been removed by means of the beginning subordinate clause. The other has been removed by means of the participial phrase, *spoiling their final year in high school.*]

The use of *so* as a conjunction is considered poor form. Its use can be avoided almost always by using a subordinate clause or a phrase expressing cause or reason.

18b

POOR USE OF <u>SO</u>   Thoreau believed in simplicity, *so* at Walden Pond he experimented with the simple life.

IMPROVED   Believing in simplicity, at Walden Pond Thoreau experimented with the simple life.

or

Because he believed in simplicity, at Walden Pond Thoreau experimented with the simple life.

STRINGY USE OF <u>SO</u>   We heard the static on the radio, *so* we were afraid of a thunderstorm, *so* we decided not to go out in the boat.

IMPROVED   Fearing a thunderstorm when we heard the static on the radio, we decided not to go out in the boat.

(2) Correct a stringy sentence by dividing it into two sentences.

STRINGY SENTENCE   I am very fond of foreign films, and so I go to the Celtic Theater more than to the other theaters, and we get only the best foreign films in this country, so I not only learn a lot, but I see better pictures.

IMPROVED   Being very fond of foreign films, I go to the Celtic Theater more than to the other theaters. Since we get only the best foreign films in this country, I not only learn a lot, but I see better pictures.   [stringiness corrected by subordination and by division into two sentences]

● EXERCISE 4.   This exercise consists of stringy sentences. Revise the sentences by one or more of the following methods: subordination, division into more than one sentence, and reduction of coordinate clauses to a compound predicate. Get rid of the monotonous use of *and* and *so*. You may add a few words of your own if the words will help you to improve the sentences.

1. The next morning most roads were impassable, so there was hardly anyone in school, so we were given a holiday.
2. Luckily at that time a tow truck came by, and we yelled to them, and they gave us a set of chains, and we put them on the car, and the chains helped us to get out of the snowbank and through the drifts on the way home.

3. To many foreigners, all Americans are rich, and they lack culture, and they are too lazy to learn any language but their own.

4. The men began their search for the lost child at once, but they had no clues to follow, and the area was wild, so they sent for some bloodhounds, but the only ones nearby were already busy trailing a bank robber.

5. Harry bowled a total of 600 in three games, and he tied the alley's three-game record, and he broke the record for a single game, so he was hailed as alley champion.

6. It was my father's summer vacation, so we drove to Mt. Washington and left the car there and hiked for a week on the Appalachian Trail, and it was the best vacation of our lives.

7. There are small cabins and open shelters along the trail, so we felt sure of night quarters, but we were civilized hikers, and we always managed to be near an inn when evening came, so we could relax in luxury.

8. The story begins with a family that came over from Europe years ago, and they started west in a wagon train, but they had trouble with their wagon, so they told their friends to go ahead, but then it was hard to find the wagon train again out on the prairie.

9. You have an hour for lunch, so you plow through the crowds and finally get pushed into a cheap hamburger stand, and then you wait a half hour for a seat and another twenty minutes for them to kill and warm the meat, and you get back to work five minutes late, so you get a scolding from the boss.

10. I asked Sue for a date, but she had already accepted an invitation, so I asked Barbara, but she had heard that I had asked Sue first, so she wouldn't go with me.

● EXERCISE 5. The style of the following items is choppy and stringy. Rewrite each item, making the style varied and smooth. Combine and subordinate ideas through phrases, appositives, subordinate clauses, and compound predicates. Vary the beginnings of sentences, the structure, and the length of sentences. You may add a few words of your own if the words will help you to improve the sentences.

1. Byrd's second expedition landed on Little America, and they proceeded to dig out the underground quarters left by the first expedition, but the buildings were twenty feet below the snow level, and so it took a lot of work to dig them out.

2. We took three empty oil drums for our raft and laid them in the water, and we took an old packing crate and made a frame to enclose the drums, and then the fun began. We slipped the frame over the drums and had visions of a leisurely sail down the river on our raft, but when we got aboard, the raft turned over, so we were wet and discouraged but patiently began rebuilding operations.

3. Our group was scheduled for a mountain-climbing expedition. We drove thirty-five miles in the camp truck over bumpy roads, and we arrived at Mt. Kearsarge and put our bed rolls on the ground and started to tramp up the mountain, but we chose the harder trail at the branching-off place halfway up, so we got very tired and stopped to rest in a clearing.

4. It was Monday morning in history class, and I looked around at my classmates and saw that they were as sleepy as I was. Someone was reading, and she had the kind of voice that made me want to go to sleep, so I gave in and rested my forehead on my hand and closed my eyes. I was just settling down for a nap when the teacher's voice boomed out my name, and I was so startled that I dropped my book from my lap and looked up stupidly into his face.

CHAPTER 19

Effective Diction

Appropriate Choice of Words

The quality of the words you select to express your ideas is just as important in composition as the quality of your sentence structure. The words you choose constitute your diction. For years, your teachers have urged you to enlarge your vocabulary. A large vocabulary is indeed a great asset in both reading and writing. But the acquisition of a large vocabulary, acquiring control of a number of big words, is only one way to improve your diction. Actually, it is not at all a guarantee of effective expression, because the effectiveness of a word does not depend on the number of its syllables or its rareness. The best word to use is the one that conveys the exact meaning you intend. Careful attention to the instruction given in this chapter will help you to select your words wisely.

TRITE EXPRESSIONS

19a. Avoid trite expressions.

Trite expressions, sometimes called *clichés*, are expressions which have grown stale through too frequent use. Originally fresh and effective, they have been used so much that they have lost any freshness and originality they once

19a

had. No doubt, the first time someone described the sensation of stage fright as "butterflies in my stomach," the description was strikingly apt, but overuse has made it too commonplace to be arresting. Similarly, such basically effective comparisons as *blanket of snow, busy as a bee, on the fence*, while still generally used in conversation, are so well known that they make writing dull rather than bright. Clichés suggest laziness and a lack of originality in the writer who uses them. They come to mind so easily when you are writing that unless you consciously guard against them, they will seriously weaken your style. The simple, straightforward statement of an idea is preferable to the use of a worn-out expression.

TRITE	SIMPLE, STRAIGHTFORWARD
bury the hatchet	stop fighting, make peace
at loose ends	disorganized
on speaking terms	friendly
fair and square	completely honest
at death's door	near death

You have probably noticed that some clichés are comparisons (*busy as a bee*), while others are simply commonplace ways of stating an idea (*fair and square*). Study the following far-from-complete list of clichés. Reading it will make you sensitive to trite expressions. You and your classmates can add to the list.

TRITE EXPRESSIONS

a good time was had by all	blushing bride
accidents will happen	break the ice
add insult to injury	brown as a berry
after all is said and done	budding genius
at death's door	bury the hatchet
at loose ends	busy as a bee
beat a hasty retreat	by the sweat of one's brow
beautiful but dumb	calm before the storm
beyond the shadow of a doubt	clear as crystal
bite off more than you can chew	depths of despair

TRITE EXPRESSIONS, continued

diamond in the rough
discreet silence
doomed to disappointment
each and every
easier said than done
eternal triangle
fair sex
Father Time
few and far between
fond parents
gala occasion
green with envy
hale and hearty
in no uncertain terms
in this day and age
irony of fate
last but not least
long arm of the law
make a long story short

none the worse for wear
on speaking terms
on the fence
out of the frying pan into the fire
point with pride
quick as a flash
ripe old age
sadder but wiser
silence reigned
straight and narrow path
supreme sacrifice
to the bitter end
trials and tribulations
view with alarm
viselike grip
weaker sex
white as a sheet
word to the wise

● EXERCISE 1. Rewrite each of the following sentences, substituting simple, straightforward language for the trite expressions.

1. After our sumptuous repast, we agreed that a good time had been had by all.
2. In this day and age, political figures who remain on the fence when burning questions are argued, will be doomed to disappointment on Election Day.
3. Although warned not to bite off more than I could chew, I signed up for six courses with the result that after all was said and done I was a sadder but wiser boy.
4. To make a long story short, I failed two courses, and to add insult to injury, my parents sent me to summer school.
5. Among the novel's characters are two members of the fair sex who wander from the straight and narrow path and are eventually embraced by the long arm of the law.
6. In the depths of despair, each and every one of us maintained a discreet silence.

7. Sensing that Mr. Stern's pleasant greeting was only the calm before the storm, I tried to beat a hasty retreat, which was nipped in the bud as, with a viselike grip, he led me into his office.

8. Busy as a bee in his ripe old age, Grandfather always pointed with pride to the beautiful garden he had made by the sweat of his brow.

9. Knowing what trials and tribulations they faced, Bill viewed with alarm the tendency of his friends to succumb to the wiles of the weaker sex.

10. Green with envy, Nancy watched the blushing bride with stars in her eyes hurry up the aisle.

JARGON

19b. Use a vocabulary that is free of jargon.

Jargon has two meanings. First, it means "the technical language used by specialists in the same profession." An engineer may use engineering jargon in a report to other engineers. An educator may use educational jargon in an article in a teacher's magazine. Jargon of this kind is an expected and usually acceptable feature of the style of a specialist writing for other specialists in the same field. There is always the danger, however, that a writer may carry his use of jargon to such an extreme that it will obscure rather than clarify meaning, even for other members of his profession. When this happens, professional jargon becomes a stylistic fault. The specialist should, whenever possible, use simple, everyday language rather than his professional jargon. As a high school student you may encounter the specialist's jargon in your reading, but you will not be likely to use it in your writing.

EXAMPLE OF PROFESSIONAL JARGON

Both equalitarianism and achievement are dominant values intimately articulated in existing institutional structures. Though they manifest certain contradictory features, neither value seems likely to cease playing a significant role. It is strange that in an age in which all the empirical evidence demonstrates that there is more upward social mobility than at any time in our history—in which large numbers of workers respond to a reduction of the work week by taking second jobs, in which more married women continue their careers after marriage on both the working-class and middle-class level, and in which the advertising industry, which most typifies an America oriented to mass consumption, demands and secures a prolonged work week from its creative personnel—it is strange that in such an age men see the norms of hard work and achievement as dead. A systematic examination of the available evidence suggests, as we shall see, that both equalitarianism and achievement have remained the dominant values in most existing institutional structures. Actually, a study of the available evidence bears most eloquent testimony to the thesis that America was and has remained a revolutionary country, more equalitarian in manners and opportunity than anyplace else in the world.[1]

The second meaning of jargon is "vague, puffed-up, pretentious language that tends to confuse the reader." The writer of this kind of jargon uses words so general in meaning that they mean practically nothing. Examples of words dear to the writer of jargon are *case, factor, field, aspect, matter, concept,* etc. Vague and unnecessary phrases like the following usually characterize jargon: *as for the fact that, under the circumstances pertaining, along the line of, in the case of, relative to the matter, as to whether, with reference to,* etc. Perhaps these examples show why jargon has been called "fuzzy language."

The writer of jargon usually overwrites. He prefers the big word to the simple word, the unusual word to the ordinary one. To him, knives are cutlery; table napkins are

[1] From "Trends in American Society" by Seymour M. Lipset from *An Outline of Man's Knowledge of the Modern World*, edited by Lyman Bryson. Copyright © 1960 by Catherine McGrattan Bryson, Executrix of the Estate of Lyman Bryson. Reprinted by permission of Doubleday & Company, Inc. and published by McGraw-Hill Book Company, Inc.

19b

napery; dogs are canines; a trailer truck is a behemoth of the highways; he rarely starts or begins—he initiates or commences. In short, the "jargonist," in using a vague, wordy, overwritten language, not only obscures meaning but also confuses and irritates his reader.

EXAMPLE OF COMMON JARGON

In spite of the fact that government aviation agencies were not in agreement with respect to the question of the cause of the accident at Kennedy Airport, the court decided that one of the contributing factors was a propeller that had been structurally weakened.

REWRITTEN WITHOUT JARGON

Although government aviation agencies disagreed on the causes of the accident at Kennedy Airport, the court decided that one cause was a structurally weakened propeller.

● EXERCISE 2.   In the following passage, the meaning is somewhat obscured by jargon. Read the passage several times until you are sure what the writer was trying to say. Then write a jargon-free revision.

Owing to the fact that a number of social factors along the line of unemployment and dislocation follow consequentially from the automation of industry, government, as well as labor and management, must concern itself with the implementation of the processes of adjustment of affected persons.

FIGURATIVE LANGUAGE

19c. Use figures of speech to make writing interesting and vivid.

In reading literature, especially in your study of poetry, you encounter many figures of speech. Those most commonly found are metaphor, simile, and personification. In each of these, the writer draws a comparison. He compares two things which are not really alike but which he finds similar in one respect at least. By making the comparison, he is able to express his meaning more clearly, vividly, and convincingly than he could by writing a literal description or explanation.

D. H. Lawrence describes a row of distant houses on a ridge at night, "The homes stood . . . black against the sky, *like wild beasts glaring curiously with yellow eyes down into the darkness.*" Lawrence knows, of course, that houses and beasts are literally quite unlike, but the houses with lighted windows suggest to his imagination beasts with yellow eyes. This figurative description makes you see the scene as he saw it and as he thought of it. It is more arresting than would be a literal statement—"The lighted houses were black against the sky."

Note the striking effect of the four figures of speech used by Pearl Buck in describing a suddenly revealed handful of precious jewels: "There were such a mass of jewels as we had never dreamed could be together, jewels *red as the inner flesh of watermelons, golden as wheat, green as young leaves in spring, clear as water trickling out of the earth.*"

Simile

19d. A *simile* is a comparison between things essentially unlike, expressed directly through the use of a comparing word such as *like* or *as*.

EXAMPLES   He had eyes **like** little dollars.
He was thin **as** a stick.

If the things compared are really alike, the comparison is not a figure of speech, not a simile.

NOT A SIMILE   He wore a hat like mine.
SIMILE   He wore a hat **like an overturned pail.**

NOT A SIMILE   His sister was like his mother.
SIMILE   His sister was **like an angel.**

19 c-d

Metaphor

19e. A *metaphor* is a comparison between things essentially unlike, expressed without a comparing word such as *like* or *as*. The comparison is implied rather than directly stated.

EXAMPLES   The silver lace of the branches above the river. . . .

The road was a ribbon of moonlight. — NOYES

Personification

19f. Personification is a figure of speech in which the characteristics of a human being are attributed to an animal, a thing, or an idea.

EXAMPLES   The **room spoke** to us of former days.

But, look, **the morn in russet mantle clad
Walks** o'er the dew of yon high eastern hill.

— SHAKESPEARE

He looked out of his lofty window and was conscious of the world below: bright roofs, **jubilant towers,** and a high-decked **sound steamer swaggering up** the glassy river. — S. LEWIS

◆ NOTE   Other figures of speech which you will find more useful in literary appreciation than in composition are *antithesis*, *apostrophe*, *hyperbole*, *irony*, *paradox*, and *metonymy*. The dictionary will give you definitions of these.

● EXERCISE 3.   Copy the figures of speech from the following passages. After each tell whether it is simile, metaphor, or personification. Be prepared to explain the figure and to evaluate its effectiveness. You should find fifteen figures.

1. When Alma went down into the audience room, in the midst of the chattering singers, who seemed to have descended like birds, from song flights to chirps, the minister approached her.—MARY E. WILKINS FREEMAN
2. The silence is cloven by alarm as by an arrow.—JAMES JOYCE

3. Spring was a very flame of green.—D. H. LAWRENCE
4. The edge of the colossal jungle, so dark green as to be almost black, fringed with white surf, ran straight, like a ruled line, far, far away along a blue sea whose glitter was blurred by a creeping mist.—JOSEPH CONRAD
5. Are there no water-lilies, smooth as cream
   With long stems dripping crystal?—ELINOR WYLIE
6. I felt like a small bubble on the surface of a mighty thing like the sea.—ROBERT P. TRISTRAM COFFIN
7. Night's candles are burnt out, and jocund day
   Stands tiptoe on the misty mountain tops.—SHAKESPEARE
8. The exhilarating ripple of her voice was a wild tonic in the rain.—F. SCOTT FITZGERALD
9. Some cut-glass vases threw jagged rainbows across the piano's field of dust, while Father in his pince-nez upon the wall looked down like a scandalized God.—LAURIE LEE
10. Maternally the great tree protected us, sighing and groaning, as she lowered her arms to shield us from the storm.

● EXERCISE 4.   Select five of the following that you think you can suggest by using simile, metaphor, or personification. For each write a sentence with the figure of speech.

1. hot August scene on a city street
2. sensations while walking in a hurricane or a blizzard
3. a person's reaction to sudden fear
4. a fruit tree in bloom
5. cars bumper-to-bumper in traffic
6. emerging from a stuffy room into a cold, clear night
7. stubbornness
8. a drink of cool water after hours of thirst
9. birds sitting on a telephone wire
10. a plane taking off

Hazards of Figurative Language

19g. Avoid strained or commonplace figures of speech.

The habit of thinking metaphorically, of seeing life in terms of comparisons, can help a writer—in prose as well

**19
e-g**

as in poetry—to enliven style and make his meaning clear.

A writer, however, must be aware of three pitfalls that lie in wait for the glib or careless user of figurative language. The first is the use of similes and metaphors which, though much used, have become so commonplace that they weaken style. Such figures are clichés: *clear as crystal, ran like the wind, silence reigned, white as a sheet,* etc. The second pitfall is the use of figures which are strained. They give the reader the feeling that the writer is trying too hard. They attract attention because they are inappropriate or farfetched: "Like a boiling lobster, the dawn turned from black to red." This fault, more common in verse than in prose, need not concern you much in your attempts to use the figures of speech. As a young writer, you are quite likely to show evidence of trying too hard, and you may be forgiven for a few strained metaphors.

The third pitfall, however, is one which you can easily avoid provided you understand it. This is the error of mixing your figures of speech.

19h. Avoid mixed figures of speech.

A mixed figure of speech—sometimes referred to as a "mixed metaphor"—is one in which the writer starts with a comparison and then shifts to another comparison that is not consistent with the first. A few examples will make clear how a careless writer mixes his metaphors.

MIXED   Flailing both wings, Miss McCall flew to the platform and barked for silence.   [The first metaphors compare Miss McCall to a bird, and the last to a dog.]

BETTER   Flailing both wings, Miss McCall **flew** to the platform and **screeched** for silence.

MIXED   His face reddened as mountainous waves of embarrassment broke over him, all but drying up the little confidence he had.   [Mountainous waves suggest water; they would hardly "dry up" anything.]

BETTER His face reddened as mountainous **waves** of embarrassment broke over him, all but **washing away** the little confidence he had.

● EXERCISE 5. Seven of the following sentences contain mixed figures of speech. Revise the sentences to remove the mixed figures. If the figure is consistently maintained, write + after its number on your paper.

1. After enduring an hour of Carl's insane driving, we ordered him into the asylum of the back seat.

2. Their struggle for power was like a championship fight between two heavyweights, and when the governor lowered his guard, the senator scored the deciding goal.

3. Bionics researchers are on a small island of knowledge in the midst of a sea of ignorance, but, like corals, they are building reefs, extending their knowledge in all directions.

4. Unfortunately the speaker did not know that he was flying too high over the heads of his audience until their general restlessness made him realize that he had better get out of the depths into the shallower water where they were.

5. In college, he changed course abruptly, and instead of foundering on the submerged rocks of low grades and expulsion from school, he got on the beam, which eventually led him to a safe landing.

6. George dived into his studies, afraid that he would never reach the top of the heap, but determined not to give up before the round started.

7. The productive field of psychiatry, once considered a pseudoscience, has now achieved respectability and may become a most important branch of medical research.

8. Every morning a chorus of starlings in the trees outside his window awakened him, their dissonances and harsh voices jangling his nerves unbearably.

9. He spent the morning of his career groping through the dark halls of obscurity until the publication of his third novel thrust him above the surface of the black waters into the brilliant noonday sun.

10. Unless the mayor sets a new course, our city is likely to be buried beneath a mound of debt.

● EXERCISE 6.   Each item in the following exercise contains a figure of speech and a space where a portion of the sentence has been omitted. Beneath the sentence four wordings are suggested for this space, one of which is preferable if the figure of speech is to be consistently maintained. After the proper number, write the letter of the wording which best fits the blank space.

1. Mr. Gross, who was up to his neck in debt, . . . when his company went on strike.
   a. collapsed
   b. nearly went under
   c. was caught off base
   d. suffered a setback

2. His path was strewn with serious problems which threatened . . .
   a. to drop on him with crippling effect.
   b. to engulf him completely.
   c. to trip him up at every step.
   d. to wreck his career.

3. The book is a treasure chest of wisdom in which you will find . . .
   a. a rich supply of bonbons to sweeten your speech.
   b. a greenhouse of rare flowers to decorate your speech.
   c. new clothes to dress up your speech.
   d. a hoard of verbal gems to adorn your speech.

4. Heavy income taxes, which exert a stranglehold on the economy, have . . . sources of new investment capital.
   a. crippled
   b. choked off
   c. tied up
   d. destroyed

5. Like a man tenderly raking leaves from a new lawn, we must always be careful that in removing the old and unwanted, we do not . . . the new.
   a. uproot
   b. bury
   c. undermine
   d. drown out

6. Mr. Browne behaves in the classroom like a tough top sergeant, . . .
   a. shouting from his pulpit and frightening even the most devout worshippers.
   b. calling all plays and carrying the ball himself.
   c. shouting out orders and brutally exaggerating the details of discipline.
   d. beating his slaves with the lash of long assignments and low grades.

7. In the character of Willie Stark, fiction has been draped about the bones of fact, and, in places . . .
   a. the truth emerges.
   b. one can recognize the original.
   c. the skeleton shows through.
   d. the model becomes clear.

8. The moon had just risen, very golden, over the hill, and like a bright, watching spirit . . . the bars of an ash tree's naked boughs.
   a. towered above
   b. rolled behind
   c. obscured
   d. peered through

9. The characters weave the pattern of the book, . . . of motives and cross-purposes, that looks like a triangle, but is really a quadrangle.
   a. an edifice
   b. a vehicle
   c. a fabric
   d. a structure

10. After bounding around the bases like a frightened kangaroo, Mills was . . . at home plate by Smith's shot from center field.
    a. winged
    b. snared
    c. pinned
    d. dropped

SLANG AND INFORMAL ENGLISH

19i. **Use diction that is appropriate to the kind of composition you are writing—avoid slang in written composition; use extremely informal English sparingly in formal writing.**

Slang

Slang consists of new words, or old words in new uses, that have made their way into the language because they are vivid or colorful. High school and college students enjoy adopting the latest slang. Most slang is short-lived. It enjoys a brief popularity and then is forgotten. Therefore, it is always difficult to compile an illustrative list of slang terms which will be meaningful even a year later. Nevertheless, the following seem to show enough endurance to be familiar to you and to serve to make clear what slang is.

TYPICAL SLANG

boo-boo (a mistake)	hack around
broke (no money)	lousy
corny	nuts (crazy)
dope (a nitwit)	oddball
goof off	square
gung-ho (enthusiastic)	stinker

Occasionally a slang expression makes its way up the usage ladder and becomes acceptable even in formal writing, whereupon, of course, it is no longer slang. Slang should rarely be used in writing, except in reproducing dialogue.

Informal English

As explained in Chapter 5, there are two kinds of standard English—formal and informal. Informal English is good English. We use it in all our conversation and in most of our writing. Within the general category of informal English, however, there are degrees of informality. Expressions typical of the most extreme degree of informality are never "bad" English, but they are sometimes inappropriate English. Because it is light in tone and sometimes very close to slang, extremely informal English should be carefully limited in serious composition.

TYPICAL INFORMAL EXPRESSIONS

flabbergast	harum-scarum	out on a limb
in a jam	kid (child)	workout

Although dictionaries label words *informal* or *slang*, you cannot rely on their arbitrarily drawn distinctions as a means of deciding whether a word is appropriate to your composition. You need to understand the basic point that any word which is inappropriate to the general *tone* of your composition should not be used, regardless of its dictionary label. You should control your natural tendency to rely too much on informal English. The deciding factor is, of course, the degree of formality of your composition, which, in turn, determines the appropriateness of the words used. In a research paper extremely informal English should be used very sparingly. In an informal essay, it may be used as frequently as in conversation.

Read the following sentences taken from formal compositions and note the inappropriateness of the italicized words.

In any eighth-grade classroom where *kids* of the same chronological age are grouped together, we expect to find a physiological-age range of six or seven years.

There is a grave danger that we may expose far too many students of only medium ability to the long course of professional study in our universities. For the employment situation in some professional areas, we must admit, is *not so hot*.

Dickens was *hipped* on the idea that by revealing the social evils of the day he could destroy them one by one.

● EXERCISE 7.   Point out the words and expressions in the following passage which are slang or so informal as to be inappropriate to the general tone.

19i

While it is true that the students in the top ten percent of any grade are capable of doing good work in the grade above them, to undertake a general upward transfer of these boys and girls would produce more socially maladjusted kids than you could shake a stick at. Efforts to meet the problem by cutting out the arbitrary division of a school into grades have been successful in small schools, where the need to classify and control has not been great and where parents couldn't care less what grade their children are in. Today the schools which allow children to go at their own speed, with a child doing sixth-grade work in one subject and third- or fourth-grade work in another, are considered pretty far out. Eventually this method of school organization may become general practice.

MEANING AND CONNOTATION

19j. Use a vocabulary which is specific. Select words with due regard for their varied meanings and their connotations.

A word is a symbol. A word has no meaning for you unless you know what it stands for. The thing or idea that a word stands for, or refers to, is known as its *referent*. You are able to understand a word only if you know what its referent is. The referent of a word should be the same for the person using the word as for the person reading or hearing it. When two persons have in mind different referents for the same word, the word is useless for communication between them until they recognize the problem and agree on the same referent.

If your teacher says, "Please give me the chalk," you immediately understand his request. You know what action *give* refers to, whom *me* refers to, and what the symbol *chalk* refers to. Had your teacher said, "Please give me the *glub*," however, you would have been confused. *Glub*, which looks and sounds like a word, is not customarily used to refer to anything. Since for you it has no referent, it is not, so far as you are concerned, a word at all.

Concrete Words and Abstract Words

Words may be divided into two groups—*concrete* words and *abstract* words. A concrete word is one whose referent can be touched or seen: *book, cloud, car, chalk.* An abstract word is one whose referent is an idea, something which cannot be touched or seen: *peace, need, love, freedom.*

(1) For clearness in description, choose the concrete word with the most specific referent.

Concrete words vary in definiteness. For example, the word *vehicle*, while its referent is something which can be seen and touched, is not at all specific. You probably do not have a clear mental picture of a *vehicle*. The word *car* is more specific; the word *convertible* is still more specific. "John was driving a dilapidated vehicle" will not convey as clear a picture as "John was driving a dilapidated convertible." As description, the second sentence is clearer. In all your writing, whenever you are considering several different words to express a particular meaning, select the most specific one.

● EXERCISE 8.   Arrange the words in each group so that the word with the least specific referent will come first, and the word with the most specific referent will come last.

1. seat, desk chair, chair, furniture, swivel chair
2. quadruped, creature, mammal, spaniel, dog
3. crack-up, plane crash, event, accident
4. storm at sea, typhoon, occurrence, storm
5. laborer, longshoreman, employee, human being, man

● EXERCISE 9.   For each of the following general words, list three words which have a more specific referent:

1. food	3. elevation	5. educational institution
2. boat	4. punishment	6. restaurant

19j

Synonyms

(2) **For clearness, choose the synonym that expresses your meaning exactly.**

Synonyms are words which are similar, but rarely identical, in meaning. A careful writer selects the word which has the exact referent that he has in mind. For example, the words *disciple*, *partisan*, and *satellite* are synonyms in that each refers to a person who is a *follower* of a leader. Yet each has its own meaning somewhat different from the others. *Follower*, the most general in meaning, may be used in place of any of the other three, but for the writer who has a specific kind of follower in mind, it lacks exactness. A writer who has in mind the followers of a professor or a religious leader, for instance, would probably use the word *disciples*. If he wishes to refer to the blindly devoted followers of a political or military leader, he might prefer the word *partisans*. To refer to the kind of followers who continuously and obsequiously circulate about a powerful leader, perhaps in hope of favors, he could use the word *satellites*. Do not be satisfied with the first synonym that occurs to you.

● EXERCISE 10. Without using the dictionary, explain the difference in meaning of the words in each group. Describe a situation in which each would be properly used.

1. highway, road, street, boulevard, expressway, path, trail
2. compel, coerce, force, constrain
3. reveal, divulge, tell, betray
4. repulsive, obnoxious, abhorrent, distasteful
5. laughing, giggling, snickering, guffawing

Exact Meaning of Abstract Words

(3) **Make clear the referent of an abstract word by definition or example.**

Abstract words, which usually refer to general ideas, must always be used with care. A great many misunderstandings are caused by abstract words which have not been carefully defined. Unless two persons agree on the meaning (referent) of an abstract word, communication between them may break down. An abstract word may have many referents.

The word *freedom*, for example, has only a very vague referent until you define it. To a prisoner behind bars, *freedom* means getting out of jail. To Mr. Barnes, who resents the neighbors' criticism of his noisy family, *freedom* means the right of his family to make as much noise as they wish. Franklin D. Roosevelt defined the freedoms in which America believes as freedom of speech, freedom of worship, freedom from want, and freedom from fear. Each of these definitions provides a more specific referent for the word *freedom*, and each, in turn, could be more narrowly defined.

Sometimes an example will help to clarify the meaning of an abstract word. In the following passage the meaning of *quality* in the context "a man of quality" is made clear by an example.

> Mansfield was a man of quality. Although he never pushed himself forward or tried to assert his superiority, you could tell by his bearing, his quiet sense of humor, and his manner of speaking that he was a superior person.

● EXERCISE 11.   Without using a dictionary, write a one- or two-sentence definition of each of the following words. Compare your definitions with those of your classmates. In discussion, you may find it helpful to clarify your meaning by means of an example.

1. fairness	3. success	5. skill
2. beauty	4. failure	6. happiness

(4) In reading and writing, distinguish between the denotative and the connotative meanings of a word.

Compare the meaning of the following sentences:

Ray's persistence surprised everyone.
Ray's stubbornness surprised everyone.

Of course, the meaning of the two sentences may be the same. *Persistence* is another word for *stubbornness*, the quality of not giving up easily. This is the *denotative* meaning of the words. But the *effect* of the words on reader or listener is very different. *Stubbornness* suggests that Ray is unreasonable, narrow-minded, unwilling to listen to others. This *suggestive* meaning of a word is its *connotation*, or *connotative* meaning. Many words have connotations. There is nothing wrong in choosing a word for its connotations, but you must be aware of the connotations lest you say or write something you did not intend.

● EXERCISE 12.   Number in a column 1–20. As you read each word in the following list, write *F* after its number if the word has favorable, pleasing connotations for you. Write *U* if it has unfavorable connotations. Write *N* if the connotations are neutral, that is, if the words do not stir any feeling in you. Compare your answers with those of your classmates.

1. liberal	8. bureaucrat	15. grand opera
2. propaganda	9. saloon	16. Americanism
3. mother	10. stars and stripes	17. Yankee
4. tavern	11. conservative	18. tycoon
5. atheist	12. communism	19. egghead
6. home	13. bar and grill	20. rebel
7. church	14. reactionary	

Loaded Words

A word which, through its connotations, carries strong feelings is said to be "loaded." The propagandist, the newspaper columnist, the political speaker are likely to use loaded words. They are trying to appeal to the emotions of people. When used deliberately, loaded words are a form of persuasion which clear thinkers disapprove of.

● EXERCISE 13.   Compare the following reports of the same speech. Both reports contain loaded words. One is loaded against Senator Blank; the other is loaded in his favor. List the loaded words and compare them with their counterparts in the other report.

1	2
Senator Blank today blasted opponents of his highway expansion program in a blistering attack from the Senate floor. In a long-winded tirade, the aging politician made a desperate bid for support but succeeded in frightening only a few senators into backing his program.	Senator Blank today criticized opponents of his highway expansion program in a powerful statement from the Senate floor. In a thorough discussion, the venerable legislator made another strong bid for support, which apparently convinced several senators that they should back the program.

● EXERCISE 14. Discuss with your classmates and teacher the connotations of the following words.

1. plump, fat, pot-bellied, stout
2. visionary, crackpot, idealist
3. crowd, gang, mob, assemblage
4. aging, venerable, senior, mature, graying
5. determined, persevering, dogged, resolute, relentless, tenacious

Exercises in Sentence Revision

This chapter contains exercises only. The exercises will help you in two ways: (1) they will test your understanding of sentence correctness, clearness, and smoothness; (2) they will give you practice in repairing faulty sentence structure. The theory behind the inclusion of exercises in any textbook is that if you learn to criticize and revise the awkward sentences in the book, most of which have been taken from student compositions, you will be able to criticize and revise your own awkward sentences.

Use the exercises in this chapter to "keep your hand in" the skills of good writing. The exercises are of various kinds, and every exercise is devoted to more than one kind of skill.

Identifying and Correcting Errors

● EXERCISE 1. Immediately below these directions you will find a list of errors in sentence structure. Each faulty sentence in the exercise illustrates one of these errors. Some of the sentences are correct. You are to do two things: (1) write *before* the number of the sentence on your paper the letter of the error illustrated in the sentence; (2) write *after* the number of the sentence a revision which eliminates the error. How you remove the error is not important, provided your sentence is correct, clear, and smooth. If the sentence is correct as it stands, write a + before its number

A Lack of agreement (subject and verb, or pronoun and antecedent)

B Incorrect case of pronoun

C Dangling modifier

D Lack of parallelism or faulty parallelism

E Unclear reference of pronoun (ambiguous, general, weak)

EXAMPLE 1. Do you know whom it was?

B 1. *Do you know who it was?*

1. A person may disapprove of a law, but they should not violate it.
2. She is a splendid athlete, a beautiful dancer, and as a student receives excellent grades in school.
3. In the obedience trials each trainer gave his dog a series of commands, and, to my surprise, he did them faultlessly.
4. Lacking sufficient capital to weather the depression, a rival firm with greater resources bought him out.
5. The editor of the paper, as well as many of its readers, was worried about recent attacks on its editorial policy.
6. The selection of stories in both books were extremely good.
7. Because the dishes burned his fingers, he dropped them.
8. The satellite has many instruments sending back reports and to record important data to be analyzed later.
9. Do you think you and him can run as fast as Jack and me?
10. Jack is a boy who, I believe, will become a good student.
11. The complexity of today's educational programs reflect the complexity of society.
12. When the child gets too big for the crib, set it on end and make a wardrobe out of it.
13. Expecting bad news at any moment, the fact that long distance was calling me nearly frightened me to death.
14. Playing without sufficient practice, the team had neither the necessary skill nor enough stamina to win the game.
15. My brother and me agreed only to tell you and she.
16. If students do not call for their notebooks this week, they will be destroyed.
17. Asking one absurd question after another, Bob's teacher was soon made to dislike him.

18. I think that you and me will get along better than Laura and her.
19. One of the nation's most serious concerns are the health and happiness of its citizens.
20. Europe was plagued by the lack of adequate production facilities, and unemployment was widespread.

● EXERCISE 2.   Follow the directions for Exercise 1.

    A Sentence fragment
    B Run-on sentence
    C Incorrect tense or verb form
    D Misplaced modifier
    E Unclear relationship between sentence ideas (lack of subordination, faulty coordination)

1. Our camp, which lays at the north end of the lake, is overshadowed by the cliffs which raise steeply above it.
2. Team teaching offers teachers at least one important advantage, it enables each teacher on the team to teach his specialty.
3. Since it has nine returning lettermen, this year's football team should win the championship.
4. The car was driven by a stunning girl with whitewall tires.
5. The band in its new uniforms and the high-stepping majorette with her twirling baton as well as the stirring music.
6. A compromise is a settlement of differences reached by mutual concessions between two parties.
7. Secret police with hidden cameras that were trying to take pictures at the meeting were physically ejected by angry students.
8. She had intended to have gone to the dance with her brother.
9. At home we suffer the constant interference of our parents, at college we will be free to make our own decisions.
10. Tickets for matinees will cost $1.50, and matinees will be given on Wednesdays and Saturdays.
11. These experiences will be valuable in my career as a social worker, and it is a career in which I shall work with people from all walks of life.
12. I found that, except for literature selections, each English course covered the same material I had the year before.

13. During negotiations between labor and management, work in the factory continued as usual.

14. The five junior high school buildings will cost eight million dollars, and they were approved by the taxpayers in yesterday's balloting.

15. We found several of the boys in the shop very busy. Learning how to take a motor apart and put it together again.

16. The senator denied the many charges that had been made against him briefly and categorically.

17. In high school I have been unable to take some courses I wanted and have been required to take others I did not want.

18. Twenty percent of the students said they were satisfied with their own study habits, fifty-four percent said they wished they knew how to study more effectively.

19. If you would have come earlier, you could have seen the first act.

20. The demand for good television material exceeds the supply, and some of the best material, important news events, is not being fully used, and the reason is that news telecasts are not profitable.

Selecting the Best Expression

● EXERCISE 3. Number your paper 1–25. After each of the following sentences, the italicized part of the sentence is rephrased in two ways. If you consider one of these rephrasings an improvement, write the letter of the better one (*a* or *b*) after the proper number on your paper. If you consider the sentence correct as it stands, write +.

1. Behind one of the doors waits a tiger, *and the other has a beautiful lady behind it.*

   a. . . . and behind the other waits a beautiful lady.

   b. . . . and a beautiful lady waits behind the other.

2. If you go on a trip, *it will give you an excellent chance to practice your camera technique.*

   a. . . . you will have an excellent chance to practice your camera technique.

   b. . . . an excellent chance to practice your camera technique will be yours.

3. When developing films, *a darkroom will be needed.*
   a. ... one thing you will need is a darkroom.
   b. ... you will need a darkroom.
4. A deep-sea fisherman needs an outboard motor much larger *than a fisherman who fishes in sheltered waters.*
   a. ... than that used by a fisherman who fishes in sheltered waters.
   b. ... than one fishing in sheltered waters.
5. This discovery had a bad effect on the mind of *Usher, he thought he buried his sister alive.*
   a. ... Usher, for he thought he had buried his sister alive.
   b. Usher. He thought he buried his sister alive.
6. Although they listen to several news broadcasts each day, *most people continue to buy a daily paper.*
   a. ... a daily paper continues to be bought by most people.
   b. ... the buying of a daily paper by most people continues.
7. It had been stated earlier in the press that representatives of union and management *would either meet around the clock until they reached an agreement or accepted government arbitration.*
   a. ... would meet around the clock until either they reached an agreement or government arbitration was accepted by them.
   b. ... would meet around the clock until they either reached an agreement or accepted government arbitration.
8. During the winter *Anderson both developed his skill in skiing and ice skating.*
   a. ... Anderson developed his skill in both skiing and ice skating.
   b. ... Anderson developed both his skill in skiing and in ice skating.
9. *Pat and him told Mike and I* the answers to the homework problems.
   a. Pat and him told Mike and me ...
   b. Pat and he told Mike and me ...
10. Ever since the accident, *driving past that spot,* the whole experience has returned.
    a. ... while driving past that spot, ...
    b. ... as I have driven past that spot, ...

11. The Governor sent his budget message to the legislature yesterday, conferred with the director of the budget this morning, *and a conference with the press was held this afternoon.*

    a. . . . and held a conference with the press this afternoon.

    b. . . . and this afternoon held a conference with the press.

12. *Was it he who* you thought stole the money?

    a. Was it he whom . . .

    b. Was it him whom . . .

13. When one of the girls *have completed their report, ask them* to bring it to me.

    a. . . . has completed their report, ask them . . .

    b. . . . has completed her report, ask her . . .

14. Don't expect *Paul and I to be as good as her* in English.

    a. . . . Paul and me to be as good as she . . .

    b. . . . Paul and I to be as good as she . . .

15. Plans for the P.T.A. party *include not only dancing but also* a floor show and a buffet supper.

    a. . . . not only include dancing but also . . .

    b. . . . include not only dancing, but also the guests will enjoy . . .

16. Jim had been in jail for safecracking *but because of good behavior was paroled.*

    a. . . . but because of good behavior had been paroled.

    b. . . . but had been paroled for good behavior.

17. To my complete surprise the students *accepted the new type of examination which the teachers had prepared without a complaint.*

    a. . . . accepted the new type of examination without a complaint, which the teachers had prepared.

    b. . . . accepted without a complaint the new type of examination which the teachers had prepared.

18. The mayor's economy committee *has been investigating street-cleaning costs, and it has published a report on its findings.*

    a. . . . , which has been investigating street-cleaning costs, has published a report on its findings.

    b. . . . has been investigating street-cleaning costs, and a report has been published on its findings.

19. The two causes of "college neurosis" are trying to get into college *and then you try to stay there.*
    a. ... and then to try to stay there.
    b. ... and then trying to stay there.

20. *The students received the new yearbook*, which came out on the last day of school, *with enthusiasm.*
    a. The students received with enthusiasm the new year book ...
    b. The students with enthusiasm received the new year-book ...

21. *The telegram reached me too late advising against going to Washington.*
    a. Too late the telegram advising against going to Washington reached me.
    b. The telegram advising against going to Washington reached me too late.

22. *It is not the cost of a gift but its appropriateness that matters.*
    a. The cost of a gift does not matter, but the appropriateness of it does.
    b. It is not the cost that matters of a gift, but its appropriateness.

23. After being reprimanded twice, *the teacher, for further punishment, sent Tom to the principal.*
    a. ... by the teacher, Tom was sent to the principal for further punishment.
    b. ... the teacher sent Tom to the principal for further punishment.

24. Public figures must learn to take *the reporters' questions and the flashing of camera bulbs calmly.*
    a. ... the questions of reporters and the flashing of camera bulbs calmly.
    b. ... calmly the questioning of reporters and the flashing of camera bulbs.

25. *Driving through the mountains, we were impressed by the engineering achievements of road builders.*
    a. We were impressed by the engineering achievements of road builders, driving through the mountains.
    b. We were impressed by the engineering achievements, driving through the mountains, of road builders.

Revising Awkward Sentences

● EXERCISE 4. This exercise is composed of awkward sentences which you are to rewrite. The sentences may be rearranged in any way that will make them clearer and smoother. Your purpose is to express the same idea in a better way. The faults in a sentence may not always be specific errors; they may be generally clumsy constructions. You may add words or omit words wherever you wish, provided you do not alter the meaning. Remove wordy passages. Eliminate errors in usage. Each problem can be handled in a single sentence, but your teacher may allow you to divide some of the problems into two sentences.

1. He tried to find out the girl's name that he was to take out.
2. Featherbedding is one result of automation, which is the practice of keeping men on the job, which is unnecessary, because the job has been made obsolete by new machines.
3. The dean was more impressed by the candidate's scholastic record than his athletic record impressed him.
4. There are many persons who have jobs part of the year, and a job is not held by them the rest of the year, being among the unemployed.
5. There is a great deal of Franklin's philosophy which certainly everyone who reads it can benefit from in his *Autobiography*.
6. Soon many families will have helicopters just like cars today and able to go from place to place much more easier than by car since there will be a direct route and the traffic will be much less.
7. Since we hadn't no tire repair kit, the motorcycle was pushed to the nearest gas station where we had a patch put on it.
8. Trotter was an optimist, easygoing, and nothing ever seemed to trouble him no matter what happened.
9. Opening the curtain, an empty stage was revealed, but the stage crew arrived a moment later and, busily working and talking, the set was soon up for the first act.
10. In a child a negative attitude may come from the natural desire for recognition and independence, but when an adult shows a negative attitude, it may be a symptom of neurosis.

● EXERCISE 5.   Follow the directions for Exercise 4.

1. Mrs. Turnbull is a good author and through experience has found out what a reader wants and has given them it in this book.

2. From my own standpoint, gardening, whether flowers or vegetables, is a lot of fun, good exercise, and the experience it provides is valuable.

3. There are many ways to show loyalty to a friend that you can use, and one of these is not to talk about them behind their back.

4. In some countries the biggest problem of the people is getting enough food, but the biggest problem of some people in America is dieting which is when you keep yourself from eating too much food.

5. Psychologists have proved that a child's mind is often more active than an adult, and they are usually eager to learn.

6. The mechanic working for the airline that failed to check the landing gear was not only guilty of negligence, but, in effect, he was a murderer as well.

7. After the dances in the gymnasium, of which we have a reasonable amount, many couples go to some eating place which is not too far away to have a bite to eat.

8. I found out that shopping quickly weakens a man's patience when I went to a department store with Mother one day.

9. The clash between East and West of ideals were blocking world unity at a time when war might be led to if unity could not be achieved.

10. By the time you have got the children into bed, you are so exhausted that all ambition to study has been lost by you, and television is all that is left as the only entertainment until the return of the parents is made.

11. A single goal may dominate an individual so that it is the only thing they live for and they work so hard that they miss the fun in life and he is never satisfied.

12. Being the first author to make a strong case for complete independence from England, Paine's book was a big seller, and it was about American independence.

13. Going even further into the effects of not having any more petroleum would have on the world is the realization that the thousands of factories in the world which use oil would have to close down.

14. After graduating from high school the learning we have attained may be lost or become hazy in a year of military training and it also adds another year to the time we will graduate from college to get a job.

15. There should be required by the school a pre-season physical examination, and there should be enforced a law to prevent anyone from playing football with a history of heart abnormalities.

PART FOUR

Composition: Paragraphs and Longer Papers

The Effective Paragraph

Developing Unified, Coherent Paragraphs [1]

No matter how long an essay is, it really consists of a series of short compositions. Each of these helps to develop the essay, and, at the same time, develops its own topic. These small compositions are paragraphs.

21a. A *paragraph* is a series of sentences developing one topic.

In your review of paragraph writing in this chapter, you will practice techniques that are applicable to all writing. In many ways a paragraph is a complete composition on a small scale. It deals with one subject which it introduces, develops, and concludes. The ideas in a paragraph, like those in a longer piece of writing, must be arranged according to a definite plan and should follow one another clearly and smoothly. The topic of the paragraph must be fully developed. In other words, the planning and writing of one-paragraph themes give you excellent practice in important techniques of composition.

[1] This chapter is concerned primarily with the paragraph in relatively formal expository writing. The student should realize that the rules for paragraph organization and development given here do not apply to the paragraph in narrative writing or in very informal personal essays or in news writing.

THE TOPIC SENTENCE

21b. The topic of a paragraph should be stated in a sentence somewhere in the paragraph.

In the sample paragraph which follows, the topic sentence is the opening sentence, printed in bold-faced type. The author develops the idea in this sentence by listing supporting details. Most paragraphs are developed in this way.

The thirty years after the outbreak of the Civil War were to disclose the mineral wealth and organic treasure concealed by the "desert." The earth's most productive wheat lands, once the secret of their cultivation was learned, covered the Dakotas and eastern Montana. In the farther reaches of these states, and in future states to the south and west, spread seemingly boundless grazing lands soon to become the source of most of the world's beef, mutton, hides, and wool. Other plains and mountain regions held some of the world's largest and purest veins of copper and iron ore, some of its most extensive deposits of lead and zinc, and valuable seams of coal. Beneath the lands of Texas (and elsewhere in the West, as time proved), lay incredibly large fields of petroleum and natural gas.[1]

21c. In general, place the topic sentence at or near the beginning of the paragraph.

A topic sentence may be placed at any point in a paragraph, but the most effective position for it in most paragraphs is at or near the beginning. Placing the topic sentence at the beginning helps the reader by giving him a clear idea of what is going to be said; it helps the writer by requiring him to formulate clearly his main point before going on to develop it.

In a composition of several paragraphs it would, of

[1] From *A New History of the United States* by William Miller. Copyright © 1958 by William Miller. Reprinted by permission of George Braziller, Inc.

21
a-c

course, be unwise to begin every paragraph with the topic sentence; to do so might give a monotonous effect.

If you should try to find a topic sentence in every paragraph of a magazine article or a book, you would soon discover that experienced writers do not always state in any one sentence the topics of their paragraphs. They may *imply* the central point so strongly that they do not need to give a statement of it. But as an inexperienced writer, you should actually include topic sentences in your paragraphs.

PARAGRAPH WITH THE TOPIC SENTENCE IN THE MIDDLE

By 1893, the United States had the immense total of 170,000 miles of railroad capitalized at almost $10,000,000,000. In 1867 the railroads did a total of $330,000,000 worth of business; by 1893 this figure was $1,200,000,000. **Along with the growth in mileage, investment, and volume came many improvements in service and safety.** In 1864 George M. Pullman built the first sleeping car. Four years later, George Westinghouse introduced the air brake. By 1875 the refrigerator car had been developed, especially for carrying meat. Succeeding years saw the acceptance of the standard gauge throughout the country, the shift from wood-burning to coal-burning engines, from iron to heavy steel rails.[1]

PARAGRAPH WITH TOPIC SENTENCE AT THE END

Young people do not spend all their time in school. Their elders commonly spend none of it there. Yet their elders are, we hope, constantly growing in practical wisdom. They are, at least, having experience. If we can teach them while they are being educated how to reason, they may be able to comprehend and assimilate their experience. It is a good principle because a college or university has a vast and complicated job if it does what only it can do. **In general education, therefore, we may wisely leave experience to life and set about our job of intellectual training.**[2]

[1] From *A New History of the United States*, by William Miller, George Braziller, Inc., New York, 1958. Reprinted by permission.

[2] From "What Is a General Education?" by Robert M. Hutchins, *Harper's Magazine*, November 1963. Reprinted by permission.

The Concluding, or Clincher, Sentence

At the end of a paragraph, particularly a long one, a writer will sometimes summarize by restating, in different words, the topic sentence he used at the beginning. A concluding sentence of this kind is sometimes called a "clincher" sentence because it clinches the point made in the paragraph.

You should be warned against overuse of the clincher sentence and against tacking it on artificially when it is not of any value. Avoid such weak and unnecessary concluding sentences as "Those are the three reasons why I like baseball" or "Now I have told you why I like baseball." It is better not to attempt a clincher sentence than to write one which is ineffective. In the following example both topic and concluding sentences are in bold-faced type.

> **The interpretation of words is a never-ending task for any citizen in modern society.** We now have, as the result of modern means of communication, hundreds of thousands of words flung at us daily. We are constantly being talked at, by teachers, preachers, salesmen, public officials, and moving-picture sound tracks. The cries of the hawkers of soft drinks, soap chips, and laxatives pursue us into our very homes, thanks to the radio—and in some houses the radio is never turned off from morning to night. Daily the newsboy brings us, in large cities, from thirty to fifty enormous pages of print, and almost three times that amount on Sundays. The mailman brings magazines and direct-mail advertising. We go out and get more words at bookstores and libraries. Billboards confront us on the highways, and we even take portable radios with us to the seashore. **Words fill our lives.**[1]

● EXERCISE 1. Each of the following subjects can be treated in a paragraph. Select three subjects from the list; think through your ideas on each of the three, and write a

[1] From *Language in Action* by S. I. Hayakawa. Copyright 1941 by Harcourt, Brace and Company. Reprinted by permission of the publishers.

topic sentence you could use to introduce a paragraph on it. You will write three topic sentences.

1. Self-discipline
2. Signs of immaturity in behavior
3. How pride affects our behavior
4. The latest venture into space
5. Human traits that advertisers appeal to
6. Dialogue in Hemingway, Salinger, or another author
7. Short stories with trick endings
8. Description of a favorite place
9. Rules for safe driving
10. The importance of atmosphere in Poe's short stories

● EXERCISE 2. Develop one of the topic sentences written for Exercise 1 into a paragraph of approximately 150 words.

Development of the Topic Sentence

21d. Develop a paragraph by giving additional, detailed information in support of the idea expressed in the topic sentence.

No skill acquired in your English course is more important in the improvement of your writing than the ability to develop a topic sentence into a good paragraph. An effective paragraph cannot be made out of nothing. You must have in mind the details with which to develop it. These details may be of many kinds. They may be facts or examples or incidents or arguments. The kind of detail is not especially important, but the details themselves are all-important.

Study the following sample paragraphs. Each of them is developed by a different kind of detail.

(1) A topic sentence may be developed by *facts*.

In the following paragraph, the details used to develop the topic sentence are facts that give meaning to the opening statement.

Of all organs in the body the liver is most extraordinary. **In its versatility and in the indispensable nature of its func-tions it has no equal.** It presides over so many vital activities that even the slightest damage to it is fraught with serious consequences. Not only does it provide bile for the digestion of fats, but because of its location and the special circula-tory pathways that converge upon it, the liver receives blood directly from the digestive tract and is deeply involved in the metabolism of all the principal foodstuffs. It stores sugar in the form of glycogen and releases it as glucose in care-fully measured quantities to keep the blood sugar at a normal level. It builds body proteins, including some essential ele-ments of blood plasma concerned with blood clotting. It maintains cholesterol at its proper level in the blood plasma, and it inactivates the male and female hormones when they reach excessive levels. It is a storehouse of many vitamins, some of which in turn contribute to its own proper function-ing.[1]

(2) A topic sentence may be developed by *examples*.

Sometimes a topic sentence may be developed by one or more examples. An example is one kind of fact. It may name names—persons, places, events. Frequently it is preceded by the expression *for example*. The point made in the second sentence of the following paragraph (the topic sentence) is supported and clarified by an example.

Children seem to learn all languages with equal facility. **What is even more amazing, a child from three to six can learn several different languages at the same time without apparent difficulty and can keep them all straight as long as individuals with whom he has significant relationships consistently speak the same language or languages to him.** Conceivably, for exam-ple, a child's father might speak to him an equal amount of time in both English and German, his mother might use only French to him and his nurse only Chinese. If he were, say, in a Spanish-speaking country, he would soon speak Spanish with

21c

[1] From *Silent Spring* by Rachel Carson, Houghton Mifflin Com-pany.

the children with whom he played and have no trouble keeping all the languages apart or in switching from one to the other as he spoke with the proper person. Difficulty would arise only if the father should unexpectedly switch to French, or the mother and the child's playmates try English or the nurse German. How people talk and what language they use seems to be very early associated by human beings with the relationships which "significant others" bear to them.[1]

(3) A topic sentence may be developed by an incident.

A brief story, an incident or anecdote, is sometimes used in support of the topic sentence. An incident is, of course, a particular type of example. To illustrate his point that even sophisticated people sometimes make the mistake of thinking that an object and its name are the same thing, the author of the following paragraph tells a story.

Although this identification of the word with the object is avoided by more sophisticated minds, they often slip just one peg down into the deeply rooted notion that the word inevitably and unalterably belongs to a particular thing or person. A name is like a label chained around the object by God's order, which nobody must presume to detach. An Englishman was lunching in a Paris restaurant. He knew no French, the waiter little English. They engaged in the friendly task of giving names in their respective languages to things at which the Englishman pointed. Eventually he pointed at the bread. "Pain," said the waiter; and the Englishman burst out laughing. "What you call it, M'sieur?" "Bread"—and the waiter laughed. At this the Englishman got angry. "M'sieur," expostulated the waiter, "you laugh when I say 'Pain,' I laugh when you say 'Bread.'" Back came the Englishman, "But it *is* bread, you know."[2]

[1] From "Linguistics: A Modern View of Language" by Henry Lee Smith from *An Outline of Man's Knowledge of the Modern World,* edited by Lyman Bryson. Copyright © 1960 by Catherine McGrattan Bryson, Executrix of the Estate of Lyman Bryson. Reprinted by permission of Doubleday & Company, Inc. and published by McGraw-Hill Book Company, Inc.

[2] From "The Disorderly Conduct of Words," by Zechariah Chafee, Jr., *Columbia Law Review,* Vol. 41, March, 1941.

(4) A topic sentence may be developed by arguments in a line of reasoning.

A paragraph which states and then explains a point of view or one side of an argument may be developed by a logical train of thought, one point leading to another until the position of the writer has been effectively supported. In a paragraph of this kind, the details used to develop the topic sentence are the reasons for, or arguments in favor of, the author's point. These reasons and arguments, of course, may themselves be supported by facts, examples, or incidents.

Study the following paragraph. Note that the argument is advanced by a line of reasoning logically presented. When you read the topic sentence, your immediate reaction is to ask why? The paragraph consists of the author's reasons for thinking as he does.

> **Now, to be properly enjoyed, a walking tour should be gone upon alone.** If you go in a company, or even in pairs, it is no longer a walking tour in anything but name; it is something else and more in the nature of a picnic. A walking tour should be gone upon alone, because freedom is of the essence; because you should be able to stop and go on, and follow this way and that, as the freak takes you; and because you must have your own pace, and neither trot alongside a champion walker, nor mince in time with a girl. And then you must be open to all impressions and let your thoughts take color from what you see. You should be as a pipe for any wind to play upon. "I cannot see the wit," says Hazlitt, "of walking and talking at the same time. When I am in the country, I wish to vegetate like the country"—which is the gist of all that can be said upon the matter. There should be no cackle of voices at your elbow to jar on the meditative silence of the morning. And so long as a man is reasoning he cannot surrender himself to that fine intoxication that comes of much motion in the open air, that begins in a sort of dazzle and sluggishness of the brain, and ends in a peace that passes comprehension.[1]

[1] From "Walking Tours" by Robert Louis Stevenson.

(5) A topic sentence may be developed by comparison and contrast.

The idea in a topic sentence can sometimes be clarified by comparing or contrasting two things or ideas. A paragraph developed in this way may clarify one idea by comparing it with a similar, more familiar, idea. To make clear how studying strengthens the mind, Mr. Martin compares it to the way training strengthens the body.[1]

> **Your mind, like your body, is a thing whereof the powers are developed by effort.** That is a principal use, as I see it, of hard work in studies. Unless you train your body you can't be an athlete, and unless you train your mind you can't be much of a scholar. The four miles an oarsman covers at top speed is in itself nothing to the good, but the physical capacity to hold out over the course is thought to be of some worth. So a good part of what you learn by hard study may not be permanently retained and may not seem to be of much final value, but your mind is a better and more powerful instrument because you have learned it. "Knowledge is power," but still more the faculty of acquiring and using knowledge is power. If you have a trained and powerful mind, you are bound to have stored it with something, but its value is more in what it can do, what it can grasp and use, than in what it contains; and if it were possible, as it is not, to come out of college with a trained and disciplined mind and nothing useful in it, you would still be ahead, and still, in a manner, educated. Think of your mind as a muscle to be developed.[2]

The following paragraph is developed by contrast. In it Mr. Hutchins presents opposite sides of a debatable issue — the value of membership in a college fraternity.

> As one who has been a "fraternity man" in his day, I think I appreciate the advantages and the evils of this ancient form

---

[1] For further discussion of reasoning by comparisons, see Analogy on pages 390–92.

[2] From "A Father to His Freshman Son" by Edward S. Martin. *Atlantic Monthly*. Reprinted by permission of George W. Martin.

of comradeship. On the credit side, it may be said that no fraternity ever made a bum of a man. The man who leaves college a bum brought his taste for being a bum to college with him. His character or lack of it, was already crystallized when he arrived at the age of eighteen. If he had the impulse to "bull" all day and play poker all night, he devoted himself to these arts whether his base of operation was a fraternity house, a dormitory or a saloon. On the debit side, it may be said that fraternities—and, of course, sororities—emphasize external possessions such as money, and trivialities such as appearances or "family." Their tradition of snobbishness inflates the ego of ordinary individuals who "make" them and too often breaks the hearts of those who do not. **Fraternities are neither a menace nor a boon, and parents and students would both be better off if they regarded them as unimportant.**[1]

(6) A topic sentence may be developed by definition.

Sometimes in the course of a composition it becomes necessary to define terms, to make clear to our reader the meaning of a word or a phrase as we understand it. Usually a quick one-sentence definition is not adequate, and we find ourselves devoting a paragraph to the definition. Writing such a definition may involve explanations and description; it may require development by the citing of examples.[2] Developing a paragraph by definition should produce a clear and useful statement of the author's idea of the meaning of a term.

In the following paragraph the writer defines romantic fiction. He gives his definition in a general way in the first sentence, the topic sentence. Then he develops it by giving a great many facts and examples which make clear the phrase "escape from reality."

[1] From "Why Go to College?" by Robert M. Hutchins. *Saturday Evening Post*. Reprinted by permission of the author.

[2] For more detailed discussion of how to write a definition, see pages 367–70.

Romantic fiction is primarily the kind which offers the reader an escape from reality. It often deals with distant lands and times. The things that happen in it are more exciting or mysterious or adventurous or strange than the things that happen in real life. Often it deals with such things as tournaments and besieged castles and perilous journeys through hostile country. Sometimes its characters have long journeys to go alone through forests infested with "pesky redskins," are besieged in lonely old houses, or are shut up on islands in the midst of faraway lakes, or lie in hushed hiding while a mortal foe treads close by. Sometimes there are pirates, hidden treasures, shipwrecks, thrilling flights from a close-pursuing enemy, last-minute rescues, ominous prophecies, missing heirs, disguised princes, intrigue, murder, breathless suspense. Again, romance is often pervaded by an atmosphere of strange things about to be revealed; often it deals with places and people now changed or forgotten or long since passed away. In short, romance shows life not just as it is, but as we like to imagine it to be.[1]

(7) A topic sentence may be developed by a combination of methods.

When you are practicing paragraph-writing, you will do well to decide when you begin a paragraph by which one of the several methods your topic sentence can be best developed. This concentration on one method at a time is excellent training. You should realize, however, that a paragraph need not be developed in only one way. In fact, experienced writers do not try to limit themselves to one method—examples or definitions or incidents; they simply use any combination of methods that will be effective. For example, a writer presenting arguments in a paragraph may use examples, an incident, and definitions. This does not mean that he is writing badly. The important point to remember is that the topic of the paragraph must be fully and effectively developed; the method is incidental. The following paragraph is developed by facts and by examples.

[1] From *The Enjoyment of Literature* by Ralph P. Boas and Edwin Smith. Reprinted by permission of Harcourt, Brace & World, Inc.

Basic to all the Greek achievement was freedom. **topic sentence** The Athenians were the only free people in the world. In the great empires of antiquity—Egypt, Babylon, Assyria, Persia—splendid though they were, with riches beyond reckoning and immense power, freedom was unknown. The idea of it never dawned in any of them. It was born in **facts** Greece, a poor little country, but with it able to remain unconquered no matter what manpower and what wealth were arrayed against her. At Marathon and at Salamis overwhelming numbers of Persians had been defeated by small Greek forces. It had been proved that **example** one free man was superior to many submissively obedient subjects of a tyrant. Athens was the leader in that amazing victory, and to the Athenians freedom was their dearest possession. Demosthenes said that they would not **concluding** think it worth their while to live if they **sentence** could not do so as free men, and years later a great teacher said, "Athenians, if you deprive them of their liberty, will die." [1]

---

[1] From *The Ever-Present Past* by Edith Hamilton. Reprinted by permission of W. W. Norton & Company, Inc., New York.

● EXERCISE 3.   Read carefully each of the following paragraphs. Find the topic sentence in each and write it on your paper. After each topic sentence indicate by the rule numbers—(1), (2), (3), (4), (5), (6)—the method by which the paragraph is developed:

(1) facts
(2) examples (one or more)
(3) incidents (one or more)
(4) arguments or reasons
(5) comparison or contrast
(6) definition

1

If you travel over regions where the buildings were made in earlier times, you will notice great differences from north to south. In the north the roofs are steep to shed the snow, the windows small to keep out the cold, the building materials often easily worked soft woods provided by the abundant nearby forests. The ceilings are low to conserve heat, the chimneys numerous or large, the doors and windows arranged to baffle chilling drafts, and the hearth is the focus of the dwelling. As you move south the roofs flatten, the windows grow larger, the ceilings rise, so that houses on the steamy James River, in Virginia, for example, have very high ceilings and also a through hall to permit easy cooling of the rooms. As you near the tropics the woods become harder to work and more vulnerable to dampness and insects. The roofs may get still flatter unless the rainfall is torrential, in which case they steepen again as in Celebes. The patio usually replaces the hearth, and the walls of adobe or stone become thicker in order to preserve coolness; now the windows are small and deeply recessed to keep the hot direct sun from penetrating the interiors. All these practical arrangements were worked out empirically long ago.[1]

[1] From "Architecture and Building" by John Burchard from *An Outline of Man's Knowledge of the Modern World*, edited by Lyman Bryson. Copyright © by Catherine McGrattan Bryson, Executrix of the Estate of Lyman Bryson. Reprinted by permission of Doubleday & Company, Inc. and published by McGraw-Hill Book Company, Inc.

2

In learning a second language, you will find that vocabulary is comparatively easy, in spite of the fact that it is vocabulary that students fear most. The harder part is mastering new structures in both content and expression. You may have to free yourself from the bondage of thinking of everything as either singular or plural. Perhaps the new language will organize content into singular, dual, and plural (here meaning "three or more"). Or perhaps the new language will not give routine consideration to the matter. English speakers can never make a statement without saying something about the number of every object mentioned. This is compulsory, whether it is relevant or not. In Chinese, objects are noted as singular or plural only when the speaker judges the information to be relevant. The Chinese experience suggests that it actually seldom is, for that language operates with only occasional references to number.[1]

3

Uniform standards for admission to college are impossible in the United States for a number of reasons. Even the degree of uniformity existing among the colleges that used the College Entrance Examination system of fifty years ago cannot be reestablished. High school people naturally resist any attempt on the part of college admission officers to prescribe the content of courses or even the pattern of courses. And it must be remembered that from some communities many boys and girls of only average academic ability are propelled by social pressures toward a four-year college. For better or worse, in many sections of the country this type of student must be given at least an opportunity to try college work. In some states practically the only requirement for admission to the state-supported institutions of higher learning is the possession of a high school diploma. Private colleges exist that have no higher requirements for admission and in which those with little preparation and only a modicum of ability can obtain a bachelor's degree. In a word, the idea is

[1] From *An Introduction to Descriptive Linguistics*, Revised Edition, by H. A. Gleason, Jr. Reprinted by permission of Holt, Rinehart and Winston, Inc.

completely illusory that the high school curriculum might be stiffened by agreement as to entrance requirements on the part of colleges and universities.[1]

4

Clay is an earthy or stony mineral consisting essentially of hydrous silicates of alumina, the result of years of "abuse" by nature. It is plastic when sufficiently pulverized and wetted, rigid when dry and vitreous when fired at a sufficiently high temperature. It is an enduring material that remains after sun, frost, rain, ice and snow have worn away the rocks of our mountains. It has been washed, bleached, and subjected to nature's violent heat, cold and chemical action until it cannot be reduced further. Hence, it is nature's own chemically inert material. But the results vary and there is more than one kind of clay. It is a tricky and temperamental material to process, as deposits may differ widely in chemical composition and physical characteristics.[2]

5

A native of the Nile, the Egyptian mouthbreeder is a translucent brown in color. The largest specimens are rarely over two and one-half inches in length. At breeding time the male scoops up the eggs and places them in a small indentation in the sand. As soon as the spawning is completed, the female scoops all the eggs into her mouth. For the next fifteen days she carries them about, going without food to avoid swallowing her future children. When the eggs hatch, the children are allowed to swim out of their mother's mouth, but at the first sign of danger, all of them rush back. This behavior continues until the children grow too large to fit in. The mouthbreeder is truly an exotic fish.

6

The value of biologists and engineers working together on basic biological research was demonstrated recently at the Max-

[1] From *The American High School Today* by James B. Conant, McGraw-Hill Book Company, Inc. Reprinted by permission of Conant Studies, Educational Testing Service, Princeton, New Jersey.

[2] Reprinted by permission of Holiday House, Inc. from *Homes: America's Building Business* by Pauline Arnold and Percival White. Copyright, 1960.

Planck-Institut in Tübingen, Germany. A team consisting of a zoologist, a physicist, an electrical engineer and a mathematician has spent several years studying a beetle's response to moving light patterns. When the experiments were analyzed from the engineering viewpoint, it appeared from the beetle's behavior that he could gather from his environment clues to his speed. The team was able electronically to mimic the beetle's ability, and an immediate application suggested itself. The researchers have designed a new ground-speed indicator for airplanes which works like the beetle's eye.[1]

7

Your school boards raise their own money by direct taxes, or at least the greater part of it. In England about 70 per cent of the expenditure of the local education authorities is met out of grants from the central government in London. There are advantages and disadvantages in this. It means that we do not have the enormous range in standards between rich areas and poor areas that you do. It means a much greater degree of standardization of conditions of employment among the teachers, and therefore of interchangeability between school and school and between area and area. But it also inevitably means a greater degree of uniformity imposed from the center. We think our system is decentralized, because it allows much more local freedom and variety than exist in the school systems of most Continental European countries. But there is no doubt that it is much more highly centralized than the American system.[2]

8

Most of Shakespeare's plays are more successful in their opening scenes. *Julius Caesar* begins with a scene of bustling horseplay and confusion and pageantry, all dear to Elizabethan audiences, which at the same time makes clear without delay, time, place, and principal characters. Notice how our attention is first directed

[1] From "New Science That Copies Life" by Ruth Sheldon Knowles, *Saturday Evening Post*, January 5–12, 1963. Reprinted by permission of the author.

[2] From "English and American Education" by Sir Geoffrey Crowther, *Atlantic Monthly*, April 1960.

to the common people, who are to have a decisive influence on the play, then to Caesar and Antony, and finally to Brutus and Cassius. The proud, sad isolation of Brutus is skillfully suggested at the moment of his first appearance. *Hamlet* has a masterly opening scene with the bitter cold night, the shivering sentries ready to start at the slightest sound, the dark shadow of the castle, and the sense of impending, supernatural disaster. The first scene of *Macbeth*, if well acted, holds the imagination of the audience spellbound and at the same time strikes the keynote of the play. *Othello* opens on a dark night in a deserted street with two men plotting in the shadows, thus giving at once an atmosphere of treachery. *Romeo and Juliet* opens with the sudden violence of a street brawl between the Capulets and the Montagues—a significant suggestion of a drama of quick passions.[1]

9

(The picaresque novel is) a chronicle, usually autobiographical, presenting the life story of a rascal of low degree engaged in menial tasks and making his living more through his wits than his industry. Episodic in nature, the picaresque novel is, in the usual sense of the term, structureless. It presents little more than a series of thrilling incidents impossible to conceive as happening in one life. The *picaro*, or central figure, through the nature of his various pranks and predicaments and by virtue of his associations with people of varying degree, affords the author an opportunity for satire on the social classes. Romantic in the sense of being a story of adventure, the picaresque novel nevertheless is strongly marked by realistic methods in its faithfulness to petty detail, its utter frankness of expression, and its drawing of incidents from low life.[2]

10

Luck is sometimes the deciding factor in a game. In the eighth inning of the deciding game of the World Series of 1924, the Giants were leading the Senators by the fairly comfortable mar-

[1] From *Enjoyment of Literature* by Ralph P. Boas and Edwin Smith. Reprinted by permission of Harcourt, Brace & World, Inc.

[2] From *A Handbook to Literature* by William Flint Thrall and Addison Hibbard, revised and enlarged by C. Hugh Holman. © 1960 by The Odyssey Press, Inc. Reprinted by permission of the publisher.

gin of 3–1. A hard-hit ground ball struck a pebble, bounded over the head of third-baseman Fred Lindstrom, and two runs came in, tying up the game. The contest went into extra innings. In the last of the twelfth, the Giant catcher, about to dash for a pop fly behind the plate, caught his foot in his mask and, to free himself, missed an easy out. The batter, given another chance, then doubled. The next man up hit another grounder toward third base. The ball again struck a pebble, soared over the third baseman, and the game and series were won by the Senators.

● EXERCISE 4. Choose one topic sentence from the list below and, using the method (or methods) of development you think best suited, develop it into an interesting paragraph of about 150 words. State by which method you developed it.

1. Part-time jobs have given me valuable experience.
2. What is a gentleman?
3. Some improvements should be made in our cafeteria.
4. The eye (hand) is a remarkable organ.
5. A slip of the tongue may be embarrassing.
6. Seniors should (should not) be allowed to sit in cars in the parking lot during lunch period.
7. The day was full of surprises.
8. I enjoy traveling by plane.
9. What does it mean to be well groomed?
10. In fishing, equipment is important.
11. Our football coach and our basketball coach are different in personality and methods.
12. Some parental restrictions do more harm than good.
13. First impressions of people are often proved wrong.
14. Teen-agers are conformists.
15. In basketball, skill is more important than strength.

Adequate Development of the Topic Sentence

Since a paragraph is the development of an idea, it must give enough details to make the idea clear and convincing. A common fault in one-paragraph compositions, such as you are writing in your study of this chapter, is the failure to provide enough information. Although there can be no strict rule as to paragraph length, a one-paragraph composition of only two sentences or of less than 100 words is likely to be thin. Because most students have difficulty in developing rather than in limiting their paragraphs, it is hardly necessary to set a maximum number of words; but if you find your paragraph running above 300 words, you are taking the risk of destroying its unity. Long paragraphs are likely, in other words, to contain details not closely related to the topic sentence.

21e. In developing a paragraph, supply enough information to insure adequate development. Avoid the thinness which results from merely repeating in different words the idea in the topic sentence.

PARAGRAPH LACKING SUFFICIENT DEVELOPMENT

Every student should engage in some extracurricular activity. A student needs experience in such an activity if he is to succeed in life. If you include athletics, there are enough activities to provide everyone with something to do in addition to his regular schoolwork. No boy or girl should leave school every day when the final bell rings and have no definite interest to follow in the after-school hours. Everyone can benefit educationally and socially by extracurricular work. No one should think of school as solely a matter of subjects to study and classes to attend.

ADEQUATELY DEVELOPED PARAGRAPH

Every student should engage in some extracurricular activity because from extracurricular work you learn a great many valuable things that you won't learn in a classroom. School is not just a matter of learning the difference between *lie* and *lay*, or what caused the War Between the States; it is learning to live and work with others. You learn to work and play with others harmoniously, to give and take, win and lose. When, as a member of a club, you are given a job to do, you learn to assume responsibility and to work un-selfishly for the good of the group. In a radio club or a photography club you get additional knowledge which may be more valuable in the long run than the knowledge you get from doing homework or attending classes. Furthermore, if you work hard in dramatics or in musical organizations you will develop talents which will be satisfying to you all your life, talents which might never have been discovered had you thought of school as confined to the hours of the daily schedule. Finally, extracurricular activities broaden your circle of acquaintants. No amount of ordinary schoolwork can take the place of friends acquired in the informal familiarity of activities.

UNITY IN THE PARAGRAPH

21f. A paragraph should be unified. Unity is achieved by discussing only one topic in a paragraph, the topic stated in the topic sentence.

● EXERCISE 5. The unity of the paragraphs which follow has been weakened by inclusion of ideas not closely related to the topic of the paragraph. The topic sentences are in bold type. Point out which sentences in each paragraph should be omitted because they do not deal with the topic.

1

Most boys do not like girls who use too much make-up and overdecorate themselves with costume jewelry and flashy clothes. Boys are self-conscious. They don't want the girl they take on a date to attract excessive attention. If a girl is pretty, she shouldn't hide her good looks under layers of make-up. If she needs a little make-up, she should apply it carefully and sparingly. Make-up should not call attention to itself. Some girls are always combing their hair in public. Inexpensive costume jewelry, like make-up, is all right if it is kept to a minimum. Since a girl's taste is reflected in what she wears, heavy necklaces and bracelets shining and jangling on her wrists suggest that she is trying to show off, which is bad taste. Neatness and fit in clothes are much better than gaudy colors.

2

Sometimes a family argument is caused not by selfishness but by the desire to please the rest of the family. On Saturday, after the four of us had spent the morning downtown shopping, Dad asked my sister and me where we would like to go for lunch. I know that Jane loves Chinese food, and so I suggested the China Inn. Jane knows I love Italian food. She suggested an Italian restaurant. We argued back and forth, both denying our true taste in food, both accusing the other of not being sincere. We had just about reached the name-calling stage when Dad asked Mother to settle the argument. Knowing Dad likes Stan's Barbecue, Mother said we'd eat there. Dad knew why she said it and started to argue with her, but he soon gave in. Dad, at least, was happy about the choice, and we were all pleased because he was. Not all our family quarrels are unselfish. On another day this argument might have been entirely selfish with everybody fighting for his own favorite restaurant.

3

From the standpoint of suitability and adaptability, English has thoroughly proven itself as a world language. It is precise and concise for commercial use, at the same time that it is capable of infinite distinction of shades of meaning for literary purposes. Its vocabulary is not only the most abundant in the world, but also the most international of all existing major national languages—more international, in fact, than that of Esperanto. Its speakers are more numerous than those of any other tongue save Chinese, and widely and strategically distributed over the earth's surface. French was once considered the language of diplomacy. English is *par excellence* the language of science and technological progress. Its popularity among non-English speakers is such that if it came to a vote today it would undoubtedly gather more second-choice votes than any other national language.[1]

[1] From *The Story of English* by Mario Pei. Copyright 1952, by Mario Pei. Published by J. B. Lippincott Company.

4

A dishonest newspaper may warp the day's news either by hiding a story or by slanting headlines. A paper with a strong political bias may hide a story favorable to the opposing party by placing it in an inconspicuous position. On the other hand, it may give large headlines and a front-page position to news favorable to its own party. Although newspapers do not change the facts in the stories which come to them, they may, if it serves their political purpose, change the total effect of a story by giving it a headline which is deliberately misleading or slanted. Headlines are written by men highly skilled in their jobs. Once the drudges of the newspaper office, these men in recent years have been accorded greater respect as reflected in easier hours and higher pay. A headline may be made misleading simply by means of the kinds of words used. MAYOR JONES REPLIES TO CRITICS gives a quite different impression from MAYOR JONES CRACKS DOWN ON CRITICS.

5

The book-buying habits of the American people reflect the human desire to be "in the know." The woman who would rather stay at home than go out in last year's hat will also rather read, or have read, the latest popular book, regardless of its quality, than a better book published a year ago. She wants to impress others with the fact that she is up to date in her reading. The weekly publication of best-seller lists stems from this desire, as does the widespread membership in such organizations as the Book-of-the-Month Club and the Literary Guild. Lending-library employees are always being rushed by avid seekers of the latest novel, who wish to be the first to spring it at the next tea party. Lending libraries can now be found in drug and stationery stores as well as in bookstores. Of course, the demand for twenty-five cent books, which are not current best sellers, is attributable to another human characteristic, the desire for a bargain.

● EXERCISE 6.   Select one of the following topic sentences and develop it into a paragraph of approximately 150 words. Insure adequate development of the topic by (1) gathering enough ideas, (2) avoiding commonplace ideas, and (3) resisting the tendency to restate the topic sentence again and again in different words. Insure unity by including only ideas which support the topic sentence.

1. Our school's athletic program puts too much (too little) emphasis on the varsity team.
2. I believe in conservatism (liberalism) in politics.
3. A good novel has three important qualities.
4. A person's little mannerisms may alienate others.
5. Education goes on outside as well as inside school.
6. Judged by any standard, —— is an excellent team sport.
7. Three qualities characterize the good citizen.
8. Parents should spend more time with their children.
9. For several reasons I have chosen —— as my life work.

COHERENCE IN THE PARAGRAPH

Arrangement of Details

A paragraph is coherent when its sentences are logically and clearly related to one another and their total effect is the clear development of the paragraph topic. One way of achieving coherence is by arranging the details in a paragraph in a clear and logical order.

21g. To insure that the details in a paragraph will follow one another logically and smoothly, arrange them in order according to some definite plan.

Four plans, or orders, for the arrangement of the details in a paragraph are *chronological order, spatial order, the order of importance,* and *the order required to bring out a comparison or contrast.*

(1) The details in a paragraph may be arranged in *chronological* order.

Chronological order, the order of time, is followed in two kinds of paragraphs. It is followed in the *narrative* paragraph, in which events are given in the order in which they happened; and it is followed in the *expository* paragraph, in which a *process* is described from beginning to end. The paragraph on page 318 about the Englishman in the French restaurant will serve as an illustration of the time order in a narrative paragraph. The following paragraph illustrates chronological order used in explaining a process.

All the products of erosion which reach the coast finally settle down on the sea floor, but rivers also deposit in their beds a great deal of the material they bring down from the mountains. What usually happens **first** is that frost and rain conspire to wash in the sides and form a valley, and the vast bulk of rock disintegrated by these agents is carried away as mud, sand, and pebbles by the stream at the bottom. **As the valley gets older,** it grows wider and may **presently** be so wide in its lower reaches as to have a virtually level bottom, over which the river slowly winds toward the sea. The river has **now** lost speed, and begins to distribute its mud and sand over its widened valley floor. **Once a river begins** to flow in a curve, a cycle of events is started which results in a steady and systematic covering of the whole valley floor with sediment. The water naturally moves most rapidly round the outside of the curve, where its increased speed causes it to remove a quantity of mud from its bank. It may actually scoop out a little cliff for itself. But on the inside of the curve the water is moving extra slowly, and because mud settles down in still water it is here that some of the mud it is already carrying is deposited. **As the river goes on** scooping out mud from one bank and depositing it on the other, so it moves sideways across its valley, leaving a carpet of alluvium in its trail.[1]

(2) The details in a paragraph may be arranged in *spatial* **order.**

Spatial order, the order of position in space, is frequently followed in descriptive writing. A word picture is clear and

[1] Adapted from *Science Marches On* by Walter Shepherd. Reprinted by permission of Harcourt, Brace & World, Inc.

coherent when the writer shows exactly where the various items in the picture are located. Usually he does this by setting up and following a logical plan which takes him smoothly and naturally from one part of the scene to another. He also may make effective use of such expressions as "in the foreground," "to the left," "in the distance," etc. It is not necessary to describe methodically from left to right or top to bottom as though "panning" a scene with a moving picture camera. Such slavish adherence to spatial order may produce an artificial style. But it is advisable to follow some plan which will make clear in an orderly fashion exactly how the parts of the picture are related spatially.

In describing the Van Tassel farmhouse, Washington Irving follows a clear plan. He first gives a general impression of the house as an approaching visitor would see it. The porch or piazza is logically next, then the hall, or living room, and through the door beyond, a view of the parlor. Notice the frequent use of expressions which give the location of the things described. Irving's attention to spatial order makes his paragraph coherent and therefore easier to follow.

It was one of those spacious farmhouses with high-ridged but low-sloping roofs, built in the style handed down from the first Dutch settlers, the low projecting eaves forming a piazza **along the front** capable of being closed up in bad weather. **Under this** were hung flails, harness, various utensils of husbandry, and nets for fishing in the neighboring river. Benches were built **along the sides** for summer use, and a great spinningwheel **at one end** and a churn **at the other** showed the various uses to which this important porch might be devoted. From this piazza the wondering Ichabod entered the hall, which formed the center of the mansion and the place of usual residence. Here rows of resplendent pewter, **ranged on a long dresser,** dazzled his eyes. **In one corner** stood a huge bag of wool ready to be spun; **in another** a quantity of linsey-woolsey just from the loom; ears of Indian corn and strings of dried apples and peaches hung in gay festoons **along the walls,** mingled with the gaud of red peppers; and **a door left ajar gave him a peep into the best parlor,** where the clawfooted chairs and dark mahogany tables shone like mirrors; andirons, with their accompanying shovel and tongs, glistened from their covert of asparagus tops; mock-oranges and conch-shells decorated **the mantelpiece;** strings of various-colored birds' eggs were suspended **above it;** a great ostrich egg was hung from **the center of the room,** and a corner cupboard, knowingly left open, displayed immense treasures of old silver and well-mended china.[1]

(3) The details in a paragraph may be arranged in the order of importance.

Order of importance usually means proceeding from the least important to the most important. This order may be profitably followed in any paragraph which presents evidence in support of an opinion or an argument. For instance, in the following example, the author, after stating her preference for a coeducational college, gives three reasons for her opinion. You will note that the reasons are given in the order of importance, the least important coming first, the most important last.

In spite of the many arguments offered by those who favor women's colleges, I have decided to go to a coeducational school. There are three main reasons for my decision. The **first,** and admittedly the **least important** consideration, is that I think I will have more fun at a coeducational college. I have always enjoyed mixed company more than "hen parties," and I'm afraid that I'd be bored in the company of girls four or five days a week for four years. **Also,** I think that we ought to have the male viewpoint in our classes. It's one thing to read what men say and what their attitudes are toward a subject, but it's quite another to hear it firsthand. In high school the boys often contribute the most original ideas to our

[1] From "The Legend of Sleepy Hollow" by Washington Irving.

class discussions. Mixed classes are more interesting and more enlightening. **Finally,** education is supposed to be a preparation for life. How can you prepare for life in a world where both sexes are constantly together, by living largely in a woman's world all through college?

(4) The details in a paragraph may be arranged to bring out a *comparison* or a *contrast*.

Occasionally a writer wishes to use a paragraph to compare or contrast two things or ideas. Naturally he will arrange his details in such a way as to bring out clearly the nature of the comparison or contrast.

In bringing out a comparison or a contrast, a writer may follow one of two arrangements: (1) details supporting one point of view may be presented first, followed by details supporting the opposite point of view; (2) details of similarity or difference may be compared or contrasted one by one, rather than being grouped into two complete parts as in the first method. These two arrangements are illustrated by the following paragraphs. In the first paragraph, one point of view is presented first, followed by the other. In the second, the differences are contrasted in pairs.

There are many advantages and some disadvantages involved in working part-time while you are in school. — topic sentence On the one hand, part-time work can offer you an interesting experience that contributes to your education. It helps you to be more independent of your family. For advantages many students, a job provides needed spending money and helps cover many of the hidden costs of a high school education. Thus part-time work helps many students to remain in school. The experience that you gain through part-time work may be of great help to you in making a decision as to the type of occupational career you would like to follow. On the other hand, you may gain temporary advantages at the expense of values that are more important from the long-range point of view. For example, you may lose time needed for sleep, rest, study, club activities, and play. As a result, you may find it hard to adjust to what the school expects from you as well as to what your employer has a right to expect. It is obvious that, if you work five hours a day in school and five or six hours a day on the job, you are carrying too much of a load. Work experience is most desirable—but you have to strike a balance between school and the job.[1]

disadvantages

concluding sentence

The difference between democracy and communism in practice is clearly shown by the differences between the United States and Russia. In the United States the people are supreme, and the government is their servant. In Russia, the government is supreme, and the people are its servants. The United

topic sentence

contrast 1

[1] From *Points for Decision* by Harold J. Mahoney and T. L. Engle. Reprinted by permission of Harcourt, Brace & World, Inc.

States Constitution guarantees to American citizens the right to choose their leaders. The two-party system insures them a choice. Control of the government in Russia rests in the hands of a small group of leaders. Voting is a farce because there is only one party—the Communist party, and any citizen who dares to oppose the ruling group receives harsh treatment. ⎱ — contrast 2

In America the government guarantees the people complete freedom to worship as they please, but in Russia the leaders discourage religion and religious worship ⎱ — contrast 3

Freedom of speech in America gives everyone the privilege of saying exactly what he thinks, even to the point of criticizing his government. Freedom of ⎱ — contrast 4

speech does not exist in Russia. The people, living in constant fear of their government, are afraid to express any views contrary to those of the party.

● EXERCISE 7. Each of the following items suggests a comparison or contrast that can be developed into an interesting paragraph. Select one and fashion a topic sentence stating your point. Using one of the two methods of arranging material in a paragraph of this kind, write a paragraph of about 150 words which will bring out clearly the point in the topic sentence. You will be developing a paragraph by means of comparison or contrast.

1. A novel or book of short stories (your preference and why)
2. Two families of neighbors or two neighbors

3. A school you formerly attended and the one you attend now
4. Marc Antony and Brutus
5. Power boating and sailing
6. The book version of a novel and the movie or TV version
7. Two kinds of fishing
8. Romantic and realistic views of life
9. Trail riding and show riding
10. A good loser and a bad loser
11. Liberal and conservative
12. Democrat and Republican

Linking Expressions and Connectives [1]

21h. Strengthen the coherence of a paragraph by using linking expressions and connectives which help the reader to follow the line of thought from one idea to the next.

The linking expressions are usually pronouns which refer to words or ideas in the preceding sentences. They serve to carry the reader back to what has just been said. The pronouns commonly used in this way are *he, they, this, that, these, those, them, it*. When they are used as adjectives, the words *this, that, these,* and *those* serve as linking expressions just as well as when they are used as pronouns.

(1) Keep the thought of a paragraph flowing smoothly from sentence to sentence by using pronouns which refer to words or ideas in preceding sentences.

One final effect of radio and TV on the language must be noted. There is no doubt that **these** great media of information have cut down considerably the time that used to be devoted to reading, both of newspapers and of books. **This** means

[1] Methods of making smooth transitions from one paragraph to another are described on pages 355–59 in the chapter on "The Whole Composition."

21h

in turn that while radio and TV may enhance the spoken language (if indeed they do) they also tend to make of us a nation of functional illiterates, absorbing our language through the ear rather than the eye. Some may view **this** as a return of language to its original form and function; others may consider it a reversal, pure and simple, to the semi-literate Middle Ages.[1]

(2) Keep the thought of a paragraph flowing smoothly from sentence to sentence by the use of connectives.

The second kind of transitional device is the word or expression which *connects* what has preceded with what is to follow. Devices of this kind may be referred to simply as *connectives*. Judicious use of connectives makes writing coherent, but you must not overuse them, for too many will make your writing artificial and cumbersome.

Study the following list of common connectives. Notice that some express spatial relationship (*above*, *beyond*); some express chronological order (*first*, *finally*); and others indicate a logical relationship of ideas (*accordingly*, *on the contrary*). With a few exceptions, connectives are equally useful in all kinds of discourse: description, narration, exposition, argument.[2]

CONNECTIVES

above	at last	finally
accordingly	at the same time	first
across from	before me	for example
adjacent to	below me	for instance
again	beside me	further
also	besides	furthermore
although	beyond	hence
another	consequently	here
as a result	equally important	if this be true

[1] From *The Story of English*, by Mario Pei. J. B. Lippincott. Reprinted by permission.

[2] For work on the careful selection of the proper connective, see pages 207–09, 211–13.

in addition	next to	such
in fact	on my left	then
in short	on my right	then too
in the distance	on the contrary	therefore
likewise	on the other hand	thus
moreover	opposite to	to sum up
nearby	otherwise	to the left
nevertheless	second	to the right
next	similarly	whereas

● EXERCISE 8. Select one of the following topics and write a paragraph of approximately 150 words. Begin with your topic sentence. Then develop it, paying special attention to such matters as having enough details to develop the idea adequately, sticking to the subject, following a definite arrangement, and using pronouns and connectives to keep the thought running smoothly.

1. An educational TV program
2. Overcoming a personal handicap
3. Characteristics of high school students' speech
4. Housewife and/or career woman
5. Privileges and responsibilities
6. Some decisions a senior must make
7. The lot of an understudy
8. A good friend and a bad friend
9. A Shakespearean clown
10. Causes of family quarrels
11. Comparison of two sonnets (Shakespeare's 18 and 55, for example)
12. Criticisms of this school
13. Pictorial art and abstract art
14. Regional differences in the United States
15. The meaning of sportsmanship
16. Ways to entertain children
17. A good citizen
18. The theme of Shaw's *Pygmalion* (*Our Town*, *Macbeth*, etc.)
19. Irony in *Macbeth* (or another work)
20. A great man

Expository Writing

The Whole Composition

The literal meaning of *compose* is "to form by *putting together*." A composition is a piece of writing formed by putting together the ideas you have on a subject. This suggests two important points about writing a composition. The first is that you must have some ideas on the subject about which you are going to write. The second is that you must be able to put these ideas together in such a way that they will form an effective whole. In your study of Chapter 21, you had a good deal of practice in composing paragraphs. In this and the chapters immediately following, you will gain practice in writing longer compositions.

The emphasis will be on expository writing. In general, the purpose of expository writing is not primarily to amuse or entertain (although it may do both), but to enlighten and instruct. Its essential quality is clearness. Most of the writing you are required to do in school—tests, reports, essays—is expository, and most of the writing you will do after you leave school will be of this kind.

No matter what you are writing about, the basic steps involved in writing are almost always the same. They should become so familiar that you will follow them habitually whenever you write.

PLANNING THE COMPOSITION

The steps in writing a composition fall into two main stages: planning and writing. Planning includes the first three steps: selecting and limiting the subject, assembling materials, and organizing (outlining).

Selecting and Limiting the Subject

22a. Select a subject that can be adequately treated within the limits of your composition.

Unless your teacher specifies what you are to write about, your first problem is the choice of a subject. Of course, you will choose one in which you are interested. You will choose one, too, on which you either have or can find enough information to make a worth-while composition. You should know before you select your subject how long your composition is going to be. On this basis you must limit your subject so that you will be able to cover it adequately in the space at your disposal. Study the following examples of how a subject may be limited for treatment in compositions of different length.

NOT LIMITED	Politics
SLIGHTLY LIMITED	American Politics Today
MORE LIMITED	How a Political Party Functions
FURTHER LIMITATIONS	The Work of a Ward Politician
	The Most Important Issue in the Campaign
	How I Helped My Party

Limiting your subject must always be done with reference to your purpose. The purpose of your composition, in fact, determines its scope. Your teacher may ask you to precede your composition with a statement of your purpose, or, at least, to state the purpose in the introductory paragraph. In any event, for your own benefit you will do well to write the

22a

purpose in a one-sentence statement so that you will be able to keep it clearly before you as you plan and write. "My purpose in this composition is to explain my objections to some TV commercials."

Assembling Materials

22b. List all the ideas you may wish to use in your composition.

Some compositions can be written "out of your head" without recourse to the library or to the opinions of others. Many compositions, however, will send you on a hunt for information.[1] In both instances Step 2 is the same. It is the listing of the ideas you think you can use in your paper. In this step, it does not matter in what order you list the ideas; the important thing is to get them down where you can look at them, evaluate them, and arrange them.

In order to illustrate the steps in planning and writing a composition, the next few pages are devoted to showing you, through a specific example, how the steps should be followed.

Imagine that you have been asked to write as a composition assignment a critical essay on some aspect of modern living. You have decided to write about TV commercials. For a long time, the common commercials have bothered you, and so you will use this writing assignment to state why. Writing your criticisms is the best way to clarify them. Since the materials for this composition are your own, you begin by searching your mind for them. You do not need to go to the library or to consult other people. You begin Step 2 by making a list of things you might include in your essay.

[1] For detailed discussion of writing a long research paper, see Chapter 25.

When you have jotted down your ideas in the order and form in which they occur to you, you will end up with a list like the following:

necessity for

interrupt programs too often

irritating ads

too much repetition

singing commercials

romantic touch

he-man approach

cure-all medicines

my favorite TV programs

meaningless terms

tiresome slogans

meaningless testimonials

insulting ads

dangerous ads

15-second ads *

misleading

false impressions of life

no commercials in some other countries *

some good commercials *

emphasize luxuries

no reasons given why product is best

dramatic *

banks and finance companies

cigarettes

detergents

cosmetics

pretty girls and handsome men

keeping up with the Joneses

false scientific *

magazine ads *

applies to radio, too *

children (box tops, etc.) *

pressures on Mother *

After the list has been completed, you should go over it carefully and remove any items that, on second thought, seem unrelated to the subject, or that, if included, would make the composition too long. For example, in going over this list, you decide to eliminate certain items (marked by an asterisk). The total absence of TV advertising in some other countries does not seem essential to a composition about American television. There seems little point in singling out the 15-second commercial or the commercials on children's programs because they have the same characteristics as all the others. To discuss the good commercials would lead away from your subject. Proceeding in this way, you reduce your list until you think it is manageable. You next perform the all-important step of organizing the ideas—putting them together according to a plan.

22b

Organizing Materials—Outlining

22c. Group related ideas together. Arrange the groups in a logical order. Make an outline.

As you group the related ideas, you are really making an outline. In making an outline, you must make major decisions concerning the content and the organization of your composition. It is no exaggeration to say that more than half the work on a composition has been done when the outline has been completed.

The Topic Outline

Two kinds of outline are in common use: the topic outline and the sentence outline. In a topic outline each item is merely a topic to be discussed in the paper; it is not a sentence. For most of the outlining that you will do, the topic outline will be adequate; in fact, it will be preferable because it is easier to make and is clear enough to serve its purpose. The following outline of the first part of the essay on TV commercials is of this kind.

  I. Necessary
     A. To pay for broadcasts
     B. To sell sponsor's products
 II. Irritating
     A. Repetitious
     B. Frequent

The Sentence Outline

There are some occasions, however, when you may prefer to use the sentence outline, which is always clearer because it gives in more detail the exact meaning of each topic. A sentence outline is the better kind if you are outlining for someone else who may not grasp the full meaning of the short headings in a topic outline. A comparison of the sentence outline below with the topic outline above will indicate the advantage of the sentence form.

I. Commercials are necessary.
    A. The sponsors pay for the broadcasts to sell their products.
    B. It is the commercials that sell the sponsors' products.

II. Commercials are irritating.
    A. The constant repetition is irritating.
    B. The too-frequent interruption of programs is irritating.

Outline Form

22d. Observe rules for form in making an outline.

(1) Place the title above the outline. It is not one of the numbered or lettered topics.

(2) The terms *Introduction*, *Body*, *Conclusion* should not be included in the outline. They are not topics to be discussed in the composition. They are merely organizational units in the author's mind as he plans.

(3) Use Roman numerals for the main topics. Subtopics are given letters and numbers as follows: capital letters, Arabic numerals, small letters, Arabic numerals in parentheses, small letters in parentheses.

CORRECT ARRANGEMENT OF NUMBERS AND LETTERS

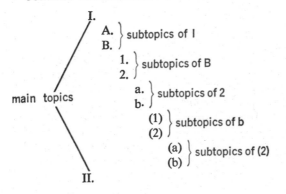

main topics

I.
  A. } subtopics of I
  B.
    1. } subtopics of B
    2.
      a. } subtopics of 2
      b.
        (1) } subtopics of b
        (2)
          (a) } subtopics of (2)
          (b)
II.

22
c-d

(4) Indent subtopics so that all letters or numbers of the same kind will come directly under one another in a vertical line.

(5) Begin each topic with a capital letter. Do not capitalize words other than the first in a topic or subtopic unless they are proper nouns or proper adjectives.

(6) In a topic outline do not follow topics with a period.

(7) There must never be, under any topic, a lone sub-topic; there must be either two or more subtopics or none at all. Subtopics are divisions of the topic above them. A topic cannot be divided into fewer than two parts.

(8) As a rule, main topics should be parallel in form, and subtopics under the same topic should be parallel in form. If in a list of topics, the first is a noun, the others should be nouns; if it is an adjective, the others should be adjectives, etc. Topics in the form of phrases should not be mixed with topics in the form of nouns or a noun and its modifiers. Subtopics need not be parallel with main topics.

The second half of the outline for the composition on television commercials is given below to show parallelism of topics.

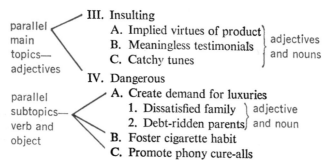

parallel
main
topics—
adjectives

III. Insulting
   A. Implied virtues of product ⎫
   B. Meaningless testimonials ⎬ adjectives and nouns
   C. Catchy tunes ⎭

IV. Dangerous

parallel
subtopics—
verb and
object

   A. Create demand for luxuries
      1. Dissatisfied family ⎫ adjective and noun
      2. Debt-ridden parents ⎭
   B. Foster cigarette habit
   C. Promote phony cure-alls

A violation of the parallelism of topics is illustrated by the following part of the outline, incorrectly phrased.

FAULTY PARALLELISM

    IV. Dangerous
        A. Create demand for luxuries [verb and object with modifying phrase]
            1. Dissatisfied family [adjective and noun]
            2. Parents in debt [noun and phrase]
        C. Promotion of phony cure-alls [noun and phrase]

(9) Do not mix the topic and sentence forms of outline.

MIXED FORMS

    IV. Dangerous [topic]
        A. Commercials create a demand for luxuries. [sentence]
            1. The family becomes dissatisfied without all the advertised products. [sentence]
            2. Debt-ridden parents [topic]
        B. Foster cigarette habit [topic]
        C. People are misled by phony cure-alls. [sentence]

(10) For each number or letter in an outline there must be a topic. Never place an *a*, for instance, next to *1* like this: *1a*.

The complete outline for the composition on TV Commercials is given below. Note that all ten points about correct outlining have been carefully observed. Note also the number of main topics. For a 500-word composition, you should not have more than five main topics. A minimum of three is a sound general rule but an outline with two main topics is sometimes acceptable.

Compare this outline with the original list of topics on page 347. You can see how the writer was able to group the desirable topics under four main topics. The changes in wording are necessary to make the outline clear and consistent in form.

TELEVISION COMMERCIALS

I. Necessary
   A. To pay for broadcasts
   B. To sell sponsor's products
II. Irritating
   A. Repetitious
   B. Frequent
III. Insulting
   A. Unexplained virtues of the product
   B. Meaningless testimonials
   C. Catchy tunes
IV. Dangerous
   A. Create demand for luxuries
      1. Dissatisfied families
      2. Debt-ridden parents
   B. Foster cigarette habit
   C. Promote phony cure-alls

● EXERCISE 1. Demonstrate that you understand the rules on pages 349–51 by correcting the following faulty outline. Make parallel the main topics and subtopics under the same main topic. Change sentences to topics, and be sure there are no isolated subtopics. Omit topics if necessary. Write the outline with proper alignment and number-letter designations.

HOW TO STUDY

I. The conditions for studying must be right.
   1. You should allow enough time
   2. Quiet Place
   3. Proper Equipment
      a. textbooks
      b. reference books
II. The Techniques
   A. Assignments that are mainly reading
      a. How to take notes
      b. Memorizing
   B. Writing Assignments
      1. Term papers
III. Conclusion

● EXERCISE 2.   Arrange the items in the following list in a correct topic outline. Begin by placing the title, which is included in the list, at the top of your paper. Then group related topics and find a main topic for each group. The topics are correctly phrased so that if properly grouped, they will be parallel. Finally, place and letter the subtopics correctly and copy the outline neatly in perfect arrangement.

counselor at summer camp
indoor work
from tips
summer jobs
heavy work
assures an outdoor life
making extra money

stock boy in a supermarket
requires an interest in children
waiter at a summer hotel
confines one to camp
from baby-sitting for guests
enjoying hotel's social life
close to home

WRITING THE COMPOSITION

If you have completed the planning stage carefully, many of the problems involved in the actual writing will already be solved. The writing stage begins with the composing of the first draft and includes all of the revisions necessary in achieving a satisfactory final draft.

The First Draft

22e. With the outline before you, write the first draft of your composition. Include an introduction and a conclusion. Pay careful attention to the division into paragraphs.

The Introduction

Before you present the first point in your composition, you will introduce the subject. Whether or not the introduction is a separate paragraph depends upon the length of the entire paper. In a composition of 500 words or more, you will probably devote the first paragraph to introducing the subject.

22e

(1) Write an introduction which will make clear the purpose of your composition and arouse the interest of the reader.

A good introductory paragraph should make clear the purpose of the composition. It may give facts that will explain the choice of subject, and it may give information necessary to the understanding of the subject. It should, if possible, arouse the interest of the reader so that he will want to read further. The following is the final form of the introductory paragraph in the composition on TV commercials.

> Spin filters are better because they spin the smoke. Micronite filters are best because they are Micronite. Instant coffee is now made in a new way that "locks the flavor in." Only Aloha Sealines Super-duper jets will fly you upside down to Hawaii! Thus the barrage of TV commercials continues day and night in almost every American home. I think most of the commercials are irritating or insulting or dangerous. I believe they can be improved so that they will be not only less offensive to the public but also more effective as advertisements.

Write your first draft rapidly. Do not worry unduly about details of punctuation and sentence structure. These can be taken care of later in your revision.

Paragraphing

(2) Paragraph a composition in such a way that the various phases of the subject will stand out clearly.

As you write the first draft, you must decide at what points new paragraphs should be started. By paragraphing you indicate to your reader the main divisions of your composition. By indention of the first line and by spacing, you set apart each paragraph as a unit developing a single aspect of your subject. Whenever you begin a paragraph, you notify the reader that you are taking up another phase of your subject. In a brief composition you may find it advisable to devote one paragraph to each of the major (Roman numeral) topics in your outline. For example, if you have three main topics, you will have three main paragraphs. Add to these an introductory paragraph and a concluding paragraph and you will have a five-paragraph composition. In the sample composition on pages 362–67, which is written from an outline with four major topics, there are eight paragraphs. Two of these are the introductory paragraph and the concluding paragraph. The six others are necessary because two of the four major topics require two paragraphs each for proper development.

In a longer paper, a research paper, for instance, you cannot follow a simple formula for paragraphing; indeed, you may wish to devote several paragraphs to a subtopic.

(3) Avoid the overlong and the very short paragraph.

When paragraphing your writing, bear in mind the fact that your reader will be able to follow you more easily if your paragraphs are not too long. Paragraphs of 300 words are probably too long for high school writers to handle effectively. On the other hand, a number of paragraphs of less than 100 words may indicate poor planning. Such paragraphs show that the writer is not taking time to support his topic sentence, and they give the composition a broken-up appearance which is confusing because it does not emphasize the major ideas.

Transitions Between Paragraphs

(4) Make the transition between paragraphs clear and smooth by using a transitional device at the beginning of a paragraph.

Because the beginning of a paragraph signifies a shift to another phase of your subject, you should make your train of thought clear to the reader by showing the relationship between this new phase and the phase discussed in the preceding paragraph. There are several devices for accomplishing this transition between paragraphs. These devices help to keep the thought flowing smoothly from paragraph to paragraph in the same way that linking words and connectives (see the section beginning on page 341) keep the thought flowing from sentence to sentence.

Some frequently used transitional devices are explained and illustrated on the following pages.

Pronouns as transitional devices

A pronoun that refers to a person or an idea mentioned in the preceding paragraph often provides a smooth transition between paragraphs. The pronouns most commonly used in this way are *he, they, this, that, these, those, them, it.* The use of these words carries the reader back to their antecedents, helping him to bridge the gap between the two paragraphs. *This, that, these, those,* when used as adjectives, are employed in the same way.

> Yet if you *didn't* nose down during the approach, you could, with a small misjudgment of your gliding angle, arrive over the edge of the airport with 200 feet of altitude and "overshoot" the whole field! Or again, in trying to avoid these errors, you could fall into their opposites: instead of overshooting, you could "undershoot"; instead of floating you might "pancake."
>
> All *this* is now wiped out. With the new gear, you can slobber it on anyhow, it makes no difference: there is no bounce. The moment the wheels touch the ground, the airplane assumes a level, no-lift attitude and clings to the ground.[1] [The pronoun *this* in the sentence *All this is now wiped out* accomplishes the transition between paragraphs.]

Each of the following sentences is the opening sentence of a paragraph. Note how the word in bold-faced type (a

[1] From "The Revolution in Small Plane Flying" by Wolfgang Langewiesche, *Harper's Magazine*, August 1960.

pronoun or an adjective) reflects something in the preceding paragraph.

And **that's** still not all.

What is **this** new formula?

A day or so later, **they** began to notice that a number of rather valuable objects were missing.

And just at **that** instant there arose from the bowels of the earth a light not of this world, the light of many suns in one.

You will understand **this** better, perhaps, if I give you some familiar examples.

Some of **these** feelings may lead to practical follies, but that is not the point.

Repetition of a key word

By repeating in the first sentence of a paragraph a key word used in the preceding paragraph, you help the reader over the gap between paragraphs.

1

For what does the ordinary man strive if not for a wife, a home, children, permanence of tenure and affection under one roof? And if these prove to be but an illusion, if the husband becomes an alimony payer, the father a stranger to his children, the seeker for permanency a wanderer, is not ours a matrimonial **anarchy**?

Why should such **anarchy** prevail? There is no easy answer to this question.[1]   [The repetition of the word *anarchy* carries the thought across the gap between paragraphs.]

2

. . . They are still wrestling with the limitations and ambiguities of mathematics, but they have been able to pin down with a fair degree of certainty what their **uncertainties** are.

One of the most basic of the **uncertainties** was introduced by Einstein's theory of relativity.

[1] From "Moonlight and Poison Ivy" by David L. Cohn, *Atlantic Monthly*, January 1949. Reprinted by permission of Mrs. David L. Cohn.

Direct reference

A preceding idea may be referred to directly, often in summary form.

1

. . . This congressional committee literally worked itself out of existence by accomplishing efficiently the job for which it had been appointed.

How the **committee accomplished its job so efficiently** makes an interesting story. . . .

2

. . . Today a computer, sorting checks and printing figures faster than the eye can follow, can handle a whole day's work for one of the bank's thirty branches in fifteen minutes.

But the incredible efficiency of computers and their remorseless logic, based on pure mathematics, may be eliminating jobs as well as problems.

Connectives

Most of the connectives listed for use in linking sentences (see pages 342–43) may also serve as transitional expressions between paragraphs. The following connectives are commonly used in this way:

accordingly	for example	on the other hand
also	for instance	otherwise
another	furthermore	similarly
as a result	however	such
at last	in fact	then
consequently	moreover	therefore
finally	nevertheless	thus

1

. . . To the writer, writing is more than communication. It is the revelation, to oneself as writer, of things that have been hidden, now forced into expression.

On the other side, the side of the reader, it is the revelation of one person to another, a personal communication in an impersonal world.

2

...It predicts a population of 50 billions (the highest estimate of the population-carrying capacity of the globe ever calculated by a responsible scholar) in less than 200 years.

The United Nations estimates of future world population, **moreover,** indicate even further acceleration in the rate of world population growth during the remainder of this century.

● EXERCISE 3. Each of the following sentences is the opening sentence of a paragraph. Point out the device or devices used in each sentence to effect a transition from what had been discussed in the preceding paragraph.[1]

1. This, then, is the family of planets of which our world is a rather junior member.
2. As we have already mentioned, the atmosphere is both a help and a hindrance.
3. The atmosphere, however, does not come to an end at the level where balloons will rise no further.
4. This thin blanket of air, without which life as we know it would be impossible, is held tightly to the Earth by the force of gravity.
5. If we ever hope to build spaceships, therefore, we must bear in mind two fundamental points.

● EXERCISE 4. Examine a daily newspaper or a current magazine to find further examples of transitional devices used by professional writers. Copy onto your paper five paragraph openings which contain such devices. Underline the transitional expressions.

The Transitional Paragraph

Sometimes, especially in a long paper, you may wish to let your reader know that you have completed your discus-

[1] Sentences are from *Space and the Spirit of War* by Arthur C. Clarke. Reprinted from *Horizon*, A Magazine of the Arts, by permission of the author and the author's agents. Scott Meredith Literary Agency, Inc.

sion of one phase of the subject and are now about to take up another. A brief paragraph will easily accomplish this purpose. Such a paragraph is called a transitional paragraph.

1

So much, then, by way of proof that the method of establishing laws in science is exactly the same as that pursued in common life. Let us now turn to another matter (though really it is but another phase of the same question), and that is, the method by which, from the relations of certain phenomena, we prove that some stand in the position of causes toward the others.[1]

2

We must now return to Earth, which for a long time to come will be the starting point for all our voyages, and consider what obstacles we will have to overcome if we wish to leave it.[2]

3

Apart from these general differences, an outline of the British system reveals special ones which are potentially useful.[3]

The Conclusion

(5) Write a conclusion which will summarize or re-emphasize the major point of the composition.

A whole paragraph of summary or conclusion may not be necessary. But you should make an effort to remind the reader at the end of the composition what it is that you have

[1] From "The Method of Scientific Investigation" by Thomas Henry Huxley.

[2] From *The Exploration of Space* by Arthur Charles Clarke. Reprinted by permission of Harper & Row, Publishers, Incorporated.

[3] From "British and American Schools" by Derek Colville, *Harper's Magazine*, October 1957. Reprinted by permission of the author.

said. In a short paper one or two concluding sentences will usually be enough. Read on page 367 the concluding paragraph in the sample composition.

Revising the First Draft

22f. Read over the first draft. Eliminate or add ideas; change the order of ideas if advisable; revise sentences to improve their structure; check spelling and punctuation.

The revision of your first draft is extremely important. The student who lazily chooses to hand in this draft as a completed composition is doing himself a great injustice. Professional writers are thorough revisers. They are rarely satisfied with the first draft of their work. A student should not claim an ability which an experienced writer would never claim.

A study of the first draft may reveal faults in the original outline. Do not hesitate, in such a case, to change the outline. *No aspect of the composition should be considered unchangeable until the final draft has been completed.*

Revision Checklist

As you revise, ask yourself the following questions:
1. Have I made my purpose clear at the start?
2. Is the paragraphing correct? Does it reveal the major points in the composition? Is each paragraph unified and coherent? Are the paragraphs clearly related to one another by transitional devices?
3. Are the sentences varied in structure? Can more complex sentences be used?
4. Is the style wordy? What expressions can be eliminated?
5. Are all words spelled correctly?
6. Where is punctuation needed to make the meaning clear?

22f

Preparing the Final Draft

22g. When the revision has been completed, copy the composition neatly. If you can, typewrite this copy.

The final draft of the composition you have seen taking shape throughout this chapter is given below. Read it through, noting the general organization, the adherence to the outline (page 352), the paragraphing, the transitions, the introduction, and the conclusion.

TELEVISION COMMERCIALS

Spin filters are better because they spin the smoke. Micronite filters are best because they are Micronite. Instant coffee is now made in a new way that "locks the flavor in." Only Aloha Sealines Super-duper jets will fly you upside down to Hawaii! Thus the barrage of TV commercials continues day and night in almost every American home. I think most of the commercials are irritating or insulting or dangerous. I believe they can be improved so that they will be not only less offensive to the public but also more effective as advertisements.

introduction

statement of purpose

Even while I am registering my objections to <u>commercials</u>, I recognize that commercials are necessary. Without them we would have no television programs, for it is the sponsor who pays

transition—key word

the bill. Since the money which pays for a TV program comes from the sale of the sponsor's products, the sponsor must have air-time in which to advertise. Americans must put up with the hourly brainwashing, and they must buy the sponsor's products if they want to enjoy television. They should not, however, have to endure the kind of advertising that accompanies most of the programs.

(compare outline: I, A and B)

<u>This advertising</u> is objectionable, first, because it is irritating. The two sources of irritation are the endless repetition of the same commercial and the too frequent interruption of programs. I suppose that once an advertiser has a slogan that has proved effective, he is reluctant to give it up, but if he realized how meaningless the familiar words become after a thousand repetitions, maybe he would find that an occasional change would be effective. My parents say that some of the ads commonly heard today, like "a combination of medically proved and tested ingredients," were used in radio advertising in the thirties. The truth is that no one pays any attention to the worn-out slogans, and everyone is irritated rather than interested when the familiar lines begin.

transition—direct reference

(compare outline: II, A)

22g

I think, _too_, that advertisers lose more than they gain when they insist on interrupting a program every ten minutes to plug their wares. Irritation of the viewer-buyer is surely not the way to sell anything. Just as the bad guys are about to destroy the good guys—for the first time in television history—the picture stops, and you are taken into a sparkling kitchen to observe the wonders of a floor wax or a detergent or a hand lotion, wonders you have already heard proclaimed night after night. As you are poised deliciously on the brink of disaster in an adventure film or carried away by the immortal lines of Shakespeare, the illusion is shattered by the shouted advice that only by banking at National can you end up a millionaire. If sponsors would all agree to confine commercials to the beginning and the end of programs, the public's appreciation would be reflected in its buying. If they would realize how weary we get of the same old commercials, they might find an occasional change to be surprisingly effective.

<u>Another kind</u> of objectionable commercial is the kind that insults our mentality with its meaningless claims.

transitional word

(compare outline: II, B)

transitional expression

Analyze the claims made by many TV commercials, and you will find yourself asking, quite logically, "Well, so what?" We are never told why smoke that spins is less harmful than smoke that follows a straight path. Just how does Micronite improve a filter or Gardol a toothpaste? In our simple-minded way, we are expected to accept the word of a cowpuncher or a water skier as sure proof of the quality of a soft drink. Every Little Leaguer knows that the leading hitter in the American League has not really achieved his enviable record because of the breakfast food he eats. And Dad knows that not all family problems will be solved by his downing a couple of headache pills. Claims that are completely without reason are insulting to thinking people. The writers of commercials should give their viewers credit for some brains.

(compare outline: III, A, B)

Finally, TV commercials can be dangerous. They can endanger the finances of the American family. The goal of advertisers is to create a demand if none exists. You should have the latest dishwasher, the newest electric hair dryer, a second car, and such status symbols as a backyard swimming pool and a winter vacation. To listen to the

transitional word

(compare outline: IV, A, 1 and 2)

honeyed pleas of the handsome, sun-
tanned, obviously happy announcers,
you wonder how any of us can possibly
live another minute without all the
luxuries of a millionaire. But, then, the
solution is so easy. Just apply for a
personal loan—fast, courteous, no questions asked—and let the Easy Loan
Finance Company pay all your bills at
once. "We'll even write the checks."
This lure could be irresistible to a young
father trying to keep up with the standard of living fostered by the commercials his family watches every night as
they try to catch a program in between.

Commercials endanger our health as
well as our budgets. Cigarette advertisers say their ads are addressed only to
people who already smoke, but their
ads try to make a boy believe that if he
wants to win that beautiful girl in the
bikini suit, he had better smoke and had
better choose the right brand. The
hypochondriac must go crazy after a
day of television. He is presented with
a sure cure for every ailment. He can
fill his medicine cabinet until it is
bursting with cure-alls, fill his objecting
stomach with pills, and cover his body
with creams until he is either dead or
unrecognizable. Certainly the daily

transition-direct
reference

compare outline:
IV, B)

(compare outline:
IV, C)

bombardment leads many people into a way of living that is dangerous to both pocketbook and health.

I have tried to make a case for the TV commercial which appeals to the intelligence of its audience. I have tried to show that commercials should be improved so that they will arouse the approval instead of the antagonism of the viewer. I myself run to the refrigerator every time I feel a commercial coming, and as a result I am getting dangerously fat!

conclusion

SPECIFIC KINDS OF EXPOSITORY WRITING

The essential steps in preparing a composition apply to all kinds of writing with the possible exception of narration. You may find it helpful, however, to consider a few additional facts about expository writing. The planning of an expository composition is affected by the particular kind of exposition being planned. In general, there are three kinds: exposition that defines, exposition that informs, and exposition that explains. Often one composition contains all three kinds, but for the sake of practice, try your hand at writing some compositions each of which will be devoted primarily to a different one of the three kinds. Follow the suggestions on the next few pages.

Exposition that Defines

Planning a definition always involves two stages. First, you must place the subject, the term to be defined, in its general class. Second, you must differentiate it from other members of that class. This is the genus-species method familiar to you from your study of biology.

To make clear what a puffin is, a dictionary tells you first that it is a sea bird and then differentiates it from other sea birds by listing its distinguishing characteristics.

puf·fin \'pəf-ən\ *n* [ME *pophyn*] **:** any of several sea birds (genera *Fratercula* and *Lunda*) having a short neck and a deep grooved parti-colored laterally compressed bill

puffin

You follow this two-stage method also in defining an abstract term. Suppose, for example, that you wish to define *sportsmanship*. You must ask yourself first to what general class of things sportsmanship belongs. Is it an attitude, a belief, or a kind of conduct? If you should decide that it is an attitude, you must then show what kind of attitude it is by giving its differentiating characteristics, those which distinguish it from all other attitudes. In other words, in the general class *attitude*, sportsmanship has characteristics which make it unique, a particular kind of attitude. It could require a long composition to give these characteristics, which comprise the second stage in definition.

22h. Plan a definition in two stages: (1) classification; (2) differentiation.

Limited Definition

Limited definition is the kind represented by the definition of *puffin*. It is a dictionary-type definition—brief and readily usable in reading and writing. The ability to write a clear limited definition is important because vague or ambiguous words obscure meaning. One way to overcome the faults of vagueness and ambiguity is to define, whenever necessary, the important, or key, words you use so that your reader will get from them the meaning you want him to get. You may have been asked by your opponent in an argument to "define your terms." This is always a reasonable request, for you cannot communicate effectively unless both you and your listener or reader have the same meaning in mind.

● EXERCISE 5.   Select five of the words listed below and write a limited definition of each in two or three sentences. Decide the general class to which the subject belongs; then, giving more information, differentiate it from other members of the class. Try this first without a dictionary.

1. a mansion
2. a chapel
3. a bat
4. a dog
5. an optimist
6. grammar
7. a canoe
8. a dictionary
9. radar
10. golf

Extended Definition

A really meaningful definition of an abstract term like *happiness*, *liberty*, or *democracy* may require a much more extensive piece of writing than a limited, dictionary-type definition. Writing such an extended definition is a valuable exercise because it requires careful planning and thinking and always serves to clarify your own thoughts. Most of an extended definition consists of a statement or description of the specific characteristics that differentiate the term from others in its class. When you have defined *happiness* as a state of mind, you have merely taken the first step. You have placed the word in its general class. The second step, differentiation, may be extended indefinitely as you give the distinguishing characteristics of happiness, perhaps by telling how it can be achieved, what it is not, how it can be recognized, and what its effects are. This kind of defining is sometimes called "descriptive definition." An extended definition may be as long as a book, but you will find that a fully developed paragraph (150 words) is often adequate.

22h

● Exercise 6. Select one of the following words and write an extended definition of approximately 200 words. Your definition may be a very personal one if you wish. That is, it may quite deliberately give your own concept of the meaning of the word rather than a dictionary-type concept which must give the meaning most generally accepted. Whenever possible, try to use examples and incidents to make your meaning clear.

1. integrity
2. success
3. love
4. maturity
5. immaturity

6. wealth
7. wit
8. freedom
9. jealousy
10. charm

● Exercise 7. Define one of the following in a full-length composition—400–500 words.

1. a good student
2. a poor student
3. a natural leader
4. a snob
5. a competent teacher (mechanic, coach, etc.)

6. a natural athlete
7. a flirt
8. a gentleman
9. a novel
10. a poem

Exposition that Informs

A common purpose of expository writing is to inform. Essay questions on an examination, reports on library reading, accounts of experiments and other research usually call for informational writing. In planning an informational composition, you do two things. First, you analyze your subject; that is, you take a careful over-all look at it to see exactly what it consists of. As you analyze the subject, you will find that the information you have tends to break up into a number of fairly distinct parts or divisions. Your second step, then, is to determine these logical divisions of the subject. When listed in order, they constitute the main topics in your outline. When you have completed the two steps—analysis and division—you have arrived at your basic plan. This process is the same as Steps 2 and 3 of the essential steps in the preparation of a composition which you studied earlier.

22i. Plan an informational composition in two stages: (1) analyze the subject; (2) divide the subject into its logical parts or divisions.

To take a simple example of this analysis-division method, suppose that you are going to write an informational article on a place you used to live, perhaps on one of the states you lived in for several years. Keeping in mind that your purpose is to inform others about a state they may not be familiar with, you analyze the subject, asking yourself what facts the members of your audience should learn. You recognize certain indispensable items of information: location, size, population, geography, climate, natural resources. Following the dictates of your purpose and your readers' interests, you may add other facts: industries, educational facilities, sociological characteristics, highways, recreation areas, political character, etc. Your analysis thus yields a number of divisions. If you find you have too many divisions, you can reduce the number of main topics by combining some of them, relegating some divisions to the status of subtopics.

● EXERCISE 8. Select from the following list a subject upon which you can write an informational composition. Analyze the subject and divide it into a number of (4 or 5) logical divisions, or main topics. Write the composition in about 300–500 words.

1. The city in which you live
2. Your school's extracurricular program
3. A summer (winter) resort
4. A person you admire
5. A new type of car (plane, boat, rocket)
6. The new styles (clothing, hairdos, etc.)

22

7. An interesting animal
8. Facts about the moon (Mars, Venus, etc.)
9. An important event
10. A relatively unknown country (area of the world)

Exposition that Explains

While exposition that defines and exposition that informs are common enough, a more common kind of exposition is that which explains. It is not often, of course, that these three kinds of exposition occur in a pure form. Usually you will use all three within one piece of expository writing. Thus, although your primary purpose in a piece of writing may be to explain, you will find that in the course of the explanation, you must both define and inform.

Analysis and Division

In planning an explanatory composition, you follow the same steps you follow in planning an informative composition. You (1) analyze your subject and (2) divide it or break it down into a number of divisions.

For example, in planning an explanation of the work done by the Student Council in your school, you begin by analyzing the Council. Your analysis reveals that the work of the Council is done by a number of standing committees. This fact is a clue to a possible plan for your essay. By describing the responsibilities and activities of each committee, you can give a clear explanation of the Council's functions. These committees, then, become the divisions of your composition.

In one school the Student Council has the following committees: Student Citizenship Board, Student Court, Handbook Committee, Activities Committee, Assembly Committee, Orientation Committee, Social Committee, Budget Committee, Student-Faculty Relations Committee. A plan for a composition which would explain the Council's functions would have too many divisions if a separate section were devoted to each of these; therefore, the writer would probably combine some which are closely related, for instance, the Student Citizenship Board, which is primarily disciplinary, and the Student Court. Also, the Orientation and Social committees could be considered together since they are, at least in part, concerned with students' social adjustment and social activities.

Similarly, to explain how a jet engine works, you begin by analyzing the engine and dividing it into its important parts. Then, by explaining the functions of each part, you can cover the operation of the engine as a whole. Your plan, again, is achieved through analysis and division.

● EXERCISE 9.   Plan and write a composition (300–500 words) explaining one of the following:

1. How to drive (or any other appropriate activity)
2. Fundamental tactics in basketball (or any other sport)
3. A traffic plan to avoid tie-ups
4. The structure of a space ship
5. Why we are prejudiced (have prejudices)
6. Abstract art
7. A concert band (symphony, dance band, etc.)
8. Why an airplane flies
9. Why my allowance is insufficient
10. The influence of climate on our lives
11. Directing a play
12. Synthetic fabrics
13. Weather forecasting
14. The dangers of smoking
15. Causes of international dissension

Explanation of a Process

A common kind of explanatory essay is that which explains or describes a process. This type of composition requires a different kind of plan. Because a process is a chronological thing, you divide your explanation according to the steps in the process and explain them in the order in which they occur.

● EXERCISE 10. Choose one of the following topics and write a composition explaining the process in chronological order. Write 300–500 words.

1. How to develop photographs
2. How to make a dress
3. How to plant a new lawn
4. How to prepare a field for planting
5. How to train a dog
6. How to administer first aid
7. How to study
8. How to prepare a meal
9. How to redecorate a room
10. How to write a short story (poem, essay, etc.)

SUGGESTED TOPICS FOR COMPOSITION

Put into practice the techniques described in this chapter as you write compositions assigned to you. If you are not assigned a definite subject on which to write, the topics in the following list may provide suggestions. Many will require limiting if you are to treat them in a composition of two or three pages. Many can be handled either informally or formally, humorously or seriously.

The Arts

1. American music
2. A definition of jazz
3. What is folk music?
4. The charm of folk music
5. Good music on the radio
6. Adolescents' taste in popular music
7. Music and moods
8. The music of George Gershwin (any other composer)
9. A great musical work (work of art)
10. How to judge a painting
11. Abstract painting
12. A comparison of media (oil, water color, pastel, etc.)
13. The work of a commercial artist
14. Effective poster making
15. My favorite artist (composer, singer, poet, etc.)
16. Modern furniture design
17. How to refinish furniture
18. Principles of home decoration

19. The ceramic process
20. Modern home architecture
21. How to arrange flowers
22. What poetry (music, art, etc.) means to me
23. Ballet or modern dance?
24. Designing and building a stage set

Family and social life

1. Why families quarrel
2. Mistakes parents make
3. Discipline in the home
4. Teen-age marriage
5. Preserving the family as a unit
6. Television and family life
7. Should both parents work?
8. Living on a budget
9. On being the oldest (youngest)
10. On being an only child
11. Traveling with the family
12. Parents' prerogatives
13. Family customs
14. My family doesn't understand me
15. What I want in a husband (wife)
16. Dates without money
17. Good manners
18. Definition of a gentleman
19. Going steady
20. On following the crowd
21. It's hard to be yourself
22. How to plan a party
23. A good youth center
24. The teen-age rebel
25. The price of popularity

People

1. A person who has influenced me
2. Student types
3. A good teacher
4. Our doctor (minister, priest, etc.)
5. The school politician
6. A great sports figure
7. Our neighbors
8. My father (mother)
9. An old friend
10. A funny person
11. A handicapped person
12. A person prominent in recent news
13. A colorful character from history (fiction, drama, etc.)

Personal

1. Pressures that force conformity
2. Decisions I must make
3. A senior's worries
4. Traits I wish I didn't have
5. On being an outsider
6. On being average
7. Facing the truth about oneself
8. How to be unpopular
9. On being spoiled
10. Beliefs changed by experience
11. After-school jobs
12. Rules I could do without
13. My biggest mistake
14. My greatest success

15. Living up to or living down a reputation
16. The meaning of "well dressed"

School and education

1. Homework
2. Is the marking system fair?
3. College Board Examinations
4. What education ought to be
5. The extracurricular burden
6. Too many standardized tests
7. How to get a scholarship
8. Needed improvements in this school
9. Who should go to college?
10. Why we have drop-outs
11. Teaching as a career
12. The ideal teacher
13. Teachers' faults
14. Bookworm vs. playboy
15. Co-education or not?
16. How to choose a college
17. Large college vs. small college
18. Four-year college vs. junior college
19. Experiences with the Guidance Department
20. New educational techniques (devices)
21. Wasteful educational practices
22. Federal aid to education
23. Education and civil rights
24. Social classes in high school
25. Our student government

Social studies

1. America's image abroad
2. Democracy vs. communism
3. The importance of the U.N.
4. Problems of a new nation
5. A threat to international peace
6. Our dependence on other nations
7. If we had no Bill of Rights
8. A lesson from history
9. The importance of the minority
10. Propaganda techniques
11. States' rights
12. Socialized medicine
13. Care of the aged
14. Urban renewal
15. Facts about the population of this community
16. The geography of this community
17. Censorship
18. The importance of a free press
19. Cause and cure of juvenile delinquency
20. Should 18-year-olds vote?
21. How to vote intelligently
22. Characteristics of a good citizen
23. A significant news event of the past week

24. Government support of farm prices
25. On second-class citizens
26. Coping with the effects of automation
27. Why such heavy defense spending?

Science

1. A recent conservation project
2. Prevention of soil erosion
3. Science aids the hunter and fisherman.
4. New drugs and their uses
5. Pesticides and health
6. Smoking, cancer, and heart disease
7. Causes of heart disease
8. Scientific dieting
9. New uses of plastics
10. The scientist aids the detective.
11. Photography, a scientific tool
12. The scientist looks at cosmetics.
13. A scientist looks at the comics.
14. Wind storms
15. Chemical aids to agriculture
16. Predicting the weather
17. Effects of science on our amusements
18. Lengthening the life span
19. New knowledge about space
20. Moon shots

21. Types of missiles
22. An electronic marvel
23. My research project
24. On science fiction
25. Correcting the world's water shortage
26. Weather prediction by satellite
27. Telemetry and space probes
28. Science and automation
29. An astronaut's capsule environment
30. Food from the sea
31. The atom as a source of energy
32. The uses and dangers of radioactivity
33. Human factors in space travel
34. Life in a drop of water
35. Wildlife management and preservation
36. Growing plants without soil (hydroponics)
37. Better plants and animals (breeding and heredity)
38. Unconquered fields in science

Sports

1. Is a varsity position worth the cost?
2. Professional vs. amateur sports
3. A great sports performance
4. Good sportsmanship
5. Bench warming

6. My best sports performance
7. Winter fishing
8. The hunter's equipment
9. Tennis tips (any sport)
10. Coaches' nightmares
11. My favorite team
12. A great sports figure
13. How to sail (any sport)
14. How to train
15. A strange sport

General

1. Keeping physically fit
2. The wise use of leisure
3. How to shop economically
4. Popular superstitions
5. Gifts
6. Experiences as a tourist
7. Living in the North vs. living in the South (East–West)
8. Life in another country
9. On friendship
10. A definition of happiness
11. Why I prefer farm life (*or* city or suburban life)

12. What is success?
13. Living your religion
14. Immorality in the movies
15. My encounters with prejudice
16. My chosen vocation
17. Values of 4-H Club work (Scouting, etc.)
18. The duties of the chairman of a meeting
19. Qualities of a good salesman (salesgirl)
20. Causes of highway accidents
21. The teen-age driver
22. Considerations in buying a car
23. How to train a dog
24. How to judge a newspaper
25. Our dependence on machines
26. My life one year from now
27. Our changing fashions
28. High school slang
29. American speech mannerisms
30. Teen-age fads

Literature

Literature offers an almost unlimited supply of ideas, characters, and technical matters to write about. Naturally, composition topics on specific literary works will be of no use to you unless you have read the particular works on which they are based. You can, however, choose a general subject and develop it by reference to works with which you are familiar. The following general subjects are intended merely to suggest the kinds of composition topics that can be drawn from your reading of literature.

1. A great novel and what makes it great
2. A social-problem play
3. The difference between theme and plot (specific examples)
4. A comparison of attitudes toward love (death, nature, war) in two poems (novels, plays, essays)
5. Three interesting characters portrayed by modern poets
6. Characterization and/or caricature in a novel (play)
7. A comparison of the style of two writers (fiction, poetry)
8. A comparison of two historical novels (plays) about the same period or the same person
9. Comparison of a novel and its movie version (play version or musical version)
10. The typical Western (detective story, romance, etc.)
11. The influence of the setting in a novel
12. The philosophy of a writer you know well
13. Irony in a piece of literature (short story, novel, play, lyric)
14. Satire in a piece of literature
15. The use of symbols in a piece of literature

Although specific works and authors are mentioned in the following topics, a great many other works and authors may be substituted for them. You may wish to use the general idea in a topic but apply it to other literary works.

1. Shakespeare's *Julius Caesar* and modern politics
2. Some Shakespearian clowns
3. Recurrent themes in Shakespeare's sonnets
4. A comparison of *West Side Story* and *Romeo and Juliet*
5. The whale as a symbol in *Moby Dick*
6. Adolescent psychology in *The Red Badge of Courage*
7. The Puritan strain in Hawthorne's stories
8. Dickens as a caricaturist
9. Chaucer as a portrayer of character
10. Satire in the novels of Sinclair Lewis
11. A comparison of *My Fair Lady* and Shaw's *Pygmalion*
12. Huxley's *Brave New World* and Orwell's *1984*
13. A comparison of Arthurian legends in Malory's *Morte d'Arthur* and White's *The Once and Future King*
14. The detective story—Poe and Doyle
15. The typical setting of Faulkner's novels

Language and Logic

Propositions, Evidence, Reasoning

Argument is a familiar feature of your daily conversation. In class you argue about history, current events, literature. Essay-type examination questions often ask your opinion and expect you to support it with knowledge. People in all kinds of work—scientists, teachers, salesmen, journalists, politicians, lawyers—know the importance of being able to argue convincingly.

In argumentative writing your purpose is to persuade the reader to accept your views on a debatable subject. You try to prove that you are right. In its simplest form, argumentative writing is a statement of personal opinion backed up by facts and reasons. In its more elaborate form, it is a skillfully planned, tightly reasoned kind of writing frequently designed not only to convince an audience but also to persuade it to action. It may appeal to the emotions as well as to the reason.

THE PROPOSITION

The statement of the point to be argued is called *the proposition*. It either states something as a fact or states that a particular course of action should or should not be followed. In either case, the proposition makes a definite assertion and is usually stated in a declarative sentence.

EXAMPLES   My client is innocent.

High school fraternities and sororities should be abolished.

Capital punishment does not deter crime.

All of the statements above can be believed, doubted, or disbelieved. The way each is stated causes us to expect reasons to be presented in support of the proposition. The reasons, or evidence, in support of a proposition are an essential part of argument. But before we consider them, we must understand what makes a good proposition and how it should be stated.

The Arguable Proposition

23a. Formulate in a proposition the point to be argued.

While there is little likelihood of your writing an argumentative composition on an "unarguable" subject, you should be warned against two kinds of futile arguing that occur in our daily conversation.

One kind of futile argument is that in which the issue is a matter of verifiable fact. How familiar does the following argument sound?

"Mary is older than Bob."   (Proposition)

"No, she isn't."

"Yes, she is. Her birthday is in April. Bob's is in July.

"But in different years."

"No, they were born the same year."

"They were not!"

These two people are getting nowhere at all. They are arguing instead of finding out the truth, something which they can easily ascertain. A statement of verifiable fact is not an arguable proposition.

23a

Like verifiable facts, personal tastes are frequent, but poor, subjects of argument. "Blue is a more beautiful color than red." "Tennis is more fun than golf." These are not sound propositions because, as matters of taste, they cannot be resolved by presenting evidence. To be sure, you could write an interesting composition in support of your taste, but no amount of arguing will ever establish a proposition of this kind as true or not true. A statement of personal taste is an expression of opinion, but it is not an arguable proposition.

Stating the Proposition

A proposition should be so worded that its meaning is definite and its terms are not ambiguous. When the editor of the school newspaper begins his editorial with the proposition "Seniors with a B average should be excused from examinations," he is probably not saying what he means. The phrase "with a B average" is ambiguous. Does it mean an overall B average for all subjects, or does it mean seniors will be excused from examinations in only those subjects in which they have a B average? Also the word *examinations* is too general. The editor certainly does not mean all examinations. He probably means only semester and final examinations. Rewording the proposition will make it clear and get the editor's argument off to a better start: "Seniors should be excused from semester and final examinations in courses in which they have a B average."

Sometimes a proposition, even though well phrased, requires explanation, or definition of some of its terms. These explanations and definitions can be given in the first paragraph of the composition.

A proposition should not in its wording assume the truth of something that has to be proved. Consider, for example, the proposition "This unfair tax should be repealed." The inclusion of the word *unfair* implies that everyone can, or should be able to, see that the tax is unreasonable, when in fact this is something that must be proved in the argument. Similarly, if you are setting out to prove that professional boxing should be outlawed because it is dangerous, it is not fair to state your proposition this way: "The *dangerous* sport of professional boxing should be outlawed." Making this kind of statement is called "begging the question."

To summarize, a proposition should be on a point that can sensibly be argued; it should be clearly stated; and it should not imply that the point to be proved is a foregone conclusion.

● EXERCISE 1. Some of the following are sound, arguable propositions; others are not. Label each proposition *P* if it is both sound and arguable or *NP* if it is not both sound and arguable. Be able to explain your answers in class discussion.

1. Dickens' novels are too old-fashioned to interest a modern reader.
2. In 1956 Don Larsen pitched the only perfect game in the history of the World Series.
3. Our high school should provide recreation rooms for juniors and seniors.
4. You should vote for Tom Winter for class president.
5. Capital punishment should be abolished.
6. Central should adopt the honor system for all examinations.
7. Wisconsin won the Big Ten football championship in 1962.
8. Abstract art is less satisfying than realistic art.
9. The school year should be extended to eleven months.
10. Our inadequate school library should be enlarged.

Minor Propositions

23b. List the points (minor propositions) you intend to use to support your proposition.

Having set up your proposition, write down in order the points you will make in support of it. These points, many of which are themselves debatable, are sometimes called minor propositions.

23b

For example, read the points listed as *minor propositions* below the following main proposition.

MAIN PROPOSITION   Seniors should be excused from semester and final examinations in courses in which they have a B average.

MINOR PROPOSITIONS

1. The B student has already shown that he knows the material of the course.
2. Students will work harder to get a B if they have the inducement of being excused from examinations.
3. Since they will not be able to raise their course grade by getting a high mark on the final examination, students will study as they go instead of depending on cramming at the end of the semester.
4. Except in borderline cases, the examination is not weighted heavily enough to lower or raise the final grade.

23c. Prepare to answer arguments on the other side of the proposition.

While it is possible to write an argument without answering the points that will be made by a writer with opposite views, it is much better to refute those points in the course of your composition. Ignoring a major argument of the other side leaves you in a weak position. Your success in persuasion may depend entirely on how well you can answer opposing arguments. Therefore, in planning an argumentative article, consider carefully what can be said against your views, and prepare a strong reply.

A writer supporting the proposition about excusing seniors from examinations should list and try to answer the following points on the other side of the issue:

1. Examinations assure learning because they force the student to review material he may have forgotten.
2. Examinations assure better learning because preparation for a final examination affords the student an overall view of the course.

3. Since even good students study only when they are forced to, removing the forcing power of the examination will encourage laziness.

● EXERCISE 2.   The following questions are arguable issues. Select one or use a subject of your own choosing and (1) state it in a clear proposition, (2) list at least three minor propositions in support, and (3) list at least two arguments that might be offered by someone arguing against the proposition.

1. Should high school students be allowed greater freedom in electing courses?
2. Should high school students be allowed to elect the teachers they want?
3. Should the intramural athletic program be expanded?
4. Should more modern literature be taught in English courses?
5. Is air travel safe?
6. Is homework necessary?
7. Should the sale of cigarettes to minors be illegal?
8. Should Americans tour the United States before touring abroad?
9. Should the state government give financial aid to private and parochial schools?
10. Should the state university charge tuition fees for students who are residents of the state?

EVIDENCE

When you have formulated your proposition and listed points in support of both sides of it, you should turn to the problem of gathering the material you will use in support. This material is called evidence.

23d. Gather sufficient evidence to prove main and minor propositions and refute opposing views.

According to the dictionary, *evidence* is "that which tends to prove or disprove something." Hence it is the

23
c-d

essence of argument. Two kinds of evidence are usually used to establish proof: (1) facts, (2) authoritative statements (testimony).

Facts as Evidence

A fact is something that can be demonstrated to be true, or *verified*. That a certain number of births were recorded in the United States last year, that it was raining on a particular night at Kennedy Airport, that water boils at 212 degrees Fahrenheit—all these are facts that can be verified beyond a reasonable doubt. Obviously, the appropriate facts provide the strongest possible support for an argument.

Two cautions are to be observed in using facts as evidence. First, the facts must be accurate. Unfortunately, there can be dishonesty in argument, and the writer who does not check his facts carefully is dishonest. Second, the facts must be plentiful enough to be convincing. How many facts it takes to convince your reader will depend on the nature of the subject and the impressiveness of the facts themselves, but, in general, the more facts you have the stronger your argument will be.

Note the use of facts in the following paragraphs in which the writer is trying to establish the need for federal aid to education.

At the present rate of growth and expansion the annual outlay for public schools will probably reach $30 billion by 1970. The costs could be considerably more, but several responsible groups, including President Eisenhower's Commission on National Goals, have estimated costs by the end of this decade should be at least double their present level. . . .

Not many people in this country fully realize what a tremendous load this $30 billion is going to be on local and state revenue programs. Ten years from now public elementary and secondary schools will be costing two thirds as much as national defense is costing now. In another decade these schools will be requiring almost as much revenue as all state and local services, including education, cost in 1959.[1]

Authoritative Statements as Evidence

Important as facts are, we cannot depend exclusively upon them in argument. In the courtroom, for example, expert opinions may be admitted as evidence: a doctor may be asked to give his opinion about a matter relating to medicine; a handwriting expert may be asked to compare two letters, and so on. Of course it is always possible that the expert may be wrong; his opinion is not verifiable in the same way that a fact is. Yet, if he is a respected figure in his field and if it cannot be demonstrated that he has a special interest in saying what he does on the matter at hand, his opinion should carry a good deal of weight.

The important question, then, is whether a particular authority is really an authority. There are no certain ways of telling, but caution and common sense will take us a long way. We may ask ourselves what obvious qualifications the person has. Doctors and lawyers display certificates showing they have attended a particular school and passed intensive examinations in their field. A scholar in another field is also likely to have degrees and is probably connected with a well-known college or university. A correspondent who has lived for years in India and has won journalistic honors for his objective reporting, a technician working for a reputable testing company, a man with long experience in the training of horses—all of these men have qualifications that are easy to check and that tell us about which matters their opinions will be most reliable.

[1] From a statement of the National Education Association in support of bills S. 1021 and H.R. 4970, delivered on March 14, 1961, by Sam M. Lambert. In *Federal Aid to Education;* hearing, March 13–20, 1961, before the General Subcommittee on Education. U.S. House of Representatives Commission on Education and Labor. 87th Congress, 1st session.

Note the use of an authority in the following paragraph:

Actually, there is impressive evidence that the states and communities can meet public school requirements in the decade ahead, if their citizens are not burdened—and beguiled—by Federal solutions. In his recent book, *Taxes for the Schools*, Roger A. Freeman, a well known authority in school finance, suggests that what we need is not just more money for the schools but more schools for the money. Even so he concedes that expenditures for the public schools may well have to rise from $12 billion in 1957 to some $24 billion in 1970—an estimate in line with that of the Rockefeller Report. About half of this increase, Freeman argues, can be handled by present state and local taxes if the economy continues to expand at a moderate and normal rate of 3.5 per cent a year. The remaining $6 billion, he shows, could be obtained by an increase in state income and sales taxes, plus a moderate increase in local property taxes. . . .[1]

The Testimonial

One kind of "evidence" loosely related to the authoritative statement is the *testimonial*. Some testimonials may be convincing. If you wish to make up your mind about installing a merit system for good conduct in your school, you will naturally be persuaded by the opinions of students in schools where such a system is in use. The testimonial used commonly in advertising, however, is not to be taken very seriously. Usually the movie star who uses Glow face cream and the professional athlete who drives a Speedo sports car have been well paid for their testimonials and would have endorsed another product if paid enough money.

REASONING

A common way to convince and persuade others is to reason with them. Reasoning must, of course, be logical;

[1] From "A 'Deeper Commitment' to Public Schools," *Fortune* Magazine, April 1961. Courtesy of *Fortune* Magazine.

that is, the thinking must be clear. In the following pages you will study several common kinds of reasoning. Each has its pitfalls into which an unclear thinker may easily fall. Study the kinds of reasoning and note the pitfalls so that you can detect them in the arguments of others and avoid them in your own compositions.

Inductive Reasoning

In inductive reasoning you begin with evidence—facts, statistics, instances, etc., and after studying the evidence, you arrive at a conclusion or generalization. For example, suppose that you have a box of chocolate creams all of which are identical in appearance. You bite into one of the chocolates and find it to be a peppermint cream. You taste a second and find it to be peppermint, too. You try a third, which is also peppermint. Now, reasoning inductively, you are about to say, "This box contains only peppermint creams." Of course, your generalization may be wrong because you have not tested every piece of candy in the box. The chances are, however, that you may be right. The more creams you sample, the more reliable your generalization becomes. You can easily see that the more evidence you have in favor of your generalization, the more likely it is that the generalization will be true.

23e. Avoid generalizations based on insufficient evidence.

Hasty Generalization

When you make a generalization based on insufficient evidence, you are committing a major error in reasoning. This error is called *hasty generalization*. All your life you will hear people make it.

An understandably angry motorist wrote the following letter to his newspaper:

23e

About midnight Saturday I was going through the inter-section of Haven Boulevard and Elm Street on a green light when my car was rammed at a right angle by a car which had obviously passed through the red light. The driver of this car was seventeen years old. He had six other teen-agers in the car with him, one of whom was badly injured in the collision. A month ago I was forced off the highway by a car driven by a high school student who insisted on passing even though there was not enough room to pass. To avoid a sideswipe, I drove into the ditch. These experiences have convinced me that teen-age drivers are a menace and that the driving age in this state should be raised to twenty-one.

The validity of this motorist's generalization is highly doubtful because the generalization is based on only two instances. It could be true, but it certainly has not been proved true by the evidence given.

Now suppose that a large insurance company decides to find out whether teen-age drivers, in proportion to their number, are involved in more accidents than are adult drivers. The insurance company has access to a vast amount of information. Its research department conducts an exten-sive investigation. If, after studying thousands of accident reports, the company finds that the percentage of teen-age drivers involved is greater than the percentage of adult drivers involved, the company may draw a generalization which will probably be true. There is always the possibility that further research may disprove the generalization, but until that happens, the company would be justified in making a generalization on the basis of its research.

Analogy

Sometimes during an argument a person, in order to clarify a point, may use an *analogy*. An analogy is a com-parison. Reasoning by analogy is the kind of reasoning that compares one situation with another. Suppose, for example, that the president of the Student Council of a school is impatient with the students for not cooperating with their student monitors, who are charged with keeping order in corridors, cafeteria, assembly, and at athletic events. In an address before the school he tries, by drawing an analogy, to persuade the students to be more cooperative. He says that a school is like an army. Just as soldiers must obey their officers, students must obey their monitors. If soldiers ignore their officers' orders, the battle may be lost. If students ignore their monitors' orders, the school will not function smoothly and its educational and social programs will be affected. It is the function of an army to win battles; it is the function of a school to provide effective educational and social programs for its students. The success of a school, like the success of an army, depends upon good discipline and respect for authority. Like good soldiers, all students should obey orders.

By drawing this analogy between a school and an army, the speaker hoped to persuade his listeners to be more co-operative, more obedient. Since discipline is essential in both an army and a school, there is some point in the analogy, and this point may have been persuasive. However, you will recognize at once that the analogy is really very weak because there are many more dissimilarities than similarities between an army and a school. Is military discipline the kind we want in a school? Is the job of an army officer like that of a school monitor? Is winning a battle really much like furthering an educational program? The analogy grows weaker the longer you study it, a fact which is true of many analogies.

Nevertheless, analogies have their place in argument. If a good one occurs to you, use it for its clarifying effect. Almost invariably it will be interesting to your reader and will help him to understand your argument better. Be ready, of course, to have an analogy attacked by people of opposing views.

23f. The soundness of an analogy depends upon the number of points in common between the things being compared.

When an analogy will not stand careful examination, it is called a *false analogy*. That is, when the points of similarity are found to be very few or even nonexistent, the analogy is false.

● EXERCISE 3.   Discuss the following examples of argument by analogy. How strong are the analogies?

1. A large vocabulary and the ability to use it with ease will not make you a great writer. Joseph Conrad said, "The gift of words is no such great matter; a man is not made a hunter or a warrior by the mere possession of a firearm."

2. In the Bible the Devil tempts Christ with bread, with power over all the kingdoms of the world, and with miracles. So the totalitarian state offers its followers economic security, political power, and sensational technological progress—all in return for one thing: absolute subservience to the high priest of these gods, the party.[1]

3. At this moment in time, at the very beginning of the centuries-long gold rush into ever expanding fields of knowledge, we must realize that there is no hope of understanding our universe until we have examined a fairly large sample of it—certainly a good deal more than one small planet out of billions. Though this cautious attitude may disappoint many who are hot for certainties, any other policy would be utterly naïve. It would put us in the same position as Pacific islanders who have never yet had any contact with the world beyond their coral reef, yet who attempt to construct a picture of the whole Earth and its peoples from the view from their highest palm tree.[2]

[1] From "The Devil and Soviet Russia" by Harold J. Berman. Reprinted from *The American Scholar*, Volume 27, Number 2, Spring, 1958. Copyright © 1958 by the United Chapters of Phi Beta Kappa. By permission of the publishers.

[2] From *Space and the Spirit of War* by Arthur C. Clarke. Reprinted from *Horizon*, A Magazine of the Arts, by permission of the author and the author's agents, Scott Meredith Literary Agency, Inc.

4. Like the manager of a wild animal circus, the principal of a high school is engaged in the business of training animals. His success depends on the performance of his charges. He will not hold his position long if they fail standardized tests, just as an animal trainer will soon go out of business if his seals cannot bounce balls on their noses and his tigers won't leap through a fiery hoop. There is always the strain, too, of having to keep the animals under control. A school can no more permit students complete freedom than a circus can release its wild animals. In both instances, the public would protest with equal vigor.

5. Although nuclear war is unthinkable, a country like ours must be prepared to wage it. In this preparedness, which accounts for more than half our national budget, lies the only sure deterrent we have. We have no choice. We are like a bank which must build a great vault with heavy steel doors, a combination time lock, and the best electrical alarm system engineers can devise. The banker regrets the enormous cost of this vault; he hopes never to have to use the alarm. But he knows the installation is the only deterrent to criminals. It would be unrealistic for a bank to reduce expenses by using a kitchen cupboard for the storage of money. It would be equally ridiculous for our country to cut its budget in half by abandoning all preparedness measures.

Deductive Reasoning

You have seen that inductive reasoning works by assembling evidence and making a generalization about it. By this method we arrive at judgments that are *probably* true. Until the last item of evidence is in, we cannot be sure.

Deductive reasoning, on the other hand, starts out from a generalization that is assumed to be true and by logical steps leads to a conclusion about a particular situation.

The Syllogism

A deductive argument can be stated in a three-part form called a *syllogism*. The first part is the generalization with

23f

which the argument begins. It is called the *major premise*. The second part states the particular situation to which the major premise is to be applied. It is called the *minor premise*. The third part states the *conclusion*.

SYLLOGISM   All sweet apples are ripe.   [major premise]
This apple is sweet.   [minor premise]
(Therefore) This apple is ripe.   [conclusion]

If the major and minor premises in this syllogism are true, the conclusion is sound. It is possible for a conclusion to be valid but not sound. A conclusion is valid if it is correctly reasoned regardless of its truth. For example, the reasoning in the following syllogism is perfectly correct, making the conclusion valid. No one, however, would accept the conclusion as sound because it is simply not true.

All two-legged animals are human beings.
A monkey is a two-legged animal.
A monkey is a human being.

If you grant the truth of the first premise and the minor premise, your conclusion follows with unquestionable logic —it is a *valid*, correctly reasoned conclusion. However, the first premise is not true: not all two-legged animals are human beings. Hence the conclusion is unsound, or false.

Testing a Syllogism

There are many complicated ways of testing the soundness of a syllogism, but for ordinary purposes, you may test a syllogism by asking three questions.

23g.   Test a syllogism by asking:

(1) Are the premises true? That is, has the major premise been arrived at inductively from enough instances? And is the fact stated in the minor premise true?

(2) Does the major premise ignore any significant fact?

(3) Does the conclusion follow logically?

False Syllogisms

When you apply the three-question test to the following false syllogisms, you will see why they are false.

All ripe apples are sweet. [major premise]
This apple is ripe. [minor premise]
(Therefore) This apple is sweet. [conclusion]

This syllogism is false because it does not stand up under the test of the first question. It is not true that all ripe apples are sweet.

Red apples are ripe. [major premise]
This apple is green. [minor premise]
(Therefore) This apple is not ripe. [conclusion]

This syllogism can be shown to be false when the second test question is applied to it. The generalization (major premise) ignores a very significant fact, which is that some green apples are also ripe.

All sweet apples are ripe. [major premise]
This apple is ripe. [minor premise]
(Therefore) This apple is sweet. [conclusion]

The syllogism is false because it does not pass the test of the third question. The conclusion does not follow logically. It is based on a misunderstanding of what the major premise says. The major premise does not say that all ripe apples are sweet.

The falseness of these simple "apple" syllogisms is easy to understand. Yet deductive reasoning of the kind they illustrate is all too common. Have you ever heard arguments like this:

Communists believe in government ownership of natural resources.
Mr. Doe believes in government ownership of the coal mines.
(Therefore) Mr. Doe is a Communist.

23g

Here the premises are true, but the major premise ignores the important fact that some people who are not Communists also believe in government ownership of coal mines.

An unsound deductive conclusion reached in this way is like a hasty generalization in inductive reasoning. It is too quickly arrived at. We call it "jumping to a conclusion," for the argument literally "jumps" over (ignores) an important fact.

● EXERCISE 4.   This exercise is a series of examples of both inductive and deductive reasoning. Number your paper 1–10. After studying each item, write after the corresponding number on your paper the kind of reasoning it represents (inductive or deductive). If the reasoning is valid, add a plus (+); if it is not valid, add a zero (0). Be able to explain your answers.

1. Only Eastern Airlines flies nonstop between here and Atlanta. Carl said he was coming from Atlanta on a nonstop flight, so he must be coming on Eastern.
2. Dad says he won't buy another station wagon because the last one we had developed too many rattles.
3. Look at the shining cars parked outside handsome fraternity houses. Look at the number of college students who spend their weekends at ski resorts and their summers abroad. You can see that college students these days are a pretty rich group.
4. To commit a burglary, one has to be at the scene of the burglary. Roy Maxwell admits that he was at the scene. Roy Maxwell is the burglar.
5. Every girl I know who comes from a wealthy home is a spoiled brat. The children of rich people are always spoiled.
6. Socialists believe in socialized medicine. Mr. Cross believes in socialized medicine. I guess Mr. Cross is a Socialist.
7. The per pupil cost of education is greater in the high school than in the elementary school. In the future a greater proportion of pupils will be in high school than has been true in the past. The cost of education, therefore, is sure to increase.

8. In the long run machinery has improved our national economy. Since 1850, when the machine age began in earnest, our population has grown $7\frac{1}{2}$ times, but jobs have grown $8\frac{1}{2}$ times, and goods and services, 34 times. Apparently we really have no reason to fear automation.

9. When an hour-long interview with Dwight D. Eisenhower on the problems of the Presidency was broadcast in prime evening time, six million people watched it, while twenty-one million were watching a suspense drama and twenty-six million were watching a popular-song program on other networks. The majority of the American people prefer entertainment to enlightenment.

10. In the last five years, while the world total of ships of 1,000 or more deadweight tons rose from 15,615 to 17,426, the number of active ships of this type registered under the U.S. flag dropped by nearly one fourth, to around 900, most of them approaching obsolescence. Only 45 percent of the cargo capacity of the United States fleet is in use. In shipbuilding, United States yards have reached the lowest ebb in years. Unless the trend is reversed, the United States will have practically no merchant marine at all.

Clear Thinking

We have already discussed some of the pitfalls in reasoning—the use of a dubious authority, hasty generalization, and the false analogy. These came up naturally in connection with the kind of reasoning in which they are most likely to occur. There are also some other important errors in reasoning that may come up in a variety of situations. Being aware of them will help you to be sure that your reasoning is clear and logical.

Cause and Effect

The purpose of much of our discussion and writing is to find remedies and preventive measures for existing evils. As any physician knows, the first step in assigning a remedy for an illness is to find the cause, and it is important that the true cause be found. In our effort to explain an event or a situation, we naturally examine the events which preceded it. We look for the cause. In so doing, however, we must not make the mistake of assuming that just because one event preceded another, it caused the second event. A Latin phrase is commonly used to describe this kind of thinking: *post hoc, ergo propter hoc,* which means "after this, therefore because of this."

A simple example of this kind of error in thinking derives from our superstitions. For instance, you may slip on the stairs and sprain your ankle so badly that you are on crutches for weeks. Looking back on events preceding the accident, you recall that when you were on your way home from school earlier in the day, a black cat crossed your path. You say, "Now that explains it. That cat was the cause of my bad luck."

23h. The fact that an event or a condition follows another event or condition does not necessarily mean that the second was caused by the first. Before ascribing a result to a certain cause, consider other possible causes.

Suppose that the basketball team at your school has won the regional championship and is therefore going to the state tournament, a day's journey away. The team travels by bus and must play its first tournament game the same night. It loses the game to a team which eventually wins the tournament. The sports columnist in your school paper, looking for the cause of the defeat, seizes upon the bus ride which preceded the game: "If the boys hadn't been exhausted from the tiring trip, they would have won the game and the championship." Of course, the columnist could be right, but there were other factors which he should have considered before deciding on the cause of defeat. The winning team also made a long trip the day of the game. The winners won by a margin of 16 points. The winning team had a better season record than the losing team. Finally, they went on to win the tournament. In the light of these considerations, it looks as though the columnist was guilty of *post hoc, ergo propter hoc* thinking.

The Irrelevant Fact—"Off-the-Subject" Arguments

The word *relevant* means "related to." A relevant argument is one which is related to the issue being argued. An *irrelevant* argument is one which is not related to the issue. When introduced into a discussion, irrelevant facts or arguments may throw the discussion "off the track." You have probably heard the chairman of a meeting accuse the participants of "getting off the subject." Clever but dishonest people may deliberately try to sidetrack a discussion when they find the argument going against them.

A common form of irrelevant argument is the one which attacks the person offering an argument rather than attacking the argument itself. For example, a nervous father advises his son at the wheel of the family car not to drive above the legal speed limit. The son's answer is that since he has often seen his father drive above the limit, it is all right for him to do so.

23i. Do not let an argument or discussion be confused by an irrelevant point.

An irrelevant point is one which simply has no bearing on the discussion. For example, a Democrat and a Republican are arguing the merits of their party platforms in an election year. The Republican says, "The American people have elected more Republican Presidents than Democratic Presidents." You can see, of course, that this statement, although true, is irrelevant so far as the merits of the current party platforms are concerned.

23
h-i

● EXERCISE 5. A student-faculty committee is discussing the question, "Should boys trying out for varsity sports be excused from last-period study halls?" Arguments presented by both sides are listed below. Study the arguments and identify those which are irrelevant, likely to lead the discussion off the subject.

Arguments in favor of excusing the boys:

1. It will relieve locker-room congestion after school.
2. Outdoor exercise is better for the boys than studying in a stuffy classroom.
3. Recently four boys on the varsity were sent to the office from last-period study because they created a discipline problem.
4. The boys will have more time for practice. The more they practice, the better the varsity teams will be.
5. Study halls should be eliminated anyway so that the school day can be shortened.
6. Athletics are as important as studies.
7. Last year our teams were the worst in years.

Arguments against excusing the boys:

1. The boys would waste the extra time because the coaches cannot join them until after school.
2. Those who are excused would have an unfair advantage over those who have a class the last period.
3. Sometimes the weather is bad, and the boys could not go outdoors.
4. It is better for the boys to study in school before practice because they will be too tired after practice to study at home.
5. We don't excuse students for other outdoor activities like fishing or playing golf, or playing outdoors at home.
6. Girls need athletics just as much as boys.

Rationalizing

When you fool yourself by attributing your behavior to reasons or motives which are not your true reasons or motives, you are rationalizing. All of us are guilty at times of rationalizing actions for which we cannot give a truly reasonable defense. The following paragraph illustrates the kind of reasoning by which a student explains his failure to make the honor roll. He is fooling himself. The truth probably is that he hasn't the ability, or he is too lazy, but he does not want to admit either of these.

> I could have made the honor roll if I had wanted to be called a brain or an egghead. I'd rather be a normal boy and enjoy life. The students who knocked themselves out to get on the honor roll aren't too popular. Who wants a brain for a friend? Lots of us are just as smart. We just don't want to spend our whole lives studying.

Wishful Thinking

People sometimes argue that a thing is true or may become true simply because they wish it to be true. Their evidence may be weak, but they believe it because they want to believe it. This kind of thinking is called wishful thinking. A simple illustration is Henry, whose former "steady" has been dating Bill for several months. Henry says, "I can wait. Bill is not the kind of friend who wears well. Betty will get tired of him, and then she'll come back to me."

● EXERCISE 6. Each of the following items illustrates an error in thinking. Number your paper 1–15. Analyze the thinking in each item. After its corresponding number write the letter of the kind of unclear thinking it represents.

A hasty generalization
B unsound deductive reasoning (false syllogism)
C unclear thinking about cause and effect
D weak or false analogy
E irrelevant (off-the-subject) argument
F rationalizing
G wishful thinking

1. Both Mary and Joe told me that Mr. Hilton is a hard marker. I need to raise my marks to get into college, and so I hope I don't get Mr. Hilton for English.

2. Lazy, ignorant people use a great deal of slang. Jane's speech, which is full of slang, shows her to be lazy and ignorant.

3. When asked about the cause of the fire, Chief Charles Waterman said he understood that Mr. Slaglé, in whose apartment the blaze started, had a bad habit of smoking cigarettes while reading in bed.

4. The President states that education must remain a matter of state and local control. But should a responsible Federal Government help pay the piper without being expected to call some of the tunes?

5. Someone is ill at the Hartmans'. I saw a car with a doctor's license plates parked outside their house this morning.

6. When Ellen Smith appeared before the Student Court to answer to the charge of running in the halls, she pleaded not guilty because she said lots of other kids were running in the halls, too, and they didn't have to appear in court.

7. World War I, World War II, and the Korean War all came when the United States was governed by a Democratic administration. To avoid war, vote Republican.

8. Automobile mechanics do not need to know good English. I intend to become an automobile mechanic. Teaching me correct English makes as much sense as teaching a polar bear how to catch an alligator.

9. Dr. Kimball advised me not to smoke because, he said, it is bad for my health. I didn't pay any attention because I noticed that he smokes all the time.

10. In the free competition of a capitalist society, business which cannot compete must be allowed to fail. In the United States the railroads have been unable to compete successfully with other modes of transportation. They should be abandoned, not subsidized by the federal government.

11. For a long time the West has based its attitude toward the East on the assumption that the fundamental goal of Russia and Communist China is to force communism upon the entire world. Recent conciliations made by Russia, however, give us hope that her attitude has changed and that the East may be ready to join us in accepting peaceful coexistence as a permanent compromise.

12. Jack wrote a short story which his classmates selected as the best short story written during the school term. Allan objected to the vote on the ground that Jack's stories were always chosen as best. He said no one else ever had a chance.

13. A man shouldn't work all the time. He needs recreation to keep him fit and help him to do his work better. Although I have not finished my homework for tomorrow, I'm going bowling tonight with Sam and Jack. I've been working so hard that I need the change and recreation. I'll feel much more like working and do a better job after a night off.

14. People who are so conscientious that they always do more work than the teacher assigned make it hard for the rest of us to get good grades. If it weren't for these people, I'd be getting an A instead of a C in English.

15. At noon on Friday, Mr. Beatty, my science teacher, saw some students leaning on his car in the faculty parking lot. After school he was unable to start the car and discovered a battery cable had come loose. Mr. Beatty accused the boys of detaching it.

● EXERCISE 7. Using the propositions prepared for Exercise 2 (p. 385), write an argumentative composition of 300–500 words incorporating these propositions, supporting your views with appropriate evidence: facts, authoritative statements, logical reasoning. Test your reasoning to be sure you have not fallen into any of the common pitfalls described on the preceding pages.

Argument and Propaganda

When an organized group—a government, an institution, a business concern—embarks upon a program to win over the public, the ideas and arguments it uses in its favor are called propaganda. Thus we refer to political propaganda, Russian propaganda, labor propaganda, advertising propaganda, etc. Propaganda is a kind of argument. Its purpose is to convince and persuade to action.

Nowadays the word *propaganda* has unpleasant associations. It suggests wily and deceitful means of swaying people's minds. But propaganda may be used for purposes we approve as well as for ones we disapprove. A physician who tries to persuade an audience to stop smoking cigarettes because there is a positive relationship between cigarette smoking and lung cancer is a propagandist, but he is unselfish in his efforts. He is seeking a result which will be beneficial to his listeners.

An individual or group that tries to influence others' opinions or actions for selfish ends is engaging in propaganda which may be harmful. The professional propagandist is promoting his own welfare regardless of whether or not his effect on you is beneficial to you.

Recognizing Propaganda

In your own argumentative writing, you probably will not be tempted to use the tricks of the propagandist. Nevertheless, you should, as part of your study of argument, learn to recognize and resist commonly used propaganda devices.

23j. Learn to recognize and evaluate propaganda.

The propagandist is a skillful user of most of the kinds of faulty reasoning you have studied on the preceding pages. He is given to frequent use of the hasty generalization; he jumps to conclusions; he reasons by analogy; he attributes an effect to the wrong cause; he diverts you from the real issue by an irrelevant fact or an off-the-subject argument. Loaded words (see page 298) and doubtful testimonials (see page 388) are his stock in trade.

In addition to all of these, the propagandist has other ways of trying to arouse your support. Some of the most common of these are described below.

Name-Calling

This is a device by which a speaker attempts to defeat an opponent not by rational arguments but by calling him names or smearing his reputation. Mudslinging of this sort is not worthy of anyone. Do not repeat a smear and do not believe it until the person under attack has had a full opportunity to reply or until you have examined the evidence.

Slogans

Propagandists know the value of a slogan. It is simple, catchy, and easily remembered. An involved train of thought is hard to follow. A series of arguments is hard to remember. A slogan makes thinking unnecessary. It oversimplifies by reducing a chain of arguments to a few words.

Slogans play an important part in politics and advertising. When you hear a slogan, remember that it does not tell a complete story. It is a device to capture your attention and memory. Here are some examples of effective slogans:

> The life you save may be your own!
> Make the world safe for democracy.
> The right is more precious than the peace.
> Go west, young man!
> Liberty, equality, fraternity!

The Unproved Assertion

Repetition is not proof. Unless the restatement is accompanied by reasons, statistics, examples, or the statements of competent and unprejudiced authorities, it is no stronger than the original utterance.

The following declaration seems to prove a point. Actually it does not because there is no evidence offered.

> My candidate is the best qualified of all. In character, experience, education, and intellectual ability he is superior to everyone who is running for this office. No one even remotely approaches his qualifications for the position. He stands head and shoulders above the other candidates. Everyone admits his superior merits. Therefore he deserves your vote.

23j

The Band Wagon

Most people like to do what others are doing and believe as others believe. Propagandists know and capitalize on this human tendency.

"Everybody is joining our cause," they say. "Come along or you'll find yourself alone."

It requires will power and the ability to think for oneself, to resist hopping on the band wagon. Do not be fooled into joining a movement simply because "others are doing it."

● EXERCISE 8. Out of your experience as a reader or listener, give an example of five of the following propaganda devices or errors in thinking.

Hasty generalization	Slogans
Unsound deduction	Name-calling
The wrong cause	The band wagon
Weak analogy	The unproved assertion
Irrelevant argument	Wishful thinking
Loaded words	Rationalizing

● EXERCISE 9. As a form of propaganda, advertising uses many of the common propaganda devices as evidence. In magazine advertisements and radio or television commercials find and report on examples of the following:

Loaded words	Slogans
Testimonials	Band wagon

Summary

In preparing an argumentative paper, observe the following:

1. Formulate a proposition that is arguable and clear.
3. List supporting points—minor propositions.
3. Prepare to refute the arguments on the other side.
4. Gather sufficient evidence: facts, authoritative statements, logical reasoning.

● EXERCISE 10. Select a controversial subject currently being argued in your school or community. State it in the form of a proposition. List minor propositions on both sides. Write a paper (300–500 words) using all the evidence you can gather. Watch for pitfalls in your reasoning.

● EXERCISE 11. Select a controversial subject of national interest currently in the news—or in the news within the past two weeks. State your views in an argumentative essay (300–500 words). Support your views with evidence. Watch for the common pitfalls in reasoning.

● EXERCISE 12. Select one of the following issues on which you have definite opinions. Limit the subject so that you can support one side (and refute the other) in an argumentative composition of 300–500 words. Prepare carefully, following the four steps discussed in this chapter. Supply plenty of evidence. Keep your reasoning sound.

1. Is the quality of television programs as high as it could practically be?
2. Are labor unions becoming too powerful?
3. Are the requirements for a driver's license in this state adequate?
4. Should mothers take a job outside the home?
5. Is life in the suburbs a good life?
6. Should high school reading be censored?
7. Should federal farm subsidies be continued?
8. Are comic books harmful?
9. Is foreign language study worthwhile?
10. Is modern advertising harmful?
11. Should the legal drinking age be raised? lowered?
12. Do we have true equality of opportunity in America?
13. Should college education, like elementary and secondary education, be free?
14. Should guided individual study replace classes in schools?
15. Do interscholastic athletics destroy sportsmanship?
16. Should the government assume the responsibility for care of the aged?
17. Are the advantages of living in a small town greater than the disadvantages?

Exercises in Composition

The Précis, The Factual Report

The exercises in this chapter will provide valuable practice in composition. In many of them the subject matter for writing has been supplied for you so that you may concentrate entirely on the writing. Do not attempt to work straight through the chapter in one stretch of a few weeks, for that plan would soon grow tiresome. Use the exercises from time to time during the year as your teacher assigns them, working on one type of exercise for a while and then on another. This plan will afford regular reviews of writing skills.

Although it is quite possible that you may do well on these composition exercises without having studied other chapters in this book, you will certainly get more help from the practice they provide if you bring to the work an understanding of the composition principles presented in Chapters 11 through 19 and especially in Chapters 21 and 22.

The kind of writing required by these exercises is rather formal expository writing. This is the kind of writing you are most often expected to do in your other classes, and the kind expected of you in business and in college.

Since in doing these exercises every member of the class faces the same composition problems, you will find it to your advantage to compare papers and, in class discussion, to evaluate the various methods of solving these problems.

THE GARBLED PARAGRAPH

A garbled paragraph is one in which the ideas have been scrambled to conceal their original logical relationships. In such an exercise, your job is to rewrite the paragraph in a form as nearly perfect as you can achieve. The garbled paragraph has been so designed that revising it will test your ability to write in a clear, smooth style. The rewriting provides excellent practice in many composition skills.

In each of the following paragraphs the first sentence is satisfactory. The other sentences may or may not be faulty. Follow these steps in rewriting the paragraph:

1. Read the paragraph through thoughtfully several times. You must have a clear idea of the meaning the author intended.

2. The order in which the ideas are arranged may not be the best. Study the order and decide whether it should be changed and in what respects. Note any points at which ideas may be profitably combined into one sentence, or one sentence divided into two sentences.

3. On scratch paper, copy the opening sentence exactly as it stands. Write the idea which, in your opinion, should come next, revising the style as you think advisable. Then turn to the idea which you think should come next in order, and continue in this way.

4. You may make changes in style and word choice but *do not omit any ideas* and *do not add any ideas of your own*.

5. Copy the revised paragraph neatly in ink.

Before beginning work, read the following list of composition skills. Not every paragraph will require all of these skills, but you may be expected to use many of them. Refer to the list occasionally as you work.

1. Arranging ideas in logical order
2. Writing complete sentences
3. Supplying proper links (connectives) between ideas
4. Subordinating ideas
5. Expressing parallel ideas in parallel form
6. Avoiding shifts in subject and verb forms
7. Improving the choice of words
8. Using correct grammar
9. Eliminating vague pronouns
10. Avoiding wordiness
11. Varying sentence structure
12. Punctuating for clearness
13. Placing modifiers clearly

● EXERCISE 1.   As your teacher directs, use the following paragraphs for practice in composition skills.

1

1   Some high school seniors who are grown up physically are
2   still immature emotionally. After studying a little psychology,
3   immature behavior can be recognized by anyone. Except
4   perhaps the childish person himself. Two obvious character-
5   istics of the childish person is his tendency to blame anyone
6   but himself for his failures and he desires to be noticed by
7   his peers. The boy who excuses his failure in English on the
8   grounds that the teacher doesn't like him, for instance. He
9   reveals the tendency to blame others. The desire of the
10   senior that is childish to be noticed by his peers frequently
11   leads him to make a fool of himself. The need for the atten-
12   tion of others are common to all of us, and we need their
13   respect. The difference between being noticed and respect
14   is not often recognized by the immature person, however.
15   He gets attention when he drives a car, for example, reck-
16   lessly to show how daring he is, endangering the lives of
17   others. He makes trouble in class because he knows the
18   bad boy always gets attention. What him and his kind don't
19   realize is that although they do get attention it is the kind
20   we give to criminals and people who are crazy. It does not
21   mean that you are respected.

2

1 Some experts believe that before we can develop an ade-
2 quate program for the reduction of crime, we must change
3 our criminal codes to conform to new concepts of punish-
4 ment. Here is an illustration. Assume that two men are
5 charged with the same offense. Assault with a ball bat.
6 The record reveals that Smith is a drunkard who beats his
7 wife and his family is not supported by him. Jones, the other
8 defendant, is clean-living; he works steady and his home life
9 is excellent. Smith also provokes brawls and fights in liquor
10 taverns. Should Smith and Jones receive equal punishment?
11 The idea of making punishment fit the crime by "giving
12 the criminal what's coming to him" is the old eye-for-an-eye
13 concept. The reports of social workers reveal that these two
14 men have different personalities and it should be taken into
15 account. The new scientific approach is that punishment
16 should fit the person. For both the good of Smith and
17 society the treatment Smith receives should be of a different
18 nature from Jones.

3

1 The adolescent has three psychological problems. First,
2 he wishes to become self-directing. He wants to get himself
3 mentally free from dependence on his parents. The achieve-
4 ment of a satisfactory relationship with the opposite sex is
5 the second thing he wants. There is too the desire to become
6 self-supporting or at least prepared for it. On the one hand
7 he enjoys being watched over by his parents and supported
8 by them. He faces these problems and he is torn between
9 the desire to remain a child and the fact that he has a strong
10 desire to be an adult and treated in that way. On the other
11 hand he craves to be independent, to escape from parental
12 restraints and so that he can prove he is grown up. His
13 wishes pull him in opposite directions. His behavior is not
14 consistent. He wavers between acceptance and rejecting
15 responsibility and independence and depending on adults.

4

1 The advantages of being the oldest child in the family
2 are outweighed by the disadvantages. In fact the advantages

3 are only a few that the oldest child enjoys and which are
4 unimportant. Having been born first, his parents give him
5 their undivided attention before the second child is born
6 during his early years. He holds a favored position from the
7 beginning. Which he may continue to enjoy the rest of his
8 life. Or suffer from, as the case may be. At the time when
9 he is the only child, his parents spoil him, and later on when
10 there are other children, they give him special privileges
11 because of being the oldest. Parents have their first ex-
12 periences as parents with a child's school life and social
13 life through him. First experiences are more interesting than
14 later ones of the same kind, so parents give more time to
15 the activities of the oldest and more interest than can be
16 afforded to be given to the later children. His toys, clothes,
17 and sports equipment are always brand new while they
18 must be content with hand-me-downs. On the other hand,
19 the other side of the story is that these very advantages bring
20 with them things that are disadvantages. For example, if a
21 child is too closely watched, too carefully brought up. It is
22 a disadvantage to him. Special privileges are often accom-
23 panied by annoying responsibilities. The oldest is expected
24 to be a model to follow for the younger brothers and sisters
25 of good behavior. He is expected to help his parents disci-
26 pline and care for the younger children behaving like an
27 adult. Always held up to them as a model and always bossing
28 them around, the younger ones resent the oldest very often.
29 It is better to be the youngest than the oldest child.

5

1   Poe's stories deal with mysterious situations and with
2 the still more mysterious effects that situations have upon the
3 mind. The detective story was created by him long before
4 Sherlock Holmes was born or Arsène Lupin. His interest
5 in what it is now the fashion to call psychological was an
6 absorbing interest with him. Whether a criminal was caught
7 and punished was not at all to him the important question
8 in a detective story, it was wholly a question of how the
9 logical part of the mind acts in the presence of a fact. Poe
10 was very vain of his own power of ratiocination as he
11 called it. Believing and proving that any puzzle which one

12 mind can contrive another mind can disentangle. It not
13 mattering whether the puzzle is mechanical or not. Poe
14 invented not only detective stories like "The Purloined
15 Letter" and "The Murders in the Rue Morgue" and these
16 are the best of their kind, but an actual case which at the
17 time when he wrote remained unsolved was taken by him
18 and he turned it into a piece of fiction "The Mystery of
19 Marie Roget" and the plot later was proved to be almost
20 an exact parallel of the real events.

THE PRÉCIS

A précis is a brief summary. Writing a précis is valuable training in composition. Since the writing requires you to be clear and concise, you must choose your words carefully and arrange them skillfully to get the maximum amount of meaning into the minimum space.

In addition to its value as a writing exercise, précis work is excellent reading practice. In order to summarize another's ideas in your own words, you must understand the ideas thoroughly.

In school and in life after school, there are many situations that call for the writing of a brief, accurate summary of your reading. You are frequently asked to prepare a summary of what you have read in your textbook or in the library. Answers on examinations often require a brief summary. People in business, in club work, and in social work must prepare short digests of articles and reports.

Study the following facts about a précis and the basic steps in précis writing.

1. *A précis is a short summary.* It is not a paraphrase, which merely says in different and simpler words exactly what the passage being paraphrased has to say. A paraphrase may be as long as the passage itself. A précis rarely is more than one-third the length of the original selection and may be only one-fourth as long.

2. *A précis gives only the "heart" of a passage.* It omits repetitions and such details as examples, illustrations, and adjectives unless they are of unusual importance.

3. *A précis is written entirely in the words of the person writing it, not in the words of the original selection.* Avoid the temptation to lift long phrases and whole sentences from the original.

4. *A précis is written from the point of view of the author whose work is being summarized.* Do not begin with such expressions as "This author says" or "The paragraph means." Begin as though you were summarizing your own writing.

In writing a précis proceed as follows:

1. Read carefully, sentence by sentence, the passage to be summarized. Try to grasp the writer's main point. Spotting the topic sentence will help. Look up in the dictionary any words whose meaning is not absolutely clear. As you read, take brief notes to be used in your writing.

2. When you have finally decided what the author's main point is, write it out in your own words. Do not use the wording of the original except for certain key words which you may find indispensable. If you cannot translate the ideas into language of your own, you do not understand them very well. Be especially careful not to rely too much on the topic sentence. Do not add any opinions or ideas of your own.

3. Revise your writing until you are sure that you have given an accurate summary.

4. Usually you will find your précis is too long—more than one-third the length of the original. Continue your revision until you have reduced the précis to the proper length. In this careful revision lies the principal value of the précis as a composition exercise. The work on "reduction" on pages 258–65 will be helpful to you in shortening your précis. Don't try to get the précis into a single sentence unless the passage is very short.

● EXERCISE 2. Read the following paragraph two or three times. Then read the four précis of it given below. Each of them illustrates one major error in précis writing.

The first thing that strikes the critical minority, as it looks at the whole cultural picture, is that ours is a nation of new-rich people, well washed, all dressed up, rather pathetically unsure just what it is washed and dressed up for; a nation convinced that a multitude of material goods, standardized, furiously and expensively advertised by appeals to greed and vanity, will in themselves make life worth the living. Because we are new-rich, we overvalue possessions. Almost any individual who makes a great deal of money very rapidly supposes that mere possession of wealth is evidence of worth. He also is apt to imagine that with his means he can buy happiness. These mistakes usually seem folly to the old-rich, to one who was born to property, whose father and mother were bred with it. Such a one knows that merely because he or his friends have it, is no sign that they are worth it, but quite commonly the contrary. He has learned through experience that money is not in itself very valuable stuff. Happiness, which is what all men desire, cannot be purchased; it is an illusive something not for sale. The old-rich know these things well enough, but the new-rich rarely discover them until they too have grown accustomed to possessions. So it seems to be with our society. We go in, almost without question and in all classes, for the sordid nonsense of supposing that externalities possessed ennoble the owners, that a full fist invariably indicates a fine spirit.[1]   [275 words]

FAULTY PRÉCIS

1. Ours is a nation of new-rich people convinced that material goods will in themselves make life worth the living. Any individual who makes a great deal of money rapidly supposes that wealth is evidence of worth. He imagines that with his means he can buy happiness. These mistakes seem folly to one born

phrases and sentences merely copied from original

[1] From *Crowd Culture* by Bernard Iddings Bell. Reprinted by permission of Harper & Row, Publishers, Incorporated.

to property. He knows that because he or his friends have it, is no sign that they are worth it. Happiness, which all men desire, cannot be purchased. We go in for the nonsense that a full fist indicates a fine spirit.   [95 words]

2. On the whole we are a nation of new-rich people who are well washed and well dressed, but we don't know what we're washed and dressed for. Our material goods are all standardized and expensively advertised. Advertisers appeal to our greed and vanity. We think these material goods are the means to wealth and happiness. The old-rich know that their friends aren't worth the money they have, but the new-rich don't know this until they have been rich for a while.   [82 words]

précis misses point of original and emphasizes unimportant points

3. First, the critical minority says that we are a nation of new-rich people all dressed up with no place to go. We think the material goods advertised by appeals to our greed and vanity are what makes life worth living. Anyone who makes a lot of money thinks his money shows his worth and believes that it will make him happy. The old-rich, however, think that these ideas are foolish. Born into a rich family with

précis is too long— nearly two-thirds the length of original

property, these people know that money and property don't make them any better people. They know that the opposite is frequently true. They know that money in itself isn't worth much and that it won't buy happiness, which is the thing everyone wants. The new-rich, however, don't know these things until they have been rich long enough to find them out. Almost everyone, regardless of social class, believes that possessions make their owners better, and the more you have the more worthy you are. This is nonsense. [152 words]

4. The critical minority says we are a nation of new-rich people who are victims of newspaper, magazine, and television advertising which, by appealing to our greed and vanity, tries to convince us that all we need for happiness is a lot of possessions. We don't need most of the advertised stuff like appliances, big cars, and fur coats, but the rest of the world judges our worth by what we have. In many other countries, people don't have the material goods we have. We can't all be as lucky as the old-rich, who don't have to worry about money because they already have it.   [104 words]

writer of précis has injected his own ideas

ACCEPTABLE PRÉCIS

Critics of American culture see us as a new-rich people who, because we are new-rich, think that material goods make life worth living. We think that money is an indication of worth and that wealth brings happiness. The old-rich know better. Born to property, they do not believe that just because they have it, they are worth it. They know that happiness cannot be bought. The new-rich, however, make the mistake of believing possessions indicate the worth of their owner.   [81 words]

idea stated in précis writer's words

less than one-third of length of original

● EXERCISE 3.   As your teacher directs, use the following passages for practice in précis writing.

1

Rapidity in reading has an obvious direct bearing on success in college work, because of the large amount of reading which must be covered in nearly all college courses. But it is probably also a direct measure of the special kind of aptitude which I am calling bookish, because rapidity of reading usually correlates with comprehension and retention. Generally speaking, the more rapidly a reader reads, the more effectively he grasps and retains. The median reading speed of college freshmen has been found to be around 250 words a minute on ordinary reading matter, and a student who reads more slowly than that will certainly have difficulty in completing his college tasks within reasonable study periods. To be a really good college risk under this criterion one should readily and habitually cover not fewer than 300 words a minute on ordinary reading matter.[1]   [143 words]

[1] From "Who Should Go to College?" in *Our Children*, edited by Sidonie Matsner Gruenberg, published by Viking Press.

2

Americans are immensely concerned with amusement; but their desire is not so much to amuse themselves as to be amused by someone else. Take music, for instance. Despite a growth in musical appreciation in this century which has been more than considerable, though perhaps it has not been so great as is sometimes supposed, we do not make nearly as much music today as our grandparents did. Instead, we are content to sit back and listen to someone else make music for us. Perhaps we are too lazy to sing and play instruments. Perhaps we are unwilling to go through the discipline necessary to acquire musical facility. Perhaps we are overawed by professional expertness, unaware that much more enjoyment is gained by singing or playing oneself, even though one does it badly, than from hearing it done, however perfectly. Our musical experience is largely receptive, not creative.[1]   [147 words]

3

Ever since a group of men first developed a government, there have been two opposing ideas of the relation between the state and its members. One view puts the state above the individual. The individual has no existence except as a member of the community, carrying out its will, living for its welfare, ready to die in its service. He is not supposed to separate his identity or his personal profit from that of the nation. The community has a right to interfere in all of his affairs; he has no private life in which it is bound not to interfere. The state is more than the sum of its members. Its continuance must be assured at whatever cost to them. The state is a *totality* in which they are completely submerged. This view of the state is held by all absolute rulers, including modern dictators. We usually speak of it as *totalitarianism* or *fascism*. It prevails over a large part of the world.

The other view puts the individual above the state. The state exists for the individual, not the individual for the state. The government has no other purpose than to serve the people; they may alter its form or, if need be, revolt against it, should it fail

[1] From *Crowd Culture* by Bernard Iddings Bell. Reprinted by permission of Harper & Row, Publishers, Incorporated.

to carry out their wishes. Public and private life are quite distinct. The state may not interfere with the individual's private life so long as he does no injury to others. The individual has numerous rights which the state may not restrict except to protect the rights of other individuals. This view came to be widely held in England and northern Europe in the 1600's and 1700's; from there it spread to the New World. It took shape in the democratic form of government.[1]   [319 words]

4

The sole end for which mankind are warranted, individually or collectively, in interfering with the liberty of action of any of their number, is self-protection. The only purpose for which power can be rightfully exercised over any member of a civilized community, against his will, is to prevent harm to others. His own good, either physical or moral, is not a sufficient warrant. He cannot rightfully be compelled to do or forbear because it will be better for him to do so, because it will make him happier, because, in the opinions of others, to do so would be wise, or even right. These are good reasons for remonstrating with him, or reasoning with him, or persuading him, or entreating him, but not for compelling him, or visiting him with any evil, in case he do otherwise. To justify that, the conduct from which it is desired to deter him must be calculated to produce evil to someone else. The only part of the conduct of anyone, for which he is amenable to society, is that which concerns others. In the part which merely concerns himself, his independence is, of right, absolute. Over himself, over his own body and mind, the individual is sovereign.

It is, perhaps, hardly necessary to say that this doctrine is meant to apply only to human beings in the maturity of their faculties. We are not speaking of children, or of young persons below the age which the law may fix as that of manhood or womanhood. Those who are still in a state to require being taken care of by others must be protected against their own actions as well as against external injury.[2]   [281 words]

[1] From *Our Changing Social Order* by Ruth Wood Gavian, A. A. Gray, and Ernest R. Groves. Reprinted by permission of D. C. Heath and Company.
[2] From *On Liberty* by John Stuart Mill.

5

One of the most significant facts that came out of the atomic meeting at Geneva was the willingness of all nations, including the Soviet Union, to exchange knowledge and experience on the peaceful uses of atomic energy. This in itself promises to go a long way toward eliminating the danger of an atomic war, as it marks a big step forward toward the eventual international control of atomic energy. But the most significant fact of all for the future of mankind was the assurance that, for the first time in his existence on earth, man at last has at his disposal an unlimited supply of energy, a supply great enough to satisfy all his needs for all time.

In one scientific report after another, presented by world authorities in the field, it was made evident that the nightmare of a future without energy was a thing of the past. The highly industrialized countries need no longer worry about the exhaustion of coal and oil within a century or less. And the peoples of Asia, Africa and other underdeveloped countries need no longer worry about not being able to raise their standards of living. For the nuclear fuels, uranium and thorium—until recently believed to be rather rare—have now been found to be present in many parts of the world in relative abundance, enough to last thousands, and more likely millions, of years. And beyond that, scientists believe they will find in the relatively near future, possibly no more than twenty years from now, a way to tame the power of the hydrogen bomb for industrial power. When that day comes, and it will surely come long before the uranium and thorium supplies are exhausted, the waters of the oceans of the world will supply man with energy from their practically limitless supply of the heavy variety of hydrogen, a store estimated by authorities to be great enough to last a billion years.

It thus became clear at the Geneva atomic conference that man was on the eve of the greatest industrial, social and economic revolution in the million years of his evolution on earth. From a civilization limited and controlled by scarcity, he is about to enter a new world based on peace, a world built to order with no limit to the realization of his vast potentialities, physically, intellectually and spiritually.[1] [393 words]

[1] From *Men and Atoms* by William A. Laurence, 1959. Reprinted by permission of Simon and Schuster, Inc., Publishers.

THE ONE–PARAGRAPH FACTUAL REPORT

The two exercises which follow will give you practice in summarizing factual material in a brief and clear paragraph. The material is presented graphically. You are to study the graphs and write out the significant facts which they present. You must support convincingly whatever conclusions you draw.

To insure clear organization, make a brief outline of your paragraph before you write. Fashion a generalization and write a topic sentence expressing it. You will find it advisable to write two drafts of your paragraphs. In the first you will be primarily concerned with getting the supporting facts down on paper; in the second you will be concerned with matters of style. This kind of writing must be especially clear and concise.

● EXERCISE 4.   Study the left-hand graph on page 423. It shows clearly the facts and trends in employment over a sixty-five year period. In a one-paragraph report (150 words) state for the benefit of high school students who will soon be choosing a vocation the significant facts revealed by the graph.

Do not begin by saying "The graph shows. . . ." Begin with a generalization about employment trends, and then support the generalization by the facts shown in the graph.

● EXERCISE 5.   The three right-hand graphs on page 423 indicate some significant and, perhaps, frightening facts about world population trends. These facts have enormous economic and political significance for your generation. In a one-paragraph report state the facts and your interpretation of them.

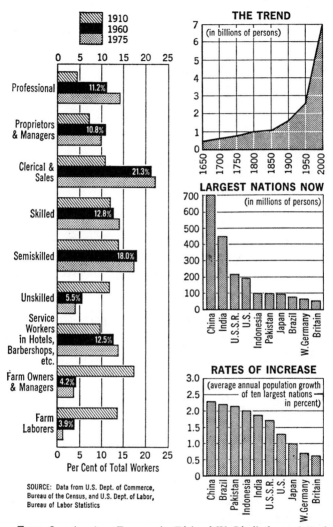

SOURCE: Data from U.S. Dept. of Commerce, Bureau of the Census, and U.S. Dept. of Labor, Bureau of Labor Statistics

From *Our American Economy* by Richard W. Lindholm and Paul Driscoll. Reprinted by permission of Harcourt, Brace & World, Inc.

Right-hand graphs from Chart on Population, The *New York Times*, December 22, 1963. © 1963 by The New York Times Company. Reprinted by permission.

The Research Paper

**Research Techniques,
The Formal Composition**

A research paper is an extensive, formal composition giving information gleaned from reading in a number of sources. The purpose of research is to discover the facts about a subject. The research paper itself is a summary of the facts discovered.

Although many research papers are purely informational, some attempt to draw a conclusion from the facts they reveal. Typical of the purely informational kind would be a paper on medieval cathedrals or American folk music or rocketry. Typical of the paper that attempts to reach a conclusion would be a paper on a controversial subject, or one that seeks the answer to a question. For example: Should capital punishment be abolished? How can the world's growing population be fed? Have our federal Indian policies been sound? Whether your purpose is merely to state the facts or to go a step further and draw a conclusion from the facts, your procedure is the same; in both instances, you must find out what the facts are.

Like any extensive undertaking requiring sustained concentration over a period of several weeks, the preparation of a research paper requires self-discipline. If you have good study habits, can stick to a schedule, and are not one who lets everything go until the last minute, you will find the job relatively easy; you may even enjoy it! If, on the contrary, you have not learned how to study efficiently and if you are a procrastinator, you may find the work frustrating. It is more than likely that the preparation of a research paper will do more to sharpen your study techniques and strengthen your self-discipline than any other single assignment of the year.

Plan to devote to your research paper enough time to insure that your work will be thorough and unhurried. Research work is careful work. Do not be satisfied with a paper that will merely "get by." Take pride in the amount of information you can give in approximately 2,000 words (or whatever length your teacher specifies); take pride in the accuracy of your work and in the neatness of its appearance.

Approach your subject with an open mind, especially if the subject is controversial. A research paper is the result of an attempt to find out the truth. Personal opinion and prejudice are completely out of place. You do not even use the pronoun *I*. Your paper is completely impersonal.

The preparation of a research paper provides a valuable review of the following skills: using the library and reference tools, note taking, organizing and outlining, paragraphing, footnoting, compiling and writing a bibliography, writing correct, clear sentences. Before beginning work, study Chapters 27 and 28, which deal with the library and reference books.

From the experience of thousands of students, a standard method of preparing a research paper and a standard form for the paper have been developed. This method and this form are described on the following pages, which you should read through rapidly before starting work on your paper in order to get some idea of the nature and the proportions of the job ahead; then begin work, following the seven-step method.

THE SEVEN STEPS IN WRITING A RESEARCH PAPER

1. Selecting and limiting the subject.
2. Preparing a working bibliography—a list of available sources
3. Preparing a preliminary outline
4. Reading and taking notes
5. Assembling notes and writing the final outline
6. Writing the first draft
7. Writing the revised final draft with footnotes and the bibliography

♦ NOTE The steps to be followed in writing a research paper are essentially the same as those for the whole composition (pages 345–62). The main difference is that in writing the research paper you must give more thought to research and the acknowledgment of sources.

FINDING THE RIGHT SUBJECT

25a. Select a subject which is interesting to you and suitable for research in the libraries at your disposal.

Since you are to do a large amount of reading, you owe it to yourself to choose a subject you really want to know more about. In a small way, you are to become an authority on this subject; choose a topic which will hold your interest.

Availability of Source Material

Other considerations are involved in the selection of a subject. The subject must lend itself to research in several sources, and the sources must be available in the libraries you use. Your autobiography would not be a suitable subject for a research paper because you could not look up material on it. It is not a research subject. Even the life of a famous person in whom you are interested would be of doubtful value for research because a complete life has probably already been published in one book, and you would tend to rely too much on just this one source. The best kind of subject is one on which information can be found in many different sources.

No matter how interesting to you a subject may be or how suitable for research, it will not be usable unless you can get the source material. If you find that your library does not have enough information on your chosen subject, you will have to choose another subject. Of course, the library is not the only source of material available to you. You may find that some excellent books on your subject are not in your school or public library but are available in inexpensive paperback editions. Government publications are also inexpensive. Students sometimes get information from personal interviews or correspondence with authorities on the subject. For example, if you were writing a history of your community, you could arrange to interview one of the older residents. If you were writing on conservation, you could interview a local conservation officer or write to the State Commissioner.

Typical Areas for Research

The following lists suggest general areas in which high school research papers may be successfully written. The lists are intended to give you an idea of the kind of subject matter that is suitable for research. To be used, most of the following subjects would have to be considerably limited.

SOCIAL HISTORY   Social customs in the eighteenth century; costume in Elizabethan England; medieval arms and armor; amusements in the Middle Ages; family life in the Victorian period; American colonial life; child labor in the nineteenth century; life in the Congo today; superstition in primitive societies; one of the world's great religions; the Great Depression; the Prohibition Era; the 1890's; the changing role of women; the way of life in ancient Greece; the outlawing of prize fights.

25a

POLITICAL HISTORY   The Crusades; early invaders of England; early history of the Republican party; the French Revolution; the pioneer in American history; Pan-Americanism; the United Nations; the League of Nations; the Monroe Doctrine in American history; socialism; communism; the communist menace in Latin America; the Lincoln-Douglas debates; third parties in America; the Supreme Court; the Electoral College; the European Common Market; labor unions.

LITERARY HISTORY   Poetry of Robert Frost; modern American essayists; experimental theaters; Shakespearean playhouses; satire in eighteenth-century literature; the frontier in literature; romanticism and realism; transcendentalism; Brook Farm; modern experimental poets; World War II novels; existentialism; censorship; movies, yesterday and today; Puritanism.

MODERN PROBLEMS   Juvenile delinquency; modern race problems; labor unions; education; conservation of natural resources; the farm problem; NATO; rise of nationalism; the "new" nations; civil defense; nuclear testing; automation; foreign aid; the Peace Corps; space exploration; care of the aged; socialized medicine; the communist menace in Latin America; the population explosion; housing; the Cold War; peaceful co-existence; the United States' image abroad; the conservative right.

SCIENCE   Medieval medicine; history of anesthesia; peacetime uses of atomic energy; electronics; chemistry in agriculture; dairying; the manufacture of steel; plastics; synthetic clothing; interplanetary travel; prolonging life; drugs and mental therapy; advances in surgery; wonder drugs; recent advances in communication; rocketry; pesticides; progress in the fight against cancer; exploration by telescope; food substitutes; controlling the weather; computers.

ART   The Pre-Raphaelite painters; Gothic architecture; abstract art; modern sculpture; new home designs; history of opera; furniture materials and design; the story of jazz; art in advertising; modern architecture; modern experimental artists; modern dance.

Limiting the Subject

It should be obvious that your subject must be sufficiently limited to enable you to treat it adequately within the scope

of your paper. Your paper will be a better piece of work if
you go deeply into a narrow subject rather than treat a
broad one superficially. The following examples show how
a subject may be limited.

Education
Federal Aid to Education
Federal Aid to Non-public Schools
Should Federal Aid Be Given to Non-public Schools?

The American Indian
The history of the American Indian
Federal policies concerning the American Indian
Have our federal Indian policies been sound?

RESEARCH

25b. Use library tools to look up available sources of information. Prepare a working bibliography on cards.

When you have selected a subject for your research paper,
limited it, and had it approved by your teacher, you are
ready to look over the field. You begin by equipping yourself with a package of 3 × 5-inch cards.

The Working Bibliography

With index cards in hand, you go to the card catalogue,
the *Readers' Guide*, the vertical file, and appropriate reference books, and compile a list of all books and articles in
the library which promise to be useful to you. Record each
book or article on a card—one source to a card. For reasons
which will be clear later you must write on the card *complete*
information about the source. For books, this information
can be obtained from the card catalogue; for magazines, it
can be obtained from the *Readers' Guide*. For other sources
(pamphlets, newspapers), you must get the information
from the source itself.

25b

Books

1. Call number in upper left-hand corner
2. Author or editor, last name first for alphabetizing later. (Indicate editor by placing *ed.* after his name.) If a book has two or more authors, only the name of the first author is given last name first. The names of the others are given first name first.
3. Title, underlined (volume, if necessary). Pamphlets only: series and number, if any, in parentheses
4. Place of publication
5. Publisher
6. Year of publication (or date for some pamphlets)

Magazine, Newspaper, and Encyclopedia Articles

1. Author (unless article is unsigned)
2. Title of article, enclosed in quotation marks
3. Name of magazine, newspaper, or encyclopedia, underlined
4. For magazines: volume and page numbers as in *Readers' Guide.* For newspapers: page number. For encyclopedias: volume and page numbers
5. For magazines and newspapers: date. For encyclopedias: place of publication, publisher, year of publication

While the card catalogue will give you, for a book, all the information you need for your working bibliography card, it will not tell you much about the contents of the book. One way to examine quickly a number of possibly useful books is to go to the shelf in the library where, according to its call number, a book on your subject will be found. Since nonfiction books are classified by subject, you will also find on this and neighboring shelves most of the books the library has on your subject. A glance at the table of contents and the index in these books will tell you how useful the books will probably be.

If you were writing on Shakespeare's Globe Theater, for example, and you found listed in the table of contents a chapter on the Globe or a chapter on Elizabethan theaters, including the Globe, you would list the book in your work-

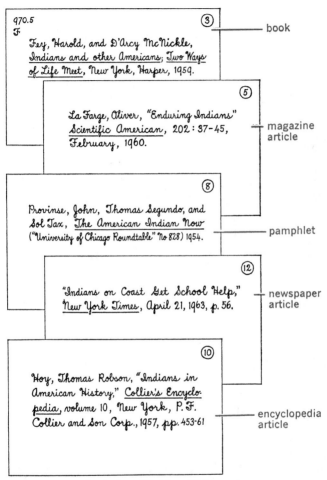

970.5
F   ③

Fey, Harold, and D'Arcy McNickle,
*Indians and other Americans; Two Ways
of Life Meet*, New York, Harper, 1959.

— book

⑤

La Farge, Oliver, "Enduring Indians"
Scientific American, 202 : 37-45,
February, 1960.

— magazine article

⑧

Provinse, John, Thomas Segundo, and
Sol Tax, *The American Indian Now*
("University of Chicago Roundtable" No 828) 1954.

— pamphlet

⑫

"Indians on Coast Get School Help,"
New York Times, April 21, 1963, p. 56.

— newspaper article

⑩

Hoy, Thomas Robson, "Indians in
American History," *Collier's Encyclo-
pedia*, volume 10, New York, P. F.
Collier and Son Corp., 1957, pp. 453-61

— encyclopedia article

Cards in a Working Bibliography

ing bibliography. Even if the table of contents does not reveal information on your subject, such information may still be in the book. Look in the index and judge the usefulness of the book by the number of pages devoted to your subject. A listing like "Globe Theater, 250–275," for instance, would certainly suggest that the book would be worth including in your working bibliography.

At the conclusion of Step 2, you will have a stack of cards—a working bibliography—representing the sources you plan to read. *Number the cards clearly in the upper right-hand corner*. The card numbers will be used later when you are taking notes, saving you the task of identifying the source in detail for each note you take.

The Preliminary Outline

25c. Prepare a preliminary outline to guide you in note-taking.

Before you can take notes in an organized way, you must have some idea of the topics on which you will need information. To formulate a list of such topics, begin your reading with a few general articles which give an overall survey. If your subject is treated in an encyclopedia, the article there will be excellent for this purpose. Another way to approach such an outline is to try to anticipate the important questions your paper will have to answer. Jot down what seem to be the major divisions of the subject.

The preliminary outline is not an outline of your paper as it will finally be organized. It is, rather, a guide for use in your reading and note-taking. It represents the topics which, at this point in your work, you think you will want to cover. As your reading suggests new topics, insert them in the outline; as you find that some of your topics cannot or should not be treated in your paper, remove them from the outline.

HAVE OUR FEDERAL INDIAN POLICIES BEEN SOUND?

   I. History of the Indian problem
  II. Federal policies
      A. Legislation
      B. Administrative policies
 III. Work of federal agencies
 IV. Problems of the Indians today
  V. Solutions

The Note Card

25d. Read and take notes on cards.

With a package of 4×6 index cards, your working bibliography, and your preliminary outline, you are ready to turn to the major task of reading your sources. The note cards should be larger than the working bibliography cards for two reasons: first, the cards will accommodate more notes; and second, you will be able to distinguish them from your smaller bibliography cards. Since you will be working with both kinds of cards at the same time, it is important that you be able to distinguish them at a glance.

At the top of a note card write the topic the notes deal with. The notes you take will fall under one or another of the topics in your preliminary outline. As you can see in the outline above, these topics will be very broad at the start of your reading. As you read further, you will find new topics or subtopics for your outline, and these, in turn, will be used as headings for your note cards. At the top of each note card write the outline topic with which the notes deal. This topic is called a *slug*. See the sample note card on page 435.

Use a separate card for each source. In the upper right-hand corner of the card, write the number of the source as you have indicated it on the card in the working bibliography. You will find that several sources will provide information on the same topic; hence you will have several

**25
c-d**

cards with the same heading, each card representing a different source.

Always write the page number either before or after every idea you jot down. You will need this number for the footnotes in your paper.

Take notes in your own words. The best way to acquire skill in note-taking is to start right in taking down information which you think may be usable. As you progress, you will develop judgment as to what you are likely to use. You will develop judgment, too, as to when you should copy word-for-word from your sources and when you should write the information in your own words. In general, you should do very little copying. A research paper should not consist of a mere list of quotations. You are expected to gather facts and ideas from your sources, digest them thoroughly, and write them in your own words. Quote verbatim only when the words of the source are especially important and especially well chosen.

Develop your own shorthand to save time in note-taking. Common ways of getting ideas down quickly are (1) abbreviate as many words as you can without affecting the clarity of your notes, (2) use symbols for short words—& for *and*, for example, (3) write phrases rather than whole sentences. Always write legibly, for if you do not use your notes for a week or two, you will find that penmanship that was perfectly clear to you when you wrote it has become surprisingly baffling.

Acknowledge your sources. No fault is more common and more serious in high school research papers than the use of quotations without acknowledgment of the sources. Teachers are quick to detect quotations that are not enclosed in quotation marks, and they are impatient with papers written not in your own style, but in the style of your sources. The danger here is that, in spite of good intentions, you may be led into copying the style of your sources without realizing that you are doing so. A "derived" style results from copying word for word everything you place on your note cards. The cure for this fault is always to take notes in your own words. Don't copy unless you intend to quote exactly. The use of the words of others as though they were your own is called plagiarism, and it is a serious offense. When you do copy, be sure to copy accurately, without abbreviating, and to enclose the copied material in quotation marks.

Learn to judge the reliability of your sources. You should develop a critical attitude toward your sources, especially when you are writing on a controversial subject. Ask yourself these questions: What do I know about this author? By what right does he claim to be an authority? Is there any ulterior motive behind his writing? When was this book or article published? If you are working on a current topic which forces you to rely largely on newspaper stories and magazine articles, which vary widely in quality, you should be especially alert to distinguish the truly dependable from the mere potboilers or the biased.

slug—from preliminary outline

number of working bibliography card

⑩

Legislation
General Allotment Act – 1887
broke up reservations into
individually owned tracts
25 yrs. later, after gov't restrictions
removed, tracts dwindled away,
split up & sold. p. 23

The Final Outline

25e. Assemble your notes and write the final outline.

When you are satisfied that you have enough notes to insure adequate treatment of your subject, your next job is arranging the notes in the order in which you will use them. Since each note card has a slug, your first step is to assemble in one pile all cards bearing the same slug. This simple mechanical task actually carries you a long way toward the organization of your paper. You will have before you a number of piles of information, each pile treating one division of your subject as represented in the preliminary outline. You now have to consider such matters as the order of topics in your paper and the possibility of various subdivisions of the slug topics.

You will find it necessary at this point to prepare your final outline in rough form. This final outline will take shape readily as you skim through your note cards. Before writing the outline, review the techniques of outlining described on pages 349–51. Follow your teacher's instructions as to whether you are to write a sentence or a topic outline. You will find that many of your slugs will become subtopics, while others may become major topics. Some may be discarded. You should probably have no more than six major topics. Using too many of these Roman numeral divisions suggests poor organization.

WRITING THE RESEARCH PAPER

25f. Write the first draft.

The writing of your paper, toward which all your work has been directed should go smoothly if you have followed directions. With your outline to guide you and your notes on each topic conveniently arranged, you are ready to write.

The First Draft

The first draft of your paper is a step in the whole process of creating a research paper; it is for your use only, not for anyone else to read. Do not worry unduly over details of style and mechanics. Do not delay your work trying to think of a clever introduction. You may start anywhere you wish; the important thing is to make a start, to put your ideas on paper, even though eventually you may revise extensively.

As you incorporate in your paper the ideas on your note cards, be careful to indicate the source on your manuscript, *whether you are giving the ideas in your own words or quoting the words of the source.* You do not need to give the source of information which is a matter of general knowledge. For instance, it would not be necessary to give a source for the fact that the Indian preceded the white man in North America or that the Bureau of Indian Affairs operates under the Department of the Interior. In writing this rough draft it will be sufficient to indicate the source of material by simply writing down after each idea the source number from the working-bibliography card, and the page number. You need not bother to copy long quotations from your note cards into this rough draft; merely jot down enough information to help you find the quotation later when writing your final draft. Write rapidly.

The Final Draft

25g. Write the revised final draft with footnotes and a bibliography.

If you have planned your work so that you are not pressed for time, the writing of the final draft should be relatively easy. Having solved troublesome problems of organization and expression, you are now concerned primarily with form. The following matters must be carefully handled.

25
e-g

Style

Having studied the chapters on usage and sentence structure in this textbook, you should apply what you have learned to your own sentences. Revise them just as you revised the exercise sentences in the chapters on correct, clear, and smooth sentences. Also check your mechanics: capital letters, puncutation, and spelling.

Appearance

Allow ample margins on both sides and at the top and bottom of each page. If you are typing your paper, type it double spaced and on only one side of the paper. Long quotations (more than five lines) should be typed single space and set off by wider margins than the rest of the paper.

Transitions

Use transitional devices to keep the thought moving smoothly from paragraph to paragraph and from one major division to another. See pages 355–59. An occasional transitional paragraph will help the reader to follow your organization. See pages 359–60.

Do not divide your paper into chapters. Chapter divisions in a 2,000-word paper tend to break it up and destroy its unity. The paper becomes five or six research papers instead of one.

Footnotes

To avoid constantly interrupting your paper with the citation of sources, you use footnotes. To the right and above the final word in a quotation or an idea taken from one of your sources, you will write a number. Write number 1 for the first source, 2 for the second, etc. These numbers refer the reader to their counterparts at the foot of the page, where the source is given. Follow your teacher's instructions as to whether you are to renumber footnotes with each page or number them consecutively straight through the paper. A footnote is followed by a period. Each page must be so planned that there will be enough space at the bottom to accommodate the footnotes for sources cited on that page.

You must give footnotes for all ideas taken from sources even though the ideas are, as they should be, written in your own words. Do not make the mistake of using footnotes only for quoted matter.

Footnote Form

The footnote for a book or a pamphlet gives the name of the author (first name first), the title of the book (underlined), and the page number. Underlining in a manuscript is the equivalent of italicizing in print. Since you will have a complete bibliography (list of sources used) at the end of your paper, you need not give facts about publication in the footnotes.

The footnote for a magazine or newspaper article gives the author (unless the article is anonymous), the title of the article (in quotation marks), the name of the magazine or newspaper (underlined), the volume (for magazines only), date and page number. All items in a footnote are separated by commas. The following are sample footnotes.

[1] William T. Hagan, <u>American Indians</u>, p. 63. [footnote for a book]

[2] Oliver La Farge, "Enduring Indian," <u>Scientific American</u>, 202, February, 1960, p. 38. [footnote for a magazine article]

[3] "Indians on Coast Get School Help," <u>New York Times</u>, April 21, 1963, p. 56. [footnote for an unsigned newspaper article]

[4] Hildegarde Thompson, "Education of the Indians," <u>Encyclopedia Americana</u>, 1961 Ed., Vol. 15, p. 61. [footnote for signed encyclopedia article]

Ibid.

When two or more consecutive footnotes refer to the same source, writers use the Latin abbreviation *Ibid.* for footnotes after the first. *Ibid.* represents the Latin word *ibidem*, meaning "in the same place." The use of *Ibid.* is efficient because it makes it unnecessary to repeat the same author, title, etc., for a footnote which has been given immediately before. Suppose, for example, that you have referred three times in succession to the same source; you have, however, referred to a different page each time. Your footnotes will appear as follows:

[1] William T. Hagan, <u>American Indians</u>, p. 63.
[2] <u>Ibid</u>., p. 70.
[3] <u>Ibid</u>., p. 73.

Notice that *Ibid.* must be underlined and followed by a period. If the reference is to the same page as that referred to by the preceding footnote, the comma and page number are not necessary.

When a footnote reference to another source comes between two references to the same source, you do not use *Ibid.* to avoid repetition because *Ibid.* always refers to the footnote immediately preceding. Instead of *Ibid.*, you use the last name of the author of the work already footnoted earlier in your paper and follow it with the page number. If the source is anonymous, you repeat the title only and follow it with the page number. For instance, had the footnotes listed above been separated by a footnote referring to a different source, the result would appear as follows:

[1] William T. Hagan, <u>American Indians</u>, p. 63.
[2] Oliver La Farge, "Enduring Indian," <u>Scientific American</u>, 202, February, 1960, p. 38.
[3] Hagan, p. 70.
[4] <u>Ibid</u>., p. 73.

Of course, if you have referred previously in your paper

to more than one work by the same author, you must, in addition to giving his last name, give the title, followed by the page number.[1]

> 3 Hagan, <u>American Indians</u>, p. 70.

Footnoting "Second-hand" Quotations

The question may arise as to how to footnote a quotation or an idea which the author you were reading had, in turn, taken from another author. The following sample shows how to give credit to both sources.

> 1 Theodore Haas, "Indian Uprising—New Style," <u>The Survey</u>, February, 1949, quoted in Petersen, Helen L., "American Indian Political Participation," <u>Annals of the American Academy of Political and Social Science</u>, 311, May, 1957, p. 123.

The Explanatory Footnote

The principal use of footnotes is to cite sources. Occasionally, however, they are used for comments by the author or for additional, interesting information which is not of first importance and which, if included in the paper itself, would constitute a confusing interruption. This kind of footnote, while sometimes useful, should be sparingly used.

● EXERCISE 1.   Each of the following items contains complete information for a footnote. Write the footnotes in correct form in the order in which they are given.

---

[1] In footnoting a source previously footnoted after other footnotes have intervened, writers formerly used another Latin abbreviation in place of the title. This abbreviation, *op. cit.*, represents the Latin words *opere citato*, meaning "in the work cited." Thus footnote 3 in the first series of footnotes above would appear as follows:

> 3 Hagan, *op. cit.*, p. 63.

You should understand the meaning of *op. cit.*, because you may encounter it in the writing of others, but you need not use the abbreviation yourself.

1. A magazine article entitled Indian Administration in the United States. Written by P. Nash. Appeared in Vital Speeches for February 15, 1963, vol. 29, page 279.
2. The same article as above, same page.
3. Book by Charles Hamilton entitled Cry of the Thunderbird, page 41.
4. Article in the New York Times for April 21, 1963, page 57. No author. Title of article: Navajos Install Tribal Chairman.
5. Same as item 3 above, page 50.
6. An article by Willard W. Beatty, in volume 15 of the Encyclopedia Americana, page 28L, entitled Indian Affairs.

The Bibliography

In order to give the reader complete information as to your sources, you must attach to your paper a bibliography, a list of the sources you used. This final bibliography differs from the working bibliography, which you prepared first, in that it includes only the books and articles you actually used. The bibliography is an important part of a research paper. Prepare it with great care. Be sure that it is complete, accurate, and consistent in form.

In writing a bibliography, observe the following details of form:

1. Items are arranged in alphabetical order according to the last names of authors. Hence, unlike footnotes, which are not arranged alphabetically, bibliographical items give the author's last name first. This applies only to the first author if the book has more than one author. The names of a second and third author are written first name first. It is not necessary to number the items. Anonymous items are placed alphabetically by the first word of their titles, unless the first word is *the*, *an*, or *a*, in which case the second word determines the alphabetical position. Alphabetizing can be done easily by arranging the working-bibliography cards in alphabetical order.

2. If the bibliography includes more than one work by the same author, it is not necessary to repeat the author's

name with each. Use a long dash in place of the name in all listings after the first.

3. When an item occupies more than one line, the second line should be indented so that the names of authors will stand out on the page.

4. Commas are used between all parts of a bibliographical item. A period at the end is optional.

5. If you type your paper, type your bibliography entries single space, but leave a double space between entries.

Study the following bibliography. The items in it were selected from a longer bibliography to illustrate the correct form for various kinds of listings.

BIBLIOGRAPHY

Brown, A. A., "America Keeps a 165-Year-Old Promise," <u>American Mercury</u>, 91:113-15, September, 1960.

Driver, Harold, <u>Indians of North America</u>, Chicago, University of Chicago Press, 1961.

Fey, Harold Edward and D'Arcy McNickle, <u>Indians and Other Americans; Two Ways of Life Meet</u>, New York, Harper, 1959.

"Indians on Coast Get School Help," <u>New York Times</u>, April 21, 1963, p. 56.

La Farge, Oliver, "Chronic Peculiarity: Indians Surrounding Santa Fe," <u>New Yorker</u>, 33:89-90+, March 16, 1957.

———— "Termination of Federal Supervision; Disintegration and the American Indians," <u>Annals of the American Academy of Political and Social Science</u>, 311:41-46, May, 1957.

"United States of America: Racial Composition," <u>Encyclopaedia Britannica</u>, Chicago, Encyclopaedia Britannica, 1937.

<u>Who's on First? Fair Play for All Americans</u>, ("Public Affairs Pamphlet," No. 233), New York, Public Affairs Pamphlets, April, 1956.

● EXERCISE 2.   Each of the items in this exercise gives complete bibliographical information about a book or an article. Revise the items so that they are correct in form and in the proper order and arrangement for a bibliography.

1. Magazine article by M. Mann entitled Slow Drivers Can Kill You appeared in Popular Science Monthly, volume 182, pages 77–79+, April, 1963.
2. Magazine article, unsigned, entitled Reading, Writing, and Driving appeared in Senior Scholastic for March 21, 1962, volume 80, page 9.
3. A book Highway Jungle by E. A. Tenney, published by Exposition Press, New York, 1962.
4. A book by R. Ward and B. W. Yates entitled Rodger Ward's Guide to Good Driving, published by Harper, New York, 1962.

Charts, Diagrams and Illustrations

Charts and diagrams may be included in your paper where they are of real value. Always give with each the source from which you copied it. Illustrations cut out from sources may be looked upon with suspicion as attempts at padding, or as evidence of vandalism in the treatment of source material.

Checklist for Research Paper

1. **Cover.**   Give your research paper a stiff cover, bearing the title of the paper. Make it attractive.
2. **Title page.**   The title page should give the title, your name, the name of the course, and the date. The first two will occupy the center of the page; the last two will be placed at the bottom, centered or at the right.
3. **Final outline.**   This, in its revised form, is the outline you followed in writing your paper.
4. **The paper itself.**   All material taken from your sources must be footnoted unless it is common knowledge. Check footnotes for accuracy and correct form.
5. **The bibliography.**   Check for accuracy and correct form, including punctuation.

ABBREVIATIONS USED IN SOURCE MATERIALS

In your reading you may encounter some of the abbreviations listed below. The meanings are given here as an aid to your understanding of your sources. Learn to recognize them at once.

c or ©	*copyright;* used before a copyright date (c1935) to indicate when copyright was obtained. (The circled *c* is the international copyright symbol.)
c., ca.	*about* (from the Latin *circa, circum*); used with dates—"*ca.* 1732" means "about 1732."
cf.	*compare* (from the Latin *confer*); "*cf.* the Atlantic Treaty" means "compare with the Atlantic Treaty."
ed.	*editor, edited, edition*
e.g.	*for example* (from the Latin *exempli gratia*)
et al.	*and others* (from the Latin *et alii*); also *and elsewhere* (from the Latin *et alibi*)
f., ff.	*following page, pages;* "p. 25f." means "page 25 and the following page"; "p. 25ff." means "page 25 and following pages."
ibid.	*in the same place* (from the Latin *ibidem*)
id.	*the same* (from the Latin *idem*)
i.e.	*that is* (from the Latin *id est*)
l., ll.	*line, lines*
loc. cit.	*in the place cited* (from the Latin *loco citato*)
ms., mss.	*manuscript, manuscripts*
N.B.	*note well* (from the Latin *nota bene*)
n.d.	*no date;* publication date not given in book
op. cit.	*in the work cited* (from the Latin *opere citato*)
p., pp.	*page, pages*
q.v.	*which see, whom see* (from the Latin *quod vide*)
sic	*thus* (from the Latin); when a writer quotes a passage containing an error (wrong date, misspelling, etc.) and he wishes to make clear that he has copied the original accurately, he inserts [*sic*] beside the error.
vide	*see* (from the Latin)

HAVE OUR FEDERAL INDIAN POLICIES BEEN SOUND?

Nancy Ambrose

[The following are sample
pages from a high school student's
research paper. Use them as a model
in preparing your own paper.]

Social Studies XII
Mr. Tegnall
April 8, 1963

OUTLINE

Have Our Federal Indian Policies Been Sound?

As everyone knows, dealing with the American Indian was one of the major problems faced by the earliest colonists. Later, settlers moving westward fought the Indian, driving him from his land and sometimes destroying his sources of food. From the establishment of a federal government in 1789, a major problem has been the formulation of policies which would both enable Indians to live peaceably with their neighbors and raise the Indian standard of living.

A concern with trading regulations first involved the federal government in Indian affairs. Policies regulating trade led eventually to concern for the Indian's welfare. The Indian Removal Act of 1830 called for the relocation of between twenty and thirty tribes from the region east of the Mississippi. The Appropriations Act of 1871 brought about greater federal legislative control of the Indians. Because Indian lands were tax exempt, the states were unwilling to contribute funds for Indian welfare. Consequently, Indian problems became the responsibility of the federal government.[1]

---

[1] "Congress Should Vote New Indian Policy," Christian Century, 76, August 19, 1959, p. 940.

By 1880, the government had assumed the role of trustee over Indian lands and people. The Indians were considered wards of the government and were subject to government control, although theoretically they had self-government on their reservations.[1]

In 1887 the reservation system was made obsolete under a new concept of treatment of the Indian. This concept held that the Indian's traditional society should be crushed and he should be absorbed into American life.[2] [transitional paragraph]

This idea was implemented by the General Allotment Act of 1887, which divided tribal land among members of the tribe. The head of each family was given eighty acres of farming land or one hundred sixty acres of grazing land. Single persons and orphans received half this amount.[3] The Secretary of

---

[1] Oliver La Farge, "Indians Want a New Frontier," New York Times Magazine, June 11, 1961, p. 70.

[2] A Sketch of the Development of the Bureau of Indian Affairs and of Indian Policy, p. 583.

[3] Theodore Haas, "The Legal Aspects of Indian Affairs from 1887 to 1957," Annals of the American Academy of Political and Social Science, 311, May, 1957, p. 12.

the Interior acted as trustee for the land and held the land title for twenty-five years or until the Indian owner was thought capable of managing the land by himself.[1]

The General Allotment Act had two objectives. First, it substituted individual ownership of land for communal ownership, which was considered savage. The hope was that individual ownership would create in the Indian a feeling of pride and self-respect. Second, it would enable an Indian to sell some of his land.[2] The sale would be beneficial because in theory at least, the Indian would sell to white settlers, who, being industrious ranchers and farmers, would set good examples for the Indian to follow.[3] The Act did not accomplish its purpose. The Indians sold millions of acres, but the hoped-for results did not occur. Theodore Roosevelt called the Act "a mighty pulverizing engine to break up the tribal mass."[4]   [direct quotation]

---

[1] Haas, p. 14.

[2] La Farge, p. 70.

[3] Ibid.

[4] Haas, p. 16.

[pages 4–8 omitted]

Although there are these various organizations handling Indian affairs, the work,
in some instances, is being transferred to
the states. State laws apply to the Indians
only if the federal government agrees.[1] Some
non-Indian citizens feel that the states are
responsible for the living conditions and
welfare of the Indian.[2] In several states
federal supervision has been terminated. For
example, Oregon has worked with the federal
government to end federal supervision in
that state. Now its policy is "not to give
sympathy to the Indians but to give them a
helping hand."[3] [direct quotation]

The Indian problem is very much the same
today as it was in 1900, when it was characterized by Chief Standing Bear of the
Sioux tribe as follows:

---

[1] Haas, p. 18.

[2] C. D. Ebersole, "Reply to: It's Almost
Never Too Late," Christian Century, 74, April 3,
1957, p. 426.

[3] A. H. Wright, chairman of the Governor's
Advisory Committee on Indian Affairs, reply to a
letter requesting information concerning Oregon's
Indian policies.

10

The attempted transformation of the Indian by the white man and the chaos that has resulted are but the fruits of the white man's disobedience of a fundamental and spiritual law. The pressure that has been brought to bear upon the native people, since the cessation of armed conflict, in the attempt to force conformity of custom and habit has caused a reaction more destructive than war, and the injury has not only affected the Indian, but has extended to the white population as well. Tyranny, stupidity and lack of vision have brought about the situation alluded to as the "Indian Problem."[1]

Major divisions of the "Indian Problem" are land usage, education, employment, discrimination, health, and standards of living.

[pages 11-14 omitted]

A sound policy is one which is both fair and effective. Judged by this definition, our federal Indian policies have not, until recent years, been sound. Although the federal government has tried to help the Indian, its policies have often done him gross injustice. Some federal legislation, the

---

[1] Charles Hamilton, Cry of the Thunderbird, p. 244.

General Allotment Act, for example, benefited the non-Indian more than the Indian.

The unsound policies of the past, however, have gradually been replaced by sounder policies under recent administrations. Before 1900, the policy was to get rid of the Indian problem by getting rid of the Indian, either through the reservation system or through absorption. Today it is more fully realized that the Indian is an Indian with his own cultural heritage, different from ours. If he chooses to accept our standards, he should be encouraged. Yet he should be free not to accept them if he so chooses.

The Indian problem can be solved by careful cooperation between the states and the federal government. The responsibility for financing should remain with the federal government, which should continue to develop more adequate programs in agriculture, health, housing, and education. The unfair and inadequate federal policies of the past are giving way to new policies based on a sincere desire to improve the general welfare of our Indian citizens.

BIBLIOGRAPHY

nswers to Your Questions on the American
Indians, Washington, D.C., United States
Department of the Interior, Bureau of Indian
Affairs, n.d.

Beatty, Willard W., "Indian Affairs,"
Encyclopedia Americana, volume 15, New York,
Americana Corporation, 1961.

"Congress Should Vote New Indian Policy,"
Christian Century, 76:940, August 19, 1959.

Ebersole, C. D., "Reply to: It's Almost Never
Too Late," Christian Century, 74:426,
April 3, 1957.

Embree, Edwin R., Indians of the Americas,
Boston, Houghton, Mifflin, 1939.

Fey, Harold Edward and D'Arcy McNickle, Indians
and Other Americans; Two Ways of Life Meet,
New York, Harper, 1959.

Haas, Theodore, "The Legal Aspects of Indian
Affairs from 1887 to 1957," Annals of the
American Academy of Political and Social
Science, 311:12–22, May, 1957.

Hagan, William T., American Indians, Chicago,
University of Chicago Press, 1961.

Hamilton, Charles, Cry of the Thunderbird,
New York, Macmillan, 1950.

"Indian Point Four," Nation, 192:158–59,
February 25, 1961.

"Indians on Coast Get School Help," New York
Times, April 21, 1963, p. 56.

La Farge, Oliver, "Enduring Indian," _Scientific American_, 202:37–45, February, 1960.

_____ "Indians Want a New Frontier," _New York Times Magazine_, June 11, 1961, p. 12+.

Neuberger, R. L., "Senator Surveys the Land of the Braves," _Saturday Review_, 42:14–15, May 9, 1959.

Provinse, John, Thomas Segundo, and Sol Tax, _The American Indian Now_, ("University of Chicago Roundtable" No. 828), 1954.

Roland, Albert, _The American Indians_, Washington, D.C., United States Information Agency, 1962.

Sketch of the Development of the Bureau of Indian Affairs and of Indian Policy, Washington, D.C., United States Department of the Interior, Bureau of Indian Affairs, n.d.

Wright, A. H., chairman of the Governor's Advisory Committee on Indian Affairs, reply to a letter requesting information concerning Oregon's Indian policies, February 11, 1963.

CHAPTER 26

Letter Writing

Standard Practice in Friendly and Business Letters

THE FRIENDLY LETTER

When you wrote your first friendly letters back in elementary school days, you probably tried to follow the instructions given you by your teachers. Certainly you put into practice what they had taught you about the proper form of a letter. You thought about ways of making your letter interesting. Your teachers gave some helpful advice such as to write about things your friend would like to know about, to be specific in telling your experiences, to avoid commonplace and dull remarks, to describe vividly, to show a sense of humor. These bits of advice still apply, but now that you are more mature, you hardly need a textbook to tell you what to say in a friendly letter. A textbook cannot and should not try to tell you what to say in an intimate letter, or how to say it, any more than it can tell you how to chat with your friends on the way home from school. A friendly letter is as natural, informal, and intimate as a conversation.

Even some details of form may be safely ignored. For example, when writing to close friends and relatives who know very well where you live, you need not give your address in the heading. Remember, however, that like standard practice in usage, grammar, and punctuation, standard practice in the writing of friendly letters recognizes a difference between informal and formal situations. While you need not observe all details of standard letter form in writing the more informal of your letters, you will surely want to observe them carefully in writing to a new acquaintance or to your aunt in Alaska whom you have never seen, for such people may judge you very largely by your letters.

Just as you have learned the characteristics of formal English even though you use informal English most of the time, so you should learn the characteristics of the more formal type of friendly letter, even though most of the letters you write are very informal. Of course, a friendly letter, like any social contact, should reveal an understanding of good manners. Considerations of neatness, attractive arrangement, and proper stationery are important in all letters.

Form in Friendly Letters

26a. **Observe standard practice in writing friendly letters.**

(1) Use appropriate stationery and ink.

Appropriate stationery is stationery that displays good taste. The fact that white stationery is always in good taste need not rule out tinted varieties. If you feel the need to express your personality in purple or green ink, do so only in letters to friends who know you well. Never write letters in pencil, and never use ruled paper as letter stationery.

If you know how to typewrite, you may type friendly letters. Do not, however, subject your reader to the arduous task of reading a letter which has been badly typed. Unless you have had experience in typing, use longhand.

(2) Be neat.

Even the most informal letters, like the most informal dress, should be neat. Avoid cross-outs, ink blots, uphill

26a

writing, crowded lines. A messy letter is an insult to its receiver.

(3) Make the margins equal.

A letter always looks better when the margins are wide and equal. Remember that the margins at the top and bottom of the page are just as important as those at the sides.

(4) Follow standard practice in page order.

If your stationery is a folded sheet and your letter will be three or four pages long, follow the regular order of book paging, writing the second page on the back of the first page. If the letter is to be only two pages long, use the third page of the stationery for the second page of the letter.

Parts of a Friendly Letter

(5) Make the five parts of the letter conform to standard practice.

While you are studying the following descriptions of the five parts of a friendly letter, refer frequently to the model form on page 460.

The Heading

Placed usually in the upper right-hand corner of the first page, the heading gives in three lines three pieces of information in which your correspondent may be interested: your street address; your city and state, separated by a comma and followed by your ZIP code number; [1] the date, with a comma between the day and the year. In order to afford an attractive margin, do not crowd the heading. It should

---

[1] If you are still using a zone number, write it after the city and place a comma after it—St. Louis 7, Missouri. It is not necessary to give *both* the zone number and ZIP code number.

not be placed at the very top of the page nor should it reach to the right-hand edge of the paper. Of course, if you have personal stationery bearing your name and address, you need write only the date.

An alternative position for your address and the date is flush with the left-hand margin just below the signature, as shown below.

> *Sincerely yours,*
> *Helen*
>
> *14 Hathaway Drive*
> *Troy, New York 12184*
> *October 3, 1965*

The indented form shown in the example below and the block form, as in the model letter on page 460, are equally acceptable. The indented form is not customary in typewritten letters.

EXAMPLE *14 Hathaway Drive*
Troy, New York 12184
October 3, 1965

The Salutation

The salutation is placed a short distance down the page from the heading, and it is begun at the left-hand margin. It is followed by a comma, not a colon. In a friendly letter almost any salutation is permissible, but *Dear* ——, is always proper.

The Body

The body of a friendly letter, the letter itself, should begin either directly below the end of the salutation, or after an indention of an inch from the left margin. Subsequent paragraphs should be indented uniformly with the first para-

14 Hathaway Drive
Troy, New York 12184 — heading
October 3, 1965

Dear Barbara, —————————— salutation

—————— body

Sincerely yours, ——— closing
Helen ——— signature

Model Friendly Letter

graph. At the end of the letter avoid such outmoded formalities as "Hoping to hear from you, I remain," or "I am," etc.

The Closing

The closing, or leave-taking, follows just below the final line of the letter. It is begun just to the right of the middle of the page and is usually followed by a comma. Although you may use whatever closing you wish, *Sincerely*, or *Sincerely yours*, is always proper. *Yours truly*, and *Very truly yours*, should be used only in business letters.

The Signature

Write your name below the closing. Since you usually sign only your first name, center it under the closing. Even though the letter is typed, your name should always be written in longhand.

(6) Make the envelope conform to standard practice.

Note in the following model that your name and address are placed in the upper left-hand corner of the envelope and the name and address of the person to whom the letter is going are placed just below the middle and begun a little to the left of the center. The person's name should be preceded by a title (Mr., Miss, Mrs., Dr., etc.). Always include the initials or the first name: *Mr. G. H. Bryce* or *Mr. George Bryce*, not *George Bryce* or *Mr. Bryce*. Your own name in the return address is not preceded by a title.

```
Helen O'Neill
14 Hathaway Drive
Troy, New York 12184


              Miss Barbara Blomquist
              336 East High Street
              Grand Rapids
              Michigan 59522
```

● EXERCISE 1. On a page of personal stationery, lay out a friendly letter as the model on page 460 is laid out. Use your own address in the heading; arrange the five parts of the letter attractively according to the instructions given above. Use neatly drawn lines for the body of the letter.

Place the letter in its envelope and write correctly on the envelope the return address and the address. Do not seal the envelope.

SOCIAL NOTES

Social notes are written to meet the demands of certain social situations. Four main types are described on the following pages: the informal invitation; the reply to an informal invitation; the thank-you note; the "bread-and-butter" note.

Social notes are written on personal stationery (preferably white) or, if they are very brief, on correspondence cards. They generally follow the form of a friendly letter. Information that is known to the receiver of the letter may be omitted from the heading of a social note. Social notes are always handwritten, not typed.

The Informal Invitation

The telephone and the increased informality of modern living have reduced the number of social occasions calling for written invitations; nevertheless, there are still some occasions for which a written invitation is desirable. When an organization like a school club or class wishes to invite a number of guests to a social event, the invitations are written. When you are giving a party at your home and you wish your invitations to be somewhat more formal than they would be if given over the telephone or passed casually in the corridors at school, a brief note is appropriate.

When you write an invitation to a married faculty member and you wish him to bring his wife, or her to bring her husband, you should make this clear either by addressing the invitation to both or by saying in the invitation that you would like to have them both come. It is not, as a rule, good manners to invite a married faculty member to a dance or other affair to which guests come in couples, without including the husband or wife in the invitation.

Room 22
Cranford High School
November 10, 1965

Dear Mr. and Mrs. Smith,

The Library Club is giving a tea in the library from three to four-thirty on Tuesday afternoon, November 16. We should be pleased to have you come.

Sincerely yours,

Jean Thomas
Secretary

Room 22
Cranford High School
October 10, 1965

Dear Mr. Long,

The French Club cordially invites you to attend its meeting on Monday afternoon, October 22, at three o'clock in Room 301 to hear an illustrated lecture by M. René Mosher, secretary of the French Consulate in New York City.

Sincerely yours,

Sarah Gilbert
Secretary

---

160 Locust Street
May 3, 1965

Dear Sue,

Mother and I are giving a buffet supper on Sunday May 10, at six o'clock in honor of my aunt Mrs. John Lamberg and my cousin Julia Lamberg from Denver. We hope that you can come.

Sincerely yours,

Betty Hamilton

Model Informal Invitations

The Informal Reply

Whether you can accept an invitation or not, you must answer it promptly—the day you receive it. Your reply, if you can accept, need not be long and chatty. Your acceptance should indicate to your hostess, however, that you have understood correctly the time, place, and nature of the occasion. If you must decline the invitation, you will wish to give some explanation.

125 Cambridge Avenue
Cranford
November 11, 1965

Dear Jean,

Thank you for your invitation to the Library Club tea from three to four-thirty on Tuesday afternoon, November 16. Mr. Smith and I are delighted to accept.

Sincerely yours,

Grace Smith

Dear Betty,

Thank you for your invitation for Sunday evening. Unfortunately, I shall be out of town with the family that weekend and Dad says we will not be home until late at night. I hope I shall have another opportunity to meet your aunt and cousin.

Sincerely yours,

Sue Wright

13 Meadbrook Road
Stamford
May 4, 1965

Model Informal Replies

● EXERCISE 2.   Assume that you are secretary of a school club that is giving a social affair to which you wish to invite certain members of the faculty. Write on appropriate stationery an informal invitation. Then, imagining that you are one of the faculty members, write a reply.

The Thank-You Note

After Christmas, your birthday, and, if you are lucky, at other times when you receive gifts from friends and relatives who live some distance away, you must write thank-you notes. A thank-you note becomes more formidable every time you put it off. Write it promptly and save yourself worry. In many instances you should use the occasion to write a full letter; it will be appreciated. On the other hand, a brief thank-you note is often sufficient.

A thank-you note should not be gushy. Make it sound enthusiastic and sincere, even though you may not have been exactly thrilled with the gift. Here is an example of an adequate thank-you note.

October 20, 1965

Dear Uncle Ned,

Thanks for the dozen golf balls. They're a lot better quality than the ones I can afford. Maybe they'll even improve my game, which can stand some improvement right now.

Mom let me order my birthday dinner, as usual. She said she really didn't have to ask me because I always order the same old steak and potatoes and apple pie.

Everybody's trying frantically to find a college that might accept me next fall. Both Dad and my counselor at school think that I should try for State. I'd like to go where you and Dad went, and so I'm going to apply. It's the second and third choices that have me worried. Any suggestions?

School keeps me so busy that I haven't played golf for nearly a month, but I'm going out this weekend and use your generous gift.

Sincerely,
Bill

The Bread-and-Butter Note

The bread-and-butter note is the note you write to your hostess to thank her for her hospitality. Often such a note becomes a full-length letter but, depending on the circumstances, it may or may not be long.

A bread-and-butter note is a "must" after you have been entertained out of town in someone's home overnight or longer. Like the reply to an invitation, it should be written promptly, immediately after your return home. It is good manners to tell your hostess that you enjoyed your stay. Make her feel that you appreciate the things she did to insure your comfort and enjoyment. Be specific. You may appropriately mention your return trip, which will be of interest to your hostess. Study the following example of a bread-and-butter note.

621 Roosevelt Street
Boonton, New Jersey   07005
July 1, 1965

Dear Mrs. Kingsbury,

Since my wonderful three days at your cottage I have spent my time remembering the good fun we had. I am sure that you and Mr. Kingsbury could have had no doubt about how very much I enjoyed my visit. I appreciated especially the trouble you took to arrange the big fishing trip on Saturday and the party Saturday night. You'll understand how I envy Jimmy his summer at such a grand place and with such a good crowd of friends.

The bus trip was hot but otherwise all right. I kept wishing all the way home that I was in the surf at Seaside.

Sincerely yours,

John

A bread-and-butter note always goes to your hostess. You may have been the guest of her son or daughter, and while you should write to your friend, too, you should write a note to his mother first.

The Formal Invitation and Reply

The formal invitation is used for formal social affairs and customarily for commencements and weddings. Since it is usually printed or engraved, you can rely on the printer to use the proper form. There is little likelihood of your having to write one yourself, but if you should have to do so, look up the correct form in a handbook or book of etiquette.

Below is an example of a wedding invitation.

Mr. and Mrs. John Barker Main
request the honor of your presence
at the marriage of their daughter
Jean Marie
to
Mr. Harold McLean Porter
Saturday, the twenty-first of June
at four o'clock
St. Andrews Church
Centerville

Although you may never have to write a formal invitation, it is entirely possible that you will receive one and have to reply to it. The letters *R.S.V.P.*, which appear on some invitations, stand for the French phrase *répondez s'il vous plaît*, which means "please reply." Your reply will be hand-written in a special form as illustrated on page 468. It must always follow the exact wording of the invitation. The acceptance should repeat the date; it is always written in the third person; numbers are spelled out.

A wedding invitation like that illustrated above inviting you to the ceremony at the church, does not require a reply unless included with it is a card inviting you to a reception after the wedding. An invitation to the reception will bear the letters R.S.V.P. The following examples of formal replies illustrate correct form for any formal social event; the first is an acceptance, the second conveys regrets.

Miss Sally Jones
accepts with pleasure
Mr. and Mrs. Smith's
kind invitation for
Thursday, the sixth of July

———————————

Miss Sally Jones
regrets that she is unable to accept
Mr. and Mrs. Smith's
kind invitation for
Thursday, the sixth of July

THE BUSINESS LETTER

Whether formal or informal in tone, the business letter is always written according to a standard form.

Form in Business Letters

26b. Observe standard practice in the writing of business letters.

(1) Use appropriate stationery.

Standard business stationery comes in two sizes, either of which is subject to slight variations by individual firms. The larger of the standard sizes is $8\frac{1}{2} \times 11$ inches; the smaller is $5\frac{1}{2} \times 8\frac{1}{2}$ inches, used for very short letters.

(2) Make an attractive "letter picture."

The "letter picture" is the over-all picture a letter presents to the reader at first glance. Businessmen insist that their letters make a favorable first impression. To make the picture attractive, you must center the letter on the page, leaving equal margins on the sides and at the top and bottom—the margins are the frame around your "picture"; space the letter parts carefully; follow consistently a standard pattern of indention and punctuation; and make the letter absolutely free of strike-overs, erasures, and other marks which mar its appearance.

On page 470 four business letters have been reproduced in miniature. Note that the letters are carefully placed in the center of the page. The side margins are equal and the top and bottom margins are equal. Two popular styles are represented: the block style without paragraph indentions and the block style with paragraph indentions. In all four letters the closing begins in the middle of the page. Note also that the letters are placed attractively in relation to the letterheads.

(3) Follow standard practice in continuing a letter on a second page.

A business letter should be as short as possible without being abrupt or confusing. However, if a letter must be continued on a second page, use a second sheet; never write on the reverse side of a page. If a letter is to run over, you must anticipate the fact and so arrange the material that at least three lines can be written on the second page. Never complete a letter on one page and put just the leave-taking and signature on the next.

The first line on the second page of a business letter on $8\frac{1}{2} \times 11$-inch stationery should be about two inches from the top. The page number should be centered about four lines above the first line of writing.

26b

Standard Oil Company
INCORPORATED IN New Jersey

44 ROCKEFELLER PLAZA, NEW YORK, N. Y. 10020

August 13,

Mr. Henry F. Myers
361 North Pine Street
Columbia, South Carolina 29203

Dear Mr. Myers:

Your letter requesting information on the history of Standard Oil Co (New Jersey) before 1911 has been referred to this office. We hope enclosed material will be of help in preparing your term paper.

The definitive and exhaustive history of the company from its format in 1882 to 1911, however, is contained in a book, "Pioneering in Big Business," by Ralph W. Hidy and Muriel E. Hidy, published by Harper Brothers, New York, in 1955. The purchase price of the book is $7.5 but I am sure you will find it in your local public library, or poss bly your school library.

It is worth noting that Jersey Standard was formed as one of the un of the Standard Oil Trust, a business organization that existed for twenty years prior to the incorporation of our company. This is exp ed fully on pages 4 through 39 of the Hidy book. The Jersey compan been completely independent, however, since 1911.

Good luck with your project!

Sincerely yours,

Eric Hanke
Eric Hanke

EH:lub

Encl.

IBM

Armonk, New York 10504
Telephone: 765-1900 (Code 914)

International Business Machines Corporation

August 25, 1964

Mr. William Zaput
Box 8092
Arizona State College
Flagstaff, Arizona

Dear Mr. Zaput:

Thank you for your recent letter describing the corporate finance course you plan to enroll in at your school. In response to your request, I am enclosing our company's 1963 annual report along with our latest quarterly earnings reports. I am also sending a copy of our booklet, "New Methods for Knowing," which I hope will be helpful in connection with your course project.

We very much appreciate your interest in our company and hope that you will not hesitate to let us know if we can be of any additional assistance.

Sincerely,

William Winger
William Winger
Supervisor
Information Services

WW/lob
Enclosure

The Museum of Modern Art

11 West 53 Street, New York, N.Y. 10019 Circle 5-8900 Cable: Modernart

September 3, 1964

Miss Alice Hoffman
201 East Thirtieth Street
New York, New York 10016

Dear Miss Hoffman:

Thank you for your letter requesting information about the Museum. Enclosed is a selection of brochures which I think will be of interest to you.

I hope that you will be able to visit the Museum in the near future.

Sincerely,

Elizabeth Shaw
Elizabeth Shaw
Director
Department of Public Information

ES:klb
enc.

ENCYCLOPÆDIA BRITANNICA

425 NORTH MICHIGAN AVENUE · CHICAGO 11, ILLINOIS

May 15, 1964

Linda Jackson
P.O. Box 242
Denver, Colorado

Dear Linda Jackson:

Your letter requesting four themes has been passed on to me for reply.

Encyclopaedia Britannica does not provide themes for students. We have this rule partly because it would be impossible to prepare in advance and keep on hand the many thousands necessary to comply with all the requests which come in, but also, more importantly, the theme written by us and submitted by you would not be your work and would not be one in which you could take pride of authorship.

Within the past ten years, excellent biographies have appeared of both Sinclair Lewis and Mark Twain, and excellent autobiographical material appears in Thurber's account of the Ageonte editor of The New Yorker, entitled The Years with Ross. I do not know of a biography of Pearl Buck, but you would easily check with your public librarian on Miss Buck, as well as on the others.

I wish you good luck in any original work you do on this project.

Sincerely,

Fred A. Krueger
Fred A. Krueger
Director of Community Relations

FAK/ed

Parts of a Business Letter

(4) Make the six parts of the letter conform to standard practice.

While you are studying the following descriptions of the six parts of a business letter, refer frequently to the model letter below.

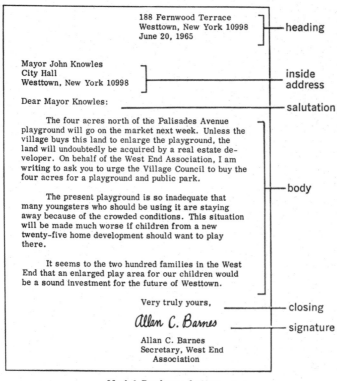

188 Fernwood Terrace
Westtown, New York 10998
June 20, 1965 ⎬— **heading**

Mayor John Knowles
City Hall
Westtown, New York 10998 ⎬— **inside address**

Dear Mayor Knowles: ——— **salutation**

    The four acres north of the Palisades Avenue playground will go on the market next week. Unless the village buys this land to enlarge the playground, the land will undoubtedly be acquired by a real estate developer. On behalf of the West End Association, I am writing to ask you to urge the Village Council to buy the four acres for a playground and public park.

    The present playground is so inadequate that many youngsters who should be using it are staying away because of the crowded conditions. This situation will be made much worse if children from a new twenty-five home development should want to play there.

    It seems to the two hundred families in the West End that an enlarged play area for our children would be a sound investment for the future of Westtown. ⎬— **body**

Very truly yours, ——— **closing**

Allan C. Barnes ——— **signature**

Allan C. Barnes
Secretary, West End
Association

Model Business Letter

The Heading

Business firms use stationery bearing their letterhead, which makes it unnecessary for the writer to supply anything but the date in the heading. When you write a business letter without a letterhead, you must give a complete heading: street address on the first line; city, state, and ZIP code on the second line with a comma between the city and state; date on the third line with a comma between the day and the year. If you use abbreviations, use them consistently.

The Inside Address

This is the part of a business letter which is not a part of a friendly letter. In the inside address you give the name of the person or the firm (or both) to whom you are writing and the address with the usual comma between city and state. Business firms file copies of the letters they write. Since the copies are filed under the name of the person or firm to which they are written, it is necessary to have an inside address on each letter. Ordinarily the inside address is placed four typewriter spaces below the heading or date and flush with the left-hand margin. If you wish to include the title or position of the person to whom you are writing, you may give his title after his name on the same line or, if the title is long, on a separate line below.

EXAMPLES   Mr. James Moore, Principal
Westbend High School
Westbend, Iowa   50597

Mr. James Moore
Plant Supervisor
King Products, Inc.
1420 Havens Blvd.
Chicago, Illinois   60636

The Salutation

The salutation, or greeting, is placed below the inside address (two spaces on the typewriter) and flush with the left-hand margin. It is always followed by a colon. The salutation varies with the nature of the inside address as follows:

1. If you are writing to a firm or a group, not to any specific individual, the proper salutation is *Gentlemen:* (*Ladies:* or, rarely, *Mesdames:* for an exclusively female concern).

EXAMPLES   Soundcraft Corporation
10 East 52nd Street
New York, New York   10022

Gentlemen:

Scholarship Board
Harvard Club of New York
33 West 44th Street
New York, New York   10018

Gentlemen:

2. If you are writing to a specific person but know only his official position and not his name, the correct salutation is *Dear Sir:* (or *Dear Madam:*).

EXAMPLE   Personnel Manager
Airborne Instruments Laboratories, Inc.
160 Old Country Road
Mineola, New York   11501

Dear Sir:

3. If you are writing to an individual and have used his name in the inside address, the proper salutation is *Dear Mr. ——:* or *My dear Mr. ——:* (The *My dear* form is considered somewhat more formal. Note that the *dear* is not capitalized in this case.)

EXAMPLES   Mr. D. H. White, Manager
Eastern Oil Company
60 East 42nd Street
New York, New York   10017

Dear Mr. White:

Mr. Scott Farnum, Director of Advertising
The Bigelow Company
74 Fourth Avenue
Grand Isle, Maine   04746

My dear Mr. Farnum:

In an address always use a title with a person's name.
Permissible abbreviations are *Mr.*, *Messrs.*, *Mrs.*, *Dr.*, *Hon.*
Others should be spelled out: *Professor* Roger Keane,
Reverend Thomas E. Haupt, etc.

4. High government officials may be addressed as follows:

THE PRESIDENT

The President
The White House
Washington, D.C.   20015

Dear Mr. President:

SENATOR

The Honorable John W. Smith
United States Senate
Washington, D.C.   20015

Dear Senator Smith:

REPRESENTATIVE

The Honorable John W. Smith
House of Representatives
Washington, D.C.   20015

Dear Mr. Smith:

GOVERNOR

The Honorable John W. Smith
Governor of New Jersey
Trenton, New Jersey   08608

Dear Governor Smith:

The Body

A business letter obviously is a means toward achieving a particular result. Businessmen are busy men. There is little room for chat and discursiveness in business letters, but there is room for courtesy. Use simple language, clearly and directly phrased. The following trite phrasings, once in common use, are no longer considered good form: *Yours of the 5th inst. received and contents noted; beg to advise (remain, state, etc.); enclosed please find; please be advised that; thanking you in advance.* For discussion of the contents of particular kinds of letters, see the treatment of the order letter, the letter of inquiry, the adjustment letter, and the letter of application on pages 477–484.

The first line of the body of a business letter is placed two typewriter spaces below the salutation. It may be indented either the usual five spaces of a typed manuscript or as far as the length of the salutation (see the letter pictures on page 470). In the pure block style, indentions are not used. Subsequent paragraph indentions will be uniform with the first one.

The Closing

In a business letter the standard form for the closing, or leave-taking, is *Yours truly* or *Very truly yours*. Less formal but frequently used is *Sincerely yours*. In writing to high government and church officials, you may use *Respectfully yours*, but avoid this in ordinary correspondence.

The closing is begun just to the right of the middle of the page and is followed by a comma. Note that only the first word is capitalized.

The Signature

The signature is written in ink immediately below the closing and flush with it. Directly below the signature the writer's name should be typewritten, a wise custom in the light of the illegibility of many signatures. This type-written repetition of the writer's name may be accompanied by his official position.

EXAMPLE   Very truly yours,

James MacPherson

James MacPherson
President

When writing to a stranger, an unmarried woman should place (*Miss*) in parentheses before her signature so that her correspondent will address her properly in his reply. A married woman may write her full married name in parentheses beneath her signature.

EXAMPLES   Very truly yours,

(*Miss*) *Virginia Shaw*

Very truly yours,

Elizabeth Blake

(Mrs. Henry G. Blake)

In general, however, do not put a title before a signature.

EXAMPLE   Very truly yours,

Thomas Strong   [not *Mr.* Thomas Strong]

(5) Make the envelope conform to standard practice.

The correct form for the return address and the address on the envelope of a business letter is the same as that for the friendly letter (see page 461). The address on the envelope should be identical with the inside address.

(6) Fold the letter according to standard practice.

The folding of a letter is determined by the size of the envelope. If a letter written on standard $8\frac{1}{2} \times 11$-inch stationery is to be placed in a long envelope, the letter is folded twice: up from the bottom about a third of the way, then down from the top so that when unfolded it will be right side up. If it is to be placed in a small envelope, the letter should be folded up from the bottom to within a quarter of an inch of the top; then the right side is folded over a third of the way and the left side folded over that fold. Insert the letter in the envelope with the fold at the bottom of the envelope.

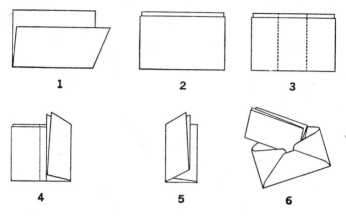

Kinds of Business Letters

26c. Learn the requirements for various types of business letters.

A busy office will turn out in a single day a dozen different kinds of business letters, but the average person, in carrying on his private affairs, will have occasion to write only three or four types of letters. You will almost certainly have need at some time for the four types described on the following pages: the order letter, the letter of inquiry or request, the letter of adjustment or complaint, and the letter of application.

The Order Letter

The order letter is being outmoded by the prevalent use of printed order forms. However, there are occasions when it is necessary to write out an order in letter form. Study

26c

21 Cranberry Road
Harmon, Illinois 61042
November 20, 1965

New Fashions Shop
187 Main Street
Castleton, Illinois 61426

Gentlemen:

Please send me the following articles advertised in the _Journal_ for November 19.

1 Heatherland tweed skirt, size 24 waist	$10.95
2 prs. Slimfit slacks, gray, size 10 long @ $6.95	13.90
1 Hemper blouse, white, Style A, size 34	3.95
Total	$28.80

I am enclosing a money order for $29.45 to cover the order and parcel post charges of $.65.

Very truly yours,

Judy Abbott

(Miss) Judy Abbott

Model Order Letter

the model order letter above and the four requirements which follow.

1. Set the list of ordered items off from the rest of the letter in a column arrangement.

2. Include all appropriate details as to quantity, catalogue number, size, style, and price. The symbol @ means *each* or *apiece:* 3 boxes @ $1.25 = $3.75. It is usually wise to specify

from what advertisement (magazine or paper and date) you have taken the information for your order.

3. Indicate how you are paying for the order: by check, money order, C.O.D., or charge account. Include money for postage if you think it is expected.

4. If you wish the merchandise sent to an address different from the address in the heading, give the address in the letter.

A simple kind of order letter is that in which only one type of thing is ordered—theater tickets, a book, a fountain pen, etc. Such a letter is illustrated below.

---

345 Graham Road
Bellmore, New York 11710
October 10, 1965

Box Office
Majestic Theater
245 West Forty-fourth Street
New York, New York 10018

Gentlemen:

    Please send me three tickets @ $3.80 for the matinee performance of <u>Hamlet</u> on Saturday, November 20. Acceptable alternate dates are November 27, December 4.

    I am enclosing a check for $11.40 and a self-addressed, stamped envelope.

                Very truly yours,

                Albert Armstrong

                Albert Armstrong

The Letter of Inquiry or Request

Occasionally you may require information which can be obtained only by writing a letter. Writing for material to use in a research paper, for facts about travel in a certain locality, for a college catalogue, etc., are common situations of this kind. Be brief and direct. Make clear immediately what you wish; then stop.

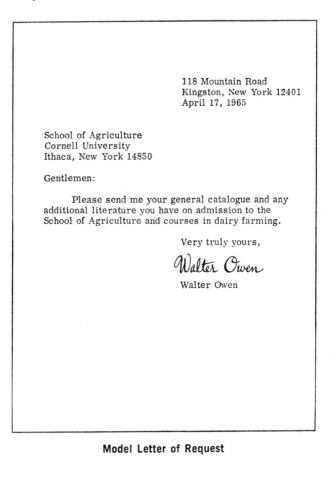

118 Mountain Road
Kingston, New York 12401
April 17, 1965

School of Agriculture
Cornell University
Ithaca, New York 14850

Gentlemen:

    Please send me your general catalogue and any additional literature you have on admission to the School of Agriculture and courses in dairy farming.

Very truly yours,

Walter Owen

Walter Owen

Model Letter of Request

348 Converse Avenue
Masonville, Iowa 50654
February 15, 1965

Bonar Plastics Corporation
1835 Washington Street
St. Louis, Missouri 63110

Gentlemen:

For my Chemistry II class I am writing a research paper on the manufacture of plastics. I should
appreciate very much your sending me any literature
on this subject that you may have for free distribution.

Very truly yours,

Mary Robinson

Mary Robinson

Model Letter of Inquiry

The Letter of Adjustment or Complaint

When you write to a business firm to ask for correction
of an error or to register a complaint of any kind, you will
get better results if you restrain your annoyance and adopt a
courteous tone. This is true also when you write to a government official complaining about poor service being given
by municipal, state, or government employees.

14 Oklahoma Avenue
Tulsa, Oklahoma 74106
May 24, 1965

Guerber's Sports Equipment Company
85 Court Street
Maysville, Oklahoma 73057

Gentlemen:

On May 14 I sent you an order which included two
white T-shirts, No. 86, size 36, @ $1.00. When the
shipment arrived I found that you had neglected to send
the shirts. I assume that this was merely an oversight
in packing and will appreciate your sending me the
shirts.

Very truly yours,

Ralph Gray

Ralph Gray

Model Adjustment Letter

The Letter of Application

The letter of application is most important for you who
are about to leave high school. Whether you wish a permanent job or temporary employment for the summer months,
you will want to make a favorable impression with your
letter. Since the letter will undoubtedly be one of many
received by your prospective employer, you must make

sure that it is correct in every detail and sufficiently convincing to make the reader consider your application further. It should, if possible, be typewritten.

---

321 Fifth Street
Riverside, Missouri
March 2, 1965

Personnel Director
Central Insurance Company
41 Bank Street
Riverside, Missouri

Dear Sir:

    Please consider me an applicant for the secretarial position advertised in Sunday's <u>Herald</u>.

    I am eighteen years old and graduated last June from Riverside High School. Since then I have completed a six-months' course in secretarial training at the Clarkson Business Institute. In high school I completed two years of courses in shorthand and typing and worked as a student assistant for two years in the office. At Clarkson I studied office practice, business machines, business English, and bookkeeping.

    For the past two summers I was employed as a fill-in stenographer by the Moore Trucking Company, where I did filing and billing as well as regular stenographic work. I feel at home in a business office and enjoy being given extra duties and responsibilities.

    The following people have given me permission to use their names as references:

    Miss Catherine Greenberg
    Head of the Commercial Department
    Riverside High School

    Mr. Stanley Williams
    Moore Trucking Company
    Riverside, Missouri

    I shall be glad to come for a personal interview at your convenience. My telephone number is 592-3107.

Very truly yours,

Jane Parkman

Jane Parkman

Model Letter of Application

There are certain clearly definable requirements for a good letter of application.

1. Begin with a statement of the position for which you are applying. Mention how you learned about it.

2. State all the facts an employer would certainly want to know: your age, education, experience.

3. Indicate, if you can do so naturally, that you are familiar with the requirements of the position and explain why you believe you can meet them.

4. Give references (three, if possible) with addresses. If you have held other jobs, be sure to include among your references one of your former employers. Include also an adult who is acquainted with you and your family. Since you are still in school, a recommendation from a member of the faculty is appropriate. Before giving someone's name as a reference, ask his permission.

5. Request an interview at the employer's convenience.

6. Be especially careful with all the details of letter form, neatness, spelling, grammar, etc. You would not wish to lose a good position simply because you were too lazy to look up the spelling of a word or to copy your letter a third or fourth time to insure its being perfect.

● EXERCISE 3.   *The letter picture.* Following the models on pages 470 and 471, lay out on a piece of typewriting paper a perfectly arranged business letter, using neatly drawn lines for the body of the letter. Use your own address and the present date in the heading. Make up an inside address. Be sure the salutation is proper.

● EXERCISE 4.   *The inside address and salutation.* The following inside addresses are mixed up. Rewrite them in correct block form. Beneath each, write the proper salutation.

1. Fred Emerson, a professor at Columbia University, West 116th Street, New York City   10027

2. Miami University, Director of Admissions, Oxford, Ohio

3. 49 East 33rd Street, Harper and Brothers, New York City 10016
4. Representative from your district in the House of Representatives in Washington, D.C., Robert E. Thomas
5. Personnel Director of the Bradley Manufacturing Company, Cass City, 82–84 South Avenue, Illinois, John T. Brooks

● EXERCISE 5. *Order letters.*

1. Write a letter to the Board in Control of Intercollegiate Athletics, Yost Field House, Ann Arbor, Michigan 48103, ordering two tickets for the Michigan–Minnesota game on November 7. The tickets cost $4.00 each.

2. Write to any firm you wish, ordering at least three different articles advertised in a magazine or newspaper. Order more than one of some of the articles. Follow the model order letter on page 478.

● EXERCISE 6. *Request letter.* Write a letter to the Dean of Admissions of any college or university stating that you wish to apply for admission at a certain date and requesting an application blank and other necessary information.

● EXERCISE 7. *Adjustment letter.* Write a letter to a business firm asking why you have received a bill for an order for which you have already paid C.O.D. Give all important details, dates, etc.

● EXERCISE 8. *Letters of application.*

1. Using your local newspaper, select a help-wanted advertisement and answer it with a letter of application. Clip the advertisement to your letter when you hand it in.

2. Write to the manager of a summer camp, applying for a position as a counselor on the camp staff during the coming summer.

3. If you are going to work immediately upon graduation from high school, you probably have in mind the kind of position you intend to apply for. Write an imaginary letter of application for such a position.

PART FIVE

Aids to Good English

Information in the Library

Arrangement and Resources of the Library

How often do you use your school library and public library? Do you go to the library only when you have an assignment that requires you to go there or do you go regularly to satisfy your love of reading and to keep yourself well informed? If you aspire to be an alert, curious, informed person, you should acquire the library habit. Whether you go to college or not, you should make regular use of the rich resources of the libraries available to you. They are the open door to a vast amount of personal satisfaction and to a successful life both while you are in school and after you have graduated.

Libraries are sufficiently alike so that when you have become familiar with one library, you can easily find your way in others. You should understand the following.

1. The arrangement of books in the library
2. The uses of the card catalogue
3. The names and functions of the parts of a book
4. The use of the *Readers' Guide*
5. The use of the vertical file
6. The location of items in your library

ARRANGEMENT OF BOOKS IN THE LIBRARY

27a.   Learn the arrangement of books.

Fiction

Books of fiction (novels and stories) are usually arranged on the shelves alphabetically by authors. By this time you know where in your library the books of fiction are located. It is a simple matter, if you know the author of a book, to go directly to the book on the fiction shelves.

You can find out whether or not the library owns a certain book by looking it up in the card catalogue (page 491). If the book you want is listed in the catalogue but is not on the shelf, ask the librarian about it. It may be "out" in circulation, or it may be "on reserve." If possible, the librarian will reserve the book for you by placing your name on the reserve list. When your name comes up, the librarian will notify you.

Nonfiction: The Dewey Decimal System

The arrangement of nonfiction books is accomplished through an amazingly efficient system developed by Melvil Dewey, an American librarian.[1] Although only librarians need to know all the details of the Dewey system, every user of a library should understand the principle on which the system is based. If you are not familiar with it, study the description and outline below.

In the Dewey system, every nonfiction book receives a number. The number, which is written on the back of the book, is determined by the particular classification of the book in the system. There are ten subject classifications, and any book can be fitted into one of them.

---

[1] The Library of Congress system of cataloguing is not described here because it is not common in high school libraries.

27a

Within these broad divisions there can be an unlimited number of subdivisions. Since a decimal point plays an important part in the numbering of books, the plan is called the Dewey decimal system. A valuable feature of this method of classifying books is that all books on the same subject are given the same class number and may be placed together on the library shelves. Once you have learned the class number of the subject you are interested in, you can find most of the books in the library on this subject grouped together in one place.

000–099	General Works (encyclopedias, periodicals, etc.)
100–199	Philosophy (includes psychology, conduct, etc.)
200–299	Religion (includes mythology)
300–399	Social Sciences (economics, government, law, etc.)
400–499	Language (dictionaries, grammars, etc.)
500–599	Science (mathematics, chemistry, physics, etc.)
600–699	Technology (agriculture, engineering, aviation, etc.)
700–799	The Arts (sculpture, painting, music, etc.)
800–899	Literature (poetry, plays, orations, etc.)
900–909 930–999	History
910–919	Travel
920–929	Biography (arranged alphabetically by name of subject of biography)

Books having the same class number may be distinguished from one another by the author's name. For instance, all books on aviation are given the number 629.1. This number appears on the back of the book. With the number appears the first letter of the author's name: if the author is Hood, the book's complete number is $\frac{629.1}{H}$. This number, including the first letter of the author's name, is known as the book's *call number*. To find the call number of a book, you look up the book in the card catalogue.

LOCATING INFORMATION IN THE LIBRARY

The Card Catalogue

Undoubtedly you have used the card catalogue in your school or town library. You may not, however, know as much about it as you need to know in order to get the most help from it.

27b. Learn the uses of the card catalogue.

The card catalogue is a cabinet containing drawers filled with alphabetically arranged cards. In most libraries, the catalogue holds at least three cards for each book in the library: one or more *author cards*, the *title card*, and one or more *subject cards*.

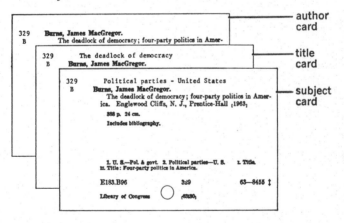

The Author Card

The *author card* has the name of the author at the top. In the case of joint authorship, there will be a card for each author. You may look up any book in the library by looking under the author's name. Since the cards for all books by an author will be placed together, you have the additional

27b

advantage of being able to find out what other books by the author the library owns. Cards for books *about* an author follow the cards for books *by* an author.

The Title Card

The *title card* has the book's title at the top. The quickest way to find a book in the catalogue is to look it up under its title. Cards for books whose titles begin with *a, an,* or *the* will be arranged alphabetically by the second word in the title. For example, the title card for a book entitled *The Writing of Fiction* would be found under *W*.

The Subject Card

The *subject card* has at the top the subject with which the book deals. Subject cards are invaluable when you wish to find a number of books on a subject but do not know specific titles or authors. Under the subject heading "Political parties—United States" for instance, you will find a card for every book in the library on this subject. In fact, you may find a card for every book that contains as little as one article or chapter on United States political parties, so thoroughly is the cataloguing done.

Information Given on a Catalogue Card

Brief study of the sample catalogue cards reproduced on page 491 will show you that a complete card gives a great deal of information. In addition to the title, author, and call number of a book, the card may give the following information:

1. *Facts about authorship:* full name of the author; names of joint authors and illustrators, if any.

2. *Facts about publication:* the place of publication; the name of the publisher; the date of publication.

3. *Facts about the book:* number of pages; whether the book contains illustrations, diagrams, etc.; height of the book in centimeters.

"See" and "See Also" Cards

An important feature of a complete card catalogue is the cross-reference cards which it contains. These are of two kinds—"see" cards and "see also" cards. The "see" card refers you to a subject heading under which you will find the material you wish. Suppose, for instance, that you wish to look up some books on World War I. You look under "World War I" in the card catalogue. The card headed "World War I," however, says "see European War 1914–1918." This means that books on World War I are catalogued under the heading "European War 1914–1918." The "see" card tells you, in effect, "There is nothing here. You will find what you want under this other heading."

A second type of cross-reference card is the "see also" card, which refers you to places in the catalogue where you may find additional titles on your subject. For instance, if you are looking for books about detectives and have found some listed under the subject heading "Detectives," you may find a "see also" card advising you to look also under the subject headings "Police" and "Secret service." A "see also" card says, "There is more material in these places."

```
World War I, see
European War 1914-1918
```

```
Detectives, see also
Police
Secret service
```

Summary

The card catalogue is a valuable library tool which may be used for the following purposes:

(1) To find the call number of a book
(2) To find out whether a certain book is owned by the library
(3) To find out what books by a certain author are in the library
(4) To find out what books on a certain subject are in the library
(5) To find out such facts about a book as may be given on a catalogue card: facts about authorship, publication, number of pages, illustrations, etc.

● EXERCISE 1.   Using the card catalogue in your library, find the title, author, and call number of the following. Write them on your paper.

1. A history of American literature
2. A book about South America
3. A book by Samuel Clemens (Mark Twain)
4. A book giving information about Samuel Clemens
5. A book about baseball

Using the card catalogue, find answers to the following questions. Write the answers.

6. Does the library own any books by Stephen Vincent Benét? If so, give the title and call number of one of them.
7. Give the title, author, publisher, and publication date of a book about John F. Kennedy.
8. Does the library own the complete plays of Shakespeare in one volume? If so, give the exact title and the publisher of the book.
9. Give the title, author, and date of publication of a book of American poetry.
10. Does the library own a copy of Nathaniel Hawthorne's *The Scarlet Letter*? If so, give the publisher.

The Parts of a Book

Once you have found the right book, it is a great advantage to be able to make use of the various aids that the author and publisher have provided. To do so, you need to know the important parts of a book and the uses of each.

27c. Learn the names and functions of the parts of a book.

The Frontispiece

The frontispiece is a full-page illustration. If the book has a frontispiece, it faces the title page.

The Title Page

The first important page in a book, the title page gives the complete title, the subtitle, if there is one, the name of the author or editor (sometimes his position, especially in a textbook), the name of the publisher, and the place of publication.

The Copyright Page

The reverse side of the title page is the copyright page. Here you find the year in which the book was copyrighted; i.e., registered in the government copyright office in Washington. Before a publisher releases a new book, he sends two copies to the United States Copyright Office along with certain required information. The office then issues a copyright, which gives to the copyright owner exclusive right to print the book or any part of it for a period of twenty-eight years. At the end of that time the copyright may be renewed for another twenty-eight years. Sometimes publishers secure a copyright in their own name, sometimes in the name of the author. The purpose of the copyright is to protect the author and publisher, who have invested their work and money in the book. Reprinting copyrighted

27c

materials without the permission of the copyright owner is a criminal offense.

Often you will find more than one date listed on the copyright page: "Copyright 1946, 1949, 1955." This means that the first edition of the book was copyrighted in 1946. In 1949 and 1955 new material was added and a new copyright secured to cover the new material. In books published since September, 1957, the international copyright symbol is used: © 1965. The date of copyright is very important when you wish to know whether the material in a book is sufficiently up to date to be reliable.

Publishers sometimes indicate on this page which printing of the book this particular volume represents. Note the distinction between a new copyright date and a new printing date. The former tells when the book was last revised; the latter, when it was merely reprinted.

The Preface, Foreword, Introduction

These terms are now used interchangeably to refer to matter at the beginning of a book in which the author, editor, or publisher explains the purpose and scope of the book, gives information which aids the reader in understanding the book, acknowledges indebtedness, etc.

The Table of Contents

The table of contents appears at the front of the book and consists of a list of the chapters and subdivisions with their page numbers. It provides a quick view of the content and organization of the entire book.

The table of contents may tell you how much information the book contains on a particular topic, but the index is a more reliable guide for this purpose. For example, a book on the History of Aviation may or may not have a chapter title referring to fighter planes of World War I, but some mention of this topic is almost certain to be included in such a book. If it is, you will find it listed in the index.

List of Illustrations (Maps, Diagrams, Charts, etc.)

A list of illustrations with page numbers is sometimes included in books that give a prominent place to illustrations. Such a list would be of obvious value in an atlas, a history of art, or a book on fashions, for example.

The Appendix

The appendix contains additional material which the author did not wish to include in the body of the book. It may include long quotations from other works on the subject, lists, diagrams and tables, etc.

The Glossary

A glossary is usually a list of definitions of technical words used in the book. It is placed near the close of the book.

The Bibliography

The bibliography is a list of books consulted by the author in writing his book or recommended to the reader who wishes more information.

The Index

The index is an alphabetical list of topics treated in the book, given with page numbers. It is much more detailed than the table of contents. The index lists every reference to a topic and tells you exactly how many pages are devoted to it. When you have found a book that seems likely to provide information on your topic, the index will tell you how much information there is and exactly where to find it.

The End Papers

The pages pasted inside the front and back covers of the book are the end papers. Sometimes they are used for a map or an illustration or to give a kind of summary of the contents.

● Exercise 2. Write answers to the following questions. You will notice that the last 6 items refer to this book (*English Grammar and Composition: Complete Course*).

1. List the parts of a book of nonfiction that you would not find in a book of fiction.
2. In a sentence or two distinguish between printing date and copyright date.
3. Explain the purpose of a glossary.
4. Distinguish between a table of contents and an index.
5. Write the date when this book was printed.
6. Write the date when this book was copyrighted.
7. By what firm was this book published?
8. Where is this firm located?
9. Skim the Preface of this book and in a sentence or two state its primary purpose.
10. What use has been made of the end papers of this book?

The Readers' Guide

A large part of the library reference work you will do in high school will deal with subjects of a contemporary rather than a historical nature. The best source of information, indeed very often the only source of information, on truly current subjects is the magazine. Without some sort of guide, you would have to spend hours hunting through magazines in search of articles on a subject. However, the *Readers' Guide* solves this problem for you.

27d. Learn how to use the *Readers' Guide* to *Periodical Literature.*

In the *Readers' Guide*, articles from more than 100 magazines are indexed alphabetically by subjects and by authors. You may look up the subject in which you are interested and find the articles that have been written on it and the magazines in which they appeared.

Magazine stories are listed by title and by author; the

MCGINLEY, Phyllis   —author entry
Are children people? excerpts from Profession: housewife. Ladies Home J 80:78-9+ Je '63
Little girl's room; poem. McCalls 90:74-83 Je '63
Profession: housewife; excerpts. Ladies Home J 80:87+ Ja; 82+ Mr; 60+ Ap; 26+ My; 78-9+ Je; 43+ Jl '63

about   —article about an author
Open letter to the New Yorker. R. M. Brown. Christian Cent 80:956-7 Jl 31 '63

MCGOVERN, George S.
Is Castro an obsession with us? N Y Times —title of article
Mag p9+ My 19 '63

MCGOWAN, J. A. See Fager, E. W. jt. auth.

MCGRADY, Pat
Leukemia: key to the cancer puzzle! Sci —name of magazine
Digest 53:31-6 Je '63

MCGRATH, Earl J.
Plea for the year-round college. N Y Times Mag p52+ Ap 28 '63

MCGRATH, Edward H.
Aid for Indian steel. America 109:108 Ag 3 '63

MCGRATTY, Arthur R.
That the blind may read. America 108:792-3 —volume number
Je 1 '63

MCGRAW, Gerald
I get 100 lbs. pork from 331 lbs. feed. por Suc Farm 61:42 Ag '63

MCGRAW-HIll publishing company
Flexible spaces, for paper work, in the country; Hightstown, N.J. buildings. il Arch Rec 133:189-93 Ap '63 —page reference

MCGRORY, Mary
Washington front. See issues of America

MCGUINESS, Kenneth C.
Is Kennedy board rewriting labor law? il por U S News 55:91-2 Jl 8 '63

MCGURN, Barrett
Newsman's tribute; John XXIII. America 108: 857-8 Je 15 '63 —date of magazine

MACHADO, Gustavo
With impunity & immunity. por Time 82:37 Jl 5 '63

MACHATTIE, Lorne A. and others
Fragment sizes produced from T5 bacteriophage DNA molecules by acid deoxyribonuclease. bibliog Science 141:59-60 Jl 5 '63

MACHEN, Eddie
Case of the frustrated fighter. M. Morgan. il pors Sat Eve Post 236:71-2 My 18 '63 —"see" cross reference

MACHINE in politics. See Boss rule

MACHINE tool industry and trade
Tooling up. Time 81:89-90 My 10 '63
Unplanned obsolescence. il Newsweek 61:83-4 My 13 '63 —subject entry

MACHINE tools
Machine tools show their age; survey of metalworking equipment. il Bsns W p65-6+ My 4 '63
Shop talk. S. M. Gallager. See issues of Popular science
Tools you need for pipe jobs. R. Treves. il Pop Sci 183:98-100+ Ag '63
See also
Lathes
Machine tool industry and trade —"see also" cross reference

27c

complete entry is given with the author listing only. Poems and plays are listed by author.

Articles *about* moving pictures and plays are listed under the subject headings MOVING PICTURE PLAYS and DRAMAS, beneath the subheading *Criticisms, plots, etc.*

The *Readers' Guide* is published in paper-bound pamphlets twice a month from September to June and monthly in July and August. Occasionally during the year a cumulative issue is published including the articles listed in preceding months as well as those for the current month. At the end of a year, a large volume is published containing all entries for the year, and every two years a volume covering a two-year period is published.

You must remember, however, that the usefulness of the *Readers' Guide* is limited by the availability to you of the magazines to which it refers you. When you are taking down references from the *Readers' Guide*, you should know what magazines your library has. You should know, too, whether the library has kept back issues of all these magazines or only of certain ones, and for how many years back it has the magazines.

A sample excerpt from the *Readers' Guide* is reproduced on page 499. You can probably understand the many abbreviations used, but if you cannot, you will find them explained in the front of the *Readers' Guide* itself.

● EXERCISE 3.   Write answers to the following questions.

1. Is there in your library a list of the magazines to which the library subscribes? Does the list give the dates of back numbers on file? If so, for what years does the library have back numbers of either the *Atlantic* or *Harper's Magazine?*

2. Where are the back numbers of magazines stored in your library? How do you get the particular number you want?

3. What is the date of the latest *Readers' Guide* in your library? What period does it cover?

4, 5, 6. Select one of the following subjects, look it up in the *Readers' Guide*, and list on your paper three articles *that you could get in your library* on the subject. Give the complete listing in the *Readers' Guide*. Show that you understand the abbreviations by spelling out all of them.

Housing	Aviation	Photography
Education	Taxation	Labor

7. Select a prominent person of today and look for an article about him in the *Readers' Guide*. Give the complete listing.
8. Find and copy a "see" reference from the *Readers' Guide*.
9. Copy from the *Readers' Guide* the complete listing of a review of a motion picture.
10. Copy from the *Readers' Guide* the complete listing of a review of a play.

The Vertical File

27e. Learn the nature and proper use of the vertical file.

Useful information on current topics is often to be found in pamphlets, usually paper-bound. They are published by government agencies, industrial concerns, museums, colleges and universities, radio stations, welfare organizations, etc. The librarian files pamphlets in a special cabinet, usually referred to as the vertical file, and can help you find material on your subject, especially if it is of contemporary interest.

In the vertical file the librarian also stores interesting pictures and significant clippings from newspapers.

27f. Learn the location of items in your library.

Your use of a library will be more efficient if you know the exact location of the principal items you may wish to use. If you will remember the information the following exercise calls for, you will save both the librarian and yourself a great deal of time.

27
e-f

● EXERCISE 4.   Be prepared to state the location in your school or public library of each of the following:

1. The desk where books are charged out
2. The card catalogue
3. The *Readers' Guide*
4. The magazine rack and the newspaper rack
5. The pamphlet file
6. The fiction shelves
7. The encyclopedias
8. The biography shelves
9. The unabridged dictionaries
10. The reserved-book shelf or the new-book shelf

Reference Books

Special Sources of Information

Libraries vary in the number and kinds of reference books they own, but almost any library will have some, if not all, of the standard reference books described here. Familiarity with these useful books will increase your efficiency in looking up information. You may be surprised to find how easily you can acquire the information you need simply by knowing that there is a reference book that is specifically designed to provide it.

Studying the descriptions given on the following pages will not be an adequate substitute for actually having the books in your hands and working with them. If possible, go to the library and spend a few minutes with each book. One member of the class may be assigned to each of the reference works listed on the following pages. Have him find out whether the work is in your school or public library. If it is, have him skim the preface and read here and there in the book in order to report to the class any additional information about it. If practical, have him bring the book (one volume of a many-volumed work) to class so that everyone may see it.

Every class member should study carefully the descriptions of the books given here and do the exercises on pages 515–18. Even though you do not have access to a particular reference work now, you should know that the book exists and what its principal uses are.

ENCYCLOPEDIAS

28a. Become familiar with the content and organization of encyclopedias.

Probably you have already used encyclopedias in your schoolwork. You know that an encyclopedia is a collection of articles on every phase of knowledge. Makers of encyclopedias are very careful to publish only authoritative articles written by eminent scholars. When you were younger, you tended to rely on an encyclopedia article alone for the information you sought. Now, however, you realize that while an encyclopedia article provides an excellent general view of a subject, it cannot treat the subject in great detail. An encyclopedia treatment makes a good starting point for research because it is general. Do not make the mistake, however, of thinking you have adequately investigated a subject when you have read only an encyclopedia article on it.

Although encyclopedias are arranged alphabetically like a dictionary, many also have an index. The reason for this is that a topic may be discussed in several widely separated articles. To find in one place a list of all the articles containing information on a topic, use the index (usually in the last volume).

For example, suppose that you were looking up information about the Olympic games. If you looked in the *Encyclopædia Britannica* volume containing the entry "Olympic Games," you would find an article several columns long. Then, if you looked in the index, you would find the volume and page number of over twenty entries in the *Britannica* giving additional information about the games. Without the index you might not have known about these other entries.

Most encyclopedias are kept up to date in two ways. First, they are constantly being revised as the world's knowledge expands, so that each printing represents some revision. Second, they are kept up to date through publication of an annual, or yearbook, giving the important events, statistics, and developments in each phase of knowledge during that year.

Encyclopedias in Many Volumes

Collier's Encyclopedia

24 volumes
Bibliography and Index in Volume 24
Publishes *Collier's Yearbook*

Encyclopedia Americana

30 volumes
Index in Volume 30
Publishes the *Americana Annual*

Encyclopædia Britannica

24 volumes
Index and atlas in Volume 24
Publishes the *Britannica Book of the Year*

Encyclopedia International

20 volumes
Index in Volume 20

World Book Encyclopedia

19 volumes
Reading and Study Guide in Volume 19
Publishes an annual supplement

One-Volume Encyclopedias

Very often you may wish a brief, handy account of a subject. To meet this need, the one-volume "desk" encyclopedias are adequate. There are three well-known works of this kind. The *Columbia Encyclopedia* and the *Columbia-Viking Concise Encyclopedia* are arranged alphabetically like a dictionary. The *Lincoln Library of Essential Information* is arranged in broad divisions of knowledge with many subdivision articles and an index. Typical of the broad

28a

divisions covered are "The English Language," "Literature," "History," etc.

GENERAL REFERENCE BOOKS

There are two kinds of general reference books that you will be using most frequently: almanacs, or yearbooks, and atlases. These offer a variety of information on many subjects—from statistics on sports to the amount of rainfall in a given year—and have complete indexes that make the books easy to use for quick reference.

Yearbooks and Almanacs

World Almanac and Book of Facts

Most popular of the desk reference books on the world today, the *World Almanac* gives, in one handy volume, facts and statistics which are frequently in demand. Typical items in the *Almanac* are sports records, exports and imports of principal countries, statistics of population, officials of the governments of the world, Nobel and other prize winners, a summary of important events of the year, etc. Although the *Almanac* is published annually to cover one year at a time, many of its statistical tables cover data for preceding years. Remember that the *Almanac* for a certain year covers the year before; thus the 1965 issue covers the year 1964. The *Almanac* has its index in the front.

Information Please Almanac

The contents of the *Information Please Almanac* are arranged somewhat differently from those of the *World Almanac*, but by using the index at the back, you can find much of the same kind of information. The book is written in an informal style, easy to understand, and discusses in a more leisurely way a smaller number of subjects than the *World Almanac*.

Statesman's Yearbook

Self-characterized as a "statistical and historical annual of the states of the world" the *Statesman's Yearbook* gives the kind of information that is of interest to government officials, diplomats, and statesmen. Beginning with accounts of important *international* governing bodies, the *Yearbook* takes up each country, giving facts about each under the following headings: government, area and population, religion, education, welfare, justice, defense, finance, production, communications, currency and banking, and diplomatic representatives. The index is at the back of the book.

Atlases

An atlas is much more than a book of maps. It gives valuable data about the topography and climate of countries, important places of interest, crops, exports and imports, and historical information. There are many excellent atlases. Find out which ones are in your library and where they are located. Since in our uncertain world the international scene changes so rapidly, the date of publication of an atlas is of great importance. Before relying on the accuracy of an atlas, look at its copyright date.

In addition to atlases of the present world, there are atlases showing the world in preceding times. These are valuable for students of history and are known as historical atlases.

The following atlases are commonly found in high school libraries:

GENERAL ATLASES

Collier's World Atlas and Geography
The Encyclopædia Britannica Atlas
Goode's World Atlas
Hammond's Universal World Atlas
National Geographic World Atlas
Rand McNally Cosmopolitan World Atlas

HISTORICAL ATLASES

Lord's *Historical Atlas of the United States*
Shepherd's *Historical Atlas*

BIOGRAPHICAL REFERENCE BOOKS

28b. Learn to use biographical reference books.

The reference shelves of your library will contain many,
if not all, of the following biographical reference books.
Since these books vary in their functions, you should be
acquainted with the particular purpose served by each.

General Biography

Biography Index (1946 to date)

This work contains no biographies. It tells you where you
can find biographical accounts of almost anyone about
whom a book or an article has been written. It indexes
current biographical books in the English language and
biographical material in more than 1,500 periodicals. Like
the *Readers' Guide*, the *Biography Index* is published
regularly and in cumulative editions. Specifically, it appears
quarterly (November, February, May, and August). One
bound volume published annually includes the year's listings. Arrangement is of two kinds: (1) straight alphabetical
listing of persons written about, and (2) alphabetical listing
of names under broad divisions of professions or occupa-
tions. Remember that this is an *index* to biographical
books and articles, not a book of biographies.

Current Biography

As indicated by its own slogan, "who's news and why,"
this regularly published reference work prints each month
short biographies of persons prominent in the news. It is

picture. Each article gives a list of the author's works with their dates, and a bibliography for further reading.

American Authors 1600–1900 by Kunitz and Haycraft
British Authors Before 1800 by Kunitz and Haycraft
British Authors of the Nineteenth Century by Kunitz and Haycraft
Twentieth Century Authors by Kunitz and Haycraft
Twentieth Century Authors: First Supplement 1955

For authors from countries other than the United States and England, as well as for world-famous American and English writers, Magill's *Cyclopedia of World Authors* is a popular reference. It gives biographical facts for each author and a critical sketch characterizing his works.

LITERATURE REFERENCE BOOKS

28c. Acquaint yourself with reference books on literature.

You have already learned something about the available biographical reference works on authors. For information about literary works, including material on plots, characters, sources, and quotations, the following books are helpful.

General

Benét's *The Reader's Encyclopedia*

Self-characterized as "an encyclopedia of all the things you encounter in reading," *The Reader's Encyclopedia* provides a great variety of information. In it you will find plots and characters in fiction, summaries of poems, brief biographies of writers, mythological, classical, and Biblical allusions, literary terms, descriptions of works of art, musical compositions, etc.

28c

Books of Quotations

Everyone, at some time or other, wishes to locate the source of a quotation. There are many books of quotations; you may find three or four in your school library. Since they are arranged in various ways, you should ascertain the particular arrangement of the book you are using and its fitness for your purpose.

Bartlett's *Familiar Quotations*

Bartlett's *Quotations* is probably the best-known source of information about quotations. The book may be used to find the following four kinds of information: (1) the author of a quotation; (2) the source or literary work in which a quotation appeared; (3) the complete quotation of which you know only a part; (4) a few famous lines from any author.

To find the author and source of a quotation, you must use the index at the back of the book. This index is arranged alphabetically according to important words in the quotation. To find the source of

> "Ill fares the land, to hastening ills a prey,
> Where wealth accumulates, and men decay."

you could look under any one of the following: *ill, fares, land, wealth, men.*

Since Bartlett's *Quotations* is arranged by authors in chronological order, you can find a great many famous quotations from a well-known author simply by turning to his name in the author index and then to the page on which quotations from his works appear.

Stevenson's *Home Book of Quotations* and *Home Book of Proverbs, Maxims, and Familiar Phrases*

Representing another kind of arrangement, these books group quotations according to the subjects with which the

● EXERCISE 3.   Number your paper 1–18. From the books and reference works given in brackets, select the one you would use to get the specified information. Write the title after the proper number on your paper. Be prepared to explain your choices.

1. Names of the senators in Congress from your state. [encyclopedia, *Who's Who in America*, *World Almanac*]
2. Quotations on the subject of love. [Bartlett's *Familiar Quotations*, Stevenson's *Home Book of Quotations*]
3. Books in your library about reptiles. [*Readers' Guide*, card catalogue, vertical file]
4. A description of the present government of France. [encyclopedia, *Statesman's Yearbook*]
5. The life of Thomas Jefferson. [*Biography Index*, *Twentieth Century Authors*, *Dictionary of American Biography*]
6. A list of magazine articles on education published during the past few months. [*World Almanac*, *Readers' Guide*, card catalogue]
7. Life of the Secretary-General of the United Nations. [*Current Biography*, *Dictionary of American Biography*, *Webster's Biographical Dictionary*]
8. Which book would probably contain Poe's poem "The Raven"? [*Granger's Index*, Bartlett's *Familiar Quotations*, Stevenson's *Home Book of Verse*]
9. A description and history of the rubber industry. [*Britannica Book of the Year*, *World Almanac*, encyclopedia]
10. International records in track events. [*Information Please Almanac*, *Statesman's Yearbook*, *Readers' Guide*]
11. The source of the common expression "All the world's a stage." [Stevenson's *Home Book of Verse*, *Webster's Dictionary of Synonyms*, Bartlett's *Familiar Quotations*]
12. Titles and authors of biographies of the President. [*Biography Index*, *Who's Who in America*, *Webster's Biographical Dictionary*]
13. A quotation about youth. [Bartlett's *Familiar Quotations*, *World Almanac*, Stevenson's *Home Book of Quotations*]
14. The copyright date of any book in your library. [encyclopedia, card catalogue, *Readers' Guide*]

15. The body of water into which the Suwannee River flows. [*Statesman's Yearbook*, *World Almanac*, atlas]
16. A picture of an author who came into prominence during the past six months. [encyclopedia, *Current Biography*, *Who's Who*]
17. Leaflets recently published by the National Safety Council. [card catalogue, *Readers' Guide*, vertical file]
18. Educational background of the president of an American university. [*Who's Who*, *Biography Index*, *Who's Who in America*]

● EXERCISE 4. Which library tool or reference book, including the encyclopedia, would you use to find the following items of information?

1. A number of magazine articles on the latest fashions in dress
2. The power for which the mythological character Aeolus was important
3. The title of a book the library owns on conservation
4. An account of the climate of Tahiti
5. The life of the author of a best-selling first novel, recently published
6. The pronunciation of the name of the prime minister of Kenya
7. Biographies (books and articles) of a famous person in today's world
8. The latest magazine articles about automobile accidents
9. An article on the life and work of a Spanish author
10. The native state of the Vice-President of the United States
11. The publisher and copyright date of a book in the library
12. The ten largest cities in the United States
13. An illustrated article on the American Indian
14. A history of the past year in sports
15. Pamphlets published by the Foreign Policy Association
16. Any books the library may have on stamp collecting
17. Officials of the present government of Pakistan
18. An illustrated article on Italian art
19. The name of the novel in which Uriah Heep is a character
20. A picture of Robert Sherwood, modern dramatist

The Dictionary

Content and Uses of Dictionaries

Dictionaries vary greatly in size, purpose, and reliability. From the unabridged dictionaries with upwards of 300,000 entries to the smallest pocket-sized ones, dictionaries offer a range of possibilities that calls for judgment on the part of the user.

Although dictionaries differ from one another in number of entries and method of presenting information, they all provide a report on the way language is used. Dictionary makers do not by themselves decide what words mean or how they should be pronounced and spelled. As a result of careful scientific research, dictionary makers are able to record the way the majority of educated people use the language: the meanings such people apply to words and the ways they pronounce and spell words.

To people who want to make themselves understood and who wish to understand what they read, such a reliable report on language practice is of obvious value. No speaker of English knows all the words. Everyone needs help sometimes with the meaning, spelling, pronunciation, and use of a particular word. The dictionary records the customary language practice of other literate speakers and writers.

KINDS OF DICTIONARIES

29a. Know the kinds of dictionaries.

Excluding the many special dictionaries—dictionaries of scientific terms, foreign language dictionaries, etc.—there are two main kinds of dictionaries with which you should be familiar: the large *unabridged* dictionary, which you will probably use mainly in libraries; and the "college-size" dictionary, which you should have at hand whenever you study.

You should be warned against the small, often pocket-sized, dictionaries sold in book, stationery, and drug stores for a dollar, more or less. While these books may help you with common word meanings and spellings, they should be taken for what they are intended to be—inexpensive condensations for quick, general reference; they are not dependable as scholarly, complete, up-to-date works.

Unabridged Dictionaries

The largest dictionaries—those containing over 300,000 words—are called *unabridged* dictionaries. *Unabridged* means that a dictionary is not a cut-down version of some larger dictionary. The best known and most available of these are these one-volume dictionaries:

Webster's Third New International Dictionary, G. & C. Merriam Company, Springfield, Massachusetts

Funk and Wagnalls New Standard Dictionary of the English Language, Funk and Wagnalls, New York, New York

An unabridged dictionary has entries for about three times as many words as a college dictionary, and the entries are likely to be longer and more detailed, and to distinguish finer shades of meaning. It simply contains more information than a college dictionary. For example, you will stand a better chance of finding in it a word that is unfamiliar to you but familiar to people in some other part of the English-speaking world, a word that has a particular meaning in a certain part of the United States, an old or obsolete meaning of a word. *Webster's Third International*, the most up-to-date of the unabridged dictionaries, also provides actual quotations showing the use of a word and identifies the person quoted. In other words, an unabridged dictionary makes available more information than can be included in any college dictionary.

College Dictionaries

The most practical dictionary for everyday use is the college dictionary. Dictionaries of this kind usually contain entries for between 80,000 and 150,000 words. Because it is easier to revise a college dictionary than an unabridged dictionary, the former is more likely to be up to date. Dictionary makers, who have students in mind when they prepare college dictionaries, are careful to include useful guides to spelling, capitalization, punctuation, research paper techniques, etc.

The college dictionaries listed below are reputable and well known.

American College Dictionary, Random House, New York, New York

Funk and Wagnalls Standard College Dictionary, text edition, Harcourt, Brace & World, Inc., New York, New York

Thorndike-Barnhart Comprehensive Dictionary, Scott, Foresman & Company, Chicago, Illinois

Webster's New World Dictionary of the American Language, World Publishing Company, College Edition, Cleveland, Ohio

Webster's Seventh New Collegiate Dictionary, G. & C. Merriam Company, Springfield, Massachusetts

29a

CONTENT AND ARRANGEMENT OF DICTIONARIES

29b. Become familiar with the kinds of information in your dictionary and the method by which the information is presented.

A dictionary is most commonly used to find out the spelling and meaning of words, but to use it exclusively for these purposes is to ignore the many other kinds of information it provides. Before making a detailed study of the treatment of individual words in the body of the dictionary, learn the kinds of information usually available in a good dictionary. The study materials and exercises on the following pages are intended to reveal to you the entire resources of your dictionary. Through your study of these pages, you should become so well acquainted with your dictionary that you will turn to it more often and use it more efficiently in the future.

Although all good dictionaries contain essentially the same kind of information, they vary in their arrangement and in their manner of presenting the information. For instance, some dictionaries list such items as names of famous persons and places in the main body of the dictionary; others list them in separate sections. Some dictionaries list common abbreviations and foreign words and phrases in the main body, while others list these in separate sections. Familiarize yourself with your dictionary.

● EXERCISE 1.   Using the dictionary with which you have been provided, write the answers to the following questions. Use the table of contents whenever it is helpful.

1. What is the full title of your dictionary?
2. Who is the publisher?
3. What is the latest copyright date? (Look on the back of the title page.)
4. Where does the complete key to pronunciation appear?
5. Is there a shorter key on each page? On every other page?

6. On what page do the explanatory notes on pronunciation begin?
7. On what page does the introductory article describing and explaining the dictionary begin?
8. Are there any special articles on the history of the language, grammar, etc.?
9. On what page does your dictionary list the abbreviations used in the dictionary?
10. Are other abbreviations, such as A.D., C.O.D., and UNESCO, explained in the body of your dictionary or in a separate section at the back?
11. Are guides to spelling, punctuation, and capitalization given? If so, list the page on which each begins.
12. Is there a section giving the meaning of commonly used signs and symbols? If so, give the page it begins on.
13. Are the names of important people and places listed in the body of your dictionary or in a separate section?
14. Does your dictionary provide derivations of words? If so, do they appear near the beginning or at the end of an entry?
15. Are the names of literary, mythological, and Biblical characters listed in the body of your dictionary or in a special section? To find out, look up Hamlet, Poseidon, and Goliath.

● EXERCISE 2. Look up in your dictionary the answers to the following questions and write the answers in a column on your paper. *After each answer write the page number on which you found it.* If any of the items are not in your dictionary, write the number of the question and leave a blank space.

1. What does the abbreviation LL.D. mean? Give the English translation.
2. What is the population of Londonderry?
3. What was the occupation of Joseph Jefferson?
4. Who was Europa?
5. Give the meaning of the French phrase *comme il faut*.
6. Give the spelling rule for retaining the silent final *e* on a word when you add a suffix.
7. Where should commas and periods be placed with relation to quotation marks—inside the quotation marks or outside?

29b

8. Give the meaning of the sign ℞ used in medical prescriptions.
9. In what play is Iago the villain?
10. Where is Prince Edward Island?

Dictionary Information about a Word

Definitions

The principal function of a dictionary is to give the meanings of words. Since a single word may have many different meanings, many dictionary entries contain a number of different definitions, which are distinguished from one another by means of letters and numbers. Numbers usually indicate important differences in meaning, and letters indicate differences within the numbered definitions.

In some dictionaries, these separate meanings are listed in historical order—the earliest recorded meaning first, the latest last. Other dictionaries give meanings in order of the frequency of their use—from the most common meaning to the least common. The following definitions illustrate these two methods of ordering meanings. The first is in historical order, and the second in order of use.

> **hi·er·ar·chy** \'hī-(ə-),rär-kē\ *n* **1 :** a division of angels **2 a :** a ruling body of clergy organized into orders or ranks each subordinate to the one above it; *specif* **:** the bishops of a province or nation **b :** church government by a hierarchy **3 :** a body of persons in authority **4 a :** arrangement into a graded series **b :** persons or other entities arranged in a series

By permission. From Webster's Seventh New Collegiate Dictionary
Copyright, 1963
by G. & C. Merriam Co., Publishers of the Merriam-Webster Dictionaries.

> **hi·er·ar·chy** (hī'ə·rär'kē) *n.*   *pl.* **·chies 1.** Any group of persons or things arranged in successive orders or classes, each of which is subject to or dependent on the one above it. **2.** A body of ecclesiastics so arranged. **3.** Government or rule by such a body of ecclesiastics. **4.** In science and logic, a series of systematic groupings in graded order, as the kingdoms, phyla, classes, orders, families, genera, and species of biology. **5.** *Theol.* **a** Any of the three ranks of angels, each of which is divided into three orders. **b** The body of angels collectively. [< LL *hierarchia* < Gk. rule of a hierarch]

Quoted by permission. From p. 632, *Funk & Wagnalls Standard* ® *College Dictionary*, Copyright 1963 by Funk & Wagnalls Company, Inc.

For each word defined, a dictionary indicates the *part of speech*, usually by means of an abbreviation at the beginning of the definition (see examples above). The abbreviations used for the parts of speech, together with all other abbreviations used in definitions, are explained in a table in the front part of your dictionary. When a word can be used as more than one part of speech, the meanings are usually grouped accordingly—noun meanings together, verb meanings together, etc. When all meanings of a word as one part of speech have been given and the dictionary begins listing its meanings as another part of speech, the numbering of definitions starts over. This is why there may be several series of numbers in the entry for one word.

When you are looking up the meaning of a word, glance through all its definitions. You cannot be sure you have found the meaning that fits the context in which you found the word until you have read all the definitions.

Even though you have looked up the meaning, you should be wary of using a word you have encountered only once. As any foreigner will tell you, a great many English words not only have more than one meaning, but they also have *implied*, or *connotative* meanings, which are not given in a dictionary. Furthermore, there may be idiomatic uses of which a young student speaker or writer is not aware. Until you have had several contacts with a word and have had a chance to observe just how it is used, you will be wise not to try to use it solely on the basis of its dictionary definition.

For example, suppose you did not know the meaning of the verb *transpire*. Looking it up, you find that it has four meanings. The first two are technical meanings in the field of physiology. The third is "to become known," and the fourth, marked *informal*, is "to happen." Now suppose that you try to use this verb in place of "happen" in the sentence "The police happened along just in time to catch the thieves." You will not make any sense if you say, "The police transpired along just in time to catch the thieves."

Knowing the dictionary definition of a word does not necessarily mean that you know how to use the word.

Spelling

The bold-faced word at the very beginning of a dictionary entry tells you the accepted spelling. When there are two or more acceptable spellings, the various spellings are given. Some dictionaries say that they give the more usual spelling first, others do not. However, you can safely use the first spelling given. No dictionary gives the more usual spelling second.

EXAMPLE   **tran·quil·li·ty, tran·quil·i·ty**

If some grammatical change in the form of a word is likely to create a spelling problem, this form is given. For example, a dictionary gives the plural of a word if the plural is formed irregularly—*hero, heroes;* it gives the present and past participle forms of *refer*, showing that the final *r* is doubled—*referring, referred;* it gives the comparative form of *nervy*, showing that the *y* is changed to *i*—*nervier.*

Capitalization

Proper nouns and proper adjectives, which are capitalized, are given with capital letters in the dictionary.

EXAMPLE

arc·tic (ärk′tik, är′tik) *adj.* **1.** Characteristic of the Arctic; extremely cold; frigid. **2.** *Biol.* Native to or inhabiting the Arctic or the regions near it: an *arctic* plant. — *n. Usually pl.* A warm, waterproof overshoe. [Earlier *artik* < OF *artique* < L *articus, arcticus* < Gk. *arktikos* of the Bear (the northern constellation *Ursa Major*), northern < *arktos* bear]
Arc·tic (ärk′tik, är′tik) *adj.* Of or relating to the region within the Arctic Circle. — **the Arctic** The region within the Arctic Circle.
Arctic Circle The parallel at 66°33′ north latitude; the boundary of the North Frigid Zone.

Sometimes a word is capitalized in only one of its many uses. In such instances, the dictionary indicates by the abbreviation *cap.* that when used in this sense, the word should be capitalized.

EXAMPLE

cap·i·tol \\'kap-ət-ᵊl,'kap-tᵊl\ *n* [L *Capitolium,* temple of Jupiter at Rome on the Capitoline hill] **1 :** a building in which a state legislative body meets **2** *cap* **:** the building in which the U. S. Congress meets at Washington

Division of Words into Syllables

When it is necessary to divide a word at the end of a line, the word should be divided between syllables. Most dictionaries indicate a break between syllables with a centered dot (com·men·ta·tor). Syllable division is indicated in the bold-faced entry word.

Pronunciation

Dictionaries indicate the pronunciation of words by means of accent marks and respellings which show clearly how the words should sound. The respellings are necessary because our alphabet uses more than two hundred combinations of letters to represent the forty sounds of English. Each letter or special symbol used in the respellings always stands for the same sound. The sounds represented by the various letters and other symbols in the respelling are shown on a key that usually appears at the front of the dictionary and at the bottom of every pair of facing pages. Since different dictionaries use different systems of indicating pronunciation, it is essential that you familiarize yourself with the key and notes on pronunciation in your own dictionary. The sample entries that follow show two different systems for representing pronunciation.

el·o·cu·tion (el/ə·kyōō/shən) *n.* **1.** The art of public speaking, including vocal delivery and gesture. **2.** Manner of speaking. [< L *elocutio, -onis* < *eloqui* < *e-* out + *loqui* to speak] — **el/o·cu/tion·ar/y** *adj.* — **el/o·cu/tion·ist** *n.*

Quoted by permission. From p. 429, *Funk & Wagnalls Standard* ® *College Dictionary*, Copyright 1963 by Funk & Wagnalls Company, Inc.

el·o·cu·tion \‚el-ə-'kyü-shən\ *n* [ME *elocucioun*, fr. L *elocution-, elocutio*, fr. *elocutus*, pp. of *eloqui*] **1 :** the art of effective public speaking **2 :** a style of speaking esp. in public — **el·o·cu·tion·ary** \-shə-‚ner-ē\ *adj* — **el·o·cu·tion·ist** \-sh(ə-)nəst\ *n*

By permission. From Webster's Seventh New Collegiate Dictionary
Copyright, 1963
by G. & C. Merriam Co., Publishers of the Merriam-Webster Dictionaries.

Notice that the two entries above differ in the way in which the accented syllables are indicated. In the first, the syllable receiving the heaviest stress is marked (′), and the syllable receiving lighter stress is marked (′). In the second entry, the heavy stress is marked (ˈ) and the light (‚).

When a word may be pronounced correctly in more than one way, dictionaries give both pronunciations.

EXAMPLE   ad′vər·tīz′mənt, ad·vûr′tĭs·mənt

Synonyms and Antonyms

Dictionaries often list other words of similar meaning (synonyms) after a definition and sometimes give a brief explanation of how these words are alike and how they may be different. The sample entries on page 529 illustrate the treatment of synonyms in two college dictionaries. Notice that both dictionaries also list words of opposite meaning (antonyms).

Inflected Forms of a Word

As explained under *Spelling* (see page 526), the dictionary gives other forms of a word whenever there is an important reason for this information. These forms, representing a change in the word, are called *inflected* or *inflectional* forms. They may be of many kinds:

gen·er·ous (jen′ər·əs) *adj.* **1.** Marked by or showing great liberality; munificent; unselfish: a *generous* contributor. **2.** Having gracious or noble qualities; magnanimous: a *generous* nature. **3.** Abundant and overflowing; large; bountiful: **a** *generous* serving. **4.** Stimulating or strong, as wine. **5.** Fertile or fruitful: *generous* soil. **6.** *Archaic* Being of noble ancestry. [< F *généreux* < L *generosus* of noble birth < *genus.* See GENUS.] **— gen′er·ous·ly** *adv.* **— gen′er·ous·ness** *n.*
  — Syn. 1. *Generous, liberal, bountiful,* and *munificent* are used to describe a person who gives freely or a gift, etc., of great worth. *Generous* emphasizes the warm feeling of sympathy, tenderness, regard, etc., that prompts the giving; *liberal* stresses the amount of the gift and points to the absence of stinginess or meanness. The *bountiful* person gives both lavishly and continuously. *Munificent* is stronger than *bountiful;* a *munificent* gift is very great in value; a *munificent* person is one who displays princely liberality. **2.** considerate, unselfish, charitable. **3.** ample, plentiful. **—Ant.** ungenerous, illiberal, close, stingy, parsimonious, meager.

brave (brāv), *adj.* [Fr.; It. *bravo,* brave, bold, orig., wild, savage < L. *barbarus;* see BARBAROUS], **1.** not afraid; having courage. **2.** showing to good effect; having a fine appearance. **3.** [Archaic], fine; superior. *n.* **1.** any brave man. **2.** [< 17th-c. N. Am. Fr.], **a** North American Indian warrior. **3.** [Archaic], a bully. *v.t.* [Fr. *braver* < the *adj.*], [BRAVED (brāvd), BRAVING], **1.** to defy; dare. **2.** to meet or undergo with courage. **3.** [Obs.], to make brave. *v.i.* [Obs.], to boast. *SYN.*—**brave** implies fearlessness in meeting danger or difficulty and has the broadest application of the words considered here; **courageous** suggests constant readiness to deal with things fearlessly by reason of a stout-hearted temperament or a resolute spirit; **bold** stresses a daring temperament, whether displayed courageously, presumptuously, or defiantly; **audacious** suggests an imprudent or reckless boldness; **valiant** emphasizes a heroic quality in the courage or fortitude shown; **intrepid** implies absolute fearlessness and especially suggests dauntlessness in facing the new or unknown; **plucky** emphasizes gameness in fighting against something when one is at a decided disadvantage. —*ANT.* craven, cowardly.

a. the plural of a word when formed irregularly: **hero;** *pl.* –ROES

b. the feminine form of a foreign word: **alumnus; alumna,** *fem.*

c. the principal parts of an irregular verb: **see;** SAW; SEEN

d. comparative and superlative forms of an adjective or adverb if formed irregularly: **good;** BETTER; BEST

e. case forms of pronouns: **who;** *possessive* WHOSE; *objective* WHOM

Derivation, or Etymology

Most dictionaries indicate the history of a word. They show by means of abbreviations what language the word originally came from and what its original meaning was. English is unusual among languages for the vast number of words it has taken from other languages. The source of newly coined words is also given. Knowing the source and original meaning of a word is often a great help to you in understanding the word's present meaning and correct use.

The abbreviations used to indicate the languages from which words derive are explained in front of your dictionary under the heading "Abbreviations Used in This Book" or another heading of essentially the same meaning. The derivation of *geography* is given as follows in the *Standard College Dictionary:*

> **ge·og·ra·phy** (jē·og′rə·fē) *n. pl.* **·phies 1.** The science that describes the surface of the earth and its associated physical, biological, economic, political, and demographic characteristics, especially in terms of large areas and the complex of interrelationships obtaining among them. **2.** The natural aspect, features, etc., of a place or area: the *geography* of the Arctic. **3.** A particular work on or system of geography. Abbr. *geog.* [< L *geographia* < Gk. < *gē* earth + *graphein* to write, describe] — **ge·og′ra·pher** *n.*

Quoted by permission. From p. 558, *Funk & Wagnalls Standard ® College Dictionary,* Copyright 1963 by Funk & Wagnalls Company, Inc.

The sign < means "from." If written out, this etymology would read "From Latin *geographia* from Greek *ge* earth and *graphein* to write, describe."

Restrictive Labels

Most of the words defined in a dictionary belong to the general vocabulary of standard English. Some words, as well as some special meanings of otherwise standard words, require special treatment, and these usually appear with a label. There are three main kinds of labels: *subject* labels, which specify that a word has a particular meaning in a certain field: *Law, Med., Aeron.* (Aeronautics); *geographi-*

cal labels, which indicate the area in which a particular word, meaning, or pronunciation is principally used: Brit., SW U.S. (Southwest U.S.); and *usage* labels, which characterize a word as to its level of usage: *informal, slang, substandard*, etc. The following examples illustrate the three kinds of labels:

> **jibe¹** (jīb), *v.*, **jibed, jibing**, *n. Naut.* —*v.i.* **1.** to shift from one side to the other when running before the wind, as a fore-and-aft sail or its boom. **2.** to alter the course so that the sail shifts in this manner. —*v.t.* **3.** to cause (a sail, etc.) to jibe. —*n.* **4.** act of jibing. Also, **gybe.** [var. of *gybe*, t. D: m. *gijben*]

Reprinted from *The American College Dictionary* (Copyright 1947, © Copyright 1963) by permission of Random House, Inc.

> **pot·latch** (pot′lach)   *n.   U.S. & Canadian*   **1.** Among American Indians of the northern Pacific coast: **a** A gift. **b** *Often cap.* A winter festival.   **2.** A ceremonial feast in which gifts are exchanged and property destroyed in a competitive show of wealth.   **3.** *Informal* A party. Also **pot′lach, pot′lache.** [< Chinook *patshatl* gift]

Quoted by permission. From p. 1056, *Funk & Wagnalls Standard ® College Dictionary*, Copyright 1963 by Funk & Wagnalls Company, Inc.

> **fink** \′fiŋk\ *n* [origin unknown]   **1** *slang* **:** INFORMER, SQUEALER   **2** *slang* **:** STRIKEBREAKER

By permission. From Webster's Seventh New Collegiate Dictionary
Copyright, 1963
by G. & C. Merriam Co., Publishers of the Merriam-Webster Dictionaries.

Usage labels provide a good general guide to usage, but every writer must learn to make judgments about these matters on the basis of his own observation. Assigning a label such as *slang* or *informal* is necessarily a subjective judgment on the part of the definer, and not all dictionaries agree about labeling the same word. For example, three widely used desk dictionaries label the noun *highbrow* as follows: (1) colloquial, (2) slang, (3) informal, and the fourth gives it no label at all.[1] Your knowledge of the connotations of a word and the situation in which you want

[1] The dictionaries are respectively, the *American College Dictionary*, *Webster's New World Dictionary*, the *Standard College Dictionary*, and *Webster's Seventh Collegiate Dictionary*.

to use it should be your guide in choosing or rejecting a particular word or meaning. If you are not sure of the appropriateness of a word without looking it up, you will do well not to use it until you know it better.

Sometimes a dictionary will provide a more detailed comment about the usage of a word than is possible in a label. For example:

> **da·ta** (dā′tə, dat′ə, dä′tə) *n. orig. pl. of* **datum** Facts or figures from which conclusions may be drawn. ◆ Those who continue to regard *data* as a Latin plural use it with a plural verb (These data *are* new), but its use with a singular verb (This data *is* new) is widespread. [< L, neut. pl. of *datus,* pp. of *dare* to give]

Quoted by permission. From p. 340, *Funk & Wagnalls Standard* ® *College Dictionary,* Copyright 1963 by Funk & Wagnalls Company, Inc.

Encyclopedic Entries

In addition to information about words, most dictionaries give a great many facts about people and places. Such information may appear as an entry in the body of the dictionary or it may be collected in a special section in the back.

Important Persons

The dictionary usually gives the following biographical data about important persons:

1. *Name:* correct spelling, pronunciation, and the first name
2. *Date of birth* (*and death if deceased*)
3. *Nationality*
4. *Why famous*

The biographical information in a dictionary cannot always be up to date for contemporary figures. A more promising source of information about contemporaries is *Who's Who* or *Who's Who in America* (see page 510).

Important Places

In listing geographical place names the dictionary usually gives the following information:

1. *Name:* spelling, pronunciation

2. *Identification:* whether a city, country, lake, mountain, river, etc.

3. *Location*

4. *Size:* population, if a city or country; area in square miles, if a country or territory or body of water; length, if a river; height, if a mountain, etc.

5. *Importance:* If a city is a capital of a state or country, this fact will be indicated, sometimes by a star or an asterisk. The capital of a country or state will also be given under the name of the country or state.

6. *Historical or other interesting information of importance:* thus, for Gettysburg, Pennsylvania, the *Standard College Dictionary* has the following entry:

> **Get·tys·burg** (get′iz·bûrg)   A town in southern Pennsylvania; scene of a Union victory in the Civil War, July 1–3, 1863; site of a national cemetery and **Gettysburg National Military Park**; 2,463 acres; established 1895.

7. *Governing or controlling country:* thus for the Bahama Islands, a dictionary entry will say "a British colony."

SPECIAL DICTIONARIES

29c. Learn the use of special dictionaries.

In addition to the general dictionaries of the English language, there are many "word books" which are useful to anyone who does much writing. These are the books of synonyms. They help you to find just the right word when you are in doubt as to which word to use, and they help you to vary your choice of words so that you do not have to keep using the same words over and over. Three of the best known books of synonyms are listed on the next page.

You do not use these books as you do a dictionary; you use them to find a substitute for a word you prefer not to use.

29c

Fernald, James C., *Funk and Wagnalls Standard Handbook of Synonyms, Antonyms, and Prepositions*

This standard book lists in alphabetical order most of the words you would wish to use, and gives synonyms and antonyms for them.

Roget's Thesaurus of the English Language in Dictionary Form

Roget's Thesaurus has long been the best known of the synonym books. Now published in an inexpensive paperback edition, it stands beside the dictionary on many student desks.

Webster's Dictionary of Synonyms

This book of synonyms and antonyms is especially valuable for its detailed explanations of the distinctions between words of similar meaning. Like the Fernald and Roget books, it is also a handy reference volume for authors in search of a word.

● EXERCISE 3. This exercise is designed to test your knowledge of the information given about a word in the dictionary. With your dictionary before you, begin work at the teacher's signal. Look up the answers to the following questions. While your speed indicates to some degree your efficiency in using the dictionary, accuracy is the more important consideration.

1. Which is the more usual spelling: *judgment* or *judgement*?
2. In the first pronunciation for *research*, is the accent on the first or second syllable?
3. Copy the correct pronunciation of the word *comely*, using the respelling and symbols.
4. Are the comparative and superlative forms of *comely* shown to be *more comely* and *most comely*, or *comelier* and *comeliest*?
5. Copy the word *automatic*, dividing it correctly into syllables.
6. How many different meanings are given in your dictionary for the word *run* as an intransitive (*v.i.*) verb?
7. What restrictive label, if any, is given the word *swell* when used to mean *first-rate*?

8. What restrictive label is given the word *shank* when used in the expression "the shank of the evening"?

9. What are the past and past participle forms of the irregular verb *burst?*

10. Distinguish between the meaning of *councilor* and *counselor.*

11. What restrictive label is given to the adverb *erstwhile?* What does the label mean?

12. What restrictive label is given to the verb *gyp?*

13. What is the origin of the word *candidate?*

14. In what literary work does the character Mrs. Malaprop appear? For what was she noted?

15. Tell the story of Hero and Leander as given in your dictionary.

● EXERCISE 4. Like the preceding exercise, this exercise will test your knowledge of the information given in a dictionary and your familiarity with the location of this information in the dictionary. At the teacher's signal look up the answers to the following questions. Accuracy is more important than speed, but speed is important.

1. Find two synonyms for the word *cowardly.*

2. Write the plural of *analysis.*

3. Write the comparative and superlative forms of *ill.*

4. What city is the capital of Burma?

5. What is the population of Dallas, Texas?

6. When did Queen Victoria reign?

7. For what is Johann Gutenberg famous?

8. What was George Eliot's real name?

9. What is the meaning of the abbreviation ROTC?

10. In the first pronunciation for *hospitable*, is the accent on the first or the second syllable?

11. What is the meaning of the symbol $\overline{AA}$ used by a doctor in writing a prescription?

12. Write two acceptable plurals of *octopus.*

13. Should you or should you not use a comma before the *and* joining the last two items of a series?

14. Give the rule for the formation of the plural of nouns ending in *o* preceded by a vowel. Give two examples.

15. What is the meaning of the Latin phrase *caveat emptor?*

CHAPTER 30

Vocabulary

Meaning Through Context and Word Analysis

Although it is likely that this may be your last year of systematic vocabulary study, the number of English words you know and are able to use will continue to be important throughout your life. Most immediately, you will see that a good vocabulary will help you to succeed in college or at a job. More important, however, your general knowledge or your knowledge of a specific field cannot be very deep or impressive unless you have a considerable stock of words at your command. The number of words a person knows is one indication of the pride he takes in his mind. You owe it to yourself to have a vocabulary that fairly reflects your interests and abilities.

Diagnostic Test

Number your paper 1–25. After the proper number, write the letter of the word or expression that comes closest to the meaning of the italicized word.

1. to *augment* the budget
   - a) increase
   - b) examine closely
   - c) reduce
   - d) disapprove of

2. to *ascertain* the facts
   - a) cover up
   - b) review
   - c) find out
   - d) testify to

3. a king known for his *avarice*
   - a) wisdom
   - b) vanity
   - c) deceitfulness
   - d) greed

4. a *biennial* event
   a) twice yearly
   b) every two weeks
   c) every two years
   d) twice daily

5. a *blithe* mood
   a) bitter
   b) proud
   c) angry
   d) carefree

6. an offer to *capitulate*
   a) confer
   b) mediate
   c) compromise
   d) surrender

7. a suspicion of *collusion*
   a) robbery
   b) foolishness
   c) mistrustfulness
   d) agreement to deceive

8. to *conjecture* about the facts
   a) talk
   b) lie
   c) guess
   d) conceal the truth

9. to *corroborate* testimony
   a) testify about
   b) confirm
   c) deny
   d) question

10. to act under *duress*
    a) compulsion
    b) misunderstanding
    c) difficulties
    d) bribery

11. an imposing *edifice*
    a) natural wonder
    b) manner
    c) speech
    d) building

12. wholesome *environment*
    a) nourishment
    b) outlook
    c) surroundings
    d) diet

13. a great man's *foible*
    a) weakness
    b) habit
    c) example
    d) follower

14. an *interminable* show
    a) worthless
    b) endless
    c) tedious
    d) difficult to describe

15. to *intimidate* a witness
    a) make disappear
    b) make fearful
    c) bribe
    d) coach

16. to *nurture* a child
    a) neglect
    b) give medicine to
    c) scold
    d) feed and bring up

17. a sign of *opulence*
    a) poverty
    b) health
    c) wealth
    d) generosity

18. a *prosaic* sight
    a) commonplace
    b) solemn
    c) stirring
    d) peaceful

19. a *prudent* action
    a) unexpected
    b) ill-mannered
    c) sensible
    d) foolish

20. good-natured *raillery*
   a) scuffling
   b) boisterousness
   c) competition
   d) mockery

21. a well-deserved *reproof*
   a) promotion
   b) reprimand
   c) apology
   d) recognition

22. an act showing *sagacity*
   a) experience
   b) feebleness
   c) good judgment
   d) old age

23. a *sanguine* outlook
   a) hopeful
   b) pessimistic
   c) quarrelsome
   d) depressing

24. the *travail* of the artist
   a) illness
   b) oppression
   c) bad luck
   d) toil

25. a *volatile* temperament
   a) changeable
   b) disagreeable
   c) sluggish
   d) easy going

CONTEXT CLUES

30a. Find clues to meaning in context.

Occasionally we encounter words in isolation—mainly in crossword puzzles and other word games—but most of the time a word that we read or hear is closely connected with other words that help to make its meaning clear. The words that surround a particular word in a sentence or paragraph are called the *verbal context* of that word. Consider this sentence, for example:

Although he continued to predict victory, General Winters was really not *sanguine* about his army's prospects.

If you are not sure of the meaning of *sanguine*, the rest of this sentence provides some important clues. The first part suggests that there is something contradictory about the general's predicting victory when he is not sanguine about his army's chances in battle. From the whole sentence, you may reasonably conclude that *sanguine* must mean "hopeful" or "optimistic." Sometimes, of course, such reasoning will lead you into a wrong guess; but more often than not you will be right.

In addition to the other words, the situation itself often provides clues to the meaning of a word. In the example above, you would expect a general to be concerned about his army's success. Thus, you would not suppose that *sanguine* meant "bored" or "disinterested." Clues provided by the situation being discussed often help in deciding between two very different meanings of the same word or of words that have the same spelling. For example, if you are reading about an argument, *retort* is likely to mean "a ready and effective reply." In a description of a scientific experiment, on the other hand, *retort* would probably mean "a vessel used in distilling." Similarly, *naiad* means "water nymph" in books about Greek mythology but "the young of the mayfly" in a biology book. Many words that are spelled and pronounced the same have different meanings. Keeping the situation in mind helps you to know which one is intended.

● EXERCISE 1. Number your paper 1–10. After each number, copy the italicized word in the sentence and write a short definition based on the clues you find in context. You may check your definitions with the dictionary later, if you wish.

1. After a good deal of coaxing, the father finally *acceded* to his children's request.
2. After a *hectic* year in the city, George was glad enough to return to the peace and quiet of the country.
3. Although the risks were great, the dissatisfied officers met and formed a *cabal* against the commander-in-chief.
4. The last two lines of the poem are so *cryptic* that no two readers can agree about what they mean.
5. Any man who was not entirely *devoid* of honor would have been outraged at the suggestion.
6. A person on a reducing diet is expected to *eschew* most fatty or greasy foods.
7. A large constrictor grabs its prey in its mouth and quickly

30a

coils itself around the victim to *immobilize* it. The harder the animal struggles, the tighter the snake constricts until all movement stops.

8. Eventually, the criminal *expiated* this murder and his many other crimes on the gallows.

9. According to Bacon, scientists should learn about nature through *empirical* observations based on experiments and on careful study of the greatest possible amount of evidence.

10. Despite the almost unlimited *fecundity* of certain fish, no single species is to be found in all of the oceans of the world.

● Exercise 2.　Number your paper 1–10 and copy the corresponding italicized word after each number. After each word write a short definition based on your understanding of the context. When you have completed the exercise, check your definitions against your dictionary.

It is not easy at this time to (1) *comprehend* the impulse given to Europe by the discovery of America. It was not the gradual (2) *acquisition* of some border territory, a province or a kingdom that had been gained, but a new world that was now thrown open to the European. The races of animals, the mineral treasures, the vegetable forms, and the varied aspects of nature, man in the different phases of civilization, filled the mind with entirely new sets of ideas, that changed the habitual current of thought and stimulated it to indefinite (3) *conjecture*. The eagerness to explore the wonderful secrets of the new hemisphere became so active that the principal cities of Spain were, in a manner, (4) *depopulated*, as (5) *emigrants* thronged one after another to take their chance upon the deep. It was a world of romance that was thrown open; for, whatever might be the luck of the adventurer, his reports on his return were tinged with a coloring of romance that stimulated still higher the sensitive fancies of his countrymen and nourished the (6) *chimerical* sentiments of an age of chivalry. They listened with attentive ears to tales of Amazons which seemed to realize the classic legends of antiquity, to stories of Patagonian giants, to flaming pictures of an El Dorado where the sands sparkled with gems and golden pebbles as large as birds' eggs were dragged in nets out of the rivers.

Yet that the adventurers were not impostors, but (7) *dupes*, too easy dupes, of their own (8) *credulous* fancies, is shown by the (9) *extravagant* character of their enterprises; by expeditions in search of the magical Fountain of Health, of the golden Temple of Doboyba, of the golden sepulchers of Sinu; for gold was ever floating before their (10) *distempered* vision, and the name of *Castilla del Oro*, Golden Castle, the most unhealthy and unprofitable region of the Isthmus, held out a bright promise to the unfortunate settler, who too frequently, instead of gold, found there only his grave.[1]

Common Clues to Meaning

Although a sentence may provide clues to the meaning of a word in a variety of ways, there are three kinds of context clues that are particularly helpful.

Words Similar in Meaning

In the sentence "The loud, *raucous* laughter of the troop irritated the lieutenant," you can guess at the meaning of *raucous* because you know the word *loud*. (*Raucous* means "harsh of voice, coarse.")

Words Used in Contrast

Contrasts often supply clues to meaning by pairing an unfamiliar word against a known one. In such a situation, you can usually assume that the unfamiliar word is more or less the opposite of the one you know.

EXAMPLES   This accidental development did not *vitiate* the theory; it strengthened it. [*Vitiate* is contrasted with *strengthened*. It probably means "weakened" or "robbed of force."]

The defendant claims he had no intention of robbing the apartment, but the state contends that the fact he had in his possession a large bag, burglar tools,

[1] From *The Conquest of Peru*, by W. H. Prescott, New American Library of World Literature, 1961.

and a floor plan of the apartment indicates *premeditation.* [The prosecutor must mean that the defendant had previously planned to commit the crime;
premeditation must mean "planning beforehand."]

Contrasts are often signaled by such words as *but,
although,* and *however.* Sometimes *or* indicates a contrast,
but you cannot assume that it always does. In the first
sentence below, two antonyms are joined and contrasted.
In the second example however, two synonyms are joined
by *or* and no contrast is indicated.

CONTRAST   *Rich* or *poor,* the people resented the tax.

NO CONTRAST No one thought his behavior *servile* or *subservient.*

In the second example, *servile* and *subservient* mean essentially the same thing: "slavish, overly submissive." Contrasts
offer many helps to meaning, but for certainty you had
better find other clues that confirm your guess or look the
word up.

Supplied Definition

When a writer anticipates that his readers may not know
the meaning of an important word, he often provides a
definition. He may introduce the definition with an expression such as *in other words,* or *that is,* or he may slip it in
without calling attention to it. The definitions or explanations in the following examples are italicized and the words
defined are in bold-faced type.

The painting clearly shows the **aegis,** or *shield,* of Athena.

A word is often defined by a **synonym**—that is, *a word of
similar meaning.*

His *observation* was *too obvious to mention*—a **truism.** [No-
tice that the explanation comes before the word defined in
this case.]

Since the days of the early Greek philosophers, **atom** has
designated *the smallest and last unit of matter that would be*

reached if a given body were divided into smaller and smaller parts.

People do not go to the trouble of explaining things unless they want to be understood. Be on the lookout for definitions of difficult words.

● EXERCISE 3. Number your paper 1–10 and after each number copy the italicized word. Give a brief definition in your own words, based on the context.

1. Along with the discovery of the properties of poisons came the discovery of substances that had properties of combatting the effects of poisons. These early *antidotes* were strange mixtures.

2. The border rebellion, *quiescent* during the winter months, broke out in renewed violence in the spring.

3. To the rest of us, the outlook just then seemed more ominous than *propitious*.

4. Most snakes are meat eaters, or *carnivores*.

5. The *salutary* effect of the new drug was obvious in the rapid improvement in the patient's condition.

6. *Subterranean* temperatures are frequently higher than those above the surface of the earth.

7. Because the official could not attend the meeting himself, he had to send a *surrogate*, or deputy.

8. The method of reasoning from the particular to the general— the *inductive* method—has played an important role in science since the time of Francis Bacon.

9. If the leaders felt any *compunction* about planning and carrying out unprovoked attacks on neighboring countries, they showed no sign of it.

10. Formerly, a doctor who found a successful cure often regarded it as a trade secret and refused to *divulge* it to others.

● EXERCISE 4. Read the following passage and then write your own definitions for the italicized words. Consult your dictionary only after you have written your own definitions from context.

Most of the doctors who had treated cases of the peculiar disease were almost certain by then that the characteristic initial (1) *lesion* was the bite of some (2) *minute* creature, but they had little reason to suspect mites of being the guilty parties. At the time, it was generally believed that mites could transmit only two serious (3) *febrile* diseases—Japanese river fever and endemic typhus. Both of these are rarely found in the United States, and anyway both had been eliminated from consideration in this instance by laboratory tests. Moreover, the mouse, unlike the rat, had never been proved to be a reservoir for disease-bearing parasites. Mr. Pomerantz admits that hitting upon the mouse as the probable (4) *host* was largely intuitive. He is persuaded, however, that in singling out mites as the carriers—or (5) *vectors*, as such agents are known—of the disease he was guided entirely by (6) *deduction*.

Mites are insectlike organisms, closely related to ticks. Both are members of the Arachnida, a class that also includes spiders and scorpions. Compared to a tick, a mite is a minute animal. A mite, when fully (7) *engorged*, is about the size of a strawberry seed. In that state, it is approximately ten times its usual, or unfed, size. So far, science has classified at least thirty families of mites, most of which are vegetarian and indifferent to man and all other animals. The majority of the (8) *parasitic*, blood-sucking mites have to feed once in every four or five days in order to live. Most mites of this type attach themselves to a host only long enough to engorge, and drop off, (9) *replete*, after fifteen or twenty minutes. No one ever feels the bite of a mite—or of a tick, either, for that matter—until the animal has dropped off. Entomologists believe that both creatures, at the instant they bite, (10) *excrete* a fluid that anesthetizes a small surrounding area of the body of the host. Mites are only infrequently found in this country and until recently were practically unknown in New York City. Consequently, very few Americans, even physicians and exterminators, have ever seen a mite. Mr. Pomerantz is one of those who have. He came across some in line of duty on three occasions in 1945.[1]

[1] From "Eleven Blue Men" from *Eleven Blue Men and Other Narratives of Medical Detection* by Berton Roueché. Copyright 1948 by Berton Roueché. Originally appeared in *The New Yorker*. Reprinted by permission of Atlantic-Little, Brown and Company.

30b. Look up unfamiliar words in your dictionary.

For those words that context does not make sufficiently clear, the dictionary will provide you with the help you need. But here, too, context is important. Most words have a number of different meanings. To find the one you want, it is a great help to keep in mind the context in which you originally encountered the word. Once you have found the meaning you want, you will do well to read on through the whole definition. Most words have a range of different meanings; to know the word well you have to know more than one of them. Moreover, learning the pronunciation, the derivation, and related forms of the word will help you to remember it. Once you take the trouble to go to the dictionary, you may as well get as much information as possible from it.

30c. Keep a vocabulary notebook.

Having learned a new word, you should not stop there. To insure that the word will become a permanent part of your vocabulary, write it in your notebook. Follow it with its pronunciation, the sentence in which you first found it, and its definition. Whenever you learn a new word, enter it in your notebook in this way; and review your list from time to time. You will find that keeping a special section of your notebook for new words will result in noticeable vocabulary growth.

WORD ANALYSIS

30d. Use your knowledge of prefixes, suffixes, and roots.

In general, English words are of two kinds: those that can be analyzed into smaller parts (*unworkable*, *impolitely*) and

30 b-d

those that cannot (*stone, money, summer*). The words of the first kind, that can be divided, are made up of parts called prefixes, roots, and suffixes. Because these parts have broad, general meanings that remain essentially the same in different words, knowing something about word analysis can help you to figure out the meaning of an unfamiliar word. However, there are some difficulties that make it unwise to depend entirely on word analysis for clues to meaning. It is not always easy to tell whether a particular group of letters is really the prefix or suffix it appears to be. The *–er* in *painter* is a suffix, but the *–er* in *summer* is not. To be certain, you have to know something about the origin of the word. Moreover, the original force of a combination of word parts may no longer have much to do with the modern meaning of a word. For these and other reasons, absolute dependence on word analysis would lead you to make as many bad guesses as good ones.

There are, however, some good reasons for having a general knowledge of the way English words are formed. Word analysis helps you to understand the peculiarities of English spelling and the connection between the related forms of a particular word. (Knowing about related forms often enables you to learn four or five new words as easily as one.) Also, word analysis gives you useful practice in taking a close look at words. In reading, you pass very quickly over words, hardly noticing more than their general shape. This is all very well for words you know well, but close examination is called for with unfamiliar ones. Most important of all, word analysis offers the key to the origin of English words. The fact that many different cultures have contributed to the vocabulary of English is one of its particular strengths. Educated people should know something about the history as well as the use of their words. After all, building a vocabulary is a kind of collecting, differing from the collection of stamps or coins in being less expensive and more useful. No collector worthy of the name is content to possess a specimen and know nothing about it. Word analysis will tell you a great deal about the words you add to your collection.

How Words Are Divided

Words that can be divided have two or more parts: a core called a *root* and one or more parts added to it. The parts that are added are called *affixes*—literally, "something fixed or attached to something else." An affix added before the root is called a *prefix;* one added after the root is called a *suffix.* A word may have one or more affixes of either kind, or several of both kinds. A root with no affixes at all is incapable of being divided. A word consisting of a root only is one like *stone* or *money* to which word analysis does not apply.

The following table shows some typical combinations of affixes (prefixes and suffixes) and roots.

PREFIX (ES)	ROOT	SUFFIX (ES)	EXAMPLE
un–	work	–able	unworkable
post–	–pone		postpone
	friend	–ly	friendly
	fright	–en, –ing	frightening
il–	–leg–	–al	illegal
under	take	–er	undertaker
	truth	–ful	truthful
	child	like	childlike

Some of the affixes and roots in English are recognizable as complete words in themselves (*fright* in *frighten; child* and *like* in *childlike*). Most other affixes and roots were also once separate words, though the original words may no longer exist in our modern language. For example, *post* in *postpone* was a Latin word meaning *after*, and *pone* (*pono, ponere*) was the Latin word for *put*.

The Origins of English Words

In the lists that appear later in this chapter, prefixes and roots are grouped according to the language in which they originated: Old English, Latin (or Latin-French), and Greek. Although it is not possible here to give a detailed account of the contribution of these three sources to modern English, a brief discussion of word borrowing will make the lists more useful.

Old English

Old English, or Anglo-Saxon, is the earliest recorded form of the English language. It was spoken from about A.D. 600 until about A.D. 1100, and most of its words had been part of a still earlier form of the language. Many of the common words of modern English, like *home, stone,* and *meat* are native, or Old English, words. Most of the irregular verbs in English derive from Old English (*speak, swim, drive, ride, sing*), as do most of our shorter numerals (*two, three, six, ten*) and most of our pronouns (*I, you, we, who*). Many Old English words can be traced back to Indo-European, a prehistoric language that was the common ancestor of Greek and Latin as well. Others came into Old English as it was becoming a separate language.

As the speakers of Old English became acquainted with Latin, chiefly through contact with Christianity, they began to borrow Latin words for things for which no native word existed. Some common words borrowed at this time were *abbot, altar, priest, shrine, fever,* and *master.*

Many other Latin words came into English through French. In 1066, toward the end of the Old English period, the French under William the Conqueror invaded England and defeated the Anglo-Saxons under King Harold. For the next three hundred years, French was the language of the ruling classes in England. During this period, thousands of new words came into English, many of them words relating to upper class pursuits: *baron, attorney, ermine, luxury.* English has continued to borrow words from French right down to the present, with the result that over a third of our modern English vocabulary derives from French.

Many words from Greek, the other major source of English words, came into English by way of French and Latin. Others were borrowed directly in the sixteenth century when interest in classic culture was at its height. Directly or indirectly, Greek contributed *athlete, acrobat, elastic, magic, rhythm,* and many others.

In the modern period, English has borrowed from every important language in the world. The etymologies in your dictionary trace the origins of words, often providing insights into their present meanings and into history as well.

● EXERCISE 5.   Find out from your dictionary the origins of each of the following words. (For help in interpreting the etymology, see page 530 of this book.)

abscond	demon	quart
air	legal	tyrant
chase	loyal	votary

Prefixes

In addition to independent words, English borrowed from Greek, Latin, and French a number of word parts for use as affixes and roots. These sources are indicated in the following list of prefixes and in the list of roots on pages 555–58.

Prefixes have broad general meanings like *not, under,* and *against,* and a particular one of them may appear in hundreds of different words. In general, a knowledge of prefixes will help you to know when to double consonants in such words as *misspell, overrun,* and *interrupt.* Notice that many of the prefixes in the following list have several different spellings in order to fit with various roots.

PREFIX	MEANING	EXAMPLES

Old English

a–	in, on, of, up, to	afoot, asleep
be–	around, about, away	beset, behead
for–	away, off, from	forsake, forget
mis–	badly, poorly, not	misfit, misspell
over–	over, excessively	overdo, overtake
un–	not, opposing	untrue, unfold

Latin (and *Latin-French*)

ab–, a–, abs–	from, off away	abduct, absent
ante–	before	antedate
bi–	two, twice	bimonthly, bisect
circum–	around	circumnavigate
com–, co–, col–, con–, cor–	with, together	compare, coexist collide, convene
contra	against	contradict
de–	away, from, off, down	defect, desert
dis–, dif–	away, off, opposing	dissent, differ
ex–, e–, ef–	away from, out	excise, efface
in–, il–, im–, ir–	in, into, within	incapable, illegal, impious
inter–	among, between	intercede, intersperse
intro–, intra–	inward, to the inside, within	introduce, intravenous
non–	not	nonentity, nonessential
post–	after, following	postpone, postscript
pre–	before	prevent, preclude
pro–	forward, in place of, favoring	protract, proceed, pronoun
re–	back, backward, again	revoke, recede, recur
retro–	back, backward	retroactive, retrospect
semi–	half	semiannual, semicircular
sub–, suf–, sum–, sup–, sus–	under, beneath	subjugate, suffuse summon, suppose, suspect

PREFIX	MEANING	EXAMPLES
super–	over, above, extra	supersede, supervise
trans–	across, beyond	transfuse, transport
ultra–	beyond, excessively	ultramodern, ultraviolet

Greek

a–	lacking, without	amorphous, atheistic
anti–	against, opposing	antipathy, antithesis
cata–	down, away, thoroughly	cataclysm, catastrophe
dia–	through, across, apart	diameter, diagnose
eu–	good, pleasant	eulogy, euphemism
hemi–	half	hemisphere, hemiplegic
hyper–	excessive, over	hypercritical, hypertension
hypo–	under, beneath	hypodermic, hypothesis
para–	beside, beyond	parallel, paradox
peri–	around, near	periscope, perimeter
pro–	before	prognosis, program
syn–, sym–, syl–, sys–	together, with	synchronize, sympathy, syllable, system

● EXERCISE 6.   Divide the following words into prefix and root, putting a slant line (/) at the point of division. Then give the meaning of the English word. Be ready to explain the connection between the meaning of the prefix and the present meaning of the word.

EXAMPLE   1. circumnavigate
          1. *circum/navigate*   (*to sail around*)

1. absolve
2. amorphous
3. antipodes
4. biennial
5. circumspect
6. compunction
7. excise
8. hypodermic
9. impolite
10. subordinate

● EXERCISE 7.   Find and write on your paper two words that contain each of the following prefixes: *ad–, de–, dia–, mis–, pro–, re–, sub–, trans–, syn–, ultra–.*

Suffixes

Suffixes, you will recall, are affixes added after the root, or at the end of a word. There are two main kinds of suffixes: those that provide a grammatical signal of some kind but do not greatly alter the basic meaning of the word and those that, by being added, create new words. The endings *–s*, *–ed*, and *–ing* are suffixes of the first kind; by adding them to *work* (*works, worked, working*) we indicate something about number and tense, but we do not change the essential meaning of the word. This kind of suffix is a *grammatical* suffix.

Grammatical suffixes are important in grammar, but in vocabulary we are more concerned with the second kind of suffixes—those that make new words. By adding *–ful* to *thank*, we get a different word: *thankful*. Adding *–hood* to *girl* gives us *girlhood*, again a different word. Suffixes that change meaning in this way are called *derivational* suffixes. Notice in the following examples that the addition of a derivational suffix often gives a new part of speech as well as a new meaning.

ROOT	DERIVATIONAL SUFFIX	RESULT
acid (n. or adj.)	–ity	acidity (n. only)
free (adj.)	–dom	freedom (n.)
accept (v.)	–ance	acceptance (n.)

Since derivational suffixes so often determine the part of speech of English words, we can conveniently classify them according to parts of speech. The meanings given for the suffixes are very broad. Often they have little connection with the meaning of the resulting word.

NOUN SUFFIXES	MEANING	EXAMPLES
Old English		
–dom	state, rank, condition	freedom, wisdom
–er	doer, maker	hunter, writer, thinker
–hood	state, condition	manhood, statehood
–ness	quality, state	softness, shortness

NOUN SUFFIXES	MEANING	EXAMPLES
Foreign (Latin, French, Greek):		
–age	process, state, rank	passage, bondage
–ance, –ancy	act, condition, fact	acceptance, vigilance, hesitancy
–ard, –art	one that does (esp. excessively)	coward, drunkard, braggart
–ate	rank, office	delegate, primate
–ation	action, state, result	occupation, starvation
–cy	state, condition	accuracy, captaincy
–ee	one receiving action	employee, refugee
–eer	doer, worker at	engineer, racketeer
–ence	act, condition, fact	evidence, patience
–er	doer, dealer in, result	baker, diner, rejoinder
–ery	skill, action, collection	surgery, robbery, crockery
–ess	feminine	waitress, lioness
–et, –ette	little, feminine	cigarette, islet, majorette
–ion	action, result, state	union, fusion, action
–ism	act, manner, doctrine	baptism, barbarism, socialism
–ist	doer, believer	monopolist, socialist
–ition	action, state, result	sedition, expedition
–ity	state, quality, condition	acidity, civility
–ment	means, result, action	refreshment, disappointment
–or	doer, office, action	juror, elevator, honor
–ry	condition, practice, collection	dentistry, jewelry
–tion	action, condition	creation, relation
–tude	quality, state, result	fortitude, multitude
–ty	quality, state	enmity, activity
–ure	act, result, means	culture, signature
–y	result, action, quality	jealousy, inquiry

ADJECTIVE SUFFIXES	MEANING	EXAMPLES
Old English		
–en	made of, like	wooden, golden
–ful	full of, marked by	thankful, masterful

–ish	suggesting, like	girlish, devilish
–less	lacking, without	helpless, hopeless
–like	like, similar	childlike, dreamlike
–ly	like, of the nature of	friendly, cowardly
–some	apt to, showing	tiresome, lonesome
–ward	in the direction of	backward, homeward
–y	showing, suggesting	hilly, sticky, wavy

Foreign

–able	able, likely	capable, affable
–ate	having, showing	animate, separate
–escent	becoming, growing	obsolescent, quiescent
–esque	in the style of, like	picturesque, statuesque
–fic	making, causing	terrific, soporific
–ible	able, likely, fit	edible, possible, divisible
–ose	marked by, given to	comatose, bellicose
–ous	marked by, given to	religious, furious

ADJECTIVE OR NOUN SUFFIXES	MEANING	EXAMPLES
–al	doer, pertaining to	rival, animal, autumnal
–an	one belonging to, pertaining to	human, European
–ant	actor, agent, showing	servant, observant
–ary	belonging to, one connected with	primary, adversary, auxiliary
–ent	doing, showing, actor	confident, adherent
–ese	of a place or style, style	Chinese, journalese
–ian	pertaining to, one belonging to	barbarian, reptilian
–ic	dealing with, caused by, person or thing, showing	classic, alcoholic

ADJECTIVE OR NOUN SUFFIXES	MEANING	EXAMPLES
–ile	marked by, one marked by	juvenile, missile
–ine	marked by, dealing with,	marine, canine, divine

	one marked by	
–ite	formed, showing, one marked by	favorite, composite
–ive	belonging or tending to, one belonging to	detective, native
–ory	doing, pertaining to, place or thing for	accessory, contributory

VERB SUFFIXES	MEANING	EXAMPLES
Old English		
–en	cause to be, become	deepen, darken
Foreign		
–ate	become, form, treat	separate, animate
–esce	become, grow, continue	convalesce, acquiesce
–fy	make, cause, cause to have	glorify, fortify
–ish	do, make, perform	punish, finish
–ize	make, cause to be	sterilize, motorize

Some of the words in the above lists make independent sense without the suffix (*employee, employ*). Others, however, do not (*delegate, deleg–*).

Because the English language has been exposed to so many different influences, the patterns of adding suffixes to form related words is often inconsistent. Things made of wood are *wooden*, but things made of stone are not *stonen*. We do have some regularities: verbs ending in *–ate* usually have a related noun ending *–ation* (*prostrate, prostration*). We have such regular patterns as *differ, difference, differential, exist, existence, existential,* etc., but we have many other cases that are not so systematic. This irregularity is one reason why it is so important to learn related forms of the new words you add to your vocabulary. You cannot derive the noun form of *reject* (*rejection*) by knowing the noun form of *accept* (*acceptance*). You have to learn it separately. In a sense, you do not really know a word until you know its important related forms.

● EXERCISE 8.   What nouns, if any, are companion forms of the following verbs? Write the noun after the proper number. If there isn't a noun form, write 0. Do not use gerunds.

EXAMPLES   1. intervene   2. abscond
           1. *intervention*   2. *0*   [not *absconding*]

1. cavil   6. intervene
2. collate   7. prescribe
3. demur   8. proscribe
4. disburse   9. stultify
5. intercede   10. verify

● EXERCISE 9.   Number your paper 1–10. Give a related verb for each noun below if there is one. If there is no verb form, write 0 after the proper number.

1. asperity   6. raillery
2. austerity   7. remission
3. complaisance   8. remuneration
4. defection   9. turpitude
5. notation   10. verification

● EXERCISE 10.   Number your paper 1–10. Give a related adjective for each of the following nouns and verbs.

1. austerity   6. essence
2. complaisance   7. excess
3. deduce   8. prescience
4. increment   9. prescribe
5. environment   10. vituperate

Roots

A root is the core of a word—the part to which prefixes and suffixes are added. To find the root, you have only to remove any affix there may be. For example, removal of the affixes *a–* and *–ous* from *amorphous* leaves us with *–morph–*, a root meaning "form or shape." The root *–clysm*, meaning "falling," remains after we remove the prefix *cata–*, meaning "down," from *cataclysm.*

Roots have more specific and definite meanings than either prefixes or suffixes and appear in fewer different words. The following list contains some of the common foreign roots in English words.

ROOT	MEANING	EXAMPLES
Latin		
–ag–, –act–	do, drive, impel	agitate, transact
–agr–	field	agriculture, agrarian
–am–, –amic–	friend, love	amatory, amicable
–aqu–	water	aquatic, aqueduct, aquarium
–aud–, –audit–	hear	audible, auditorium
–ben–, –bene–	well, good	benefit, benediction
–brev–	short, brief	abbreviate, breviary
–cand–	white, glowing	candor, incandescent
–capit–	head	capital, decapitate
–cent–	hundred	century, centennial
–cid–, –cis–	kill, cut	suicide, regicide, incision
–clin–	bend, lean	decline, inclination
–cogn–	know	recognize, cognizant
–cred–	belief, trust	incredible, credulity
–crypt–	hidden, secret	crypt, cryptic
–culp–	fault, blame	culpable, exculpate
–duc–, –duct–	lead	educate, conductor
–equ–	equal	equation, equanimity
–err–	wander, stray	erratic, aberration
–fac–, –fact–, –fect–, –fic–	do, make	facile, manufacture, defective, efficient
–fer–	bear, yield	transfer, fertile
–fid–	belief, faith	fidelity, perfidious
–fin–	end, limit	final, indefinite
–frag–, –fract–	break	fragment, fracture
–fus–	pour	transfuse, effusive
–gen–	birth, kind, origin	generate, generic
–jac–, –ject–	throw, hurl, cast	adjacent, eject
–junct–	join	junction, disjunctive

ROOT	MEANING	EXAMPLES
–jud–	judge	prejudice, adjudicate
–jug–	join, yoke	conjugal, conjugate
–jur–	swear, plead	adjure, perjury
–leg–, –lig–, –lect–	choose, read	eligible, legible, lectern
–loc–	place	locus, locale
–loqu–, –loc–	talk, speech	colloquial, locution
–magn–	large	magnitude, magnify
–mal–	bad	malady, malevolent
–man–, –manu–	hand	manicure, manual
–mit–, –miss–	send	remit, emissary
–mor–, –mort–	die, death	mortuary, immortal
–omni–	all	omnipotent, omniscient
–pater–, –patr–	father	paternal, patrimony
–ped–	foot	pedal, quadruped
–pend–, –pens–	hang, weigh	appendix, suspense
–pon–, –pos–	place, put	postpone, interpose
–port–	carry, bear	transport, importation
–prim–	first, early	primitive, primordial
–punct–	point	punctuation, punctilious
–reg–, –rig–, –rect–	rule, straight, right	regent, incorrigible, rectangular
–rupt–	break	rupture, interrupt
–sang–	blood	sanguine, consanguinity
–sci–	know, knowledge	omniscient, prescience
–scrib–, –script–	write	inscribe, proscribe, manuscript
–sent–, –sens–	feel	presentiment, sensitive
–sequ–, –secut–	follow	sequel, persecute
–son–	sound	consonant, sonorous
–spir–	breath, breathe	expire, inspiration
–string–, –strict–	bind tight	constrict, stricture
–tract–	draw, pull	traction, extractor
–uni–	one	unity, uniform
–verb–	word	verbal, verbiage

ROOT	MEANING	EXAMPLES
–ven–, –vent–	come	intervene, supervene
–vid–, –vis–	see	evident, television
–vit–	life	vitality, vitamin

Greek

ROOT	MEANING	EXAMPLES
–anthrop–	man	anthropology, misanthropic
–arch–	ancient, chief	archeology, monarch
–astr–, –aster–	star	astronomy, asterisk
–auto–	self	automatic, autonomy
–bibli–	book	bibliography, bibliophile
–bio–	life	biology, autobiography
–chrom–	color	chromatic, chromosome
–chron–	time	chronometer, synchronize
–cosm–	world, order	cosmos, microcosm
–cycl–	wheel, circle	cyclone, bicycle
–dem–	people	democracy, epidemic
–gen–	kind, race	eugenics, genesis
–geo–	earth	geography, geology
–gram–	write, writing	grammar, epigram
–graph–	write, writing	orthography, geography
–hydr–	water	hydrogen, dehydrate
–log–	word, study	epilogue, theology, logic
–micr–	small	microbe, microscope
–mon–	one, single	monogamy, monologue
–morph–	form	amorphous, metamorphosis
–neo–	new	neologism, neolithic
–orth–	straight, correct	orthodox, orthography
–pan–	all, entire	panorama, pandemonium
–path–	feeling	apathy, pathology, sympathy
–phil–	like, love	philanthropic, philosophy
–phon–	sound	phonology, euphony
–poly–	many	polygon, polygamy
–proto–	first	prototype
–psych–	mind	psychology, psychosomatic
–soph–	wise, wisdom	philosophy, sophomore
–tele–	far, distant	telegram, telepathy
–zo–	animal	zoology, protozoa

● EXERCISE 11.   List two English words (other than those given as examples above) containing each of the following roots.

EXAMPLE   1. –verb–
                    1. *adverb, verbose*

1. –aud– (hear)
2. –crypt– (hidden, secret)
3. –duc– (lead)
4. –fin– (end, limit)
5. –junct– (join)

6. –man–, –manu– (hand)
7. –mor–, –mort– (death)
8. –port– (carry)
9. –vid–, –vis– (see)
10. –vit– (life)

● EXERCISE 12.   Follow the instructions for Exercise 11.

1. –anthrop– (man)
2. –auto– (self)
3. –bio– (life)
4. –chron– (time)
5. –cycl– (wheel, circle)

6. –dem–, –demo– (people)
7. –gram– (write, writing)
8. –hydr– (water)
9. –mega– (large)
10. –poly– (many)

● REVIEW EXERCISE A.   Using slanting bars (/) to mark each separation, divide the following words into their parts. Then referring to the preceding lists of prefixes, suffixes, and roots—or, if necessary, to your dictionary—write a brief definition for each. Be prepared to explain how the parts produce the total meaning.

EXAMPLE   1. philanthropic
                    1. *phil/anthrop/ic   (loving mankind)*

1. achromatic
2. autonomy
3. bibliophile
4. cosmic
5. cryptogram
6. deduction
7. evoke
8. extortion
9. geology
10. ineligible

11. incapable
12. infidel
13. judicious
14. lucid
15. nominee
16. proponent
17. pseudonym
18. subsequent
19. transmission
20. vociferous

Limitations of Word Analysis

Knowing something of the way in which prefixes, suffixes, and roots combine to form words provides insights into the history of our words and into their meanings. However, it would be misleading to suggest that the original meanings of the parts are always clearly reflected in a modern word.

It may happen that following the method of word division will lead you to a meaning that is so far from the modern one as to be of little help. For example, the words *admonition* and *monetary* have an element (*–mon–*) in common. The first means "warning" and the second "pertaining to money." What is the connection? There is one, but it is remote: in ancient Roman times, money was coined in or near a temple of a particular god known as "the warner." This is interesting, but not much of a clue if you do not already know the meaning of both words. Word analysis can often help you to make a plausible guess at what a word may mean; it can rarely be depended upon absolutely.

Semantic Change

One obvious reason that word analysis does not always work as a way of finding meaning is that words change their meanings. This change in meaning—called *semantic change*—is extremely common.

There are several ways in which this change comes about. Sometimes a word that has had a general meaning comes to have a specific meaning. The word *starve* once meant "to die." It only later took on the special meaning of "to die for lack of food." In Old English, any crawling creature—including the dragon in *Beowulf*—could be called a *worm*. Now the word is used only to mean earthworms and the like.

Words also take on new meanings in the opposite way—from specific to general. Originally *barn* meant "a storage place for barley," and *lord* meant "loaf guard or bread keeper."

When a word acquires a new meaning, it may lose the old meaning, as *worm, starve,* and *lord* have. When this situation takes place, the word has become detached from the root meaning, although it retains the original root form. The *–jure* of *adjure* is related to *jury* and originally had to do with swearing in a legal sense. But usually the word now means "to entreat," and the meaning connection with the root has been lost.

Auspices literally means "looking at birds." The ancient Romans believed that they could tell from studying the entrails of sacrificial birds whether or not an enterprise would be successful. The word came to be used for any combination of favorable signs and then, as it is now, for a combination of protection, guidance, and patronage.

Sometimes both old and new meanings are retained. Indeed, often it works out that a word will have six, eight, or ten meanings. Some of these meanings may be close to the original meanings of the word elements, some may vary from them considerably. The word *aegis* meant originally a shield or breastplate, especially one associated with the goddess Athena; then it came to mean also "protection" and "patronage, sponsorship." Depending on the context, it can mean any of these things in modern English. As a result, we may say that a lecture or exhibit is held under either the auspices—originally, bird watching—or the aegis—originally, shield—of a certain group. *Insular* means "pertaining to an island," but it has also come to mean "isolated, detached" and also "narrow, provincial." *Sanguine* may retain the root meaning and indicate "bloody," but it is more likely to mean "quite optimistic." Because there are so many situations involving semantic change, careful use of context clues or steady use of the dictionary is likely to give a more accurate sense of word meanings than word analysis alone.

● EXERCISE 13.   List the following words and write after each its original meaning as given in the dictionary: *abey-*

ance, challenge, derive, detriment, dirge, farce, glamour, knave, lampoon, melancholy, monster, pedigree, sabotage, scandal, vegetable.

Synonyms

Word borrowing, word derivation by affixes and roots, semantic change, and other processes keep going on all the time, making English rich in synonyms. Synonyms are words that may be interchanged in given contexts. We can say "a hard task" or "a difficult task," because *hard* and *difficult* are synonyms. We can say that New York is a large city or a metropolis, and *city* and *metropolis* are therefore synonyms.

It is often said that there are very few pairs of words in English that are entirely interchangeable, because there are usually slight but important differences between synonyms. Sometimes one synonym is noticeably more learned than another; *edifice* is more learned and pretentious than *building*, *domicile* more so than *home* or *residence*. *Daily* is the ordinary English word, *diurnal* and *quotidian* quite learned. Sometimes one of a pair of synonyms is noticeably informal; *smidge* or *smidgeon* is less formal than *particle*. Often learned words are rather specific in their suggestions; the sphere in which they can be used is narrow. It is possible to analyze both *terrestrial* and *mundane* as "pertaining to the world." But *terrestrial* is likely to suggest contrast between our world and other heavenly bodies, described by words like *lunar* and *solar*, and *mundane* carries with it suggestions of the practical, routine, everyday affairs of this world, as contrasted with more spiritual matters. Synonyms may differ, too, in expressing value judgments; to be *resolute* is a virtue; to be *determined* expresses no value judgment; and to be *obstinate* is a fault.

The wealth of synonyms in English gives us a variety of ways of expressing ourselves, but challenges us to decide on the most appropriate of them.

●EXERCISE 14.   Find three synonyms apiece for each of the following words. Use your dictionary if necessary. Be prepared to discuss differences between your synonyms.

1. sick	5. dangerous	9. dislike
2. expensive	6. talk	10. work
3. pleasant	7. walk	11. enjoyment
4. hard	8. see	12. knowledge

●EXERCISE 15.   Be prepared to discuss in class differences between the following pairs of synonyms.

1. donation, gift	6. vapid, inane
2. venomous, toxic	7. void, vacuum
3. reverent, pious	8. gracious, cordial
4. lean, gaunt	9. congenital, hereditary
5. meditate, ruminate	10. handle, manipulate

Early in this chapter, you were advised to keep a vocabulary notebook in which to list new words and their meanings. If you have done so, your notebook should contain a number of new words drawn from this chapter and from the word list that follows it. Do not be content, however, to have these words in your notebook. Listen for them, and watch for them in your reading. Observing how a new word is used is the best way of learning to use it yourself. Your vocabulary notebook is like the address books people use to remind them of the names and addresses of people they don't encounter often. No one needs such a book for close acquaintances. Get into the habit of making old friends of new words.

●REVIEW EXERCISE B.   Number 1–20. After the proper number, write the letter of the word or expression that comes closest to the meaning of the italicized word.

1. *amorphous*
   a) formless
   b) romantic
   c) jar-shaped
   d) commonplace

2. under the *auspices* of the state
   a) protests
   b) sponsorship
   c) opposition
   d) observation

3. struggle for *autonomy*
   a) fair treatment
   b) free elections
   c) survival
   d) self-rule

4. the last chance to *capitulate*
   a) turn the tide
   b) surrender
   c) negotiate
   d) compromise

5. *circumspect* behavior
   a) improper
   b) cautious
   c) surprising
   d) praiseworthy

6. to *collate* two documents
   a) preserve
   b) seal up
   c) duplicate
   d) compare

7. feeling no *compunction*
   a) satisfaction
   b) ambition
   c) remorse
   d) pride

8. to *conjecture* about a motive
   a) guess
   b) conceal the truth
   c) lie
   d) find out

9. the soldier's *defection*
   a) cowardice
   b) decoration
   c) desertion
   d) wound

10. not daring to *demur*
    a) whisper
    b) appear
    c) object
    d) tell the truth

11. a man *devoid* of sympathy
    a) full
    b) without a trace
    c) deserving
    d) undeserving

12. without *divulging* the answer
    a) guessing
    b) revealing
    c) suspecting
    d) peeking at

13. to *expiate* a crime
    a) profit from
    b) witness
    c) atone for
    d) be sorry about

14. a *judicious* choice
    a) illegal
    b) required by law
    c) wise
    d) laughable

15. a *minute* creature
    a) short-lived
    b) quickly moving
    c) very small
    d) very young

16. *mundane* concerns
    a) worldly
    b) tedious
    c) religious
    d) dishonest

17. *parasitic* followers
    a) loyal
    b) living off others
    c) disloyal
    d) fanatical

18. a *propitious* start
    a) proper
    b) false
    c) sudden
    d) favorable

19. an unusual *pseudonym*
    a) last name
    b) nickname
    c) pen name
    d) honorary title

20. an act of *temerity*
    a) cowardice
    b) rage
    c) uncertainty
    d) foolish daring

WORD LIST

The 240 words in the list below may be used as the basis of your vocabulary study this year. In many of them you will recognize the Old English, Latin, and Greek word parts you have just studied. Make it a habit to learn unfamiliar words from this list regularly; ten each week is a practical number. When you consult a dictionary for the meaning of an unfamiliar word, make sure you find the meaning that fits the context you have in mind; or ask your teacher to verify the meaning.

abdicate
abeyance
abscond
accede
accessory
accost
acquisition
acrimonious
adjudge
adjure

aegis
aesthetic
allay
amorphous
antipathy
antipodes
apostasy
apposite
archive
ascertain

ascetic
ascribe
asperity
auspices
austerity

autonomy
biennial
bucolic
cabal
calumny

capricious
cataclysm
cavil
chicanery
chimerical
cognizant
collateral
complaisance
compunction
conjecture

conjugal
consanguinity
contravene
contumely
conversant
cosmic
cosmopolitan
coterie
couplet
covet

credible
credulous
cryptic
decorum
deduction
defection
demure
denizen
derive
derogatory

desiccate
desist
deteriorate
detriment
devoid
differentiate
dilatory
dirge
disburse
discursive

disparity
dissent
diurnal
divulge
doggerel

dogma
drastic
dupe
duress
dynamic

effete
eject
elegant
elite
elixir
elocution
elude
emissary
emolument
empirical

enormity
entomologist
environment
ephemeral
epicurean
equanimity
eschew
essence
eugenics
eulogy

euphony
evanescent
evoke
excise
exhort
expiate
facile
febrile
fecundity
foible

frivolous
glamour
gratuitous
humdrum
hyperbole
immutable
inane
inanimate
incarcerate
incompatible

increment
inculcate
induction
ingenuous
iniquity
insular
intercede
intervene
invidious
irony

laity
lampoon
loquacious
microcosm
modicum
mundane
nefarious
nemesis
nonentity
omniscient

opulence
panegyric
parasitic
patron
perfidious
perspicuity

pertinent
platitude
pleasantry
plebeian

plebiscite
politic
predilection
prescience
presumptuous
primordial
priority
proffer
prognostic
proletarian

propitiate
propitious
proponent
proscribe
prospective
protagonist
protege
prototype
proxy
pseudonym

puissance
punctilious
purport
pusillanimous
querulous
quiescent
raillery
raucous
reactionary
recalcitrant

reciprocate

redundant
regicide
regimen
remission
remuneration
repartee
replete
repository
repugnance

residual
restitution
retroactive
retrospect
revelation
rostrum
rotund
sagacity
salient
saline

salutary

sanguine
sardonic
saturnine
schism
scurrilous
sedentary
sedulous
solstice
somnolent

sonorous
sortie
specious
stereotype
stipend
strident
stultify
subservient
subsidiary
subterfuge

superannuate

surreptitious
synchronize
syndicate
temerity
tenable
tenuous
tenure
truism
unprecedented

venal
verify
vernacular
virulent
vitiate
vituperate
vociferous
volatile
voluminous
votary

PART SIX

Speaking
and Listening

Solving Problems Through Discussion and Debate

Types of Discussion; Elements of Debating

It is natural for people to talk things over, either to exchange information or to dispute. Both kinds of discussion can be profitable if they are conducted in an orderly way and in a form that suits the purpose. The common kinds of discussion and debate, a specialized form, are treated in this chapter.

Group Discussion

A group discussion is an attempt to solve a problem by cooperative deliberation. Societies of every kind—school clubs, civic organizations, labor unions, legislative assemblies—use discussion as a means of arriving at a solution to a particular problem or airing the opinions of members before making a decision. This method of problem-solving gives each member a voice in deciding matters which may affect his welfare and ensures the right of everyone to be heard.

31a. Learn how discussion differs from conversation and debate.

Although conversation, discussion, and debate are similar, there are marked differences.

A *conversation* is unplanned and private. It ranges over many topics, casually touching on each. It may have no purpose at all other than fellowship, or it may aim to entertain, instruct, or persuade. Usually not more than a handful of people are engaged in the same conversation at the same time.

A *discussion* is planned and public. It is focused on one topic, which is examined in depth under the direction of a chairman. Its purpose is to consider a problem, evaluate proposed solutions, and arrive at the best solution. As many as fifteen persons may participate in a discussion. A larger number is possible but unwieldy.

A *debate* considers two sides of a problem. The supporters of each side attempt to defeat their opponents by arguments set forth in carefully reasoned and extended speeches. A debate usually follows a formal procedure and involves a decision by judges. Participants in a group discussion, on the other hand, consider all aspects of a problem and have a cooperative attitude toward one another. They exchange information and opinion in a more informal manner and their statements are not so lengthy.

A debate may grow out of a discussion. Many points of view are explored in a discussion. When they are narrowed to two, debate comes into play. Debate starts where discussion ends.

31b. Know the limitations of discussion.

Discussion is an important tool of democracy, but it has limitations.

In the first place a one-man decision is a more efficient

31
a-b

means of getting action started. When decisions are made by one person, a dictator, for example, the time that would otherwise be spent in discussion is saved. A dictator issues decrees, and his followers obey. Discussion is slow. People have to meet, exchange opinions, compromise differences, and agree upon a decision. However, they will work willingly to put the decision into action because each has contributed to it and feels responsible for its success.

Another limitation is due to the participants themselves. They need to have a cooperative and fair-minded attitude. If they are belligerent or prejudiced, or if they resist change of any kind, they are not fit to carry on a discussion. Participants in a discussion ought to be flexible and responsible. They should keep their attention focused on the point at issue, defend any position they consider valid, and discard any which is proved to be weak.

Types of Group Discussion

31c. Learn the various types of group discussion.

Among the many types of group discussion, the most common are the *round table*, the *forum*, the *symposium*, and the *panel*.

A *round table* is an informal discussion in which the participants exchange views around a table—not necessarily round—under the leadership of a chairman and most often without an audience. The number of participants usually does not exceed a dozen. Members of the group speak without rising and without being recognized by the chair.

The most common example of round-table discussion is the committee meeting. Many organizations conduct a large part of their business through committees. A committee considers business referred to it and reports its findings and recommendations to the entire organization.

In a round-table discussion everyone has a feeling of

equality. This type of discussion is most likely to succeed when the participants are well informed and about equal in ability.

Possible seating plans:

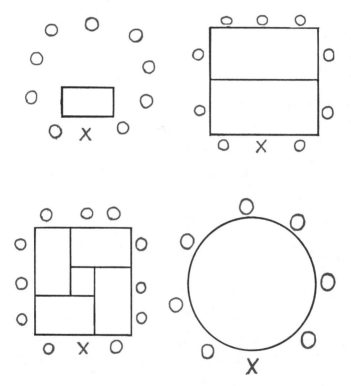

A *forum* is any type of speaking program which is followed by audience participation. For example, a lecture followed by questions from the audience is a forum. A forum is most successful when the audience is small. When the audience is large, people are reluctant to stand up and speak their minds.

A *symposium* involves several formal speeches on a single topic followed by audience participation. When the audience

31c

is large, audience participation is sometimes limited to questions; expressions of opinion from the floor are usually not allowed.

A forum may be one-sided since only one speaker is involved. A symposium seeks a more rounded consideration by means of several speakers with differing points of view.

A *panel* is a discussion by a selected group of persons under a chairman in front of an audience which joins in later. The speakers represent different viewpoints. There are usually no set speeches but sometimes speakers are asked to set forth their viewpoints in brief preliminary statements.

A panel is really an overheard conversation guided by a chairman. It may consist of four to eight members who face the audience and remain seated while talking. The chairman keeps the discussion moving forward and, at some interesting point, invites the audience to join in. The panel conversation spills over, as it were, to include the audience. At the conclusion of the discussion, the chairman summarizes what has been said and thanks the participants and the audience.

A panel should be seated this way

rather than this

so that the panelists may better communicate with one another. When tables are used, the speakers may be seated as follows:

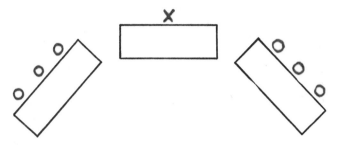

The purpose of a panel is to get important facts and opposing opinions into the open, stimulate audience thinking, and lay a basis for wide participation later.

31d. Select a topic which lends itself to profitable group discussion.

The success of a group discussion depends in no small measure on the topic. Before selecting a topic, ask yourself:

1. Is it related to the needs, interests, and experience of the listeners and speakers?
2. Is it timely?
3. Is it controversial?
4. Is it many-sided?
5. Is it stated clearly?

What are good sources of topics for group discussion? Your own experience may suggest some: for example, "Teen-age problems," "Fads in popular music," or "Learning by working after school hours." Your school courses may suggest others; for instance, "Why study mathematics and science?" "What is the most valuable subject in the curriculum?" or "Is high school too easy?" Books, magazine articles, movies, and television programs can often

31d

stimulate discussion. Newspapers are another source. The discussion of current events, especially of controversial matters, can capture and hold an audience's attention. Topics which are trivial or time-worn, have no audience appeal, do not evoke strong differences of opinion, or can be answered by *yes* or *no* are not suitable.

A topic for discussion should be a question of policy rather than fact. "Have we a supply of atomic bombs?" is a question of fact and hence not discussible. The only appropriate reply is a direct, factual answer. "Should we use atomic bombs in the event of war?" is a question of policy which should stir discussion.

● EXERCISE 1.   List five topics suitable for group discussion. Test yours and those submitted by other members of the class against the criteria listed above. The topics may be related to school, community, state, national, or international affairs.

● EXERCISE 2.   Conduct a round-table discussion on a topic which concerns all the participants. The student chairman, appointed beforehand, will end the discussion after 20 minutes, summarize, and invite class discussion. Suggested topics:

High school fraternities and sororities

City vs. country living

Improving the student organization

Improving the school cafeteria

The school yearbook

Assembly programs

Building school spirit

Teen-age fads

● EXERCISE 3.   Conduct a forum. A student will lecture on a current, vital problem, and propose a solution for it. At the end of his lecture the class will ask questions.

● EXERCISE 4.   Conduct a symposium on discipline. The speakers should represent the viewpoints of a young person, a parent, a law enforcement officer, an educator, and a community leader.

● EXERCISE 5.   Divide the class into groups. Each group will select a chairman and present a panel discussion before the class on any one of the following topics. (The list is suggestive only. Choose a topic of your own if you prefer; be sure it is of interest and concern to all.) Each panel should meet beforehand to settle matters of procedure and scope.

Modern manners	Prejudice—and how to overcome it.
Radio and television advertising	Should 18-year-olds be permitted to vote?
Youthful crime	The kind of world I'd like to live in
The ideal school	
Choosing a vocation	
The honor system of conducting examinations	Extracurricular activities
	Our foreign policy
Professional vs. amateur sports	Problems of the small farmer
Vandalism	Ways of preventing war
Should Latin be dropped from the curriculum?	Selecting a college

31e. Prepare for group discussion by thinking, talking, and reading about the topic.

Many discussions fail because of insufficient preparation by the participants.

If a discussion is to be more than a pooling of misinformation or ignorance, everyone must think, talk, and read about the subject before the discussion takes place. When the topic is announced:

1. Think about it. Do your own thinking. If you simply swallow what you see, hear, and read without analyzing it, you are not acting intelligently. Make sure that there is sufficient evidence to substantiate the truth of every major point. Think things through and avoid making rash or erroneous judgments.

2. Talk to others about it. Discuss it with your friends and parents. If you know someone who is an authority on

31e

the subject, discuss it with him. Be ready to modify your previous opinion in the light of your new knowledge.

3. Consult reference books, recent publications, magazine articles and editorials. Inform yourself as thoroughly as you can about the topic. Investigate the facts before arriving at a decision, for otherwise you may delude others as well as yourself.

4. In problem-solving discussions, follow the steps of logical thinking. When you are confronted by a problem, your mind follows certain logical steps. For example, if your ball point pen fails to write, you ask yourself:

- a. What is the trouble?   [You define the problem.]
- b. What *might be* the cause?   [You mentally list various causes: a clogged point, defective mechanism, exhausted ink cartridge.]
- c. What *is* the cause?   [You consider each of the previously listed possibilities. The point is not clogged, the mechanism works smoothly, the cartridge is used up.]
- d. What should be done about it?   [Obviously you need a new cartridge or a new pen.]

This simple example illustrates the steps in problem-solving. They are as follows:

1. Define the problem.
2. Find the possible causes.
3. Examine the proposed solutions.   [What would be the effects of each? To what extent would each solve the problem?]
4. Select the best solution.
5. Put the best solution into operation.   [What obstacles will be encountered and how will they be overcome?]

When participants and chairman are familiar with these five steps, they follow them in their individual and group thinking and an orderly discussion results. The discussion does not remain static and pointless. It marches forward.

● EXERCISE 6. Listen to a TV or radio discussion program and report on it orally to your class. Did the discussion follow the steps in problem-solving listed above? If not, what order or sequence did it follow?

Participating in Group Discussion

The success of a group discussion depends on the attitudes of the participants and the quality of their participation, the leadership of the chairman, and the response of the audience.

31f. Learn the responsibilities of a speaker in a group discussion.

As a speaker in a group discussion, you should have a cooperative attitude, recognizing that the common good of the group supersedes your own concerns.

Know your subject well. To have an adequate knowledge of the topic, prepare thoroughly by reflecting on it and by talking and reading about it.

Contribute willingly. Some of your ideas will come from previous reflection and others on the spur of the moment, stimulated by what someone else has said. Don't hesitate to express tentative ideas for the other participants to consider, for these ideas may be just what are needed, but be careful not to monopolize the discussion. Everyone should have a chance to be heard.

Listen intelligently. When you agree with another speaker, listen to increase your store of information. When you disagree, listen to accept a different viewpoint if it is supported by sufficient evidence or to refute it by sound reasons if it is fallacious.

Speak so that all may hear—not only the participants but the audience too, if there is one.

Recognize and admit the truth of what others say. There

31f

is no need, however, to pass judgment on every statement made by someone else.

Be courteous always. Sarcasm and ridicule are out of place. Self-control is a mark of maturity. Disagree reasonably—and with reasons.

31g. Learn the responsibilities of a chairman of a discussion.

The skill and personality of the chairman of a discussion are important. If you are chosen to lead a discussion, considered yourself complimented. Your teacher and classmates have recognized your leadership ability.

As chairman, you should familiarize yourself with the subject and the special interests and backgrounds of the participants. If the discussion is to be held before an audience, arrange a preliminary meeting of the speakers to decide on procedure and the order in which the various aspects of the topic will be discussed.

Decide on the seating plan. "Set the stage" with an arc of chairs and tables on a slightly raised platform close to the audience. Do not seat members with similar viewpoints together; mix them up. Seat lively talkers on the ends, quieter ones near the center so you can encourage them.

Introduce the speakers to the audience, telling something of each one's background or the point of view he represents.

Arouse the audience's interest in the topic by a brief introductory statement. Say just enough to spotlight the problem and throw out the first question.

Address your questions to the group as a whole. Don't question individual members, as a rule. Let participation be as free and spontaneous as possible. Ask challenging questions—not the *yes* and *no* kind, but *why?* and *how?*

Dig out points of differences, not as in debate but in a friendly, united pursuit of a solution. Work to find the common meeting ground.

Take time for occasional summaries. People like to know what progress is being made. In your final summary mention the loose ends, if any.

Keep your own viewpoint out of the discussion. Break in only to ask clarifying questions, bring the discussion back on the track, advance to the next point, or summarize. Be impartial.

Keep the discussion on the track. Encourage the give-and-take of opinion among the participants. Try to have it

THIS WAY

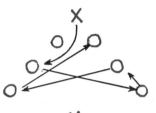

NOT THIS WAY

Invite audience participation at a point of high interest, usually about the half-way mark. Speakers from the floor may describe their own experience, state their opinions, or ask questions. As the chairman, do not answer questions; refer them to the panel.

Before closing, thank the speakers and the audience.

31h. Learn the responsibilities of a member of the audience.

The audience plays a larger role in group discussion than is generally supposed. By listening attentively, asking questions, and making clarifying statements, an audience can help make a group discussion stimulating.

31
g-h

As a member of the audience, you also have an obligation to prepare for the discussion by thinking, talking, and reading about the topic.

Listen with an alert mind. Ask yourself: What proof is offered in support of each important argument?

Join in when the chairman invites the audience to participate. Speak freely, briefly, sincerely. A discussion in which there is general participation is more stimulating and interesting than one in which only a few take part.

Focus on the main issues. Minor points of fact or opinion should be overlooked.

Speak audibly. While your remarks are addressed to the chairman, speak so that all may hear.

● EXERCISE 7.   Bring in newspaper announcements of discussions to be held in your community. Note the forms of discussion and the questions to be discussed. If you can attend one of these discussions, do so and report on it orally to the class.

● EXERCISE 8.   Divide the class into groups of 6–8 members. Each group, under the direction of a chairman, will select a question for discussion and phrase it properly. The discussions will be carried on simultaneously in separated areas of the room with the instructor moving from one to another. After a designated time, the class will reassemble and the chairman of each group will report on the problems his group faced in its discussion, how they were handled, and where improvement is needed.

● EXERCISE 9.   If one of your class discussions is especially interesting, arrange to present it before another class or at a school assembly.

Listening

As a chairman, speaker, or member of the audience you must not only have ideas that you can express well, but you must be able to understand and evaluate the ideas of others in the discussion. In other words you must *listen* to what is said, not just *hear* it.

31i. **Learn to listen efficiently.**

Do you know that most of us do not listen efficiently? Studies show that the average listener recalls only a little more than half of what a speaker says. By understanding and applying the following points you can close this communication gap between speaker and listener.

1. *Listen to acquire information and evaluate it.* A witty author once remarked, "A good listener is not only popular everywhere, but after a while he knows something." As you hear a speaker present ideas, you interpret them and pass judgment on them as sound or weak. In effect, you are talking back in your own mind. Ask yourself: "Has the speaker presented enough evidence to justify his opinions? Is the evidence from reliable sources? Is his reasoning valid?"

2. *Listen with the right attitude.* To listen efficiently you must be unbiased and cooperative. People with fixed ideas find it difficult to listen to viewpoints different from their own. They develop a mental deafness to ideas that do not sit well with them. They only "tune in" on ideas that they like to hear, even if they are half-truths or not truths at all. An intelligent listener, on the other hand, is fair-minded and receptive to all ideas which are supported by convincing evidence.

Do not strongly agree or disagree with a speaker early in his talk. Withhold final judgment until he develops his topic.

3. *Listen with attention.* Concentration is hard work. We all have a tendency to listen for a few minutes, daydream for a while, and then turn our attention again to the speaker. To overcome this tendency, be aware of it and make an effort to concentrate continuously on the speaker's message.

4. *Listen for the main ideas.* Usually only a few main

31i

points are presented in a discussion, although many minor points and some digressions creep in. Listen with the purpose of discovering the central ideas and fastening attention upon them.

5. *Listen for supporting information.* A speaker should support his assertions by offering evidence in the form of facts, statements of authorities, and logical reasoning.[1] The evidence must be sufficient to justify what has been said or else the assertion fails for lack of proof. Whatever is asserted without proof can be denied without proof.

6. *Listen for faulty reasoning.* In Chapter 27 you learned about faulty cause and effect arguments, irrelevant arguments, rationalizing, and wishful thinking.

As you listen to discussions, you may hear faulty reasoning of this sort, for this mistake is more common in oral than in written presentations.

7. *Listen for loaded words.*[2] The use of emotionally loaded words is natural in free discussion, particularly when the speakers are committed to a viewpoint. The active listener is aware of this danger and discounts arguments that are directed at his emotions, not his reason.

● Exercise 10.   Listen carefully to a social studies or science lesson, or to any other lesson in which there is general class discussion. Prepare a report telling what main ideas were developed and what minor points were also developed. Explain how you were able to distinguish between major and minor matters. Were there any digressions? If so, were these digressions helpful or confusing to class and teacher?

● Exercise 11.   Report on a radio or television discussion on a controversial question. Did the speakers present both sides of the question fairly? What evidence did they offer to support their opinion? What objections can you pose?

[1] For a discussion of evidence, see pp. 385–88.
[2] For a discussion of loaded words, see pp. 298–99.

Evaluating Group Discussion

By considering the merits and deficiencies of a group discussion after it is over, you can learn to improve future discussion programs. In your evaluation, consider the group as a whole, the individual participants, the chairman, and the outcome of the discussion.

31j. Evaluate a group discussion by asking key questions about it.

The following questions will help you estimate the worth of a group discussion.

1. Was the discussion purposeful? Were the causes of the problem considered? Were various solutions proposed and analyzed? Did the discussion ramble or did it proceed in an orderly fashion? If the discussion was concerned with solving a problem, did it follow the steps of logical thinking?

2. Was the outcome worthwhile? A group discussion need not reach a solution or agreement. It may be successful if it brings areas of disagreement into the open.

3. Were the participants thoroughly familiar with the problem? Did they present facts, statements of competent and unbiased authorities, and statistics to support their opinions?

4. Was the discussion lively and general? Was there a give-and-take of opinion in an atmosphere of mutual respect? Did all participate? Did anyone monopolize the meeting, or did everyone speak briefly and to the point?

5. Were the audience's questions thought-provoking? Did the speakers answer them directly and fully?

6. Was the discussion courteous? Did each speaker exercise self-control by refraining from interrupting when another was speaking? Were statements and objections phrased courteously?

7. Was the chairman competent? Did he arouse interest by his introductory remarks? Did he guide the discussion

31j

so as to prevent pointless digressions? Did he encourage everyone to join in? Did he summarize?

● EXERCISE 12. Prepare a rating sheet for use by class and teacher in rating group discussions.

● EXERCISE 13. Record a class discussion on a tape recorder. Play the recording to the class so that the participants may analyze their effectiveness or ineffectiveness.

DEBATING

A debate is a contest in which arguments are used instead of physical strength. It is a form of argument in which two sides publicly dispute a question in a systematic way.

Debating focuses attention on controversial questions, particularly those affecting the public interest. It stimulates thinking, develops ability in speaking, provides training in research, and encourages the habit of suspending judgment until all facts are at hand.

The team supporting the question or proposition is called the affirmative; the opposing team, the negative. Each team consists of two (or, rarely, three) speakers, who are called *first affirmative* (or *negative*), *second affirmative*, etc.

A debate is divided into two parts. During the first part (constructive speeches) both sides present their arguments for or against the proposition. After an intermission, both sides try to refute (with rebuttal speeches) the opposing arguments.

The order of speaking is as follows:

CONSTRUCTIVE SPEECHES	REBUTTAL SPEECHES
First affirmative	First negative
First negative	First affirmative
Second affirmative	Second negative
Second negative	Second affirmative

Notice that the affirmative side opens and closes the debate and that the first rebuttal is made by the negative side.

The Proposition

The characteristics of a proposition are discussed in Chapter 23, page 380. The following review should recall the main points in that discussion.

31k. A proposition is a topic stated in debatable form.

It may be phrased either as a resolution or as a question.

EXAMPLES   Should football be prohibited as a high school sport?
Resolved: Football should be prohibited as a high school sport.

(1) A proposition should contain only one central idea.

WRONG   Resolved: Fraternities and sororities should be banned in high schools and every high school student should be required to participate in at least one extracurricular activity.   [two ideas]

RIGHT   Resolved: Fraternities and sororities should be banned in high schools.

RIGHT   Resolved: Every high school student should be required to participate in at least one extracurricular activity.

(2) A proposition should be debatable. It should have two sides.

NOT DEBATABLE   Resolved: The automobile has greatly affected the way we live.   [This is so obviously true that it cannot be debated.]

NOT DEBATABLE   Resolved: Through space flights man obtains valuable scientific information to aid human progress.   [Since nearly all the arguments are on the affirmative, this is too one-sided to be debatable.]

31k

(3) A proposition should be stated fairly.

UNFAIR   Resolved: That the unjust and harmful compulsory military service law should be abolished. [This assumes what has to be proved—that compulsory military service is unjust and harmful.]

FAIR   Resolved: That the compulsory military service law should be abolished.

(4) A proposition should be timely.

Current problems are more exciting than dead ones. For example, few people today would be interested in debating our entry into the Spanish-American War, although at the time that question stirred widespread interest. There are hundreds of vital questions relating to young people, schools, local conditions, state, national, and international affairs which stimulate controversy.

(5) A proposition should be stated affirmatively.

WRONG   Resolved: Capital punishment should not be abolished. [The affirmative side would have to argue, "Yes, it should not be abolished," a confusing position.]

RIGHT   Resolved: Capital punishment should be abolished.

(6) A proposition should put the burden of proof on the affirmative.

Anyone who makes an assertion should be ready and able to prove it. The affirmative side, which asserts the truth of a proposition, must present enough proof to establish its case beyond a reasonable doubt.

The affirmative side must show a need for a change; for example, that high school football should be prohibited or that a government lottery should be established. Existing conditions—called the *status quo*—are presumed to be satisfactory until the affirmative offers sufficient proof to show that a change is necessary.

WRONG Resolved: That our government should continue to negotiate with communist countries. [This makes the affirmative defend the *status quo* and the negative advocate a change.]

RIGHT Resolved: That our government should break off relations with communist countries.

The negative has only to prove that the affirmative case is false or unsound. It does not have to offer an alternative solution.

(7) A proposition should contain no words of uncertain meaning.

For example, "Resolved: That oil is more valuable than steel in modern civilization" is not debatable because "valuable" has no exact meaning. Does it mean essential? Costly? Efficient? Useful?

● EXERCISE 14. Compose five propositions for class debate. Be sure that each of your propositions satisfies all the requirements listed above.

The Issue

311. An issue is a point of disagreement.

The points in a debate on which there are clashes of opinion are called *issues*.[1] A proposition rests on several issues. If they are proved, the proposition is proved. An issue is stated as a question which can be answered by *yes* or *no*.

PROPOSITION Resolved: That the voting age should be lowered to 18.

ISSUES 1. Are those between 18 and 21 really ready for the responsibility of voting?

[1] An *issue* in debate corresponds to the minor proposition in other kinds of argument.

311

2. Is the vote of youth needed to strengthen and preserve democracy?
3. Should a person who is old enough to fight in the armed services be considered old enough to vote?

Issues often deal with the need for a change, the practicability of a proposed solution, and the desirability of adopting a different solution.

● EXERCISE 18.   List at least three issues for one of the propositions you submitted in Exercise 14.

The Brief

31m. A brief is an outline for debate.

In Chapter 27, you learned the principles of argumentation. Those principles are as valid in debating as in writing. Debating is simply oral argumentation.

In a debate, arguments are not written in consecutive prose. They are prepared in the form of a detailed logical outline called a *brief*. A brief is an orderly arrangement of all the arguments needed to prove or disprove a proposition. All the statements in a brief are complete sentences.

The introduction summarizes the history of the question and defines terms. Sometimes, it sets forth issues and mentions any matters that are excluded from discussion by mutual agreement.

In the brief proper the issues are taken up one by one and the evidence in support of each is given in the form of facts, figures, examples, authority, and logical reasoning.

The conclusion summarizes the main arguments and reasserts or denies the proposition.

The example that follows illustrates the form and content of a brief.

Should 18-Year-Olds Be Allowed to Vote? [1]

Affirmative

I. The 18-year-olds deserve to vote.
   A. They are entitled to a voice in determining foreign policy because they are the ones most likely to be called into active service in the event of war.
   B. They are entitled to a voice in determining domestic policies because, as workers, they are directly affected by the government's economic, social, and political policies.

II. They are qualified to vote.
   A. They are prepared educationally.
      1. They have had a longer period of schooling than young people of previous generations.
      2. They have taken part in activities and studied subjects, such as social studies, designed to prepare them for citizenship.
   B. They are prepared by practical experience.
      1. In the early days of the republic, a young man served as an apprentice until age 21, and his every act was dominated by his employer.
      2. Young workers today exercise their own judgment and initiative.

III. Our nation would benefit if 18-year-olds were allowed to vote.
   A. The present three-year interval between school and voting leads to a loss of interest.
      1. The poorest voting record is that of the age group 21–30 as Professor James K. Pollack of the University of Michigan has pointed out.
      2. If a citizen were permitted to vote at age 18, he would form the voting habit from the beginning.
   B. To add the 18–20 group to the electorate would help solve some of our most pressing problems.
      1. Because the percentage of older people in our popula-

[1] From "Should 18-Year-Olds Be Allowed to Vote?" by Oliver Clinton Carpenter in *Debate Outlines on Public Questions*. Reprinted by permission of Mail and Express Printing Company, Inc.

tion is constantly increasing, the voting balance favors older ages.

2. The addition of 18-year-olds would establish a balance of age groups.

3. Older people tend to be settled in their opinions; younger people tend towards fresh and unprejudiced viewpoints.

4. Such questions as the atomic bomb, our relations with the Soviet Union, and our position in world affairs require new points of view if they are to be settled.

Negative

I. The 18-year-olds do not necessarily "deserve" to vote.

A. They do not "deserve" to vote because "they are old enough to fight."

1. The draft age of 18 was selected because of military necessity.

2. The factors that make an 18-year-old a good soldier have nothing to do with his voting qualifications.

B. They do not "deserve" to vote because they are subject to governmental policies and pay taxes.

1. Governmental policies affect an individual from infancy, not from age 18.

2. Every individual with sufficient earning power pays taxes, regardless of age; there is no connection between the obligation to pay taxes and the right to vote.

II. They are not qualified to vote.

A. They lack independent judgment.

1. The law guards young people from the need of exercising independent judgment until age 21.

a. They cannot obligate themselves for debts or bind themselves to a contract.

b. In school and at home their actions are governed by obedience.

2. Their experience is inadequate.

a. Political decisions affect personal freedom and property rights.

     b. The only experience young people have in these matters is limited to what they have read in books or have been told by others.

III. It would be against the nation's best interests to have them vote.

    A. It would encourage impractical schemes.

    B. It would give strength to demagogues and dangerous groups.

      1. Dictators always start by appealing to youth.

      2. Selfish groups would try to mislead young people.

The Rebuttal

31n. Plan the rebuttal while preparing the debate.

The rebuttal is the most interesting phase of a debate because it tests a debater's ability to analyze and answer his opponent's arguments. To refute effectively, a debater must be able to think on his feet and speak extemporaneously.

Prepare for the rebuttal weeks before the debate, at the time you are gathering material and thinking about your case. As you learned in Chapter 27, you will be in a weak position if you ignore a major argument of the other side. Your success as a debater may rest on your ability to answer your opponents' arguments. As you prepare your brief, consider the arguments they will use, confer with your colleagues about them, and assemble arguments to refute them. Summarize each opposing argument and your answer to it on a separate card. Have your cards available for reference during the debate.

Refutation can start during the constructive speeches. Reply to your opponent's arguments when your turn comes to speak. Because of time limitations, however, most of your reply must wait until the rebuttal period.

When refuting, state your opponent's arguments clearly and fairly, in his own words if possible. Then present

31n

evidence to show that his argument is illogical, misleading, or unproved.

In rebuttal, limit yourself to the main arguments of the opposition. It is wasteful to spend time refuting minor points of fact or opinion. If you can demolish the opposition's main contentions, the minor arguments can be ignored.

Participating in Debate

31o. Observe the conventions of debate.

Address the chairman as "Mr. Chairman" or "Madam Chairman." Refer to the judges as "Honorable judges."

Instead of referring to participants by name, use the customary terms, "The first affirmative speaker," "My worthy opponents," "The gentlemen of the opposition," "My colleagues," or "My teammates."

Ridicule, sarcasm, and personal attacks have no place in debating. A debate should be won or lost on the basis of reasoned argument and convincing delivery.

31p. The judges' decision is based on the skill of the debaters, not on the truth or falsity of the proposition.

The most common method of determining the winner of a debate is by decision of three appointed judges. The judges base their decision on the merits of the debate and not upon their own views of the question.

Another method is by decision of a critic judge who announces the winning team and gives the reasons for his decision.

A third method is by means of a shift-of-opinion poll. Before the debate a ballot is distributed to each listener on which he records his opinion with respect to the proposition. At the end of the debate he records his opinion again.

A tally is taken. Only ballots showing a change of opinion are counted. The decision is awarded to the team that caused the greater number of listeners to change their opinion.

● EXERCISE 16. Divide the class into groups of four or six. Each group will decide on a proposition for debate, divide into affirmative and negative teams, prepare briefs, and on the appointed date present the debate in class under a chairman appointed by the teacher or elected by the class. If desired, another class may be invited to attend the debate. The following topics, which should be phrased as propositions, are only suggestive.

Coeducation
Homework
Jury system
Tipping
Freedom of the press
Censorship of motion pictures
Communism
Elective courses
Professional boxing
Nuclear energy
Abolition of the UN
U.S. foreign policy
Abolition of interscholastic athletics
Federal aid to schools
Honor system of examinations

High school fraternities
Abolition of football
Government control of radio and TV
Electoral college
Compulsory voting
Eleven-month school year
Raising (Lowering) the driving age
Conservation
Labor unions
Comic books
Youthful crime
Compulsory military service
Lagging school spirit
Reorganization of Congress

CHAPTER 32

Effective Speech

Pronunciation and Enunciation

If you want to communicate your ideas and feelings to others so that they understand, feel, and act as you want them to, you must know how to speak effectively. Poor speech interferes with communication. It diverts attention from *what* is being said to *how* it is being said. Listeners who hear a speaker pronounce *theater* as *the-AY-ter* and habitually say *dese, dose, dem, gimme, gunna, lemme,* and *wanna* will be distracted by his slovenly speech habits from the thoughts he is uttering. You must learn to avoid any peculiarity of speech that draws attention from your message. "Mend your speech," said Shakespeare, "lest it mar your fortunes."

PRONUNCIATION

Some think that the best speech is that used by the upper class in England or by cultured speakers in a particular city such as Oxford, Dublin, or New York. Others try to imitate stage speech or the speech of the Atlantic coast from New York to Canada. Which speech is best for you?

32a. Use the speech of educated speakers in your region as a model.

The United States has several speech regions, each with its own standard of pronunciation. Fortunately, American regional differences are not great enough to hinder communication. The speech of one region is easily understandable in another. Throughout this country educated people pronounce most words in the same way, although some pronunciations accepted in Boston and other eastern or northern cities may sound odd or affected to a native of New Orleans or Denver.

Speak the speech of your home region without trying to imitate the speech of other regions. Use the speech of educated persons in your area as your model—radio and TV announcers, teachers, executives, legislators, lawyers, and other persons of education and culture. Good speech does not attract attention to itself. Avoid the extreme pronunciation of any region, including your own. You will be understood anywhere if your pronunciation does not deviate too much from the common usage of your area.

● Exercise 1.   List several well-known persons whom you consider models of good speech in your region. Discuss your choices, giving reasons.

● Exercise 2.   Give examples of expressions heard in other sections of the country which are not commonly heard in your region. Do you know of any expressions that are peculiar to your own area? If so, give examples of them.

32b.   Recognize the difference between standard and substandard pronunciation.

Every region has two main levels of usage,[1] *standard* English and *substandard* English. Standard English has two sub levels—formal and informal.

[1] For further discussion of usage levels, see pages 72–78.

**32
a-b**

Formal English is the speech of educated people when they are speaking carefully, especially in a formal situation such as a commencement or public debate.

Informal English is the speech of educated people in informal situations such as social conversations. It is the kind normally used in everyday conversation by teachers and students in classrooms and by businessmen in their offices.

The pronunciation of both formal and informal English is the same. Both observe regional standards.

Substandard English is the language of persons who have had only a little education. It is ungrammatical in form and careless in pronunciation. Substandard English is not ordinarily acceptable in educated circles. Examples of substandard pronunciation are

athaletics	*for*	athletics
acrost	*for*	across
heighth	*for*	height
northren	*for*	northern
libary	*for*	library
filum	*for*	film
umberella	*for*	umbrella

● EXERCISE 3.   List several common examples of substandard pronunciation and give the correct form for each.

32c. Be particularly careful about stress or accent.

No pronunciation fault is quite so obvious as stressing the wrong syllable.

It occurs most often with words we encounter in books but rarely hear. For such words, a dictionary is usually a reliable guide to pronunciation. For the pronunciation of commonly used words, of course, careful speakers in your own area are your best guides.

There are a few general rules governing stress but they

have so many exceptions that you must be careful in applying them.

1. *Stress tends to be recessive in English; it recedes, or backs away from the final syllable.*

When *automobile* came into English from the French, it was pronounced *automoBILE*. Later it became *autoMObile*. Today it is commonly *AUtomobile*.

Chauffeur and *menu*, once stressed on the last syllable, are now stressed on the first.

Balcony and *confiscate* were formerly stressed on the second syllable only. *Retail, detail,* and *address,* formerly accented on the second syllable only, may now receive a stress on the initial syllable.

2. *Words that contain the suffix* –able *do not usually put the accent on the syllable immediately preceding* –able.

EXAMPLES

ádmirable	inéxplicable
ápplicable	inéxtricable
disréputable	inhóspitable
fórmidable	irréfutable
incómparable	préferable

3. *In words ending in* –ity *and* –ety, *stress the third syllable from the end.*

EXAMPLES

aménity	satíety
anonýmity	spontanéity
inebríety	

4. *The final syllable is stressed in many words taken from the French.* In nearly every case these words have not been fully naturalized.

EXAMPLES   bourgeoisíe

entrepreneúr

ragoút (rhyme this with "Drag who?")

32c

5. *Words ending in* –iacal *have a long* i *sound and are stressed on the* i.

EXAMPLES hypochondríacal   maníacal

6. *Stress is sometimes used to distinguish parts of speech.* A word that has the same form when used as a noun, adjective, or verb, is usually stressed on the first syllable when used as a noun or adjective and on the second syllable when used as a verb.

NOUNS OR VERBS	ADJECTIVES OR VERBS
affix	absent
compress	frequent
contract	perfect
insult	present
rebel	subject
survey	
torment	

7. *Compound nouns and adjectives usually receive primary stress on the first part of the compound; compound verbs are usually stressed on the second part.*

NOUNS bláckbirds, lóoking-glass, móonshine, síxpence, éarthquake

VERBS outdó, overcóme, counteráct, underráte

● EXERCISE 4. The following words are often stressed on the wrong syllable. Check each in a dictionary and write it with an accent mark over the stressed syllable. Note that in some cases two pronunciations are permissible.

acumen	contrary	eczema
admirable	conversant	equitable
adult	curator	formidable
alias	debate	gondola
awry	decorous	grimace
combatant	desultory	herculean
condolence	dirigible	horizon

hospitable	infamous	prestige
impious	integral	recess
impotent	lamentable	respite
incognito	mischievous	robust
incomparable	municipal	secretive
indefatigable	orchestra	superfluous
inexorable	peremptory	theater

● EXERCISE 5. Here are some foreign words frequently used in English. Look up their pronunciation in a dictionary.

French apropos, blasé, bon voyage, cuisine, de luxe, elite, en masse, en route, hors d'oeuvre, lingerie, née, petite, première, rapport, sabotage, trousseau.

Italian adagio, concerto, fiasco, maestro, maraschino, cognoscenti, sotto voce.

Spanish guitar, mesa, rodeo.

Latin ad infinitum, ad nauseam, de facto, gratis, facsimile, status quo, data, via, vice versa.

● EXERCISE 6. Each of the following words can be used as a noun or verb. The accented syllable is shifted to denote the parts of speech. Read the list aloud, accenting the correct syllable in each case.

perfume (n.)	rebel (n.)	refuse (n.)
perfume (v.)	rebel (v.)	refuse (v.)
object (n.)	present (n.)	insult (n.)
object (v.)	present (v.)	insult (v.)
survey (n.)	torment (n.)	contract (n.)
survey (v.)	torment (v.)	contract (v.)

32d. Avoid the omission or addition of syllables and the switching of sounds.

A quite common error is the elimination of a syllable as, for example, *s'pose* for *suppose*, *champeen* for *champion*, and *jool* for *jewel*.

32c

An equally common error is the addition of a sound or syllable as *umberella* for *umbrella*, and *athalete* for *athlete*.

In certain cases, sounds may be switched or transposed; for example, *calvary* for *cavalry*, *irrevelant* for *irrelevant*, *prespiration* for *perspiration*, and *bronical* for *bronchial*.

● Exercise 7.   Careless speakers frequently omit a syllable or a sound in each of the following words. Practice saying this list aloud, taking care not to omit a syllable.

government	probably	cigarette
ideal	geography	finally
library	policeman	literature
company	poetry	particular
giant	geometry	ridiculous

● Exercise 8.   Practice each of the following words aloud, being careful not to add a sound or syllable.

elm	extraordinary	laundry
film	idea	burglar
helm	chimney	translate
athlete	lightning	grievous
athletics	hindrance	mischievous
ticklish	banana oil	law

● Exercise 9.   Practice each of the following words aloud, being careful not to transpose sounds.

perspiration	modern	western
southern	cavalry	irrelevant
hundred	larynx	prescription
prodigy	poinsettia	bronchial

32e. **Learn the rules for pronouncing *ng*.**

The *ng* sound causes much confusion. You can eliminate any difficulty by learning three simple rules.

1. *All words ending in –ng and all words derived from them are pronounced with the final sound in* sing.

EXAMPLES   bring, bringer, wing, winging

EXCEPTIONS   Use the sound in *finger* in the following words:

longer, longest, stronger, strongest, younger, youngest

2. *The combination* nge *at the end of a word is pronounced* nj.

EXAMPLES   hinge, flange

3. *In all other words,* ng *is pronounced as in* finger.

EXAMPLES   hunger, anger, finger

EXCEPTIONS   gingham, Bingham

● EXERCISE 10. Practice the following words and sentences aloud. In every case *ng* is pronounced as in *sing*.

tongue	among	harangue
ringlet	fangless	songbird
springier	thronging	prongless
slangy	clingy	twangy

The slangy singer sang a song.
The bringer of good news came from Long Island.
He was coming in, not going out.
The youngish singer put the hanger in the closet.
The throng gathered around the bell ringer.
The young and lovely child had a ringlet on her forehead.

● EXERCISE 11. Practice the following words and sentences aloud. In every case *ng* is pronounced as in *finger*.

anger	hunger	tangle
finger	jingle	dangle
single	jangle	Englishman
bangle	English	fungus
bungle	language	spangled
linger	younger	elongate
longer	stronger	angry

When I was single, my pockets did jingle,
I wish I was single again.
Linger longer.

The English language is difficult to learn.
The angler hurt his finger.
Because the Englishman was hungry, he did not linger.

ENUNCIATION

Enunciation is the process of forming, uniting, and separating speech sounds. It has to do with distinctness of utterance.

When you enunciate correctly, your words are clearly shaped and easily understood, yet not overly precise. Here are some typical enunciation errors:

gimme	gunna	wanna
whyncha	dunno	wit' (for *with*)
wonnerful	gen'lman	gover'ment

32f. Enunciate clearly.

Vigorous lip and tongue action is essential for clear enunciation. Indistinct articulation results from a sluggish tongue and lazy lips.

If your friends often have difficulty in understanding what you say or if telephone operators often ask you to repeat a number or message, your enunciation may be faulty.

The exercises that follow are useful in correcting the habit of mumbling. Practice them with exaggerated vigor, precision, and speed.

● EXERCISE 12.   Practice the following sound and word combinations before a mirror. Exaggerate your lip movements.

bah-bay-bee-baw-boh-boo	bool-ah, bool-ah
mah-may-mee-maw-moh-moo	raw beet, raw beet
mee-maw, mee-maw	meat ball, meat ball

● EXERCISE 13.   Place the tip of the tongue on the gum ridge behind the upper teeth. Lightly and agilely practice:

t-t-t   d-d-d   t-t-t   d-d-d
tah-tay-tee-taw-toh-too
dah-day-dee-daw-doh-doo
lah-lay-lee-law-loh-loo

● EXERCISE 14.   Old-fashioned tongue twisters are lots of fun—and good enunciation drills, too. Practice the following, at first slowly and then with increasing speed. Exaggerate your lip and tongue movements.

The big black bug bit the big black bear.
Fanny Finch fried five floundering fish for Francis' father.
Lemon liniment, lemon liniment.
Prunes and prisms, prunes and prisms.
Rude food makes man brood.
The seething sea ceaseth and thus sufficeth us.
She sells sea shells by the seashore.
The sixth sheik's sixth sheep's sick.
Truly rural, truly rural.
She stood at the door of Burgess' fish-sauce shop welcoming him in.

● EXERCISE 15.   Pronounce the following lists of words, giving special attention to the enunciation problem indicated for each list.

INITIAL SOUNDS

about	electric	exact
America	eleven	huge
because	eraser	remember

MEDIAL SOUNDS

accidentally	February	library
all right	finally	mystery
already	geography	poem
automobile	giant	poetry
champion	government	really
company	history	recognize
cruel	interesting	shouldn't
diamond	jewel	wonderful

FINAL SOUNDS

child	East side	meant
gold	West side	nest
hand	abrupt	past
kind	chest	post
second	last	left

DIFFICULT CONSONANT COMBINATIONS

cts: conflicts, facts, respects, restricts, tracts
dths: widths, breadths, hundredths
fts: lefts, shafts, shifts, tufts
lds: builds, fields, folds
pts: accepts, precepts, concepts
sks: asks, desks, disks, risks
sps: clasps, lisps, rasps, wasps
sts: adjusts, frosts, digests, insists, lists, mists, rests, tastes, tests

32g. Avoid substituting one sound for another.

The substitution of one sound for another is a frequent fault: *ciddy* for *city*, *dis* for *this*, *tree* for *three*.

● EXERCISE 16. Practice the following pairs of words, taking care to distinguish between them.

T–D		T–TH		D–TH	
beating	beading	boat	both	bayed	bathe
bitter	bidder	tree	three	breed	breathe
matter	madder	true	through	dare	there
metal	medal	taught	thought	day	they
latter	ladder	tinker	thinker	doze	those
writing	riding	tin	thin	read	wreathe

PART SEVEN

Mechanics

CHAPTER **33**

Capitalization

Standard Uses of Capital Letters

Capital letters serve many purposes. They indicate the beginnings of sentences, an important aid to the reader; they distinguish names, titles, etc., from the rest of the sentence (*The Black River divides Port Huron*); they show respect (*the worship of God*). On the other hand, many uses of capital letters are merely conventions; i.e., they are usages customarily observed by educated people for no other reason than that they are customary. Readers expect capital letters to be used according to rules established by custom; in other words, according to *standard usage*. A writer should follow the conventional usage expected of him just as he follows the conventions of correct spelling, grammatical usage, and punctuation.

In the use of capital letters, as in all matters pertaining to language usage, variations and inconsistencies are common. In standard usage, for instance, the names of the seasons are not capitalized, but some newspapers do capitalize them. Newspapers also may adopt what they call the "down style" of capitalization in which words like *street*, *high school*, *club* are not capitalized as they are in standard usage when used with a particular name.

STANDARD USAGE	"DOWN STYLE"
Twenty-first Street	Twenty-first street
Bellmore High School	Bellmore high school
Hunting and Fishing Club	Hunting and Fishing club

608

The usage described in this book is standard ("up style") usage, which is followed in books and magazines. Review the rules and do the exercises so that you will be able to check accurately the capitalization in your own writing.

33a. Capitalize the first word in any sentence.

If failure to use a capital letter at the beginning of a sentence is one of your faults, you should review Chapter 11, because the error is almost invariably due to failure to recognize the end of one sentence and the beginning of the next.

(1) Capitalize the first word of a formal statement following a colon.

EXAMPLE The following statement was released to the press: For reasons of national security, details of the defense program cannot be given to the general public at this time.

(2) Capitalize the first word of a resolution following the word *Resolved*.

EXAMPLE Resolved: That American aid to underdeveloped countries should be increased.

(3) Capitalize the first word of a direct quotation.

EXAMPLE Mr. Jackson said, "Your sister is her own worst enemy."

Do not capitalize the first word of a quoted sentence fragment.

EXAMPLE I agree with Mr. Jackson's remark that my sister is "her own worst enemy."

(4) Capitalize the first word of a statement or question inserted in a sentence without quotation marks.

EXAMPLE Our problem is, How can we get somebody to help us?

◆ NOTE Traditionally, poets capitalize the first word in a line of poetry. This use of capitals, while by no means as common today as it once was, is still usually observed.

33a

33b. Capitalize the pronoun *I* and the interjection *O*.

You will probably have little use for the interjection *O*, which is used only in such rare expressions as "O happy day, come soon!" The common interjection *oh* ("Oh, what a beautiful morning!") is capitalized only when it appears at the beginning of a sentence. *Oh* is usually followed by a mark of punctuation, but *O* is rarely followed by punctuation.

EXAMPLES   Help us, **O** mightiest of all!
He said he was sorry, **oh,** so sorry!

33c. Capitalize proper nouns and proper adjectives.

A proper noun is the name of a particular person, place, thing, or idea. The opposite of a proper noun is a common noun, which is not capitalized.

PROPER NOUNS	COMMON NOUNS
James McCall	man
Canada	country
Mohawk River	river

◆ NOTE   Words which name a kind or a type (*spaniel, sloop, sonnet*) are not capitalized. Names given to individuals within the type are proper nouns and are capitalized (Fido, *Wave-Rider*, "Sonnet XXI").

A proper adjective is an adjective formed from a proper noun.

PROPER NOUNS	PROPER ADJECTIVES
England	English
Europe	European

Study the following classifications of proper nouns.

(1) Capitalize the names of persons.

Before writing names beginning with *Mc* or *Mac* (meaning "son of"), find out whether or not the person spells his name with two capitals. Custom varies: McDonald, MacNutt, Macdonald, Macmillan, Macbeth, etc. Names beginning with *O'* (meaning "of the family of") usually contain two capitals: **O'Reilly, O'Neill.**

The abbreviations *Sr.* and *Jr.* following a name are capitalized: Henry Morgan, **Sr.**; Robert Lawton, **Jr.**

(2) Capitalize geographical names.

Cities, townships, counties, states, countries, continents   Garden City, Hempstead Township, Nassau County, New York, United States of America, North America

Islands, peninsulas, straits, beaches   Sea Island, Iberian Peninsula, Strait of Gibraltar, Silver Beach

Bodies of water   Arrowhead Lake, Lake Superior, Red River, Atlantic Ocean, Baltic Sea, Cedar Pond, Peconic Bay

Mountains   Rocky Mountains, Pikes Peak

Streets   Washington Avenue, Whitehall Boulevard, Dover Parkway, Pennsylvania Turnpike, Forty-second Street   [In a hyphenated street number, the second word begins with a small letter.]

Parks, forests, canyons, dams   Yosemite National Park, Belmont State Forest, Grand Canyon, Hoover Dam

Recognized sections of the country or world   the South, the Northwest, the Far East

◆ NOTE   Do not capitalize *east*, *west*, *north*, and *south* when they indicate directions. Do capitalize them when they refer to recognized sections of the country.

EXAMPLES   Turn east at the next corner, and you will see the church on the north side of the street.

To understand America, visit the Middle West.

We were going south, and the car that hit us was going east.

We are going South for the winter.

33 b-c

The modern tendency is to write nouns and adjectives derived from *East, West, North,* and *South* without capital letters (a *southerner, southern* hospitality, *northern* cities, *middle-western* customs, *western* clothes), but in the light of conflicting authorities, the capitalization of such words is also correct.

Adjectives specifying direction are not capitalized unless they are part of the name of a country: southern Ohio, eastern Russia, but West Germany, South Korea.

In spite of their origin, some nouns and adjectives derived from proper names are not capitalized: mackintosh, macadam, morocco leather, china dishes. Most words of this nature, however, may be written with or without capital letters: roman (Roman) numerals, plaster of paris (Paris), venetian (Venetian) blinds, turkish (Turkish) bath, gothic (Gothic) style, etc. When you are in doubt about the capitalization of words of this kind, refer to your dictionary.

● EXERCISE 1.   Number your paper 1–24. In each of the following items you are to choose the correct one of two forms. After the proper number on your paper, write the letter of the correct form (*a* or *b*). In two of the items, both forms are correct; write both *a* and *b*.

1. a. the Amazon river
   b. the Amazon River
2. a. He said, "Wait for me."
   b. He said, "wait for me."
3. a. strait of Magellan
   b. Strait of Magellan
4. a. Oxford boulevard
   b. Oxford Boulevard
5. a. I heard him say he was "tired of being good."
   b. I heard him say he was "Tired of being good."
6. a. Norwegian settlers
   b. Norwegian Settlers
7. a. Aegean sea
   b. Aegean Sea
8. a. an American Citizen
   b. an American citizen
9. a. Westchester County roads
   b. Westchester County Roads
10. a. north of the barn
    b. North of the barn
11. a. the Malay peninsula
    b. the Malay Peninsula
12. a. Twenty-Third Street
    b. Twenty-third Street

13. a. Grand Coulee Dam
    b. Grand Coulee dam
14. a. William Winter, Jr.
    b. William Winter, jr.
15. a. people of the Far East
    b. people of the far east
16. a. the Verrazano Bridge
    b. the Verrazano bridge
17. a. a French poodle
    b. a French Poodle
18. a. Clearwater Beach
    b. Clearwater beach
19. a. valley of the Ohio
    b. Valley of the Ohio

20. a. Grand Teton national Park
    b. Grand Teton National Park
21. a. Go south for three miles.
    b. Go South for three miles.
22. a. Jericho Turnpike
    b. Jericho turnpike
23. a Western Pennsylvania
    b. western Pennsylvania
24. a. Timothy O'neill
    b. Timothy O'Neill

● EXERCISE 2. Copy the following, using capital letters wherever they are required; or, prepare to write them from your teacher's dictation.

1. essex county
2. an african village
3. dallas, texas
4. latin america
5. two miles west
6. pioneering in the west
7. thirty-fourth street
8. great salt lake
9. glacier national park
10. the indian ocean
11. the catskill mountains
12. a city like san francisco
13. a popular british composer
14. an english bulldog
15. mackinac island
16. german composer
17. farragut boulevard
18. elmore county
19. the canadian wilderness
20. george o'connor, jr.

(3) Capitalize names of organizations, business firms, institutions, and government bodies.

Organizations Spanish Club, League of Women Voters, Veterans of Foreign Wars

Business firms American Airlines, Minnesota Mining and Manufacturing Company, General Motors Corporation, Americana Hotel, Plaza Theater

Institutions Princeton University, Arizona State College, Franklin High School, Ford Foundation, First Methodist Church, English Department

Government bodies   Congress, House of Representatives, Securities and Exchange Commission, Department of Defense

◆ NOTE   The names of government bodies are capitalized when they are exact names. Do not capitalize such general names as the following: *the state legislature, the latest department meeting.*

◆ NOTE   Do not capitalize such words as *hotel, theater, church, high school, college,* and *university* unless they are part of a proper name.

Onondaga Hotel	a hotel in Syracuse
University of Michigan	a university in Michigan
Emerson High School	a high school textbook
United States Post Office	the local post office

(4) Capitalize the names of historical events and periods, special events, and calendar items.

Historical events   Battle of the Coral Sea, Middle Ages, French Revolution, World War II

Special events   National Open Golf Championships, World Series, American Legion Convention, Junior Prom

Calendar items   Sunday, November, Christmas Eve, Labor Day, Book Week

◆ NOTE   Names of the seasons are not capitalized unless personified.

a late spring
Spring in her green dress

(5) Capitalize the names of nationalities, races, and religions.

EXAMPLES   Caucasian, Negro, Semitic, Roman Catholic, Baptist, Indian, Australian

(6) Capitalize the brand names of business products.

EXAMPLES   Coca-Cola, Chemstrand, Fritos

◆ NOTE   The common noun which often follows a brand name is not capitalized except in advertising displays.

Tip-Top bread, Royal typewriter, Rambler station wagon

(7) Capitalize the names of ships, planes, monuments, awards, and any other particular places, things, or events.

EXAMPLES   the *Constitution* (ship), Lincoln Memorial, Purple Heart

◆ NOTE   Do not capitalize the names of school subjects, except the languages and course names followed by a number.

EXAMPLES   English, French, German, Latin, Italian, math, art, chemistry, home economics, Chemistry II, History III, Art 102

◆ NOTE   Schoolrooms and other nouns followed by a numeral or letter are usually capitalized.

EXAMPLES   Room 31, Parlor B, School District 18, Chapter 4

◆ NOTE   Names of school classes may or may not be capitalized, but the modern tendency is to capitalize them; however, the words *senior, junior, sophomore, freshman* are not capitalized when used to refer to a student.

A freshman attended the meeting of the Senior Class.

● EXERCISE 3.   Number your paper 1–25. Copy after the proper number all items to which capitals must be added. Write *C* after the number of a correct item.

1. cambridge university
2. room 134
3. a neighborhood theater
4. parkview high school
5. He is a sophomore.
6. a negro orchestra
7. an underwood typewriter
8. summer vacation
9. the arcade theater
10. geometry
11. interstate commerce commission
12. biology II
13. the shafer hotel
14. memorial day
15. chemistry department
16. skippy peanut butter
17. five college freshmen
18. bureau of internal revenue
19. *sunset limited* (train)
20. members of the department
21. the american revolution
22. the battle of bunker hill
23. the kentucky derby
24. fairview country club
25. a swedish restaurant

● EXERCISE 4. This exercise covers all capitalization rules presented to this point. Write in order in a list the words which should be capitalized in each sentence. When the capitalized words belong in one phrase, write them as a phrase: *Sunrise Highway, Jefferson Memorial Library.* Indicate in which sentence each word or word group appears.

EXAMPLE 1. As a child in montclair, new jersey, I used to play in anderson park.

    1. *Montclair, New Jersey*
       Anderson Park

1. Mr. glenn, our science teacher, took his sophomore biology classes to willow creek to collect specimens for the high school laboratories.
2. This winter we have been studying in social studies III the pioneers who settled in the west during the years following the war between the states.
3. The university of wisconsin is situated on lake mendota in madison, the capital of the state.
4. Residents of five school districts in shannon county voted to build a new high school and junior college as recommended by the state department of education.
5. In washington, d.c., during the annual spring trip of the senior class, those seniors who are members of the art club visited the national gallery of art.
6. The massachusetts mutual building stands on the former site of the st. nicholas collegiate reformed church next to rockefeller center on the corner of fifth avenue and forty-eighth street.
7. Mr. frank mills, jr., is faculty adviser to the upper classes and is personally acquainted with every junior and senior in the high school.
8. One mile north of the village of turnerville, the lincoln highway crosses salt creek near the entrance to cameron state park.
9. The state theater and the park hotel on main street will be torn down to make room for the approach to the new marlborough bridge.

10. Harry mcdonald, who has a natural scottish accent, read some of robert burns's poems to our english class on monday afternoon.
11. Hamilton gardner, owner of the gardner baking company, makers of tasty crust bread and pastries, endowed the city's new hospital, which will be built in avon park and known as the gardner general hospital.

33d. Capitalize titles.

(1) Capitalize the title of a person when it comes before a name.

EXAMPLES   Superintendent Williams, Dean Marsh, General Bradley, President Drake

(2) Capitalize a title used alone or following a person's name only if it refers to a high government official or someone else to whom you wish to show special respect.

EXAMPLES   Dr. John Williams, superintendent of schools; Miss Marsh, dean of girls; John Drake, president of our class; *but* DeWitt Clinton, Governor of New York; Charles Evans Hughes, Chief Justice of the Supreme Court   [titles of high government officials]
the Senator, *but* the work of a senator; the General's orders, *but* the insignia of a general; the Chief Justice, the Secretary of Agriculture, the Prince of Wales

♦ NOTE   When used to refer to the head of a nation, the word *president* is usually capitalized. Two capitals are required in *vice-president* when it refers to the vice-president of a nation. The words *ex–* and *–elect* used with a title are not capitalized: *ex*-President, Governor-*elect*.

♦ NOTE   When a title is used in place of a person's name, it is usually capitalized.

Hello, Doctor.
I'll find out, Coach.

33d

(3) Capitalize a word showing family relationship when used with a person's name but *not* when preceded by a possessive (unless it is part of the name).

EXAMPLES   Uncle Tom, Cousin Jim, my cousin Jim, your mother, Bill's sister, *but* my Aunt Mary

◆ NOTE   Words of family relationship are usually, but not always, capitalized when used in place of a person's name.

Someone told Mother.

(4) Capitalize the first word and all important words in titles of books, periodicals, poems, stories, articles, documents, movies, paintings and other works of art, etc. [The important words are the first and last words and all other words except the articles (*a, an, the*) and conjunctions and prepositions of fewer than five letters.]

EXAMPLES   *A Tale of Two Cities, Saturday Review, New York Times,* "The Fall of the House of Usher," Treaty of Paris, *Winter in New England*   [painting]

◆ NOTE   The words *a, an, the,* written before a title, are capitalized only when they are part of the title. Before the names of magazines and newspapers, they are not capitalized.

The Last of the Mohicans, An Island Voyage   [*The* and *An* are part of the title.]

Have you read the *First Principles* of Herbert Spencer?   [*The* is not part of the title.]

the *Saturday Evening Post,* the *Los Angeles Times*

(5) Capitalize words referring to the Deity.

God, the Almighty, Lord

Pronouns referring to God (*he, him* and, rarely, *who, whom*) are often capitalized.

EXAMPLE   Joel said he was sure that God would make His wishes known to him.

The word *god*, when used to refer to pagan deities, is not capitalized.

EXAMPLE   Achilles' mother asked the gods to help her son.

● EXERCISE 5.   Number your paper 1–25. Copy after the proper number all items to which capitals must be added. Write *C* after the number of a correct item.

1. captain Blake
2. a congressman rose to speak
3. Mrs. Goldberg, the librarian
4. our class president
5. the club secretary
6. the vice-president of the United States
7. Father Casey, an Army chaplain
8. ex-president Hoover
9. the leader of the guerrillas
10. a captain in an army
11. The lord in his wisdom
12. aunt Louise
13. senator Feinberg
14. mayor Lane of Stamford
15. W. S. Thompson, one of the principals
16. *the case of the missing mail* [book title]
17. the *new republic* [magazine]
18. the monroe doctrine
19. Mr. Lane, a former mayor of Stamford
20. your uncle
21. the *Washington post* [newspaper]
22. responsibilities of a senator
23. god whom we worship for his goodness
24. Ben Hogan, former national champion
25. "mending wall" [poem]

● REVIEW EXERCISE   This exercise covers all capitalization rules in the chapter. Write in order in a list the words which should be capitalized in each sentence as you did in Exercise 4.

1. The rotary club of edgemont county has established an office in the Roosevelt hotel.
2. In their english classes this term the juniors have read *giants in the earth*, a novel about the norwegian immigrants who settled in the dakotas.
3. According to professor Schwartz, Tennyson's *idylls of the king* was published in 1859, the same year that saw the

publication of Darwin's *origin of species*, Fitzgerald's translation of the *rubáiyát of omar khayyám*, and Dickens' *a tale of two cities*.

4. The president went to Dulles international airport to bid farewell to the secretary of state who was taking off for europe on an important mission.

5. Since he is not a high school graduate, Russell is taking courses at Springfield vocational school to prepare for a position with the Bowman engineering company, manufacturers of everlast electric motors.

6. After spending several winters in the northwest, my father sought a warm climate and moved to the south, finally entering the real estate business in madeira beach, florida, on the east side of the gulf of mexico.

7. The early christian missionaries to north America succeeded in converting the indians from the worship of their pagan gods.

8. Dr. Eugene Walker, jr., principal of the high school, explained why all sophomores are required to take history II and biology.

9. The treaty of versailles, which followed world war I, specified that germany should lose its colonies, the african colonies being made french and english mandates under the league of nations.

10. The site proposed for the new high school is on the shore of clear lake about two miles north of here on highway 101.

11. My grandmother, who grew up in the south, cooks southern fried chicken much better than my mother does.

12. Mary Mckay, who is president of the riding club, owns a beautiful horse, which she keeps at the Johnson farm on River road to the west of town.

13. The vice-president of the United States is customarily selected by the president at the time of his nomination by his party.

14. Most of the boys in my cabin at camp this summer were from junior high schools in suburban communities outside New York and Boston and a few other large cities in the east.

15. Shea stadium, which was built near the site of the New York world's fair of 1964–1965, is the home of the mets, the national league team in New York.

Summary Style Sheet

Mexico City	a city in Mexico
Ocala National Forest	our national forests
Twenty-ninth Street	across the street
Houghton Lake	a shallow lake
the South	a mile south (north, east, west)
North America	northern Wisconsin
the Explorers' Club	a club for explorers
Ford Motor Company	an automobile company
Central High School	a new high school
Pomona College	four years in college
the American Revolution	a successful revolution
the Wrigley Building	a Chicago building
the Fourth of July	the fifth of July
the Senior Ball	a ball given by seniors
the Freshman Class	freshman classes
English, French, Latin	social studies, physics, art
History II	a course in world history
Winter's frosty breath	spring, summer, winter, fall
Principal Langley	Mr. Langley, the principal
the President (U.S.)	the president of our club
Senator Dodds	a senator's duties
God made His will known.	tribal gods of the Indians
Don't tell Mother (or mother).	Don't tell my mother.
Uncle Bill	my uncle
Ivory soap	
a Negro, a Presbyterian, a Swede	
The Last of the Mohicans	
the Reader's Digest	

CHAPTER 34

Punctuation

End Marks and Commas

Punctuation is used to make the meaning of a sentence clear to the reader. Some marks of punctuation are used to indicate in written English the pauses and stops which the voice makes in spoken English. They indicate not only where a pause should come but also the extent of the pause; the comma standing for a slight hesitation, the period for a longer one. Other vocal inflections are conveyed by the question mark and the exclamation point.

A complete statement of the correct uses of all punctuation marks is provided in this chapter and the one that follows, together with exercises to help you fix these uses in your mind. Punctuating exercises is at best an artificial activity, however, and you must be very careful to carry over into your writing the punctuation principles you have learned. Since punctuation is so closely related to meaning, you probably should punctuate as you write, for while you are writing you continually use punctuation to group certain ideas together and to separate other ideas from each other. On the other hand, many writers prefer to concentrate first on getting their ideas onto paper; then they go back over what they have written and insert whatever punctuation is necessary to make the writing clear to others and conventionally correct. This latter process, known as proofreading, is a very important part of writing. Never consider a piece of writing finished unless you have proofread it carefully.

Using too much punctuation is just as bad as using too little. Do not overpunctuate. Use a mark of punctuation for only two reasons: (1) because meaning demands it, or (2) because conventional usage requires it. Otherwise omit punctuation.

END MARKS

34a. A statement is followed by a period.

EXAMPLE   Summer vacation begins June 26.

34b. An abbreviation is followed by a period.[1]

EXAMPLES   Ave.   Dec.
A.D.   Dr.

34c. A question is followed by a question mark.

(1) Distinguish between a statement containing an indirect question and a sentence which asks a question directly.

EXAMPLES   She wants to know what the assignment is.   [statement containing an indirect question—followed by a period]

Do you know what the assignment is?   [a direct question—followed by a question mark]

(2) Polite requests in question form (frequently used in business letters) may be followed by a period; a question mark would, of course, be perfectly correct.

EXAMPLES   Will you please ship this order three weeks before Christmas.

Will you please ship this order three weeks before Christmas?

34
a-c

[1] For fuller discussion of abbreviations see page 667.

(3) A question mark should be placed inside quotation marks when the quotation is a question. Otherwise, it should be placed outside the quotation marks.

EXAMPLES   John asked, "Have you heard from Joe?"   [The quotation is a question.]

Did you say, "Meet me at eight o'clock"?   [The quotation is not a question. The whole sentence, however, is a question.]

34d. An exclamation is followed by an exclamation point.

EXAMPLES   What a beautiful dress!
How expensive!
For goodness' sake!
You're kidding!
How about that!

(1) Many exclamations begin either with "What a . . ." or "How . . . " as in the first two of the preceding examples. When you begin a sentence with these words, check your end mark carefully.

(2) An interjection at the beginning of a sentence is usually followed by a comma.

CUSTOMARY   Ah, there you have me!
RARE   Ah! There you have me!

(3) An exclamation point should be placed inside quotation marks when the quotation is an exclamation. Otherwise, it should be placed outside the quotation marks.

EXAMPLES   "What a game that was!" exclaimed the coach as he entered the lockerroom.

How foolish of him to say in the fifth inning, "The game is won"!

34e. An imperative sentence may be followed by either a period or an exclamation point, depending upon the force intended.

EXAMPLES Please reply by return mail.
Block that kick!

● EXERCISE 1. Many periods and all exclamation and question marks have been omitted from the following passage. Copy in a column on your paper all words which you think should be followed by end marks. After each word write the end mark required. If a new sentence should begin after the end mark, write the first word of the sentence, giving it a capital letter. Before each word write the number of the line in which it appears.

EXAMPLE 1 "What an exciting picture" exclaimed my com-
2 panion as we left the theater wasn't it too bad
3 I couldn't agree with him the picture had been ...

1. *picture!*
2. *theater. Wasn't*
3. *him? The*

1 Janet Smith, wife of Herman T Smith, M D, stopped
2 her car behind an enormous truck "Whew" she sighed.
3 "What a lot of traffic" Presently the cars at her right moved
4 forward, but not the truck ahead although in a hurry, she
5 accepted the fact that Sixth St at this hour was an over-
6 crowded thoroughfare, and she decided to be patient. The
7 taxi driver behind her, however, had a different idea he
8 honked his horn the sound startled Mrs Smith, but what
9 could she do anyone could see the truck was blocking her
10 way. "How stupid some drivers are" she thought. The
11 insistent honking continued, and Mrs Smith became an-
12 noyed when the truck moved on, she deliberately made a
13 slow start and felt rewarded when the horn behind her broke
14 into a deluge of noise.
15 When the light turned green at the next corner, she was
16 about to press the accelerator when another horn, of deeper
17 tone but just as unpleasant, broke out in the rear "All right

**34
d-e**

18 All right" she exclaimed. "Hold your horses" When, after
19 a number of similar incidents, she turned into her own drive,
20 she was thoroughly sick of horns and ill-mannered drivers.
21   That evening, as Mrs Smith settled down to her favorite
22 television program, her nerves were shattered again by a
23 too familiar sound. "Good heavens" she exclaimed. "Will
24 I never have any peace" Looking across the front lawn, she
25 saw Hal Jordan's jalopy at the curb Hal was calling for
26 Jimmy Smith. "Jimmy," she shouted, "come here at once"
27 Jimmy stopped short in the second of his usual two leaps
28 from stairway to door. "Jimmy, you tell that Hal Jordan
29 he is never to honk that horn in front of this house again
30 can't he walk up to the door and ask for you is he a cripple"
31 Her words were drowned by Hal's obliging repetition of
32 the two long and three short blasts Jimmy escaped, leaving
33 his mother still talking but inaudible.
34   "Cut it out" she heard him yell "Do you love the sound
35 of that horn"
36   When Dr Smith came in from a late call, his wife gave
37 him an account of her experience with hornblowers "I
38 will propose to the Governor tomorrow morning," he
39 said, "that auto horns be made inoperable when the car is
40 not in motion wouldn't that be a good law" Mrs Smith
41 stood in speechless admiration of her sensible husband.

THE COMMA

The comma—the most frequently used mark of punctuation—is used mainly to group words that belong together and to separate those that do not. Some other uses have little to do with meaning but are simply customary ways of punctuating sentences.

Items in a Series

34f. Use commas to separate items in a series.

EXAMPLES He was formerly on the staff of the embassies in
Moscow, Berlin, Vienna, and Madrid.

There were toys for the children, tools for Father, and books for Mother.

♦ NOTE Do not place a comma before the first item or after the last item in a series.

WRONG During the summer the workmen had installed, a new gymnasium floor, an improved heating system, and green chalkboards, in the high school building.

RIGHT During the summer the workmen had installed a new gymnasium floor, an improved heating system, and green chalkboards in the high school building.

It is permissible to omit the comma before the *and* joining the last two items in a series if the comma is not needed to make the meaning clear. There are some constructions in which the inclusion or omission of this comma affects the meaning of the sentence.

American folk songs may be classified in the following categories: marching songs, work songs, ballads, hymns, and spirituals. [five categories]

American folk songs may be classified in the following categories: marching songs, work songs, ballads, hymns and spirituals. [four categories]

♦ NOTE Words customarily used in pairs are set off as one item in a series: *bag and baggage, pen and ink, hat and coat, pork and beans, bread and butter,* etc.

For lunch she served a fruit cup, macaroni and cheese, salad, ice cream and cake, and coffee.

(1) If all items in a series are joined by *and* or *or*, do not use commas to separate them.

EXAMPLE The weatherman predicted rain or sleet or snow.

(2) Independent clauses in a series are usually separated by a semicolon. Short independent clauses, however, may be separated by commas.

EXAMPLE We walked, we played, we ate, and we gained weight.

34f

34g. Use a comma to separate two or more adjectives preceding a noun.

EXAMPLES She is a pretty, vivacious girl.

We patiently sat through a long, dull, amateurish performance.

(1) Do not use a comma before the final adjective in a series if the adjective is thought of as part of the noun.

WRONG It was a cold, raw, dark, November day.

RIGHT It was a cold, raw, dark November day. [*November day* is considered as one word, one item. The adjectives modify *November day*, not *day*.]

RIGHT She is a pretty, charming, talented young woman. [*Young woman* is thought of as one word.]

(2) If one of the words in a series modifies another word in the series, do not separate them by a comma.

EXAMPLE She wore a **bright blue** gown.

Comma Between Independent Clauses

34h. Use a comma before *and, but, or, nor, for, yet* when they join independent clauses, unless the clauses are very short.

EXAMPLES Saturday's Council meeting was unusually harmonious, for no one raised any objections.

The first two acts were slow moving, but the third act was full of action and suspense.

You go ahead and I'll follow. [independent clauses too short to require punctuation]

When the conjunction joins two verbs, not two main clauses, a comma is not used.

EXAMPLES I gave some good advice to Gerald and got some from him in return. [The conjunction joins the verbs *gave* and *got*.]

I gave some good advice to Gerald, and he gave me some in return. [The conjunction joins two independent clauses.]

◆ NOTE   You are allowed some freedom in the application of this rule. Many writers use the comma before these conjunctions—as they use the comma before *and* between the last two items in a series—only when necessary to keep the meaning clear.

NOT CLEAR   I grabbed the dog and the woodchuck limped away.

CLEAR   I grabbed the dog, and the woodchuck limped away.

NOT CLEAR   I didn't know whether or not to wait longer for the postman had brought no word from you.

CLEAR   I didn't know whether or not to wait longer, for the postman had brought no word from you.

As you can see from the preceding examples, a reader may easily be confused if the comma is omitted. This is especially true of the comma before the conjunction *for*, which should always be preceded by a comma when it means *because*.

● EXERCISE 2.   The following sentences cover rules 34f–h. Number your paper 1–15. Copy after the proper number the words in each sentence which should be followed by a comma, placing the comma after the word. Since the meaning of some sentences may be determined by the punctuation, you should be prepared to explain the punctuation you use.

1. I revealed your secret to no one but Alice probably did.
2. Mr. James asked the waiter for coffee beans and ham and eggs.
3. States included in the Japanese beetle area are New York New Jersey Maryland and Delaware.
4. Apply to the librarian for a library card and the world of books will be opened to you.
5. Everyone turned to watch the large pale yellow moon.

34 g·h

6. This policy covers medical expenses iron-lung rental hospitalization and transportation to a center of treatment.
7. The train pulled out and left me in a strange town without my luggage hat and coat or credentials.
8. The school administration is responsible for these disciplinary problems stem from rules made in the office.
9. This poet did not use capital letters and his punctuation was frequently unconventional.
10. The wagon train was approaching lonely wild Indian country.
11. The wind froze us the rain soaked us and the waves tossed us.
12. We are learning more and more about space through our new and stronger telescopes our huge radar installations and our instrument-packed rockets.
13. He found that it was a friendly unsophisticated little town that he had chosen for his home.
14. Soldiers were stationed at frequent intervals along the curb and the sidewalks behind them were jammed with onlookers.
15. She is pretty tall and blonde; her sister is small and dark and beautiful.

Nonessential Elements

34i. Use commas to set off nonessential clauses and nonessential participial phrases.

A nonessential (nonrestrictive) clause is a subordinate clause that is not essential to the meaning of the sentence but merely adds an idea to the sentence.

NONESSENTIAL   Joan Thomas, **who was offered scholarships to three colleges,** will go to Mt. Holyoke in September.

The basic meaning of this sentence is *Joan Thomas will go to Mt. Holyoke in September.* The subordinate clause does not affect this basic meaning; it merely adds an idea to the sentence. It is a nonessential clause because it does not limit in any way the word it modifies—*Joan Thomas.*

Clauses which modify proper nouns are nearly always non-essential.

The opposite of a nonessential clause is an essential (restrictive) clause.

ESSENTIAL   Joan Thomas is the only senior **who won scholarships to three colleges.**

Here the subordinate clause is essential to the sentence, for without it the sentence would mean something else: *Joan Thomas is the only senior.* The subordinate clause limits the meaning of *senior—senior who won scholarships to three colleges.*

Study the following examples of essential and non-essential clauses until you understand the terms. Note the punctuation: *essential—no punctuation; nonessential—set off by commas.*

ESSENTIAL   The city **which interests me most** is Hollywood.
NONESSENTIAL   Bismarck**, which is the capital of North Dakota,** is in the south central part of the state.

ESSENTIAL   The man **who spoke to me** is my science teacher.
NONESSENTIAL   Mr. Orban**, who is my science teacher,** spoke to me.

Sometimes a clause may be interpreted as either essential or nonessential. In such instances the writer must decide which interpretation he wishes the reader to give to the clause and punctuate it accordingly.

The boys took their problem to the librarian who is an authority on reference books.   [interpreted as essential]
The boys took their problem to the librarian, who is an authority on reference books.   [interpreted as nonessential]

We may assume from the first sentence, which contains an essential clause, that there is more than one librarian. The boys chose the one who is an authority on reference books.

From the second sentence we may assume that there is

34i

only one librarian and that he is an authority on reference books.

> My uncle who works at the Union Trust Company lives in New Jersey.   [one of several uncles]

> My uncle, who works at the Union Trust Company, lives in New Jersey.   [only one uncle, no others]

● EXERCISE 3.   Some of the sentences in this exercise contain essential clauses; others contain nonessential clauses. Number your paper 1–20. If the italicized clause is essential, write *E* after the proper number; if it is nonessential, write *Commas* to indicate that you would use commas in this sentence.

1. Friends *who do favors for you* may expect you to do favors for them.
2. The Welcoming Committee *who made us feel at home in a strange school* helped us through the first confusing days of the term.
3. Our new Buick *which Dad bought in Detroit* is a four-door model.
4. The Buick *which Mr. Burton drives* is like the one we saw on television.
5. She is wearing the sweater *that she received for Christmas.*
6. Her new sweater *which was a Christmas gift* is two sizes too large.
7. Men *who are timid* do not make good detectives.
8. Men *who are supposed to be the stronger sex* cannot stand pain as well as women.
9. American cities *that are outwardly very much alike* may show distinctive characteristics on more intimate acquaintance.
10. Cities *that have great financial problems* levy a sales tax.
11. The Sault Sainte Marie Canals *which connect Lakes Superior and Huron* would be a prime target in wartime.
12. I do not like girls *who apply make-up in public.*
13. These antiquated tariffs *which were necessary during the depression* are shutting off foreign markets from American manufacturers.
14. Many people *who settled America* came to escape tyranny.

15. The Hudson's Bay Company *which is one of the oldest trading firms in the world* was founded in 1670.
16. Sir Isaac Newton *who was an English mathematician* is generally considered the father of modern science.
17. The book *that I have read for this report* is a novel about World War II.
18. On my return I found that the people *that I had expected to see* had moved away.
19. Mr. French *who does his own gardening* says he exhausts himself trying to keep up with his power lawnmower.
20. All the tickets *that had been sold* were recalled.

A participial phrase is a group of related words containing a participle (see page 42). Present participles end in *–ing;* past participles of regular verbs end in *–ed* or *–d.*

Like a nonessential clause, a nonessential participial phrase is set off by commas because it is not necessary to the meaning of the sentence.

NONESSENTIAL   My little brother, **playing in the street,** was struck by a car.

ESSENTIAL   A child **playing in the street** may be struck by a car.

NONESSENTIAL   Mrs. Hampton, **frightened by the thunder,** locked herself in a closet.

ESSENTIAL   People **frightened by thunder** often try to hide.

NONESSENTIAL   The crowd broke up suddenly, **dispersing rapidly in all directions.**

ESSENTIAL   I watched the crowd **dispersing rapidly in all directions.**

● EXERCISE 4.   This exercise covers all comma rules given up to this point in the chapter. After the proper number write all words in the sentence which should be followed by a comma. Write the comma after each word. Be prepared to explain your answers.

1. Anyone who has so many talents should excel on the stage in the classroom and on the athletic field.

2. The butler was responsible for the silver and the maids were responsible for the linen.

3. A person who has received a liberal education is better able to make intelligent personal public and business decisions.

4. The Senator leaving the committee room stopped to talk with some reporters who had clustered eagerly around him.

5. We received favorable reactions from everyone but our parents were especially enthusiastic.

6. Astronomy which is a study of the heavens has always interested me more than geography which is a study of the earth.

7. People living in the north west and south parts of the city tend to look down on those living in the east which is highly industrialized.

8. The Stevens' yacht which Mr. Stein and his men had not quite completed lay at anchor looking sleek graceful and shipshape.

9. A tired-looking old man who had been helped on the plane at the last minute took the seat beside me and having settled himself promptly fell asleep.

10. A plan which will clear up traffic snarls has been submitted to the Traffic Control Board which will consider it at Monday's meeting.

Introductory Elements

34j. Use a comma after certain introductory elements.

(1) Use a comma after words such as *well, yes, no, why*, etc., when they begin a sentence.

EXAMPLES   Yes, you were elected.
Oh, I wouldn't be too sure about that.
Why, the entire argument is false!

(2) Use a comma after an introductory participial phrase.

EXAMPLE   **Behaving like a spoiled child,** he pouted and sulked.

◆ NOTE   Do not confuse a gerund ending in *–ing* and used as the subject of the sentence with an introductory participial phrase.

EXAMPLES   **Washing and polishing the car** is fun.   [gerunds used as subjects—not followed by a comma]

Washing and polishing the car, I developed sore muscles.   [introductory participial phrase—followed by a comma]

(3) Use a comma after a succession of introductory prepositional phrases.

EXAMPLE   **At the edge of the deep woods near Lakeville in Cumberland County,** he built a small log cabin.

◆ NOTE   A single introductory prepositional phrase need not be followed by a comma unless it is parenthetical (*by the way*, *on the contrary*, etc.) or the comma is necessary to prevent confusion.

EXAMPLES   By the way, I had a letter from Frances.
With the weak, competition is unpopular.
In the morning I am never wide awake.

(4) Use a comma after an introductory adverb clause.

EXAMPLE   **While Mario put the costume on,** his accompanist played "Deep Purple."

An adverbial clause at the end of a sentence is not usually set off:

His accompanist played "Deep Purple" **while Mario put the costume on.**

● EXERCISE 5.   This exercise covers all comma rules to this point in the chapter. Number your paper 1–10. Copy after the proper number the words in each sentence which should be followed by a comma, placing a comma after each word.

1. One look at the assignment is not enough for most students will need to study it carefully.
2. When we had finished playing the piano was rolled offstage to make room for the next act.

34j

3. On the afternoon of the first day of school the halls were still filled with lost confused or frightened freshmen.

4. Well if you need help please don't hesitate to ask me or Mrs. Seil or Mr. Faust.

5. In the second half of the third period Johnson evaded the defense caught a twenty-yard pass and raced into the end zone.

6. Speaking in assembly yesterday Pete Stover urged students to obey the new rules governing conduct in the cafeteria the school corridors and the parking lot.

7. Having studied the tax proposals of both political parties Governor Ross who was not satisfied rejected both and then presented a plan of his own.

8. Marchers in the long orderly picket line appeared to have the support of everyone in the crowd but the police carrying out their orders broke up the demonstration.

9. Legitimate theaters are prospering in many American cities but the New York stage is still the goal of young actors dancers and musicians.

10. When Bill was driving our truck lurched unexplainably and we wondered whether he was falling asleep at the wheel.

Interrupters

34k. Use commas to set off expressions that interrupt the sentence.

To set off an expression takes two commas unless the expression comes first or last in the sentence.

(1) Appositives and appositive phrases are usually set off by commas.

An appositive is a word—with or without modifiers—that follows a noun or pronoun and identifies or explains it. An appositive phrase consists of an appositive and its modifiers.

EXAMPLE   A syndicated column by Bernard Silverman, **the noted author,** will appear in the *Times-News*, **a local paper.**

When an appositive is so closely related to the word it modifies that it appears to be part of that word, no comma is necessary. An appositive of this kind is called a restrictive appositive. Usually it is one word.

EXAMPLES His cousin Arthur
The novel *Windswept*
Your friend Jean
William the Conqueror
The conjunction *and*

(2) Words used in direct address are set off by commas.

EXAMPLES I don't know, **Alice,** where your brother is.
Sam, please come here.
Your grades are disappointing, **my boy.**

(3) Parenthetical expressions are set off by commas.

The following expressions are commonly used parenthetically: *I believe (think, know, hope,* etc.), *I am sure, on the contrary, on the other hand, after all, by the way, incidentally, in fact, indeed, naturally, of course, in my opinion, for example, however, nevertheless, to tell the truth.*

EXAMPLES My father will, **I am sure,** let me have the car tonight.
The weight of the car, **of course,** determines the price of the license.
On the contrary, colonialism is dead.
Jenkins was doing things the hard way, **naturally.**

Knowledge of the above rule and of the expressions commonly used parenthetically is helpful in punctuating, but you should understand that the author's intention is the determining factor governing the punctuation. If he wishes the reader to pause, to regard an expression as parenthetical, he sets it off; if not, he leaves it unpunctuated. Sometimes, however, the placement of the expression in the sentence determines the punctuation. Study the following examples, noting the cases in which the comma is a matter of choice

34k

and the cases in which the placement of the expression governs the punctuation. All the examples given illustrate correct usage.

This is **indeed** a great piece of news.

This is**,** **indeed,** a great piece of news.

Indeed, this is a great piece of news.   [comma required by placement]

We **therefore** agreed to sign the petition.

We**,** **therefore,** agreed to sign the petition.

We agreed**,** **therefore,** to sign the petition.   [comma required by placement]

I hope this raise in salary will relieve your financial distress. [no comma because of placement]

This raise in salary will**,** **I hope,** relieve your financial distress. [comma required by placement]

● EXERCISE 6.   The following exercise covers all comma rules to this point in the chapter. Number your paper 1–20. Copy after the proper number the words in each sentence that should be followed by a comma, placing a comma after each word. Write *C* if the item is correct.

1. The final act a general free-for-all had the first-night audience a dignified crowd holding their sides.
2. Indeed if I knew the answer my friend I would not be asking you for it.
3. The authors of this book a volume of bitter criticism have in my opinion been most unfair.
4. This shark Betty was caught twenty miles offshore by your grandfather an experienced deep-sea fisherman.
5. Russian artists on the other hand must promote Communist doctrines for everyone in Russia works for the state.
6. Our aerial attack I knew would have to be a success or failure would be certain.
7. The story *Markheim* which was written by Stevenson is on the other hand a psychological study of the thoughts of a murderer.

8. Imprisoned without warning or explanation the two reporters were held if I remember correctly for two months in spite of efforts by England France and the United States to effect their release.

9. If you are prompt in getting your order in our office will guarantee delivery before Christmas which is only ten days off.

10. You should understand my good friend that much as I should like to do so I cannot give money to every organization that thinks it needs help.

11. Passengers riding in the front of the wrecked bus were the ones who were most severely injured.

12. This school composed largely of boys and girls from farm homes must offer courses in agriculture the occupation that most of the boys will enter.

13. Looking for a sports car at a bargain price Henry who is car-crazy spent the day hanging around the North Country Motor Company which buys sells and services all makes of foreign cars.

14. Bob and Jim left alone in the house immediately raided the refrigerator which was full of tasty items for the party that Jim's mother was giving the next day.

15. Napoleon's brothers Joseph and Lucian tried to prevent him from selling Louisiana but Richard Livingston and James Monroe the American representatives succeeded in making the purchase.

16. Well having tried all morning to reach me the boys delivered the message and I gave them a written reply which I hoped would be satisfactory.

17. In spite of their coach's warning Al and Steve who should have known better went to the dance the night before the game and didn't get home they admitted until two o'clock.

18. Taking an afternoon stroll in the park my little brother Bobby befriended a retriever a spaniel and a mutt that followed him home.

19. Before you start taking anything apart David I hope you will be sure that you can if necessary put it together again.

20. When Jimmie had finished the cake and pie were all gone and left untouched were the steak potatoes and salad.

Conventional Uses

34 l. Use a comma in certain conventional situations.

(1) Use a comma to separate items in dates and addresses.

EXAMPLES   Our sentimental idea was to hold a class reunion on June 18, 1969, at the old high school.

Address me at 222 Twin Oaks Road, Akron, Ohio, after the first of March.

Their son was born on Monday, May 1, 1949, in Baltimore, Maryland.

♦ NOTE   When only the month and day are given, no punctuation is necessary.

It was on May 10 that we began work.

When the items are joined by a preposition, do not use commas.

He lived at 331 Main Street in Passaic, New Jersey.

(2) Use a comma after the salutation of a friendly letter and after the closing of any letter.

EXAMPLES   Dear Joe,   Sincerely yours,

(3) Use a comma after a name followed by *Jr., Sr., Ph.D.*, etc.

EXAMPLES   Frank Lehman, Jr.   Martin Sellers, Ph.D.

Unnecessary Commas

34m. Do not use unnecessary commas.

Commas are not to be sprinkled about in a composition as though, like salt, to add flavor. The tendency of modern writers is to use commas sparingly. You should be able to show either that the commas you use help the reader to read what you have written or that they are required by custom—as in a date or address, for example. Using commas just for the fun of it is as bad as not using them when they are necessary. Your teacher will surely question your competence if you use them in places where they cannot be justified.

● REVIEW EXERCISE This exercise covers end marks and all comma uses. Copy the sentences, inserting punctuation and capitalization where necessary.

1. Trapped on a sand bar by the incoming tide the amateur clam diggers Pete and Don who could not swim had to be rescued.
2. In the first semester the following courses in homemaking will be offered: cooking sewing interior decoration baby care and feeding.
3. Our house at 2125 Northern Boulevard Flushing New York was sold and we moved to 433 West Thirty-fourth Street New York City.
4. John Carr Jr the only Eagle Scout in the troop organized the parade selected the flag-bearers hired the band and generally substituted for the scoutmaster.
5. In 1935 putting the *Herald Tribune* on microfilm was begun and we now have on microfilm copies of every issue of the *Tribune* from April 19 1841 up to last month.
6. When Chuck who was driving tried to show off his friend Lucille fearing an accident threatened never to ride with him again.
7. In violation of school rules Phil who owns a car skipped band rehearsal on Friday and went to see Jan his girl friend who had stayed home with a cold.
8. When the general called Stackpole a major in the RAF and an official of the Kenyan government were standing at the table watching an experiment.
9. Some of the men were eating others were cleaning their guns and the sheriff was conferring with the troopers who had just arrived to assist in the hunt.
10. Our company which has a representative in your area will gladly submit designs for a ranch-type split-level or colonial house.

34
l·m

11. Ruth had moved to Tampa Florida on November 19 1965 and in 1966 she moved again to Columbus Ohio.

12. Our research papers on which we had worked for weeks were destroyed in the fire at school, how disappointed we were to find that Mr. Walker had not yet read them.

13. When the school on the one hand had refused us the use of a bus and our parents on the other hand had refused us their cars what other solution was open to us.

14. In an address delivered on Friday March 5 in Miami Florida he said that the way to peace is through international economic cooperation political understanding and disarmament.

15. Although the crossbar had trembled as he passed over the judges declared he had not touched it and declared him the winner.

Summary of Uses of the Comma

34f. Use commas to separate items in a series.

34g. Use a comma to separate two or more adjectives preceding a noun.

34h. Use a comma before <u>and</u>, <u>but</u>, <u>or</u>, <u>nor</u>, <u>for</u>, <u>yet</u> when they join independent clauses, unless very short.

34i. Use commas to set off nonessential clauses and nonessential participial phrases.

34j. Use a comma after certain introductory elements.
   (1) After words such as <u>well</u>, <u>yes</u>, <u>no</u>, <u>why</u>, etc., when they begin a sentence
   (2) After an introductory participial phrase
   (3) After a succession of introductory prepositional phrases
   (4) After an introductory adverb clause

34k. Use commas to set off expressions that interrupt the sentence.
   (1) Appositives
   (2) Words in direct address
   (3) Parenthetical expressions

34l. Use a comma in certain conventional situations.
   (1) To separate items in dates and addresses
   (2) After the salutation of a friendly letter
   (3) After a name followed by <u>Jr.</u>, <u>Sr.</u>, <u>Ph.D.</u>, etc.

34m. Do not use unnecessary commas.

CHAPTER 35

Punctuation

Other Marks of Punctuation

Although the marks of punctuation treated in this chapter are used less frequently than the period and comma, they are often important. Just as you have learned to follow certain conventions in grammar and usage and spelling, you should observe the conventional uses of the punctuation marks described in this chapter.

THE SEMICOLON

35a. Use a semicolon between independent clauses not joined by *and, but, or, nor, for, yet*.

EXAMPLES   Representatives of seventy-five nations attended the spring meeting of the General Assembly; they remained in session from April 5 to May 18.

Take with you only indispensable things; leave behind all heavy and bulky items.

A writer must have some basis for deciding whether to use two independent clauses with a semicolon between them, or two sentences with a period (and capital letter). In most writing the division into sentences is preferable. A semicolon is used only when the ideas in the two clauses are so closely related that a period would make too distinct a break between them.

35a

35b. Use a semicolon between independent clauses joined by such words as *for example, for instance, that is, besides, accordingly, moreover, nevertheless, furthermore, otherwise, therefore, however, consequently, instead, hence.*

EXAMPLES   Holiday traffic has always been a menace to safety; **for instance,** on one Fourth of July weekend, four hundred persons were killed in traffic accidents.

Tension rose rapidly during yesterday's meeting; **nevertheless,** most of the Council members remained calm.

Matters involving Germany and Italy were discussed; **therefore** representatives from these countries were invited to attend the preliminary planning sessions.

When the connectives mentioned in this rule are placed at the beginning of a clause, the use of a comma after them is frequently a matter of taste. When they are clearly parenthetical (interrupters) they are followed by a comma. The words *for example, for instance,* and *that is* are always followed by a comma. The word *however* is almost always followed by a comma.

EXAMPLES   The foreign situation was deteriorating rapidly; **that is,** governments could find no basis for agreement.

The foreign situation was deteriorating rapidly; **however,** all governments remained optimistic.   [. . . all governments, *however,* remained optimistic.]

Most of the words listed in this rule, however, are rarely used at the beginning of a clause. They are usually placed later in the clause.

EXAMPLE   Matters involving Germany and Italy were discussed; representatives from these countries were **therefore** invited to attend.

35c. A semicolon (rather than a comma) may be needed to separate independent clauses if there are commas within the clauses.

EXAMPLE   The Canby, the new theater on Bank Street, announced programs of Westerns, gangster pictures, and re-releases of horror and blood-and-thunder movies; and the crowds, surprisingly enough, were enormous.

♦   NOTE   As suggested in Rule 35c by the words "may be needed," you are allowed considerable leeway in applying this rule. When there are only one or two commas in the independent clauses, the semicolon is not needed. It is required when there are so many commas, as in the example above, that the sentence would be confusing without the semicolon because the reader could not immediately see where the first clause ended.

35d. Use a semicolon between items in a series if the items contain commas.

EXAMPLE   The following are members of the new committee: Bob Bates, president of the Student Council; Allan Drew, president of the Senior Class; Helen Berger, vice-president of the Honor Society; and James Green, who, as a member of the Student Council, proposed that the committee be formed.

THE COLON

35e. Use a colon to mean "note what follows."

(1) Use a colon before a list of items, especially after expressions like *as follows* and *the following*.

EXAMPLES   The car trunk was large enough for everything: rackets, golf clubs, fishing supplies, suitcases, a picnic basket, and heavy clothing.

**35
b-e**

You will probably have to answer the following questions : How long have you been unemployed? Why did you leave your last position? What experience have you had? [list introduced by "the following"]

♦ NOTE   When a list comes immediately after a verb or a preposition, do not use a colon.

EXAMPLES   Foreign aid organizations **sent** food, clothing, medical supplies, toys, and books.   [list follows the verb *sent*]

He has always had an interest **in** snakes, lizards, mice, and other small animals.   [list follows the preposition *in*]

(2) Use a colon before a long, formal statement or quotation.

EXAMPLE   Dr. Stoddard made the following observation : The time is coming when a general college education will be as common as a high school education is today . . . [Note that a formal statement like this need not be enclosed in quotation marks.]

(3) Use a colon between independent clauses when the second clause explains or restates the idea in the first.

EXAMPLE   These seat covers are the most durable kind : they are reinforced with double stitching and covered with a heavy plastic coating.

35f. Use a colon in certain conventional situations.

(1) Use a colon between the hour and the minute when you write the time.

EXAMPLE   4 : 30 P.M.

6. Mr. Graham frequently gives assignments in current magazines for example, a typical assignment would run as follows
the Atlantic, 210 41–46 Senior Scholastic, 78 4 Commonweal,
74 17.

7. According to an editorial in the Times-News, the election
indicates a change in the public's attitude toward tariffs the
candidate who favored protective tariffs was defeated.

8. Mrs. Johnson had me revise my composition three times first,
to correct the spelling second, to revise some sentences third,
to remove all so's and and so's.

9. The smaller colleges are in a difficult position their income
has been cut, but their expenses have increased.

10. At the book store I bought the following gifts a copy of
Sandburg's Complete Poems for my father, a framed print
of duck hunters, entitled In the Blind, for my uncle and for
my sister, a new album called Folksong Favorites.

QUOTATION MARKS

35i. Use quotation marks to enclose a direct quotation—a person's exact words.

DIRECT QUOTATION   Mother said, "You may have the car until
noon."

Do not use quotation marks to enclose an indirect quotation—one that does not give a person's exact words.

INDIRECT QUOTATION   Mother said I could have the car until
noon.

Enclose means to place quotation marks at both the
beginning and the end of a quotation. Omission of quotation marks at the end of a quotation is a common error.

(1) A direct quotation begins with a capital letter.

EXAMPLE   I heard her say, "Complete the lesson at home."

EXCEPTION   If the quotation is only a fragment of a sentence,
do not begin it with a capital letter:

EXAMPLE   One critic called the book "an appalling waste of
paper."

**35
h-i**

(2) When a quoted sentence is divided into two parts by an interrupting expression such as *he said* or *Mother asked*, the second part begins with a small letter.

EXAMPLES "Go home," he pleaded, "before you cause more trouble."

"Have you," she asked, "been working this summer?"

If the second part of a broken quotation is a new sentence, it begins with a capital letter.

EXAMPLE "Drive carefully," he warned. "Speed is the cause of most accidents."

(3) A direct quotation is set off from the rest of the sentence by commas or by a question mark or exclamation point.

EXAMPLES She said, "We can reach them by telephone."
"What did you say about me?" she asked.

♦ NOTE If the quotation is only a phrase, do not set it off by commas.

EXAMPLE Apparently he does not believe in government "of the people, by the people, and for the people."

(4) Other marks of punctuation when used with quotation marks are placed according to the following rules:

1. *Commas and periods are always placed inside the closing quotation marks.*

EXAMPLE "I know," he said, "that we can finish the job today."

2. *Semicolons and colons are always placed outside the closing quotation marks.*

EXAMPLES "Jim," my grandfather said, "you should stop being a burden on your family"; then he suggested that I leave school and get a job.

The following are what Mr. Sims describes as "highbrow reading": Homer, Shakespeare, the Bible, and Milton.

3. *Question marks and exclamation points are placed inside the closing quotation marks if the quotation is a question or an exclamation, otherwise they are placed outside.*

EXAMPLES   "Are the players ready?" asked the referee.

"How trying you are sometimes!" she exclaimed.

Were you surprised when he said, "Hop in"?

How disappointing it was to hear him say, "Your train has left"!

No more than one comma or one end mark is used at the end of a quotation.

WRONG   "Who," asked Mrs. Regan, "said, 'Life is a flight of uncarpeted stairs.'?" [two end marks, period and question mark]

RIGHT   "Who," asked Mrs. Regan, "said, 'Life is a flight of uncarpeted stairs'?" [question mark only]

WRONG   Helen inquired, "Did you hear him ask, 'Who are you?'?"

RIGHT   Helen inquired, "Did you hear him ask, 'Who are you?'"

(5) When you write dialogue, begin a new paragraph every time the speaker changes.

EXAMPLE   "Hi, kids. Have you heard about Sandra and Bob?" Betty and I knew it was Sally Howe with some more gossip, and we also knew Sandra was on the other side of the row of lockers.

"Hi, Sally. How'd you like that French exam?" Betty was trying to change the subject fast.

"Oh, who cares about French?" she said. "Have you heard about Sandra and Bob?"

"Sally," I said in a feeble attempt to sidetrack her, "where did you get that cute pin? I've never seen one like it."

"Say, what goes on here?" Sally persisted. "I'm trying to tell you a story I heard about Sandra and that Bob Sharp and—oh, hello, Sandra. I didn't know you were here!"

"Serves you right, you little gossip!" Sandra approached menacingly. "Now what's that story?"

(6) When a quoted passage consists of more than one paragraph, place quotation marks at the beginning of each paragraph and at the end of the entire passage, not at the end of each paragraph.

♦ NOTE   Usually such a long quotation will be set off from the rest of the paper by indention and single spacing. In such a case, no quotation marks will be necessary.

(7) Use single quotation marks to enclose a quotation within a quotation.

EXAMPLE   I remember her exact words, "For tomorrow read Frost's poem 'Mending Wall.'"

35j. Use quotation marks to enclose titles of chapters, articles, short stories, poems, songs, and other parts of books and periodicals.

EXAMPLES   Read Chapter 37, "Victorian Poetry."

I enjoyed Hollis Alpert's story, "The Home of a Stranger," in the *New Yorker*.

♦ NOTE   Book titles and names of magazines are indicated by underlining (italics) (see page 647).

35k. Use quotation marks to enclose slang words, technical terms, and other expressions that are unusual in standard English.

Use this device sparingly.

EXAMPLES   I heard him characterized as a "loony" and a "screwball."

These units of speech are referred to by linguists as "phonemes."

Because his first name was Fiorello, Mayor La-Guardia was known as the "little flower."

● EXERCISE 2. Copy the following sentences, inserting quotation marks and other required punctuation.

1. Do you think Miss Shapiro asked that you can be ready at four
2. Let's go Jean was all I heard you say.
3. What she asked have you done with the children
4. This is a mighty long job groaned Alice we should have started earlier.
5. He asked how old I was, and I replied I'm old enough to know better.
6. Mr. Seegar said does everyone know the beginning of Alexander Pope's line which ends with the words where angels fear to tread.
7. I think that Shakespeare's phrase the primrose path appears in both Macbeth and Hamlet Mr. Stone replied.
8. Why John Morgan she exclaimed how dare you
9. Well they asked what about us are we what you mean by the lunatic fringe of the class
10. We'll be glad to help you Mrs. Riley I said the job won't take long if we all work at it.

THE APOSTROPHE

35 l. To form the possessive case of a singular noun, add an apostrophe and an s.

EXAMPLES Father's opinion
man's coat
Gus's hat

In words of more than one syllable which end in an s-sound, it is permissible to form the singular possessive by adding the apostrophe without the s. This is done to avoid too many s-sounds.

35
j-l

EXAMPLES   Mr. Furness' car
                 the princess' wedding
                 Odysseus' travels

◆ NOTE Since writers vary in the use of the apostrophe, it is not possible to make a hard and fast rule about the apostrophe in singular words ending in *s*. Thus *Burns' poetry* and *Burns's poetry* are equally acceptable. Punctuate according to your pronunciation. If you say "Burnses" or "Dickenses," you would write "Burns's" and "Dickens's." If you say "Burns" poems or "Dickens" novels, you would write "Burns'" and "Dickens'."

(1) To form the possessive case of a plural noun ending in *s*, add only the apostrophe.

EXAMPLES   boys' gymnasium
                 the Joneses' tennis court

◆ NOTE The few plural nouns that do not end in *s* form the possessive by adding an apostrophe and an *s* just as singular nouns do.

EXAMPLES   women's fashions
                 children's games

(2) Personal pronouns in the possessive case (*his, hers, its, ours, yours, theirs, whose*) do not require an apostrophe.

WRONG   I thought the scarf was her's.
RIGHT   I thought the scarf was **hers.**

WRONG   You have seen baseball at it's best.
RIGHT   You have seen baseball at **its** best.

WRONG   Do you know who's book this is?
RIGHT   Do you know **whose** book this is?

(3) Indefinite pronouns (*one, everyone, everybody*, etc.) in the possessive case require an apostrophe and *s*.[1]

EXAMPLES   **Everyone's** prediction was wrong.
                 He objected to **everybody's** getting a prize.

[1] Note the correct form of such words used with *else:* everyone *else's;* somebody *else's*. Note that there is no apostrophe in *oneself.*

● EXERCISE 3.   Number your paper 1–10. After the proper number, write both the singular and plural possessive of the italicized word.

EXAMPLE   1. *citizen* privilege
1. *citizen's, citizens'*

1. *city* water sup-
ply
2. *girl* dresses
3. *friend* opinions
4. *deer* horns
5. *laborer* wages
6. *man* neckties
7. *dog* collars
8. *fox* tricks
9. *student* books
10. *church* doc-
trines

● EXERCISE 4.   Number your paper 1–20. If the possessive case in each item in the list has been correctly formed, write a + after the proper number. If it has been incorrectly formed, write the correct form.

1. everyone's friend
2. bus' brakes
3. childrens' toys
4. this school's reputation
5. spectacles' rims
6. Is this your's?
7. Is it a girl's or a boy's school?
8. made it's way to port
9. tree's trunk
10. Victory is our's.
11. a street of worker's homes
12. in the Brown's yard
13. that nation's business
14. women's objections
15. broke it's back
16. travelers' passports
17. marines bravery
18. did its best
19. babie's bottles
20. the actors' parts

(4) In hyphenated words, names of organizations and business firms, and words showing joint posses-sion, only the last word is possessive in form.

EXAMPLES   **Mother-in-law's visit
commander-in-chief's order**

ORGANIZATIONS   **the Food and Agriculture Organization's work
Dun and Bradstreet's publications
Proctor and Gamble's products**

JOINT POSSESSION   **Dorothy and Ann's room
Jack and Tom's responsibility**

EXCEPTION   When the second word is a possessive pronoun, the first word is also possessive.

WRONG   Dorothy and my room
RIGHT   **Dorothy's and my** room

WRONG   his friend and his reasons
RIGHT   his **friend's and his** reasons

(5) When two or more persons possess something individually, each of their names is possessive in form.

EXAMPLE   **Jack's** and **Tom's** sweaters

(6) The words *minute, hour, day, week, month, year*, etc., when used as possessive adjectives, require an apostrophe. Words indicating amount in cents or dollars, when used as possessive adjectives, require apostrophes.

EXAMPLES   a minute's work, five minutes' work
a day's rest, three days' rest [1]
one cent's worth, five cents' worth

● EXERCISE 5.   In the following list the possessive relationship is expressed by means of a phrase. Change each so that the possessive case of the noun or pronoun will be used to express the same relationship. Write your answers.

EXAMPLE   1. a vacation of two weeks
1. *a two weeks' vacation*

1. gloves of David and Pat
2. locker room of the boys
3. home of my brother-in-law
4. personality of a person
5. boat of Charles and Bob
6. opinion of the editor-in-chief
7. worth of three dollars
8. store of Barton and McLean
9. novels of Kenneth Roberts
10. top of it
11. fears of the witnesses
12. a delay of a week
13. worth of ten cents
14. events of the day
15. wraps of the ladies
16. authority of the sergeant-at-arms
17. car of Bruce and Bill
18. a wait of ten minutes
19. rays of the moon
20. products of Johnson and Johnson

[1] Also correct: a three-day rest, etc.

35m. Use an apostrophe to show where letters have been omitted in a contraction.

A contraction is a word made up of two words combined into one by omitting one or more letters.

EXAMPLES For *do not* the contraction is **don't**. [the letter *o* omitted]

For *it is* the contraction is **it's**. [the letter *i* omitted]

For *they are* the contraction is **they're**. [the letter *a* omitted]

◆ NOTE The most common error in the use of the apostrophe in a contraction (except the failure to use it at all) comes from the confusion of *it's*, which means *it is*, with the possessive form *its* (*its* appearance), which has no apostrophe. Another common error, probably the result of carelessness, is the insertion of the apostrophe in the wrong place: *ca'nt* for *can't*, *does'nt* for *doesn't*, etc. Also note especially that *let's* in such an expression as "Let's go!" is a contraction of *let us* and requires an apostrophe for the omitted *u*.

35n. Use the apostrophe and *s* to form the plural of letters, numbers, and signs, and of words referred to as words.

EXAMPLES Mississippi is spelled with four *s*'s, four *i*'s, and two *p*'s.

Instead of a *3* and an *8* he had written two *3*'s.

How many +'s in this exercise?

Count the number of *and*'s in that paragraph.

● EXERCISE 6. Number your paper 1–25. Copy the following, inserting apostrophes where they are needed and changing the phrasal possessives to the possessive case. Some of the items are correct.

1. girls locker room
2. guns of a man-of-war
3. Its quite true, isnt it?
4. wind in its rigging
5. Lets find out whats up.
6. Ive found cryings no use.
7. firm of Stengel and Ford
8. mens shoes

35
m-n

9. Whats its meaning?
10. a days fun
11. football of Fred and Herb
12. Whos in Jeans car?
13. this chains links
14. Im sure its early.
15. Theyll play if he lets them.
16. Her parents opinions are the same as hers.
17. Arent there two *rs* in *embarrass?*
18. womens handbags
19. boys magazine
20. Her numbers two *3s* and two *0s.*
21. publications of Bennett and Osborne
22. One works by oneself.
23. office of the boss
24. notebooks of Grace and Marie
25. Lets see whos here.

THE HYPHEN

35o. Use a hyphen to divide a word at the end of a line.

Division of words at the end of a line in order to maintain an even margin should be avoided, but it is sometimes necessary. For rules that will help you in deciding where to place the hyphen see "Manuscript Form," pages 669–70.

35p. Use a hyphen with compound numbers from *twenty-one* to *ninety-nine* and with fractions used as adjectives.

EXAMPLES **thirty-three** students
a **two-thirds** majority, *but*
two thirds of the students

35q. Use a hyphen with the prefixes *ex-*, *self-*, *all-*, with the suffix *-elect*, and with all prefixes before a proper noun or proper adjective.

EXAMPLES   ex-president   un-American
           self-imposed   anti-Russian
           all-star   pro-British
           governor-elect   Pan-American

35r. Hyphenate a compound adjective when it precedes the word it modifies.

a second-story room   a room on the second story
an after-school meeting   a meeting after school
dark-colored glasses   glasses of a dark color
door-to-door selling   selling from door to door
well-planned program   The program was well planned.

◆ NOTE Do not use a hyphen if one of the modifiers is an adverb ending in *–ly*.

EXAMPLES   beautifully made table
           quietly prepared meal

35s. Use a hyphen to prevent confusion or awkwardness.

EXAMPLES   re-collect   [prevents confusion with *recollect*]
           re-form   [prevents confusion with *reform*]
           re-enlist   [avoids the awkwardness of *reenlist*]
           semi-invalid   [avoids the awkwardness of *semiinvalid*]

THE DASH

35t. Use a dash to indicate an abrupt break in thought.

EXAMPLES   He might — and according to plans, should — have reinforced the Second Division.

The title — if, indeed, the poem had a title — has escaped me.

35u. Use a dash to mean *namely, in other words, that is,* etc. before an explanation.

EXAMPLE   The referees had it in their power to prevent the fracas — they could have stopped the game at any time.   [dash means *that is*]

35
o-u

In this use the colon and the dash are frequently inter-changeable.

EXAMPLE   The referees had it in their power to prevent the fracas : they could have stopped the game at any time.

PARENTHESES

35v. **Use parentheses to enclose incidental ex-planatory matter which is added to a sentence but is not considered of major importance.**

EXAMPLES   Senator Saltonstall (Massachusetts) is chairman of the committee.

The results of the recent election affected the stock market (see Diagram A) only temporarily.

◆ NOTE   For setting off incidental matter, commas, dashes, and parentheses are frequently interchangeable. Commas and dashes are more common than parentheses.

(1) Be sure that any material within parentheses can be omitted without changing the basic meaning or structure of the sentence.

IMPROPER USE OF PARENTHESES

Harry had been working (in a book store) for many years. [The idea in parentheses is too important to the meaning of the sentence to be placed in parentheses.]

(2) Punctuation marks are used within parentheses when they belong with the parenthetical matter. Punctuation marks which belong with the main part of the sentence are placed after a closing parenthesis.

EXAMPLES   Mr. Baker asked him (What a tactless question !) whether he had been fired.

If the petition is signed by Alyson (Does she spell her name that way?), others will probably sign it.

BRACKETS

In ordinary composition you will have practically no use for brackets. Commas, dashes, and parentheses are preferable as means of setting off parenthetical matter.

35w. **Use brackets to enclose explanations within parentheses or in quoted material when the explanation is not part of the quotation.**

EXAMPLES   The following is a quotation from Mr. Gray's address of acceptance: "I am honored by it [the appointment], but I am also aware of the responsibilities which accompany it."

The court of appeals upheld the lower court's decision by a vote of 3–2. (See the explanation on page 217 [Chart B] of the system of *lower* and *higher* courts.)

● REVIEW EXERCISE.   Most of the necessary punctuation and capital letters have been omitted from the following passages. When a passage is assigned, copy it, making it as mechanically perfect as you can. The only changes you need to make in paragraphing are those required by dialogue. Some of the punctuation is incorrect, but in most instances you need only *add* punctuation and capitals. When you are in doubt as to a particular punctuation or capitalization problem, don't guess. Look up the rule.

1

In any discussion of the thrilling unbelievable deeds of Americas sports immortals the feats of Ty Cobb the georgia peach are sure to play a prominent part. In his twenty three years in the major leagues Cobb scored more runs made more hits and stole more bases than any other player in history. His lifetime batting average the highest ever made was .367 he finished three seasons with an average better than .400 won the american league batting championship twelve times a feat never equaled and stole ninety-six bases in one season 1915 more than entire teams now steal. To increase his speed Cobb used to wear heavy shoes in

35
V-W

training so that his playing shoes would feel light he was the first player to swing three bats while warming up pitchers who usually walk dangerous hitters didnt dare walk Cobb he was too dangerous on the bases, he played twenty-one years with the Detroit tigers taking time out in 1918 to join the chemical warfare division of the army. He was the first of baseballs heroes to be represented when in 1939 the baseball hall of fame was opened in Cooperstown New York.

2

At 9 30 A M on columbus day which is not a school holiday in indiana a fire broke out in the chemistry laboratory of emerson high school the big new fireproof brick building on the north side of oxford boulevard. The third period chemistry II class which is composed of seniors happened to be in the laboratory displaying a seniors presence of mind the students seized their chemistry notes their english texts and their french notebooks and shouting with glee hurled them into the flames. It was Jerry Montague I believe who at this exciting moment appeared in the doorway carrying one of the schools fire extinguishers. wow what a splendid conflagration he exclaimed whats cooking as he prepared to warm himself at the literary bonfire someone I am sure it was an accident knocked a bottle of sodium into a sink which was full of water. During the ensuing weeks the principals squad of detectives did its duty but didnt succeed in finding the pyromaniac who had caused all the excitement.

3

I was sitting in the front row of the bleachers Wednesday afternoon waiting for the start of the fifth inning of our game with plainfield high. These are Ann Wrights books Sue, she asked me to keep them while she went back to the high school for a minute but Ive got to go home. Will you watch them until she gets back This unexpected outburst from Jan Cunningham was accompanied by the arrival in my lap of a pile of literature science math and French textbooks a notebook and a pencil case I wondered why some girls carry so many books home. I dropped Anns library under the seat and turned back to the game. Someones voice bellowed in my ear knock the cover off it Pug,

Pug you know is our best hitter. I forgot everything but the game at 8 30 that night Jan telephoned she wanted to know what Id done with Anns books. Anns books I asked vaguely oh yes I guess I left them there. where did you leave them Jan sounded desperate. Under the bleachers, Ann didnt come for them I said. Yes she did Jan explained, she looked for me and when she couldnt find me she thought Id taken the books home now she hasnt her books and its pouring outside.

I was sorry when I saw the books the next morning they had been swollen by the rain to twice their normal size, Jan said Ann and she were angry but it wasnt my fault was it.

CHAPTER 36

Manuscript Form

Standard Practices in
Preparing and Revising Compositions

A neat, properly prepared manuscript is the mark of a careful writer. While it is possible that a sloppy, hard-to-read manuscript may show evidence of thorough research and good thinking, it is not very likely. A writer who has gone to the work of doing research and writing a good composition is usually willing to go to the extra pains of making his work presentable to his reader. By following the simple procedures described in this chapter you can make sure that your manuscript is clear and acceptable as far as form is concerned.

THE MANUSCRIPT

Paper and ink. Write compositions on standard size ($8 \times 10\frac{1}{2}''$) lined paper. Use black, blue, or blue-black ink. Write on only one side of the paper.

If you type, use standard size ($8\frac{1}{2} \times 11''$) white typewriting paper. Double space and use only one side of the paper.

Labeling and numbering pages. Follow the school policy concerning labeling and numbering of pages. The common practice is to write your name, the subject (English IV), and the date in that order, one below the other, in the upper right-hand corner of the first page. Number all pages, except the first, with Arabic numerals in the upper right-hand corner. It is a good plan to write your name beneath the page number on each sheet.

Margins. Leave a margin of at least one and a quarter inches at the left and one inch at the right side of the paper. The left-hand margin must be even; the right-hand margin may be slightly uneven. In typewritten manuscripts, place the first line of all pages after the first at least one inch below the top of the paper and leave a one-inch margin at the bottom of all pages.

The title. Place the title of the composition in the center of the first line of a ruled page, and skip a line between the title and the first paragraph. The title of a typewritten composition should be placed about two inches below the top of the page. Composition titles should not be underlined or placed in quotation marks, except in rare instances when the title is itself a quotation.

Indention. Indent the first line of every paragraph the same distance—about one inch in handwritten papers; five spaces in typewritten papers.

Long quoted passages may be made to stand out by indenting the entire passage. In typescript such indented passages are single-spaced and written without quotation marks.

Neatness. Do not mar the appearance of a composition by cross-outs, insertions between lines, and afterthought additions in the margins. If changes must be made in the final copy, make them neatly or rewrite the entire page. Strike-overs and messy erasures mar the neatness of typewritten work.

Never begin any line with a comma, dash, or other punctuation mark, with the exception of opening quotation marks.

REVISING THE FIRST DRAFT

All compositions should be written twice. The first draft of a composition is your own copy and need not conform to the manuscript standards noted above. Mark up this first draft with your revisions and corrections. When you are satisfied that you have made all necessary changes, write your final draft to be handed to your teacher.

Revision is an extremely important step in the composition process. You should look upon each theme, whether written for English or for any other class, as an attempt at perfection. Revision of a first draft should be done in three steps: (1) Evaluate the general organization of the whole composition. (2) Eliminate badly constructed sentences and poorly chosen words. (3) Check the mechanics.

Use the following checklist each time you revise the first draft of a composition.

Checklist for Revision

Evaluate:
> Quality of material (effectiveness, relevance, interest, etc.)
> General organization (sequence of ideas)
> Division into paragraphs (topic sentences)
> Transitions (within and between paragraphs)
> Variety of sentence structure

Eliminate:
> Errors in grammatical usage
> Sentence fragments and run-on sentences
> Awkward sentences
> Confusing sentences
> Wordy passages
> Clichés

Check:
> Spelling
> Punctuation (Don't forget the apostrophe!)
> Capital letters
> Hyphenated words at the ends of lines

Abbreviations

36a. In compositions do not use abbreviations except in certain special instances in which abbreviations are customary.

WRONG   One cold Mon. A.M. in Feb., as I was crossing a downtown st., a man rushed from a bldg. directly ahead of me and leaped into a car bearing a Cal. license.

RIGHT   One cold **Monday morning** in **February,** as I was crossing a downtown **street,** a man rushed from a **building** directly ahead of me and leaped into a car bearing a **California** license.

(1) The following abbreviations are customary before a name: *Mr., Messrs., Mrs., Dr., Rev., St.* **(Saint). The following are abbreviated after a name:** *Jr., Sr.,* **and the college degrees** *A.B., Ph.D.,* **etc. With the exception of the college degrees, these abbreviations are used only with a name.**

WRONG   We called a Dr. for the sr. member of the firm.
RIGHT   We called a doctor for John Parsons, Sr.

(2) The following abbreviations are acceptable in all writing: *A.D.* **(***A.D.* **485);** *B.C.* **(271** *B.C.***);** *A.M.* **(before noon);** *P.M.* **(after noon);** *etc.* **(and so forth);** *i.e.* **(that is);** *e.g.* **(for example). Generally understood abbreviations for government agencies are acceptable:** *FBI, TVA, SEC, NLRB.* **Periods are not used with abbreviations of this kind for government agencies.**

(3) Do not use the symbol & or ⅏ for *and.*

Numbers

36b. Do not begin a sentence with a numeral.

WRONG   8 students crowded into the car.
RIGHT   **Eight** students crowded into the car.

36
a-b

36c. Numbers of more than two words should be written in numerals.

EXAMPLES   1,450,280; $125.75; 1965

two dollars; forty cents; thirty-three

Expenditures on roads and highways rose to over a billion dollars.

Be consistent in your use of words and numerals.

WRONG   My brother makes forty dollars a week, but I make only $35.00.

RIGHT   My brother makes **forty** dollars a week, but I make only **thirty-five.**

◆ NOTE   Rule 36c applies to ordinary writing. In mathematical, scientific, and statistical writing, most numbers are written as numerals, not spelled out.

Never spell out the year or page numbers following the word *page.*

36d. Hyphenate all compound numbers from *twenty-one* to *ninety-nine* and fractions used as adjectives.

EXAMPLES   He spent **twenty-three** days in the hospital.

a **two-thirds** majority, but **two thirds** of the people

36e. Write out numbers like *second, twenty-fifth*, etc., instead of writing them as numerals with letter endings: *2nd, 25th*, etc.

EXAMPLE   I was standing **tenth** (not 10th) in the **third** (not 3rd) line.

The number of the day when given with the month is not used with the letter endings *st, nd, rd, th.* The name of a street, however, may be written with these endings.

EXAMPLES   On June **25** we sail for Europe, and on August **21** we return.

133 West **34th** Street (also 34 Street or Thirty-fourth Street)

Dividing Words at the End of a Line

Division of words at the end of a line in order to maintain an even margin should be avoided but is sometimes necessary. A hyphen is used between parts of words divided in this way. Words should be divided between syllables, but accurate division of words into syllables is a technical matter. When you are in doubt, consult the dictionary. A few simple rules may be helpful in deciding where to place the hyphen.

36f. Divide a word at the end of a line between pronounceable parts only. One-syllable words should never be divided.

WRONG   stay-ed   [one-syllable word]
RIGHT   **stayed**
WRONG   underst-and   [parts not pronounceable]
RIGHT   **under-stand**

36g. A word having double consonants should be divided between the consonants.

EXAMPLES   hap-py
            recom-mend

Words like *bill-ing* and *toss-ing* are exceptions. See rule 36j regarding prefixes and suffixes.

36h. Do not divide a word so that a single letter stands alone. If possible do not divide a word so that only two letters are carried over to the next line.

WRONG   e-normous, priva-cy
RIGHT   enor-mous, pri-vacy

36
c-h

36i. Do not divide proper names or separate title, initials, or first name from a last name.

WRONG .... we were delighted to have Mr. Russel as our guest................................

RIGHT .... we were delighted to have Mr. Russel as our guest...........................

36j. Words having prefixes and suffixes should usually be divided between the prefix and the root of the word or between the root of the word and the suffix.

EXAMPLES   pre-fer, actual-ly, jump-ing, call-ing

CORRECTING COMPOSITIONS

The marking symbols and other corrections your teacher writes on your composition will teach you little unless you do something about them. What you are to do about each marking symbol, or marked error, is explained in the list of symbols below.

All errors requiring rewriting of one or more sentences should be numbered (①,②, etc.) in the margin where the symbol occurs and then rewritten, marked with the same number, on a separate "correction sheet" or, if there is space, on the final page of your composition. As indicated below, errors which do not require rewriting a whole sentence are to be corrected on the composition at the place where the error appears.

Study the marked and corrected passages on pages 672–73.

CORRECTION SYMBOLS WITH INSTRUCTIONS

ms   *error in manuscript form or neatness*
Rewrite the sentence or paragraph neatly on correction sheet.

cap   *error in use of capital letter*
Cross out the incorrect letter and write the correct form above it.

p   *error in punctuation*
Insert punctuation, remove it, or change it as required.

sp   *error in spelling*
Cross out the word; write the correct spelling above it; write the word five times correctly spelled on your correction sheet.

frag   *sentence fragment*
Correct it by changing punctuation and capital or by rewriting on correction sheet.

rs   *run-on sentence*
Correct it by inserting the necessary end mark and capital.

ss   *error in sentence structure*
Rewrite the sentence on your correction sheet.

k   *awkward sentence or passage*
Rewrite the sentence or passage on your correction sheet.

nc   *not clear*
Rewrite the sentence or sentences on your correction sheet.

ref   *unclear reference of pronoun*
Cross out the error and write the correction above it.

gr   *error in grammar*
Cross out the error and write the correct form above it.

w   *error in word choice*
Cross out the word and write a better one above it.

¶   *Begin a new paragraph here.*
This will not be corrected but should be carefully noted.

t   *error in tense*
Cross out the error and write the correct form above it.

∧   *You have omitted something.*
Insert omitted words above the line.

COMPOSITION PASSAGE MARKED BY THE TEACHER

p
gr
sp

cap

W ref

p

r–s

frag

K

nc

        A repertory company, with it's com-
mand of a number of plays, are quite
different from a cast which preforms
only one play for a run and then breaks
up. The usual company on broadway consists of actors brought together to produce one (thing.) If (it) is a success, the
actors repeat the same roles night after
night. A repertory company on the other
hand produces a number of plays, it may
produce three or four different plays
in the course of one week. Each actor
thus playing a different role each night.
At any time a repertory company is able
to revive an old play with as many as
twenty-five plays in its repertoire.
The parts are all ready and the scenery,
properties, and costumes.

PASSAGE CORRECTED BY THE STUDENT

p
gr
sp

cap

        A repertory company, with it's com-
mand of a number of plays, ~~are~~ *is* quite
different from a cast which ~~preforms~~ *performs*
only one play for a run and then breaks
up. The usual company on *B*roadway con-

sists of actors brought together to pro-
duce one ~~thing.~~ *play* If ~~it~~ *the play* is a success, the
actors repeat the same roles night after
night. A repertory company, on the other
hand, produces a number of plays. It may
produce three or four different plays
in the course of one week, ~~E~~each actor
thus playing a different role each night.
At any time a repertory company is able
to revive an old play with as many as
twenty-five plays in its repertoire.
The parts are all ready and the scenery,
properties, and costumes.

CORRECTION SHEET ATTACHED TO COMPOSITION

perform, perform, perform, perform, perform
① *A repertory company, with as many as twenty-five plays in its repertoire, is able to revive an old play at any time.*
② *The actors are familiar with their parts, and the scenery, properties, and costumes are ready in the company's storeroom.*

CHAPTER 37

Spelling

Improving Your Spelling

This chapter suggests a number of things you can do to improve your spelling:

1. Be careful.
2. Use the dictionary.
3. Keep a list of your own spelling errors.
4. Learn to spell words by syllables.
5. Learn a few helpful spelling rules.
6. Learn to distinguish between homonyms.
7. Learn lists of commonly misspelled words.

GOOD SPELLING HABITS

1. *Be careful.* Care in writing and in proofreading your compositions will eliminate errors in the spelling of simple words like *to, there, its,* which account for so many of the teacher's corrections on students' themes.

2. *Use the dictionary.* Some students apparently think themselves allergic to the dictionary. They would rather take a chance on guessing than expose themselves to the truth. But the only sure way to find out how to spell a word is to look it up.

3. *Keep a list of your own spelling errors.* We do not all misspell the same words. Although it is a difficult habit to

establish, the habit of recording in your notebook the words you misspell in your compositions will pay you a large return on the investment of a little time and patience.

4. *Learn to spell words by syllables.* This is the "divide and conquer" technique used with success by invading armies. It is equally effective in attacking a long and troublesome word. Dividing a long word into syllables gives a number of short parts. Short parts are simpler to spell than long ones; hence you can simplify your spelling problem by acquiring the habit of dividing words into syllables and spelling them part by part.

Two common causes of spelling mistakes are the omission of a letter or syllable and the addition of an extra letter or syllable. A student who spells *probably* as though it were *probaly* has made the first kind of mistake. If he spells *lightning* as though it were *lightening*, he has made the second kind. Errors like these are errors in pronunciation which, in turn, are the result of not knowing the exact syllables in the word.

Dividing a word into its pronounceable parts (syllables) will help you to pronounce and to spell the word correctly.

● Exercise 1. Write each of the following words in syllables—place a hyphen between syllables. When you have completed the exercise and studied the words, take a test on them from dictation. Whether your divisions correspond exactly with the dictionary syllabication is not important, provided the words are divided into pronounceable parts and all letters are included and no letters are added.

1. modern	7. boundary
2. similar	8. candidate
3. library	9. representative
4. surprise	10. entrance
5. privilege	11. lightning
6. perspiration	12. accidentally

● EXERCISE 2.   Follow directions for the preceding exercise.

1. athletics
2. disastrous
3. government
4. undoubtedly
5. equipment
6. temperament

7. recognize
8. business
9. sophomore
10. quiet
11. mischievous
12. curiosity

SPELLING RULES

5. *Learn a few helpful spelling rules.* Although some spelling rules are hopelessly complicated, a few are simple enough and important enough to justify the effort required to master them. Study the following rules and apply them whenever possible in your writing.

ie and ei

37a. Write *ie* when the sound is $\bar{e}$, except after *c*.

EXAMPLES   believe, thief, fierce,   ceiling, receive, deceive
EXCEPTIONS   seize, either, weird, leisure, neither

Write *ei* when the sound is not $\bar{e}$, especially when the sound is $\bar{a}$.

EXAMPLES   freight, neighbor, weigh; height
EXCEPTIONS   friend, mischief

● EXERCISE 3.   Write the following words, supplying the missing letters (*e* and *i*) in the correct order. Be able to explain how the rule applies to each.

1. for...gn
2. br...f
3. rel...ve
4. conc...ve
5. v...l
6. n...ce
7. c...ling
8. gr...f

9. p...ce
10. rec...ve
11. retr...ve
12. sl...gh
13. ach...ve
14. handkerch...f
15. perc...ve
16. th...f

17. s...ge
18. s...ze
19. bel...ve
20. w...rd
21. rec...pt
22. bel...f
23. f...nd
24. l...sure

–cede, –ceed, and –sede

37b. Only one English word ends in *–sede*— *supersede;* only three words end in *–ceed*— *exceed, proceed, succeed;* all other words of similar sound end in *–cede.*

EXAMPLES   precede, recede, secede, accede, concede

Adding Prefixes

A *prefix* is one or more letters or syllables added to the beginning of a word to change its meaning.

37c. When a prefix is added to a word, the spelling of the word itself remains the same.

il + legal = **il**legal
in + elegant = **in**elegant
im + movable = **im**movable
un + necessary = **un**necessary
un + excused = **un**excused
dis + satisfied = **dis**satisfied

mis + understood = **mis**understood
mis + spell = **mis**spell
re + commend = **re**commend
over + run = **over**run
over + eat = **over**eat

Adding Suffixes

A *suffix* is one or more letters or syllables added to the end of a word to change its meaning.

37d. When the suffixes *–ness* and *–ly* are added to a word, the spelling of the word itself is not changed.

EXAMPLES   mean + ness = mean**ness**
final + ly = final**ly**

EXCEPTIONS   Words ending in *y* usually change the *y* to *i* before *–ness* and *–ly:* ready—readily; heavy—heaviness; happy—happiness. One-syllable adjectives ending in *y*, however, generally follow Rule 37d: dry—dryness; shy—shyly.

37
a-d

● EXERCISE 4.   Spell correctly the words indicated.

1. *rate* with the prefix *over*
2. *habitual* with the suffix *ly*
3. *agree* with the prefix *dis*
4. *green* with the suffix *ness*
5. *material* with the prefix *im*
6. *appoint* with the prefix *dis*
7. *apprehend* with the prefix *mis*
8. *practical* with the suffix *ly*
9. *abated* with the prefix *un*
10. *casual* with the suffix *ly*
11. *natural* with the prefix *un*
12. *stubborn* with the suffix *ness*
13. *legal* with the prefix *il*
14. *appropriate* with the prefix *in*
15. *appear* with the prefix *dis*
16. *movable* with the prefix *im*
17. *construct* with the prefix *re*
18. *animate* with the prefix *in*
19. *similar* with the prefix *dis*
20. *keen* with the suffix *ness*
21. *spell* with the prefix *mis*
22. *use* with the prefix *mis*
23. *avoidable* with the prefix *un*
24. *merry* with the suffix *ly*

37e. Drop the final *e* before a suffix beginning with a vowel.

EXAMPLES   care + ing = car**ing**   use + able = us**able**

EXCEPTIONS   Keep the final *e* before *a* or *o* if necessary to retain the soft sound of *c* or *g* preceding the *e*: noti**ce**able, coura**ge**ous

37f. Keep the final *e* before a suffix beginning with a consonant.

EXAMPLES   care + ful = care**ful**   care + less = care**less**

EXCEPTIONS   true + ly = truly   argue + ment = argu**ment**
acknowledge + ment = acknowled**gment** [more usual spelling]

37g. With words ending in *y* preceded by a consonant, change the *y* to *i* before any suffix not beginning with *i*.

EXAMPLES   funny—funnier; hurry—hurried; hurry—hurrying

37h. **Double the final consonant before a suffix that begins with a vowel if both of the following conditions exist: (1) the word has only one syllable or is accented on the last syllable; (2) the word ends in a single consonant preceded by a single vowel.**

EXAMPLES   plan + ing = planning [one-syllable word]

forget + ing = forgetting [accent on last syllable; single consonant and single vowel]

cancel + ed = canceled [accent not on last syllable]

prefer + able = pref'erable [accent shifts; not on last syllable]

● EXERCISE 5. Write correctly the words formed as follows:

1. defer + ed
2. defer + ence
3. hope + ing
4. approve + al
5. benefit + ed
6. nine + ty
7. prepare + ing
8. profit + ing
9. write + ing
10. propel + ing
11. desire + able
12. control + ed
13. hope + less
14. move + ing
15. true + ly
16. run + ing
17. singe + ing
18. fame + ous
19. name + less
20. red + est

The Plural of Nouns

37i. **Observe the rules for spelling the plural of nouns.**

(1) The regular way to form the plural of a noun is to add s.

EXAMPLES chair, chairs   book, books

37
e-i

(2) The plural of some nouns is formed by adding *es*.

The *e* represents the extra sound heard when −*s* is added to words ending in *s*, *sh*, *ch*, and *x*.

EXAMPLES   dress, dresses   bush, bushes
               birch, birches   box, boxes

(3) The plural of nouns ending in *y preceded by a consonant* is formed by changing the *y* to *i* and adding *es*.

EXAMPLES   fly, flies   lady, ladies
               enemy, enemies   salary, salaries

(4) The plural of nouns ending in *y preceded by a vowel* is formed by adding an *s*.

EXAMPLES   monkey, monkeys   donkey, donkeys

(5) The plural of most nouns ending in *f* or *fe* is formed by adding *s*. The plural of some nouns ending in *f* or *fe* is formed by changing the *f* to *v* and adding *s* or *es*.

EXAMPLES   Add *s*: roof, roofs   dwarf, dwarfs
                     chief, chiefs

               Change *f* to *v* and add *s* or *es*:

                    knife, knives   calf, calves
                    loaf, loaves   wharf, wharves
                    leaf, leaves

(6) The plural of nouns ending in *o preceded by a vowel* is formed by adding *s*. The plural of nouns ending in *o preceded by a consonant* is formed by adding either *s* or *es*.

EXAMPLES   *o* following a vowel:

                    rodeo, rodeos   radio, radios

               o following a consonant:

                    hero, heroes   potato, potatoes
                    mosquito, mosquitoes

EXCEPTIONS Words ending in *o* that refer to music form the plural by adding *s*: piano, pianos; soprano, sopranos; solo, solos.

(7) The plural of a few nouns is formed by irregular methods.

EXAMPLES   child, children   ox, oxen
                  mouse, mice   woman, women
                  tooth, teeth   goose, geese

(8) The plural of compound nouns written as one word is formed by adding *s* or *es*.

EXAMPLES   cupful, cupfuls
                  leftover, leftovers
                  strongbox, strongboxes

(9) The plural of compound nouns consisting of a noun plus a modifier is formed by making the noun plural.

In the following examples, the phrases *in-law* and *of-war* and the adjectives *martial, general,* and *by* are all modifiers. It is the nouns modified by them that are made plural.

EXAMPLES   mother-in-law, mothers-in-law
                  man-of-war, men-of-war
                  court martial, courts martial
                  secretary-general, secretaries-general
                  passer-by, passers-by

(10) The plural of a few compound nouns is formed in irregular ways.

EXAMPLES   drive-in, drive-ins
                  standby, standbys
                  six-year-old, six-year-olds

(11) Some nouns are the same in the singular and the plural.

EXAMPLES   sheep, deer, trout, species, Chinese

(12) The plural of some foreign words is formed as in the original language.

EXAMPLES   alumnus (*man*), alumni (*men*)
            alumna (*woman*), alumnae (*women*)
            datum, data
            crisis, crises

(13) The plural of other foreign words may be formed either as in the foreign language or by adding *s* or *es*.

EXAMPLES   index, indices *or* indexes
            appendix, appendices *or* appendixes

◆ NOTE   In certain words the English plural is the preferred one, for example, *formulas* not *formulae*. Whenever there is any doubt about which plural to use, consult the dictionary.

(14) The plural of numbers, letters, signs, and words considered as words is formed by adding an apostrophe and *s*.

EXAMPLES   If you think there are ten 5's in that column, you'd better count again.

            There are two *s*'s in *necessary*.

            My last paper was full of 0's, not +'s.

            Don't use too many *I*'s in writing your paper.

● EXERCISE 6.   Write the plural form of each of the following nouns. Be able to explain your spelling on the basis of the rules.

1. candy	11. fly
2. sheep	12. alto
3. piano	13. brother-in-law
4. valley	14. shelf
5. alumnus	15. bench
6. cameo	16. editor-in-chief
7. torch	17. spoonful
8. chief	18. hero
9. tomato	19. knife
10. gas	20. goose

● EXERCISE 7. By referring to the rules on the preceding pages, explain the spelling of each of the following:

1. regretted
2. receive
3. illegible
4. coming (*e* dropped)
5. conferring
6. niece
7. contraltos
8. misstate
9. drunkenness
10. peaceable
11. ladies
12. conference
13. alumnae
14. leisure
15. occurred
16. writing (*e* dropped)
17. roofs
18. weigh
19. disappear
20. naturally

Words that Sound Alike

6. *Learn to distinguish between words that sound alike.* These words present problems because they sound alike but have different meanings and different spellings. You have probably had trouble distinguishing between *principle* and *principal*, *capital* and *capitol*, and other such pairs. Most of the paired words in the following lists sound alike. Some pairs, however, are confused even though they are not pronounced exactly alike.

already	*previously* I had *already* seen the movie twice.
all ready	*all are ready* (or *wholly ready*) Give the signal when you are *all ready*.
all right	[This word really does not belong in this list, but it is included here because many persons think there is a word spelled *alright*, as though *all right* did have a homonym. There is no word *alright*. The correct spelling is always *all right*.]
altar	*a table or stand in a church* or *a place for outdoor offerings* The priest was standing beside the *altar*.
alter	*to change* If we are late, we will *alter* our plans.

altogether	*entirely*
	He doesn't *altogether* approve of me.
all together	*everyone in the same place*
	We were *all together* at Christmas.

born	*given birth*
	When were you *born?*
borne	*carried*
	He has *borne* his hardships bravely.

brake	*device to stop a machine*
	A defective *brake* caused the accident.
break	*to fracture, shatter*
	Try not to *break* any dishes.

capital	*city;* also as an adjective, *punishable by death* or *of major importance*
	Washington is the *capital* of this country.
	Murder is a *capital* offense.
	That is a *capital* idea.
capitol	*building*
	The *capitol* faces a park.

cloths	*pieces of cloth*
	Try the new cleaning *cloths.*
clothes	*wearing apparel*
	Her *clothes* are expensive.

● EXERCISE 8. Number your paper 1–20. Write after the proper number the correct one of the words given in parentheses in the sentences below.

1. The damage has (already, all ready) been done.
2. Father was (all together, altogether) too surprised to protest.
3. Events have (born, borne) out my predictions.
4. Pete is an (altar, alter) boy at St. Anne's Church.

5. If you (brake, break) a window, you will pay for it.
6. When you are (already, all ready) I will help you.
7. Belgrade is the (capital, capitol) of Yugoslavia.
8. If you will (altar, alter) the neckline, I will buy the dress.
9. My mother was (born, borne) in France.
10. Was his work (alright, all right)?
11. We use old sheets for cleaning (cloths, clothes).
12. We will (altar, alter) the building to suit tenants.
13. The dome on the (capital, capitol) is illuminated at night.
14. The club members have been (all together, altogether) only once.
15. Cars are (born, borne) across the river on a ferry.
16. Everyone was wearing his best (cloths, clothes).
17. How many states in this country have abandoned (capital, capitol) punishment?
18. I applied the (brakes, breaks) immediately.
19. Are you feeling (all right, alright)?
20. The family were (all together, altogether) on my birthday.

---

coarse	*rough, crude*
	He wore a suit of *coarse* cloth and used *coarse* language.
course	*path of action; part of a meal; a series of studies*
	He followed a straight *course*.
	The golf *course* and the race *course* are outside of town.
	Soup was the first *course*.
	I am taking a *course* in cooking.

---

complement	*something that completes* or *makes perfect*
	The *complement* of 50° is 40°. [*completes* a 90° angle]
	His part of the job *complements* mine. [Together they *complete* the job.]
compliment	*a remark that says something good about a person; to say something good*
	I am pleased by your *compliment*.
	She *complimented* me on my cooking.

consul	*representative of a foreign country* The American *consul* in Quito helped us during our visit.
council, councilor	*a group called together to accomplish a job;* a member of such a group is a *councilor* The *council* met to welcome a new *councilor*.
counsel, counselor	*advice; the giving of advice;* one who gives advice is a *counselor* I accepted the wise *counsel* of my *counselor*.

des′ert	*a dry region* We flew across the *desert*.
desert′	*to leave* He *deserted* his family.
dessert′	*the final course of a meal* The *dessert* was ice cream.

formally	*conventionally, properly, according to strict rules* He spoke *formally* and with great dignity.
formerly	*in the past, previously* I was *formerly* a member of that church.

its	[possessive] The village is proud of *its* school.
it's	*it is* *It's* a long way.

later	*more late* We will arrive *later*.
latter	*the second of two* When he gave me my choice of a football or a tennis racket, I chose the *latter*.

lead	[present tense] *to go first* You *lead* and we will follow.
led	[past tense] He *led* the army to victory.

lead   [pronounced **lĕd**] *a heavy metal;* also *graphite in a pencil*
The industrial uses of *lead* are many.

● EXERCISE 9. Number your paper 1–20. Write after the proper number the correct one of the words given in parentheses in the sentences below.

1. Our (consul, counsel) in Romania has returned to Washington.
2. I enjoyed the dinner but not the (dessert, desert).
3. Avoid (course, coarse) language.
4. Mr. Abrams was (formally, formerly) vice-president of the bank.
5. No (councilor, counselor) may serve more than three years on the council.
6. I do not enjoy parties conducted as (formally, formerly) as this one.
7. The walls of the room were papered but (its, it's) ceiling had been painted.
8. Some people are distrustful of (compliments, complements).
9. We are not sure which (course, coarse) to follow.
10. (Desert, Dessert) soil is often fertile if irrigated.
11. Are you sure (its, it's) not too late?
12. I spent five summers working as a camp (councilor, counselor).
13. A golf (course, coarse) requires continual care.
14. I spoke to the mayor and the superintendent; the (later, latter) was more helpful.
15. I can't recall his ever giving me a (complement, compliment) on my writing.
16. The soldiers who (deserted, desserted) were finally caught.
17. The guidance (councilor, counselor) advised me to take the test.
18. During his senior year, Albert (lead, led) the team to a championship.
19. Have you finished your (course, coarse) in hygiene?
20. These supplies will (complement, compliment) those you already have.

loose   *free, not close together*
   The animals broke *loose*.
   He stumbled in the *loose* sand.

lose   [pronounced **lōoz**] *to suffer loss*
   When did you *lose* your books?

---

miner   *worker in a mine*
   A *miner's* job is sometimes dangerous.

minor   *under legal age; less important*
   A *minor* cannot vote.
   He raised only *minor* objections.

---

moral   *good;* also *a lesson of conduct*
   His good conduct showed him to be a *moral* person.
   The class understood the *moral* of the story.

morale   *mental condition, spirit*
   The *morale* of the army is high.

---

passed   *verb*
   He *passed* me at the finish line.

past   *noun* or *adjective* or *preposition*
   Some persons prefer to live in the *past* (n.) because
      past (adj.) events seem more interesting than
      present ones.
   I went *past* (prep.) your house without realizing it.

---

peace   *opposite of strife*
   Everyone prefers *peace* to war.

piece   *a part of something*
   They ate every *piece* of cake.

---

personal   *individual*
   He gave his *personal* opinion.

personnel   *a group of people employed in the same place*
   The *personnel* of the company ranged in age from
      16 to 64.

plain	*not fancy;* also *a flat area of land;* also *clear* She lives in a very *plain* home. We crossed the *plains* in two days. Our problem is *plain.*
plane	*a flat surface;* also *a tool;* also *an airplane* *Plane* geometry is a study of imaginary flat surfaces. The carpenter used a *plane.* A *plane* circled the airport.

principal	*head of a school;* also *the main one of several things* He went to the *principal's* office. The *principal* cause of accidents is carelessness.
principle	*a rule of conduct;* also *a main fact* or *law* The judge accused the criminal of having no *principles.* He understands the *principles* of mathematics.

quiet	*still, silent* A study hall should be *quiet.*
quite	*completely, wholly;* also *to a great extent* or *degree* I had *quite* forgotten his advice. Bob is *quite* tall.

● EXERCISE 10. Number your paper 1–20. Write after the proper number the correct one of the words given in parentheses in the sentences below.

1. The judge regarded the crime as a (miner, minor) one.
2. A series of unexpected defeats destroyed the team's (moral, morale).
3. (Peace, Piece) had been maintained by the UN.
4. The meaning of his remark was perfectly (plain, plane).
5. These trucks are used for military (personnel, personal).
6. Word that the (principle, principal) wished to see me made me uncomfortable.
7. Do you understand the (principle, principal) of the gasoline motor?

8. If you don't wish to (lose, loose) the camera, keep it in the case.

9. The library was unusually (quite, quiet).

10. He had been a (minor, miner) in the Pennsylvania mines for many years.

11. The (principal, principle) characteristic of his poetry is its rhythm.

12. A (piece, peace) of the ship's mast was found.

13. Joe told me to (loose, lose) the dog from its leash.

14. A (personal, personnel) director is supposed to keep employees happy.

15. It was impossible to make the students be (quite, quiet).

16. When he (passed, past) me, I was going sixty miles an hour.

17. The (moral, morale) of the story was clear.

18. He went (passed, past) me like a flash.

19. You are a (miner, minor) in this state until the age of twenty-one.

20. He is a man who acts according to the highest (principles, principals).

---

stationary	*in a fixed position* The classroom desks are *stationary*.
stationery	*writing paper* I received three boxes of *stationery* at Christmas.

---

than	[a conjunction] I am stronger *than* she.
then	adverb meaning *at that time* Wear a green hat; *then* I'll recognize you.

---

there	*a place;* also used as an expletive (see page 26) We were *there* at two o'clock. *There* were four of us.
their	[possession] The pupils bring *their* own lunches.
they're	*they are* *They're* going with us.

to	[a preposition or part of the infinitive form of a verb]
	Give the book *to* me, please.
	We will have *to* leave early.
too	adverb meaning *also* or *too much*
	George is a sophomore, *too*.
	It is *too* late to go now.
two	*one plus one*
	We had only *two* dollars.

waist	*middle part of the body*
	She wore a wide belt around her *waist*.
waste	*unused material;* also *to squander*
	Please empty the *waste*baskets.
	Don't *waste* your time.

who's	*who is, who has*
	Who's coming?
	Who's been here?
whose	[possessive]
	Whose coat is this?

your	[possessive]
	Is this *your* coat?
you're	*you are*
	You're a true friend.

● EXERCISE 11.   Number your paper 1–20. Write after the proper number the correct one of the words given in parentheses in the sentences below.

1. The boys had neglected to lock (there, their) lockers.
2. I wanted to go to camp, (to, two, too).
3. Tie the rope around your (waist, waste).
4. The platform, we discovered when we tried to move it, was (stationary, stationery).

5. No one could remember (whose, who's) name had been drawn first.
6. This year's annual will be larger (than, then) last year's.
7. Where do you think (your, you're) going?
8. Some students regard the class as a (waist, waste) of time.
9. The work was (to, too) strenuous for me.
10. I used school (stationary, stationery) for my letters.
11. When (you're, your) homework has been finished, call me.
12. I do not know (whose, who's) going to solve the problem.
13. As soon as (their, they're) printed, we will ship the books.
14. Write your letters on business (stationary, stationery).
15. (Your, You're) lucky to have such a good job.
16. I cannot do any more (then, than) I have done.
17. Before we knew what the job was, (to, two, too) dollars an hour seemed to be good pay.
18. I'd like to know (who's, whose) responsible for this mess.
19. I was surprised at (you're, your) taking that attitude.
20. Chemistry has converted many (waste, waist) products into valuable commodities.

● REVIEW EXERCISE. Number your paper 1–40. After the proper number write the correct one of the words in parentheses in the sentences below.

1. Columbia is the (capital, capitol) of South Carolina.
2. Everything seemed to be (alright, all right).
3. Mr. Starkey (complemented, complimented) me on my English grade.
4. Have you discussed this problem with your guidance (councilor, counselor)?
5. We were blown several miles from our (course, coarse).
6. The letters have (all ready, already) been mailed.
7. The amount of vegetation in the (dessert, desert) surprised us.
8. Mrs. Crane (formally, formerly) taught here.
9. Every nation must conserve (its, it's) resources.
10. My companion (lead, led) me down a dark passage.
11. We were (all ready, already) to start before dawn.
12. Try not to (lose, loose) your temper.
13. Success is the best (moral, morale) builder.
14. His (coarse, course) manners were not amusing.

15. We had been told not to ask for a second (piece, peace) of pie.
16. The new (altar, alter) is made of white marble.
17. I have read all of Steinbeck and Hemingway, and I prefer the (later, latter).
18. You must go to the (principal, principle) to get a working permit.
19. (Its, It's) time to think about getting a job.
20. There was (all together, altogether) no truth in the accusations.
21. Members of the (counsel, council) are elected annually.
22. A (capital, capitol) offense will cost you your life.
23. Everyone is (all ready, already).
24. (Course, Coarse) wood absorbs more paint than fine-grained wood.
25. His work and mine are (complimentary, complementary).
26. Jack (past, passed) the ball to Joe.
27. When you are (all together, altogether), I'll take a group picture.
28. The mission was accomplished without loss of (personal, personnel).
29. The company embarked on the strongest advertising campaign in (its, it's) history.
30. What are the (principal, principle) products of Puerto Rico?
31. Some teachers prefer (stationary, stationery) seats in their classrooms.
32. There's a boy (whose, who's) going to succeed.
33. His performance was not outstanding, but it was (alright, all right).
34. Her (plain, plane) clothes did not detract from her beauty.
35. When we had cleaned our lockers, the (waistpaper, wastepaper) littered the floor.
36. The (principals, principles) of democracy have always been attacked.
37. Do you know (they're, their, there) new address?
38. Why didn't the campers follow their (counselor's, councilor's) instructions?
39. (Who's, Whose) pen is this?
40. Mrs. Smith gave us (complimentary, complementary) tickets.

COMMONLY MISSPELLED WORDS

7. *Learn lists of commonly misspelled words.* Frequent short spelling tests are an effective means of fixing correct spellings in your mind. On the following pages you will find a list of 300 commonly misspelled words. Taking no more than twenty at a time, have these words dictated to you. Study the ones you miss and record them in your list of spelling errors. When you have studied them (divided them into syllables and practiced writing each word several times), write them again from dictation. Spelling tests should be written, not oral.

THREE HUNDRED SPELLING WORDS [1]

abundant	alliance	biscuit
academically	allotting	blasphemy
accelerator	annihilate	boulevard
accessible	anonymous	bracelet
accidentally	apologetically	buffet
acclimated	apparatus	bureaucrat
accommodation	apparent	burial
accompaniment	arousing	calculation
accomplishment	arrangement	camouflage
accuracy	atheistic	capitalism
acknowledge	attendance	carburetor
acquaintance	awfully	caricature
adequately	ballet	catalogue
admittance	bankruptcy	catastrophe
admission	barbarian	cellar
adolescent	basketball	cemetery
advantageous	beggar	changeable
aerial	behavior	chassis
allege	beneficial	Christianity
allegiance	bibliography	circumstantial

[1] The list does not include the homonyms listed on pages 683 to 691.

colossal
communist
comparative
competition
complexion
conceivable
connoisseur
conscientious
consciousness
consistency

controlling
controversy
cruelty
curriculum
debacle
decadent
deceitful
deference
descendant
desirable

despair
detrimental
devastation
devise
dilemma
diligence
disastrous
disciple
discrimination
diseased

dissatisfied
division
ecstasy
efficiency
embarrassment
emperor

emphasize
endeavor
enormous
enthusiastically

entertainment
entrance
environment
espionage
exhaustion
exhibition
exhilaration
expensive
exuberant
familiarize

fascination
fascism
feminine
financier
fission
forfeit
fulfill
fundamentally
gaiety
galaxy

gauge
grammatically
guidance
harassment
hereditary
hindrance
hospital
horizontal
hygiene
hypocrisy

ideally

idiomatic
incidentally
independent
indispensable
inevitable
influential
ingenious
initiative
innocent

inoculate
institution
intellectual
interference
irrelevant
irresistible
kerosene
laborious
larynx
leisurely

license
livelihood
liquor
luxurious
magistrate
magnificence
maintenance
malicious
manageable
maneuver

marriageable
martyrdom
materialism
meadow
mediocre
melancholy
melodious

metaphor
miniature
mischievous

misspelled
mortgage
mosquito
municipal
mysterious
naive
necessity
neurotic
novelist
noticeable

nucleus
nuisance
nutritious
obedience
occasionally
occurrence
omitting
opportunity
orchestra
outrageous

pageant
pamphlet
paralysis
parliament
pastime
peasant
pedestal
penicillin
perceive
permanent

permissible
persistent

perspiration
phenomenon
physician
picnicking
playwright
pneumonia
politician
precede

presence
presumption
prestige
prevalent
privilege
procedure
propaganda
propagate
prophesy
prove

psychoanalysis
pursue
quietly
rebellion
receive
recommendation
reference
referred
rehearsal
relieve

reminiscent
remittance
representative
resources
responsibility
reveal
safety
seize

separation
sergeant

siege
significance
souvenir
specimen
sponsor
statistics
strategic
stubbornness
succeed
succession

summed
superintendent
supersede
suppress
surroundings
susceptible
symbolic
symmetrical
symphonic
synonymous

tariff
temperament
temperature
tendency
theoretical
tolerance
tomorrow
tortoise
traffic
tragedy

transcend
transparent
tried

twelfth

tyranny

undoubtedly

universal

unmistakable

unnatural

unnecessary

unscrupulous

vaccine

vacuum

valedictory

variation

vaudeville

vehicle

vengeance

versatile

vigilance

villain

vinegar

welcome

whisper

whistle

withhold

yacht

yawn

PART EIGHT

A New Look at Grammar

CHAPTER 38

A New Look at Grammar

Structural and Transformational Grammars

Unless you plan to major in English or some other language in college, the chances are that this year will be the last in which you study formal grammar. Perhaps you find this prospect pleasing. Whatever your feelings about grammar, you have invested hundreds of hours in its study. In addition to the facts and skills that you have learned in this time, you should have a general notion of what the subject is about and why people think it is important. You should also know that there are other "grammars of English" than the one you have been studying and have a general idea of what they are like.

WHAT GRAMMAR IS

It may seem odd at this stage to consider what grammar is. Yet the question is important and not so easy to answer. It is possible to become so engrossed with the details of a subject that we lose sight of the ideas that make the details meaningful. It is especially easy to form misconceptions about grammar because the word is commonly used in several closely related but different ways. One meaning is illustrated by the sentence *His grammar could be better*, which means that the person referred to makes some slips in speaking or writing that careful users of English look down on and avoid. Perhaps he habitually uses expressions like *it don't, have went, hisself*, etc. That is one meaning of *grammar*, but it is not the one that we are concerned with in this chapter.

Grammar may also mean the system of a language—the way in which words are put together to make phrases and sentences—or the study of this subject or a book about it. These three meanings, all of which have to do with language as a system for communicating, are the ones that this chapter is about. Most often we will use *grammar* to mean simply "the system of English."

In one sense—at least if you are a native speaker of English—you have known this system since early childhood. If you had not, you would not have been able to ask nearly so many questions as you did at three or four or understand the answers or been able to let people know when you wanted something. Learning to speak English means learning its system. Any speaker of English has an unconscious grasp of the principles of the language; the study of grammar makes you consciously aware of these principles. We study grammar partly because it is interesting and partly because it can be put consciously to use in solving language problems. If you have a close friend, you can recognize him on the street or in school without giving a thought to how you do it. Suppose, however, that you want to tell someone else how to recognize your friend. You would have to consider what features or qualities you unconsciously note in distinguishing your friend from everyone else. It is much the same with your familiarity with language. It is often important to know how we do the things that we do.

In grammar, then, we study a description of the system of a language. The description you have been studying is one of several ways of looking at English. Because it is the oldest way, it is usually called *traditional grammar*. Although men of many different times have contributed to it, traditional grammar has a single point of view that is reflected in all of its rules and statements: the point of view of a person observing and explaining something extremely close and familiar to him—his native language. It corresponds roughly with the description of your friend—a collection of details and observations that puts into words information of which you usually make unconscious use. Traditional grammar is based on the user's feelings about his language—what sounds correct or reasonable to him. It makes constant reference to meaning, because after all it is to express meaning that languages exist. Although its explanations are sometimes extremely complicated, traditional grammar always ends up saying "We say it that way because that's what we mean."

In the last hundred years or so, another point of view toward language has produced descriptions of language that are quite different from traditional grammar. This new way of looking at language regards it as a system that can be studied without reference to what is going on inside a speaker's head at a given time. Instead of asking himself *why* he puts words together in a certain way, the grammarian holding this view will examine many different sentences and try to figure out the system by means of observation and experiment. If this seems an odd way of proceeding, remember that it is often the most familiar things that are difficult to talk sensibly about. We all know a question when we hear one, but are we able to describe exactly what a question is?

There are many features of our language that we are so accustomed to that we hardly notice them. It is just such features that the grammarians who were not satisfied with traditional grammar paid most attention to at first. As a result, some people made fun of them for finding hard ways

PROBLEM   Is *birthday* a noun or an adjective in the sentence "It is my **birthday** and my **birthday** party"? Is it a noun both times or only the first time? If the answer is "only the first time," what does it name then that it doesn't name the second time? If it is a noun both times, not all words that modify nouns are adjectives, as the definition of that term implies.

Now we must be clear about one thing: traditional grammarians had been well aware of these problems before the structuralists came along. Some of them they solved by adding special explanations (see the explanation of nouns used as adjectives on page 9 of this book). Other problems they were willing to put up with to avoid having to give extremely complicated explanations for terms that named very obvious and easily recognized elements of English.

The traditionalists were, after all, mainly interested in providing a vocabulary with which they could talk about matters of expression. The traditional definition of adjective is a perfectly good one for understanding such a sentence as: "Try to use fewer adjectives in your descriptions." For such purposes, traditional grammar serves very well.

For purposes of scientific description, however, such definitions will not do. Therefore, the structuralists proposed to classify words and the functions of words by formal and structural means—that is, by describing changes in a word's form and the ways it can be used in sentences. The following exercise will help you to see how this is done.

● EXERCISE 1.   The words listed below are from Swahili, a language of East Africa. Swahili has a kind of word that is much like an English noun. Like English nouns, these Swahili nouns have a singular and a plural form. Study the following columns until you can state how these particular Swahili nouns show number.[1]

---

[1] This exercise and the one that follows are based on an unpublished lesson written by H. A. Gleason, Jr. Used by permission.

SINGULAR		PLURAL	
mtu	"person"	watu	"persons"
mgeni	"stranger"	wageni	"strangers"
mvulana	"boy"	wavulana	"boys"
msichana	"girl"	wasichana	"girls"

1. How does English indicate singular and plural?
2. What similarities between the English system and the Swahili system do you notice?
3. What clue might we use in deciding whether a Swahili word like *wapishi* was a noun? If it is a noun, would it be singular or plural in form?

● EXERCISE 2.   Test your observations in Exercise 1 by supplying the appropriate form for the following numbered blanks.

1. mlinzi	"guard"	——	"guards"
2. ——	"king"	wafalme	"kings"
3. mwongo	"——"	wawongo	"liars"
4. mjane	"widow"	wajane	"——"
5. mgana	"doctor"	——	"——"

Form Classes

If you had any luck at all in Exercises 1 and 2, you already have an idea of how words can be classified by form. Words that have the same inflectional features seem to belong together. By using this principle, we can say that a noun in English is a word that has forms like these illustrated by dog: *dog, dogs; dog, dog's.* We can make a similar pattern for *boy, boys, boy, boy's* and thousands of other nouns. We may have some trouble with a few nouns like *goose, sheep,* and *child,* but at least they fit part of our pattern (*goose, goose's; child, child's*).

Another way of classifying words without resorting to meaning is by typical position in sentences. A noun for example will always fit in the position indicated by the blank in the following sentence: I was thinking of ——(s). The (*s*) may be used or omitted as necessary. Nouns like *science* and *soup* fit without the *s*; nouns like *apple* and *girl* need it. This simple positional test rules out all words that are not nouns except for a few pronouns (*some*, *him*, *everybody*, etc.), which the formal clues rule out in any case. For example, *some* fits the frame, but does not have a possessive form or a plural that adds the sound of *s* or *z*.

By applying these methods, the structuralists arrived at four large classes of words that accounted for all but a few hundred words in the language. The four large classes—called *form classes* because of their inflectional characteristics—correspond in general to the classes *noun*, *adjective*, *adverb*, and *verb* of traditional grammar.

Members of a form class can be identified simply by trying them in four characteristic test frames—a sentence with a word left out. By following a few simple rules, you can determine whether a word is a noun, adjective, adverb, or verb by using the following frames:

NOUN	I was thinking of ——(s).
ADJECTIVE	It seems ——.
ADVERB	They did it ——.
VERB	He may —— (it).

The (s), you will remember, may be used or not as needed. Similarly, the (it) following the blank in the verb frame is needed for some verbs (*admit*) but not for others (*go*). Also, as you would expect after *may*, only the infinitive form (first principal part) of the verb can be used in the testing frame.

All clear? To see how the frames work, try your hand at the following exercise—this time with English words.

● EXERCISE 3.   Using the frames above and following the simple rules for their use, label each of the following words noun, adjective, adverb, or verb, according to which blank they fit. You should not be surprised to find that some words fit more than one frame. A word can belong to more than one form class just as it can belong to more than one part of speech. If a word fits more than one frame, give more than one label.

1. scary	11. take
2. persecution	12. harmless
3. freeze	13. bowl
4. Charlie	14. fast
5. cheerfully	15. grammar
6. wrong	16. linguistics
7. aeronautics	17. education
8. the *New York Times*	18. bookish
9. fish	19. carelessly
10. ants	20. phonemes

Structure Words

The few hundred remaining words in English—mainly prepositions, conjunctions, pronouns, and a few odds and ends—are classified separately according to their uses in sentences. These words, taken altogether, give important signals about the structure of sentences. For this reason, they are often called *structure words*. The following list contains only a sampling of structure words:

a	he	about	which	enough	is	because
the	it	in	what	how	can	unless
every	them	by	that	very	have	while
some	everyone	after	as	although	may	who

Notice that all of these words have one thing in common: they do not mean much by themselves. That is, they have to be in a particular sentence to take on meaning. The words *potato*, *girl*, and *car* have a certain general meaning in isolation; *the*, *what*, and *do* do not. These empty words have one main job—to provide clues to the structure of the sentence. In a sense they provide the framework into which words from the form classes can be dropped in like cards into slots:

The ——— may ——— unless the ——— are very ———.

There are thousands of different ways in which these blanks can be filled but whatever the combinations, the general structure of the sentence remains the same.

Structure and Function

So far we have been dealing with the signals that individual words give. Certain endings tell us that a word is a noun or an adjective; certain structure words provide important connections between the form class words in sentences. The work that structure words do leads us to the central problem of any grammar: the description of the relations between one part of a sentence and another. Structural grammar offers two ways of describing this relationship. To see how they work we need to understand two important terms—*structure* and *function.*

One common meaning of structure is "the way something is put together." We use this meaning when we refer to the structure of a sentence. But there is a second common meaning that we will find useful in discussing structural grammar. This second meaning is the one we have in mind when we refer to a platform or a building as a *structure.* In this sense, the word means "something that is built or constructed." We will use this meaning of structure from now on in this chapter.

Function means "the job something does." The function of a quarterback is to call signals, and the function of a policeman is to keep order. Similarly, in grammar, the job done by words or groups of words in sentences is called their function. We will call the words and groups of words *structures,* and we will call the jobs they do in sentences their *functions.*

We have said that structural grammar provides two methods for talking about the relationship of words in sentences. The first method grows directly out of the idea of form classes and structure words. It classifies structures according to their function in sentences. Three kinds of structures can be distinguished: noun structures, verb structures, and modifier structures. The first two are named after the form class words that usually appear in them. Remember however that when we speak of a noun structure we are speaking of a structure that is doing a particular job in a sentence.

Noun Structures

A noun structure is a word from the noun form class or another word or group of words used like a noun. The bold-faced words in the following examples are noun structures:

> **Astronomy** is interesting.
> **The study of the stars** is called **astronomy.**
> It has **a long history.**
> No one denies **that the study of the stars is important.**

There are several things to notice about noun structures. They can consist of one word or more than one. When there is more than one word in a noun structure, one of them is likely to be a structure word like *the*, *a*, or *some*. The modifiers that accompany a noun are included in the noun structure. Typical functions of noun structures are subject, predicate nominative, direct and indirect object, and object of a preposition.

Verb Structures

Verb structures consist of words from the verb form class, together with certain structure words that go with them. The bold-faced words in the following examples are verb structures:

> We **agree.**
> The boys **are teasing** the dog.
> The truth of the charges **can be proved.**

Some structure words (*be, have, do*) may be the whole verb structure or only a part of it:

We **have been waiting.**
We **have** some.
We **are waiting.**
We **are** ready.

Modifier Structures

Modifier structures are either words from the adjective and adverb form classes or groups of words used as adjectives and adverbs are used. Such word groups are always introduced by structure words that mark modifier structures: *of the people, in the park, by the ears.* Certain structure words like *when, if,* and *because,* turn independent clauses into modifier structures: *when it rains, if it matters, because it's there.* The bold-faced examples below are modifier structures:

The red hen is spreading rumors **again.**
The popcorn machine is **out of order.**
Any man **who can remember the signals** can be **the** quarterback.

Notice that some of the modifier structures in the examples above are parts of larger structures. For example, *red* is a modifier structure by itself but it is also a part of the noun structure *the red hen.* The structures of English are not always strung one after another like box cars in a freight train. They often fit inside each other like Chinese boxes. For example, the following modifier structure contains another modifier structure, a verb structure, and two different noun structures:

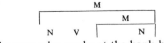

The man who works at the bank has taken a vacation.

● EXERCISE 4.   In each of the following sentences a word or group of words is italicized and numbered. Beside the appropriate number on your paper, indicate whether the word or group of words is a noun structure, verb structure, or modifier structure.

a. (1) *The people* of Pleasant Valley are (2) *famous* for (3) *their courage* and tenacity.

b. Their village is at (4) *the confluence* of (5) *two* mighty rivers.

c. (6) *During the summer*, they (7) *enjoy* boating and other water sports, and (8) *in the winter*, they (9) *skate* and (10) *fish* through the ice.

d. As spring approaches, however, (11) *they* become feverishly (12) *active*.

e. They (13) *pack* their (14) *belongings* in oil skin and carry them to caves in the hills (15) *surrounding the village*.

f. The (16) *reason* is (17) *obvious*.

g. The rivers (18) *flood* the village (19) *every spring*.

h. All of the houses (20) *are submerged* by the muddy waters.

i. The people visit (21) *their relatives* at this time.

j. When the (22) *flood* waters recede again, the villagers (23) *return*.

k. They (24) *have grown* accustomed to disaster.

l. To (25) *the women of the valley*, spring cleaning has a special meaning.

Sentence Patterns

Some linguists classify typical English sentences according to the structures they contain and the arrangement of these structures. They begin with the simplest kind of sentence, which consists of only a noun structure (functioning as the subject) and a verb structure (functioning as the predicate). In the labels, N stands for noun structure and V for verb structure.

	N	V
PATTERN 1	Bears	dance.

A PATTERN 1 sentence may consist of only these two structures or it may have a modifier structure after the verb. To show that the M may or may not occur, we will put it in parentheses:

N	V	(M)
Bears	dance	awkwardly.
Bears	dance	in circuses.

PATTERN 2 differs from PATTERN 1 in two ways. First of all, a modifier *must* follow the verb structure and the verb is of the kind that traditional grammar refers to as a linking verb:

	N	V	M
PATTERN 2	Bears	seem	awkward.
	The man	is	angry.

Notice that we do not enclose the M in parentheses when it is essential to the pattern.

PATTERN 3 is exactly like PATTERN 2, except that a noun structure instead of a modifier structure must follow the linking verb:

	N	V	N
PATTERN 3	We	are	students.
	Bears	are	entertainers.
	Two plus two	equals	four.

Notice that the noun that follows the linking verb names or defines the noun that functions as the subject.

PATTERN 4 differs from 3 in two ways. The verb cannot be a linking verb and the noun that follows it names a different person or thing than the subject:

	N	V	N
PATTERN 4	We	chose	a leader.
	Cats	eat	mice.

In traditional grammar, the parts labeled N, V, and M in the patterns are the ones that appear on the horizontal line in diagraming. Compare the four patterns and the diagrams for the same sentences on page 714:

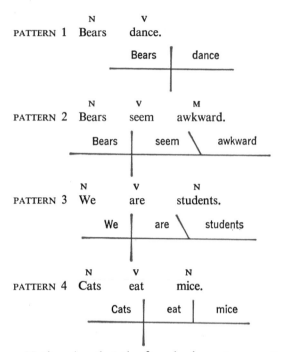

PATTERN 1

N   V
Bears   dance.

Bears | dance

PATTERN 2

N   V   M
Bears   seem   awkward.

Bears | seem \ awkward

PATTERN 3

N   V   N
We   are   students.

We | are \ students

PATTERN 4

N   V   N
Cats   eat   mice.

Cats | eat | mice

Notice also that the four basic sentence patterns given above do not contain structures within structures. They are all simple sentences. More complicated sentences are usually thought of as expansions of these basic patterns, the expansion being accomplished by the insertion of modifiers or by the substitution of a more complex noun structure for the simple one given in the pattern.

BASIC SENTENCE	Bears	dance.
EXPANSIONS	Some bears	dance.
	Some circus bears	dance.
	Bears that have been trained	can dance.
BASIC SENTENCE	We	believe it.
SUBSTITUTIONS	We	believe that it is true.
	Many of the jurors	believe that he is telling the truth.

Summary

1. Most words can be classified by their formal characteristics and by their typical positions in sentences.
2. Words are used together in sentences in structures. (A structure can consist of a single word.)
3. A structure is a word or group of words functioning as a unit.
4. One structure can contain another.
5. Structures can be classified by function: noun structures, verb structures, and modifier structures.
6. Sentences can be classified according to the arrangement, or pattern, of the structures contained in them.

● EXERCISE 5. The following sentences have one of the four basic patterns described on pages 712–13. After the proper number, give the pattern number (1, 2, 3, or 4).

1. The meek shall inherit the earth.
2. The natives are restless.
3. The party was a success.
4. The hostess seemed pleased.
5. The rain has stopped.
6. Joan dances beautifully.
7. This problem is difficult.
8. The stranger may be a spy.
9. No one suspected the butler.
10. We live here.

● EXERCISE 6. Each of the formulas below stands for a basic sentence pattern. Supply a sentence for each pattern, substituting a single word for each V and M. You may use *a, an, the,* or *some* plus a noun for each N. Label each pattern 1, 2, 3, or 4, as in Exercise 5.

1. NVN (second noun should name the same thing as the first)
2. NV
3. NV(M) (modifier may but need not be included)
4. NVN (second noun should name a different thing)
5. NVM (modifier must be included)

● EXERCISE 7. Expand the basic sentences you wrote for Exercise 6 by adding prepositional phrases (modifier structures) wherever appropriate.

EXAMPLE   1. The boy loves my sister (4)
           1. *The boy in the drug store loves my sister.*

Pattern Parts

In classifying structures according to function, we have been assuming that we always know where one structure ends and another begins. So far, however, we have not discussed ways of analyzing a sentence into the smaller structures it contains. Unless we have some objective tests for breaking sentences into their parts, we have gained little by labeling a subject as a noun structure and so on. Structural grammar does provide an objective test of this kind, and the procedure involved is one of the most important contributions of modern linguistics.

We are all accustomed to thinking that words are the main carriers of meaning in our language and that to say something we need only select the right words and string them together. On examination, however, this simple notion turns out to be far from the truth. The three words *Mary, John, love* all have some kind of meaning, yet spoken in that way they do not mean anything more together than they do separately. To make a sentence of these words we must first put them in proper order and add an appropriate ending to *love: John loves Mary* or *Mary loves John*. The difference between *Mary, John, love* and *John loves Mary* is grammatical relation. As native speakers, we have little trouble in recognizing grammatical relation when we see it. Finding ways of describing it that are not based entirely on the meaning of the sentence is a good deal harder.

To solve this problem, the structural grammarians hit upon a simple but extremely useful way of showing grammatical relation. Remember that one structure can fit inside another like Chinese boxes. Sensing that this arrangement of parts within parts was an important principle of English grammar, the structuralists worked out a system of analysis that assumes that sentences are constructed mainly of two parts, and that these parts also have two parts, and so on down to the level of individual words.

Let's begin by dividing the following sentence into two parts. Where shall we divide it?

The boy who works in the garage loves my sister.

If you are a typical native speaker, you will probably divide the sentence between the last word of the complete subject and the main verb, just as traditional grammar does:

The boy who works in the garage | loves my sister.

By making the cut between *garage* and *loves* we have divided the sentence into two parts that have a clear grammatical relation to each other—the relation of actor-action that is basic to most of the sentences in our language. If we can continue to cut this sentence up into smaller and smaller parts in such a way that each cut reveals some kind of grammatical relation, we may have the objective test we are looking for. In any case, let's try cutting in two each of the parts we already have:

The boy | who works in the garage | loves | my sister.

Again, the cuts reveal grammatical relation. To begin with the one at the left, the clause *who works in the garage* functions as a modifier structure to *the boy*. The noun structure *my sister* is a complement to the verb *loves*. (If we ignore the expansion for a moment, we have an example of PATTERN 4: *The boy loves my sister.*) So far, the cuts still reveal clear grammatical relationships.

But, you may object, the cuts are made in a completely arbitrary way. You may object further that they are made where they are because we know the grammatical relation of subject-predicate, noun-modifier to begin with. If the cuts are arbitrary or made because of an understanding of the meaning of the sentence, the procedure is of course pointless. Let's see, first of all, whether the cuts are arbitrary. If they are, they can be made anywhere.

We may try another division of the whole sentence:

The boy who works in the garage loves | my sister.

This time the cut shows no clear grammatical relationship. It is different from the second cut above because this time it divides the whole first part of the sentence from *my sister*. *My sister* is the complement of the verb *loves*, it is not the complement of the whole word group *the boy who works in the garage loves*.

To avoid making cuts that lead to such unsatisfactory results, we must follow a simple rule: make cuts in such a way that you can substitute a single word for the part on each side of the line. We can do that for the cut between *garage* and *loves*, but not for the one between *loves* and *my sister*:

He   does
The boy who works in the garage | loves my sister.

?   her
The boy who works in the garage loves | my sister.

In the second, unsatisfactory, cut we can substitute *her* for *my sister*, but there is no single word that can take the place of both the subject and the verb at the same time. To put it another way, no word can function as both noun structure and verb structure simultaneously. The same test eliminates other cuts:

He?   does?
The boy who | works in the garage loves my sister.

Neither "He works in the garage loves my sister" nor "The boy who does" makes sense. On the other hand, both *He loves my sister* and *The boy who works in the garage does* do make sense.

By following this rule, we can make successive cuts on each side of the original line until we get down to single words. (When there is nothing left to cut on one side of a line, we simply stop and cut where we can.)

```
The  boy who works  in  the garage| loves  my sister
The  boy| who works  in  the garage| loves| my sister
The| boy| who| works  in  the garage| loves| my| sister
The| boy| who| works| in  the garage| loves| my| sister
The| boy| who| works| in| the garage| loves| my| sister
The| boy| who| works| in| the| garage| loves| my| sister
```

This process, properly applied, gives us a powerful test of grammatical relationships. We can say that any two parts of a sentence that can be divided by one of our cuts stand in direct grammatical relation to each other. Thus each of the following cuts shows this kind of direct relationship:

The boy who works in the garage | loves my sister   [subject-predicate]

The boy | who works in the garage   [noun structure and modifier]

loves | my sister   [verb and complement]

the | boy   [modifier and noun structure]

who | works in the garage   [subject and predicate of subordinate clause]

my | sister   [modifier and noun structure]

works | in the garage   [verb and adverbial modifier]

We can easily see the relations of these parts. By adding the idea of subordination, we can analyze the remaining prepositional phrase:

in | the garage   [subordinator and noun structure]

By subordination, we would mean the operation of making a noun structure a non-essential element in the sentence.[1] In other words, a subordinated noun structure cannot be a subject, object, predicate nominative, etc.

● EXERCISE 8.   Copy the following sentences and draw a line between the two main pattern parts. Use the substitution rule as a general guide to the appropriate cut.

[1] In the clause *who works in the garage, who* also functions as a subordinator.

1. The last of the money is gone.
2. Recent studies confirm my findings.
3. The people who used to live there have moved away.
4. We have never doubted the man's sincerity.
5. The cake tasted a little strange.
6. Few people guessed that he was a policeman in disguise.
7. One of the qualities that a hero needs is courage.
8. Mr. Mathers has the reputation of being a hard marker.
9. The losing candidate demanded a recount.
10. None of the contestants knew the answer.

● EXERCISE 9.   The following sentences have been cut once. Copy the sentences and make a second level cut on each side of the line.

1. The man on the bench | is the coach.
2. The player beside him | plays quarterback.
3. The coach | has called him to the bench for instructions.
4. The team's failure to score | may be the reason.
5. Only a drastic change in strategy | can save the day.

● EXERCISE 10.   Copy the following items and make the best single cut in each.

1. below the bridge
2. who came to dinner
3. the suitcase containing the money
4. the statue in the park
5. under the circumstances
6. people who gossip
7. the reason is obvious
8. while you were gone
9. several boxes of candy
10. one of the boys

TRANSFORMATIONAL GRAMMAR

Traditional grammar provides an *explanation* for the way language works; structural grammar examines thousands of sentences and produces a *description* of the system of a language. Transformational grammar, the third kind of grammar that concerns us here, does something different from either of the others: it sets out to state the *process* by which English sentences are formed.

In everyday life we are accustomed to explanations and definitions given in the form of the steps in a process. A recipe may tell us what a cake is by telling us how to make one; whereas, a description of the cake would tell us whether the cake is dark or light, whether it has layers and filling, what the frosting is like, and so on. Transformational grammar gives the recipes for constructing English sentences and nothing else.

To understand how this works, try to imagine that you are in charge of a computer and that your job is to make it produce English sentences of its own. (There is no computer that can do this, but let's assume that yours can.) Your problem is to break the process of making English sentences up into simple steps that the machine can perform one at a time. You must also give these steps to the computer in the right order. To do this successfully, you would have to give the computer the whole system of English, and you would have to give it not as an explanation or a description but as a set of instructions that the machine can follow. There is only one kind of computer that can turn out an infinite number of different English sentences— a speaker of the language like yourself. To do so, you unconsciously follow a process much like the one that a mechanical computer would follow. Transformational grammar attempts to state this process in a set of rules.

This chapter can give you only the most general idea of what transformational grammar is like and what it tries to do. The system of a language is a complicated matter and therefore the process by which sentences are formed sometimes gets complicated, too. Some of these rules may seem to have little to do with what goes on inside your head when you form a sentence, but don't be too sure. Your mind is capable of performing many complicated operations that you are quite unaware of. (If you had to think about all the operations involved in walking downstairs you would probably fall from the top step.)

Kernel Sentences

Transformational grammar begins by assuming that there are a few sentence patterns that are basic to the language. These are essentially similar to the basic sentences for structural grammar on pages 712–13; in transformational grammars they are usually called *kernel sentences*. Later rules give the steps that produce more complicated sentences. These sentences that are formed by combining or adding to kernel sentences are called *transformed sentences*, or *transforms*. To understand how transformed sentences are made, however, we must begin with the kernel sentences.

The first rule for forming kernel sentences is as follows:

1. $S \rightarrow NP + VP$

The S stands for sentence. The arrow is an instruction to "rewrite S as NP + VP." Later rules will tell us what NP and VP mean. Since there is always an arrow in a transformational rule, we may as well pause now to consider its meaning carefully. The part of the formula at the right of the arrow always gives a fuller description of the part at the left of the arrow. The formula "Rewrite S as NP + VP" means that sentences must be understood in terms of units called NP's and VP's. For more information about NP's and VP's we must have additional rules.

NP in the formula means *noun phrase*—essentially the same thing as noun structure (page 710). VP means *verb phrase*. (Compare verb structure, page 710.) Taken altogether the first rule tells us that to get a clearer idea of S (sentence) we must think of it as NP + VP. The next rule will then have one of these terms on the left of the arrow:

2. $NP \rightarrow (D) + N$

NP is the term to be rewritten; the rewrite at the right gives us a statement that further explains what goes into an NP: A D and an N. We need two more rules to know what these stand for:

3. D → the, a
4. N → boy, dog, ball, etc.

Rules 3 and 4 give us the information we need to interpret Rule 2: An NP can be rewritten as *the* or *a* plus *boy*, *dog*, or any of an endless number of nouns. The parentheses around the D mean that this element may, but need not, occur. Thus, all of the following are possible equivalents of (D) + N:

the boy   [D: the]
a dog   [D: a]
science   [D: not used]

Rules 2–4 give us half of the rewrite for S. To get the other half—that is to know what a VP is—we need the following additional rules:

5. VP → verb + (NP)
6. verb → hit, took, went, barked, etc.

We already have the rewrite for NP and the parts that go into it. Therefore we have enough instructions for constructing a large number of English sentences. To see how this works out, examine the following table in which the successive steps are listed one below the other. The number in the brackets at the right indicates which rule was applied to get a particular result:

	Sentence			
NP	VP			[1]
(D) N	VP			[2]
the N	VP			[3]
the dog	VP			[4]
the dog	verb	(NP)		[5]
the dog	bit	(NP)		[6]
the dog	bit	(D) N		[2]
the dog	bit	the N		[3]
the dog	bit	the	boy	[4]

If we choose not to use the NP in parentheses we get another kind of sentence:

                        Sentence

        NP   VP   [1]
        (D) N   VP   [2]
        the   N   VP   [3]
        the dog   VP   [4]
        the dog   verb (NP)   [5]
        the dog   barked   [6]

Although many sentences can be formed from these simple rules, further refinements are needed. For example, a rule is needed to make subject and verb agree. A fullscale transformational grammar has such rules.

● EXERCISE 11.   Using the numbered rules below, complete the formulas given below. Copy the whole formula.

    1. S → NP + VP   4. N → boy, dog, ball, etc.
    2. NP → (D) + N   5. VP → verb + (NP)
    3. D → the, a   6. verb → hit, took, went, etc.

EXAMPLE   a. ——— → NP + VP
          a. *S*   → *NP + VP*

a. ——— → the, a   e. VP → verb + ———
b. ——— → hit, took, went, etc.   f. verb → ———, etc.
c. VP → ——— + (NP)   g. NP → (D) + ———
d. S → ——— + VP   h. ——— → verb + (NP)

Transformed Sentences

The kernel sentences that can be formed from rules like the six we have been studying are very similar to the basic sentences of structural grammar. All three kinds of grammar —traditional, structural, and transformational—in fact give primary importance to simple sentences of this kind. Unlike the other systems, however, transformational grammar sets out to demonstrate how all other more complicated sentences derive from kernel, or basic, sentences. The first set of transformational rules produces kernel sentences; the second set shows how elements in the kernels can be switched around and combined to produce transformed sentences.

Like the rules for forming kernel sentences, this second set of rules gives the steps in a process. Let's begin with a kernel sentence much like those we have been dealing with:

He is here.

One kind of transformation that we can apply will make a question out of this statement:

Is he here?

What has been added? Nothing. The parts of the sentence have simply been switched around: the order of *he* and *is* has been reversed.

In English we ask the *yes/no* kind of question when we want something confirmed or denied. If we want other information we usually have to use question words like *where*, *when*, *why*, etc. For example, if we want to know the location of the person we are talking about, we use *where* instead of *here:*

He is where?

We can leave the question in that form only under special circumstances: if we have already had an answer to the question which we failed to hear or understand or find hard to believe. If we are asking the question for the first time, we must move the question word to the beginning of the sentence:

where he is

But this still isn't English. We must once again apply the rule we used in forming the *yes/no* question; we have to reverse *he* and *is*. The whole process can be stated as follows:

KERNEL   He is here.

PROCESS	RESULT
1. Change *here* to *where*	he is where
2. Move *where* to beginning	where he is
3. Reverse *he* and *is*	Where is he?

In a transformational grammar these rules would be stated in formulas that would apply to all such questions, not merely a single one, but the process is essentially the same.

Similar rules tell us how to get the transformed sentence "There is food in the refrigerator" from "Food is in the refrigerator." The rule this time is to add the word *there* and once again to switch the order of subject and verb:

Food is in the refrigerator.
> *becomes*

There is food in the refrigerator.

This transformation with *there* is one that we often use when we want to emphasize the subject of a sentence. But suppose we also want to ask a question. Once again the verb *is* is moved ahead—this time ahead of *there:*

There is food in the refrigerator.
> *becomes*

Is there food in the refrigerator?

This question results from applying a transformation to a sentence that has already been transformed. Still other changes can be made. By adding *n't* to the verb, we can get the negative form of the question:

Isn't there food in the refrigerator?

By applying the rules in a different order or by using other rules we can get such results as:

Is there not food in the refrigerator?
There is food in the refrigerator, isn't there?
What is there in the refrigerator? etc.

In the kernel sentences of transformational grammar, adjectives appear only in the VP—that is, as predicate adjectives. An adjective standing before the noun it modifies is accounted for as a predicate adjective from one kernel inserted into another. For example, *The little boy cried* is considered a combination of the sentences:

The boy cried. ⎫
The boy was little. ⎭ The little boy cried.

There are many other ways of combining two or more kernel sentences. One rule for combining sentences instructs us to substitute *who* or *that* for the subject of one sentence and then to combine the results:

A. The boy loved the dog.
B. The dog bit the boy.

If we perform the operation on sentence A we get *who loved the dog* which can be added onto the end of B:

The dog bit the boy who loved the dog.

By substituting a pronoun to avoid the awkward repetition we get:

C. The dog bit the boy who loved him.

Similar steps applied to B result in:

D. The boy loved the dog that bit him.

Other transformational rules produce passive sentences, other questions, emphatic sentences, etc. The following examples illustrate a few of the transformed sentences that can be derived from "Jerry left the key in the mailbox."

The key was left in the mailbox by Jerry.
The key was left in the mailbox.
Was the key left in the mailbox?
Did Jerry leave the key in the mailbox?
What did Jerry leave in the mailbox?
Where did Jerry leave the key?
Who left the key in the mailbox?

● EXERCISE 12.   Apply the *there* transformation to the following sentences.

EXAMPLE   1. A bird is in that tree.
            1. *There is a bird in that tree.*

1. A puppy is in the pet shop window.
2. A package is on the hall table.

3. Few good books are in that library.
4. A policeman is waiting outside.
5. A message is in this bottle.

● EXERCISE 13.   Change the following sentences according to the instructions in the brackets.

1. An animal of some kind is in the cereal box. [Apply the *there* transformation.]
2. There is some reason to think so. [Make the statement into a question that can be answered *yes* or *no*.]
3. The money is here. [Make the statement into a question with *where*. Show the successive steps performed.]
4. A tree is in the backyard. [First, apply the *there* transformation. Then make the resulting statement into a *yes/no* question.]
5. Carelessness caused the delay. [Make this active sentence into a passive one. Notice what additions and changes you have to make and be able to describe them in your own words.]

Pronunciation Rules

We have had a look at two parts of a transformational grammar: the part that gives instructions for forming kernel sentences and the part that gives instructions for transforming sentences. The necessity of simplifying rules in order to present them in so short a space largely conceals the importance of the third part of a transformational grammar: the set of rules for changing the results of transformations into pronounceable English sentences.

A set of transformational rules capable of accounting for all of the complexities of English would produce results more or less like this:

the + boy + have + present + be + –en + go + –ing + to + the + dentist

The new elements in this formula are *present*, the indication of tense that must be part of the VP in a detailed presentation, and the endings *–en* and *–ing*, which may be added and switched around in sentences according to certain specific rules. After all of the transformations have been applied, a final set of rules must be applied to make the sentence pronounceable. Thus, we have rules like these:

```
have + present → has
be   + -en     → been
go   + -ing    → going
```

The application of rules like these gives us this final result:

the + boy + have + present + be + -en + go + -ing + to + the + dentist

> *becomes*

The boy has been going to the dentist.

Summary

1. A transformational grammar consists of sets of rules for forming sentences, each rule stating a single step in the process.
2. There are three main sets of rules: 1) those for forming kernel sentences: 2) those for combining or otherwise changing kernel sentences into transformed sentences; 3) rules for making the results of the various transformations into pronounceable sentences.
3. Transformational rules state in single steps the process involved in making kernel sentences into questions, passives, and other more complicated forms.

A FINAL WORD

Although brief, this chapter should have given you some idea of the new developments in grammar. Most of the details—some of them extremely important—were left out; nevertheless, you have had a chance to try your hand at some of the typical methods of structural and transformational grammars. Perhaps even this slight acquaintance with these new ideas will give you new insights into the way in which your language operates.

Quite possibly, the methods of the modern grammarians may seem overly complicated and cumbersome to you. This is because they try to arrive at statements which will apply to a large number of different sentences. To do so, they must take into account details that seem to matter little as far as a particular sentence is concerned. If they seem to spend too much time and effort in dealing with the simplest of sentences, remember that a science that cannot explain simple things is not likely to manage very well with complicated things.

Whatever you think about modern grammar, do not make the mistake of thinking it does not concern you. Everything you do involves language—your relations with others, your studies, your private thoughts. It is well worthwhile to know something about a matter so closely involved with your life. Above all, do not think of grammar as a mysterious body of knowledge that belongs to English teachers and no one else. It is your grammar because it is your language. The more you know about it the better.

PART NINE

College Entrance
and Other
Examinations

College Entrance and Other Examinations

At the present time, the percentage of young people wishing to attend college is greater than ever before. Deluged by applications for admission and for scholarship aid, colleges and other scholarship-granting agencies have been forced to become increasingly selective. If you are planning to go to college, you will probably encounter the selective process in the form of a test of your aptitude for college work and of your achievement as a high school student.

If a college is going to test you before it admits you, the chances are about eight in ten that it will test your verbal and mathematical aptitude and your skill in English composition. Verbal aptitude means your ability to deal with words, to understand them either alone or in combinations. Your skill in this area has a direct effect on your ability to do well in courses that require considerable reading and writing. Verbal aptitude is not developed in any particular courses you have had in school; on the contrary, you have been developing your verbal aptitude in all your reading, your listening, and your talking, since before you started school. Composition, however, is taught in English class. When you are tested in composition, you are being tested on skills you have learned in class.

Since both verbal aptitude tests and English composition tests try to measure abilities you have, rather than definite subject matter, there is not much that you can do in the way of specific preparation for them. You will not be tested on how well you know and can use any list of 500 or 1,000 specific words, or how glib you are in parroting ten rules of grammar.

What you can do in preparation, however, is to familiarize yourself with some of the standard ways of measuring verbal aptitude and compositional ability. The purpose of this chapter is to show you these methods. When any test you take makes use of them, you will, in a sense, be on familiar ground.

Always give careful attention to the test directions. Read them through at least twice. There may be a special way of marking your answer sheet; or there may be a slight variation from the directions you have followed in other tests. If you do not pick up these details, the chances are that you will not convey to the examiner the real knowledge that you have. In most modern tests, the means of communication between the student and the tester is the answer sheet. If you mark your answer sheet erroneously, there will be no proper communication.

TESTS OF VERBAL APTITUDE

Tests of verbal aptitude measure your knowledge of words. They test not only your understanding of single words, but also of words in context, of words in their relationship to other words, and of the meaning conveyed by whole passages of words. The commonest types of test exercises involve synonyms, antonyms (opposites), analogies, sentence completions, and reading comprehension exercises. Consideration of each individual type follows.

Synonyms and Antonyms

In a synonym test you are asked to select out of four or five choices the word most similar in meaning to the word given to you. In an antonym test, you are asked to pick out the word most nearly opposite to the word given. The test directions read about as follows:

SYNONYMS   Each of the following questions consists of a word printed in capital letters followed by five words lettered A through E. Choose the lettered word which is most nearly *similar* in meaning to the word in capital letters.

ANTONYMS   Each of the following questions consists of a word printed in capital letters followed by five words lettered A through E. Choose the lettered word which is most nearly *opposite* in meaning to the word in capital letters.

You must be careful in reading these directions to make sure whether you are being asked to choose synonyms or antonyms, since some test questions will ask for one thing, an antonym for example, and will include a synonym as a wrong choice. Careful reading of directions will keep you straight. Following are three sample questions in which you are to find a synonym for each word given in capital letters:

i. ENERVATE: A. encourage   B. enlarge   C. bemoan
     D. weaken   E. cut

ii. CATACLYSM: A. disaster   B. catacomb   C. cliff
     D. slope   E. detriment

iii. DISCLOSE: A. react   B. darken   C. resound
     D. visualize   E. announce

The answers here are i–D, ii–A, iii–E. Notice that in i a common misconception of the word's meaning is included among the choices. Many people are confused as to whether *enervate* means to take "nerve" away from a person or to put it in—hence *encourage* as a wrong choice. With ii and iii, the question forces you to a fairly accurate knowledge of the word in question. *Cataclysm* is something bad, but both *disaster* and *detriment* are bad. *Catacomb* may confuse because it has the same prefix as *cataclysm*. With iii, *visualize* may suggest looking and so be associated with one meaning of *disclose*—"to reveal." Only *announce* is a suitable choice among the possibilities given.

● Exercise 1.　Number your paper 1–5. Following the directions for antonyms on page 734, write your answers after the proper number on your paper.[1]

1. obtuse:　A. popular　B. compact　C. brief　D. light
　　E. perceptive

2. din:　A. silence　B. order　C. withdrawal　D. brightness
　　E. glamour

3. palliate:　A. deprecate　B. color　C. drop　D. aggravate
　　E. eradicate

4. effete:　A. wealthy　B. raucous　C. fresh　D. feminine
　　E. sad

5. transient:　A. radioactive　B. swift　C. polite
　　D. permanent　E. sure

Word Analogies

The analogy, which is designed to measure your understanding of the relationships existing between words, is generally set up like this:

i. yawn : ennui :: A. drink : hunger　B. shout : triumph
　　C. birds : prophecy　D. miserliness : thrift
　　E. equanimity : faith

Directions for the analogy will read about as follows:

Each of the following questions consists of two words which have a certain relationship to each other, followed by five pairs of related words. Choose the one pair of words which are related to each other in the same way as the original pair are related to each other.

[1] Answers for this and subsequent exercises are on page 767.

In the sample question given, *yawn* and *ennui* have a certain relationship to each other. It can be verbalized as *a yawn is a sign of ennui* (or, since it is not yet clear whether *yawn* is to be considered a noun or a verb, *when you feel ennui, you often yawn*). Looking at the choices to find a similar relationship, you note that A will not do, since drinking indicates thirst, not hunger. B may be all right, since a shout is often a sign of triumph. In C, birds are not at all a sign of prophecy, though the Greeks and Romans often considered bird flights good or bad omens. Miserliness and thrift, in D, have a certain relationship, but it is not the *sign-of-something* relationship we are looking for; they are, to an extent, different degrees of a particular quality. And in E, a person who has faith may or may not have equanimity. In any case, it is a state of mind rather than a physical action indicating something else. B, then, is the only relationship that will work and is the best answer.

It will probably help you in doing analogies if you will verbalize each question. Something along the following lines is as good as anything: *Yawn is to ennui as shout is to triumph;* or, *a yawn is a sign of ennui; a shout is a sign of triumph.* Here is another sample to try:

ii. GIRTH : CIRCUMFERENCE :: A. area : volume   B. length :
    width   C. height : altitude   D. rectangle : circle
    E. color : stain

The first thing to do is to get the relationship expressed. *Girth* and *circumference* are in a limited way synonyms, although one is used most frequently with people or animals and the other with geometric figures; one is a short, earthy word and the other seems more abstract. Of course, C is the right answer, since *height* and *altitude* are in a way synonyms; in addition, *altitude* seems a little more abstract and more formal than *height. Area* and *volume* make an attractive wrong choice, but they are not really synonyms, since *area* is two-dimensional and *volume* is three-dimensional. *Color* and *stain*, too, have something in common, but the best you can do there is to say that *stain* is a kind of color, usually a discoloration, different from the color that surrounds it. B and D seem designed only to catch the fancy of someone unacquainted with the meaning of one of the original pair.

● EXERCISE 2. Number your paper 1–5. Following the directions for analogies on page 735, write your answers after the proper number on your paper.

1. BRAVERY : LION :: A. shrewdness : mole   B. wisdom : owl
   C. fox : stealth   D. temper : elephant   E. shark : fish

2. THINK : MEDITATE :: A. want : yearn   B. study : scan
   C. paddle : swim   D. mutter : talk   E. hurry : run

3. RECTITUDE : CONDUCT :: A. wealth : society   B. politics : government   C. cowardice : fear   D. foibles : etiquette
   E. virtue : morals

4. STUTTER : SPEAK :: A. limp : walk   B. snore : sleep
   C. whistle : sing   D. nausea : illness   E. walk : ride

5. COMPLIMENT : SLUR :: A. jump : climb   B. master : mistress
   C. caress : blow   D. servitude : employment   E. rope : string

Words in Context

Moving on from the measurement of word relationships, the test of verbal aptitude may next examine the understanding of words in context. This is done sometimes by asking questions about words in long passages of writing, but more generally by short questions of two types. There is the type, very like the synonym, that presents the word to be tested in a phrase; and there is the full sentence with one or more words omitted. In the former, the student is simply asked to choose the word that is closest in meaning, as he did with the regular synonyms. In the latter, he is asked to choose the word (or words) that will fill the blank(s) and make a satisfactory sentence.

Here is an example of the word in context:

i. An *estimate* of the chances
   A. prophecy   B. guess   C. calculation   D. denial
   E. reversal

Follow the same procedures in doing this kind of question that you would with synonyms. The answer is C.

The directions for sentence completion (sentence with one or more blanks) run as follows:

Each of the following sentences has one or more blank spaces, each blank indicating that a word has been omitted. Beneath the sentence are five words, or pairs of words. Choose the one word, or pair of words, which, when inserted in the sentence, best fits the meaning of the sentence as a whole.

Here is an example of the sentence completion:

i. There are human beings so —— that they need drink or drugs
   to feel alive.   A. perverse   B. moribund   C. unusual
   D. attenuated   E. listless

The sense of the sentence is easy enough. Some human beings have a quality about them that makes them need drink or drugs. *Perverse* will not do, since perversity suggests a cantankerous frame of mind that is very alive, though not always pleasant. *Moribund* looks for a moment like a possibility, but a moribund person is a dying person and neither drink nor drugs will make such a person feel alive. *Unusual* doesn't explain satisfactorily why the people need something to feel alive. *Attenuated* seems to have nothing to do with the case and will probably attract only the students who don't know what it means and are guessing anyway. This leaves *listless*, which fits well. The sentence now makes complete sense, since *listless* describes a condition which can at least temporarily be relieved by artificial stimulation.

With a question as easy as this one, it will certainly not be necessary consciously to seek the answer so exhaustively. But each choice must be tried out, however quickly, to see what sense it makes; and the kind of trying out we have just gone through works as well as any. One more sample will probably suffice:

ii. The idea of giving —— credit for work done in —— school bothers many college teachers. A. upper-class . . . graduate B. legal . . . law C. full . . . marginal D. college . . . secondary E. academic . . . partial

Here we have an example of the sentence completion with two blanks. In completions of this kind you may find that the first blank, or the second, may be satisfactorily filled with more than one of the alternate choices offered. It is only when the two blanks are filled at the same time with the two words of the choice you are trying out that you can see whether you have found the right answer. Thus *upperclass, full, college,* and *academic* can all fit nicely into the sentence, and even *legal* could be forced in if necessary. Likewise, leaving the first blank empty, you could easily put *graduate, law,* and *secondary* into the second blank. But when the two blanks are filled at the same time, as they must be, A and B make little sense: graduate school work is certainly as good as upperclass work, though the demand for this kind of credit must be rare; and law school is certainly where legal credit, whatever it may be, is won. C fails because of *marginal school.* You can talk of marginal schools or colleges and be understood, but you do not speak of *marginal school.* Nor can you speak of *partial school* in E. D then is correct, as you can tell as soon as you try *college* and *secondary* in the blanks at the same time.

● EXERCISE 3. Number your paper 1–5. Following the directions for sentence completions on page 738, write your answers after the proper number on your paper.

1. Most books are painfully ——, however hopeful the author may have been of creating a lasting work.
   A. risky B. up-to-date C. transitory D. rewarding
   E. unpredictable

2. Through efforts of many different agencies, there is now a widespread practice of —— of vitamins removed during the processing of food for human consumption.
   A. growth   B. destruction   C. concentration
   D. restoration   E. exploitation

3. Advancement in —— is best acquired by intimate association with creative workers who are, through research and reflection, —— the boundaries of knowledge.
   A. understanding . . . extending   B. adaptability . . . removing   C. knowledge . . . refining   D. science . . .obliterating
   E. position . . . mapping

4. The Alexandrians labored under the difficulties that —— creative artists in an age when literature has passed one of its great periods.
   A. mold   B. beset   C. equate   D. signalize   E. inspire

5. Some students —— their colleges because they believe that only a certain group of institutions are within their reach ——.
   A. defend . . . scholastically   B. reflect . . . socially   C. corroborate . . . mentally   D. describe . . . verbally   E. choose . . . economically

Reading Comprehension

The aim of a test devoted to reading comprehension is to find out not only how well a student can understand what he has read, but also how well he can draw implications from his reading and make judgments about it. This might be called *total reading*. Reading-comprehension exercises ask the student to get all he can out of what he reads.

The reading passages you will find in your tests require no outside knowledge, aside from a knowledge of what words and sentences mean. The necessary information to answer all the questions asked is to be found in each reading passage itself.

Directions generally run something like this:

The following test (or section) consists of passages of reading material, after each of which you will find a number of questions based on the passage itself. After reading each passage, answer the questions following it by choosing the *one* best answer for each question. Answer all questions on the basis of what is *stated* or *implied* in the passage.

Here is a sample passage followed by six questions:

Being free from local political control, independent schools are free to experiment, to compete, to select their students and adapt their academic methods to the changing admissions requirements of our leading colleges. Attracting
5 boys and teachers from many sections of the country, the boarding school offers an important counterpoise to the localism of the public school and provides essential training in the give and take of community living and community responsibility. A bad independent school, like a poorly
10 run business, soon ceases to function; the good one provides, by virtue of small classes, teachers chosen for background in their fields and their understanding of boys, a twenty-four hour program of wholesome and purposeful work and recreation, an unparalleled opportunity to incul-
15 cate those intellectual, moral, spiritual, and social disciplines which make the effective citizen of the future. Several hundred such schools presently serve the country, and the records of their graduates need no embellishment.

As a group these schools serve as the consistent strong-
20 holds of the basic disciplines of the English tongue, mathematics, history, and science—at the formative level. Leading public school advocates and administrators are the first to proclaim the independent schools as the pace-setters for our great public school system, at present belabored
25 by overcrowding, a shortage of competent teachers and classrooms, and the necessity of teaching down to the mediocre in response to growing public feeling that a secondary school diploma is a right for all, not a privilege for the competent. College admissions deans can document
30 at request the demonstrated competence of independent school graduates to pursue advanced education.[1]

[1] From "The Challenge to Independent Schools" by Harold H. Corbin, Jr., in *Lake Forest Academy: The First Hundred Years 1857–1957.*

i. How does the independent school provide an "important counterpoise" to localism, according to the passage?

   A. by paying no attention to local regulations

   B. by enrolling students and securing teachers from many sections of the country

   C. by adapting academic methods to the admissions requirements of the country's colleges

   D. by experimentation and competition

   E. by a strong teaching program that forcibly broadens student outlook

ii. When the passage says "the records of their graduates need no embellishment," it means essentially that

   A. the records are known to everyone

   B. such records are uniformly good

   C. the records are better than public school records

   D. the records indicate a high degree of public service

   E. such records speak for themselves

iii. Which of the following is *not* a present worry to public schools, according to the passage?

   A. the availability of good students

   B. the availability of good teachers

   C. the availability of space

   D. the necessity of holding down the rate of teaching

   E. the necessity of graduating most students

iv. The passage implies that the real duty of the independent school is to

   A. prepare students for college

   B. provide a counterpoise to localism

   C. provide leadership for the public schools

   D. train effective citizens

   E. serve as a stronghold of learning

v. In which of the following lines do you detect an exaggeration?

   A. line 2   B. line 6   C. line 13   D. line 21   E. line 27

vi. As far as bias is concerned, how would you judge this passage?

A. It is strongly biased in favor of the independent school.
B. It is biased in favor of the independent school but attempts to be fair to public schools.
C. There seems to be no bias in the passage.
D. It is strongly biased in favor of public schools.
E. It is biased in favor of public schools but attempts to be fair to the independent school.

The questions you have just read are typical of the questions that are asked in reading comprehension exercises. Question i, for example, asks for the plain sense of the passage. The independent school, it is stated in lines 5–8, draws students and teachers from all parts of the country and thus provides an important counterpoise to localism. Hence B is the answer. You will note that some of the other choices, notably C and to some extent E, present advantages claimed by the passage for the independent school; but neither of these has any bearing on the question of localism. D is too general, and A states something that has no source in the passage and is undoubtedly not true.

Question ii, instead of asking you to find an answer in what you have read, checks to see whether you have understood a particular portion of the text. As in other questions, two or three of the choices are plausible, but only E provides the necessary paraphrase of the clause about embellishment.

Question iii again calls for the plain sense of the passage, but it does so negatively, by asking what the passage does not contain. The answer is clearly A. The passage nowhere states or implies that there are not good students in the public schools. The passage does, however, complain about the shortage of teachers and adequate classrooms and the necessity of "teaching down"; and it states that there is strong pressure to see that everyone gets a diploma, whether or not he is competent. The only thing to remember in dealing with this kind of question is to note carefully that the question is a negative one.

Question iv is an example of a question that goes somewhat beyond the passage and requires the student to draw an inference. There is nowhere in the passage an explicit statement of the essential aim of the independent, or of any, school. We know that the school does—or at least the passage says it does—everything stated in all five choices. But in lines 11–18 the primary advantages of the independent school are summarized and it is asserted that all these advantages help inculcate the disciplines that make a good citizen. The passage implies then, and the question asks you to understand, that turning out a good citizen is really the primary aim of a school.

Questions v and vi require you to get outside the passage in another way, this time to judge it. All too frequently, students—and people in general—take literally anything they read. Questions of this sort suggest to the student that authors as well as students are fallible and that it is not a good idea to swallow anything without at least taking a careful look at it. Question v, to which the answer is C, is aimed at the "twenty-four hour program," which leaves little time for necessary sleep. And question vi requires him to stand off and judge the passage as a whole. There is no doubt that the author is a backer of the independent schools, though he does take time in the second paragraph to praise the public schools. The answer then is B.

● EXERCISE 4. Number your paper 1–5. After reading the following passage, answer the questions given at the end of it. Refer to the directions for reading comprehension on page 740.

This experiment, and the others that preceded it, settled once and for all the question of spontaneous generation of bacteria. Of course, many people repeated these experiments after Pasteur, and many failed; but it was a question of technique. Nowadays, it is commonplace to prepare a sterile solution that will remain bacteria-free indefinitely.

Researches that have been carried out since Pasteur's day have shown that bacteria are not nearly so simple as had been assumed up to that time. Although they are very small, they have a very delicate organization and very complicated chemical processes go on in them. They are just as complicated chemically as the individual cells that make up the bodies of higher plants and animals, and the idea of such complicated structures originating by chance in a medium containing nothing but organic chemicals is quite fantastic. As a recent writer has said: "Imagine a factory with smoke-stacks, machinery, railroad tracks, buildings, and so on springing into existence in a moment—following some natural event like a volcanic eruption. The same sort of event is assumed when one assumes that something as complex as a bacterial cell can originate in a pot of gravy." [1]

1. Spontaneous generation of bacteria probably means the
   A. appearance of bacteria with no discernible cause
   B. automatic reproduction of bacteria by the splitting of the cells
   C. production of whole generations of bacteria in a single experiment
   D. idea that bacteria were very simple organisms
   E. production of bacteria by higher plants and animals

2. In this context, "it was a question of technique" means essentially that
   A. investigators tried these experiments to show how good their technique was
   B. since scientists knew the answer, they were interested only in how it could be arrived at
   C. investigators whose experimental technique was good would not fail
   D. many people found Pasteur's technique questionable
   E. investigators whose experimental technique was poor did most of the later experiments

[1] From "The Origin of Life" by Norman H. Horowitz in *Engineering and Science*, November, 1956, published at the California Institute of Technology.

3. The experiment mentioned at the beginning of the passage is probably an experiment to

   A. prepare a pot of gravy that produces bacteria
   B. show that bacteria are chemically complicated
   C. show that bacteria can be found in plants and animals
   D. prepare a sterile solution that would remain bacteria-free
   E. demonstrate the spontaneous generation of bacteria

4. It was once a popular assumption, the passage implies, that

   A. chemicals were the cause of bacteria
   B. complicated chemical processes went on in all matter
   C. bacteria had lives of their own
   D. decay in foods caused bacteria
   E. small things must have a simple organization

5. A possible criticism of the comparison between the factory and the bacterial cell might be that

   A. the factory appears too suddenly
   B. there is no counterpart for the volcanic eruption
   C. factories do not have their own railroad tracks
   D. the factory is too big
   E. the factory is too complex

COMPOSITION TESTS

The remainder of this chapter will be concerned with test exercises designed to measure your skill in the writing (and speaking) of English, a skill which has been developed chiefly in your work in school in a specific area. Many tests in this area are multiple-choice tests, like those we have already considered. Some allow room for individual reaction and require trained personnel to grade; and some, of course, allow the student freedom to respond as he will.

Correctness and Effectiveness

Multiple-choice tests of English composition concentrate on three areas of a student's writing ability: correctness and effectiveness, organization, and taste and sensitivity

Of these areas, correctness and effectiveness, as perhaps the easiest to test, receives the greatest stress.

Correctness and effectiveness deals with the basic mechanics of writing: the spelling, the punctuation, the capitalization, the grammar and usage. There are many different ways of testing basic mechanics objectively. This chapter will show four kinds of tests: spelling, sentence correction, error recognition, and construction shifts.

Spelling

Spelling can be tested variously. Perhaps the most common form is the question consisting of five words, one of which may be misspelled. You pick out the wrong word if there is one; if there is not, you mark a 0 or a *C* on your answer sheet. The test questions usually hit the basic rules of spelling: *ie* or *ei*, double or single consonant, drop or keep a final *e* when adding a suffix, etc. You will occasionally find trick words from a favorite list, words like *plaguy*, *kimono*, *naphtha;* but generally the questions are straightforward. Here is a sample exercise in spelling.

● EXERCISE 5. Each of the following questions consists of five words, one of which may be misspelled. Choose the one word which is misspelled, and write its letter after the proper number on your paper. If all words in a group are spelled correctly, mark that question 0.

1. A. seize
   B. percieve
   C. salutary
   D. pronunciation
   E. righteous

2. A. catalogue
   B. laughter
   C. explannatory
   D. traveler
   E. ruse

3. A. peaceable
   B. edible
   C. salable
   D. syllable
   E. changable

4. A. picnicking
   B. dyeing
   C. prejudice
   D. foreigner
   E. desiccate

5. A. mischievious
   B. grandeur
   C. gorgeous
   D. athletic
   E. important

Sentence Correction

The next type of objective question covering correctness and effectiveness of expression is a form of sentence correction. It asks you to look at a sentence of which a portion has been underlined and to determine which version of the underlined portion from among several offered you is the best. There is not always a mistake in the sentence presented and the first choice is usually the underlined portion as originally presented, or NO CHANGE. This kind of question deals mainly with grammar and usage, though punctuation, capitalization, and spelling may also be included. One caution is necessary: these questions usually indicate the part of the sentence to be queried by underlining it; be sure to notice whether the underlining includes, or does not include, the punctuation. If a question wishes to test the use of a comma after the word *there*, for example, it will look like this: there,; if it wishes to test the word only, it will look like this: there,.

The directions for sentence correction will run about as follows:

DIRECTIONS   In each of the following sentences one portion has been underlined. Beneath each sentence you will find five ways of writing the underlined part; the first of these merely repeats the original, but the other four are all different. If you think the original sentence is better than any of the suggested changes, you should choose answer A; otherwise you should mark one of the other choices. Select the best answer and blacken the corresponding space on your answer sheet.

Here is a sample question to try:

i. Eating, drinking, and to stay up late at night seemed to be the only pleasures he could enjoy.
A. to stay   B. he liked staying   C. staying   D. to remain
E. OMIT

You can often see at once the grammatical principle or rule being tested in these questions. Here, for example, it is a question of parallelism. Since *eating* and *drinking* are gerunds, quite obviously *to stay* has to be changed to a gerund to make a satisfactory sentence. The answer is C.

Many of the tests that college-bound students take these days make use of a slight variation of sentence correction. This variation presents a passage of prose rather than a single sentence and underlines several places in the text. One passage of prose thus yields many questions of the sentence-correction type. An advantage of the longer passage is that connections between sentences can be tested, as to a certain extent can sequence of thoughts—and, to a lesser extent, organization (should the third paragraph have preceded the second paragraph?). Generally, however, there is little difference between these questions and those that can be asked about single sentences.

● EXERCISE 6. Number your paper 1–5. Following the directions for sentence correction on page 748, write your answers after the proper number on your paper.

The term "metaphysical" was first applied to a school of poetry by Dryden. It got firmly established in poetical criticism by Dr. Samuel Johnson in his *Life of Abraham Cowley*, where he applied it to John Donne and his followers (one of whom was Cowley) because he said they "were men of learning, and to show their learning was their whole endeavor."

1.
A. It got firmly
B. Firmly
C. It was firmly
D. This idea was firmly
E. and was firmly (do not begin new sentence)

2.
A. they "were
B. they, "were
C. they "Were
D. they, "Were
E. they were

Dr. Johnson felt that they filled
their poetry with ingenious intellectual toys, <u>instead of</u> more funda-
                    3
mental conceptions of truth. Since
Dr. Johnson's day the word, <u>however</u>,
                                    4
has come to have in criticism a
larger and more complimentary meaning
for poetry. Today, metaphysical
poetry, including that of Donne and
his followers, <u>is that which</u> uses
                    5
complex ideas and images to give a
complex representation of a complex
life.

3. A. instead of
   B. and not
   C. in lieu of
   D. rather than
   E. rather than
      with

4. A. Leave where
      it is.
   B. Place at be-
      ginning of
      sentence.
   C. Place after
      day.
   D. Place after
      come.
   E. OMIT

5. A. is that
      which
   B. is the kind
      which
   C. is poetry,
      which
   D. is poetry
      which
   E. OMIT

Error Recognition

A third type of question testing correctness and effectiveness is error recognition. Error recognition exercises present you with sentences that have (or occasionally have not)
certain types of errors in them. There may be errors in
diction. There may be redundancy, or simply general wordiness. There may be clichés or mixed metaphors. And there
may be errors in grammar, usage, or sentence structure.
No sentence contains more than one error, and some are
correct as they stand. The student is to classify each sentence
according to the particular type of error it contains.

DIRECTIONS The following exercise contains sentences which may have certain types of errors in them. You are to read each sentence carefully and to record your answer on the answer sheet as follows:

A if the sentence contains an error in diction
B if the sentence is verbose or redundant
C if the sentence contains a cliché or a mixed metaphor
D if the sentence contains faulty grammar
E if the sentence contains none of these errors

No sentence contains more than one kind of error. Some sentences have no errors.

A typical sentence might be the following:

i. Each day it was an everyday occurrence to see them pick their way through the boulders to the sea.

This is a relatively easy example. If seeing them pick their way was an everyday occurrence, the adverbial expression *each day* is surely redundant. The sentence would be classified as having too many words.

● EXERCISE 7. Number your paper 1–5. Following the directions given above, record your verdict on the following sentences beside the proper number.

1. The young man was merry as a cricket when he rang the front doorbell.
2. The President had not been in office scarcely two months when the tax crisis arose.
3. I do not see that this mass of detail you have been giving us is penitent to the question.
4. Neither of the occupants of the runaway carriage was more than shaken up.
5. To all intents and purposes, this is the same, roughly, as the equivalent of a million dollars.

Construction Shifts

The fourth type of question testing correctness and effectiveness does not ask the student to detect errors. Rather, it tries to see whether his command of language is good enough to enable him to make certain structural changes in sentences and still keep the sentences correct and their meanings relatively intact. If a sentence is complex, for example, a student may be asked to make it compound instead. Or he may be asked to take the idea of the independent clause and make it subordinate. The altered sentence will necessarily contain certain words or phrases and the student must identify these and so mark his answer sheet.

DIRECTIONS   In each of the following questions you are given a complete sentence which you are to rephrase according to the directions which follow it. The rephrasing should be done mentally to save time, but you may make notes in your test book if you wish.

Below each sentence and its directions are listed words or phrases which may occur in your rewritten sentence. When you have thought out a good sentence, find in the answer choices that word or phrase which is included in your rewritten sentence and blacken the corresponding space on the answer sheet.

Make only those changes that the directions require; that is, keep the meaning the same, or as nearly the same as the directions permit. If you think that more than one good sentence can be made according to the directions, select the sentence that is most exact, natural in phrasing and construction, and effective.

Try the following sample:

i. SENTENCE   What has the class been doing all week but "busy work"?

DIRECTIONS   Change this sentence from interrogative to declarative.

A. nothing all week but
B. anything all week more than
C. had done
D. does
E. little

The changed sentence would read, *The class has been doing nothing all week but "busy work,"* and A is correct. B would demand a sentence such as "The class has not been doing anything all week more than 'busy work,'" which is not incorrect but is less concise and therefore less satisfactory than A. C and D have verb forms that cannot be present in the new sentence because their tense is wrong. E suggests the sentence "The class has been doing little all week but 'busy work,'" a perfectly good sentence but differing more in meaning from the original than it should.

● EXERCISE 8.   Following the directions just given, write your answers after the proper number on your paper.

1. SENTENCE   When night came and the temperature fell, my father lit the fire in our bedroom.

   DIRECTIONS   Begin with *Each night.*

   A. Each night, when the temperature
   B. Each night upon the temperature's
   C. Each night that the temperature
   D. Each night, if the temperature
   E. Each night, because the temperature

2. SENTENCE   Leaning on the arm of his grandson, the old man slowly entered the room.

   DIRECTIONS   Begin with *The old man leaned.*

   A. so that he could
   B. to slowly enter
   C. for his entrance
   D. and thus
   E. as he

3. SENTENCE   Aside from his innate dread of snakes, he was afraid of almost nothing.

   DIRECTIONS   Begin with *He had an innate dread.*

   A. and so
   B. aside from that fear
   C. still
   D. but otherwise
   E. and yet

4. SENTENCE   Despite the keen competition between the Orange
and the White teams, student-body attendance fell off mark-
edly at the games.

DIRECTIONS   Begin with *Although student-body attendance*

A. is keen
B. was kept up
C. was keen, however
D. was still keen
E. had been keen

Organization—the Scrambled Paragraph

The second of the areas of composition in which a student
is generally tested is organization. The most frequent exercise designed to measure organizational ability is the
scrambled paragraph. This exercise takes a paragraph from
any type of subject matter and presents the sentences to you
in random order. Your job is to figure out the correct order,
the order which will re-form the sentences into a well-knit
paragraph. This you do to some extent by studying the
sequence of ideas presented; but primarily you have to
concern yourself with the transitional words and phrases.

Here is the way the directions are likely to go:

DIRECTIONS   Each group of sentences in this section is actually
a paragraph presented in scrambled order. Each sentence in
the group has a place in the paragraph; no sentence is to be
left out. You are to read each group of sentences and decide
the best order in which to put the sentences so as to form a
well-organized paragraph.

Before trying to answer the questions which follow each
group of sentences, jot down the correct order of the sentences
in the margin of the test book. Then answer each of the questions by blackening the appropriate space on the answer sheet.
Remember that you will receive credit only for answers
marked on the answer sheet.

A sample paragraph follows:

P. If they came to college for the wrong reasons, they can be appealed to to work and succeed for the right reasons.

Q. But of course it has to be done realistically.

R. People in college work should not look too sharply at the motives of entering students.

S. The least promising students must sometimes be discouraged from embarking on overambitious plans.

T. This lifting of sights for all students, even the least promising, is as important as any other function in a dean's office.

   i. Which sentence did you put first?

     A. Sentence P
     B. Sentence Q
     C. Sentence R
     D. Sentence S
     E. Sentence T

  ii. Which sentence did you put after Sentence P?

     A. Sentence Q
     B. Sentence R
     C. Sentence S
     D. Sentence T
     E. None of the above. Sentence P is last.

 iii. Which sentence did you put after Sentence Q?

     A. Sentence P
     B. Sentence R
     C. Sentence S
     D. Sentence T
     E. None of the above. Sentence Q is last.

The sample paragraph is not a difficult one. Only two sentences, R and S, do not refer specifically to something that must have gone before. P refers to *they* twice, Q uses *but* and *it*, and T talks of *this lifting of sights;* all these transition elements or links show you that these sentences must be in the body of the paragraph. S could begin a paragraph perfectly well, but not *this* paragraph, since none of the other sentences carries on the idea started in S. The choice for the first sentence then is R. Next you need a sentence that carries on the idea of students' motives—and P is clearly the only one that will do. Working on from there to see what must follow P, you find that Q or T could do. But the sequence QS is a clear one that has probably struck you immediately on reading the scrambled paragraph. If you establish Q and S as following P, you are left with T; and T obviously does not follow S and is not the appropriate last sentence for this paragraph. So you look to T as a possible follower of P and realize that this *lifting of sights* refers to the appeal mentioned in P and should follow P. Once you have come this far, Q and S fall quickly into place.

The correct order for the sentences, then, is RPTQS, and this you must determine before you answer the questions. But note and keep firmly in mind that the questions will not ask you which sentence you put first, second, third, etc.; the questions will ask, for example, which sentence comes after P or Q or R. The exercises are set up in this way so that you will get credit for every correct relationship of sentences that you detect. If you were merely asked which sentence you put first, second, or third, and you had picked the wrong one for first place, all your answers would be wrong. Test-makers want to give you credit for what you do know, even if you do not get the paragraph put back completely straight.

● EXERCISE 9.   Following the directions on page 754, write the answers on your paper after the proper numbers.

1

P. There is an important difference between tests of ability and measures of interest and personality.

Q. There is no question whether you have expressed correct interests.

R. In tests of ability, there are right, or at least best, answers.

S. In measures of interest and personality, however, the only right answers are those that best describe the person tested.

T. An interest in scientific activities, for example, is no more correct than an interest in literary activities.

1. Which sentence did you put first?
   A. Sentence P
   B. Sentence Q
   C. Sentence R
   D. Sentence S
   E. Sentence T

2. Which sentence did you put after Sentence P?
   A. Sentence Q
   B. Sentence R
   C. Sentence S
   D. Sentence T
   E. None of the above. Sentence P is last.

3. Which sentence did you put after Sentence Q?
   A. Sentence P
   B. Sentence R
   C. Sentence S
   D. Sentence T
   E. None of the above. Sentence Q is last.

4. Which sentence did you put after Sentence R?
   A. Sentence P
   B. Sentence Q
   C. Sentence S
   D. Sentence T
   E. None of the above. Sentence R is last.

5. Which sentence did you put after Sentence S?
   A. Sentence P
   B. Sentence Q
   C. Sentence R
   D. Sentence T
   E. None of the above. Sentence S is last.

6. Which sentence did you put after Sentence T?
   A. Sentence P
   B. Sentence Q
   C. Sentence R
   D. Sentence S
   E. None of the above. Sentence T is last.

2

P. At first his affiliations were with the Whigs, but he found, as time went on, that the Whigs were less sympathetic with his views about ecclesiastical affairs than the Tories.

Q. In the next four years he wrote a large number of political pamphlets, becoming perhaps the greatest political pamphleteer that England has ever known.

R. As a reward for his services, he anticipated that the Tories would give him an important post in the Church of England.

S. To Swift, this was a matter of vital importance, and about 1710 he transferred his allegiance to the Tory party.

T. During his visits to England in the early part of the century, Swift occasionally tried his hand at political pamphleteering.

7. Which sentence did you put first?

    A. Sentence P
    B. Sentence Q
    C. Sentence R
    D. Sentence S
    E. Sentence T

8. Which sentence did you put after Sentence P?

    A. Sentence Q
    B. Sentence R
    C. Sentence S
    D. Sentence T
    E. None of the above. Sentence P is last.

9. Which sentence did you put after Sentence Q?

    A. Sentence P
    B. Sentence R
    C. Sentence S
    D. Sentence T
    E. None of the above. Sentence Q is last.

10. Which sentence did you put after Sentence R?

    A. Sentence P
    B. Sentence Q
    C. Sentence S
    D. Sentence T
    E. None of the above. Sentence R is last.

11. Which sentence did you put after Sentence S?

    A. Sentence P
    B. Sentence Q
    C. Sentence R
    D. Sentence T
    E. None of the above. Sentence S is last.

12. Which sentence did you put after Sentence T?

    A. Sentence P
    B. Sentence Q
    C. Sentence R
    D. Sentence S
    E. None of the above. Sentence T is last.

Taste and Sensitivity

The third area of English composition tested by objective tests is the area of taste and sensitivity. There are of course different kinds of exercises measuring ability in this area. In general, however, the student will be asked to take a small piece of writing, prose or poetry, judge the style and level of usage as well as the meaning of the author, and fill in a blank part of the passage by choosing among various offered alternatives. Not only will he be asked to choose the appropriate answer to fill in the blank space; he will also be required to make a judgment as to why the other alternatives are not proper. One will usually be at variance with the meaning of the passage, one will not fit in with the tone of the passage, one will probably contain faulty grammar or usage, and one may be too wordy.

Here are the directions for an exercise of this sort, and a sample passage follows:

DIRECTIONS   In each of the prose excerpts in this section you will find a blank space indicating that a sentence (or clause) has been omitted. Beneath each excerpt are five choices which might be inserted in the blank space. One of these is appropriate (acceptable in tone, diction, and meaning), one is inappropriate in meaning (does not fit the context), one is inappropriate in tone or diction, one is grammatically de-fective, and one is wordy (verbose or redundant). You are to determine the proper category for *each* choice.

On the answer sheet mark answer space

    A if the choice is appropriate,
    B if the choice is inappropriate in meaning,
    C if the choice is inappropriate in tone or diction,
    D if the choice is grammatically defective,
    E if the choice is wordy.

Sample

    Asem had spent his youth with men, had shared in their amusements, and had been taught to love his fellow creatures with the most ardent affection; but from the tenderness of his disposition he exhausted all his fortune in relieving the wants of the distressed. The petitioner never sued in vain; . . . .
. . . . ; he only desisted from doing good when he had no longer the power of relieving.

   i. the lonely wanderer ever found the welcome mat
  ii. the hunted stag was never further pressed
 iii. the weary traveler never passed his door
  iv. the homeless and unhoused ever found shelter, succor, and
      refuge there
   v. he the homeless waif sought daily

What you must do here, as you did with the sentence completions earlier in the chapter, is to determine the intent of the author. You will then be able to single out the one sentence that has the wrong meaning for the rest of the passage. The remaining choices are presumably satisfactory as far as meaning is concerned; but one will contain poor grammar or usage, one will have something out of keeping with the tone of the passage, and one will be unnecessarily verbose. One of course will be completely appropriate and will be what the author originally wrote.

In the sample passage, it is quite clear that another in-stance of Asem's charity to mankind is what is wanted. Four of the five choices give this, but ii shows that Asem was kind to wild animals—an admirable trait but not what the passage needs. Choice ii therefore can be marked B on the answer sheet and eliminated.

The error in grammar or usage is rarely hard to find (here of course it is choice v) nor is the verbose choice. People who are unhoused are usually homeless; and not very many need shelter, succor, and refuge all at once. Choice iv, too, therefore can be eliminated.

The choice between the appropriate answer and the sentence offending in tone may sometimes be more difficult to make. Close scrutiny will usually find something like the welcome mat, however, an element that is not only trite but also completely out of keeping (and 150 years too late) for the formal, balanced, eighteenth-century quality of the original passage. Choice i is thus inappropriate in tone, and choice iii qualifies as the right answer.

● EXERCISE 10.   Following the directions on page 759, write your answers after the proper number on your paper.

1

When I started this narrative, I knew that sooner or later I would have to have a go at Texas, and I dreaded it. ....
. . . .
It sticks its big old Panhandle up north and it plops and slouches along the Rio Grande. Once you are in Texas it seems to take forever to get out, and some people never make it.[1]

1. I could of skipped Texas about as well as a small boy can avoid the elephants at the zoo.
2. I could have bypassed Texas and gone on home without anyone's blaming me for it in the slightest.
3. I might have skipped Texas and not gone there about as well as a little boy can avoid an open jar of cookies.
4. I could have avoided Texas no more than a subject can ignore the summons of his sovereign queen.
5. I could have bypassed Texas about as easily as a space traveler can avoid the Milky Way.

[1] From *Travels with Charley* by John Steinbeck. Reprinted by permission of the Viking Press Inc.

2

Why, then, should he not recommend Stelling? His friend Tulliver had asked him for an opinion......................
.............................And if you deliver an opinion at all, it is mere stupidity not to do it with an air of conviction and well-founded knowledge. You make it your own in uttering it and naturally become fond of it.

6. It is distinctly unfriendly, something a good friend does not want to do, to refuse to give an opinion when asked.
7. It is always chilling, in friendly intercourse, to say you have no opinion to give.
8. Saying you have no opinion to give, this is always unfriendly in pleasant conversation.
9. It is incumbent on a participant in a friendly talk to perform what is asked whenever possible.
10. How could he, who knew Stelling all too well, recommend the man?

The Interlinear Exercise

Besides these multiple-choice questions testing your ability in English composition, you are increasingly likely to find free-response exercises in the English tests you take. These exercises may ask you to write single phrases, clauses, or sentences to complete a piece of writing given you; or they may ask you to write full-length essays based on topics or other materials given you as part of the directions. Special introductions to this type of test question are not necessary: all you need do is pay careful attention to the directions. The one free-response exercise you might profitably have prior familiarity with is the *interlinear*.

The interlinear exercise is a piece of prose into which some errors in grammar and usage and some infelicities and clumsy constructions have been introduced. These weak spots in the passage have not been marked in any way. The exercise is presented to the student with wide spaces between the lines and he is instructed to find and correct in his own words as many errors as he can. The grader notes the attempts at correction the student has made and marks them as to their acceptability, in accordance with the approved key he has to work with.

One point should be emphasized here, although it is covered in the test directions. There are only a certain number of errors that have been introduced into the text, and the testers are particularly interested in how the student goes about correcting them. You should look for these specific errors, or weaknesses, and make specific corrections of them rather than attempt to rewrite the whole passage. Rewriting takes up unnecessary time and frequently avoids the specific errors that you are supposed to find.

Here are the directions for the interlinear exercise and a sample paragraph for you to attempt. After you have finished, check your work against the corrected version of the passage on page 765. Be sure to read the discussion of the errors in the passage that begins on page 765.

DIRECTIONS Reprinted below is a poorly written passage. You are to treat it as though it were the first draft of a composition of your own, and revise it so that it conforms with standard formal English. Wide spaces have been left between the lines so that you may write in the necessary improvements. Do not omit any ideas and do not add any ideas not now present. You may, however, change any word which you think is expressing an idea inexactly; and you may omit words, phrases, or sentences that are unnecessary.

You are not expected to rewrite the whole passage. Trying to do so will not only waste time but will also cause you to miss many of the specific errors you are expected to correct. Much of the passage is satisfactory as it stands. Leave such parts alone and concentrate on finding weak places that need changing.

In general, corrections should be made by crossing out the word, phrase, or mark of punctuation you wish to change and writing your own version above it. Any clear method of indicating changes is satisfactory, however. Simply make sure that what you intend is clear.

The captain advanced toward the column of Indians slowly waving the flag as he walked. One rider comes forth from the main body this was Cameahwait, chief of the Shoshones. Like Lewis was, he was a young man. In the

5   center of the meadow of buttercups and Indian paintbrush, there was at last the meeting of the two. Down from the pony's bare back the secretary to the President of the United States was looked at by the savage.

The time would come when the American nation could

10   be able to pour westward many regiments of blue-coated cavalry, and there would be long charades of covered wagons. Finally, puffing locomotives on steel tracks. But now the future of the great march to the Pacific hanged upon a man in tattered buckskin facing an Indian that was feathered

15   on a paint pony.

Twelve errors appear in this short passage. They range from faulty sentence planning to misused words, and they include the dangling modifier, faulty parallelism, wrong tense, and misuse of preposition. The sample on the next page shows possible ways of correcting these. Let us take up the errors one by one and show alternative ways of correcting them. In this way, you will get an idea not only of the kind of thing the interlinear exercise generally contains, but also of the sort of correction that is expected.

The captain advanced toward the column of Indians, ~~slowly~~ waving the flag as he walked. One rider ~~comes~~ *came* forth from the main body. This was Cameahwait, chief of the Shoshones. Like Lewis ~~was~~, he was a young man. In the

5 center of the meadow of buttercups and Indian paintbrush, *the two* ~~there was~~ at last *met.* ~~the meeting of the two. Down~~ from the pony's bare back *the savage looked down at* the ~~secretary to the President of the~~

United States w~~as looked at by the savage.~~

The time would come when the American nation could

10 ~~be able to~~ pour westward many regiments of blue-coated cavalry, ~~and there would be~~ long *parades* ~~charades~~ of covered wagons, *and* ~~Finally,~~ puffing locomotives on steel tracks. But now the future of the great march to the Pacific ~~hanged~~ *depended* upon a man in tattered buckskin facing ~~an~~ *a feathered* Indian ~~that was feathered~~

15 on a paint pony.

Line 2: *Slowly* is misplaced. Now impossible to tell whether the advancing or the waving was slow. Place at beginning of sentence, or before or after *advanced*. Or leave where it is and separate with a comma from part of sentence it does not belong to.

Line 2: *Comes forth* is wrong tense. Change to *came forth*.

Line 3: Run-on sentence. *This was Cameahwait . . .* should be a new sentence.

Line 4: *Like* is a preposition, not a conjunction. Change to *Like Lewis*, or *As Lewis was*.

Line 6: *There was at last the meeting* is an awkward, flat, and unemphatic expression. Change to *In the center . . . the two at last met;* or at least, *the meeting at last took place.*

Line 6: *Down from the pony's . . .* is a dangling element—the Indian was on the pony's back. Change to *From . . ., the savage looked down at* or something similar.

Lines 9 and 10: Tautology. Use either *could*, or *would*, or *would be able to*, not *could be able to*.

Line 10 ff.: Faulty parallelism. Sentence reads much better thus: *. . . pour westward many regiments . . . , long parades . . . , and finally puffing locomotives . . . .* Partial improvements here would receive partial credit.

Line 11: Wrong word. Should be *parades*, not *charades*.

Line 12: Sentence fragment. Tie the locomotives in with what precedes.

Line 13: *Hanged* not used in this sense. *Hung* is correct form, but *depended* is a better word here.

Line 14: Wordy and confusing. Change to a *feathered Indian*.

You will have noticed that the errors inserted into the exercise are chiefly those of correctness and effectiveness. This is always the case with the interlinear exercise. It cannot measure organization, and the nuances of taste and sensitivity tend to be overlooked as students search for the grosser errors; but it is an excellent measure for testing correctness and effectiveness of expression.

These, then, are the chief types of exercises that you will find in tests of verbal aptitude and of English composition. They are not the only exercises, to be sure; but if you run into different ones, the chances are that they will only be variations on those that appear here.

Treat these exercises as they should be treated. That is, familiarize yourself with what they are and the specific things they ask for. Understand the intricacies of the directions. But do not try to cram on exercises of this kind. Tests like these measure your general preparedness for further work rather than any special material you have worked over just before examination time. Continuing to read and to write is the best way of preparing for any test of verbal aptitude or of English composition.

Answers to Exercises

EXERCISE 1, page 735 1–E; 2–A; 3–D; 4–C; 5–D
EXERCISE 2, page 737 1–B; 2–A; 3–E; 4–A; 5–C
EXERCISE 3, page 739 1–C; 2–D; 3–A; 4–B; 5–E
EXERCISE 4, page 744 1–A; 2–C; 3–D; 4–E; 5–B
EXERCISE 5, page 747 1–B; 2–C; 3–E; 4–O; 5–A
EXERCISE 6, page 749 1–C; 2–A; 3–E; 4–C; 5–D
EXERCISE 7, page 751 1–C; 2–D; 3–A; 4–E; 5–B
EXERCISE 8, page 753 1–A; 2–E; 3–D; 4–D
EXERCISE 9, page 756 1–A; 2–B; 3–D; 4–C; 5–B; 6–E
　　　　　　　　　　　7–E; 8–C; 9–B; 10–E; 11–B; 12–A
EXERCISE 10, page 761 1–D; 2–B; 3–E; 4–C; 5–A;
　　　　　　　　　　　6–E; 7–A; 8–D; 9–C; 10–B

Making Writing Interesting

Making Writing Interesting

This supplement to your study of composition explains some of the ways reporters, columnists, and other authors of articles, features, essays, and reports make their writing interesting. While these men know that the first requirement for success is to have something to say, they also know that unless they can attract and hold readers, they will not long survive as writers, no matter how good their ideas or how important their information. You probably have no aspirations toward a career as an author. But you can, by studying this supplement, learn to make your essays, articles, and reports more interesting by using some of the tricks of the journalist's trade.

MAKE WRITING INTERESTING BY USING NARRATIVE

Everyone likes a story. The interesting conversationalist is the person who always has a good tale to tell and can tell it in an entertaining way. The interesting writer is the writer who, recognizing the high interest value of narrative, intersperses his work with incidents—brief stories—that illustrate the ideas he is presenting. Using narrative in this way not only increases the reader's interest but also makes the writer's ideas easier to understand and to remember. Ministers and other public speakers know the great value of inserting a brief story in a sermon or an address. You have observed in church how quickly the congregation comes to life when the preacher starts to tell a story to illustrate a point in his sermon. Chances are that many in the congregation will remember the story first and the sermon second.

In the following article on the hazards of skiing and the incredible enthusiasm of skiers for such a dangerous sport, the author shows that he is well aware of the value of narrative as a means of arousing and holding the reader's interest. As you read the article, note the way he uses stories to clarify the points he makes.

THE SCARY, SAPPY LIFE OF SKI MANIACS
by Marshall Smith

1. The hand-crank telephone connecting strategic points in the area jangled to life. "Summit," a voice said, "there's a crack-up on the Canyon." The voice was cool and matter of fact, obviously that of a professional making a routine announcement. A second voice cut in on the line. "We got you," it said. The first voice continued, "Location just above the road . . . looks pretty bad . . . send one man and I'll swing up from here."

2. At the rescue center an occupant stirred. "I'll take this one," he said, and strapped on his leather first-aid pouch. Within five minutes the rescue team was at the scene, unloading a Thomas splint (for traction cases) and a box splint (for simple breaks). Within ten minutes the victim had been wrapped securely in blankets to prevent shock and placed head downward on a crude but effective conveyance. Expertly maneuvered by the rescuers, it moved rapidly over rough terrain. On reaching the first-aid station, the patient was examined, then transferred to a waiting ambulance which delivered him to a doctor. The voice on the telephone droned, "Mark on the board that the meat wagon is out."

3. The operation described above is neither a Strategic Air Command rescue nor a mop-up after a peacetime paratroop drop. Rather it is a routine occurrence at the ski resort of Mt. Snow, Vermont, and it happens day in and day out between December and April at any well-run ski slope in the U.S. The

rescuers are members of a ski patrol. The conveyance used to bring in the wounded is a toboggan.
The victim could be any one of about twelve thousand cheerful martyrs who will show up in classrooms and offices this winter, brandishing casts,
slings, and crutches.

4. If any other supposedly peaceful pursuit required such elaborate machinery for bringing in the
wounded, it would be banned forthwith in the name
of public safety. Not skiing. The fanatics defend
their obsession on the grounds that it is healthy and
invigorating. Furthermore, they go around trying to
talk other people into taking up skiing. They begin
with the most unsuspecting people—little children,
innocent spouses, trusting friends—and then go
after total strangers.

5. Two basic come-ons are used to enlist new
skiers. Both are destructive, but no skier is ever de-
terred by destruction.

6. Approach A lures the beginner with a sugar-
coated vision of a gala weekend: fresh air and fun
on the mountain top, hot-buttered rum afterward,
and girls—man, you have to beat 'em off with ski
poles. This approach prompted one eligible male to
set off with his friend and tempter for Stowe, Vermont.

7. The first morning the friend took him to the
top of the Nose Dive, a serpentine of snow so precipitous that even experts approach it warily. The new
recruit, standing insecurely on his new skis, studied
the trail that dropped down steeply for about fifty
yards and then veered out of sight to the right. "What
do I do when I get to that turn?" he asked. The
friend reassured him: "You've ice-skated, haven't
you? Well, just turn sideways and dig in your skis."

8. The recruit shoved off and picked up speed. The
cold air nipped at his face. His stomach had a
weightless feeling he had experienced in rapidly descending elevators and roller coasters. Boy, was this

living! When he came to the turn he dug in his skis like ice skates, just as he had been told. It was two years before he skied again. It took that long for a cracked rib, a broken shoulder, and his confidence to heal. The man, whose name is Ray O'Connell, is now not only a hopeless addict but even an enthusiastic stockholder in a ski resort.

9. Approach B is the love trap. It is deadly for either sex. A case in point is the story of a college lad whose betrothed was a honey-haired coed. The only barrier in the way of connubial bliss was the fact that she skied and he did not. So she took him to the slopes to teach him herself, the lesson beginning at the base of the T-bar lift.

10. A T-bar, which carries skiers to higher altitudes, is usually mounted while it is moving, and this got the beginner off to a bad start. The T-bar caught his ladylove just right but dumped him on his face in the snow. By the time he got himself untangled, she was far up the mountain. Undaunted, he latched onto another bar and set out in pursuit.

11. About halfway up he got interested in the scenery and forgot to keep the bar tucked firmly under his behind. Suddenly it slithered up over his back, and only by a heroic lunge was he able to catch it in his arms. Hanging on in this fashion, he was dragged upward for another hundred yards, at which point one ski came off and he lost his hold from sheer exhaustion. A passing lift-rider grabbed his wayward ski and shouted that he would leave it at the top.

12. Our hero was now abandoned on the mountain with only one ski and no knowledge of how to use it. Painfully wallowing onward and upward, he sank to the hips with every step, until at last he reached the top and found his beloved. "Where have you been?" she demanded angrily. "I could have made two runs in the time I've waited for you. Come on, let's go."

13. It so happened that the snow that day was of the "blue ice," or extremely fast, variety. Every time the beginner started to move he would reach what seemed like terminal velocity in what seemed like one-fifth of a second, then fall on the back of his head. On the first run downhill he fell forty-nine times. The only good thing about the situation was that with each spill he slid a few feet closer to warmth and safety.

14. He endured all the self-tortures that new skiers must face. His ski boots crushed his feet like Iron Maidens,[1] cutting off circulation. His arches ached terribly and his thighs, bruised and scraped on the outside, were seized by cramps. He was sweating inside his clothes but was afraid to touch his semi-frozen ears for fear they would snap off. He was frightened, frustrated, humiliated, and, above all, mad. He was mad at all the smug athletes who kept rocketing past him down the slope. The only logical thing to do on reaching the base shelter was to throw his skis in the open fire and give up the whole thing. But he did not. He gave up the girl instead—and is now an ardent skier.

15. The only way to protect most skiers is to put them in a strait jacket from December to April. But for those few who will listen to reason there are some points to bear in mind. The first is that disaster can strike anyone, novice or expert, at any time and in any manner. On every mountain it is possible to say precisely where most accidents will occur, and it is seldom on trails bearing such foreboding names as Shincracker, Suicide Six, or The Jaws of Death. Winter Park in Colorado keeps a pin map of its trails with accident locations marked. The greatest concentration of pins is right at the bottom of the practice slope.

---

[1] The Iron Maiden of Nuremberg was a famous torture instrument shaped like a human. The interior was studded with spikes which impaled the victim who was placed inside.

16. Overconfidence is the most grievous of the sins which lead to skiing accidents. It bubbles up within skiers at an alarming rate on the most ideal days, particularly with a bright sun shining on new powder snow. Then they all get to feeling frisky and acting like winterized hot-rodders.

17. Doctors and ski patrolmen can almost set their watches by the time the casualties start rolling in. The worst time is right after lunch, before the skier gets a second wind and while he is still logy from eating. Later on pure fatigue sets in, compounded by fading light and a drop in temperature which makes the snow deceptively faster. But nothing prevents the skier from taking that perilous "last run."

18. Nothing clears a slope quite so quickly as the cry "Runaway ski!" People dive headlong into the trees and take cover behind stumps and ledges. Only slightly less terrifying are runaway skis with people on them. With new recruits swarming the already overcrowded slopes, the wonder is that there are not still more collisions—and collisions, says Willy Schaeffler of the Olympic ski committee, are seldom little accidents.

19. Some are caused by courteous skiers who are legitimately out of control. But the growing menace of the slope is the hit-and-run artist who creates vast chaos and consternation. His warning cry is a wild yell, and on his mad run down the mountain he terrifies beginners by cutting across their paths. He sideswipes people, scatters small groups, discombobulates ski classes—and never stops to say "sorry." In this country he is called a "basher." In the Bavarian Alps he is called a "ski pig," and there is actually a law against him. Ski policemen issue him a summons wherever they find him, even if he is a stretcher-case being carried off the mountain.

20. In the next decade, to safeguard skiers from themselves, cops on ski-bikes will undoubtedly

patrol U.S. slopes. And if a safety movement ever gets started, it could go all the way. Then all skiers would be required to pass physical fitness tests. Lifts would operate only on cloudy days, and then only until lunchtime. There would be traffic control booths with caution blinkers marking critical points and leading down to them a series of trailside signs, spelling out the legend: "Danger Ahead!—Watch Out!—This Means You!" [1]

Mr. Smith begins his article with narrative: "The hand-crank telephone connecting strategic points in the area jangled to life." His account of the way the rescue center handles a call for help is carefully designed to arouse interest. He follows this opening story with an explanation, in paragraphs 3 and 4, of why he told it and then gets directly into the main point of his article. When he suspects that his reader's interest may be lagging, Mr. Smith tells a story about Ray O'Connell, a story that shows how a person may become a skiing enthusiast—or maniac, as Mr. Smith thinks—in spite of a most disastrous first experience. A second story shows us another beginner, this time one who was attracted by what Smith calls "Approach B, the love trap." Note that Mr. Smith attempts to dramatize the incident he writes about, just as a writer of fiction does. He knows that people in action are usually more interesting than ideas.

Narrative as a Method of Paragraph Development

As you know, a well-constructed paragraph usually begins with a general statement expressing the main idea of the paragraph. This general statement is called the topic sentence. Having begun with the topic sentence, the writer then goes on to support it by giving additional details. These details may be examples of the truth expressed by the

[1] From *Life*, February 2, 1959. © 1959 by Time, Inc. Reprinted by permission of the publisher.

topic sentence. One kind of example is the incident, a brief story that supports the opening generalization. Telling an incident, or story, dramatizes the generalization and makes it more specific.

In the following paragraph, for example, Mr. Hayakawa makes the point that quoting a writer or speaker "out of context" is a vicious practice. A person's words should be judged, not in isolation, but in relation to the situation in which they were spoken and to the content before and after the quoted passage. Read the paragraph and note how effectively the author uses narrative in the form of an incident to illustrate his idea.

It is clear, then, that the ignoring of contexts in any act of interpretation is at best a stupid practice. At its worst, it can be a vicious practice. A common example is the sensational newspaper story in which a few words by a public personage are torn out of their context and made the basis of a completely misleading account. There is the incident of an Armistice Day speaker, a university teacher, who declared before a high school assembly that the Gettysburg Address was "a powerful piece of propaganda." The context clearly revealed that "propaganda" was being used, not according to its popular meaning, but rather, as the speaker himself stated, to mean "explaining the moral purposes of a war." The context also revealed that the speaker was a very great admirer of Lincoln's. However, the local newspaper, ignoring the context, presented the account in such a way as to suggest that the speaker had called Lincoln a liar. On this basis, the newspaper began a campaign against the instructor. The speaker remonstrated with the editor of the newspaper, who replied, in effect, "I don't care what else you said. You said the Gettysburg Address was propaganda, didn't you?" This appeared to the editor complete proof that Lincoln had been maligned and that the speaker deserved to be discharged from his position at the university. Similar practices may be found in advertisements. A reviewer may be quoted on the jacket of a book as having said, "A brilliant work," while reading of the context may reveal that what he really said was, "It just falls short of being a brilliant work." There are some people who will always be able to find a defense for such a practice in saying, "But he did use the words 'a brilliant work,' didn't he?" [1]

You will find another paragraph developed by an incident on page 318, under rule (3).

● EXERCISE 1. Write a paragraph in which you use an incident (or two) to support your topic sentence. If you need suggestions, you may use one of the following as your topic sentence.

1. As graduation approaches, the star high school athlete is besieged by college coaches with fantastic offers.
2. Cheating on homework assignments and examinations sometimes backfires.
3. In summer we city children used the streets as our playground.
4. In northern climates, fishing in winter is rugged but fun.
5. Nothing teaches a family the virtues of patience and consideration for others so well as a vacation tour in the car.
6. The military draft, in spite of the government's efforts to make it fair, sometimes operates unfairly.
7. Getting accepted by the college of your choice involves more than submitting a good scholastic record.
8. When people break laws simply because they disapprove of them, they endanger the foundations of our social structure.
9. The prejudices of parents become the prejudices of their children.
10. Nonconformists are not popular.

[1] From *Language in Thought and Action* by S. I. Hayakawa. Reprinted by permission of Harcourt, Brace & World, Inc.

Narrative in Descriptive Writing—the Character Sketch

A kind of description that can be most effectively developed by narrative is the character, or personality, sketch. In a character sketch, your purpose is to show the reader the kind of person your subject is. Since a person's actions reveal his character, you can often accomplish your purpose effectively by showing your subject in action. In other words, you tell a story about him.

In the following paragraphs taken from a longer profile of Arturo Toscanini, the great Italian conductor (1867–1957), the writer uses an incident to support the point he is making about Toscanini's strong political convictions.

> Though he is modest almost to a point of shyness in private life, Toscanini, as a public personality, is as fiercely independent as an emperor. His lordly refusals to knuckle down to the Fascists in Italy and the Nazi administrators of the Bayreuth and Salzburg festivals are now a matter of history. They have, in fact, made the "old man" a political hero to millions who never would have paid him homage merely as a musician. Aside from a few painful incidents like the famous face-slapping scene in Bologna, the "old man" has enjoyed his fight, especially when he had a chance to make the enemy look ridiculous.
>
> When the Philharmonic played in Turin in the spring of 1930 before an audience including the Princess of Piedmont, Toscanini had one of these chances. A legal and temperamental impasse had been produced by three conflicting rules: the first was the traditional Italian rule that when royalty is present at a concert the Italian national anthem must be played. The second was Mussolini's rule that when the national anthem is played it must be immediately followed by the Fascist Party anthem "Giovinezza." The third was Toscanini's own private rule that he never would under any circum-

stances conduct "Giovinezza," which he had once described as musical trash unworthy of his baton. The authorities pleaded, but Toscanini was firm. The Princess could have her ceremonial national anthem, but no "Giovinezza" for Mussolini.

Finally, after much negotiation, a solution was found. While the Philharmonic waited on the stage, formal and stiff in evening dress, a ragged-looking local brass band, dressed in what looked like street cleaners' uniforms, filed out furtively in front of the footlights and gave both the Italian anthem and Mussolini's "Giovinezza" performances that sounded almost homicidal. During the whole proceeding Toscanini, with a perfectly straight face, stood with folded arms before the orchestra. When the anthems were over and the scared-looking band had filed out again, the concert began.[1]

● EXERCISE 2. Write a character sketch (three or four paragraphs) of someone whose personality interested you. You may choose a relative, a friend, a public figure, or a teacher you had in either elementary or secondary school. In the course of your sketch, tell at least one incident to illustrate a personality trait.

Narrative in Expository Writing

The principal purposes of expository writing are to inform and to explain. Both purposes can be accomplished by telling a brief story. For example, if your purpose in writing a composition is to explain how to handle a sailboat in a severe squall, you might do this by telling the story of a personal experience in which, while sailing, you were caught in a squall. By telling exactly what you did and what happened, you would, in effect, be explaining what to do

---

[1] From "The Magic of Toscanini" by Winthrop Sargeant from *Life*, January 17, 1944. © 1944 by Time, Inc. Reprinted by permission of the publisher.

and what not to do in such circumstances. Narrative would make your explanation interesting.

In the excerpt below, Charles W. Cole describes the dating customs of modern youth. He uses narrative to illustrate his discovery that dating customs today are governed by the practice of "going steady." A boy's girl is his and his alone as long as she and he have agreed to go steady. Read the following excerpt from Mr. Cole's essay and note how he uses stories to make clear what he has to say. You may find the essay dated (it was written in 1957), but you will agree that the use of narrative makes it interesting.

Youth at present is almost completely monogamous in a thoroughly established fashion, and it is aggressively sure that its customs and ways are right.

Not long ago, I was talking with three college seniors. They had been questioning me about the social customs of the twenties, which to them are as quaint (and as remote) as the nineties were to my generation, but appealing because of the good music like "Tea for Two" or "St. Louis Blues" and dances like the Charleston. I had been telling about stag lines and cutting in and getting stuck and the old story of the five-dollar bill held behind the girl's back. One of the seniors asked:

"But why did you cut in on a girl?"

I replied, "Well, maybe you knew her and she was a good dancer, or fun to talk to, or had what we called a 'good line.' Or perhaps you didn't know her and got introduced and cut in. Then if the two of you got on together you asked her for a date."

There was a hushed pause. Then another of the seniors questioned me a little timidly. "Do you mean that when another man brought the girl, you felt you could ask her for a date right at the dance?"

"Certainly," I answered. "In fact, that was the way you met new girls."

A pall of disapproving silence settled over us as the young men contemplated the immorality, the stark and blatant indecency of their parents' generation. Then one of them with visible tact changed the subject.

A boy today who seeks to make friends with a girl somebody else brings to a dance is known as a "bird-dog," and what he does is called "bird-dogging." The origin of the phrase is neither known nor obvious. But the activity is frowned on in the most thoroughgoing fashion. There was the case of Weston Brewer. He was a member of the Alpha Beta Gamma fraternity. At one of the house dances to which he had brought his own girl, he met a girl named Maureen, from Boston, who had been brought by one of the other brothers, Tim Morton. With Weston and Maureen it was love at first sight in the best romantic tradition. Weston went to Boston to see her. He went every weekend. When this fact became known, the matter was brought up at the next chapter meeting, and it was proposed that Weston be expelled from the fraternity for bird-dogging a brother's girl. But Weston's friends— though in no way condoning his actions—pointed out that Maureen was not really Tim's girl, since he had only one date with her before the dance. It concluded, therefore, that, while Weston was guilty of the worst taste, expulsion from the chapter would not be justified.[1]

The kind of expository writing that relies most heavily on narrative is the informal essay. In an informal essay the writer expresses his personal opinions and prejudices. The tone of the essay is light, often frivolous. Usually its purpose is to entertain the reader. Informal essayists recognize that narrative is entertaining. Some essays are nothing more than a series of incidents, often humorous, that support or explain the opinions of the writer.

[1] From "Youth Goes Monogamous" by Charles W. Cole from *Harper's Magazine*, March 1957. Copyright © 1957 by Harper's Magazine, Inc. Reprinted by permission of the author.

The following is an informal essay. Note, as you read, how the author uses a story to make her point.

Honesty Is the Only Policy

I aim to pick a quarrel with an old and time-honored maxim, to wit: Honesty is the best policy.

That has been a high-sounding axiom ever since Cervantes set it down in *Don Quixote*. But it is fallacious, misleading, and deceitful, not to say a snare for the feet of the unwary.

Honesty is not the best policy: Honesty is the only policy, and the sooner the old saw is amended to this effect, the fewer public officials who will languish in durance vile[1]—perhaps. It is doubtful if even Madison Square Garden could hold all the public figures now convicted or serving time for lying.

If the maxim is eventually amended, I don't want any credit. It should go, posthumously, to Papa. He was a rugged individualist who faced up to Cervantes and the third-grade schoolteacher in Caldwell, Idaho, and rewrote the old saw for home consumption.

In those far-off days, they taught penmanship and high moral precepts by making us third graders copy in faltering script such varied truisms as "Sweet mercy is nobility's true badge" and "Poverty is no sin."

So one day when I was dragging my feet at my homework, Papa glanced over my shoulder and saw that I was writing, for the eighty-ninth time "Honesty is the best policy."

Papa insisted that I start all over again and write "Honesty is the only policy," and that began his private war with Miss Grant, the third-grade teacher. Because Miss Grant fired the paper right back at me and told me to copy the maxim as written: Honesty is the best policy.

That was when Papa marched up to the Lincoln

---

[1] **durance vile:** harsh imprisonment.

School to confront Miss Grant, and the battle was joined. His argument went something like this:

"I do not want my child taught that honesty is the best policy. I want it pounded into her thick little skull that honesty is the only policy.

"If you say that honesty is the best policy, it implies that there are other policies and that there is an element of choice in the matter. But there is no choice. Either you are honest or you aren't. You can't be a 'little bit honest' without being equally dishonest at the same time." In summing up, Papa delivered his coup de grâce.

"It's this way, Miss Grant," he said, "there is no such thing as 'a little garlic' or 'a little honesty.' Either you refrain from either or you go whole hog."

Miss Grant stuck by Cervantes, but Papa stuck by honesty, and eventually he wore her down. I was permitted to write "Honesty is the only policy." And so was my sister and my brother, when they made third grade.

"If they wind up in jail," Papa told Miss Grant, "it won't be your or my or Cervantes' fault. They'll have done it on their own."

At the risk of sounding not a little stuffy, let me point out that none of us has ever been in jail—although there is yet time. None of Papa's children has ever been caught lying to a grand jury, a congressional committee, or a duly constituted court. Or doctoring the books.

It would benefit all to see Papa's reform sweep the country, to wit: Honesty is the only policy. While the politicians and public officials are out back writing this truism a hundred times in their copy books, they could very well keep their ball-point pens poised for a hundred-time go at another of Papa's favorite saws: "Tell the truth and shame the devil." Nothing else will.[1]

---

[1] From *Don't Just Stand There* by Inez Robb, 1962. Reprinted by permission of David McKay Company, Inc., New York.

● EXERCISE 3. Write an informal essay (about 300 words) in which you give your personal opinions on a subject that is not of earth-shaking consequence. Although informal essays are more likely to be humorous than serious, amusing than instructive, you need not strain to be funny. (Mrs. Robb's essay is amusing but completely serious.) You must, however, be interesting. To assure this, tell a few incidents in illustration of your opinions. If you need help in finding a suitable subject, read the list of suggested topics for composition on pages 374–78. Many of the topics can be treated informally.

Narrative in Argumentative Writing

The kinds of discourse—narration, description, exposition, and argument—rarely appear in pure form. Description is an important part of narration and exposition; narration, as you have seen, can be an important feature of both description and exposition. Narration may also be used with good effect in argument. Suppose, for example, that a former player writes an article arguing against big-time college football because of its bad effects on those who play it. He could hardly do better than to support his views by relating some of his experiences as a varsity athlete. These, of course, would take the form of narratives.

The following is the concluding portion of an essay in which Phyllis McGinley argues in favor of the northeastern portion of the Eastern Seaboard as an ideal place to live. She relates an incident. Miss McGinley knows that a single incident, one example, does not prove anything, but the brief story beautifully summarizes her argument and concludes the essay in an interesting way.

> Ungrudgingly, then, we admit to the Californian that he's a lucky fellow in the matter of weather. We tell the man from Alabama that we could certainly do with a few of those magnolias, and we agree with

the Coloradan that he possesses some mighty elegant scenery. But we know that scenery is no substitute for conversation and art galleries and windows that open on the world. There are some of us who breathe more easily in a meadow full of daisies than on top of a mountain, and some of us who would rather explore the jungles of Madison Avenue than the Carlsbad Caverns.

A friend of mine who lives in Honolulu is spending a year in the East while her professor husband takes his sabbatical leave from his university. Her family is numerous and they have lived cramped in a city apartment during one of the foulest of our recent winters. I asked her the other day if she was not longing for the return to Hawaii and its spacious amenities.

"Oh, no!" She sighed. "No, no, no. We're all so happy here. I suppose it's ungrateful of me not to miss Hawaii. But somehow I just don't want to go back to Paradise."

No, this is not Paradise or even close to it. But it is home for a certain kind of moderate heart. And while I wouldn't visit here if you gave me the place, it's a wonderful region just to live in.[1]

MAKE WRITING INTERESTING WITH ATTRACTIVE INTRODUCTIONS

Begin with a Story.

You have seen that narrative adds interest to any kind of writing. Because this is true, telling a story is an excellent way to attract your reader's attention at the beginning of a composition. Reread the beginning of Mr. Smith's article on skiers and skiing. Note how effectively the story he tells serves to introduce the article.

[1] From "The Happy Exile" from *The Province of the Heart* by Phyllis McGinley. Copyright 1956 by Phyllis McGinley. Reprinted by permission of The Viking Press, Inc.

2. In one comic book story, out of fifty-one pictures, no less than forty-five are scenes of violence and brutality.

                        Frederic Wertham

3. The past fifty years of what we call civilization have utterly ruined childhood.

                        Philip Wylie

4. Europeans have made a cliché of saying that nothing is so sad as the sight of Americans having a good time.

                        Bernard De Voto

5. Last winter a student at the Massachusetts Institute of Technology was killed while being initiated into a fraternity.

                        Sloan Wilson

Begin with a Question.

Asking a question at the beginning of a composition offers two advantages. First, it is an easy way to make clear what the article is about. The reader assumes that in the article the author will answer the opening question. Second, a question stirs an immediate response in the reader. As he wonders how to answer it, he is forced to think about the subject of the article, something that every author wants his reader to do. Here are examples of how three authors used the question in the introduction to an article.

What is a tropical jungle like, not from distant generalities or sweeping surveys, but as seen by an ordinary human on a very usual walk?

                        William Beebe

What do college grades predict? Can you forecast from the record of a young man graduating from college now how successful he's likely to be a few decades from now?

                        Sylvia Porter

The next example actually combines two kinds of opening—the startling statement and the question.

> According to the Nobel prize-winning chemist Dr. Wendell M. Stanley, the next century will find mankind able to control to a remarkable degree the hereditary traits of plants, animals, and humans. Hermann J. Muller, another Nobel laureate, has also predicted the guidance of human evolution. The notion that man may be able to manipulate his genetic endowment is at once exciting and troublesome: How accurate are such predictions likely to be, and how desirable is the prospect of their fulfillment?[1]
>
> Louis Lasagna

● EXERCISE 4.   Thumb through a number of magazines, looking at the opening paragraphs of articles. Try to find an example of a narrative beginning, a startling-statement beginning, and a question beginning. Copy them and bring them to class to share with your classmates. Note other methods that writers use to attract a reader's attention in an introduction.

MAKE WRITING INTERESTING BY USING SPECIFIC LANGUAGE

The content of a piece of writing is more important than its style. If what you have to say is not interesting, your manner of saying it, no matter how skillful, will probably not make it seem interesting to your reader. Still, given the same content for a piece of writing, one writer may produce an interesting article while another writer may produce a dull one. The difference may lie in their style of writing.

[1] From "Heredity Control: Dream or Nightmare" by Louis Lasagna from *The New York Times Magazine*, August 5, 1962. © 1962 by The New York Times Company. Reprinted by permission of the publisher and Paul R. Reynolds, Inc.

It is possible to list some of the qualities of an interesting style. You can, by studying these qualities and by trying to incorporate them into your own writing, make your writing more interesting.

Interesting Writing Is Specific.

Writing is said to be specific when it contains a great many details and examples to support its general statements. The opposite of specific is vague or general. By comparing the expressions in each of the following pairs, you will learn what is meant by specific writing.

1. vague: a beautiful day
   specific: mountainous white clouds in a pale blue sky, crisp air, bright sunshine
2. vague: He bore a bad reputation.
   specific: James had been convicted of armed robbery, car theft, and resisting the police.
3. vague: For several years the Russian delegation consistently thwarted UN efforts to achieve international cooperation.
   specific: Between 1946 and 1965, the Russian representative on the Security Council of the UN invoked the veto 103 times, while all other representatives together did so only six times.

As you compare the following three descriptions, note how, by means of additional details, the writing becomes less vague, more specific.

1. Some of the boys on the outing seemed to be more interested than others in the planned activities.
2. The younger boys at the Firemen's Picnic could hardly wait for the games and races to begin. The older boys, apparently indifferent toward sack races, the broad jump, and softball, stood around talking and watching the girls.
3. The younger boys at the Firemen's Picnic besieged Chief Barnard, jumping up and down as they circled him, clamoring for the games and races to begin. The older boys, apparently

indifferent toward sack races, the broad jump, and softball, stood in a group by themselves talking and watching the girls, who were self-consciously giggling together at one end of the bleachers.

The second example is more specific than the first.

"The younger boys" is more specific than "some of the boys."

"Firemen's Picnic" is more specific than "outing."

"The older boys" is more specific than "others."

"Sack races, the broad jump, and softball" is more specific than "planned activities."

Comparing the third example with the second, what details do you find that have been expressed more specifically in the third?

Read the following descriptions of the imperial train of Tsar Nicholas II, the last Russian Tsar. The one in the left-hand column is full of details. The one in the right-hand column, because it omits many of the specific details, is far less interesting. A comparison of the two passages should convince you of the importance of specific details in making writing interesting.

I

The imperial train which bore the Tsar and his family on these trips across Russia was a traveling miniature palace. It consisted of a string of luxurious royal-blue salon cars with a double-eagled crest emblazoned in gold on their sides, pulled by a gleaming black locomotive. The private car of Nicholas and Alexandra contained a bedroom the size of three normal compartments, a sitting room for the Empress

II

The imperial train which bore the Tsar and his family on these trips across Russia was a traveling miniature palace. It consisted of a string of luxurious cars, pulled by a gleaming black locomotive. The private car of Nicholas and Alexandra contained a bedroom, a sitting room for the Empress, and a private study for the Tsar. The bathroom boasted a tub with such ingeniously designed overupholstered in mauve and gray, and a private study for the Tsar furnished with a desk and green leather chairs. The white-tiled bathroom off the Imperial bedroom boasted a tub with such ingeniously designed overhangs that water could not slosh out even when the train was rounding a curve.

Elsewhere in the train, there was an entire car of rooms for the four Grand Duchesses and the Tsarevich, with all the furniture painted white. A mahogany-paneled lounge car with deep rugs and damask-covered chairs and sofas served as a gathering place for the ladies-in-waiting, aides-de-camp and other members of the Imperial suite, each of whom had a private compartment. One car was devoted entirely to dining. It included a kitchen equipped with three stoves, an icebox, and a wine cabinet; a dining room with a table for twenty; and a small anteroom, where before every meal *zakuski* were served. Even while traveling, the Imperial suite observed the Russian custom of standing and helping themselves from a table spread with caviar, cold salmon, sardines, reindeer tongue, sausages, pickled mushroom, radishes, smoked

hangs that water could not slosh out even when the train was rounding a curve.

Elsewhere in the train was an entire car of rooms for the four Grand Duchesses and the Tsarevich. A lounge car served as a gathering place for the ladies-in-waiting, aides-de-camp, and other members of the Imperial suite, each of whom had a private compartment. One car was devoted entirely to dining. It included a kitchen, a dining room, and a small anteroom, where before every meal *zakuski* were served. Even while traveling, the Imperial suite observed the Russian custom of standing and helping themselves from a table spread with food. At dinner Nicholas always sat at the middle of a long table with his daughters beside him, while Count Fredericks and other court functionaries sat opposite. With rare exceptions, the Empress ate alone on the train or had her meals with Alexis.

I

herring, sliced cucumber, and
other dishes. At dinner, Nicholas always sat at the middle of
a long table with his daughters
beside him, while Count Fredericks and other court functionaries sat opposite. With
rare exceptions, the Empress
ate alone on the train or had
her meals with Alexis.[1]

Specific writing is not only more interesting than vague
writing; it is also clearer. It is clearer because every general
statement, every abstraction, is followed by an example. The
example clears up any doubt as to what the writer means.

For instance, the generalization in the second sentence of
the following paragraph is clarified by the specific example
that follows it.

It is true that a price goes up because someone puts
it up. But the ultimate limit to the ability of any
seller to put up his price—assuming there is competition—is demand. Picture a seller of cotton yarn.
He has numerous competitors. Demand has been
slack, and, to get more business, he has been shaving
his price. Then his salesmen begin sending in more
orders, and he hears that the same is true of his competitors. One day he decides to "test the market" by
raising the price a little. His salesmen report grumbles
from their customers but, after a few days, no loss
of business; the other yarn mills have followed the
price rise. Demand has supported a higher price
level.[2]

[1] From *Nicholas and Alexandra* by Robert K. Massie. © 1967 by
Atheneum Publishers. Reprinted by permission of the publisher.

[2] From "A Serious Inflation Is Not in the Cards" by Edwin L.
Dale, Jr., from *The New York Times Magazine*, February 11, 1968.
© 1968 by The New York Times Company. Reprinted by permission
of the author and publisher.

Interesting Writing Is Rich in Images.

An image is usually a word picture. More accurately, it is anything that can be experienced through the senses: sight, hearing, touch, taste, and smell. "The law" is an abstraction; a policeman is an image. "Democracy" is an abstraction; a citizen casting his ballot is an image. You cannot see the law or democracy, but you can see a policeman and you can see a citizen casting his ballot. Abstract terms, of course, are necessary, but the clear and interesting writer strives to give them specific equivalents as often as possible.

The more specific an image is the more effective it is. "A policeman" is not so specific as "a heavy-set police captain, his gold badge glistening against his dark blue uniform."

Use Adjectives to Create Specific Images.

Adjectives help us to make our images specific, but adjectives themselves may be specific in varying degrees. The phrase "pretty girl" is such a vague image that it is almost meaningless. "A slender, raven-haired girl with startling blue eyes framed by long black lashes" is a far more meaningful and interesting image.

Compare the following two descriptions of the same scene. Evaluate the images.

1. From our vantage point on the mountainside, we could see several small towns scattered about the valley.
2. From the narrow rock ledge on which we stood high on the precipitous mountainside, we could see the white church spires of five tiny villages scattered across the green floor of the valley.

Use Specific Active Verbs.

Writing becomes more vivid and therefore more interesting as its verbs become more specific and active. The forms of the verb *to be*—*am, is, are, was, were, be, being, been*—

are totally colorless. Necessary and common as they are, they do nothing to enliven style. Vague verbs like *walk*, *act*, and *move* are weak in their image-making ability. You can think offhand of half a dozen more interesting substitutes for each of them.

Like nouns, verbs, if they are specific enough, do not need modifiers. When a reporter writes "The players *trotted* toward the sidelines," the verb *trotted* expresses the action so exactly that adverbs—*slowly, mechanically, dutifully*, for instance—while they may in a certain context be necessary, would in most contexts be superfluous.

● EXERCISE 5. The following passage is an account of a high school student and his father, who is a high school teacher, leaving their farmhouse home for school early on a very cold winter morning. As you read the passage, copy onto your paper at least ten examples of the writer's use of specific details and images that make the experience real to the reader. Include the specific words, especially adjectives and verbs, that make the description clear and interesting. Discuss the style of the author with your classmates.

> It was a long, heavy car, and the cylinders needed to be rebored. Also it needed a new battery. My father and I got in and he pulled out the choke and switched on the ignition and listened, head cocked, to the starter churn the stiff motor. There was frost on the windshield that made the interior dim. The resurrection felt impossible. We listened so intently that a common picture seemed crystallized between our heads, of the dutiful brown rod straining forward in its mysterious brown cavern, skidding past the zenith of its revolution, and retreating, rejected. There was not even a ghost of a spark. I closed my eyes to make a quick prayer and my father got out and frantically scraped at the windshield frost with his fingernails until he had cleared a patch for the driver's vision. I got out on my side and, heaving

together on opposite doorframes, we pushed. Once. Twice. An immense third time.

With a faint rending noise the tires came loose from the frozen earth of the barn ramp. The resistance of the car's weight diminished; sluggishly we were gliding downhill. We both hopped in, the doors slammed, and the car picked up speed on the gravel road that turned and dipped sharply around the barn. The stones crackled like slowly breaking ice under our tires. With a dignified acceleration the car swallowed the steepest part of the incline, my father let the clutch in, the chassis jerked, the motor coughed, caught, *caught*, and we were aloft, winging along the pink straightaway between a pale green meadow and a fallow flat field. Our road was so little travelled that in the center it had a mane of weeds. My father's grim lips half-relaxed. He poured shivering gasoline into the hungry motor. If we stalled now, we would be out of luck, for we were on the level and there would be no more coasting. He pushed the choke halfway in. Our motor purred in a higher key. Through the clear margins of the sheet of frost on our windshield I could see forward; we were approaching the edge of our land. Our meadow ended where the land lifted. Our gallant black hood sailed into the sharp little rise of road, gulped it down, stones and all, and spat it out behind us. On our right, Silas Schoelkopf's mailbox saluted us with a stiff red flag. We had escaped our land. I looked back: our home was a little set of buildings lodged on the fading side of the valley. The barn overhang and the chicken house were gentle red. The stuccoed cube where we had slept released like a last scrape of dreaming a twist of smoke that told blue against the purple woods. The road dipped again, our farm disappeared, and we were unpursued. Schoelkopf had a pond, and ducks the color of old piano keys were walking on the ice. On our left, Jesse Flagler's high whitewashed barn seemed to toss a mouthful of hay in our direction. I glimpsed the round brown eye of a breathing cow.

The dirt road came up to Route 122 at a treacherous grade where it was easy to stall. Here there was a row of mailboxes like a street of birdhouses, a STOP sign riddled with rusty bullet-holes, and a lop-limbed apple tree. My father glanced down the highway and guessed it was empty; without touching the brake he bounced us over the final hurdle of rutted dirt. We were high and safe on firm macadam. He went back into second gear, made the motor roar, shifted to third, and the Buick exulted. It was eleven miles to Olinger. From this point on, the journey felt downhill.[1]

Index